Software Metrics and Software Metrology

Software Metrics and Software Metrology

Editor:

Gerard Ian Prudhomme

ArclerPress

www.arclerpress.com

Software Metrics and Software Metrology

Editor: Gerard Ian Prudhomme

© 2017 Arcler Press LLC
708 3rd Avenue, 6th Floor
New York
NY 10017
United States of America
www.arclerpress.com

ISBN: 978-1-68094-468-6

Library of Congress Control Number: 2016951339

About the Editor

Gerard Ian Prudhomme

Gerard I. Prudhomme has a graduate degree (M.S.) for Computer Science from University College London (UCL). He has also worked as a software programmer and tech writer for different Fortune 500 companies, and studied at UCL, Harvard, and Oxford.

Contents

List of Contributors ... xiii

Preface ... xix

Chapter 1 **A Bridge Role Metric Model for Nodes in Software Networks ... 1**

Abstract ... 1

1. Introduction ... 1
2. Methods ... 2
3. Algorithm 1 (N,M) ... 3
4. Results and Discussion ... 3

Conclusions ... 8

Acknowledgments ... 10

Author Contributions ... 10

References ... 10

Chapter 2 **Evaluating Characteristics of De Novo Assembly Software on 454 Transcriptome Data: A Simulation Approach ... 13**

Abstract ... 13

1. Introduction ... 14
2. Results ... 15
3. Discussion ... 19

Conclusions ... 20

Materials and Methods ... 20

Acknowledgments ... 21

Author Contributions ... 21

References ... 21

Chapter 3 **Artificial Neural Networks-Based Software for Measuring Heat Collection Rate and Heat Loss Coefficient of Water-in-Glass Evacuated Tube Solar Water Heaters ... 25**

Abstract ... 25

1. Introduction ... 25
2. Materials and Methods ... 27
3. Results and Discussion ... 28

Conclusion ... 34

Supporting Information ... 34

Acknowledgments ... 36

Author Contributions ... 36

References ... 37

Chapter 4 **Load Index Metrics for an Optimized Management of Web Services: A Systematic Evaluation ... 39**

Abstract ... 39

1. Introduction ... 39
2. Materials and Methods ... 42
3. Results and Discussion ... 44

Conclusions ... 55

Acknowledgments ... 55

Author Contributions ... 56

References ... 56

Chapter 5 **Error Rates in Users of Automatic Face Recognition Software 59**
Abstract 59
1. Introduction 59
2. Experiment 1 60
3. General Discussion 65
4. Supporting Information 67
Acknowledgments 70
Author Contributions 70
References 70

Chapter 6 **Stakemeter: Value-Based Stakeholder Identification and Quantification Framework for Value-Based Software Systems 73**
Abstract 73
1. Introduction 73
2. Proposed Framework Stakemeter 76
3. Stakeholder Factor Formulation 77
4. Inclusion and Exclusion Criterion 80
5. Implementation Guidelines 81
6. Case Studies 81
7. Performance Analysis of the Stakemeter 87
8. Future Research Directions 90
Conclusion 91
Acknowledgments 91
Author Contributions 91
References 91

Chapter 7 **A Web Resource for Standardized Benchmark Datasets, Metrics, and Rosetta Protocols for Macromolecular Modeling and Design 95**
Abstract 95
1. Introduction 96
2. Benchmarks (Methods) 97
3. Design Tests 99
4. Website Description 103
5. Discussion 104
Acknowledgments 104
Author Contributions 104
References 104

Chapter 8 **Sdmdata: A Web-Based Software Tool for Collecting Species Occurrence Records 107**
Abstract 107
1. Introduction 107
2. The Basic Workflow of Sdmdata 109
3. Supporting Information 111
Acknowledgments 114
Author Contributions 114
References 114

Chapter 9 **Traceable Calibration, Performance Metrics, and Uncertainty Estimates of Minirhizotron Digital** Imagery for Fine-Root Measurements 117
Abstract 117
1. Introduction 117

2. Materials and Methods ... 118
3. Results and Discussion ... 126
Conclusions ... 131
Acknowledgments ... 132
Author Contributions ... 132
References ... 132

Chapter 10 Evaluating the Good Ontology Design Guideline (Goodod) With the Ontology Quality Requirements and Evaluation Method and Metrics (Oquare) ... 135
Abstract ... 135
1. Introduction ... 136
2. Methods ... 137
3. Discussion ... 146
Conclusion ... 147
Author Contributions ... 148
References ... 148

Chapter 11 Comprehensive Quantitative Analysis on Privacy Leak Behavior ... 151
Abstract ... 151
1. Introduction ... 151
2. Model ... 152
3. Methods ... 154
4. Results ... 157
5. Supporting Information ... 160
6. Author Contributions ... 161
References ... 161

Chapter 12 Dosimetric Verification by Using the Arccheck System and 3dvh Software for Various Target Sizes ... 163
Abstract ... 163
1. Introduction ... 164
2. Materials and Methods ... 164
3. Results ... 166
4. Discussion ... 170
Conclusions ... 171
Author Contributions ... 171
References ... 171

Chapter 13 Analysis of Lipid Experiments (Alex): A Software Framework for Analysis of High-Resolution Shotgun Lipidomics Data ... 173
Abstract ... 173
1. Introduction ... 173
2. Materials And Methods ... 174
3. Results And Discussion ... 175
Conclusions ... 184
Acknowledgments ... 184
Author Contributions ... 184
References ... 184

Chapter 14 Confocalcheck - A Software Tool for the Automated Monitoring of Confocal Microscope Performance ... 187
Abstract ... 187
1. Introduction ... 187

	2.	Materials and Methods	189
	3.	Results and Discussion	193
		Acknowledgments	195
		Author Contributions	195
		References	195
Chapter 15		**Reporting of Systematic Reviews: Better Software Required**	**199**
		References	199
Chapter 16		**The Question of Data Integrity in Article-Level Metrics**	**201**
		Abstract	201
	1.	The Price of Purpose	201
	2.	The Question of Data Integrity	202
	3.	Strategies	202
	4.	Call to Action	205
		References	206
Chapter 17		**Article-Level Metrics and the Evolution of Scientific Impact**	**207**
	1.	Measuring Impact	207
	2.	Article-Level Metrics	208
	3.	The Trouble with Comments	208
	4.	Technical Solutions to Social Problems	209
		References	212
Chapter 18		**I3drefine Software for Protein 3d Structure Refinement and its Assessment in Casp10**	**213**
		Abstract	213
	1.	Introduction	213
	2	Materials and Methods	214
	3.	Results and Discussion	216
		Conclusions	228
		Acknowledgments	228
		Author Contributions	228
		References	228
Chapter 19		**Putting the Pieces Together: Integrative Modeling Platform Software for Structure Determination of Macromolecular Assemblies**	**231**
	1.	Introduction	231
	2.	A Platform for Integrative Modeling	234
	3.	Towards Open Structure Modeling	235
		Acknowledgments	235
		References	235
Chapter 20		**Marathon: An Open Source Software Library for the Analysis of Markov-Chain Monte Carlo Algorithms**	**239**
		Abstract	239
	1.	Introduction	239
	2.	Methods and Materials	241
	3.	Experiments	246
	4.	Results.	247
		Results and Discussion	252
		Acknowledgments	252

Author Contributions 252
References 252

Chapter 21 What Do Eye Gaze Metrics Tell Us About Motor Imagery? 255
Abstract 255
1. Introduction 256
2. Materials and Methods 256
3. Results 259
4. Discussion 260
Conclusion 262
References 262

Index 265

List of Contributors

Bo Li
Key Laboratory of Intelligent Information Processing, Shan Dong Institute of Business and Technology, YanTai, Shandong, China

Yanli Feng
Key Laboratory of Intelligent Information Processing, Shan Dong Institute of Business and Technology, YanTai, Shandong, China
Department of Computer Foundation Studies, Shan Dong Institute of Business and Technology, YanTai, Shandong, China

Shiyu Ge
Department of Computer Foundation Studies, Shan Dong Institute of Business and Technology, YanTai, Shandong, China

Dashe Li
Key Laboratory of Intelligent Information Processing, Shan Dong Institute of Business and Technology, YanTai, Shandong, China

Marvin Mundry
Evolutionary Bioinformatics, Institute for Evolution and Biodiversity, Westfaelische-Wilhelms-University, Muenster, Germany

Erich Bornberg-Bauer
Evolutionary Bioinformatics, Institute for Evolution and Biodiversity, Westfaelische-Wilhelms-University, Muenster, Germany

Michael Sammeth
Functional Bioinformatics, Centre Nacional d'Ana`lisi Geno`mica (CNAG), Barcelona, Spain

Philine G. D. Feulner
Evolutionary Bioinformatics, Institute for Evolution and Biodiversity, Westfaelische-Wilhelms-University, Muenster, Germany

Zhijian Liu
Department of Power Engineering, School of Energy, Power and Mechanical Engineering, North China Electric Power University, Baoding, Hebei, 071003, PR China

Kejun Liu
College of Software Engineering, Sichuan University, Chengdu, Sichuan, 610064, PR China

Hao Li
College of Chemistry, Sichuan University, Chengdu, Sichuan, 610064, PR China

Xinyu Zhang
National Center for Quality Supervision and Testing of Solar Heating Systems (Beijing), China Academy of Building Research, Beijing, 100013, PR China

Guangya Jin
Department of Power Engineering, School of Energy, Power and Mechanical Engineering, North China Electric Power University, Baoding, Hebei, 071003, PR China

Kewei Cheng
School of Computing, Informatics, and Decision Systems Engineering (CIDSE), Ira A. Fulton Schools of Engineering, Arizona State University, Tempe, Arizona, United States of America

Paulo S. L. Souza
Computer Systems Department, University of Sao Paulo, Sao Carlos, Sao Paulo, Brazil

Regina H. C. Santana
Computer Systems Department, University of Sao Paulo, Sao Carlos, Sao Paulo, Brazil

Marcos J. Santana
Computer Systems Department, University of Sao Paulo, Sao Carlos, Sao Paulo, Brazil

Ed Zaluska
Electronic and Computer Science, University of Southampton, Southampton, United Kingdom

Bruno S. Faical
Computer Systems Department, University of Sao Paulo, Sao Carlos, Sao Paulo, Brazil

Julio C. Estrella
Computer Systems Department, University of Sao Paulo, Sao Carlos, Sao Paulo, Brazil

David White
School of Psychology, The University of New South Wales, Sydney, Australia

James D. Dunn
School of Psychology, The University of New South Wales, Sydney, Australia

Alexandra C. Schmid
School of Psychology, The University of Sydney, Sydney, Australia

Richard I. Kemp
School of Psychology, The University of New South Wales, Sydney, Australia

Muhammad Imran Babar
Department of Software Engineering, Universiti Teknologi Malaysia, Johor, Malaysia

Masitah Ghazali
Department of Software Engineering, Universiti Teknologi Malaysia, Johor, Malaysia

Dayang N. A. Jawawi
Department of Software Engineering, Universiti Teknologi Malaysia, Johor, Malaysia

Kashif Bin Zaheer
Department of Mathematical Sciences, Universiti Teknologi Malaysia, Johor, Malaysia

Shane Ó Conchúir
California Institute for Quantitative Biosciences (QB3), University of California San Francisco, San Francisco, California, United States of America
Department of Bioengineering and Therapeutic Sciences, University of California San Francisco, San Francisco, California, United States of America

Kyle A. Barlow
Graduate Program in Bioinformatics, University of California San Francisco, San Francisco, California, United States of America

Roland A. Pache
California Institute for Quantitative Biosciences (QB3), University of California San Francisco, San Francisco, California, United States of America
Department of Bioengineering and Therapeutic Sciences, University of California San Francisco, San Francisco, California, United States of America

Noah Ollikainen
Graduate Program in Bioinformatics, University of California San Francisco, San Francisco, California, United States of America

Kale Kundert
Graduate Program in Biophysics, University of California San Francisco, San Francisco, California, United States of America

Matthew J. O'Meara
Department of Pharmaceutical Chemistry, University of California San Francisco, San Francisco, California, United States of America

Colin A. Smith
California Institute for Quantitative Biosciences (QB3), University of California San Francisco, San Francisco, California, United States of America
Department of Bioengineering and Therapeutic Sciences, University of California San Francisco, San Francisco, California, United States of America
Graduate Program in Bioinformatics, University of California San Francisco, San Francisco, California, United States of America

Tanja Kortemme
California Institute for Quantitative Biosciences (QB3), University of California San Francisco, San Francisco, California, United States of America
Department of Bioengineering and Therapeutic Sciences, University of California San Francisco, San Francisco, California, United States of America
Graduate Program in Bioinformatics, University of California San Francisco, San Francisco, California, United States of America
Graduate Program in Biophysics, University of California San Francisco, San Francisco, California, United States of America

Xiaoquan Kong
Department of Life Science, Anqing Normal University, Anqing, Anhui, 246011, PR China

Minyi Huang
Department of Life Science, Anqing Normal University, Anqing, Anhui, 246011, PR China

Renyan Duan
Department of Life Science, Anqing Normal University, Anqing, Anhui, 246011, PR China

Joshua A. Roberti
National Ecological Observatory Network (NEON), Boulder, Colorado, United States of America

Michael D. SanClements
National Ecological Observatory Network (NEON), Boulder, Colorado, United States of America
Institute of Arctic and Alpine Research (INSTAAR), University of Colorado, Boulder, Colorado, United States of America

Henry W. Loescher
National Ecological Observatory Network (NEON), Boulder, Colorado, United States of America
Institute of Arctic and Alpine Research (INSTAAR), University of Colorado, Boulder, Colorado, United States of America

Edward Ayres
National Ecological Observatory Network (NEON), Boulder, Colorado, United States of America
Institute of Arctic and Alpine Research (INSTAAR), University of Colorado, Boulder, Colorado, United States of America

Astrid Duque-Ramos
Departamento de Informa´tica y Sistemas, Facultad de Informa´tica, Universidad de Murcia, Murcia, Spain

Martin Boeker
Department of Medical Biometry and Medical Informatics, University of Freiburg, Freiburg, Germany

Ludger Jansen
Department of Philosophy, University of Muenster, Muenster, Germany

Stefan Schulz
Institute of Medical Informatics, Statistics and Documentation Medical University of Graz, Graz, Austria

Miguela Iniesta
Departamento de Estadı´stica e Investigacio´n Operativa, Universidad de Murcia, Murcia, Spain

Jesualdo Toma´ s Ferna´ndez-Breis
Departamento de Informa´tica y Sistemas, Facultad de Informa´tica, Universidad de Murcia, Murcia, Spain

Lejun Fan
Institute of Computing Technology, Chinese Academy of Sciences, Beijing, China

Yuanzhuo Wang
Institute of Computing Technology, Chinese Academy of Sciences, Beijing, China

Xiaolong Jin
Institute of Computing Technology, Chinese Academy of Sciences, Beijing, China

Jingyuan Li
Institute of Computing Technology, Chinese Academy of Sciences, Beijing, China

Xueqi Cheng
Institute of Computing Technology, Chinese Academy of Sciences, Beijing, China

Shuyuan Jin
Institute of Computing Technology, Chinese Academy of Sciences, Beijing, China

Jin Ho Song
Department of Radiation Oncology, Seoul St. Mary's Hospital, College of Medicine, The Catholic University of Korea, Seoul, Republic of Korea

Hun-Joo Shin
Department of Radiation Oncology, Incheon St. Mary's Hospital, College of Medicine, The Catholic University of Korea, Seoul, Republic of Korea

Chul Seung Kay
Department of Radiation Oncology, Incheon St. Mary's Hospital, College of Medicine, The Catholic University of Korea, Seoul, Republic of Korea

Seok Hyun Son
Department of Radiation Oncology, Incheon St. Mary's Hospital, College of Medicine, The Catholic University of Korea, Seoul, Republic of Korea

Peter Husen
Department of Biochemistry and Molecular Biology, University of Southern Denmark, Odense, Denmark

Kirill Tarasov
Zora Biosciences Oy, Espoo, Finland

Maciej Katafiasz
Department of Biochemistry and Molecular Biology, University of Southern Denmark, Odense, Denmark

Elena Sokol
Department of Biochemistry and Molecular Biology, University of Southern Denmark, Odense, Denmark

Johannes Vogt
Institute for Microscopic Anatomy and Neurobiology, Johannes Gutenberg University Mainz, Mainz, Germany

Jan Baumgart
Institute for Microscopic Anatomy and Neurobiology, Johannes Gutenberg University Mainz, Mainz, Germany

Robert Nitsch
Institute for Microscopic Anatomy and Neurobiology, Johannes Gutenberg University Mainz, Mainz, Germany

Kim Ekroos
Zora Biosciences Oy, Espoo, Finland

Christer S. Ejsing
Department of Biochemistry and Molecular Biology, University of Southern Denmark, Odense, Denmark

Keng Imm Hng
MRC Clinical Sciences Centre, Faculty of Medicine, Imperial College London, London, United Kingdom

Dirk Dormann
MRC Clinical Sciences Centre, Faculty of Medicine, Imperial College London, London, United Kingdom

Jan Brogger
University of Bergen Bergen, Norway

Gregg Gordon
Social Science Research Network, Rochester, New York, United States of America

Jennifer Lin
Public Library of Science, San Francisco, California, United States of America

Richard Cave
Public Library of Science, San Francisco, California, United States of America
Independent, San Francisco, California, United States of America

Ralph Dandrea
Social Science Research Network, Rochester, New York, United States of America

Cameron Neylon
Science and Technology Facilities Council, Rutherford Appleton Laboratory, Didcot, United Kingdom

Shirley Wu
23andMe, Mountain View, California, United States of America

Debswapna Bhattacharya
Department of Computer Science, University of Missouri, Columbia, Missouri, United States of America

Jianlin Cheng
Department of Computer Science, Informatics Institute, Bond Life Science Center, University of Missouri, Columbia, Missouri, United States of America

Daniel Russel
Department of Bioengineering and Therapeutic Sciences, Department of Pharmaceutical Chemistry, California Institute for Quantitative Biosciences (QB3), University of California, San Francisco, San Francisco, California, United States of America

Keren Lasker
Department of Bioengineering and Therapeutic Sciences, Department of Pharmaceutical Chemistry, California Institute for Quantitative Biosciences (QB3), University of California, San Francisco, San Francisco, California, United States of America
Raymond and Beverly Sackler Faculty of Exact Sciences, Blavatnik School of Computer Science, Tel Aviv University, Tel-Aviv, Israel

Ben Webb
Department of Bioengineering and Therapeutic Sciences, Department of Pharmaceutical Chemistry, California Institute for Quantitative Biosciences (QB3), University of California, San Francisco, San Francisco, California, United States of America

Javier Vela´zquez-Muriel
Department of Bioengineering and Therapeutic Sciences, Department of Pharmaceutical Chemistry, California Institute for Quantitative Biosciences (QB3), University of California, San Francisco, San Francisco, California, United States of America

Elina Tjioe
Department of Bioengineering and Therapeutic Sciences, Department of Pharmaceutical Chemistry, California Institute for Quantitative Biosciences (QB3), University of California, San Francisco, San Francisco, California, United States of America

Dina SchneidmanDuhovny
Department of Bioengineering and Therapeutic Sciences, Department of Pharmaceutical Chemistry, California Institute for Quantitative Biosciences (QB3), University of California, San Francisco, San Francisco, California, United States of America

Bret Peterson
Google, Mountain View, California, United States of America

Andrej Sali
Department of Bioengineering and Therapeutic Sciences, Department of Pharmaceutical Chemistry, California Institute for Quantitative Biosciences (QB3), University of California, San Francisco, San Francisco, California, United States of America

Steffen Rechner
Institute of Computer Science, Martin Luther University Halle-Wittenberg, Halle (Saale), Germany

Annabell Berger
Institute of Computer Science, Martin Luther University Halle-Wittenberg, Halle (Saale), Germany
German Centre of Integrative Biodiversity Research (idiv) Halle-Jena-Leipzig, Leipzig, Germany

Elodie Poiroux
LUNAM, Université d'Angers, Laboratoire Angevin de Recherche en Ingénierie des Systèmes (LARIS), EA 7315 F-49000, Angers, France
LUNAM, Université d'Angers, Département de Médecine Physique et de Réadaptation, CHU d'Angers, 4 rue Larrey, 49933, Angers, Cedex 9, France

Christine Cavaro-Ménard
LUNAM, Université d'Angers, Laboratoire Angevin de Recherche en Ingénierie des Systèmes (LARIS), EA 7315 F-49000, Angers, France

Stéphanie Leruez
LUNAM, Université d'Angers, Laboratoire Angevin de Recherche en Ingénierie des Systèmes (LARIS), EA 7315 F-49000, Angers, France
LUNAM, Université d'Angers, Département d'Ophtalmologie, CHU d'Angers, 4 rue Larrey, 49933, Angers, Cedex 9, France

Jean Michel Lemée
LUNAM, Université d'Angers, Département de Neurochirurgie, CHU d'Angers, 4 rue Larrey, 49933, Angers, Cedex 9, France
LUNAM, Université d'Angers, INSERM U1066 « Micro- et nano-médecines biomimétiques », bâtiment IRIS 3e étage, CHU d'Angers, 4 rue Larrey, 49933, Angers, Cedex 9, France

Isabelle Richard
LUNAM, Université d'Angers, Département de Médecine Physique et de Réadaptation, CHU d'Angers, 4 rue Larrey, 49933, Angers, Cedex 9, France
LUNAM, Université d'Angers, Laboratoire d'épidémiologie, ergonomie et santé au travail, EA 4626 F- 49000, Angers, France

Mickael Dinomais
LUNAM, Université d'Angers, Laboratoire Angevin de Recherche en Ingénierie des Systèmes (LARIS), EA 7315 F-49000, Angers, France
LUNAM, Université d'Angers, Département de Médecine Physique et de Réadaptation, CHU d'Angers, 4 rue Larrey, 49933, Angers, Cedex 9, France

Preface

In software programming, a metric is the dimension of a specific attribute of a program's overall performance or effectiveness. Maintainability, for example, is a preferred attribute of a software program element which is referenced in most of the primary software quality models (such as the ISO 9126).

Although the software metrics criteria utilized in the past was used downstream, the total trend in the area would be to force measurement techniques upstream to the design stage. Code intricacy may be specific which enables it to be recognized by dimension, while the time required for you to repair code is only able to be calculated after the software program is in use. A few metrics are wider compared to others. The first chapter features a bridge role metric model. Chapter 2 compares metrics of assemblies. Chapter 3 scrutinizes measurements of heat collection rate. Chapter 4 suggests a model of service performance of web services. Chapter 5 puts emphasis on of automatic face recognition. Chapter 6 evaluates value-based requirements engineering. Chapter 7 peruses development of computational macromolecular modeling. Chapter 8 probes high quality species distribution data. Chapter 9 evaluates fine-root turnover. Chapter 10 gives an outline of GoodOD guideline for ontology development. Chapter 11 figures out privacy leak behavior. Chapter 12 analyzes the usefulness of the 3DVH software. Chapter 13 views global lipidomics analysis. Chapter 14 features confocal microscopy. Chapter 15 scrutinizes systematic reviews. Chapter 16 is designed to develop article-level metrics. Chapter 17 scrutinizes prepublication peer review processes. Chapter 18 deals with i3Drefine. Chapter 19 explains macromolecular assemblies. Chapter 20 analyzes sampling algorithms. Chapter 21 studies kinesthetic motor imagery.

Editor
Gerard Ian Prudhomme
Hawaii, US

CHAPTER 1

A BRIDGE ROLE METRIC MODEL FOR NODES IN SOFTWARE NETWORKS

Bo Li[1,2], Yanli Feng[1,2], Shiyu Ge[2] , Dashe Li[1]

[1] Key Laboratory of Intelligent Information Processing, Shan Dong Institute of Business and Technology, YanTai, Shandong, China

[2] Department of Computer Foundation Studies, Shan Dong Institute of Business and Technology, YanTai, Shandong, China

ABSTRACT

A bridge role metric model is put forward in this paper. Compared with previous metric models, our solution of a large-scale object-oriented software system as a complex network is inherently more realistic. To acquire nodes and links in an undirected network, a new model that presents the crucial connectivity of a module or the hub instead of only centrality as in previous metric models is presented. Two previous metric models are described for comparison. In addition, it is obvious that the fitting curve between the *Bre* results and degrees can well be fitted by a power law. The model represents many realistic characteristics of actual software structures, and a hydropower simulation system is taken as an example. This paper makes additional contributions to an accurate understanding of module design of software systems and is expected to be beneficial to software engineering practices.

INTRODUCTION

Large-scale software systems have developed quickly with the rapid development of software engineering. Hence, understanding, measuring, and controlling design are significant challenges for designers, which have attracted a significant amount of attention. There are many studies on software metric methods such as property-based [1],junction point [2],productivity [3] and combination [4], but "a common approach of using simple regression models to predict software defects [5]–[8] can lead to risk management decisions". In 2002, complex networks were applied to metric software structures by Valverde et al, where the software structure is represented by a complex network. Characteristics of scale-free and small-world networks have been determined [9], and subsequently, studies have also determined that software networks that are extracted from various software also follow power-law degree distributions [10]–[19], exhibit strong community phenomenon [10], [20], and show some complex network behavior characteristics[13], [21]–[26]. Furthermore, other studies have been analyzed in software systems, and subsequently, the methodology of dependability in software networks based on three dimensions of structure has been discussed, and the structural stability in software is analyzed on dimension of composition. Because of the reusability of design patterns in object-oriented software systems, the design patterns are regarded as a typical structure that has more effect on the whole [27], [28]. [29] has studied nine large object-oriented software networks, recovering that graphs associated

Citation: Li B, Feng Y, Ge S, Li D (2014) A Bridge Role Metric Model for Nodes in Software Networks. PLoS ONE 9(11): e111613. doi:10.1371/journal.pone.0111613.

with these software networks are self-similar. They have also studied the time evolution of fractal dimensions during software system growth, and a significant correlation is found between the complexity metrics and the fractal dimension. [30] has presented a systematic empirical analysis of the statistical properties of communities.

On the other research front, some studies are trying to develop a metric for the role of a module in software networks, but few models can describe the "bridge" role of a module more accurately. The Weighted OO Software Coupling Network as the node weight is proposed in [31], where the weight and out degree follow a power law distribution. [32], [33]have introduced main metric parameters of software networks in detail and have integrated these metrics parameters into a hierarchical metric set. The analytic results in [34] have revealed that most of the parameters in complex systems can also be used to represent properties of software structures, some efficient metrics and methods are introduced which are based on basic parameters in other complex systems, and a practical example is used to demonstrate the validity and effectiveness of the proposed metrics. [35] has described some recent algorithms that appear to work as well as some algorithms based on betweenness, which is one of the most important metrics of the centrality of a module in a software network. [36] has introduced another important metric model: closeness. It makes regular and macroscopic analysis and subsequently, utilizes the method to measure important features and characteristics. The relativity among the integral measure and identities facilitates important proofs for the qualification of software qualities.

This paper is motivated by the above considerations. [10], [32]–[33] have proposed some metric parameters and models to represent properties of software structure that are independent of the connectivity role of a module, and modules in [34]–[36] represent the centrality of a module in software networks but are different from connectivity. Hence, a new model is proposed from a new perspective. Some modules behave stronger connectivity than other modules, and if a fault occurs, neighbors of these modules cannot connect to each other. A "bridge" is used to represent the connectivity of the module in the software network; therefore, a bridge role metric model that can more accurately serve as a metric for characteristics is proposed. The remainder of this paper is outlined as follows. After describing the bridge role metric model in section 2, we compare this model with two other previous models and analyze the correlation between the *Bre* results and other fundamental metrics. In section 4, an actual hydropower system is taken as an example to demonstrate the validity of the model and the implications of design principles for software structure are discussed. In section 5, the conclusion is presented and future studies are proposed.

METHODS

Software Networks

Software is a system which is composed of many interactional and collaborative units reflecting coding, design and execution. The extraction from codes to network is displayed in Fig. 1. Particularly, some modules are reused or rely on other modules, and the dependency relations between two modules A and B include two types: inheritance and association. If A makes reference to B (either through association or inheritance) in its definition, there is an edge directed from A to B and vice versa. Hence, a software network is defined as $G=<V,E,f>$, where $V=\{v_i|i=1,......,N\}$, which represents modules, is a set of nodes and $E=\{e_{i,j}|i=1,...m;j=1...n\}(|E|=M)$, which denotes relations between modules. The repeated edges between modules are not considered. Software is regarded as an undirected network, and $e_{i,j}=e_{j,i}$. Node i is characterized by parameters such as the degree k_i, closeness $C_C(i)$, and the betweenness $C_B(i)$, which are presented in section 3. In this paper, approximately 100 randomly selected software (listed in table in Appendix S1) from the open source community (http://sourceforge.net, http://code.google.com/hosting/and http://www.oschina.net) are chosen as empirical cases.

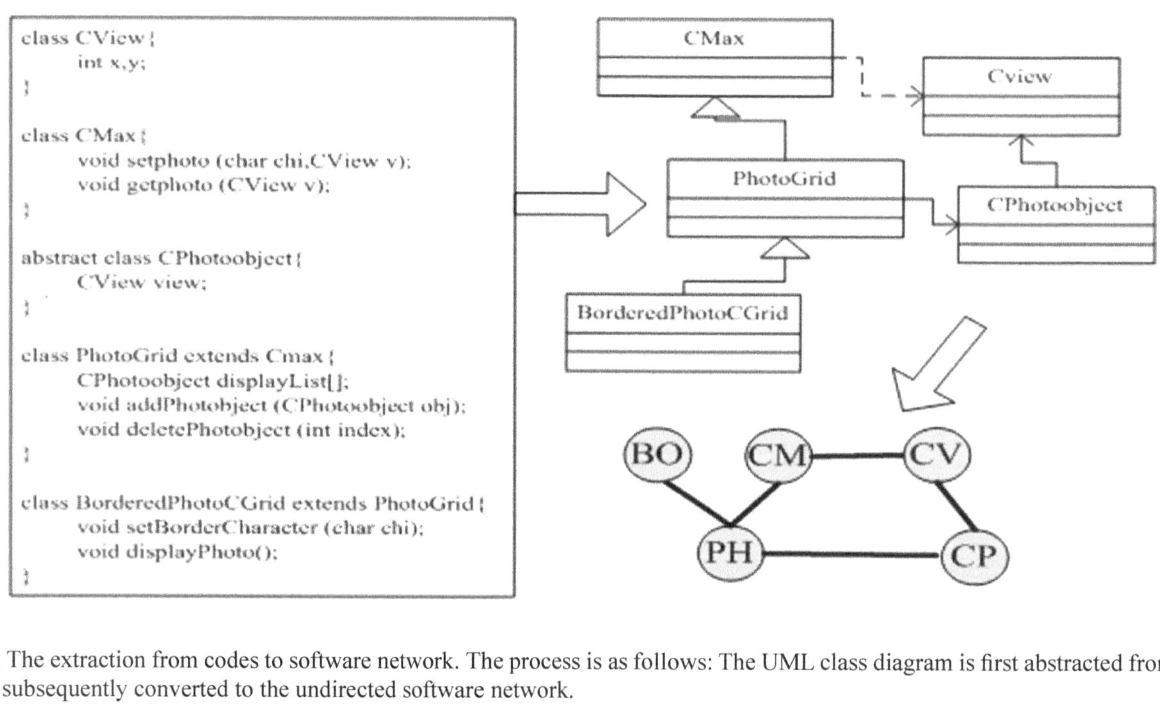

Figure 1. The extraction from codes to software network. The process is as follows: The UML class diagram is first abstracted from the source code and subsequently converted to the undirected software network.

Bridge role metric model

As mentioned above, two metric models can better measure the centrality of a node in the software network, *i.e.* the closeness $C_C(i)$ [36] and the betweenness $C_B(i)$ [35], and their definitions are as follows: $C_C(i)=(N-1)\left[\sum_{j=1}^{N} d_{ij}\right]^{-1}$, where N is the number of nodes in the software network, $i<>j$, and $d_{ij}=d_{ji}=1$ if there is an direct connection between node $i$and j; otherwise, $d_{ij}=d_{ji}=d_{iv_1}+d_{v_2v_1}+\ldots\ldots+d_{v_2v_m}+d_{v_mi}$, $m<=n$. $C_B(i)=\sum_{s\neq i\neq t\in V}\delta_{st}(i)/\delta_{st}$, where $\delta_{st}(i)=1$ if node i is located on the shortest path between node s and t, and δ_{st} is the number of shortest paths between s and t.

Conversely, closeness and betweenness cannot show the connectivity role effectively; therefore, the bridge role metric model is proposed in this paper, and comparisons with the two metric models above are executed.

The definition is as follows:

$$Bre_i=\sum_{j\neq i}(p_{ij}+\sum_{k,k\neq i,k\neq j}p_{ik}p_{kj})^2 \quad (1)$$

$$p_{ij}=\frac{d_{ij}}{\sum_k(d_{ik})} \quad (2)$$

where node j is any neighbor of node i, and $d_{ij}=1$ if there exists an edge between node $i$and node j; otherwise, $d_{ij}=0$. We now discuss the value of equation (1). We suppose the number of all neighbors of node i is n ($1\leq n\leq N-1$,); therefore, node i and all its neighbors can be considered as a community as follows: $p_{ij}=\frac{d_{ij}}{\sum_k(d_{ik})}=\frac{1}{n}$ and $Bre_i=\sum_{j\neq i}(\frac{1}{n}+\sum_{k,k\neq i,k\neq j}\frac{1}{n}p_{kj})^2$. We set the number of neighbors (including node i) of node k $(k\neq i,k\neq j)$ as $n_k(1\leq n_k\leq n)$ and the number of neighbors of node j as $n_j(1\leq n_j\leq n)$. We obtain $p_{kj}=\frac{1}{n_k}$and $Bre_i=\sum_{j\neq i}(\frac{1}{n}+\sum_{k,k\neq i,k\neq j}\frac{1}{n}\frac{1}{n_k})^2$. One of the two extreme cases is that when $n_j=1(j\neq i)$, $Bre_i=\sum_{j\neq i}(\frac{1}{n}+\sum_{k,k\neq i,k\neq j}\frac{1}{n}\times 0)^2=\sum_{j\neq i}(\frac{1}{n})^2=\frac{1}{n}(\lim_{n\to\infty}\frac{1}{n}=0)$, and the other extreme case is that when $n_k\neq n(k\neq i,k\neq j)$, *i.e.*, the community is a n+1-clique, then $Bre_i=\sum_{j\neq i}(\frac{1}{n}+\sum_{k,k\neq i,k\neq j}\frac{1}{n^2})^2=\sum_{j\neq i}(\frac{1}{n}+\frac{n-1}{n^2})^2=\sum_{j\neq i}(\frac{2n-1}{n^2})^2=(\frac{2n-1}{n^3})^2$. We set $Y=\frac{(2n-1)^2}{n^3}$, and subsequently, the solutions of equation $Y'=0$ are $n=0.5$ and $n=1.5$, but n is an integer; hence, the extremal solution is $n=2$ and $Bre_i=1.125$. When $n\geq 3$,$(2n-1)^2\leq n^3$; therefore, $Y<1$. Finally, another case should be discussed in which the community is not a star network or a clique. In these cases, the maximum can be computed with the recurrence method. Suppose that there are $\frac{n(n-1)}{2}-1$ edges between neighbors of node i, *i.e.* $M=\frac{n(n-1)}{2}-1$(if $M=\frac{n(n-1)}{2}$, the community is an $n+1$-clique). We then set $Bre_i(\frac{n(n-1)}{2}-1)$ to represent the value of the metric model.

$Bre_i(\frac{n(n-1)}{2}-1)=\sum_{j\neq i}(\frac{1}{n}+\sum_{k,k\neq i,k\neq j}\frac{1}{n}\frac{1}{n_k})^2=(n-2)(\frac{1}{n}+\frac{n-1}{n^2})^2+2(\frac{1}{n}+\frac{n-2}{n^2})^2=\frac{(n-2)(2n-1)^2}{n^4}+\frac{2(2n-2)^2}{n^4}<Bre_i(\frac{n(n-1)}{2})=\frac{(n-2)(2n-1)^2}{n^4}+\frac{2(2n-1)^2}{n^4}$; hence, we have $Bre_i(n-1)<Bre_i(n)$ and

$$Bre_i=\begin{cases}\in(0,1)\cup(1,1.125] & n\in[2,+\infty]\\ 1 & n=0,1\end{cases},$$

where $n=0$ means that the node is an isolated one.

Computing the Bre value can be described with the following algorithm. The method of creating the hierarchical network is by placing the nodes to a corresponding hierarchy based on its centralization. For example, the nodes that are in the center will be placed in the most inner, and the whole network will be similar to a multi-ring network.

ALGORITHM 1 *Bre*(*N*,*M*)

Create Hierarchical Network *H*(*N*,*M*)

If the number of nodes in the nodes set $|N|\neq\varnothing$

Computing the isolated and nodes (suppose the number of these nodes is $n1$,Bre=1)

hierarchy =1

while $|N|\neq\varnothing$ do

$|N|=|N|-n1$;

Computing the nodes of the current hierarchy

hierarchy = hierarchy+1;

Removing the nodes of the current hierarchy from $|N|$;

end while

returning results

RESULTS AND DISCUSSION

Comparisons

How does the bridge role metric model represent the connectivity of a node? Fig. 2 shows several cases with the number of edges gradually increasing, and node *1* is taken as an example to explain the function of the model. In Fig. 2(a), there are no edges between neighbors of node 1; hence, the neighbors cannot make contact with each other without node 1. In Fig. 2(b), four pair of nodes can connect to one another without node 1, and inFig. 2(c), much more of these types of nodes exist. In Fig. 2(d), any node can connect to any other one. It can be concluded that the connectivity of a node in a given community becomes stronger with Bre_i value decreasing, and it has been theoretically proved in section 2.2 with equation (3), where connectivity means the ability to make other nodes communicate with each other.

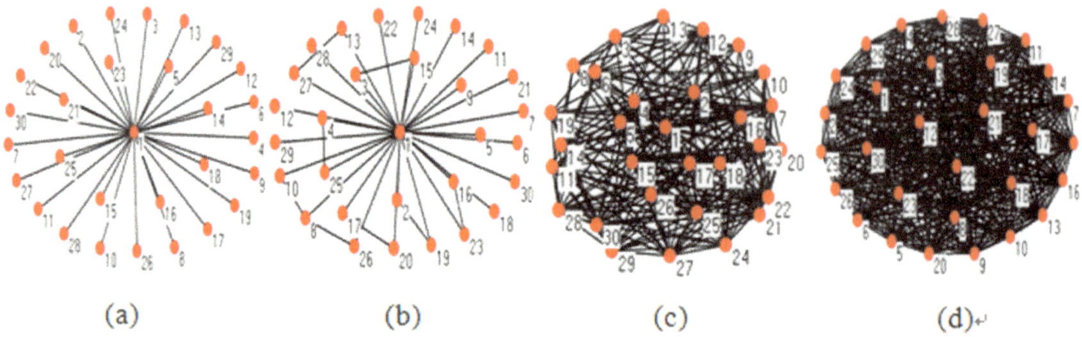

Figure 2. Several cases with number of edges gradually increasing and the fixed nodes. In Figure 2 (a), N=30, M=29, and Bre_1=0.0345. In Figure 2 (b), N=30, M=37, and Bre_1=0.0577. In Figure 2 (c), N=30, M=275, and Bre_1=0.1319. In Figure 2 (d), N=30, M=435, and Bre_1=0.1332. The value of Bre_1 reflects the connectivity of the node 1.

As mentioned in section 2.2, two previous metric model parameters are the closeness $C_C(i)$ [36] and the betweenness $C_B(i)$ [35]. How does the metric model in this paper work more effectively than these two models? Node 1 is taken as an example, and comparisons are described as follows.

In Fig.3, there are two networks that almost have the same structure except for a few edges. Node 1 is in the center of (a) and (b). In (a), nodes 2, 6, and 10 can communicate with each other only through node 1; hence, node 1 acts as a "bridge". In (b), all other nodes can connect to each other without node 1; therefore, in the latter network, the role of node 1 is not very important. The closeness of node 1 $C_C(1)$ is 0.5 in the two networks, which cannot reflect the evident different role of node 1 as an intermediate node. Nevertheless, in the former network, Bre_1 =0.3333, and Bre_1 =0.6533 in the latter network. It shows that the bridge role metric model can reflect the connectivity of a node more effectively than can the closeness.

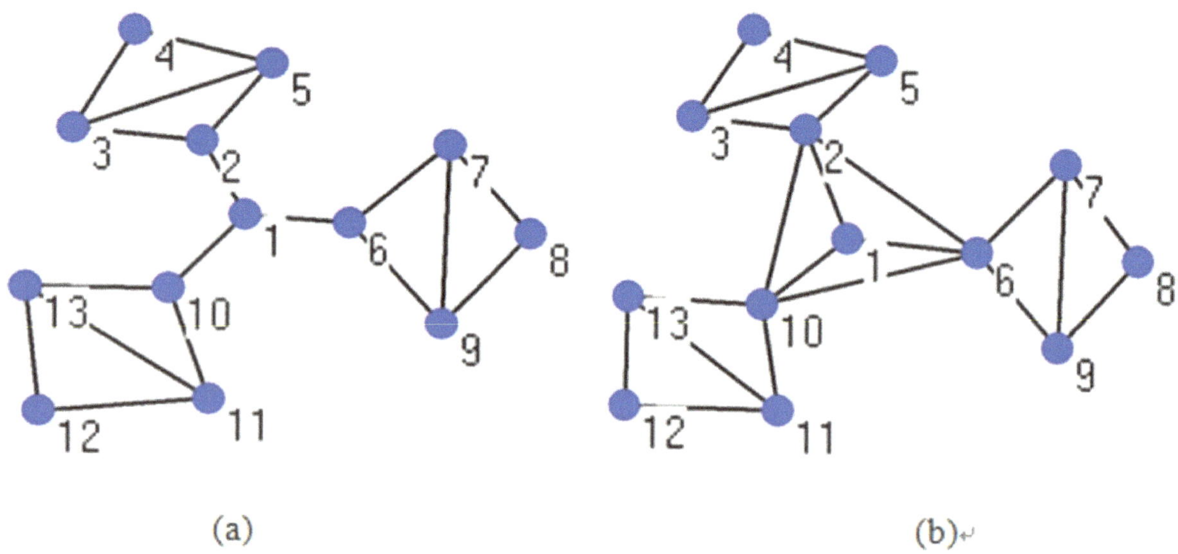

Figure 3. Comparisons of the value between closeness and bridge role in two identical networks. (a) N=13 and M=18. (b) N=13 and M=21, where there are three more edges in this network on the basis of the network in (a). Node 1 is in the center in these two networks.

We now concentrate on the other previous metric model parameter: betweenness. In addition, there are two networks in Fig. 4, where the latter one has two more edges than the former. In (a), there are a total of 66 shortest paths between the nodes excluding node 1, in which node 1 is located in 54 paths; therefore, $C_B(1)$=0.8182. Meanwhile, node 1 acts as a bridge to allow nodes 2, 6, and 10 to communicate with each other, where Bre_1 =0.25. In (b), the connectivity of node 1 for nodes 2, 6, and 10 does not change, and Bre_1 =0.25; however, the shortest paths that node 1 is located in decrease, where $C_B(1)$=0.6667. It should be noted that Bre_2,Bre_5, Bre_8 and Bre_{11} are altered because of the two extra edges.

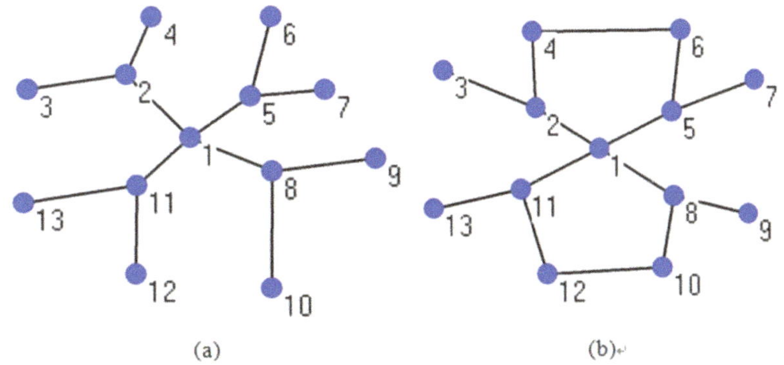

Figure 4. Comparisons of the value between the betweenness and bridge role in two identical networks. (a) N=13 and M=12. (b) N=13 and M=16. Node 1 is also in the center in these two networks as shown in Figure 3.

The conclusion can be drawn as discussed above that the metric model proposed in this paper can reflect the connectivity of nodes more effectively than the closeness or betweenness.

Simulations

Some studies have revealed that software networks follow power law distributions over an extent of degree$K$, which is the number of edges attached to the node $P(K) \sim K^{\lambda}$ [36]. It is natural to consider the correlations between the bridge role metric model and other metrics.Fig.5 shows the correlations of *Bre*, betweenness, closeness, and the degree K in four familiar software networks.

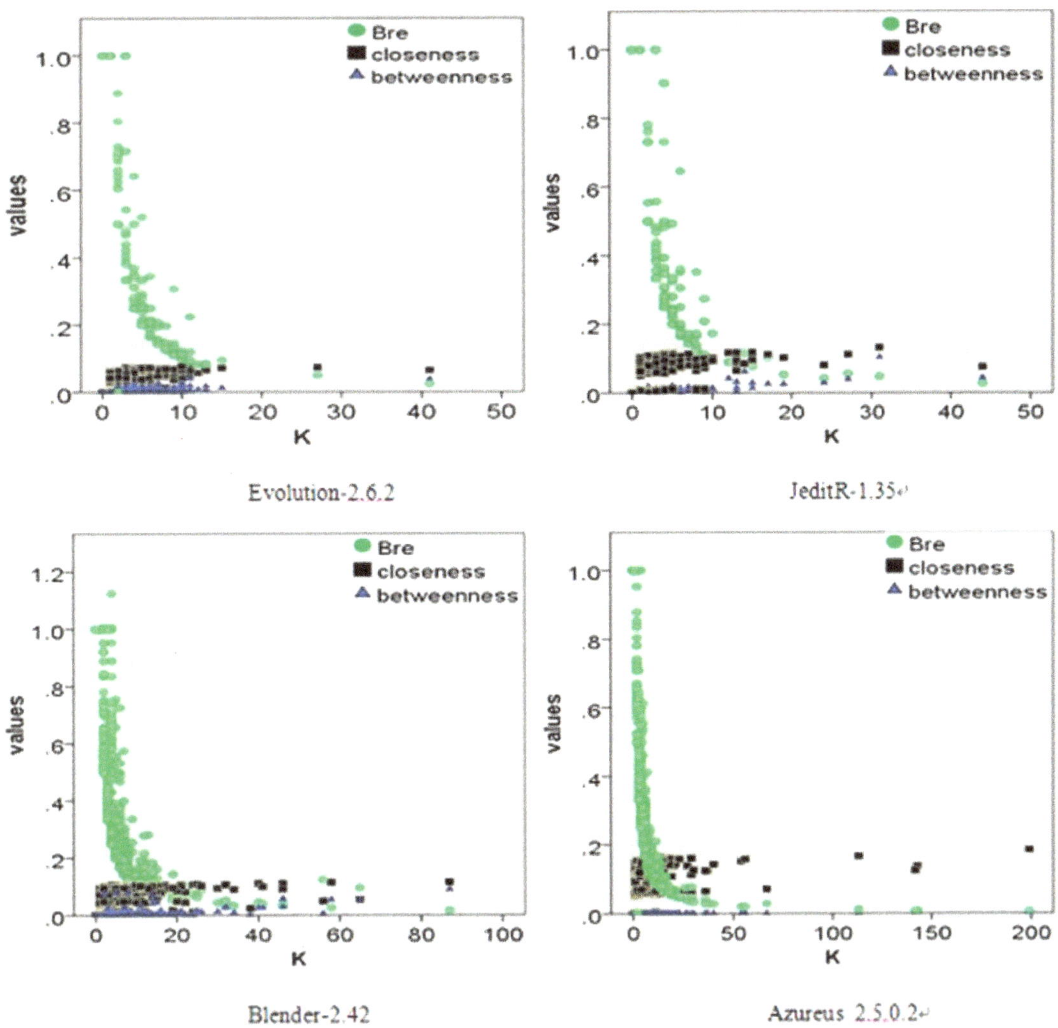

Figure 5. The correlations between the metric model *Bre* **values, closeness,** betweenness and the degree K. The corresponding data obtained from Evolution-2.6.2 (N=1445, M=1129), JeditR-1.35 (N=822, M=718), Blender-2.42 (N=2426, M=2848) and Azureus_2.5.0.2 (N=2375, M=3278), which are well-known software packages. The data points (•,▪,▴) represent measurements of the three metric models.

Typically, centrality (closeness or betweenness) has a significant correlation with the degree; nevertheless, it can be seen in Fig. 5 that the closeness or betweenness increases but is less pronounced as the degree *K* increases, and the centrality of a node does not significantly depend on its degree. Specially, it is determined that *Bre* values are logarithmic with the degrees, and it indicates that the node plays a less important connectivity role with increasing degree. Meanwhile, there are more edges between the neighbors of the corresponding node. The correlation contributes more to an accurate understanding of the module for software engineering practices. If there are some reusable modules in a software system, they will obey the engineering principle where if the reusable rate is high. The corresponding module is often redesigned as several additional modules, the neighbors often use or rely on more than one modules, and hence making the neighbors more "close".

The *Bre* values have a close relation with the edges between their neighbors; therefore, there is most likely a correlation between them and another metric model called Clustering Coefficients (*CC*2) [34], which also depends on the edges. $CC2 = \frac{E(G_1(v))}{E(G_2(v))}$, where $E(G_k(v))$ is the number of edges among nodes in the k-neighborhood of node $v(k=1,2)$. As seen in Fig.6, there is an approximately linear correlation between CC2 and *Bre*. The correlation indicates that increased use between parts of neighbors (k=1,2) will inevitably lead to a decrease of the connectivity of the corresponding module. Because of the scale-free characteristic ($P(K) \sim K^{\lambda}$) mentioned above, it is clear that $P(Bre)$ is not proportional to Bre^{λ}, which represents the difference between *Bre* and *K* from another point of view. The *Bre* distribution certainly does not reflect the scale-free [26] nature of the software system, which is shown in Fig. 7.

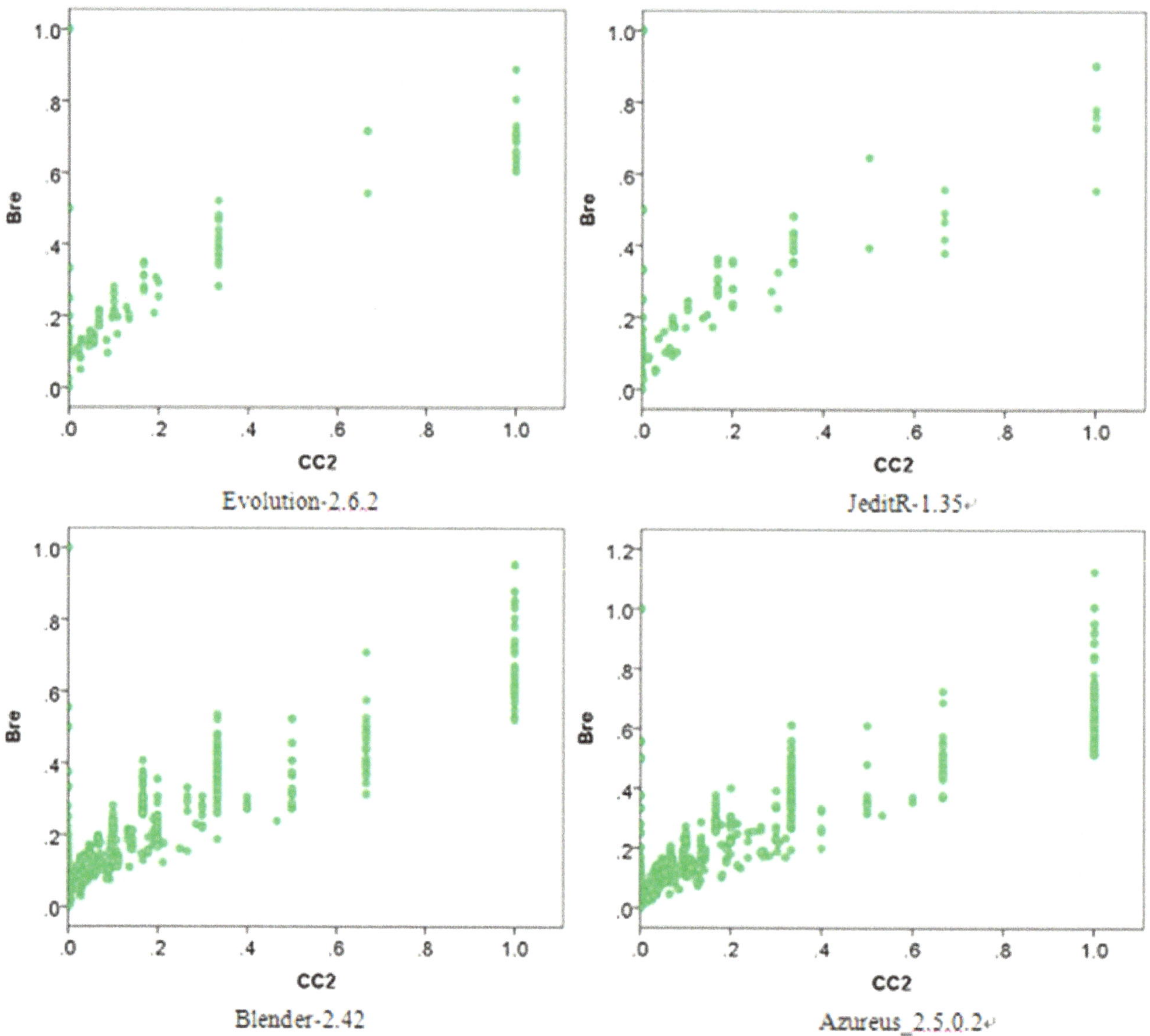

Figure 6. The correlations between the *CC*2 and *Bre* **values.** The corresponding data are also obtained from Evolution-2.6.2, JeditR-1.35, Blender-2.42 and Azureus_2.5.0.2. The data points • represent measurements of the *Bre* models.

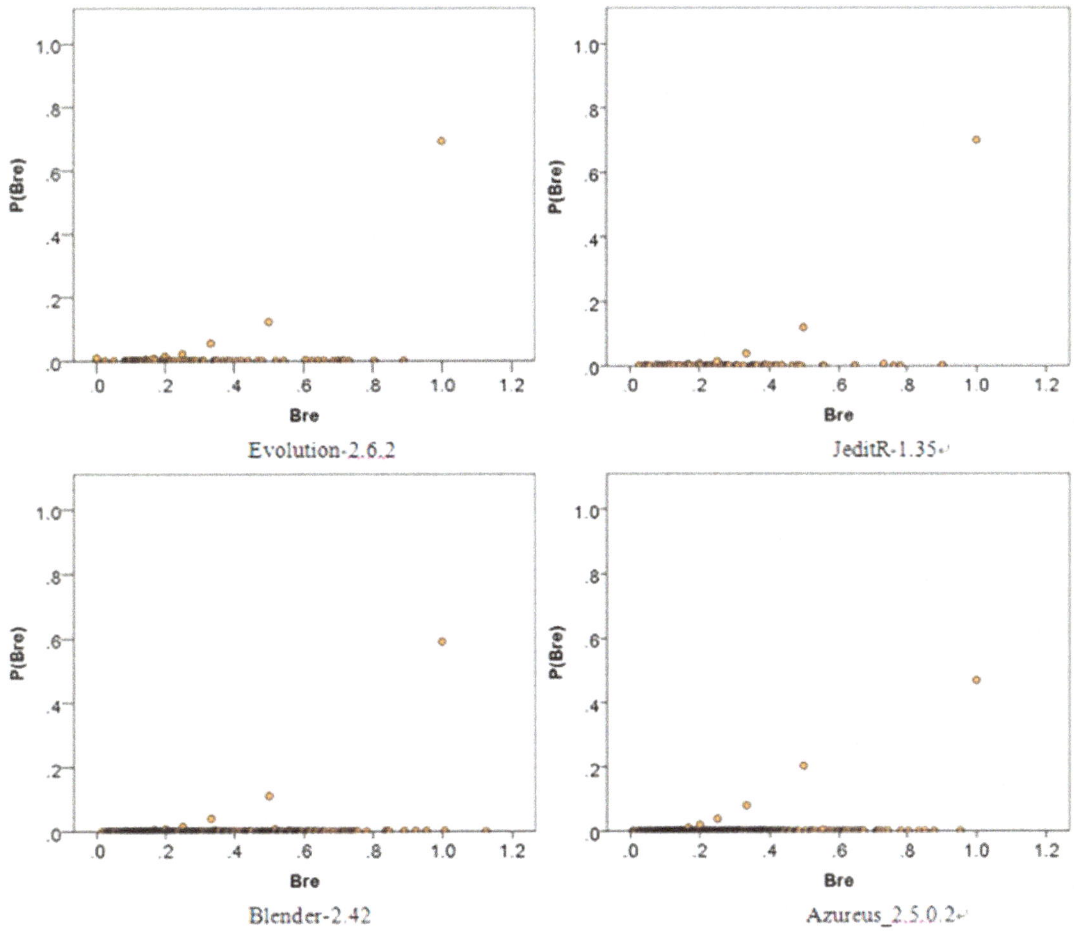

Figure 7. The distributions of the *Bre* **values.** The data points • represent $P(Bre)$. The distribution can be plotted with two branches, one of which seems to be most likely proportional to Bre but with few data points; therefore, there is no correlation between Bre and $P(Bre)$.

To verify the validity of the metric model proposed in this paper for software engineering practices, a hydropower simulation system [34] is taken as an example. The architecture and corresponding networks are shown in Fig. 8. It is developed by Embedded Technology Lab in Northeastern for the Fengman station, which was the earliest established large hydropower station. The software has access to two national software copyright studies (No. 0009448 and No. 050963) and has been working for more than ten years. The metric model in this paper is used for fault detection in developing version 2.0 software. First, modules are sorted based on the Bre values, subsequently, source codes of the modules that have lower values and are not isolated are analyzed. The studies determined that there are fault-pronesses [37] in four modules (the XJ, RD, LP and VoltCurr modules), which lead to overall instability. These modules are basic control units and plays significant bridge roles in the system because other modules inherit or use them. The studies facilitated redesigns to reduce the fault-proness and enhance stability.

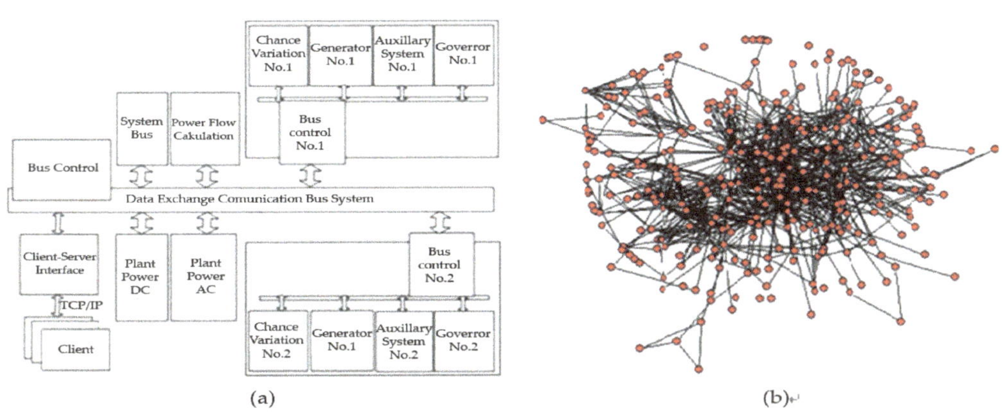

Figure 8. Architecture and network of the hydropower simulation system. (a) Architecture. (b) Network (N=310, M=850). The software system is developed by Embedded Technology Key Lab in Northeastern University (www.netology.cn) for the Fengman hydropower station in China.

CONCLUSIONS

The contribution of this paper is the proposed bridge role metric model. Because of the different connectivity role of a node in a software network, we use the *Bre* metric model instead of the previous two metric models: betweenness and closeness. After providing a definition, the range of the metric value was discussed. The metric model's function is illustrated with different cases as well as theoretically. Comparisons are also carried out, and the analysis indicates that the model can reflect the connectivity more effectively. Furthermore, it is determined that *Bre* values are logarithmic with the degrees and are proportional to another metric model-Clustering Coefficients-CC2, which indicates that the node plays a less important connectivity role as the degree increases. Nevertheless, $P(Bre)$ is not proportional to Bre^{λ}. To verify the validity of the model in software engineering practice, a hydropower simulation system is taken as an example to detect the fault-proness in modules.

However, we still require further work to improve the application of the model in software structure designs. Most likely, we can detect fault-proness through a combination of this model and others (*K*, closeness, etc.). Second, it also required some other proof, we will use some software engineering metrics such as coupling, Cohesion to support the solution proposed. Additionally, further investigations to extend the metric model to macro- and micro-structure should be carried out to emphasize estimating the role of a node in the entire software network more effectively.

The work in this paper could facilitate a better understanding of the role of modules in systems. Actually, because local instability most likely leads to global failures, the structure is very important for designers to predict the fault-proneness of a module. The metric can help us to redesign the structure of software, improve the quality of software, and subsequently shorten the development life cycle.

Supporting Information

Number	Software	Number of Nodes	Number of edges	Average Degree	Average Core	Average Shortest Path
1	amarok-1.4.1-beta1	645	665	1.3008	1.3008	3.0437
2	aMule-2.1.3	639	684	1.3177	1.3177	2.9336
3	anjuta-2.1.0	756	557	0.9272	0.9272	2.0268
4	apache-tomcat-6.0.18	1522	2140	1.6117	1.6117	2.3300
5	abiword2.2.7	2002	2978	1.2944	1.2944	1.8700
6	asterisk-1.2.9.1	465	522	1.5333	1.5333	6.6740
7	audacious-1.1.1	597	409	0.8610	0.8610	2.1126
8	Azureus_2.5.0.2	2375	3278	1.5996	1.5996	2.1924
9	beagle-2.2.0	220	288	1.4091	1.4091	2.1043
10	bibletime-1.6	159	162	1.2201	1.2201	1.5856
11	binutils-2.17.50.0.16	1583	1763	1.4327	1.4327	2.4500
12	blender-2.42	2426	2848	1.4110	1.4110	6.5993
13	cglib-src-2.0.2	1300	239	1.7931	1.7931	1.8833
14	cinelerra-cvs-20060619	2506	6391	2.7654	2.7654	5.7575
15	clucene-core-0.9.23.0-Source	320	353	1.2906	1.2906	2.6967
16	cmake-2.4.6	484	424	1.0186	1.0186	3.5686
17	coda-6.0.14	440	547	1.4614	1.4614	2.3413
18	dasher-4.0.4	213	302	1.6808	1.6808	2.6660
19	dia0.95R	459	679	1.6275	1.6275	2.7254
20	dovecot-1.0.rc5	371	729	2.3693	2.3693	3.7233
21	dxr3player-0.10	297	418	1.7172	1.7172	4.4831
22	eclipse3.1.1	14739	27576	2.0742	2.0742	1.3175
23	electric-7.00	1445	1129	2.3350	2.3350	3.9168
24	eMule0.49b	627	580	1.1053	1.1053	2.9168
25	epiphany-2.14.2.1	320	213	0.8469	0.8469	2.6902
26	f-spot-0.1.11	517	537	1.2302	1.2302	1.8813
27	fastdb-2.92IDE	200	294	1.8000	1.8000	1.3836
28	ffmpeg-0.4.9-p20060302	370	428	1.3649	1.3649	1.9929

29	fontforge-20060703IDE	522	1013	2.3640	2.3640	2.3364
30	freemind0.4	133	102	0.9023	0.9023	2.9350
31	freeradius-1.1.0	170	118	1.0235	1.0235	1.7317
32	freetype-2.1.10	329	374	1.3891	1.3891	2.9614
33	gaim-2.0.0beta3	490	379	0.9796	0.9796	0.4138
34	ganglia-3.0.2	150	156	1.3533	1.3533	2.5385
35	gedit-2.14.3	206	97	0.6311	0.6311	2.2489
36	ghc-6.4.2	133	155	1.5188	1.5188	2.1049
37	glib-2.16.5	474	391	1.0295	1.0295	1.2792
38	glibc-2.3.6	961	609	0.8606	0.8606	2.6936
39	gnokii-0.6.12	193	129	0.8394	0.8394	1.8929
40	gnome-media-2.14.2	117	69	0.7863	0.7863	1.6715
41	gnusound-0.7	100	96	1.1300	1.1300	3.3346
42	gnustep-gui-0.10.3	543	666	1.3407	1.3407	1.4575
43	gossip-0.14	159	100	0.7673	0.7673	1.4257
44	graphviz2.6R	438	521	1.4703	1.4703	2.2188
45	httpd-2.2.0	493	627	1.5801	1.5801	3.1369
46	j2sdk-1.4.2	16039	26369	1.8610	1.8610	4.7816
47	jakarta-tomcat-5.0.29	1452	1731	1.3643	1.3643	2.8701
48	jdk-1.5.0	19173	30396	1.8060	1.8060	4.7037
49	jEditR1.35	822	718	1.0438	1.0438	3.0334
50	kaffe-1.1.7	7849	12120	1.7546	1.7546	3.2603
51	kdeartwork-3.5.4	162	105	0.8827	0.8827	1.5756
52	kdebase-3.5.3	1677	1779	1.2701	1.2701	2.3612
53	kdebindings-3.5.4	2564	1811	1.4126	1.4126	3.6102
54	kdeedu-3.5.4	1010	1031	2.0416	2.0416	1.9030
55	kdegraphics-3.5.3	2014	3349	3.3257	3.3257	3.0623
56	kdemultimedia-3.5.3	1129	1077	1.9079	1.9079	2.5487
57	kdepim-3.5.3	3518	4074	2.3161	2.3161	2.7708
58	kdesdk-3.5.4	819	1063	1.5360	1.5360	2.1877
59	kdeutils-3.5.4	705	609	1.0695	1.0695	2.3159
60	kdevelop-3.4.0	1453	1434	1.1796	1.1796	3.0404
61	kicad-20060626 IDE	212	300	1.6462	1.6462	1.3020
62	kmplayer-0.9.2	203	284	1.5616	1.5616	3.5389
63	koffice-1.5.0	4580	5892	1.4915	1.4915	2.3534
64	kopete-0.12.1	1512	2009	1.5972	1.5972	1.0418
65	linux1.2.13	552	347	0.8170	0.8170	2.1574
66	maildrop-2.0.2	107	96	1.3084	1.3084	1.7100
67	mozilla3.0.11	8354	13878	1.8816	1.8816	3.0733
68	mplayer-20070814	1493	1209	1.0101	1.0101	2.0288
69	mysql-5.0.56	3132	3837	1.3956	1.3956	6.0744
70	octave2.1.73R	305	364	1.4328	1.4328	2.9059
71	ooh323c-0.8.4	773	1381	2.0129	2.0129	3.5951
72	OpenIPMI-1.4.14	379	543	1.6306	1.6306	3.9670
73	openldap-2.2.30	276	384	1.7428	1.7428	1.5290
74	openswan-2.4.5	368	364	1.2880	1.2880	2.7803
75	p7zip_4.42	531	777	1.6252	1.6252	2.1874
76	paludis-0.24.6	1093	1034	1.0393	1.0393	2.2613
77	pingus0.7.2	450	683	1.7800	1.7800	1.9765

78	pl-5.6.60	791	746	1.2111	1.2111	2.1624
79	postfix-2.5.5	190	213	1.3263	1.3263	1.6163
80	qcad-2.0.4.0-1	312	460	1.7019	1.7019	1.8086
81	qemu-0.8.1	357	237	0.9048	0.9048	1.6773
82	qtiplot-0.8.2	166	152	1.1265	1.1265	2.8714
83	resin-3.0.22	5076	7873	1.7650	1.7650	2.5690
84	rhythmbox-0.9.6	366	342	1.0820	1.0820	2.7084
85	rpm-4.4.1	1260	1294	1.2365	1.2365	3.3682
86	scim-1.4.7	277	254	1.2058	1.2058	1.8700
87	Silver.1.6	346	369	1.3671	1.3671	5.5000
88	sim-0.9.4	786	960	1.3741	1.3741	3.0026
89	strongswan-2.6.4	312	265	1.1346	1.1346	2.8284
90	subversion-1.5.6	1116	788	0.8405	0.8405	2.3000
91	synaptics-0.14.4	208	119	0.7308	0.7308	2.2139
92	tk8.4.13	363	491	1.7190	1.7190	2.8085
93	ups-3.38	246	212	1.2561	1.2561	2.3201
94	vlc-0.8.5	1250	1535	1.4288	1.4288	1.9815
95	waimea-0.5.0	116	193	1.9483	1.9483	3.7262
96	wine-1.1.5	7943	7606	1.0909	1.0909	2.6754
97	xen-3.0.2	1354	931	0.8516	0.8516	2.9500
98	xorg-server-1.1.1	1113	1183	1.3738	1.3738	1.5522
99	yasm-0.5.0rc1	150	191	1.5000	1.5000	2.9407
100	ZODB3-3.9.0a12	549	333	0.7942	0.7942	3.6561

Appendix S1. Appendix to the manuscript.

ACKNOWLEDGMENTS

The authors gratefully acknowledge the helpful comments and suggestions of the reviewers, which have improved the presentation.

AUTHOR CONTRIBUTIONS

Conceived and designed the experiments: BL YF SG DL. Performed the experiments: BL YF SG DL. Analyzed the data: BL YF SG DL. Contributed reagents/materials/analysis tools: BL YF SG DL. Wrote the paper: BL YF SG DL.

REFERENCES

1. Briand LC, Morasca S, Basili VR (1996) Property Based Software Engineering Measurement. IEEE Transaction on Software Engineering 22(1): 68–86. doi: 10. 1109/32. 481535
2. Furey S (1997) Why we should use function points. IEEE Software 14(2): 28–30. doi: 10. 1109/52. 582971
3. Arnold M, Pedross P (1998) Software Size Measurement and Productivity Rating in a Large-Scale Software Development Department. In: Proceedings of 1998 International Conference on Software Engineering[C] Kyoto: 503–506.
4. Bauer M (1999) Analysing Software Systems by Using Combinations of Metrics. In: Proceedings of ECOOP'99 Workshops[C] Lisbon: 170–171.
5. Kpodjedo S, Ricca F, Antoniol G, Galinier P (2009) Evolution and Search Based Metrics to Improve Defects Prediction. In: Proceedings of the1st International Symposium on Search Based Software Engineering, Windsor, UK: 23–32.
6. Fenton NE, Neil M (2000) Software metrics: successes, failures and new directions. Journal of Systems and Software 47(23): 149–157. doi: 10. 1016/s0164-1212(99)00035-7
7. Mens T, Demeyer S (2001) Future trends in software evolution metrics. In: Proceedings of 4th International Workshop on Principles of Software Evolution, Austria: 83–86.
8. Fenton NE, Krause P, Neil M (2002) Software Measurement: Uncertainty and Causal Modeling. IEEE Software 19(4): 116–122. doi: 10. 1109/ms. 2002. 1020298
9. Valverdes, Cancho RF, Sole RV (2002) Seale free networks from optimal design. Europhysics Letter 60: 512–517. doi: 10. 1209/epl/i2002-00248-2
10. Myers CR (2003) Software systems as complex networks: Structure, function, and evolvability of software collaboration graphs. Physics Review E 68: 1–15. doi: 10. 1103/physreve. 68. 046116
11. Valverdes S, Sole R (2003) Hierarchical small worlds, in software architecture. Working Paper of Santa Fe-institute, SFI/030744.
12. De Moura APS, Lai YC, Motter AE (2003) Signatures of small-world and scale-free properties in large computer

programs. Physical Review E 68: 017102. doi: 10. 1103/ physreve. 68. 017102

13. Barabási AL, Albert R (1999) Emergence of scaling in random networks. Science 286: 509–512. doi: 10. 1126/ science. 286. 5439. 509
14. Wen L, Dromey G, Kirk D (2009) Software engineering and scale-free networks. IEEE Transactions on Systems, Man, and Cybernatics PartB: Cybernatics 39(4): 845–854. doi: 10. 1109/tsmcb. 2009. 2020206
15. Concas G, Marchesi M, Pinna S, Serra N (2007) Power-laws in a large object-oriented software system. IEEE Transactions on Software Engineering 33(10): 687–708. doi: 10. 1109/tse. 2007. 1019
16. Clauset A, Shalizi CR, Newman ME (2009) Power-law distributions in empirical data. SIAM Review 51(4): 661–703. doi: 10. 1137/070710111
17. Ma YT, He KQ, Li B, Liu J, Zhou XY (2010) A Hybrid Set of Complexity Metrics for Large-Scale Object-Oriented Software Systems. Journal of Computer Science and Technology 25(6): 1184–1201. doi: 10. 1007/s11390-010-9398-x
18. Potanin A, Noble J, Frean M, Biddle R (2005) Scale-free geometry in OO programs. Communications of the ACM-Adaptive complex enterprises 48(5): 99–103. doi: 10. 1145/1060710. 1060716
19. Liu J, He KQ, Ma YT, Peng R (2006) Scale free in software metrics. In: Proceedings of 30th Annual International Computer Software and Applications Conference pp. 229–235.
20. Subelj S, Bajec M (2011) Community structure of complex software systems: analysis and applications. Physica A 390(16): 2968–2975. doi: 10. 1016/j. physa. 2011. 03. 036
21. Jenkins S, Kirk SR (2007) Software architecture graphs as complex networks: a novel partitioning scheme to measure stability and evolution. Information Sciences 177(12): 2587–2601.
22. Li B, Pan WF, Lu JH (2011) Multi-granularity dynamic analysis of complex software networks. in: Proceeding of IEEE International Symposium on Circuits and Systems pp. 2119–2124.
23. Pan WF, Li B, Ma YT, Qin YY, Zhou XY (2010) Measuring structural quality of object-oriented softwares via bug propagation analysis on weighted software networks. Journal of Computer Science and Technology 25(6): 1202–1213. doi: 10. 1007/s11390-010-9399-9
24. Roach C, Menezes R (2011) Using networks to understand the dynamics of software development. Communications in Computer and Information Science 116(2): 119–129. doi: 10. 1007/978-3-642-25501-4_12
25. Dabrowski R, Stencel K, Timoszuk G (2011) Software is a directed multi-graph. In: Proceedings of the 5th European conference on Software architecture pp. 360–369.
26. Zhang HH, Zhao H, Cai W, Zhao M (2008) Visualization and cognition of large-scale software structure using the k-core analysis. In: Proceedings of the 2008 International Conference on Intelligent Information Hidingand Multimedia Signal Processing, pp. 954–957.
27. Wang W, Zhao H, Li H, Zhang J, Li P, et al. (2010) Research on LFS Algorithm in Software Network. Journal of Software Engineering and Applications 3(2): 185–189. doi: 10. 4236/jsea. 2010. 32023
28. Wang W, Zhao H, Li H, Li P, Yao D, et al. (2010) Application of Design Patterns in Process of Large-scale Software Evolving. Journal of Software Engineering and Applications 3(1): 58–64. doi: 10. 4236/jsea. 2010. 31007
29. Concas G, Locci MF, Marchesi M, Pinna S, Turnu L (2006) Fractal Dimension in Software Networks. Europhysics Letters 76(6): 1221–1227. doi: 10. 1209/ epl/i2006-10384-1
30. Lancichinetti A, Kivelä M, Saramäki J, Fortunato S (2010) Characterizing the Community Structure of Complex Networks. PloS ONE 5(8): e11976. doi: 10. 1371/journal. pone. 0011976
31. Liu J, He KQ, Ma YT, Peng R (2006) Scale Free in Software Metrics. In: Proceedings of the 30th Annual International Computer Software and Applications Conference (1): 229–235.
32. Liu J, He KQ, Peng R, Ma YT (2006) A Study on the Weight and Topology Correlation of Object Oriented Software Coupling Network, In: Proceedings of the 1st International Conference on Complex Systems and Applications pp. 955–959.
33. Ma YT, He KQ, Liu J, Yan YL (2005) A Complexity Metrics Set for Large-scale Object-Oriented Software Systems. In: Proceedings of the 6th International Conference on Computer and Information Technology pp. 189.
34. Cai W, Zhao H, Zhang HH (2007) Static Structural Complexity Metrics for Large-scale Software. Special Issue on Software Engineering and Complex Networks of Dynamics of Continuous, Discrete and Impulsive Systems Series B 14(S6): 12–17.
35. Newman ME (2004) Detecting community structure in networks. Euro. Phys. J. B 38(2): 321–330. doi: 10. 1140/epjb/e2004-00124-y
36. Peng L (2011) Research on Structure Characteristics and Information Metabolism of Software Network. Shen Yang: Northeastern University. 344 p.
37. Huang P, Zhu J (2008) Predicting the fault-proneness of class hierarchy in object-oriented software using a layered kernel. Journal of Zhejiang University 9(10): 1390–1397. doi: 10. 1631/jzus. a0720073

CHAPTER 2

EVALUATING CHARACTERISTICS OF DE NOVO ASSEMBLY SOFTWARE ON 454 TRANSCRIPTOME DATA: A SIMULATION APPROACH

Marvin Mundry[1], Erich Bornberg-Bauer[1], Michael Sammeth[2], Philine G. D. Feulner[1]

[1] Evolutionary Bioinformatics, Institute for Evolution and Biodiversity, Westfaelische-Wilhelms-University, Muenster, Germany

[2] Functional Bioinformatics, Centre Nacional d'Ana`lisi Geno`mica (CNAG), Barcelona, Spain

ABSTRACT

Background

The quantity of transcriptome data is rapidly increasing for non-model organisms. As sequencing technology advances, focus shifts towards solving bioinformatic challenges, of which sequence read assembly is the first task. Recent studies have compared the performance of different software to establish a best practice for transcriptome assembly. Here, we adapted a simulation approach to evaluate specific features of assembly programs on 454 data. The novelty of our study is that the simulation allows us to calculate a model assembly as reference point for comparison.

Findings

The simulation approach allows us to compare basic metrics of assemblies computed by different software applications (CAP3, MIRA, Newbler, and Oases) to a known optimal solution. We found MIRA and CAP3 are conservative in merging reads. This resulted in comparably high number of short contigs. In contrast, Newbler more readily merged reads into longer contigs, while Oases produced the overall shortest assembly. Due to the simulation approach, reads could be traced back to their correct placement within the transcriptome. Together with mapping reads onto the assembled contigs, we were able to evaluate ambiguity in the assemblies. This analysis further supported the conservative nature of MIRA and CAP3, which resulted in low proportions of chimeric contigs, but high redundancy. Newbler produced less redundancy, but the proportion of chimeric contigs was higher.

Conclusion

Our evaluation of four assemblers suggested that MIRA and Newbler slightly outperformed the other programs, while showing contrasting characteristics. Oases did not perform very well on the 454 reads. Our evaluation indicated that the

Citation: Mundry M, Bornberg-Bauer E, Sammeth M, Feulner PGD (2012) Evaluating Characteristics of De Novo Assembly Software on 454 Transcriptome Data: A Simulation Approach. PLoS ONE 7(2): e31410. doi:10.1371/journal.pone.0031410.

software was either conservative (MIRA) or liberal (Newbler) about merging reads into contigs. This suggested that in choosing an assembly program researchers should carefully consider their follow up analysis and consequences of the chosen approach to gain an assembly.

INTRODUCTION

454 transcriptome sequencing is widely used as a cost effective sequencing method, especially for non-model organisms [1]–[31]. Concentrating the sequencing effort on the expressed part of the genome not only saves costs, it allows analysis of the expressed part of the genome, which is not easily predicted from the genome sequence alone. Splice patterns, versatile combinations of exons, can be identified, and gene expression rates can be estimated and compared. In addition, single nucleotide polymorphisms (SNPs) and simple sequence repeats (SSRs) within the coding part of the genome can be determined.

Most analyses that utilise transcriptome data require assembled reads. With next generation sequencing (NGS), DNA molecules are fragmented, size-selected, amplified, and high-throughput sequenced resulting in reads of a length which is specific for the respective NGS technology. This fragmentation procedure is reversed *in silico* by merging overlapping reads into contigs during the assembly process. The study presented here focuses on the performance of software for *de novo* assembly of cDNA reads generated by 454 sequencing. In studies lacking a sequenced genome, it is not possible to assemble the reads by mapping them onto a reference genome. Instead all reads have to be aligned against each other, i.e. *de novo* assembled. Despite the higher costs compared to other NGS technologies, 454 is still widely used because of the long reads it produces, facilitating read alignment during the *de novo* assembly. Other sequencing technologies, such as Illumina, are constantly increasing their read length and supersede 454 especially in terms of throughput and per base pair costs. In addition, new technologies being developed for example the semiconductor technology of Ion Torrent. Therefore, the assembly of around 200 bp long reads, as evaluated in the study presented here, likely will persist as a bioinformatics challenge.

For the *de novo* assembly of 454 transcriptomic reads the following assemblers are most widely used: CAP3 [32] (TGICL [33], wrapper for CAP3), MIRA [34] (est2assembly [35], wrapper for MIRA), Newbler [36], Seqman NGen© , CLC bio©, and the web application EGassembler [37] (see Table 1). Not all of these assemblers are specifically intended for transcriptome data. In contrast to a genome consisting of few long continuous stretches (linkage groups or chromosomes), the transcriptome is comprised of many transcripts that are variable in length. The complexity of assembling a transcriptome is further exacerbated by varying expression levels, resulting in an uneven distribution of reads amongst the diverse transcripts. Even if experimental cDNA normalization aims to reduce the dynamic range of expression it usually does not result in an even distribution of transcripts [8]. In addition, alternative splicing results in multiple isoforms, which share partial sequence information [38].

Table 1. Assembler software recently used for *de novo* **assembly of 454** transcriptome data.[§]

Assembler	Organism
CAP3 [31]	*Amaranthus tuberculatus* [2]; *Conyza canadensis* [3]; *Momordica charantia* [4]; *Oncopeltus fasciatus* [5]; *Oryza longistaminata* [6]; *Papaver somniferum*[*] [7]; *Pisum sativum*[*] [8]; *Pteridium aquilinum* [9]; *Trichostrongylus colubriformis* [10];
MIRA [33]	*Anguilla anguilla* [11]; *Bathymodiolus azoricus* [12]; *Cochliomyia hominivorax* [13]; *Cucurbita pepo* [14]; *Fagopyrum esculentum* and *F. tataricum* [15]; *Pisum sativum* [8]; *Pteridium aquilinum* [9]; *Schmidtea mediterranea* [16]; *Thamnophis elegans* [17]; *Trialeurodes vaporariorum*[*] [18];
Newbler [35]	*Agrilus planipennis* [19]; *Cajanus cajan* [20]; *Cimex lectularius* [21]; *Euphausia superba* [22]; *Oncopeltus fasciatus* [5]; *Paulinella chromatophora* [23]; *Phytoseiulus persimilis* [24]; *Teladorsagia circumcincta* [25]; *Thamnophis elegans* [17]; *Vigna radiata* [26];
Seqman NGen ©	*Crotalus adamanteus* [27]; *Littorina saxatilis* [28]; *Oncorhynchus mykiss* [29];
CLC bio ©	*Coregonus clupeaformis* [30]; *Tigriopus californicus* [31];
EGassembler [36]	*Amaranthus tuberculatus* [2]; *Conyza canadensis* [3];

*Utilising a wrapper TGICL [33] or est2assmbly [35].
§For more studies refer to Table 1 in [1].
doi:10.1371/journal.pone.0031410.t001

These intrinsic features of the transcriptome pose special challenges for any assembly software. A recent study by Kumar and Blaxter compared transcriptome assemblers by analysing 454 cDNA reads from *Litomosoides sigmodontis*, a nematode, and evaluated the resulting contigs [1]. The quality of read assemblies were assessed for basic assembly metrics, such as various measurements of bases used, contig number, and length. In addition, contigs were compared with previously existing sequence databases. Besides presenting a very comprehensive evaluation of different software solutions, some aspects have not been addressed exhaustively: (1) The analysis of basic assembly metrics usually suffers from the fact that optimal values are not known when only using real data. Although it may seem tempting to simply assume that longer contigs represent a better assembly, this might not necessarily be the case, e.g. if reads of different transcripts are concatenated. (2) The comparison of assemblies with pre-existing sets of reference sequences from other organisms might be misleading. The best performing assembler does not necessarily always match well with reference sequences, even when these references originate from the same species because the transcriptome varies depending on tissue, time point, and abiotic factors [39]–[42]. (3) Due to some sequence similarity between transcripts, reads originating from different transcripts can be merged into one contig during the assembly process. Without knowledge of the origin of reads, it is difficult to determine the extend to which an assembler produces chimeric contigs, i.e. contigs containing reads from different transcripts.

We used a novel approach to assess the performance of assembler software. By applying a simulation approach we circumvent some of the problems mentioned above. Given a transcriptome, the simulator carried out *in silico* gene expression, reverse transcription, fragmentation and 454 sequencing. In contrast to real 454 reads, the exact origin of each simulated read was known. Utilising this information it was possible to merge reads with a minimum of one base pair overlap, independent of sequence information. This way, we knew an ideal solution (Model Assembly MA), which was assigning all reads to their original transcripts while merging reads as efficiently as possible with the given amounts of data (one single 454 plate). Therefore the MA was the optimal solution of the assembly problem given the data. The same simulated reads were assembled using assembly software which operated on sequence information only. The resulting assemblies could be compared to the MA. The MA provided reference values for basic assembly metrics, such as contig count and contig length. Additionally, the MA could be used as a reference data set against which to compare the output contigs of the assemblers to determine specificity and sensitivity measurements. Assessing the amount of reads aligning back to multiple contigs identified alignment ambiguity and redundancy in the assemblies. As we knew from which transcript each simulated read originates, it was, in addition, possible to identify reads of different origin joined to form one chimeric contig and quantify the extent of chimera formation in the different assemblies.

In our study we created simulated reads based on a description of the human transcriptome (GRCh37.58). The human data set was chosen due to the comprehensive amount of data available and the complexity and size of the transcriptome. In addition, we used real 454 reads from a human tissue pool in order to compare the simulation approach with a realistic experimental setup. The assemblers tested in this study are CAP3 [32], MIRA [34], Newbler[36], and Oases [43]. These assemblers had been chosen as they are frequently used in non-model organism transcriptome studies and are freely distributed stand-alone applications (see Table 1). Although Oases is primarily designed for shorter Illumina reads, it was included in this study because it is specifically designed for transcriptome data.

RESULTS

The Simulated and Real Data Set

The simulation produced 3'340'245 cDNA fragments (for details see Material and Methods). We randomly discarded all but 800'000 fragments to match the amount of a "typical" single 454 sequencing run. Gene expression, reverse transcription, fragmentation, and 454 sequencing was simulated based on a human transcriptome annotation [44] in the following manner: the cell profiles are randomly assigned according to a modified Zipf's law as observed universally in RNA expression interrogations [45]. Subsequently, in silico expressed transcript molecules have been subjected to reverse transcription to recast 5′ to 3′-representation biases in libraries that are reversely transcribed before fragmentation [46]. Then simulated fragmentation was carried out employing a mechanical model of molecule breakage [47]. Fragments obtained were sub-sampled in the sequencing process, additionally mimicking errors typical for the sequencing chemistry [36], [47]. The resulting simulated reads (800'000 reads of a mean read length ~220 bp) were assembled using four different *de novo* transcriptome assembly programs, namely CAP3, MIRA, Newbler, and Oases. For comparison a "real" 454 data set (NCBI Short Read Archive Accession: SRX002932) containing 823'575 sequences (454 FLX reads with an average length of 250 bp) was obtained and assembled using the same assembly programs. For the simulation approach we generated a Model Assembly (MA) based on the origin of each read. In the MA, reads were merged into contigs using position information if they overlapped by at least a single base pair. Figure 1 illustrates the workflow (light grey) with details on the data sets and comparisons (black) made to evaluate the assemblers. We utilised the MA ultimately as a reference point for the evaluation of transcriptome assemblers (Comparison 1 in Figure 1). The simulated reads were created from the transcriptome annotation, and after assembly, compared back to it (Comparison 2 in Figure 1). Finally, real reads from an independent experiment were also assembled and compared to the transcriptome annotation (Comparison 3 in Figure 1).

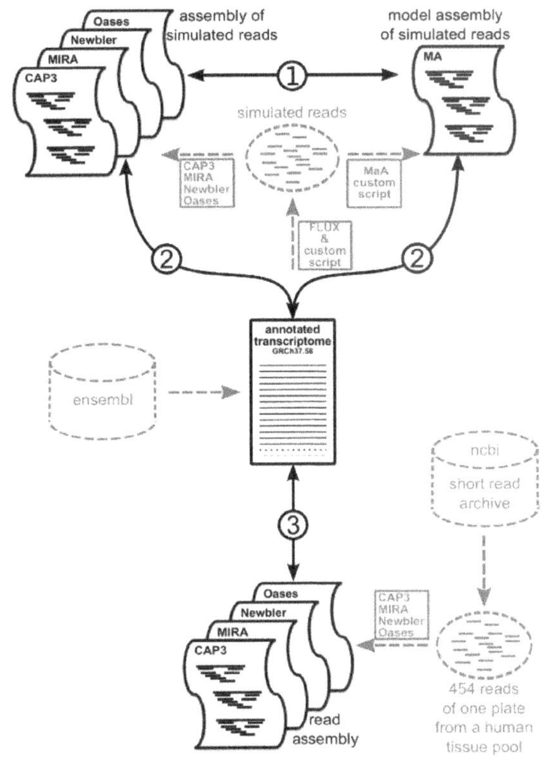

Figure 1. Workflow and comparison scheme for assembler evaluation. Workflows are shown in grey, comparisons between data sets in black. To evaluate the performance of different assemblers three comparisons were performed: 1) Different assemblies of simulated reads were compared to a Model Assembly (MA), which was based on positional information. 2) Different assemblies of simulated reads were compared to a transcriptome annotation. The MA was compared in the same way to provide reference values for the evaluated measurements. 3) Different assemblies of real reads were compared to the transcriptome annotation to compare the simulation approach to values from a real data set.

Basic Assembly Metrics

To allow comparisons between the assemblies of different assembly programs (run under default parameters for transcriptome assembly; details are given in Material and Methods), singletons and contigs shorter than 100 bp were discarded before subsequent analysis. Standard metrics describing the assembly, such as number of contigs, total bases used in the assembly, number of large contigs (>1 kbp), number of base pairs used in large contigs, maximal, average, and median contig length, and N50 value, were used to compare the assembly programs. The N50 value is defined as the contig length where half the assembly is represented by contigs of this size or longer. We included N50 values for comparison with other studies even if it is not strictly applicable for transcriptome assemblies [1].

The number of contigs produced by the algorithmically similar programs MIRA and CAP3 is about 4 times higher than the amount of contigs produced by Newbler and the algorithmically very different Oases. This was observed in the assemblies of the simulated data (Table 2) as well as of the real reads (Table 3). Newbler and Oases produced less contigs than were present in the MA, while MIRA and CAP3 produced more. Accordingly, comparing the amount of bases output into contigs by the assembly programs, MIRA and CAP3 assemblies added up about twice the number of base pairs compared to Newbler and Oases. This held for both simulated and real data sets. The number of contig bases output by CAP3 and MIRA was above but close to the amount of bases in the MA. Oases put out less than half the bases of the MA. Newbler produced on average longer contigs than other assemblers tested in this study (highest mean and median contig length), even though this did not amount to overall more base pairs. The mean and median contig length retrieved with MIRA, CAP3, and Oases were quite similar to the values of the MA. Figure 2 shows the distribution of contig lengths. CAP3 produced many short contigs and few long contigs. MIRA and both versions of Newbler produced more long contigs than CAP3, but MIRA also output a high amount of short contigs. CAP3 and Oases produced fewer long contigs, while MIRA and Newbler constructed almost as many long contigs as present in the MA. Newbler and Oases assemblies held fewer short contigs compared to the MA. Overall, the contig length comparison showed similar results for simulated and real read assemblies. Besides the current version of Newbler (2.3) we also tested a prerelease version (2.5p1 beta version as far as applicable, for details see Material and Methods), which performed very similar in all the analysis (results not shown). Wall-clock run times for each program varied between minutes to around a day on a 2.6 GHz AMD Opteron 2435 server with 16 GB RAM. At this magnitude the runtime is of less importance than the quality of an assembly, but might become relevant if one wants to explore the parameter space or analyse larger or multiple data sets [1].

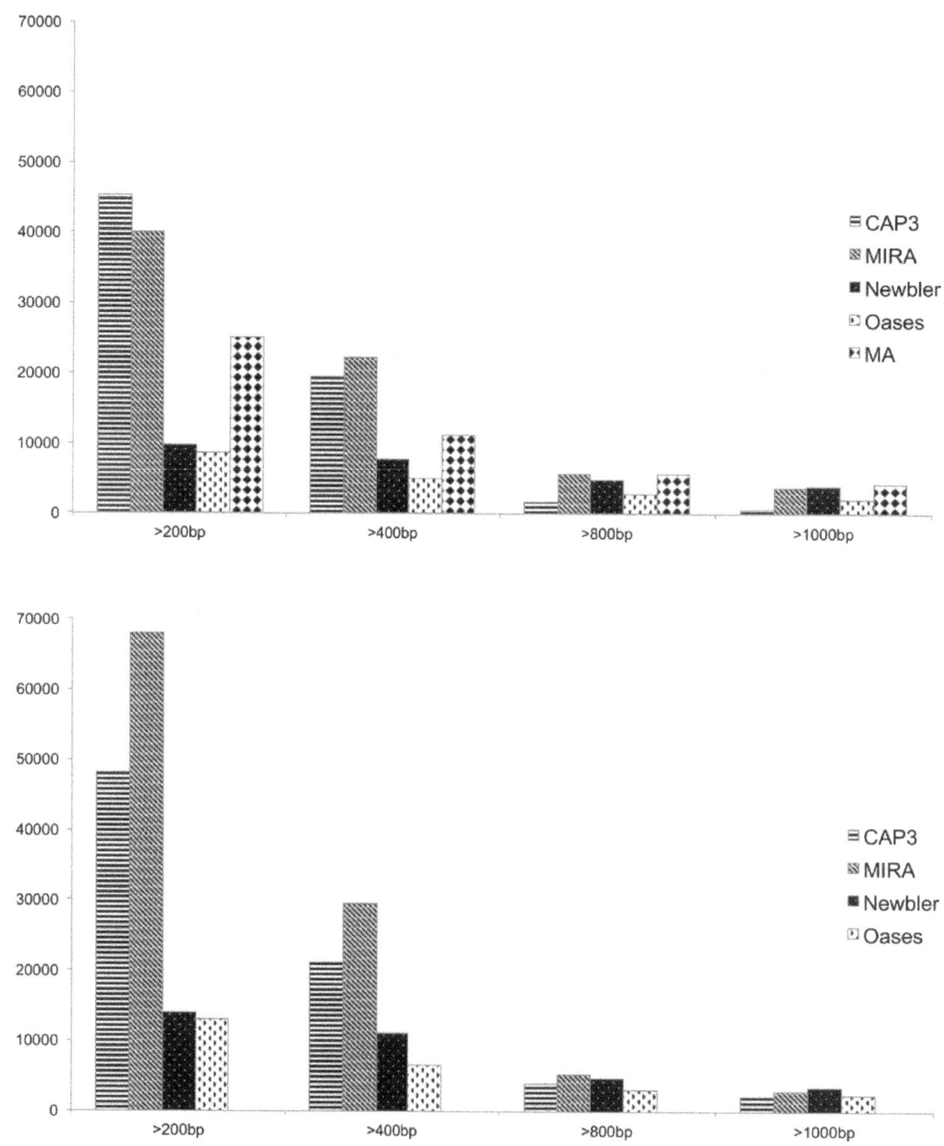

Figure 2. Cumulative contig lengths for different assemblies. Counts of contigs longer than 200, 400, 800, and 1000 base pairs for the different assemblies. Assemblies of simulated (top) and real 454 reads (bottom) are shown in separate diagrams.

Table 2. Basic assembly metrics (simulated 454 reads).

	CAP3	MIRA	Newbler	Oases	MA
Number of contigs*	45'422	40'129	9'774	11'355	24'993
Total bases*	19'147'862	22'855'498	12'764'265	7'937'884	18'152'459
Number of contigs (>=1 kbp)	606	3'683	3'938	2'138	4'337
Total bases (in contigs >=1 kbp)	779'806	6'626'729	9'614'255	4'686'216	9'935'980
Max contig length	13'981	17'958	17'915	17'906	17'958
Mean contig length	421	569	1'305	699	726
Median contig length	376	427	797	331	330
N50	425	602	2'128	1'351	1'214
Time taken	341 min	859 min	34 min	10 min**	N/A

*Only contigs >100 bp.
**Summed time for velveth, velvetg, and Oases.
doi:10.1371/journal.pone.0031410.t002

Table 3. Basic assembly metrics (real 454 reads).

	CAP3	MIRA	Newbler	Oases
Number of contigs*	50'381	76'126	14'633	16'862
Total bases	22'062'745	31'495'153	11'728'579	9'020'336
Number of contigs (>=1 kbp)	2'106	2'964	3'365	2'261
Total bases (in contigs >=1 kbp)	2'963'339	4'188'919	6'007'896	3'890'312
Max contig length	4'859	3'958	8'611	8'461
Mean contig length	437	413	801	534
Median contig length	364	337	565	300
N50	458	456	1'025	837
Time taken	1731 min	816 min	790 min	8 min**

*Only contigs >100 bp.
**Summed time for velveth, velvetg, and Oases.
doi:10.1371/journal.pone.0031410.t003

Assembly evaluation

Assemblers could also be evaluated on how well the respective assembly recaptures already known sequences. We compared the assemblies to the human transcriptome annotation from Ensembl. We aligned the assembled contigs to the transcriptome and vice versa, evaluating specificity and sensitivity of the comparison. Specificity was defined as the relative amount of contigs covering at least 80% of a respective transcript in the Ensembl annotation (BLAST e-value$<10^{-9}$ for details see Material and Methods). Specificity was high for all assemblies of the simulated reads, which were directly created out of the Ensembl transcriptome (91 to 95%; Table 4). Assuming that the Ensembl annotations were comprehensive, contigs not matching the transcriptome were either too short to cover at least 80% of a respective transcript or were potential misassembled contigs. The assemblies of real reads, which stem from RNA of different human cell lines, showed a lower and broader range of specificity (49 to 79%; Table 5). Amongst the real read assemblies Newbler and Oases scored highest, while MIRA produced the lowest amount of contigs that were contained in the transcriptome. Sensitivity was defined as the relative amount of Ensembl transcripts contained in the assemblies (for details see Material and Methods). For the assemblies of the simulated reads the sensitivity showed a broader range (2 to 13%;Table 4). This indicated performance differences between the assemblers. Newbler and MIRA were most sensitive, while CAP3 was least sensitive. The real read assemblies all showed a low sensitivity (6 to 8%; Table 5).

Table 4. Comparison between simulated 454 read assemblies and transcriptome.

	CAP3	MIRA	Newbler	Oases	MA
Specificity absolute	42'697/45'422	37'587/40'129	8'932/9'774	10'398/11'355	23'737/24'993
Specificity relative	94.00%	93.67%	91.39%	91.57%	94.97%
Sensitivity absolute	3'140/146'962	14'920/146'962	18'723/146'962	9'379/146'962	23'985/146'962
Sensitivity relative	2.14%	10.15%	12.74%	6.38%	16.32%

doi:10.1371/journal.pone.0031410.t004

Table 5. Comparison between real 454 read assemblies and transcriptome.

	CAP3	MIRA	Newbler	Oases
Specificity absolute	30'256/ 50'381	37'376/76'126	11'505/14'633	12'065/16'862
Specificity relative	60.05%	49.10%	78.62%	71.55%
Sensitivity absolute	10'487/ 146'962	11'209/146'962	11'857/ 146'962	9'543/146'962
Sensitivity relative	7.14%	7.63%	8.07%	6.49%

doi:10.1371/journal.pone.0031410.t005

Ultimately we aimed to evaluate assembler performance based on how well their assembly of the simulated reads approximates the MA (Table 6). All assemblers achieved a rather high specificity: 91 to 95% of the contigs generated by the assemblers were present in the MA. The CAP3 and MIRA assemblies had the highest specificity, while Newbler showed the lowest specificity. Sensitivity was lower than specificity: 15 to 41% of the MA contigs were found in the simulated read assemblies. The MA had the highest contig overlap with the MIRA assembly (41%) followed by Newbler (34%), CAP3 (17%), and Oases (15%). Specificity and sensitivity indicated that MIRA produced the assembly that was most similar to the MA (Table 6).

Table 6. Comparison between simulated 454 read assemblies and model assembly.

	CAP3	MIRA	Newbler	Oases
Specificity absolute	43'312/45'422	37'930/40'129	8'856/9'774	10'582/11'355
Specificity relative	95.35%	94.52%	90.61%	93.19%
Sensitivity absolute	4'202/24'993	10'329/24'993	8'530/24'993	3'671/24'993
Sensitivity relative	16.81%	41.33%	34.13%	14.69%

doi:10.1371/journal.pone.0031410.t006

Ambiguity within the assemblies was evaluated by aligning simulated reads back to assembled contigs (Table 7). The greatest majority of reads could be mapped back to MA contigs. For the MA, we knew that only reads of a common transcript had been assembled. Nevertheless, while mapping the reads to the contigs, some reads aligned to multiple contigs due to sequence similarity between transcripts. This is showing the intrinsic redundancy within the data set. A similar high proportion of aligned reads as for the MA could only be found in the MIRA contigs. For the other assemblies some reads did not find a good match in the assembled contigs. Redundancy in the assembly was revealed by reads mapping back to multiple contigs. CAP3 and MIRA had by far the most reads with multiple hits, whereas Newbler and Oases had fewer reads mapped to multiple contigs than the MA. Another form of ambiguity, chimeric contigs arose when reads, which originated from different transcripts, were assembled into the same contig. These chimeras might cause major artefacts in analysis following a transcriptome assembly, like detection of sequence or expression variation. Our simulation approach kept track of the origin of every read and allowed us to find and quantify the amount of misplaced reads forming chimeric contigs in the assemblies. Table 8 shows that MIRA and CAP3 have a high proportion of non-chimeric contigs (86% and 85%, respectively), whereas Newbler produced only 62% of non-chimeric contigs. As the Oases software did not allow tracing reads during the assembly process we could not determine with certainty which reads contributed to the contigs and therefore could not evaluate the extend of non-chimeric contigs directly. Transcriptome assemblies are especially challenging since genes with multiple transcripts are difficult to distinguish using sequence information only. Therefore, we expected these genes to be particularly prone to misalignments. Out of the 800'000 reads simulated 64'630 originate from non-alternative spliced genes. The average proportions of misplaced reads for contigs representing genes with and without alternative splicing are presented in Table 8. As expected, genes with a single transcript isoform showed a lower average proportion of misplaced reads per contig in all assemblies. This indicates, that no assembler performed particularly well in assembling genes with multiple splicing variants, reflecting the specific challenges of assembling transcriptome data. But again MIRA and CAP3 outperformed Newbler in this aspect.

Table 7. Alignment ambiguity between simulated reads and assembled contigs.

	CAP3	MIRA	Newbler	Oases	MA
Contigs hit	45'410/45'422	40'108/40'129	9'771/9'774	11'342/11'355	24'983/24'993
Reads mapped (out of 800'000)	708'344	786'490	709'680	689'079	798'768
Reads mapped to multiple contigs	609'429	611'832	202'681	223'616	294'738

doi:10.1371/journal.pone.0031410.t007

Table 8. Evaluation of chimera formation.

	CAP3	MIRA	Newbler
Non chimeric contigs absolute	38'429/45'422	34'558/40'129	6'138/9'957
Non chimeric contigs relative	85%	86%	62%
Average proportion of misplaced reads AS	5.27%	4.61%	11.70%
Average proportion of misplaced reads non-AS	0.88%	0.91%	2.82%

AS: Genes with alternative splicing.
Non-AS: Genes without alternative splicing.
doi:10.1371/journal.pone.0031410.t008

DISCUSSION

The Model Assembly as a Reference for Comparing Assembler Performance

Previous studies that evaluated assemblers for *de novo* transcriptome data, compared the assembly of different programs against previously determined EST sequences for the target species and transcriptome data of related organisms [1]. In this study we adopted a simulation approach to evaluate a given assembly and compare different assemblies. Thus, we benefited from knowing the optimal solution for the assembly problem given the data. We created a Model Assembly (MA) with a minimal overlap of one bp ensuring that no assembler outperforms the MA, therefore the MA could be used as the gold standard. First, the MA provided reference values for the diverse metrics, on which the assembler were assessed and compared to each other. Second, we evaluated how close the different assemblies match the MA. And finally, this approach allowed us to evaluate chimeric contigs in the assembly directly. As the simulation may not have captured all confounding processes involved in real experiments, e.g. PCR read chimeras, we also evaluated a comparable real data set. In assemblies of real experimental data the optimal solution was not known. Nevertheless, in the case presented in this study, the human transcriptome annotation was most likely a very good proxy. Altogether, the combination of simulated and real experimental data provided further insights on general advantages and shortcomings of different software solutions for 454 *de novo* transcriptome assembly.

Comparing the Assembly Metrics

The interpretation of assembly quality based on metrics like contig length was difficult without reference values. For example, longer contigs are not always good indicators of assembly quality; if an assembler simply concatenates all reads, the result would be an assembly with a high median contig length although it is a large chimeric sequence. The MA provided reference values for basic assembly measures so these values could be assessed accordingly. We exploited this feature to reveal Newbler produced contigs with a higher median length, average length, and N50 length, than the MA. This suggested that Newbler was merging reads into contigs that originate from different transcripts. This assumption was further strengthened by the lower number of base pairs output in the Newbler assembly compared to the MA. The higher amount of chimeric contigs and the higher average amount of misplaced reads per contig in the Newbler assembly relative to the other assemblies (Table 8), which was only possible to evaluate directly due to our simulation approach, further confirmed these conclusions. MIRA and CAP3 seemed to be more conservative in merging reads, resulting in lower median contig length but higher numbers of base pairs used in the assemblies. A large total number of bases used in the assembly pointed towards some degree of redundancy in the MIRA and CAP3 assemblies. Again our simulation approach allows us to directly show the higher redundancy in these assemblies (Table 7). Oases produced contigs of a similar length as CAP3, MIRA, and MA, but output a low number of bases in the assembly suggesting that the software discarded some read information. Comparing assembly metrics for the simulated and real data set (see Table 2 and 3), led to similar conclusions, revealing major differences between Newbler on the one side and MIRA plus CAP3 on the other side.

Specificity and Sensitivity of the Transcriptome Assemblies

As expected, the MA had the highest specificity and sensitivity (Table 3). In the simulation, 800'000 reads were produced representing the amount of sequences generated by one 454 sequencing run. Due to the amount of data used for the assembly, sensitivity was rather low (16%) and a specificity of 95% indicated that not all contigs in the MA represent complete transcripts, i.e. some transcripts were not completely covered by reads. These results confirmed that a single 454 sequencing run did not allow for a complete restoration of a whole (human) transcriptome, resulting in low sensitivity scores and incomplete specificity. However we could compare specificity and sensitivity across different software solutions to determine performance differences. We evaluated a prerelease (2.5p1) version of Newbler along with the current 2.3 version, as Kumar and Blaxter [1] showed major performance differences between versions. We only found minor differences in the performance between the two Newbler versions in any of the metrics or comparisons we evaluated (results not shown). These findings were in the line with results by Ewen-Campen et al. [5].

The specificity scores of the different assemblies for simulated reads were all very high. This might be expected as the reads have been directly generated from the transcriptome, resulting in almost every contig mapping back to the reference. For the real data set, specificity differed more between the assemblies (Table 5), and indicated that Newbler was most successful in restoring complete length transcripts. MIRA showed a low specificity, which might be caused by the conservative merging of reads. Essentially, MIRA escaped producing chimeric contigs but as a consequence failed to produce long contigs and generates redundancy in the assembly. The sensitivity scores showed slight variations due to the low amount of initial reads. For both simulated and real read sets, Newbler and MIRA were the most sensitive assemblers. The relatively low specificity, together with the low number of contigs and amount of bases used in the Oases assembly indicated that Oases might not be the right choice for transcriptome assembly of 454 reads. This might not be surprising as this software was designed for shorter reads and not for ~200 bp reads as used in this study. The Oases assembly might be improved by using a multiple k-mer strategy, but for the scope of this study we decided to evaluate software with their default settings.

CONCLUSIONS

As we used a simulation approach we were able to identify general features of different software for *de novo* 454 transcriptome assembly. In summary, our analysis indicated that Newbler performed best in restoring full-length transcripts at the cost of a higher proportion of chimeric contigs. In contrast, MIRA was particularly conservative in combining reads. This resulted in more fragmented transcripts and a certain degree of redundancy in the assembly. Depending on the analysis following the assembly, researchers might favour different features of assemblers. Downstream variation detection might suffer substantially from chimeric reads, which produce false positive variation calls. Therefore one might prefer a conservative approach as performed by MIRA. Other studies interested in the expressed sequences might prefer an optimal restoration of full-length transcripts with minimal redundancy. Here, Newbler might be the better choice for assembly, despite some degree of chimeric contigs. All assessed approaches can be assumed to benefit from experimental improvement, like e.g. normalization of expression levels, or tuning parameter settings specific for the data analysed, but the overall tendencies of characteristic differences between approaches we describe here are less expected to change. Furthermore we focus here on the *de novo* assembly of a specific human transcriptome. The assembly problem might vary depending on tissue type, expression profile, and species under consideration. Nevertheless we outline in our study how a simulation approach can guide decision on assembly strategy and support the choice of parameters. Simulations on reads obtained under similar experimental conditions in related species can also provide valuable information for the design and the analysis of RNA-Seq experiments in species with an *a priori* unknown transcriptome composition.

MATERIALS AND METHODS

Data Sets

For the qualitative evaluation of sequence assemblers, we simulated 454 ESTs *in silico*. On the basis of the human genome and transcriptome annotation (Ensembl [44] GRCh37.58) the FluxSimulator [48] (v20090831) simulated gene expression (20000 Cells, 200 Million Molecules), reverse transcription (transcription start site variation: 25, poly-A shape and scale: 0, random primers) and fragmentation (physical, lambda 900, cDNA cut-off 500–800 bp; parameters not mentioned were left at default values). The human transcriptome was chosen as a start point for the simulation due to its quality especially with respect to the knowledge about different isoforms of genes. A custom python script (available on request from the authors) resembling the approach of MetaSim [49] simulated the 454 sequencing process with 100 flow cycles. Throughout all these processes the information about which transcript a fragment/read originated from was maintained. This allowed creation of a Model Assembly (MA). The MA was not based on overlapping sequence information between reads but instead was based on the knowledge of the origin of each read. Reads were merged into contigs when they shared a common origin and overlapped by at least one base pair. Any assembler operating on sequence information could not produce a better assembly than the MA. For comparison we repeated the analysis with a real 454-FLX sequenced human transcripts [50]. The sequenced transcripts originated from the microarray quality control A sample (NCBI Short Read Archive Accession: SRX002932). It consisted of pooled RNA from different cell lines and therefore should give a good representation of the human transcriptome.

Assemblers

We compared the performance of following assemblers: CAP3 (version for Linux with an Intel processor) [32], MIRA (3.2.0rc3) [34], Newbler (2.3 and 2.5p1) [36], and Oases (0.1.18)[43]. Based on the algorithms the assembly software uses, the assemblers can be grouped into two different classes. Overlap-Layout-Consensus based assemblers (MIRA, CAP3, Newbler) are usually employed in the assembly of longer reads such as those produced by 454 sequencing. De Bruijn graph assemblers (Oases) are primarily designed for short read data, e.g. from Illumina sequencing [51]. Although we only studied long-read data sets we nevertheless evaluated the performance of Oases. We did so as Oases is explicitly designed for the assembly of transcripts. All assemblers were run under default parameters with the following required adjustments for 454 transcriptome data: MIRA: denovo,est,accurate,454 -GE:not=4; Newbler2.3,Newbler2.5: cDNAMode=True, numCPU=4; Oases: k=31. The prerelease version of Newbler 2.5 (2.5p1) used in this study contained a bug (known to the developers) that causes the software to fail on reading in certain cDNA reads in fasta format. In order to assess the software, we had to eliminate reads crashing the program manually. For the simulated reads, Newbler 2.5 was run with only 793'430 reads instead of 800'000 reads. On the real read data set, we were not able to run the software at all. After assembly, contigs less than 100 bp in length and singletons (singletons could not be determined in the Oases assembly) were discarded for subsequent analysis (this was done to ensure comparability between the output of the different assemblers as some keep while other discard singletons and/or contigs shorter 100 bp).

Comparative Evaluation of Assemblers

We compared the total number of bases in an assembled contigs, the amount of contigs longer 200 bp, 400 bp, 800 bp, and 1 kbp, mean, median, maximum, N50 contig length (the smallest contig size in which half the assembly is represented), and run times of all evaluated assemblers for both the simulated and the real data set. As Oases uses a preliminary assembly produced by velvet (specifically, the applications, velveth and velvetg) we summed run times over all steps. These statistics were collected to determine which assembler approximates the MA best.

In addition to the simulation approach, we compared the assemblies of real and simulated data to the transcriptome. We expected that the assemblers would perform comparably on the simulated and real data. We calculated the following optimality criteria to validate our simulation approach and evaluate the performance of the different assemblers: (1) Specificity: This measure described the relative amount of contigs in the assembler's output which were also contained in the transcriptome or MA. We considered a contig to be present in the transcriptome or MA if it had a BLAST [52] hit with an e-value$<10^{-9}$ and the hit covered at least 80% of the length of the transcriptome or MA sequence. (2) Sensitivity: The relative amount of transcriptome sequences or MA contigs, which were contained in the output of one assembler (BLAST) and covering at least 80% of the length of the output contig. Figure 1 illustrates performed comparisons between the different data sets. (3) Ambiguity: Aligning simulated reads back to assembled contigs, we evaluated how many reads map to multiple contigs (multiple BLAST hits above the e-value threshold of 10^{-9}) to assess redundancy in the assembled contigs. Besides, we evaluated the origin of reads joined into the same contig. Non-chimeric contigs aligned only reads of the same transcript origin. For each contig, we determined the proportion of misplaced reads (reads mapped to contigs originating from different transcripts - chimeras). We calculated the average proportion of misplaced reads over all contigs for alternatively spliced and non-alternatively spliced genes, separately.

ACKNOWLEDGMENTS

We thank Benjamin Bolte for programming support. Ewan Birney kindly hosted MM at the EMBL-EBI. Lothar Wissler is acknowledged for suggesting such a study and for helpful discussions. We thank Mahesh Panchal, Freddy Chain, and Antoine Branca for their help with critically revising the manuscript.

AUTHOR CONTRIBUTIONS

Conceived and designed the experiments: EBB PGDF MM. Performed the experiments: MM. Analyzed the data: MM PGDF MS. Contributed reagents/materials/analysis tools: EBB MS. Wrote the paper: PGDF MM EBB MS.

REFERENCES

1. Kumar S, Blaxter M (2010) Comparing de novo assemblers for 454 transcriptome data. BMC Genomics 11: 571.
2. Riggins CW, Peng Y, Stewart CN Jr, Tranel PJ (2010) Characterization of de novo transcriptome for waterhemp (*Amaranthus tuberculatus*) using GS-FLX 454 pyrosequencing and its application for studies of herbicide target-site genes. Pest Management Science 66: 1042–1052.
3. Peng Y, Abercrombie LL, Yuan JS, Riggins CW, Sammons RD, et al. (2010) Characterization of the horseweed (*Conyza canadensis*) transcriptome using GS-FLX 454 pyrosequencing and its application for expression analysis of candidate non-target herbicide resistance genes. Pest Management Science 66: 1053–1062.
4. Yang P, Li X, Shipp MJ, Shockey JM, Cahoon EB (2010) Mining the bitter melon (*Momordica charantia* l.) seed transcriptome by 454 analysis of non-normalized and normalized cDNA populations for conjugated fatty acid metabolism-related genes. BMC Plant Biol 10: 250.
5. Ewen-Campen B, Shaner N, Panfilio K, Suzuki Y, Roth S, et al. (2011) The maternal and early embryonic transcriptome of the milkweed bug *Oncopeltus fasciatus*. BMC Genomics 12: 61.
6. Yang H, Hu L, Hurek T, Reinhold-Hurek B (2010) Global characterization of the root transcriptome of a wild species of rice, *Oryza longistaminata*, by deep sequencing. BMC Genomics 11: 705.
7. Desgagne-Penix I, Khan MF, Schriemer DC, Cram D, Nowak J, et al. (2010) Integration of deep transcriptome and proteome analyses reveals the components of alkaloid metabolism in opium poppy cell cultures. BMC Plant Biol 10: 252.
8. Franssen S, Shrestha R, Brautigam A, Bornberg-Bauer E, Weber A (2011) Comprehensive transcriptome analysis of the highly complex *Pisum sativum*genome using next generation sequencing. BMC Genomics 12: 227.
9. Der JP, Barker MS, Wickett NJ, Depamphilis CW, Wolf PG (2011) De novo characterization of the gametophyte transcriptome in bracken fern, *Pteridium aquilinum*. BMC Genomics 12: 99.
10. Cantacessi C, Mitreva M, Campbell BE, Hall RS, Young ND, et al. (2010) First transcriptomic analysis of the economically important parasitic nematode,*Trichostrongylus colubriformis*, using a next-generation sequencing approach. Infection, Genetics and Evolution 10: 1199–1207.
11. Coppe A, Pujolar JM, Maes GE, Larsen PF, Hansen MM, et al. (2010) Sequencing, de novo annotation and analysis of the first *Anguilla anguilla* transcriptome: EeelBase opens new perspectives for the study of the critically endangered European eel. BMC Genomics 11: 635.
12. Bettencourt R, Pinheiro M, Egas C, Gomes P, Afonso M, et al. (2010) High-throughput sequencing and analysis of the gill tissue transcriptome from the deep-

sea hydrothermal vent mussel *Bathymodiolus azoricus*. BMC Genomics 11: 559.

13. Carvalho RA, Azeredo-Espin AM, Torres TT (2010) Deep sequencing of New World screw-worm transcripts to discover genes involved in insecticide resistance. BMC Genomics 11: 695.
14. Blanca J, Canizares J, Roig C, Ziarsolo P, Nuez F, et al. (2011) Transcriptome characterization and high throughput SSRs and SNPs discovery in *Cucurbita pepo*(Cucurbitaceae). BMC Genomics 12: 104.
15. Logacheva MD, Kasianov AS, Vinogradov DV, Samigullin TH, Gelfand MS, et al. (2011) De novo sequencing and characterization of floral transcriptome in two species of buckwheat (*Fagopyrum*). BMC Genomics 12: 30.
16. Abril JF, Cebria F, Rodriguez-Esteban G, Horn T, Fraguas S, et al. (2010) Smed454 dataset: unravelling the transcriptome of *Schmidtea mediterranea*. BMC Genomics 11: 731.
17. Schwartz TS, Tae H, Yang Y, Mockaitis K, Van Hemert JL, et al. (2010) A garter snake transcriptome: pyrosequencing, de novo assembly, and sex-specific differences. BMC Genomics 11: 694.
18. Karatolos N, Pauchet Y, Wilkinson P, Chauhan R, Denholm I, et al. (2011) Pyrosequencing the transcriptome of the greenhouse whitefly, *Trialeurodes vaporariorum* reveals multiple transcripts encoding insecticide targets and detoxifying enzymes. BMC Genomics 12: 56.
19. Mittapalli O, Bai X, Mamidala P, Rajarapu SP, Bonello P, et al. (2010) Tissue-specific transcriptomics of the exotic invasive insect pest emerald ash borer (*Agrilus planipennis*). PLoS ONE 5: e13708.
20. Dutta S, Kumawat G, Singh BP, Gupta DK, Singh S, et al. (2011) Development of genic-SSR markers by deep transcriptome sequencing in pigeonpea [*Cajanus cajan* (L.) Millspaugh]. BMC Plant Biol 11: 17.
21. Bai X, Mamidala P, Rajarapu SP, Jones SC, Mittapalli O (2011) Transcriptomics of the bed bug (*Cimex lectularius*). PLoS ONE 6: e16336.
22. Clark MS, Thorne MAS, Toullec JY, Meng Y, Guan LL, et al. (2011) Antarctic krill 454 pyrosequencing reveals chaperone and stress transcriptome. PLoS ONE 6: e15919.
23. Nowack EC, Vogel H, Groth M, Grossman AR, Melkonian M, et al. (2011) Endosymbiotic gene transfer and transcriptional regulation of transferred genes in*Paulinella chromatophora*. Molecular Biology and Evolution 28: 407–422.
24. Cabrera AR, Donohue KV, Khalil SMS, Scholl E, Opperman C, et al. (2011) New approach for the study of mite reproduction: The first transcriptome analysis of a mite, *Phytoseiulus persimilis* (Acari: Phytoseiidae). Journal of Insect Physiology 57: 52–61.
25. Dicker AJ, Nath M, Yaga R, Nisbet AJ, Lainson FA, et al. (2011) *Teladorsagia circumcincta*: The transcriptomic response of a multi-drug-resistant isolate to ivermectin exposure in vitro. Experimental Parasitology 127: 351–356.
26. Moe KT, Chung JW, Cho YI, Moon JK, Ku JH, et al. (2011) Sequence information on simple sequence repeats and single nucleotide polymorphisms through transcriptome analysis of mungbean. Journal of Integrative Plant Biology 53: 63–73.
27. Rokyta DR, Wray KP, Lemmon AR, Lemmon EM, Caudle SB (2011) A high-throughput venom-gland transcriptome for the Eastern Diamondback Rattlesnake (*Crotalus adamanteus*) and evidence for pervasive positive selection across toxin classes. Toxicon 57: 657–671.
28. Galindo J, Grahame JW, Butlin RK (2010) An EST-based genome scan using 454 sequencing in the marine snail *Littorina saxatilis*. Journal of Evolutionary Biology 23: 2004–2016.
29. Salem M, Rexroad CE 3rd, Wang J, Thorgaard GH, Yao J (2010) Characterization of the rainbow trout transcriptome using Sanger and 454-pyrosequencing approaches. BMC Genomics 11: 564.
30. Jeukens J, Renaut S, St-Cyr J, Nolte AW, Bernatchez L (2010) The transcriptomics of sympatric dwarf and normal lake whitefish (*Coregonus clupeaformis* spp. , Salmonidae) divergence as revealed by next-generation sequencing. Molecular Ecology 19: 5389–5403.
31. Barreto FS, Moy GW, Burton RS (2011) Interpopulation patterns of divergence and selection across the transcriptome of the copepod *Tigriopus californicus*. Molecular Ecology 20: 560–572.
32. Huang X, Madan A (1999) CAP3: A DNA sequence assembly program. Genome Res 9: 868–877.
33. Pertea G, Huang XQ, Liang F, Antonescu V, Sultana R, et al. (2003) TIGR Gene Indices clustering tools (TGICL): a software system for fast clustering of large EST datasets. Bioinformatics 19: 651–652.
34. Chevreux B, Pfisterer T, Drescher B, Driesel AJ, Muller WE, et al. (2004) Using the miraEST assembler for reliable and automated mRNA transcript assembly and SNP detection in sequenced ESTs. Genome Res 14: 1147–1159.
35. Papanicolaou A, Stierli R, ffrench-Constant R, Heckel D (2009) Next generation transcriptomes for next generation genomes using est2assembly. BMC Bioinformatics 10: 447.
36. Margulies M, Egholm M, Altman WE, Attiya S, Bader JS, et al. (2005) Genome sequencing in microfabricated high-density picolitre reactors. Nature 437: 376–380.
37. Masoudi-Nejad A, Tonomura K, Kawashima S, Moriya Y, Suzuki M, et al. (2006) EGassembler: online bioinformatics service for large-scale processing, clustering and assembling ESTs and genomic DNA fragments. Nucleic Acids Research 34: W459–W462.
38. Breitbart RE, Andreadis A, Nadal-Ginard B (1987) Alternative splicing: A ubiquitous mechanism for the generation of multiple protein isoforms from single genes. Annual Review of Biochemistry 56: 467–495.
39. De Boer TE, Birlutiu A, Bochdanovits Z, Timmermans MJTN, Dijkstra TMH, et al. (2011) Transcriptional plasticity of a soil arthropod across different ecological conditions. Molecular Ecology 20: 1144–1154.

40. Müller L, Hutter S, Stamboliyska R, Saminadin-Peter S, Stephan W, et al. (2011) Population transcriptomics of *Drosophila melanogaster* females. BMC Genomics 12: 81.

41. van Leeuwen H, Kliebenstein DJ, West MAL, Kim K, van Poecke R, et al. (2007) Natural Variation among *Arabidopsis thaliana* Accessions for Transcriptome Response to Exogenous Salicylic Acid. The Plant Cell Online 19: 2099–2110.

42. Whitehead A, Crawford DL (2006) Variation within and among species in gene expression: raw material for evolution. Molecular Ecology 15: 1197–1211.

43. Schulz M, Zerbino D (2010) Oases website. Available:http://www. ebi. ac. uk/~zerbino/oases/. Accessed 2011 Jun 24.

44. Hubbard TJP, Aken BL, Ayling S, Ballester B, Beal K, et al. (2009) Ensembl 2009. Nucleic Acids Research 37: D690–D697.

45. Furusawa C, Kaneko K (2003) Zipf's Law in Gene Expression. Physical Review Letters 90: 088102.

46. Iyengar SS, Quave SA (1979) A computer model for hydrodynamic shearing of DNA. Comput Programs Biomed 9: 160–168.

47. Richter DC, Ott F, Auch AF, Schmid R, Huson DH (2008) MetaSim - A Sequencing Simulator for Genomics and Metagenomics. PLoS ONE 3: e3373.

48. Sammeth M (2009) FLUX website. Available: http:// flux. sammeth. net. Accessed 2011 Oct 3.

49. Richter DC, Ott F, Auch AF, Schmid R, Huson DH (2008) MetaSim: a sequencing simulator for genomics and metagenomics. PLoS ONE 3: e3373.

50. Mane SP, Evans C, Cooper KL, Crasta OR, Folkerts O, et al. (2009) Transcriptome sequencing of the Microarray Quality Control (MAQC) RNA reference samples using next generation sequencing. BMC Genomics 10: 264.

51. Bentley DR, Balasubramanian S, Swerdlow HP, Smith GP, Milton J, et al. (2008) Accurate whole human genome sequencing using reversible terminator chemistry. Nature 456: 53–59.

52. Altschul SF, Madden TL, Schaffer AA, Zhang J, Zhang Z, et al. (1997) Gapped BLAST and PSI-BLAST: a new generation of protein database search programs. Nucleic Acids Research 25: 3389–3402.

CHAPTER 3 ARTIFICIAL NEURAL NETWORKS-BASED SOFTWARE FOR MEASURING HEAT COLLECTION RATE AND HEAT LOSS COEFFICIENT OF WATER-IN-GLASS EVACUATED TUBE SOLAR WATER HEATERS

Zhijian Liu[1], Kejun Liu[2], Hao Li[3], Xinyu Zhang[4], Guangya Jin[1], Kewei Cheng[5]

[1] Department of Power Engineering, School of Energy, Power and Mechanical Engineering, North China Electric Power University, Baoding, Hebei, 071003, PR China

[2] College of Software Engineering, Sichuan University, Chengdu, Sichuan, 610064, PR China

[3] College of Chemistry, Sichuan University, Chengdu, Sichuan, 610064, PR China

[4] National Center for Quality Supervision and Testing of Solar Heating Systems (Beijing), China Academy of Building Research, Beijing, 100013, PR China

[5] School of Computing, Informatics, and Decision Systems Engineering (CIDSE), Ira A. Fulton Schools of Engineering, Arizona State University, Tempe, Arizona, United States of America

ABSTRACT

Measurements of heat collection rate and heat loss coefficient are crucial for the evaluation of in service water-in-glass evacuated tube solar water heaters. However, conventional measurement requires expensive detection devices and undergoes a series of complicated procedures. To simplify the measurement and reduce the cost, software based on artificial neural networks for measuring heat collection rate and heat loss coefficient of water-in-glass evacuated tube solar water heaters was developed. Using multilayer feed-forward neural networks with back-propagation algorithm, we developed and tested our program on the basis of 915measuredsamples of water-in-glass evacuated tube solar water heaters. This artificial neural networks-based software program automatically obtained accurate heat collection rateand heat loss coefficient using simply "portable test instruments" acquired parameters, including tube length, number of tubes, tube center distance, heat water mass in tank, collector area, angle between tubes and ground and final temperature. Our results show that this software (on both personal computer and Android platforms) is efficient and convenient to predict the heat collection rate and heat loss coefficient due to it slow root mean square errors in prediction. The software now can be downloaded fromhttp://t.cn/RLPKF08.

INTRODUCTION

Currently, the boosting solar water heater market worldwide promotes the demand for advanced technologies and related products. The solar water heater has become one of the most efficient and economical ways to utilize solar energy. This system, including solar collectors, heat exchanger and solar concentrators, gathers and converts energy from solar radiation and transfers it into household water [1]. In China, the water-in-glass evacuated tube solar water heaters have been widely used because of their high energy efficiency and simple installation [2, 3].The solar energy industry has developed rapidly in China. By the end of 2012, around 2.57× 10^8 $m^2$of solar water heaters was installed in China, 90% of which was water-in-glass evacuated tube solar water heaters[4]. The market share

Citation: Liu Z, Liu K, Li H, Zhang X, Jin G, Cheng K (2015) Artificial Neural Networks-Based Software for Measuring Heat Collection Rate and Heat Loss Coefficient of Water-in-Glass Evacuated Tube Solar Water Heaters. PLoS ONE 10(12): e0143624. doi:10.1371/journal.pone.0143624

of all-glass evacuated tube solar collectors was about 88% in 2003, while by 2009 it increased to 95%[5]. From 2001 to 2009, the production of evacuated solar tubes increased at an annual rate of 30% in China[3]. More than twenty million evacuated solar tubes were produced in 2001, and by 2009 the production increased to350 million [6].

Studies using experimental, theoretical and computational fluid dynamics (CFD) simulation[7–10]had been performed to investigate and evaluate the heat collection rate, heat loss coefficient and energy efficiency of water-in-glass evacuated tube solar water heaters. Using the ISO9459-2 standard test methods, a previous study showed that the stagnant zone could significantly affect the water-in-glass collector tubes operation[11].A new-type all-glass evacuated tubular solar air heater coupled with compound parabolic concentrator may produce large flow heated air at above 200°C[12].The study for the heat transfer and fluid flow characteristics in one single tube heat collector by computational fluid simulation indicates that the twist tape inserts reduce velocity magnitude and make the temperature field more uniform[13]. The study for the effect of the factor of water temperature in tank on the thermal performance has also shown that as water temperature in tank increases, the net energy storage in the above system declines. The difference between required tank water temperature of 40°C and 80°C was over1,000 $Whm^{-2}d^{-1}$under the condition of a solar radiation gain of 8,000 Whm^{-2} d^{-1}[14].One other study indicates that the outlet temperature and thermal efficiency of a low temperature water-in-glass evacuated tube solar collector by employing the Boussinesq approximation model were closer to the experimental data than those obtained by using the variation of the proprieties with temperature model[15]. By a mathematical method, it is shown that the factors, including collector forms, solar tubes size, central distance between tubes, angles of azimuth and tilt, and diffuse flat reflector employment, may influence the annual collectible radiation in the single tube daily collectible radiation level of all-glass evacuated tube solar collectors[16]. One similar study of natural hydraulic circulation flow field characteristics in water-in-glass evacuated tube solar collectors, showed that the circulation flow rate was closely linked with tank temperature in tank, aspect ratio of tube, angle of collector tilt and the input of solar radiation[17].

However, the most important coefficients of thermal performance, including heat collection rate and heat loss coefficient, are very difficult to determine because the test conditions to assess the thermal performance of solar water heaters are confined by GB/T 19141–2011 standards[18]:

- the test period is 8 h, including 4 h before solar noon and 4 h after;
- the daily solar irradiation shall be higher than 16 MJ/m^2;
- the daily average surrounding temperature shall be between 8 and 39°C;
- the daily surrounding air speed shall be less than 4 m/s;
- the initial temperature in the storage tank shall be 20 ± 1°C.

According to the GB/T 19141–2011 standards, it requires15 days to obtain the heat collection rate of a new solar water heater in Beijing, China, which is time-consuming and strenuous[18]. Although the detection devices (PDT 2013–1), as shown in Fig 1 and the experimental setup schematic of measuring the thermal performance of water-in-glass evacuated tube solar water heaters, as shown in Fig 2, can acquire data precisely, the whole process is time-consuming and energy-consuming due to the necessary disassembly of the water heaters. In addition, this may cause damage to heaters and so far an effective solution to avoid the unnecessary damage is still unknown. Previously, we developed a novel method using some machine learning models such as support vector machine (SVM) for the prediction of heat collection rates and heat loss coefficients [19]. However, lacking of a well-developed software, users may find it difficult to use the method for practical measurements. Here, we propose a software based on artificial neural networks (ANNs) to predict the heat collection rate and heat loss coefficient without the disassembly of heaters based on experimental data. Parameters that can be precisely obtained by"portable test instruments", as shown in Table 1[19], were set as independent variables, which are all relevant to the values of heat collection rate and heat loss coefficient, including tube length(mm), number of tubes, tube center distance(mm), heat water mass in tank(kg), collector area(m^2), angle between tubes and ground(°)and final temperature(°C).The heat collection rate (MJ/m^2)and heat loss coefficient [(W/(Km^3)]measured from the detection device and relevant equations were set as dependent variables. Multilayer feed-forward neural networks (MLFNs) trained with back-propagation (BP)algorithm were used for training the predictive models based on the data from 915 solar water heaters. To choose the best model for the software, comparisons were made among the models with different number of training epochs, hidden nodes, learning rates and momentums.

Figure 1. Picture of the detection deviceused to measure the heat collection rate and heatloss coefficient.

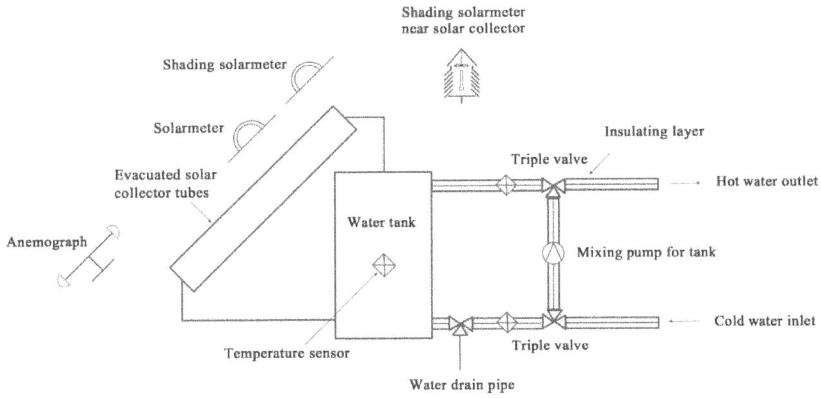

Figure 2. Experimental setupschematic of measuring the thermalperformance of water-in-glass evacuated tube solar water heaters.

Table 1. "Portable test instruments" for the determination of parameters of water-in-glass evacuated tube solar water heaters[19].

Parameters	Portable test instruments	Accuracy
Final temperature of water	Digital thermoelectric thermometer	0.5%
Hot water mass in tank	Electric platform scale	1.0%
Diameter, tube center distance, tube length, collector area	Taper ZSH-3	0.5%

doi:10.1371/journal.pone.0143624.t001

MATERIALS AND METHODS

Experiment

According to the methods for independent and dependent variable determination in this study, 915 water-in-glass evacuated tube solar water heaters (in service for one year) were precisely obtained by the "portable test instruments" and the PDT2013-1 detection device (National Center for Quality Supervision and Testing of Solar Heating Systems, Beijing).The complete data can be downloaded from http://t.cn/RLPKF08. Table 2 shows the statistical analysis of the data.

Table 2. Descriptive statistic of the variables for 915 samples of in service water-in-glass evacuated tube solar water heater.

Item	Tube length (mm)	Number of tube	Tube center distance (mm)	Tank volume (kg)	Collector area (m^2)	Angle (°)	Finaltemperature (°C)	Heat collection rate (MJ/m^2)	Heat loss coefficient [$W/(m^3K)$]
Maximum	2200	64	151	403	8.24	85	62	11.3	13
Minimum	1600	5	60	70	1.27	30	46	6.7	8
Range	600	59	91	333	6.97	55	16	4.6	5
Average	1811	21	76.2	172	2.69	46	53	8.9	10
Standard deviation	87.80	5.80	5.11	47.00	0.73	3.89	2.00	0.48	0.77

doi:10.1371/journal.pone.0143624.t002

ANNs Model

ANNs are effective machine learning approaches with functions of estimation and approximation based on input values [20–22], which are widely used in numeric predictions and pattern recognitions. In our studies, MLFNs were chosen for model development and BP algorithm was used as the training algorithm.

MLFNs

An MLFN model consists of neurons that are ordered into different layers[23–25]. The first layer is the input layer while the last layer is the output layer, and the layers between the input and output layers are the hidden layer (Fig 3). The data moves in only one direction. Each neuron in a particular layer is connected with all neurons in the next layer and each neuron is a computational unit that takes inputs, and outputs[22–24]:

$$h_{w,b}(x) = f(\xi_i) = f(\sum_{i=1}^{m} w_i x_i + b) \quad (1)$$

where $\xi_i$is the potential of the*i*th neuron and $f(\xi_i)$is called the transfer function.*w*is the weight coefficient and *b*is the threshold coefficient which can be understood as a weight coefficient of the connection with formally added neuron.

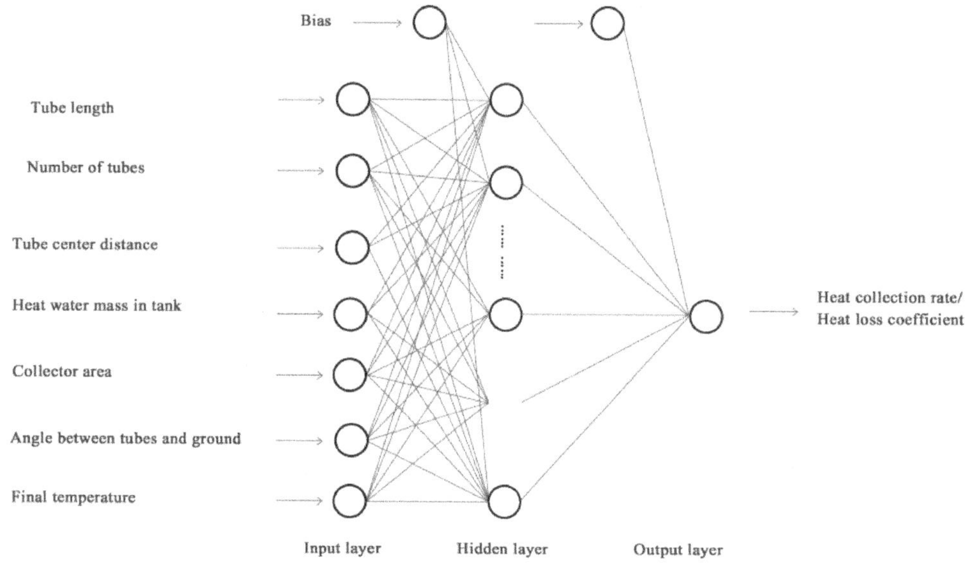

Figure 3. Schematic structure of an ANN in our study.

BP Algorithm

BP algorithm adopts gradient descent as its optimization method, in which it calculates the gradient of a loss function with respects to all weights and bias in the network[26–28]. Then the gradient is fed and used to update weights and bias, in order to minimize the loss function.

In BP algorithm, sigmoid function is widely used as the transfer function[29]:

$$f(x) = \frac{1}{1 + e^{-x}} \quad \textbf{(2)}$$

RESULTS AND DISCUSSION

Model Development

Using the "portable test instruments", for an in service water-in-glass evacuated tube solar water heater, precise values of tube length(mm), number of tubes, tube center distance(mm), heat water mass in tank(kg), collector area(m^2), angle between tubes and ground(°) and final temperature(°C)can be obtained easily from outdoors, whereas the heat collection rate(MJ/m^2) and heat loss coefficient[$W/(Km^3)$]can only be determined by the conventional detection device after being dismantled. To avoid complex disassembly and obtain the heat collection rate and heat loss coefficient in real time, here, we aim at using machine learning techniques, specifically, MLFNs to develop a series of prediction models for the heat collection rate and heat loss coefficient. Data acquired by "portable test instruments" were designated as independent variables, while the heat collection rate (MJ/m^2)and heat loss coefficient [$W/(Km^3)$]were designated as dependent variables. Models were developed for both heat collection rate (MJ/m^2) and heat loss coefficient [$W/(Km^3)$]in order to find out the best prediction model for each of these two dependent variables. 915 groups of completed experimental data were used for the model development. 815data groups were used as the training set, while 100 data groups were used as the testing set.

Before deciding the configuration of ANNs, factors which influence the performance of ANNs need to be analyzed. The values of weight and bias between layers in neural net, which are key to the performance of ANNs, are determined by data pre-processing, activation function, the number of training epochs, the number of nodes in hidden layer, learning rate, and the momentum. Data pre-processing is the process of reducing data to its canonical form in order to prevent certain feature with much bigger values than others from overshadowing other features. We adopt data normalization, specifically simple rescaling method to do data pre-processing here. In ANNs, the transfer function of a node defines the output of that node given an input or set of inputs. We uses igmoid function as the transfer function, between input layer, hidden layer and output layer. The final data vectors lie in the range [0.1,0.9].The number of training epochs determines the number of epochs the ANNs trained. Another important factor is the momentum, which is a useful technique that can help the network out of local minima. Thus, besides data pre-processing method and transfer function, the performance of ANNs is mainly influenced by training epochs, hidden nodes, learning rate and momentum.

In order to find out the best ANNs configuration, control variable method is adopted here. Different training epoch, hidden node, learning rate and momentum were set individually. To avoid missing the best configuration figure set, the experimental range of each parameter is as large as possible. The range of training epoch we set here is from 1 to 500. As the range of learning rate and momentum lies in [0.1, 0.9] themselves, they are set from 0.1 to 0.9. The hidden nodes of models were numbered from 1 to 13, from which we could track the change regulation of the ANNs when dealing with the development processes.

Root mean square error (RMS error) in testing and the required training time were used as indicators to measure the performance of the MLFNs. The RMS errors of each model were calculated by Eq (3):

$$RMSE = \sqrt{\frac{\sum_{i-1}^{n}(Z_i - O_i)^2}{n}} \quad \textbf{(3)}$$

Where Z_i is the predicted value, O_i is the actual value and n is the number of tested samples.

A runnable ANN program is written. Each time we change one particular variable in the ANN configuration figure set and run the ANN program, then the corresponding RMS errors are recorded, from which we can find the best ANNs models for heat collection rates and heat loss coefficient separately by choosing the ANNs model with the lowest RMS error.

Experiment shows that when predicting the heat collection rates, the RMS errors of the presented models vary from 0.6254 to 0.2049. The main reason for the various RMS errors is that there may be some under-fitted and over-fitted results in some configurations after trainings, leading to relatively higher RMS errors. The lowest RMS error exists in the BP with 200 epochs, 7 nodes, 0.9 learning rate, and 0.9 momentum(0.2049). Therefore, for the prediction of heat collection rate, it is reasonable to consider that the BP model with 200 epochs, 7 nodes, 0.9 learning rate and 0.9 momentum is one of the best models. Detailed results of prediction models for heat collection rate are included in S1 Table.

In terms of the prediction of heat loss coefficient, RMS errors are quite similar in different models, which vary from 1.1304to 0.9246. The reason for the variety of RMS errors is also the under-fitted and over-fitted results, which is the same as the heat collection rate models discussed above. The lowest RMS error exists in the BP with 50 epochs, 1 node, 0.1 learning rate, and 0.1 momentum (0.9246). Therefore, for the prediction of heat loss coefficient, it is reasonable to consider that the BP model with 50 epochs, 1 node, 0.1 learning rate and 0.1 momentum is one of the best models. Detailed results of prediction models for heat loss coefficient are included in S2 Table.

Model Analysis

Before the development of the packed software the model should be evaluated first. Fig 3shows the comparisons between the residual values and their actual values. Residual values were calculated by Eq (4):

$$z=y-x \quad \textbf{(4)}$$

where z is the residual value, y is the actual value and x is the predicted value.It can be seen that the prediction of heat collection rate is precise because the residual values are close to zero [Fig 4 (a)]. In terms of the prediction of heat loss coefficient, despite deviations exist when the actual values are close to 9.0, most residuals are close to zero [Fig 4 (b)]. Our results suggest that the two BP models we chose for predicting heat collection rate and heat loss coefficient respectively are applicable in actual situations.

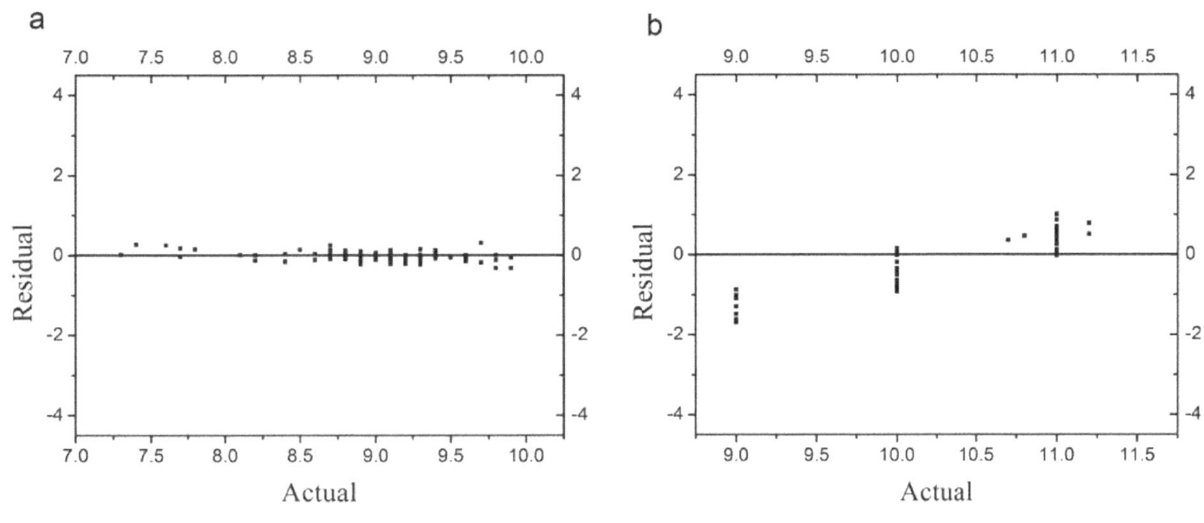

Figure 4. Residual values versus actual values in predicting. (a) Heat collection rate. (b) Heat loss coefficient.

Software Development

In order to offer great convenience for users work either in office with personal computer or outdoor with portable smartphone, two pieces of individual software are developed, including personal computer (PC) platform version and smartphone platform version. Considering that Android platform is now the world's most commonly used smartphone platform (dominated the global smartphone market with a share of 82.8% in 2015) [30], in terms of smartphone platform, we developed Android platform in particular. So users are free to adopt the PC version when dealing with analysis on computer, and can also use the Android version simply with their phone when computer is not available. Figs 5 and 6 show the overview panel of our software, *WaterHeater*. The application ranges of tube length (mm), number of tubes, tube center distance (mm), tank volume(kg), collector area (m^2), angle (°) and final temperature (°C) are[1600, 2200], [5, 64], [60,151], [70.433, 403.332], [1.27, 8.24], [30,85] and [46,68], respectively. More detailed descriptions about the design of*WaterHeater*are covered in S1 File.

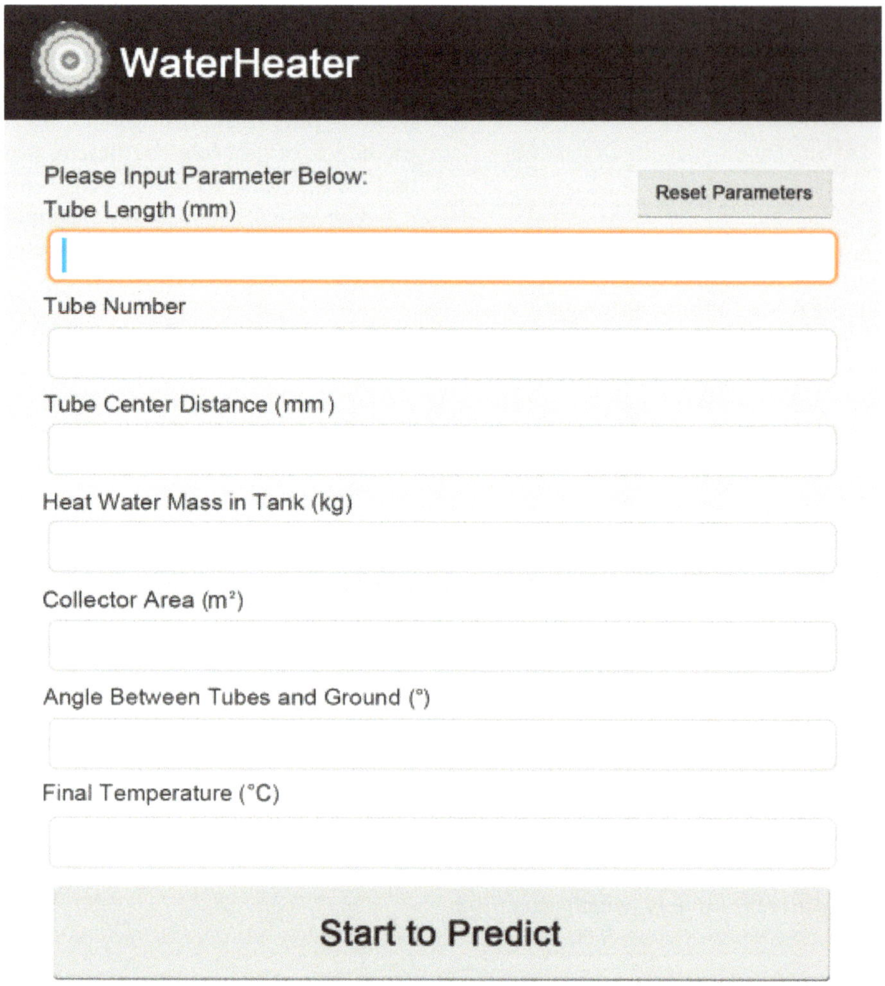

Figure 5. Overview panel of Android platform.

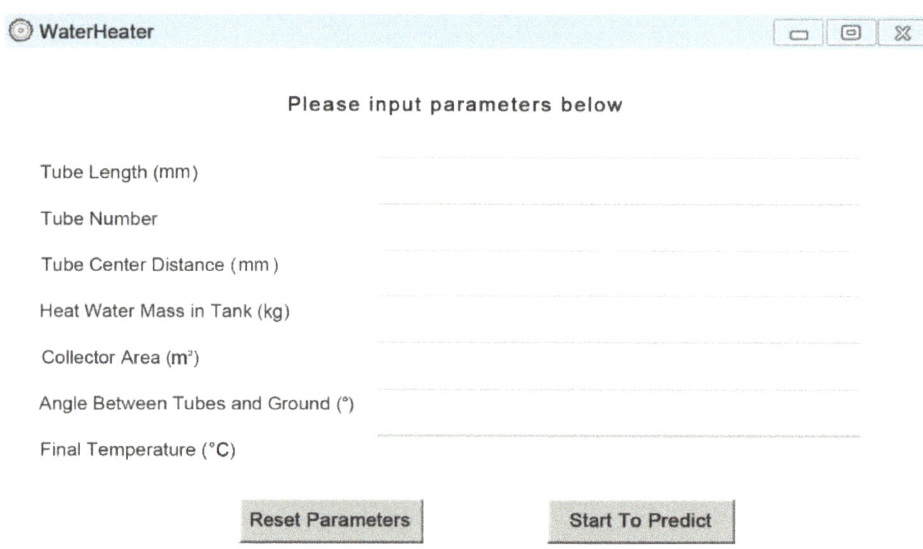

Figure 6. Overview panel of PC platform.

Comparison with Conventional Methods

Using conventional methods for determination of heat collection rate and heat loss coefficient[31], a series of steps using detection devices needs to be completed (Fig 7). The pipes of water-in-glass evacuated tube solar water heaters need to be dismantled at first. However, for the determination tothe in service heaters, the disassembly of the pipes of heater is highly inconvenient and will cause damage to the instruments. Furthermore, the whole determination process requires at least 15 days. After a complicated determination process, the heat collection rate and heat loss coefficient canbe obtained by empirical equations [Eqs (5) and (6)], which is from ISO9459-2[32].

$$q_s = \frac{a_1 H + a_2(t_a - t_i) + a_3}{S} \quad (5)$$

$$U_s = \frac{\rho_w C_{p,w} V_s}{V \Delta\tau} \ln\left[\frac{t_{is} - t_{as(av)}}{t_{fs} - t_{as(av)}}\right] \quad (6)$$

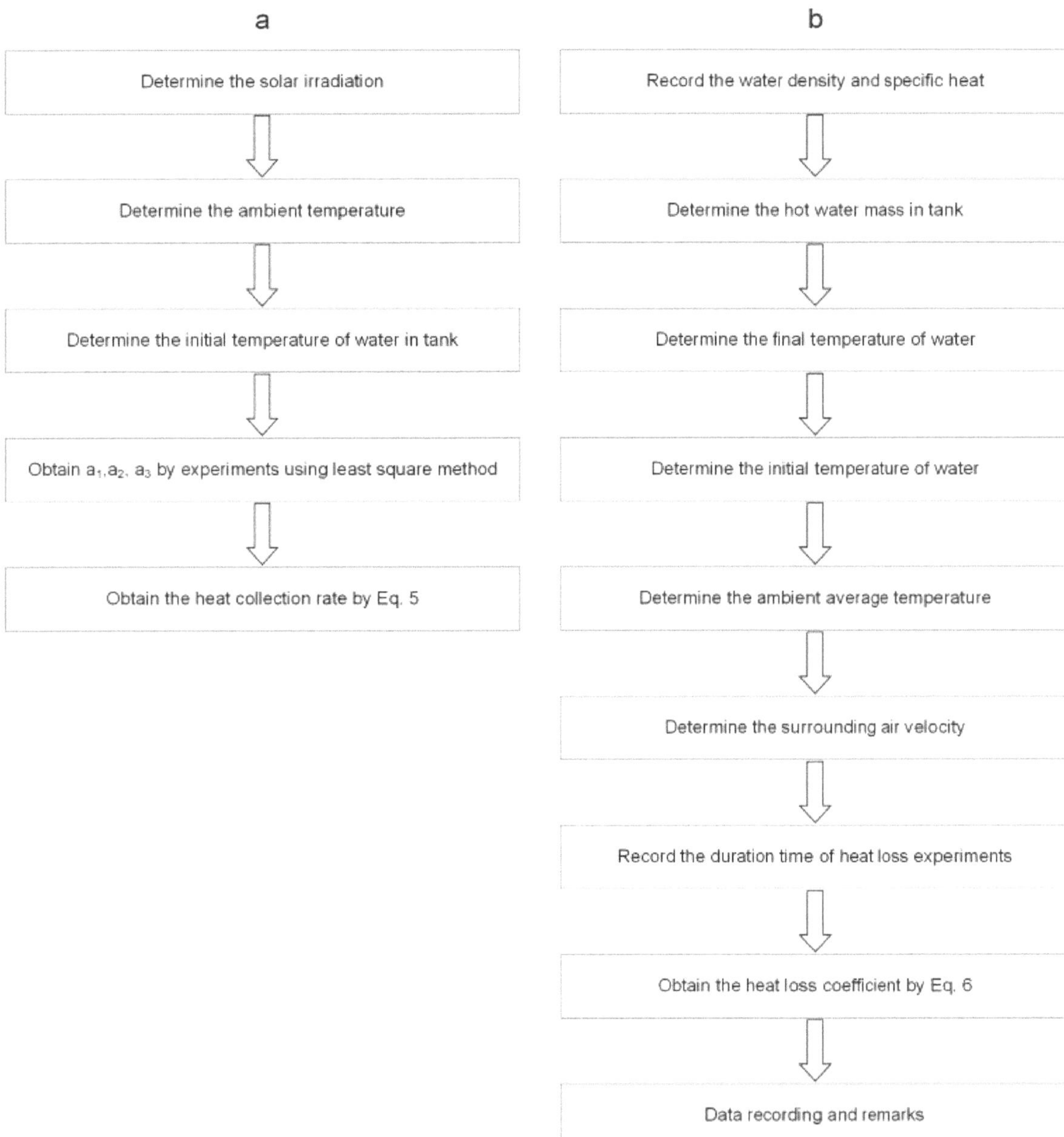

Figure 7. Flow chart of the conventional method for determining. (a) Heat collection. (b) Heat loss coefficient.

Where q_s is the heat collection rate, H is the amount of solar radiation, t_a is the ambient temperature, $t_i$is the initial temperature of water in tank, S is the area of tubes and a_1, $a_2$anda_3 are the coefficients; U_s is the heat loss coefficient, ρ_w is the water density, $C_{p,w}$ is the specific heat of water, V_s is the heat water mass in tank, t_{is} is the initial temperature of water,t_{fs} is the final temperature of water, $t_{as(av)}$ is the ambient average temperature, V is the volume of water and $\Delta\tau$ is the duration time of heat loss coefficient experiments.

To optimize the determination method, herein, we propose a novel method to avoid the disassembly of the heaters, and meanwhile, largely shorten the testing time. The determination process using our novel method shows that the independent variables obtained by the «portable test instruments» can be inputted into the ANNs (Fig 8). The predicted results of heat collection rate and heat loss coefficient can be obtained precisely from the output of the ANNs. The use of «portable test instruments» is of great briefness and the combination of ANNs can greatly save time and give highly precise predicted results.

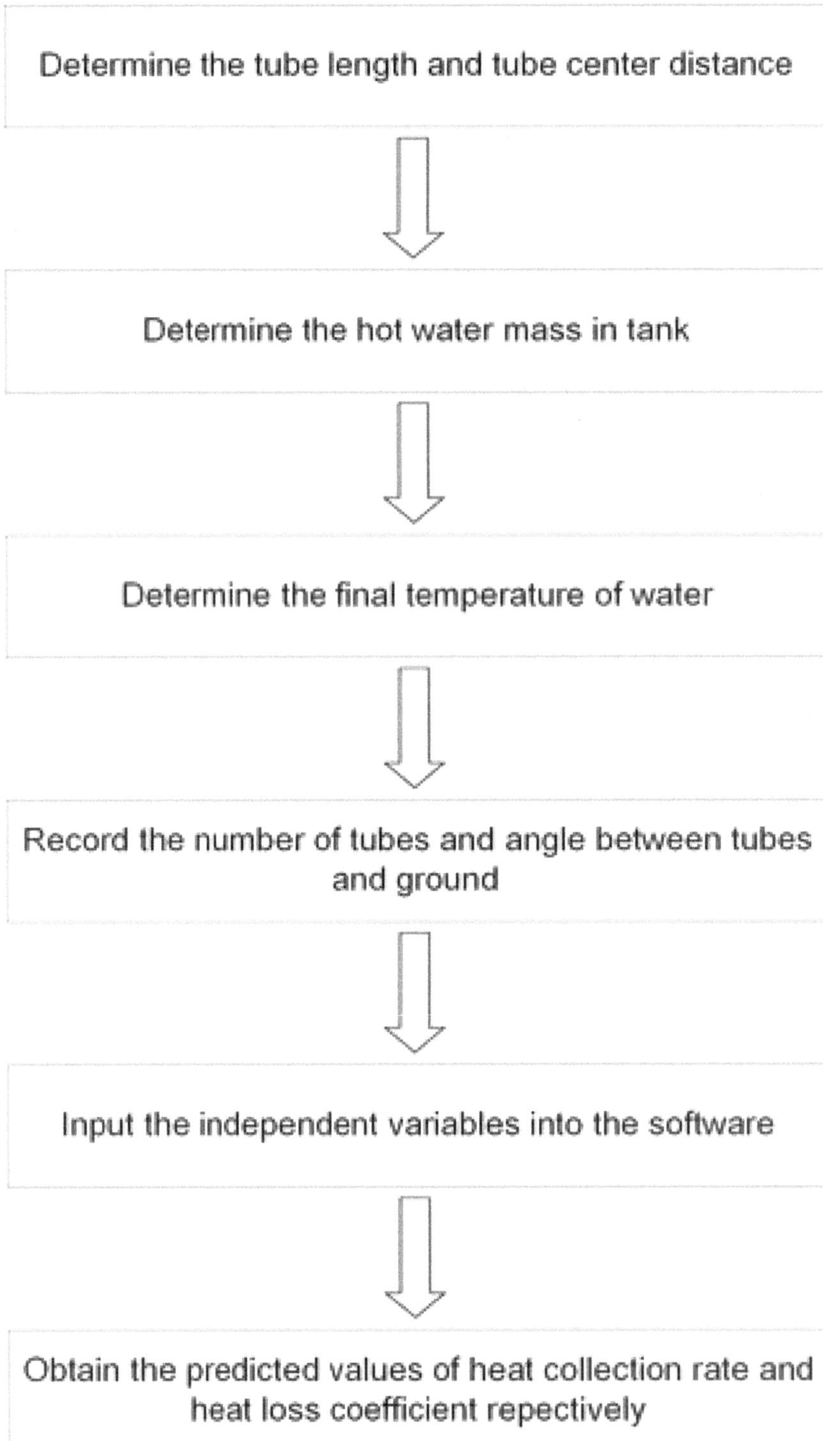

Figure 8. Flow chart of the novel method using "portable test instruments" combined with ANNs for determining heat collection rate and heat loss coefficient.

Here, we present one case using both conventional method and the new one. According to the methods for independent and dependent variable determination in this study, the values of independent variables of our chosen water-in-glass evacuated tube solar water heater are 1800 mm, 20, 75 mm, 150.599 kg, 2.45 m^2, 45°, 56°C respectively for tube length, number of tubes, tube center distance, tank volume, collector area, angle between tubes and ground and final temperature. With traditional method, the corresponding heat collection rate and heat loss coefficient are9.2 MJ/m^2 and 10 [$W/(Km^3)$] respectively, while with new method, the results are 9.225 MJ/m^2 and 10.05[$W/(Km^3)$]respectively. Figs 9 and10 show the results on both Android platform and PC platform.

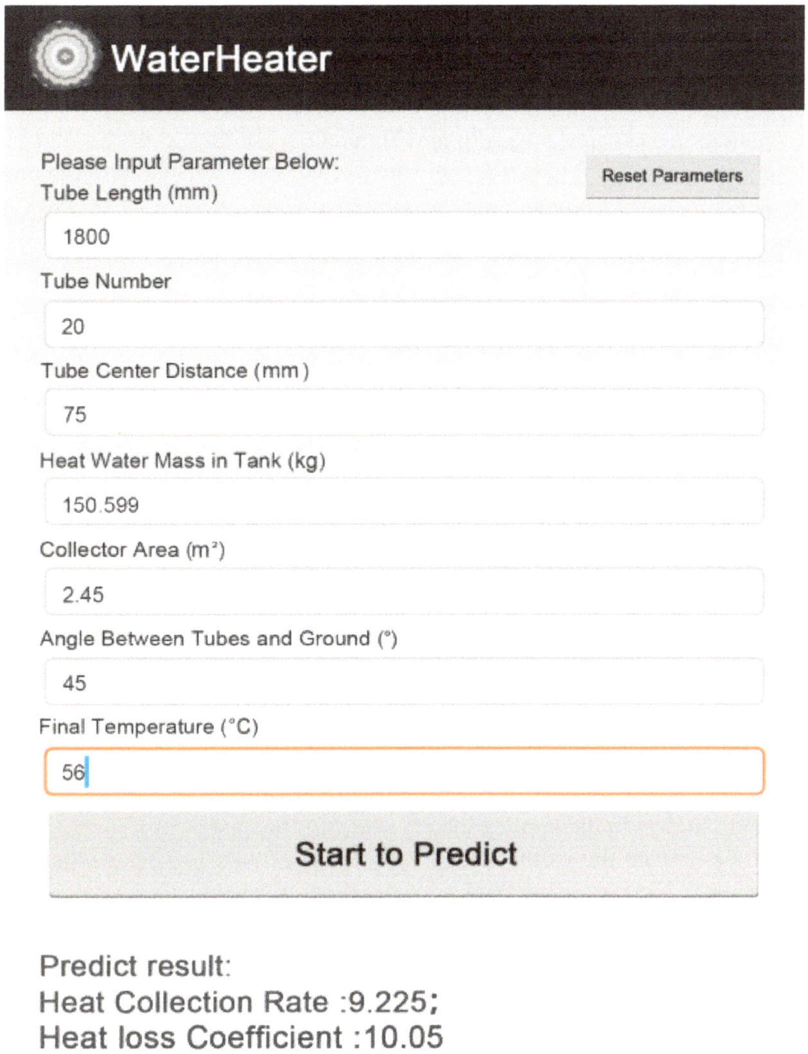

Figure 9. Results of an instance on Android platform.

Figure 10. Results of an instance on PC platform.

CONCLUSION

WaterHeater, the ANNs-based software for predicting heat collection rate and heat loss coefficient of water-in-glass evacuated tube solar water heater is now developed. Results show that the BP models have high performances in predicting the heat collection rate and heat loss coefficient. The BP model with 200 epochs, 7 nodes, 0.9 learning rate, and 0.9 momentum has the best prediction performance for heat collection rate, with an RMS error 0.2049, while the BP model with 50 epochs, 1 hidden node, 0.1 learning rate, and 0.1 momentum has the best prediction performance for heat loss coefficient, with an RMS error 0.9246.In practical applications, the determination of heat collection rate and heat loss coefficient can be conducted outdoors using "portable test instruments". Data of independent variables obtained by "portable test instruments" can be inputted into the software and the precise predicted values of heat collection rate and heat loss coefficient can be obtained rapidly from the output of the models. Therefore, using our novel techniques, the determination of heat collection rate and heat loss coefficient is not to be performed in laboratories after being dismantled, which avoids the possible damage to the instruments and reduces manpower, experimental time and unnecessary operations. The software on both PC and Android platform can be currently downloaded from:http://t.cn/RLPKF08.

Furthermore, most of previous studies in the applications of ANNs to energy systems only proposed the methodology for model developments. However, lacking of details of programming and experimental data, other scientists and users usually found that it is difficult to repeat the same model process and use the method effectively. In this study, the development of the software, *WaterHeater*, based on the trained results of ANNs can avoid this common problem. Users can input the independent variables they acquired and the two coefficients can be acquired automatically without the acquisition of experimental data for training and the complex model development process of ANNs.

SUPPORTING INFORMATION

Usability of an interface system is a measure of the amount of effort of a user must expend to learn its use and then use it to perform his or her routine in the workplace [1]. In this study, our goal is to satisfy users' requirement for predicting heat collection rate and heat loss coefficient by a convenient way, leading us to develop the software, WaterHeater, with certain key features. Firstly, WaterHeater must have high usability, measured through ease of use, ease of learning and perceived gains in using it. Considering the platforms users might use, WaterHeater should be capable in varied environments [2].

In order to apply the system to varied environments, both personal computer (PC) and mobile platform were tested. Java language, which is known for Java Object Oriented Programming [3], was used throughout the project so that the artificial neural networks (ANNs) module could be easily packed into different platforms. Android operating system, which has been widely used nowadays, was chosen as a representative of mobile platforms. In our system, the minimum sdk version for android is 9 and target sdk version is 17. In terms of the PC platform, Java Runtime Environment (allowing executing a computer program compiled into Java bytecode, designed by Oracle Corporation) has been embedded in the PC platform system, so that the system can be applied to different environments.

We used java language to preform ANNs for predicting function according to ANNs and back propagation algorithm and then encapsulated the function into a module, named class in Java, which can be packaged into both mobile and PC platforms [4]. The module was divided into two main components including reading normalized data, looking for the best bias and weight according to error. 815 groups of experimental data were firstly read into the module, and bias and weight were randomly set. One set of data was read into the input layer of the ANN each time. Values from the input layer were computed with bias and weight and transferred to the hidden layer. Hidden layer calculated values received using transfer function, computed with bias and weight and forwarded values to the output layer. After a series of 'forward' actions, ANNs output values were compared with actual output values and loss values were calculated with respects to all weights and bias in the network. Weight and bias were updated according to the loss values. The best weight and bias could be produced when the training with all 815 sets of data finished.

Android platform

The whole Android software development was conducted in Android Developer Tools including Eclipse Platform (Android Developer Tools is a plugin for Eclipse that provides a suite of tools to help developers develop Android application quickly) [5]. Firstly, the graphical layout and main logical module of software were designed and coded, respectively. Then each component in the graphical layout was bundled with corresponding function in main logical module. ANNs predicting module was related to certain function in main logical module. When particular component in graphical layout was invoked, which sometimes involved pressing buttons, related function in main module would call ANNs predicting module. Then two ANNs instances including heat collection rate and heat loss coefficient started to train using the 815 sets of data in a proper order. After training, established ANNs models received seven independent values from input boxes and output the two dependent values, heat collection rate and heat loss coefficient, which were displayed in a panel component in the graphical layout.

PC platform

We developed the PC-based software in Eclipse (an integrated development environment useful to develop applications). The user interface was designed with Java Graphical User Interface (GUI) which is a type of interface that allows users to interact with electronic devices through graphical icons and visual indicators [6]. Similar to the design in Android development, we added a particular event function on certain component in layout, named 'control' in GUI. When particular control was invoked, ANNs predicting module was woken up and two ANNs models including heat collection rate and heat loss coefficient were produced after training. Data from input boxes were imported into the established models and predicted results were displayed on the label in GUI layout.

Flow Chart of WaterHeater

Fig 1 shows the flow chart of WaterHeater. The system firstly examined the validity of input independent variables. If invalid, a new set of input was required. Else, the training part of ANNs was prompted and the valid data was stored. Then the ANNs training part starts to work. The gradient descent algorithm was used in ANNs model, which performed a feed-forward pass, computing the activations for layers and then updated the training parameters according to the errors between ANNs output and actual output in the data sets [7]. After training, the best bias and weight were used to test the data stored before. Finally, output results were displayed on the panel.

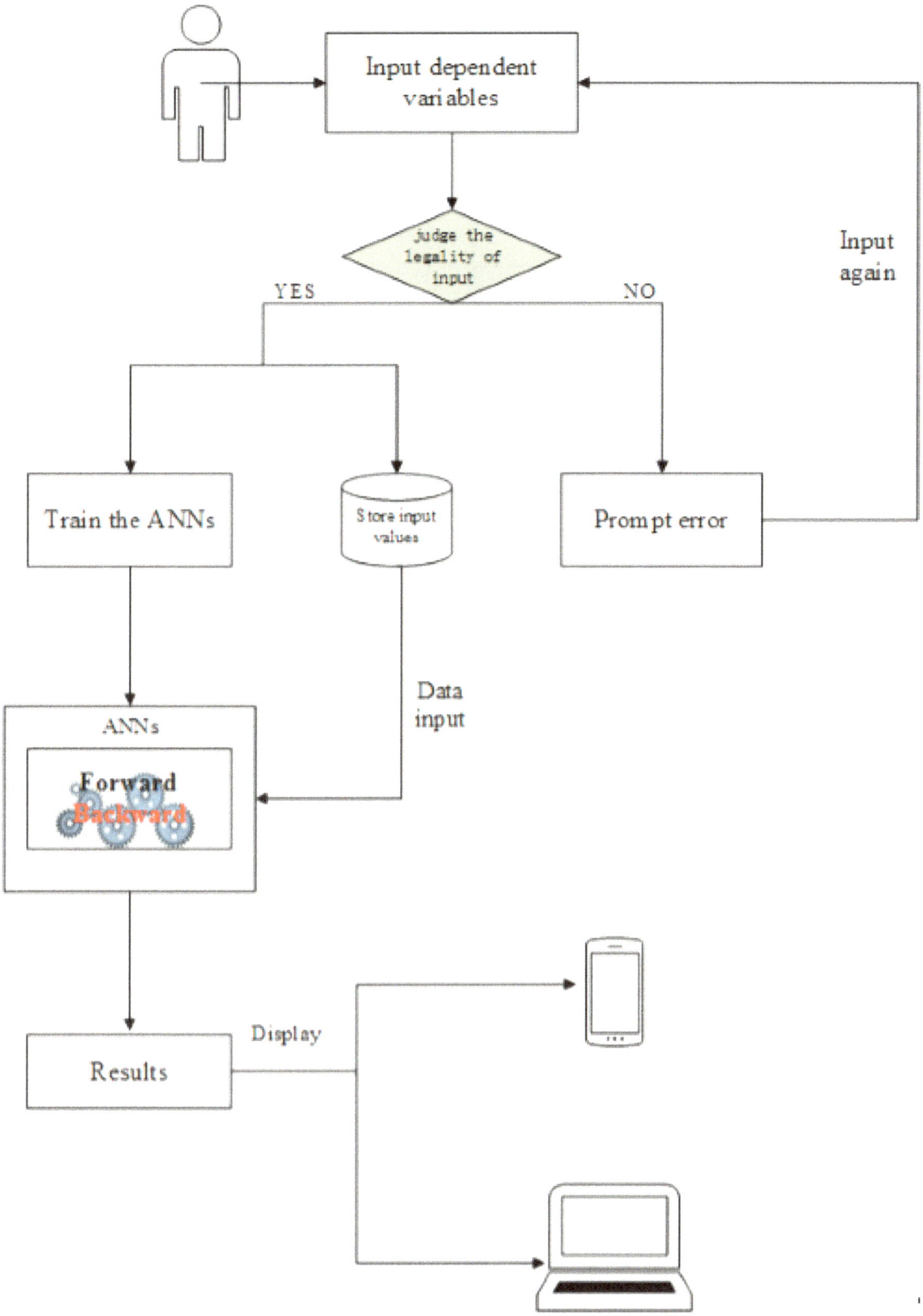

S1 File. Detailed descriptions of the design of *WaterHeater*. This also includes flow chart and user interface of *WaterHeater*.

S1 Table. Results of prediction models for heat collection rate.

1	1	0.9	0.1	0.6254
5	1	0.9	0.1	0.5979
10	1	0.9	0.1	0.5379
50	1	0.9	0.1	0.4057
100	1	0.9	0.1	0.3655
200	1	0.9	0.1	0.3659
250	1	0.9	0.1	0.3675
300	1	0.9	0.1	0.3693
400	1	0.9	0.1	0.3718
500	1	0.9	0.1	0.3736
200	2	0.9	0.1	0.3119
200	3	0.9	0.1	0.2916
200	4	0.9	0.1	0.2979
200	5	0.9	0.1	0.3291
200	6	0.9	0.1	0.3197
200	7	0.9	0.1	0.2702
200	8	0.9	0.1	0.3228
200	9	0.9	0.1	0.3393
200	10	0.9	0.1	0.3173
200	11	0.9	0.1	0.3098
200	12	0.9	0.1	0.301
200	13	0.9	0.1	0.3561
200	7	0.8	0.1	0.2869
200	7	0.7	0.1	0.3077
200	7	0.6	0.1	0.3277
200	7	0.5	0.1	0.3441
200	7	0.4	0.1	0.3564
200	7	0.3	0.1	0.3814
200	7	0.2	0.1	0.4459
200	7	0.1	0.1	0.5106
200	7	0.9	0.9	0.2049
200	7	0.9	0.8	0.2226
200	7	0.9	0.7	0.2421
200	7	0.9	0.6	0.2607
200	7	0.9	0.5	0.2651
200	7	0.9	0.4	0.2592
200	7	0.9	0.3	0.2555
200	7	0.9	0.2	0.2587

S2 Table. Results of prediction models for heat loss coefficient.

Training Epoch	Hidden Node	Learning Rate	Momen-tum	Mean RMS Error
1	1	0.9	0.1	1.1304
25	1	0.9	0.1	1.0921
50	1	0.9	0.1	1.0886
100	1	0.9	0.1	1.0976
150	1	0.9	0.1	1.1046
200	1	0.9	0.1	1.1096
300	1	0.9	0.1	1.1163
400	1	0.9	0.1	1.12
500	1	0.9	0.1	1.1216
50	2	0.9	0.1	1.1099
50	3	0.9	0.1	1.0999
50	4	0.9	0.1	1.1124
50	5	0.9	0.1	1.1097
50	6	0.9	0.1	1.1036
50	7	0.9	0.1	1.1192
50	8	0.9	0.1	1.1102
50	9	0.9	0.1	1.105
50	10	0.9	0.1	1.1082
50	11	0.9	0.1	1.1192
50	12	0.9	0.1	1.1152
50	13	0.9	0.1	1.1187
50	1	0.8	0.1	1.0822
50	1	0.7	0.1	1.0759
50	1	0.6	0.1	1.07
50	1	0.5	0.1	1.0645
50	1	0.4	0.1	1.0591
50	1	0.3	0.1	1.0502
50	1	0.2	0.1	1.0221
50	1	0.1	0.1	0.9246
50	1	0.1	0.9	1.0129

ACKNOWLEDGMENTS

This study is supported by the Fundamental Research Funds for the Central Universities, No. 2015MS108.

AUTHOR CONTRIBUTIONS

Conceived and designed the experiments: ZL. Performed the experiments: KL. Analyzed the data: HL. Contributed reagents/materials/analysis tools: XZ. Wrote the paper: GJ ZL KC.

REFERENCES

1. Mekhilef S, Saidur R, Safari A. A review on solar energy use in industries. Renewable and Sustainable Energy Reviews. 2011;15(4):1777–90. doi: 10.1016/j.rser.2010.12.018
2. Fan L, Liu G, Wang F, Geissen V, Ritsema CJ. Factors affecting domestic water consumption in rural households upon access to improved water supply: Insights from the Wei River Basin, China. PloS one. 2013;8(8):e71977. doi: 10.1371/journal.pone.0071977. pmid:23977190
3. Shah LJ, Furbo S. Theoretical flow investigations of an all glass evacuated tubular collector. Solar Energy. 2007;81(6):822–8. doi: 10.1016/j.solener.2006.09.007
4. Dowson M, Pegg I, Harrison D, Dehouche Z. Predicted and in situ performance of a solar air collector incorporating a translucent granular aerogel cover. Energy and Buildings. 2012;49:173–87. doi: 10.1016/j.enbuild.2012.02.007
5. Liu L-q, Wang Z-x, Zhang H-q, Xue Y-c. Solar energy development in China—a review. Renewable and Sustainable Energy Reviews. 2010;14(1):301–11. doi: 10.1016/j.rser.2009.08.005
6. Tang R, Li Z, Zhong H, Lan Q. Assessment of uncertainty in mean heat loss coefficient of all glass evacuated solar collector tube testing. Energy conversion and management. 2006;47(1):60–7. doi: 10.1016/j.enconman.2005.03.013
7. Kalogirou SA. Prediction of flat-plate collector performance parameters using artificial neural networks. Solar Energy. 2006;80(3):248–59. doi: 10.1016/j.solener.2005.03.003
8. Li H, Dai Y, Li Y, La D, Wang R. Case study of a two-stage rotary desiccant cooling/heating system driven by evacuated glass tube solar air collectors. Energy and Buildings. 2012;47:107–12. doi: 10.1016/j.enbuild.2011.11.035
9. Nahar N. Year round performance and potential of a natural circulation type of solar water heater in India. Energy and Buildings. 2003;35(3):239–47. doi: 10.1016/s0378-7788(02)00091-9
10. Kulkarni GN, Kedare SB, Bandyopadhyay S. Optimization of solar water heating systems through water replenishment. Energy Conversion and Management. 2009;50(3):837–46. doi: 10.1016/j.enconman.2008.09.019
11. Morrison G, Budihardjo I, Behnia M. Water-in-glass evacuated tube solar water heaters. Solar energy. 2004;76(1):135–40. doi: 10.1016/j.solener.2003.07.024
12. Wang P-Y, Guan H-Y, Liu Z-H, Wang G-S, Zhao F, Xiao H-S. High temperature collecting performance of a new all-glass evacuated tubular solar air heater with U-shaped tube heat exchanger. Energy Conversion and Management. 2014;77:315–23. doi: 10.1016/j.enconman.2013.08.019
13. Yao K, Li T, Tao H, Wei J, Feng K. Performance Evaluation of All-glass Evacuated Tube Solar Water Heater with Twist Tape Inserts Using CFD. Energy Procedia. 2015;70:332–9. doi: 10.1016/j.egypro.2015.02.131
14. Porras-Prieto CJ, Mazarrón FR, de los Mozos V, García JL. Influence of required tank water temperature on the energy performance and water withdrawal potential of a solar water heating system equipped with a heat pipe evacuated tube collector. Solar Energy. 2014;110:365–77. doi: 10.1016/j.solener.2014.09.030
15. Alfaro-Ayala JA, Martínez-Rodríguez G, Picón-Núñez M, Uribe-Ramírez AR, Gallegos-Muñoz A. Numerical study of a low temperature water-in-glass evacuated tube solar collector. Energy Conversion and Management. 2015;94:472–81. doi: 10.1016/j.enconman.2015.01.091
16. Tang R, Gao W, Yu Y, Chen H. Optimal tilt-angles of all-glass evacuated tube solar collectors. Energy. 2009;34(9):1387–95. doi: 10.1016/j.energy.2009.06.014
17. Budihardjo I, Morrison GL, Behnia M. Natural circulation flow through water-in-glass evacuated tube solar collectors. Solar Energy. 2007;81(12):1460–72. doi: 10.1016/j.solener.2007.03.002
18. Press CS. Specification of domestic solar water heating systems. Beijing 2011.
19. Liu Z, Li H, Zhang X, Jin G, Cheng K. Novel Method for Measuring the Heat Collection Rate and Heat Loss Coefficient of Water-in-Glass Evacuated Tube Solar Water Heaters Based on Artificial Neural Networks and Support Vector Machine. Energies. 2015;8(8):8814–34. doi: 10.3390/en8088814
20. Hopfield JJ. Artificial neural networks. Circuits and Devices Magazine, IEEE. 1988;4(5):3–10. doi: 10.1109/101.8118
21. Dayhoff JE, DeLeo JM. Artificial neural networks. Cancer. 2001;91(S8):1615–35. doi: 10.1002/1097-0142(20010415)91:8+<1615::aid-cncr1175>3.0.co;2-l
22. Piaggi P, Lippi C, Fierabracci P, Maffei M, Calderone A, Mauri M, et al. Artificial neural networks in the outcome prediction of adjustable gastric banding in obese women. PloS one. 2010;5(10):e13624–e. doi: 10.1371/journal.pone.0013624. pmid:21048960
23. Svozil D, Kvasnicka V, Pospichal J. Introduction to multi-layer feed-forward neural networks. Chemometrics and intelligent laboratory systems. 1997;39(1):43–62. doi: 10.1016/s0169-7439(97)00061-0
24. Johansson EM, Dowla FU, Goodman DM. Backpropagation learning for multilayer feed-forward neural networks using the conjugate gradient method. International Journal of Neural Systems. 1991;2(04):291–301. doi: 10.1142/s0129065791000261
25. Smits J, Melssen W, Buydens L, Kateman G. Using artificial neural networks for solving chemical problems: Part I. Multi-layer feed-forward networks. Chemometrics and Intelligent Laboratory Systems. 1994;22(2):165–89. doi: 10.1016/0169-7439(93)e0035-3
26. Kumar R, Aggarwal R, Sharma J. Energy analysis of a building using artificial neural network: A review. Energy and Buildings. 2013;65:352–8. doi: 10.1016/j.enbuild.2013.06.007
27. Wu J, Zhang G, Zhang Q, Zhou J, Wang Y. Artificial neural network analysis of the performance

characteristics of a reversibly used cooling tower under cross flow conditions for heat pump heating system in winter. Energy and Buildings. 2011;43(7):1685–93. doi: 10.1016/j.enbuild.2011.03.008

28. Jin W, Li ZJ, Wei LS, Zhen H, editors. The improvements of BP neural network learning algorithm. Signal Processing Proceedings, 2000 WCCC-ICSP 2000 5th International Conference on; 2000: IEEE.

29. Horikawa S-i, Furuhashi T, Uchikawa Y. On fuzzy modeling using fuzzy neural networks with the back-propagation algorithm. IEEE transactions on Neural Networks. 1992;3(5):801–6. pmid:18276479 doi: 10.1109/72.159069

30. Smartphone OS Market Share 2015 [2015]. Available:http://www.idc.com/prodserv/smartphone-os-market-share.jsp. Accessed 2015.

31. Zhang X, You S, Xu W, Wang M, He T, Zheng X. Experimental investigation of the higher coefficient of thermal performance for water-in-glass evacuated tube solar water heaters in China. Energy Conversion and Management. 2014;78:386–92. doi: 10.1016/j.enconman.2013.10.070

32. Standardization IOf. Solar heating-Domestic water heating systems[S]. Geneva:International Organization for Standardization.

CHAPTER 4

LOAD INDEX METRICS FOR AN OPTIMIZED MANAGEMENT OF WEB SERVICES: A SYSTEMATIC EVALUATION

Paulo S. L. Souza[1], Regina H. C. Santana[1], Marcos J. Santana[1], Ed Zaluska[2], Bruno S. Faical[1], Julio C. Estrella[1]

[1] Computer Systems Department, University of Sao Paulo, Sao Carlos, Sao Paulo, Brazil

[2] Electronic and Computer Science, University of Southampton, Southampton, United Kingdom

ABSTRACT

The lack of precision to predict service performance through load indices may lead to wrong decisions regarding the use of web services, compromising service performance and raising platform cost unnecessarily. This paper presents experimental studies to qualify the behaviour of load indices in the web service context. The experiments consider three services that generate controlled and significant server demands, four levels of workload for each service and six distinct execution scenarios. The evaluation considers three relevant perspectives: the capability for representing recent workloads, the capability for predicting near-future performance and finally stability. Eight different load indices were analysed, including the *JMX Average Time* index (proposed in this paper) specifically designed to address the limitations of the other indices. A systematic approach is applied to evaluate the different load indices, considering a multiple linear regression model based on the stepwise-AIC method. The results show that the load indices studied represent the workload to some extent; however, in contrast to expectations, most of them do not exhibit a coherent correlation with service performance and this can result in stability problems. The *JMX Average Time* index is an exception, showing a stable behaviour which is tightly-coupled to the service runtime for all executions. Load indices are used to predict the service runtime and therefore their inappropriate use can lead to decisions that will impact negatively on both service performance and execution cost.

INTRODUCTION

Web services are widely used in many Internet applications and comprise an essential component of SOA (Service-Orientated Architecture) systems. One major advantage is their intrinsic platform-independence, which becomes possible once the necessary web services are available from a server (or multiple servers) and accessed via the Internet [1], [2]. This paper presents a systematic evaluation of well-known load indices in the context of the load balancing of web services implemented on a cluster of servers.

Most web services seek to optimize key operational requirements such as high reliability, high security and shorter service runtime by adopting techniques such as load balancing[3], [4], [5], [6]. The individual server workload is

Citation: Souza PSL, Santana RHC, Santana MJ, Zaluska E, Faical BS, Estrella JC (2013) Load Index Metrics for an Optimized Management of Web Services: A Systematic Evaluation. PLoS ONE 8(7): e68819. doi:10.1371/journal.pone.0068819.

used by the server management software to distribute requests from the web to individual servers in a cluster of servers. The requirement is to select the most appropriate server which will maximize the target quality achieved by an individual web service [7], [8], [9], [10], [11].

Optimum load balancing is a problem of acknowledged difficulty, because of the performance levels in web service servers which track an extremely dynamic workload generated by the requested services. Moreover, the additional load generated by middleware systems (such as Apache Tomcat [12] and JBoss [13], [14]) also affects the overall system performance. The use of these middleware systems in server clusters introduces significant differences in the overall system operation when compared with other application domains, such as HPC (High-Performance Computing), distributed databases and static-content web servers.

A load index metric typically approximates the amount of workload in an individual server. The load index definition of Ferrari and Zhou [15] is adopted in this research, defining a load index as a non-negative variable, starting from zero (an idle resource) and increasing in value as the workload increases. Such a load index frequently represents the current workload and is often used to predict the server performance expected in the near future. Several alternative indices, such as the number of requests submitted, the size of the ready-processes queue, the size of the free memory and current service runtime have been adopted by web services for this purpose [16], [17], [18], [19]. However, in many cases the metric has been adopted without an accurate evaluation of its suitability and likely efficiency. Indeed, there appears to have been little or no prior work to establish the key advantages and disadvantages of the different metrics for this application.

The main objective of this paper is to analyse qualitative aspects of the different metrics under different service demands and workload levels. The results demonstrate that a good representation of the current workload can be achieved by some indices. The ability of the load index to predict the individual server service performance in the near future is also analysed, together with the stability of the index. These are important considerations when selecting the most appropriate server in a cluster to respond to a given service request.

The research reported in this paper is part of a larger project (named Jerrymouse), designed to deliver a new framework to distribute service requests to individual servers in an optimized, dynamic and transparent fashion [20]. The features of the load indices evaluated in this study have now been incorporated in the policies developed for the Jerrymouse framework.

The experiments reported in this paper consider three specific services, representative of distinct system demands - CPU-bound, memory-bound and database applications. A number of different scenarios are considered: firstly each of the three services above (CPU-bound, memory-bound and database) running by themselves. A further scenario considers a mixture of all three services and also another two more scenarios, again with a mixture of services but running on a platform with normal load (i.e. *not-overloaded*) and then a platform which has been deliberately *overloaded*. Each of these scenarios also considers four different levels of workload, with one, two, four and then eight concurrent clients requesting the services.

A number of different load indices are analysed - seven metrics that are commonly used together with an eighth metric, the *JMX Average Time*, which has been especially designed to address the disadvantages of the other metrics. The details of this new index, the *JMX Average Time* metric, are set out for the first time in this paper.

The load indices are evaluated in this paper using three different approaches. Firstly, graphs are used to compare the measured service runtime and the values of the indices generated from a real system executing the scenarios. In this paper, service runtime is the response time, i.e., the amount of user time that has passed since a particular service started until it is completed. A systematic approach to evaluate the different load indices is then applied, using a multiple linear regression model based on the stepwise-AIC (Akaike Information Criteria) method for the selection of the best models representing an index or a union of indices [21], [22]. The service runtime was also evaluated by means of the main linear models generated through the stepwise-AIC method. This runtime prediction demonstrates, in this practical example, the impact of different load indices on the performance estimate. The final evaluation presented in this paper compares the stability of the indices based on their standard deviation. The stability of an index is compared to the other indices and, in particular, to the runtime stability.

The results show that a careful selection of metrics is essential to achieve high performance and high overall server utilization. While most of the load indices studied do indeed represent the workload to some extent, the use of a less-appropriate metric will result in the selection of an inappropriate server by incorrectly assessing a node as either overloaded or idle, when in fact a significantly more suitable selection is possible. This incorrect selection impacts both on the overall quality of service and also the energy efficiency of the system (this is the so-called "green" factor).

This paper is organized as follows: 'SOA and Web Services' presents concepts of SOA and web services; 'Monitoring Web Services' discusses how to monitor web services using the Ganglia monitoring-software tool; the main properties related to load indices are highlighted in 'Load Indices'; 'Materials and Method' describes the approach used in the experiments to collect and analyse the data; 'Results and Discussion' points out the details of the main results, correlating their different aspects; finally, 'Conclusions' presents the final considerations and highlights future research directions.

SOA and Web Services

Web services are a key mechanism for the provision of remote services executing elsewhere on the web. They allow integration between computers, databases and networks by creating a logical link that can be invoked by a distant client. Services run remotely in servers, providing functionality that is both more accessible and also independent of the platform.

Services are made available to applications through standard publishing and discovery protocols. Web service providers publish descriptions of their services using discovery agents and well-defined standards [17]. Client applications interested in these services follow the description provided to establish a connection. The WSDL (Web Service Description Language) allows the description of services by means of an

XML (eXtensible Markup Language) file, which contains information about the methods supported by the service, its location and arguments. This file is stored in a broker using (for example) a UDDI (Universal Description Discovery and Integration) protocol, which defines methods to discover and publish service directories [17]. SOAP (Simple Object Access Protocol) is a protocol specification for exchanging structured information on a distributed platform, using XML content in HTTP messages. REST (Representative State Transfer) is an architectural style to build distributed applications using HTTP messages. Both REST and SOAP can be used by client applications to request remote services [23].

Web service providers are able to run in clusters, which can potentially improve a number of different aspects, such as performance, fault tolerance and availability [24], [25], [26], [27]. Apache Tomcat [12], JBoss [13], [14] and Apache Axis2 [28] are examples of web service providers. Apache Tomcat is a servlet-container fully compliant with the Oracle specification. Tomcat supports the use of clusters through automatic publication and section-replication of services which provides fault tolerance and flexibility to the client when accessing databases through dynamic pages. The automatic publication of services in different nodes assists the developer during the service publication. JBoss is designed to provide a complete solution to business-integration using Apache Tomcat and Java technology [13],[14]. Axis (Apache eXtensible Interaction System) is a framework to create clients, servers and gateways for SOAP or REST. Axis also includes a simple server to receive requests, connection with Apache Tomcat via servlets, support for WSDL updated, tools to generate classes based on WSDL and additional tools for monitoring [28].

SOA and web services have generated several new challenges in the provision of effective computing systems. These challenges can be classified into three levels: basic, composite and management [29]. The basic level refers to the details of middleware, such as publication, discovery, selection, heterogeneous platforms and security. The composite level aggregates multiple services into a single "composite" service. Orchestration and choreography are examples of interaction protocols designed to control and coordinate collaborating services. On the top of these levels is the management level, designed to provide facilities, such as service governance, monitoring, metrics and load balancing.

It is possible to organize web services in several different ways [13], [14], depending on the objectives and the choice of providers and platforms. This paper assumes that a typical platform consists of nodes acting as UDDI broker, client, front-end, back-ends and database servers. The client node hosts the application that requests services. This application searches for the service description in a UDDI broker and then sends an HTTP message with SOAP content to the front-end. The front-end can receive the HTTP message using a web server, as Apache [20] or directly through JBoss [30]. If an Apache server receives this message, it routes it to JBoss using a distributing policy to distribute requests to the back-ends. Several front-end nodes can interact and cooperate to receive requests from applications. A back-end node receives the request by using its JBoss instance, which is responsible for the actual running of the service. The back-end node returns the results to the front-end, which then sends them back to the client (back-ends may also return results directly to the client, depending on the settings). Remote database servers are usual in the web service context, where services send requests to a database in order to complete their jobs.

Monitoring Web Services

The monitoring of web services provides useful data to estimate the near-future performance, avoid potential bottlenecks, optimize the use of system resources and generally improve the overall cost-benefit ratio [31].

Ganglia is a software-monitoring tool developed by the University of Berkeley and widely used in distributed platforms [32]. It offers scalable monitoring based on hierarchical distributions of clusters known as *federations*. Ganglia has a flexible design and can collect pre-defined indices as well as allowing users to create their own indices. The standard indices built in Ganglia provide information about the node configuration, the percentage of CPU use, the number of processes in the ready (or blocked) queue, the free memory and the use of disk and network.

Gmond is a Ganglia daemon present in all nodes. It collects and publishes previously selected indices, receives information from other nodes (using multicasting) and publishes its own information for other nodes. The information is distributed in an XML document to allow other systems in the platform to access it in a straightforward fashion, using a TCP connection and an XML parser. Gmtad is a tool that groups different gmonds, creating a hierarchical structure called *federation of clusters* (the objective of the federation concept is to reduce the overall communication overhead when updating indices over a widely-distributed platform).

The gmetric tool supports the addition of new metrics into Ganglia by means of TCP/IP messages sent to gmond. It is also able to run programs developed in other languages to collect data directly from the machine where the JSP (Java Service Provider) is running through the use of JMX (Java Management Extensions). JMX manages resources (called Managed Beans or MBeans) as applications, devices and services. Some examples of data that can be obtained from JMX are the heap size, the number of loaded classes and the number of active threads. MBeans usually runs on servers with Apache Tomcat and JBoss to monitor their nodes.

The combination of JMX and Ganglia generates and publishes load indices, providing a flexible and efficient method to monitor web service servers. JMX monitors and provides JBoss information while Ganglia is responsible for the collection and publishing of metrics. A script sends the indices collected from JBoss to gmetric, which acts as a link between these two environments: JBoss/JMX and gmetric/gmond. This arrangement enables each gmetric to send indices related to the execution of web services to gmond, which broadcasts its values to the other gmonds so that the entire cluster maintains updated information about the whole platform.

The combination of Ganglia and JMX provides a very robust framework for web services, but an important question about these monitoring tools is to determine which load index to monitor in a given specific execution. This question does not have a straightforward answer because of the diversity of demands imposed by web services. In practice, different implementations have selected different load indices to represent the web service workload. The next section describes the main load indices currently used by typical web services.

Load Indices

The correct use of load indices must consider the overall platform objectives as well as the performance metrics associated with each objective. Some examples of overall objectives widely used are a reduction in the response time, an increase in the platform throughput, an improvement of load balancing and provision of enhanced fault tolerance [33]. Load indices collect data from a platform to quantify the overall system behavior in the context of the objectives. They can also estimate 'near-future' performance based on current performance and the recent past. Service runtime reduction is a common and important objective and has been selected as the key performance objective in the experiments described in this paper to evaluate the effectiveness of the load indices.

The quality of a load index can be determined by specified criteria and desirable properties[15]: 1) sufficient accuracy to represent the workload adequately, even under different computational demands; 2) a straightforward relationship with performance metrics (ideally linear) such that the load index can be easily applied to predict the probable future performance; 3) stability, in particular by smoothing out workload peaks; 4) scalability, allowing a low implementation cost to be maintained even in large platforms. The costs of gathering the load index and the strategy adopted to transmit it to other nodes are also very important because they directly affect the scalability. This paper does not address the scalability of load indices specifically, although the Results section contains some brief comments.

Besides quantitative properties, load indices should also present other qualitative properties, such as the ability to encapsulate details from architectures and Operating Systems, a capability for supporting portability among heterogeneous platforms, and an overall objective of providing transparency to applications, providers and services. It is far from trivial to satisfy all these properties simultaneously, especially because some of them are contradictory. For example, increasing the index accuracy typically increases the cost of obtaining the data and reducing the peaks in an index usually decreases both its accuracy and ability to predict future performance.

The HPC application domain traditionally uses a number of different load indices, of which many are related to the scheduling of processes and load balancing. Some classic examples are the *number of ready processes*, *percentage of idle CPU time*, *percentage of memory used* and *number of active network connections* [34], [35], [18]. The index called*ready-processes* has been widely used in the HPC context, because it can be easily extracted from the operating system and provides important information on the overall system performance [15].

Web services typically make use of load indices to predict the performance in at least two cases: during the discovery phase and when distributing requests to the back-end nodes[36]. The discovery-phase algorithms use load indices to select the best options of services registered in brokers by providers through the UDDI protocol [24], [25], [37], [26], [30], [38],[39]. Load indices are also used after the discovery phase, when the web service provider must distribute the request that has just arrived to a back-end node in a cluster of servers[34], [16], [31], [26], [30].

A number of different load indices can be found in the scientific literature for web services[9], [40], [5]. Some examples are the number of requests (received, finalized or waiting to be attended), the shortest response time, the throughput availability (an uptime percentage for a service in a period), reliability (the probability of receiving a correct answer in a maximum specified time), safety (which represents the confidentiality and authentication guaranteed), accuracy (the service error rate) and integrity (the capability for completing the correct execution of a service transaction).

In addition to the various load indices described in the literature, service providers (e.g. JBoss [13], [14] and Tomcat [12]) often use practical indices, such as the number of submitted requests, active sessions, network traffic (among web service providers) and pending requests.

MATERIALS AND METHODS

In this experimental study services were considered on a platform consisting of three nodes with Intel Core 2 Quad 2.66 GHZ processors, 6 MB cache, 4 GB DDR2 RAM and a Sata-2 Hard Disk of 500GB/7200RPM. The database used was MySQL, version 5.1. The network was a Gigabit Ethernet with TP-LINK TL-SL3428 switch and the operating system was GNU/Linux, kernel 2.6.31–22. The compilers used were gcc 4.3 and Java 1.6.0_20. The web service provider was JBoss 5.1.0.GA. Ganglia 3.1.2 was used for the monitoring and JMX 5.1.0.GA ran on the server in default configuration.

Although relatively modest, the platform can nevertheless analyse the comparative behaviour of load indices in a web service server. It supports a controlled demand generated from the execution of applications that request services hosted in monitored servers. The application sends requests to the front-end node through HTTP messages with SOAP encapsulation. The front-end forwards the HTTP message to its local JBoss, which runs the requested service. The third node hosts a database server to handle requests from services.

The experimental study considers the execution of two different services in the front-end, generating controlled and specific workloads on the CPU and memory. A third service (called database) generates workload mainly on the memory, disks and network-interface of the remote database server to simulate the typical environment when remote databases are accessed by services [41].

These three services (CPU-bound, memory-bound and database) are used in the experimental studies to produce controlled demands to analyse the behaviour of different load indices. These controlled demands enable a deeper analysis of the behaviour of the load indices, allowing, among other things, comparing an index with respect to different demands. The demands related to CPU, memory and databases were chosen because they can be clearly correlated to real services, which generate similar workloads on the servers.

The CPU-bound service executes instructions providing arithmetic operations on integer and floating-point matrices, conditional-control structures, repetition structures and also short procedure calls [42], [43]. This service avoids I/O operation requests and the matrices used are small in order to fit into the cache and therefore avoid unnecessary main memory accesses. The CPU-bound service returns the amount of interactions and the runtime.

The memory-bound service evaluates the memory bandwidth between CPU and main memory, using vector processing with vectors large enough to eliminate cache effects and allow the description of the results in terms of a continuous bandwidth [42], [43]. The main results returned by this service are throughput, average time, shortest time and longest time.

The service designed to request the database (database service for short) is based on the OSDB benchmark, an open source version of the AS^3AP benchmark originally developed by the Compaq Computer Corporation [41]. This service includes the creation and access of tables with data from text files and also the creation of indices.

The evaluation of the load index behaviour was performed under three different perspectives [15]: its accuracy in representing the workload, its relation with performance metrics (runtime in this case) and its stability.

The experiments do not consider a discovery phase, since this phase does not affect the load index behaviour in the front-end node. Each client-application runs exactly 1,000 iterations, each one executing the following sequence: request the service, wait until the result is returned and print the result. Each service takes approximately 10 s when running without competition from other services. The amount of 1,000 iterations for each client requesting a service running at 10 s has been chosen to avoid the inaccuracy of small samples, without generating excessive runtimes. The analyses considered confidence intervals of 99% for all the results.

One, two, four and eight concurrent application threads were requested for each service, each one in a different experiment. When four application threads are considered, for example, four concurrent requests were sent to the same service in the server. This strategy is designed to facilitate the analysis of the load indices under specific and homogeneous workloads, reducing the effect of any transitional period and allowing the real influence of each load to be determined.

Table 1 shows the load indices considered in the experiments. The indices *Idle CPU,Waiting I/O*, *Free Memory*, *Swap Used*, *Bytes In/Out* and *Ready Processes* were gathered directly from the operating system using the Ganglia monitoring tool. The *Amount of Requests* index represents the amount of requests recently submitted, evaluated from the difference between the last two samplings of the total amount of requests submitted, which is monitored from JMX and distributed through Ganglia.

Table 1. Load indices analysed in the experiments.

Indices	Descriptions
Idle CPU	Percentage of idle CPU time.
Waiting I/O	Percentage of CPU I/O waiting time.
Free Memory	Amount of GBytes free in the memory.
Swap Used	Amount of GBytes used for swap.
Bytes In/Out	Amount of KBytes received and sent over the network interface.
Ready Processes	Average number of processes in the ready queue (over the last minute)
Amount of Requests	Amount of requests received between the last two samples of the total amount of requests submitted, monitored by JMX.
JMX Average Time	Arithmetic average using sliding windows with the total runtime by JMX and total amount of requests submitted.
Service Runtime	Service runtime on the server (directly collected from the service code).

doi:10.1371/journal.pone.0068819.t001

The *JMX Average Time* metric is a new load index proposed in this paper and represents the average runtime of a specific service, from a JMX perspective. As shown in Eq. (1), this index is based on the average of the five most recently-collected samples, using two sliding windows with five positions each. In Eq. (1) ***N*** is the amount of total samples already performed, ***i*** is the ***i^{th}*** sample, ***n*** is the ***n^{th}*** value calculated for the *JMX Average Time*, **t** is the *Service Total Runtime* by JMX and ***r*** is the *Total Amount of Requests Submitted* by JMX. The *service total runtime* by JMX is an accumulated index, containing the sum of all service runtimes since the server started operation. The *total amount of requests* represents the accumulated number of requests sent to a specific service hosted in the server since the operation started.

$$JMXAvgTime_n = \frac{\sum_{i-N-4}^{N} t_i}{\sum_{i-N-5}^{N-1} r_i} \quad (1)$$

The experimental studies performed to determine the sliding window size considered the three services (CPU-bound, Memory-Bound and Database) and sizes of windows varying from one to twenty-five positions. The standard deviation from *JMX Average Time* results for each window size was used to compare their stability. The results show that sliding windows between two and twenty-five positions were, on average, 18.9% more stable that the sliding window with just one-position, and that from five-positions it was already possible to obtain an stability 18% better. The choice of a five-position window considered the trade-off between reducing performance peaks and maintaining recent data for the calculation of *JMX Average Time*. The *JMX Average Time* index is calculated assuming a shift of one location between the samples collected for the *amount of requests* and *service total runtime*metrics, as shown in Figure 1. The *total amount of requests* metric does not consider the last sample because it represents only the requests submitted and not those already completed while the *service total runtime* represents the runtime of finalized requests. This shift minimizes the impact of those requests submitted and not yet completed. Although this mechanism does not guarantee that the average will reflect only completed requests, nevertheless it acts to minimize this problem. The empirical results demonstrate that the *JMX Average Time* metric provides an excellent index when compared with the service runtime gathered directly from the server.

#	Service Total Runtime by JMX
n	Total $Runtime_{n}$
n-1	Total $Runtime_{n-1}$
n-2	Total $Runtime_{n-2}$
n-3	Total $Runtime_{n-3}$
n-4	Total $Runtime_{n-4}$
n-5	Total $Runtime_{n-5}$
...	...

#	Total Amount of Requests Submitted by JMX
n	Total of $Requests_{n}$
n-1	Total of $Requests_{n-1}$
n-2	Total of $Requests_{n-2}$
n-3	Total of $Requests_{n-3}$
n-4	Total of $Requests_{n-4}$
n-5	Total of $Requests_{n-5}$
...	...

Figure 1. Sliding windows used to evaluate JMX Average Time.

Service Runtime is the response variable used in the linear models (described in next section) and was used to benchmark the behaviour of the indices being studied, because the key performance objective is to reduce the overall service runtime.

Different numbers of instances from these benchmarks were considered to represent the number of users in the system at a given moment (one, two, four and eight users). While these benchmarks were requesting services for the server, the Ganglia distributed monitoring system [32] and the Java Management Extensions (JMX) [44] kept collecting distinct load indices from the server nodes. The daemon gmond, running in the front-end node, sampled the indices every 10 s and then sent the results back to the client node. A script in the client node collected all the published indices and stored them in a log file. The interval of 10 s reduces the cost of updating the load indices and thus has minimal effect on the service runtime. In summary, the requests are sent by the clients to the servers that execute the services and are monitored by the Ganglia and JMX in order to obtain the samples.

All results of the load indices presented in this paper use the EMA (Exponential Moving Average) moving average using a window covering the last five samplings [45]. The EMA presented in Eq. (2) is similar to the simple moving average, although more weight is given to the latest data. In Eq. (2) V_n is the last sampling performed at time n and N is the window size (five in this paper).

$$EMA_n = (V_n - EMA_{n-1})X\frac{2}{1+N} + EMA_{n-1} \quad (2)$$

RESULTS AND DISCUSSION

The main results from the experiments are initially organized by service in this section. They are presented with a focus on three main factors: the relationship with service runtime (the performance objective adopted), stability and capability to represent the actual workload.

The relationship between the runtime service and the eight load indices described in Table 2 was evaluated through multiple linear regression models, which helps to understand how these indices may explain the service runtimes. In models of multiple regression it is necessary to select which predictor variables (the load indices in this paper) best explain the response variable (the service runtime). In other words, the objective is to select and rank the load indices depending on how well they explain the runtime variations. The combination of load indices that best represents the service runtime was selected using the stepwise method with AIC (the Akaike Information Criteria) [21], [22]. The stepwise method uses an automatic approach to select predictor variables, instead of considering all possible regressions. It starts with no input predictor variable in the model and in each step a new variable is introduced and then tested to see if a better model has been obtained. When the model reaches three or more predictor variables, the stepwise method checks to see if a better result can be obtained by removing one of them (the AIC criterion is used to compare the quality of the models in each step). It is important to observe that the stepwise method is able to analyse both an isolated index and merged ones during its analysis. This procedure is effectively constructing a new metric that considers an average value using distinct indices.

Table 2. Significance of the indices to explain the variability in the service runtimes evaluated through the stepwise-AIC method.

Load Indices	CPU-bound Estimates (%)	Memory-bound Estimates (%)	Database Estimates (%)	All Services Estimates (%)	*Overloaded* Platform Estimates (%)	*Not-Overloaded* Platform Estimates (%)
Idle CPU	−0.218 (3.3)	−2.843 (5.4)	−0.386 (13.6)	−0.161 (0.3)	−3.495 (6.1)	−1.579 (7.1)
CPU Waiting I/O	0.248 (3.8)	2.255 (4.3)	0.181 (6.3)	3.128 (6.0)	1.949 (3.4)	0.314 (1.4)
Swap Used	0.0 (0.0)	7.929 (15.0)	0.0 (0.0)	4.558 (8.7)	16.236 (28.2)	0.0 (0.0)
Free Memory	−0.510 (7.7)	−2.334 (4.4)	−0.074 (2.6)	−0.900 (1.7)	−0.579 (1.0)	−0.886 (4.0)
Ready Processes	0.392 (6.0)	2.399 (4.5)	0.025 (0.9)	1.836 (3.5)	0.933 (1.6)	1.421 (6.4)
Bytes In/Out	0.065 (1.0)	0.841 (1.6)	0.650 (22.8)	0.0 (0.0)	5.778 (10.1)	0.230 (1.0)
JMX Average Time	5.153 (78.2)	33.773 (64.0)	1.378 (48.3)	40.665 (77.6)	26.425 (46.0)	16.375 (74.1)
Amount of Requests	0.0 (0.0)	0.383 (0.7)	0.157 (5.5)	1.132 (2.2)	2.080 (3.6)	1.285 (5.8)

doi:10.1371/journal.pone.0068819.t002

Load indices are expressed using different scales, therefore to enable a valid comparison of different indices in a common range, they were all normalized to be between -1 (lowest) and 1 (highest). The results presented in this paper for linear regression models were obtained using the *Action* statistical software package [46].

The stepwise method with AIC applied to the load indices estimates the best models to represent the service runtime. Table 2 shows the results of the influence estimated for each index, quantifying how significant the indices are (in relation to other ones) to explain the variability of the service runtimes. In this case, the higher the absolute value the more significant an index is. A positive sign indicates a direct correlation between the index and the service runtime; a negative sign indicates an inverse correlation. The load indices with estimates 0.0 (zero) in Table 2 mean that they have been discarded by the linear regression model, as they have not contributed to the service runtime prediction.

The coefficients of determination (R^2) shown in Table 3 quantify the amount of the variability, i.e. the extent that the runtime services (y-axis) can be predicted by the load indices (x-axis). R^2 ranges from 0 to 1, where values close to 1 represent the best predictions. Figure 2complements Table 3 showing graphically how the predicted service runtimes fit to the real service runtimes, using the multiple linear regression model evaluated for each one of the six scenarios.

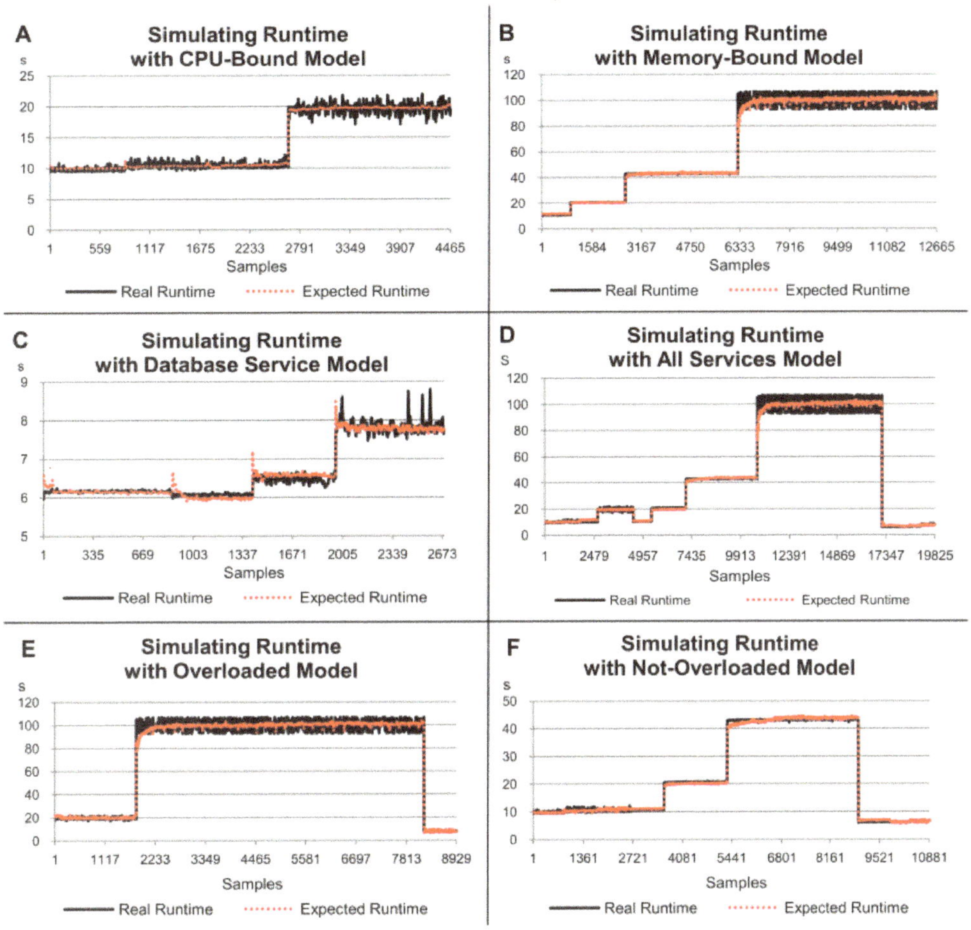

Figure 2. Graphs showing the relation between the predicted runtimes based on multiple linear models (used in the six scenarios) and the actual runtimes. The x-axis represents the samples collected every 10 s by Ganglia and JMX while the benchmarks were requesting services for the server.

Table 3. Coefficient of determination (R^2) obtained from the stepwise-AIC method.

Scenarios	R^2
CPU-bound	0.986
Memory-bound	0.993
Database	0.963
All services	0.996
All services with *overloaded* platform	0.991
All services with *not-overloaded* platform	0.998

doi:10.1371/journal.pone.0068819.t003

The experiments described in this paper were based on six distinct execution scenarios. Firstly, the selection of models was applied separately to the results of each service: CPU-bound, memory-bound and database (the first, second and third scenarios). The objective was to identify significant differences in the behaviour of load indices when the demand requested by the service is previously known. The results from all services were then grouped and a new selection of the linear model was conducted, aiming at verifying the behaviour of the indices when requests are performed for services whose demand is heterogeneous and normally unknown in advance (the fourth scenario). In this case, the evaluation considered all the results of the services with one, two, four and eight concurrent clients. A final evaluation was conducted with all three services executing in both*overloaded* and *not-overloaded* platforms (the fifth and sixth scenarios). The *overloaded*platform was based on the results from eight concurrent clients requesting the three services. In contrast, the *not-overloaded* platform used results from one, two and four concurrent clients. The term *not-overloaded* is used instead of *idle* because the platform is actually executing services requested by four concurrent clients, although it is operating normally and is not yet overloaded. During our experiments, the *overloaded* platform had on average: 73% of CPU usage, 600 MB of swap utilization, 5.3 requests being processed and 6.5 ready processes waiting in the queue. In contrast, the *not-overloaded* platform had around 48% of CPU usage, 2.2 requests being processed, 2.9 ready processes waiting in the queue and no swap space was required.

The stability of the indices was analysed with their standard deviations, using the normalized values as a basis (Table 4). These normalized values were used to permit the comparison of the standard deviations obtained for each load index and also for the service runtime. The standard deviation for a specific service represents the arithmetic average of the standard deviations from each group of clients (one, two, four and eight). Analogously, the standard deviation for all services is the arithmetic average of their standard deviation; for an *overloaded* platform it is the average of standard deviation from the results from all services with only eight concurrent clients and for the *not-overloaded* platform it is the average of standard deviation from all services with one, two and four clients.

Table 4. Standard deviation (SD) representing the stability of the load indices.

Scenarios	Clients	Service Runtime	Idle CPU	CPU Waiting I/O	Swap Used	Free Memory	Ready Processes	Bytes In/Out	JMX Average Time	Amount of Requests
CPU-bound	1	0.005	0.012	0.000	0.000	0.009	0.042	0.005	0.001	0.021
	2	0.009	0.059	0.001	0.000	0.011	0.058	0.017	0.001	0.041
	4	0.007	0.128	0.001	0.000	0.014	0.131	0.027	0.002	0.079
	8	0.014	0.075	0.003	0.000	0.029	0.141	0.103	0.002	0.140
	Average SD	0.009	0.069	0.001	0.000	0.016	0.093	0.038	0.001	0.070
Memory-bound	1	0.001	0.015	0.001	0.000	0.023	0.047	0.009	0.001	0.020
	2	0.002	0.016	0.001	0.000	0.043	0.061	0.009	0.004	0.035
	4	0.002	0.029	0.004	0.000	0.091	0.099	0.023	0.024	0.065
	8	0.071	0.157	0.329	0.068	0.330	0.277	0.019	0.057	0.178
	Average SD	0.019	0.054	0.084	0.068	0.122	0.121	0.015	0.021	0.074
Database	1	0.000	0.038	0.045	0.000	0.044	0.052	0.011	0.000	0.020
	2	0.001	0.024	0.000	0.000	0.013	0.061	0.006	0.002	0.053
	4	0.002	0.034	0.001	0.000	0.011	0.096	0.037	0.001	0.089
	8	0.004	0.043	0.006	0.000	0.012	0.134	0.094	0.001	0.168
	Average SD	0.002	0.035	0.013	0.000	0.020	0.086	0.037	0.001	0.083
All services		0.010	0.053	0.033	0.068	0.052	0.100	0.030	0.008	0.076
Overloaded		0.030	0.092	0.112	0.068	0.124	0.184	0.072	0.020	0.162
Not- Overloaded		0.003	0.039	0.006	0.000	0.029	0.072	0.016	0.004	0.047

doi:10.1371/journal.pone.0068819.t004

The standard deviations could also be used to compose new load indices, in order to include the variability of them when estimating future runtimes. However, this would require new experimental studies with an extra dimension of complexity. Given our initial objectives and the results already achieved, this additional complexity is outside the scope of the current paper.

The analysis of the capability of load indices to represent the workload, independently of their correlation with the runtime service, was done observing the behaviour of each index when there was variation in the workload arising from changes in the number of concurrent clients.

Finally, the results are shown with the use of different (and specific) load indices to predict the service runtime. The main objective here is to demonstrate the impact of the load indices on the quality of the decisions made by the policies controlling the distribution of requests for web services. This simulation of the service runtime also verifies the coherence of the load index representation (as pointed out with the linear models). According to the multiple regression models, the more significant indices are expected to estimate the service runtimes more precisely.

The data for the indices was collected without any specific instrumentation of services, providers or applications. This approach provides for a high portability among different platforms, since these indices are the usual ones normally available in a variety of different architectures and operating systems.

Scalability and the overall costs necessary to obtain the load indices are not considered in this paper. Ganglia gathered the indices locally from the Operating System or JMX and then the normal hierarchical federation structure was used to minimize the publishing costs to remote nodes.

CPU-Bound Service Scenario

The runtimes for the CPU-bound service showed significant changes only when eight concurrent requests arrived in the server (Figure 3). The times observed scale from approximately 10 s for one, two and four clients to approximately 20 s for eight clients. This can be explained by the use of a CPU with four cores in the server hosting the service. Considering a demand located inside the CPU, each core executes a service separately up to four simultaneous requests, without any significant changes in the runtime. When there was a larger amount of services than cores (two services per core on average), the runtime doubled.

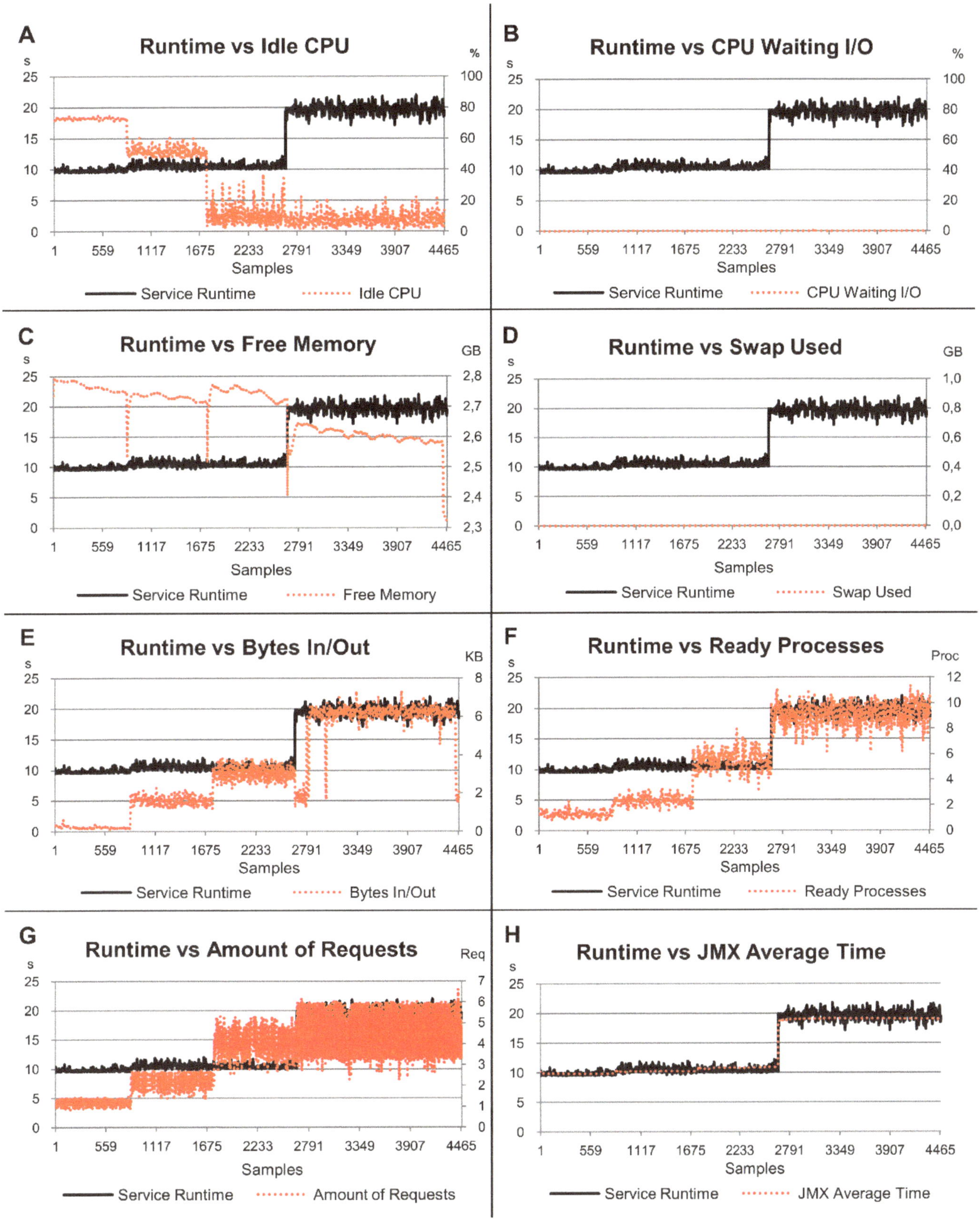

Figure 3. Relation of the service runtime versus eight load indices, considering the first scenario (CPU-bound service). The left-hand scale of the y-axis always represents the service runtimes in seconds (s). The right-hand scale of the y-axis, where necessary, represents the metric used by the load index. The x-axis represents the samples collected every 10 s by Ganglia and JMX while the benchmarks were requesting services for the server.

The R^2 value for this CPU-bound service indicates that 98.6% of the runtimes can be explained by the analysed load indices (Table 3). The *JMX Average Time* load index has a strong weight in the evaluation and represents 78% of the estimates, when compared to other indices (which have a much smaller significance compared with the *JMX Average Time* metric).

This small significance is, in part, due to the behaviour of these indices when the workload changes, as a consequence of the number of concurrent clients. It is possible to observe in the graphs that the variability in the indices, excluding the *JMX Average Time*, do not follow the same behaviour as the service runtime. In contrast to expectations, even load indices strongly related to the CPU use, such as *Idle CPU* and *Ready Processes*, had a low correlation. Again, the CPU with four cores in the server was responsible for this gap, when considering CPU indices. Another aspect related to *Idle CPU* and *Ready Processes* is their low stability, according to the standard deviation given in Table 4. Similarly, the *Amount of Requests* index demonstrated high instability in this experiment and was not significant to justify most of the runtimes.

In respect of the stability, the *JMX Average Time* index also provided the best result (0.001), with an even better value than the one observed for the service runtimes. Another index with a similar result is the *CPU Waiting I/O*, mainly due to the small number of memory accesses. The standard deviation for the *Swap Used* index was zero because it was not used, hence there was no variation during executions (Table 4). The most unstable index was the *Ready Processes* index (0.093), being 10 times more unstable than the service runtime.

The load indices exhibited distinct behaviours, when analysed under the perspective of workload representation and independently of the service runtime. The *CPU Waiting I/O*,*Free Memory* and *Swap Used* indices were not able to represent the workload variations imposed by CPU-bound service. They remained at around the same level for all workloads. The *Idle CPU* index was not able to represent the change of workload from four to eight clients, since the percentage of idleness approached zero. The *Bytes In/Out*, *Ready Processes* and *Amount of Requests* indices showed variations according to the workloads submitted, although such variations did not always represent changes in the service performance in terms of runtime. As expected, the *JMX Average Time* index followed the runtime and represented the workload variation only when it affected the service performance.

Memory-Bound Service Scenario

Figure 4 shows that the runtimes for the memory-bound service exhibited variations for all the different amounts of concurrent clients executed. The average times were 11 s for one client, 20 s for two clients, 43 s for four clients and 100 s for eight clients. These variations occur mainly because the runtimes of the services executed in the CPU with four cores depended on the memory response, which is unique and shared by all cores. Therefore there is a gradual variation in the runtime according to the number of concurrent services in the cores.

The linear models associated with the indices analysed for the memory-bound service show that 99.3% of the runtimes can be explained by the variability in the indices (Table 3). In this context, the *JMX Average Time* index represented 64% of the estimates made and *Swap Used* 15%. These results are expected, especially the *Swap Used*, given the high memory demand generated by eight concurrent clients. However, differently from what was expected, the *Free Memory* index did not provide a good service runtime estimate, representing only 4.4%. Although the *Free Memory* index has exhibited good behaviour in respect of the computational workload, the lack of stability with four and mainly eight clients reduces its significance.

The most stable indices for the memory-bound service were *Bytes In/Out* and *JMX Average Time*, with standard deviations of 0.015 and 0.021 respectively (Table 4). These results are close to the Service Runtime stability, whose standard deviation was 0.019. A high instability of the load indices was observed, mainly when the platform remained *overloaded*. The*Swap Used* index, for example, did not show any variation with one, two and four clients; however, it presented a high instability with 8 clients (0.068). The memory-bound service with eight concurrent clients was the only case in which any memory swap was necessary in the experiments. The most unstable indices were the *Free Memory*, *Ready Processes* and the *CPU Waiting I/O* indices with standard deviation of 0.122, 0.121 and 0.084 respectively. Note that these values are up to 5.4 times higher than that observed for the service runtime (0.019). One positive aspect of this high instability is the potential ability to use it as a heuristic to detect computer overload with high-memory-demand applications.

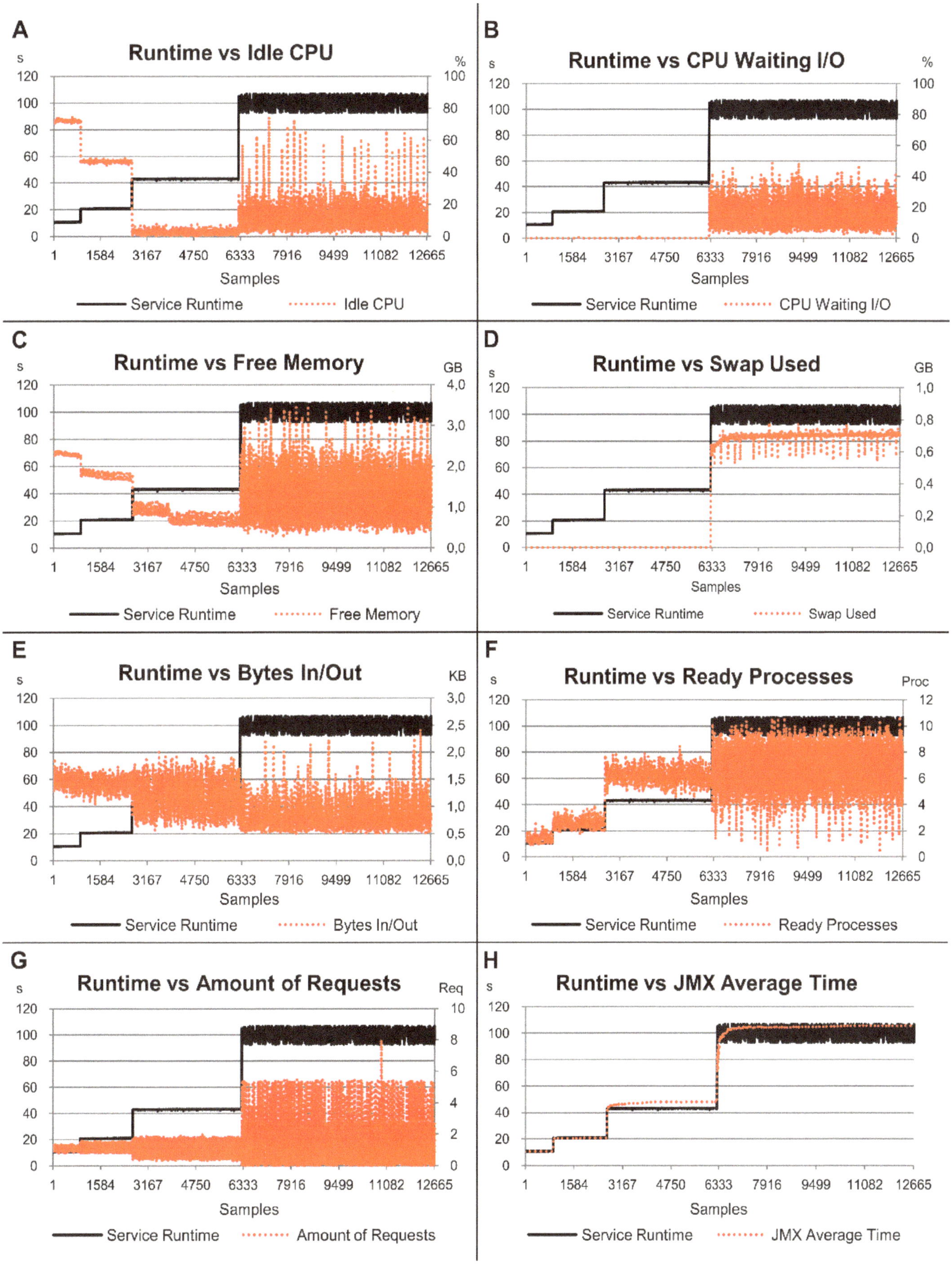

Figure 4. Relation of the service runtime versus eight load indices, considering the second scenario (memory-bound service). The left-hand scale of the y-axis always represents the service runtimes in seconds (s). The right-hand scale of the y-axis, where necessary, represents the metric used by the load index. The x-axis represents the samples collected every 10 s by Ganglia and JMX while the benchmarks were requesting services for the server.

In respect of the workload variation, the *Idle CPU*, *Free Memory*, *Ready Processes* and *JMX Average Time* indices exhibited behaviour according to the workload submitted (Figures 4–A, 4–C, 4–F and 4–H). On the other hand, the *CPU Waiting I/O*, *Swap Used* and *Amount of Requests* indices (Figures 4–B, 4–D and 4–G) remained at their normal levels with one, two and four clients, presenting a significant variability only with eight concurrent clients, when a high instability could be observed. The *Bytes In/Out* index (Figure 4–E) remained at the same level until there were four concurrent clients, however it was possible to observe a higher instability for four and eight clients.

Database Service Scenario

The service runtimes for the database service were, on average, 6.2 s, 6.1 s, 6.5 s and 7.8 s for one, two, four and eight concurrent clients respectively (Figure 5). The runtimes for one and two clients were similar mainly due to the persistent connections used by OSDB [41]. The service runtime with one and two clients is determined by the establishment of this connection and from four simultaneous accesses the demand generated was capable of affecting the service runtime.

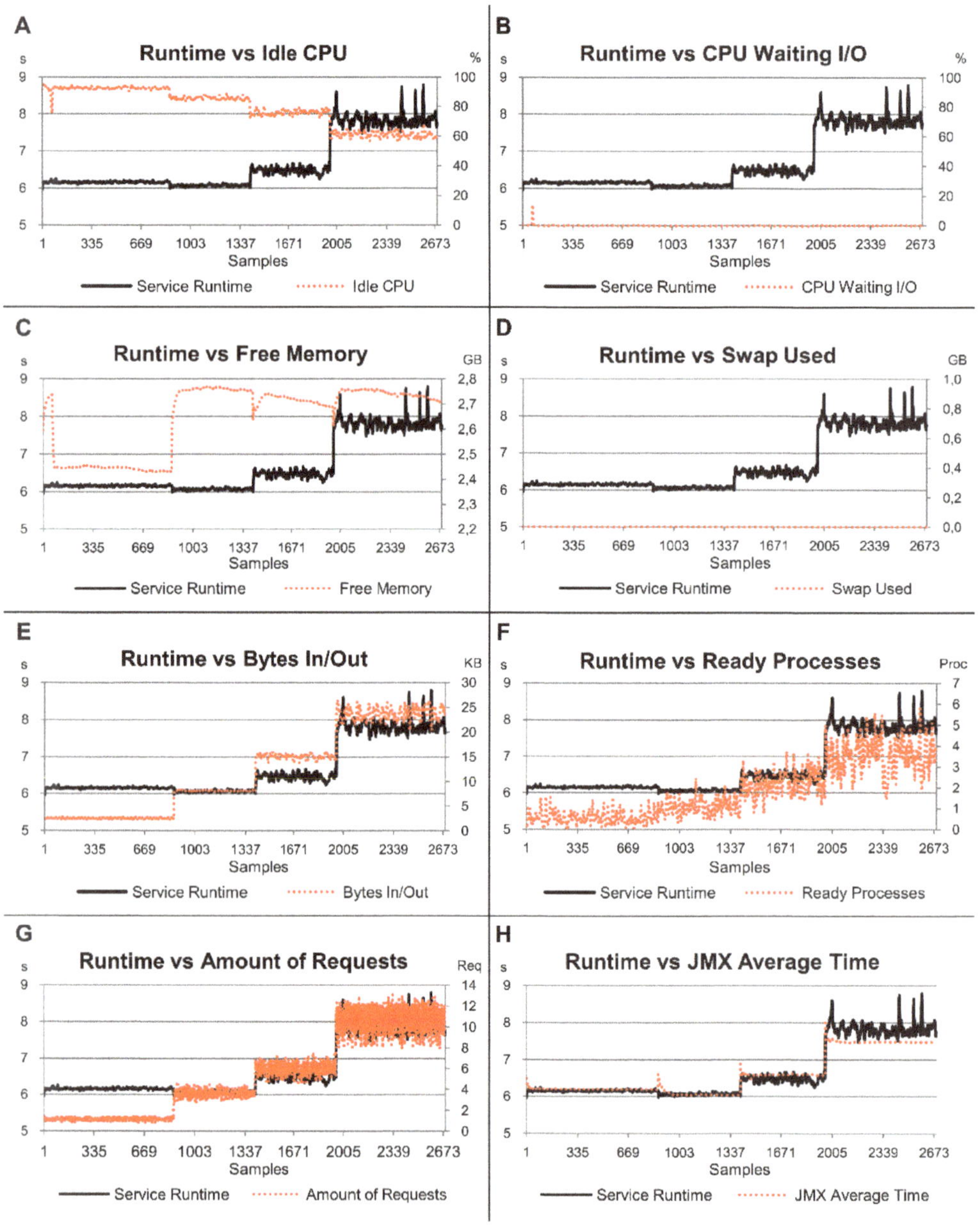

Figure 5. Relation of the service runtime versus eight load indices, considering the third scenario (database-bound service). The left-hand scale of the y-axis always represents the service runtimes in seconds (s). The right-hand scale of the y-axis, where necessary, represents the metric used by the load index. The x-axis represents the samples collected every 10 s by Ganglia and JMX while the benchmarks were requesting services for the server.

The R^2 for the database service indicates that 96.3% of the service runtimes are explained by the load indices analysed (Table 3). The *JMX Average Time* index had the largest representation of the estimates with 48.2%, followed by *Bytes In/Out* with 22.8%. Together these indices represent 71% of the estimates. The more significant value reached by *Bytes In/Out* for this service is coherent with the demand generated, since the database server is in a remote computer. The model also showed a representation of 13.6% for *Idle CPU* (the best result for this index) probably due to the stability observed (when comparing its stability with other services). All other indices showed a lower representation due to their behaviour in relation to the respective runtime changes (see *CPU Waiting I/O*, *Free Memory* and *Swap Used*) and their instability (see *Ready Processes* and *Amount of Requests*).

Considering only the stability (Table 4), the *JMX Average Time* index demonstrated the best standard deviation (0.001), with a value close to the service runtime (0.002). The *Swap Used* index did not show any variation during the executions with database service and therefore its value is zero. The most unstable indices were *Ready Processes* and *Amount of Requests*, with 0.086 and 0.083, respectively. These values are up to 42 times higher than that observed for the service runtime.

The *Idle CPU*, *Bytes In/Out*, *Ready Processes*, *Amount of Requests* and *JMX Average Time*indices were all able to represent the workload variation (Figures 5–A, 5–E, 5–F, 5–G and 5–H). The *CPU Waiting I/O* and *Swap Used* indices did not show any variability during the execution of the service (Figures 5–B and 5–D). The behaviour of the *Free Memory* index was not consistent with the variability in the workload (Figure 5–C).

All Services Scenario

The graphs relating runtimes of all services with the load indices are shown in Figure 6. The workload plotted in Figure 6 changes according to the service being executed (samples 1 to 4467 represent the CPU-bound service workload, samples 4468 to 17141 represent the memory-bound service workload and samples 17142 to 19825 represent the database service workload). The R^2 resulting from the linear model with all services indicates that 99.6% of the service runtimes can be explained by the variability in the indices (Table 3). The most significant index for the estimates was again the *JMX Average Time* index, responsible for 77.6% of them. Figure 6–H shows the behaviour of this index in relation to service runtime. Despite the lower significance, the *Swap Used* index was the second best index, with 8.7%, due to its behaviour when the platform remained *overloaded.*

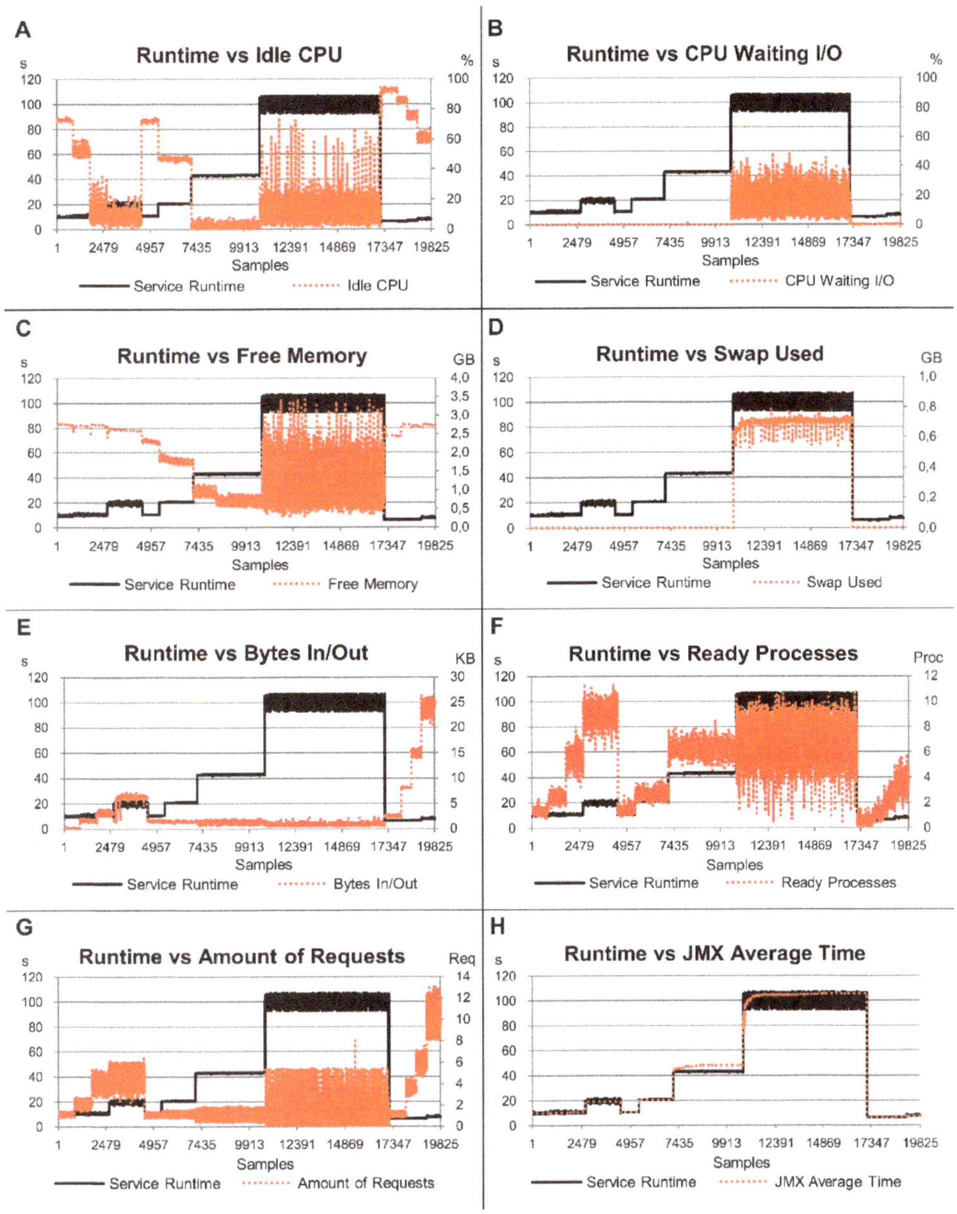

Figure 6. Relation of the service runtime versus eight load indices, considering the fourth scenario (all services). The left-hand scale of the y-axis always represents the service runtimes in seconds (s). The right-hand scale of the y-axis, where necessary, represents the metric used by the load index. The x-axis represents the samples collected every 10 s by Ganglia and JMX while the benchmarks were requesting services for the server.

The most stable index for all-services was *JMX Average Time*, with a standard deviation of 0.008 (Table 4). This stability is close (and even better) to that observed for service runtime (0.010). The most unstable indices were *Ready Processes* and *Amount of Requests*, with values of 0.1 and 0.076, respectively.

Overloaded and Not-Overloaded Platforms Scenarios

R^2 for the *overloaded* platform indicates that 99.1% of the variability in the indices explain the runtimes (see Table 3 and Figure 7). The *JMX Average Time* index corresponds to 46% of these estimates, followed by *Swap Used* with 28.2%. These results were as expected, due to the tight-coupling of the *JMX Average Time* index with the service runtime and the behaviour of the *Swap Used* index when executing the memory-bound service with the*overloaded* platform. It is important to point out that *Swap Used* indicated that there was no variability for the CPU-bound and database services, even with an *overloaded* platform. Another aspect verified in the experiments was the relative instability of the indices in this high-demand scenario. *Ready Processes* and *Amount of Requests* were the more unstable indices, 0.184 and 0.162 respectively (Table 4). These results are up to 8 times higher than that of the standard deviation for *JMX Average Time* (0.020). The relationships of service runtimes with *Ready Processes* and *JMX Average Time* for *overloaded* platforms are shown in Figures 7–F and 7–H.

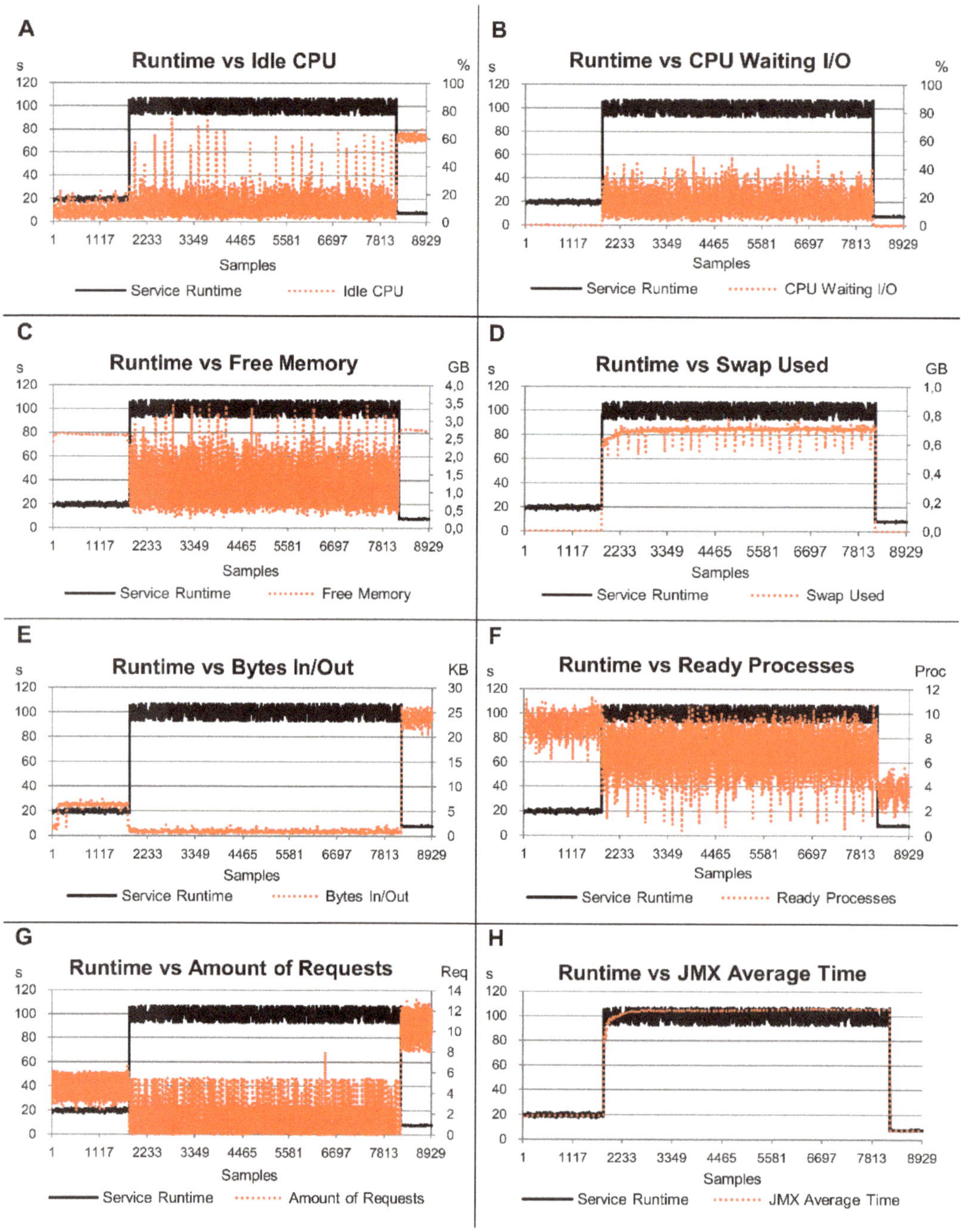

Figure 7. Relation of the service runtime versus eight load indices, considering the fifth scenario (overloaded platform). The left-hand scale of the y-axis always represents the service runtimes in seconds (s). The right-hand scale of the y-axis, where necessary, represents the metric used by the load index. The x-axis represents the samples collected every 10 s by Ganglia and JMX while the benchmarks were requesting services for the server.

The value of R^2 for the *not-overloaded* platform was 99.8% and the *JMX Average Time*index was responsible for 74.1% of the estimates. Its significance was much larger than that of other indices in this scenario (see Figure 8 and Table 2).

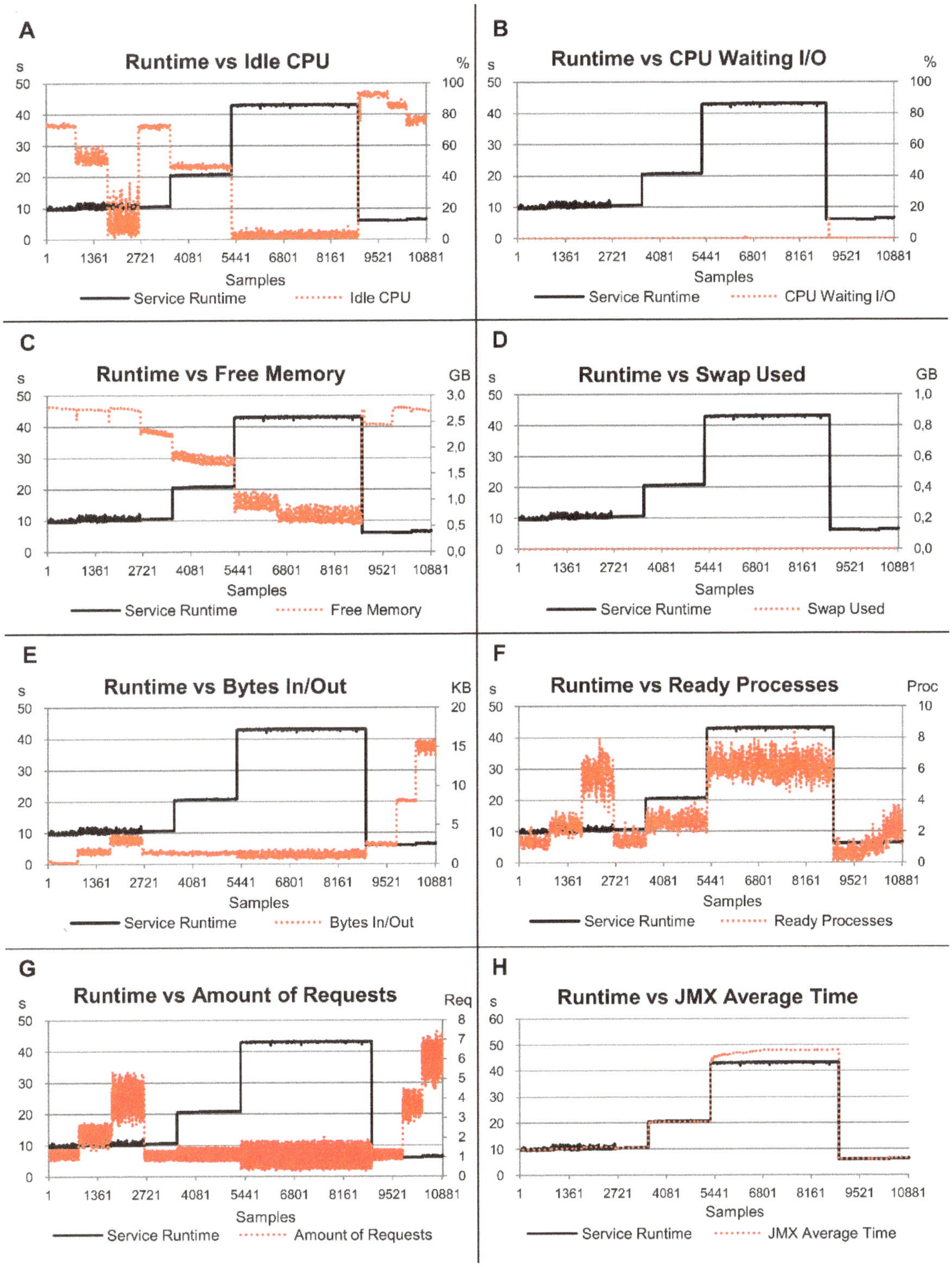

Figure 8. Relation of the service runtime versus eight load indices, considering the sixth scenario (not-overloaded platform). The left-hand scale of the y-axis always represents the service runtimes in seconds (s). The right-hand scale of the y-axis, where necessary, represents the metric used by the load index. The x-axis represents the samples collected every 10 s by Ganglia and JMX while the benchmarks were requesting services for the server.

In relation to stability, the *JMX Average Time* index showed a stable behaviour with a standard deviation of 0.004 (Table 4). This stability was close to that observed for the service runtime (0.003). The *CPU Waiting I/O* index also showed a stable behaviour for *not-overloaded* platforms, with a standard deviation of 0.006. However, this index presented a significance of just 1.4% to explain the variability of service runtimes. The instability of the other indices was high when executing on a *not-overloaded* platform, if compared to the variability of the service runtime. *Bytes In/Out* was 4.3 times more unstable and *Ready Processes* was 23 times more unstable than service runtime. The graphs for *JMX Average Time*, *Bytes In/Out* and *Ready Processes* (Figures 8–E, 8–F and 8–H) demonstrate the relation of these indices with service runtime.

Predicting Service Runtimes

Future service runtimes were simulated in this study using simple linear models based on load indices and the correlation between these simulated times with the actual ones was analysed using the R^2 values. The linear equations used in this simulation and the R^2 for each of them are given in Table 5. Figure 9 shows the relation between the real service runtime (measured from the system) and the estimated service runtime (obtained from linear equations) graphically. As in this case the indices are considered individually, the normalization applied in the previous section is not necessary and the equations presented in Table 5 use the original data.

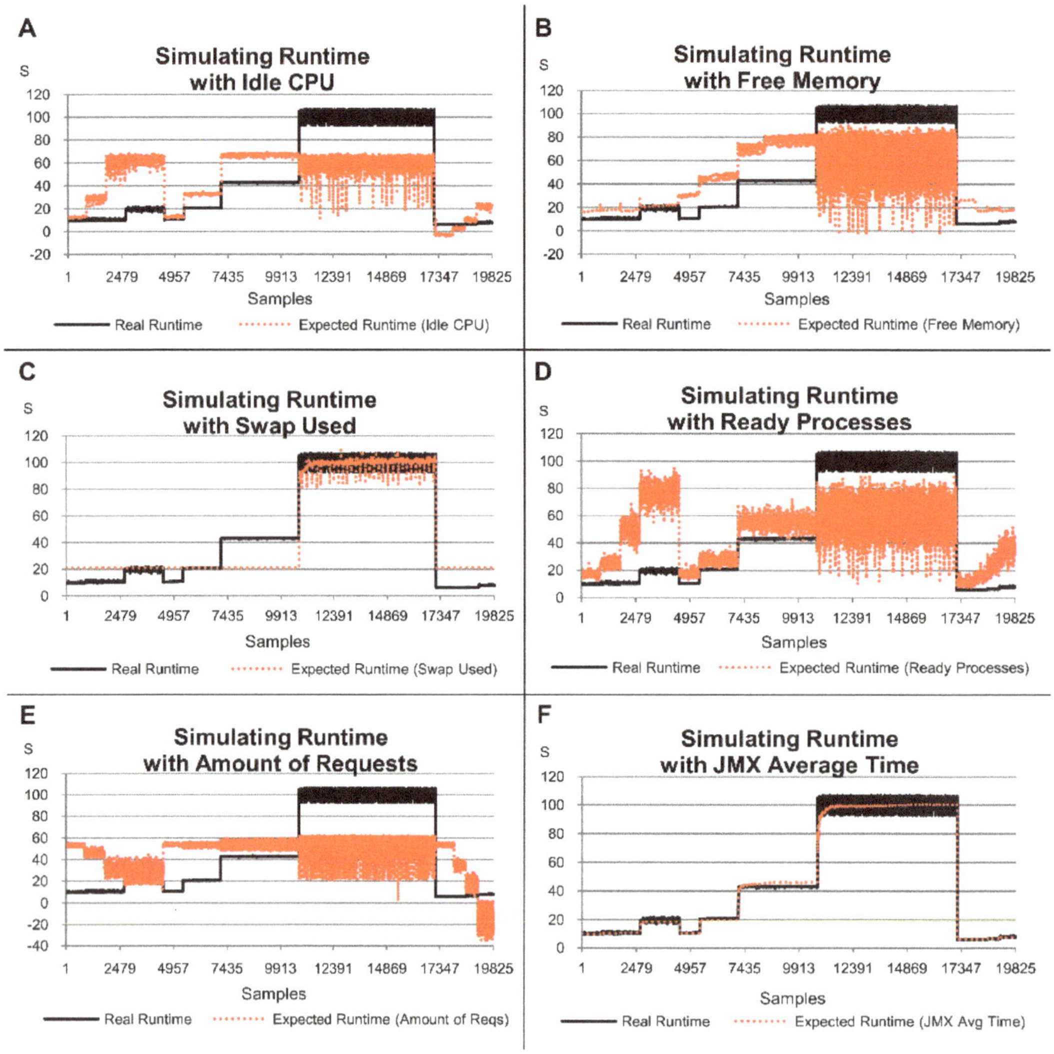

Figure 9. Graphs showing the relation between actual runtimes and the predicted ones. The x-axis represents the samples collected every 10 s by Ganglia and JMX while the benchmarks were requesting services for the server.

Table 5. Linear equations used to estimate the service runtimes and their coefficients of determination.

Load Indices	Linear Equations	R^2
JMX Average Time	0.9473 * JMX Average Time +0.3677	0.995
Swap Used	112.9882 * Swap Used +21.0953	0.903
Idle CPU	−0.7736 * Idle CPU +68.9285	0.353
Free Memory	−29.3253 * Free Memory +97.9967	0.400
Ready Processes	7.7600 * Ready Processes +6.7807	0.301
Amount of Requests	−7.5027 * Amount of Requests +61.8613	0.201

doi:10.1371/journal.pone.0068819.t005

The main objective is to demonstrate how efficient each load index would be when applied to a distributing policy to select the best server to execute a web service. Although the load indices can be used in different ways by distributing policies, this simulation shows a usable result when predicting the near-future performance, assuming a linear relation between the runtime and indices.

The service runtime simulation is based on the execution of different services generating heterogeneous demands with distinct workloads (one, two, four and eight concurrent clients). Six load indices were chosen according to their importance in relation to the estimates evaluated in the previous section. Another factor considered was the constant use of such indices as metrics by policies to distribute requests on clusters of web services.

The indices chosen were *JMX Average Time* and *Swap Used* (these were the more significant according to the linear model); *Idle CPU* and *Free Memory* (less significant according to the linear model) and *Ready Processes* and *Amount of Requests* (frequently associated with the request distributing policies).

The simulations of runtime service using *JMX Average Time* and *Swap Used* provided the best results, according to R^2 (Table 5 and Figure 9). These results are consistent with the preliminary results from the linear regression. The simulations resulting from the *Idle CPU*and *Free Memory* indices are significantly different from the actual values observed for the service runtime, with a R^2 of 0.353 and 0.4, respectively. The simulations resulting from*Ready Processes* and *Amount of Requests* showed results even more different from real ones, with R^2 of 0.301 and 0.201 respectively. Divergent results mean that the policies are highly likely to make incorrect decisions, over or under estimating the host performance. These cases affect the service performance adversely and increase the overall cost of execution.

CONCLUSIONS

This paper has described experimental studies carried out to evaluate the behaviour of eight load indices widely used for web service servers. Three perspectives were considered: 1) the capability for predicting near-future performance (using the service runtime to determine performance), 2) the workload representation and 3) index stability.

The experiments considered three different types of services that generated controlled demands on the server, four levels of workload for each service and six distinct execution scenarios, where each scenario involves: one type of service by itself, all services operating together and the level of workload in the node (*overloaded* and *not-overloaded*).

The results demonstrate that most of the indices do not have a close relation to the actual service runtime. This means that the use of such indices as driving metrics for heuristics to optimize the performance can have serious drawbacks and platforms can be wrongly assessed to be overloaded or idle. This can reduce the overall performance of the services significantly, since requests can be sent in error to supposedly idle servers, which are actually overloaded. Alternatively, nodes can be considered overloaded where in fact they are not. In this case, unnecessary nodes may be used raising both the execution costs and the overall energy consumption.

The *JMX Average Time* index proved to be the best in terms of significance to estimate the service runtime, considering all the six scenarios of the experiments and the multiple linear regression model based on the stepwise-AIC method. Its significance changed from 46.0% up to 78.2% (64.7% on average) in those scenarios. The *JMX Average Time* index was also able to simulate the service runtime with high accuracy in relation to real runtime, obtaining an excellent coefficient of determination equivalent to 99.5%. *Swap Used* showed a good coefficient of determination equivalent to 90.3%, due to the scenario with the *overloaded*platform executing the memory-bound service. It also showed a null variation for other scenarios.

Other indices showed a smaller significance compared to *JMX Average Time* in the same scenarios. In some cases the significance was only smaller, as in the case of the *Swap Used* for all services with the *overloaded* platform. However, in other cases (*Amount of Requests* for the CPU-bound service, for instance), *Swap Used* was null. The simulations of the service runtime using some of these indices confirmed their relatively limited importance, with coefficients of determination indicating significance from 20% to 40%.

The *JMX Average Time* index is more stable than the other indices studied in most cases. It is stable for all scenarios that were considered, being in some cases even better than the stability of the runtime service. The stability of the other indices changed significantly depending on the scenario used. This stability behaviour for the other indices in different scenarios restricts the practical use of such indices because they are not able to correlate to runtime service, a more stable metric, in an appropriate way. The instability could be attenuated by using a larger window of samples in the EMA. However, all results in this paper used EMA and increasing the sample window size will also reduce the accuracy of the index, since it will introduce a longer delay before changes in the current workload are reflected in the index.

The main contribution of this paper is to demonstrate by means of experimental studies that the metrics commonly used by performance-estimating heuristics do not reflect, in practice, the actual performance. The results show that the mistaken use of such indices can lead to decisions that will have a negative impact on both service performance and execution cost.

Another contribution of this paper is the proposal of the *JMX Average Time* metric, a novel load index which is independent of the platform and to the demand generated by services. The *JMX Average Time* index is tightly-coupled to the service runtime, a widely used performance metric for computing platforms.

Future work will be directed to the following objectives: 1) applying the results of this paper to the ***Jerrymouse*** project [20] for the development of advanced request distributing policies on web service clusters; and 2) establishing a methodology to evaluate load indices in a comparable and standardized way.

ACKNOWLEDGMENTS

The authors acknowledge the assistance of Dr. Dorival Leao Pinto Junior (Department of Applied Mathematics and Statistics, ICMC-USP) with the linear regression model.

AUTHOR CONTRIBUTIONS

Conceived and designed the experiments: PSLS RHCS. Performed the experiments: BSF. Analyzed the data: PSLS RHCS MJS. Wrote the paper: PSLS RHCS. Contributed to the interpretation of results and finalized manuscript: EZ MJS JCE.

REFERENCES

1. Bichler M, Lin K (2006) Service-Oriented Computing, Computer. 39(3): 99–101. doi: 10. 1109/mc. 2006. 102
2. Huhns MN, Singh MP (2005) Service-oriented computing: key concepts and principles, IEEE Internet Computing. 9(1): 75–81. doi: 10. 1109/mic. 2005. 21
3. Rosenberg F, Platzer C, Dustdar S (2006) Bootstrapping Performance and Dependability Attributes of Web Services. In Proceedings of the IEEE International Conference on Web Services (ICWS '06). IEEE Computer Society, Washington, USA, 205–212.
4. Rud D, Schmietendorf A, Dumke R (2006) Performance Modelling of WS-BPEL-Based Web Service Compositions. In Proceedings of the IEEE Services Computing Workshops (SCW '06). IEEE Computer Society, Washington, USA, 140–147.
5. Song HG, Ryu Y, Chung T, Jou W, Lee K (2005) Metrics, Methodology, and Tool for Performance-Considered Web Service Composition. Computer and Information Sciences (ISCIS2005), Lecture Notes in Computer Science 3733: 392–401. doi: 10. 1007/11569596_42
6. Xiong P, Fan Y (2007) QoS-aware Web Service Selection by a Synthetic Weight. In Proceedings of the Fourth International Conference on Fuzzy Systems and Knowledge Discovery (FSKD '07), IEEE Computer Society Washington, USA 3: 632–637. doi: 10. 1109/ fskd. 2007. 462
7. Ardagna D, Pernici B (2006) Global and Local QoS Guarantee in Web Service Selection. Business Process Management Workshops. Lecture Notes in Computer Science 3812: 32–46. doi: 10. 1007/11678564_4
8. Grundy J, Hosking J, Li L, Liu N (2006) Performance Engineering of Service Compositions. In Proceedings of the International Workshop on Service-Oriented Software Engineering (SOSE '06), ACM, New York, USA, 26–32.
9. Liu Y, Gorton I, Zhu L (2007) Performance Prediction of Service-Oriented Applications based on an Enterprise Service Bus, In Proceedings of 31st Annual International Computer Software and Applications Conference(COMPSAC 2007), Beijing, China. 1: 327–334. doi: 10. 1109/compsac. 2007. 166
10. Schopfl JM, Raicu I, Pearlman L, Miller N, Kesselman C, et al. (2006) Monitoring and Discovery in a Web Services Framework: Functionality and Performance of Globus Toolkit MDS4. Argonne National Laboratory Tech Report ANL/MCS-P1248–0405, 1–6.
11. Tu S, Flanagin M, Wu Y, Abdelguerfi M, Normand E, et al. (2004) Design Strategies to Improve Performance of GIS Web Services. In Proceedings of the International Conference on Information Technology: Coding and Computing (ITCC'04) IEEE Computer Society, Washington, DC, USA 2: 444–448. doi: 10. 1109/itcc. 2004. 1286692
12. The Apache Software Foundation (1999) Apache Tomcat. Available:http://tomcat. apache. org/Accessed 11 October 2012.
13. Red Hat (2005) JBoss Application Server Documentation. Available:http://www. jboss. org/jbossas/docs/7-x. html Accessed 11 October 2012.
14. Marchioni F (2010) JBoss AS 5 Development. Packt Publishing.
15. Ferrari D, Zhou S (1987) An Empirical Investigation of Load Indices for Load Balancing Applications. In Proceedings of the 12th IFIP WG 7. 3 International Symposium on Computer Performance Modelling, Measurement and Evaluation (Performance '87), North-Holland Publishing Co. , Amsterdam, Netherlands, 515–528.
16. Dyachuk D. , Deters R (2007) Optimizing Performance of Web Service Providers. In Proceedings of the 21st International Conference on Advanced Networking and Applications (AINA '07). IEEE Computer Society, Washington, USA, 46–53.
17. Papazoglou MP, van den Heuvel W-J (2005) Web Services Management: A Survey. IEEE Internet Computing 9(6): 58–64. doi: 10. 1109/mic. 2005. 137
18. Qin X (2008) Performance comparisons of load balancing algorithms for I/O-intensive workloads on clusters. Journal of Network and Computer Applications 31(1): 32–46. doi: 10. 1016/j. jnca. 2006. 07. 001
19. Saddik AE (2006) Performance Measurements of Web Services-Based Applications. IEEE Transactions on Instrumentation and Measurement 55(5): 1599–1605. doi: 10. 1109/tim. 2006. 880288
20. Souza PSL, Faical BS, Matos J, Santana MJ, Santana RHC, et al. . (2011) Jerrymouse: a tool for a flexible and dynamic distribution of web service requests. In Proceedings of the 8th IEEE 2011 International Conference on Services Computing (SCC 2011), Washington, USA, 520–527.
21. Yamashita T, Yamashita K, Kamimura R (2007) A Stepwise AIC Method for Variable Selection in Linear Regression. Communications in Statistics–Theory and Methods 36(1): 2395–2403. doi: 10. 1080/03610920701215639
22. Montgomery DC, Peck EA, Vining GG (2012) Introduction to Linear Regression Analysis. 5th edition, New Jersey: John Wiley & Sons, Inc. , 672 p.
23. Josuttis NM (2007) SOA in Practice: Art of Distributed System Design. O'Reilly and associates.
24. Al-Masri E, Mahmoud QH (2007) Discovering the Best Web Service. In Proceedings of the 16th international conference on World Wide Web (WWW '07). ACM, New York, USA, 1257–1258.
25. Kalepu S, Krishnaswamy S, Loke SW (2003) Verity: A QoS Metric for Selecting Web Services and Providers, In Proceedings of the Fourth International Conference

on Web Information Systems Engineering Workshops (WISEW'03), San Diego, California, USA, 131–139.

26. Pacifici G, Spreitzer M, Tantawi AN, Youssef A (2005) Performance Management for Cluster-Based Web Services. IEEE Journal on Selected Areas in Communications 23(12): 2333–2343. doi: 10. 1109/jsac. 2005. 857208
27. Schultheiss SJ, Münch M-C, Andreeva GD, Rätsch G (2011) Persistence and Availability of Web Services in Computational Biology. PLoS ONE 6(9): e24914 doi:10. 1371/journal. pone. 0024914.
28. Apache Software Foundation (2009) WebServices - Axis. Available athttp://ws. apache. org/axis/Accessed 11 October 2012.
29. Papazoglou MP, Traverso P, Dustdar S, Leymann F (2007) Service-Oriented Computing: State of the Art and Research Challenges. IEEE Computer 40(11): 38–45. doi: 10. 1109/mc. 2007. 400
30. Raimondi F, Skene J, Emmerich W (2008) Efficient online monitoring of web-service SLAs. In Proceedings of the 16th ACM SIGSOFT International Symposium on Foundations of software engineering (SIGSOFT '08/ FSE-16). ACM, New York, USA, 170–180.
31. Li Z, Jin Y, Han J (2006) A Runtime Monitoring and Validation Framework for Web Service Interactions. In *Proceedings of the Australian Software Engineering Conference* (ASWEC '06). IEEE Computer Society, Washington, USA, 70–79.
32. Massie ML, Chun BN, Culler DE (2004) The ganglia distributed monitoring system: design, implementation, and experience. Parallel Computing 30(7): 817–840. doi: 10. 1016/j. parco. 2004. 04. 001
33. Porter G, Katz RH (2006) Effective Web Service Load balancing through Statistical Monitoring. Communications of ACM 49(3): 48–54. doi: 10. 1145/1118178. 1118201
34. Chen G, He W, Liu J, Nath S, Rigas L, et al. . (2008) Energy-Aware Server Provisioning and Load Dispatching for Connection-Intensive Internet Services. In Proceedings of the 5th USENIX Symposium on Networked Systems Design and Implementation, Berkeley, CA, USA, 337–350.
35. Muszala SP, Connors DA (2006) The Promise of Load Balancing the Parameterization of Moist Convection Using a Model Data Load Index. Journal of Atmospheric and Oceanic Technology 23(4): 525–537. doi: 10. 1175/ jtech1865. 1
36. Marzolla M, Mirandola R (2007) Performance prediction of web service workflows. In Proceedings of the Quality of Software Architectures 3rd International Conference on Software Architectures, Components, and Applications (QoSA'07). Springer-Verlag, Berlin, Heidelberg, 127–144.
37. Mani A, Nagarajan A (2002) Understanding quality of service for Web services. Available: http://www. ibm. com/developerworks/webservices/library/ws-quality/ index. html Accessed 11 October 2012.
38. Sherchan W, Krishnaswamy S, Loke SW (2005) Relevant Past Performance for Selecting Web Services. In Proceedings of the Fifth International Conference on Quality Software (QSIC '05). IEEE Computer Society, Washington, USA, 493–445.
39. Yu T, Zhang Y, Lin K (2007) Efficient Algorithms for Web Services Selection with End-to-End QoS Constraints. ACM Transactions on the Web, 1(1): Article Number 6.
40. Schaefer J (2006) An Approach for Fine-Grained Web Service Performance Monitoring. Distributed Applications and Interoperable Systems, Lecture Notes in Computer Science 4025: 169–180. doi: 10. 1007/11773887_13
41. OSDB (2011) The Open Source Database Benchmark. Available:http://osdb. sourceforge. net/Accessed 11 October 2012.
42. Sabetta A, Koziolek H (2008) Measuring Performance Metrics: Techniques and Tools (book chapter). Dependability Metrics, Lecture Notes in Computer Science 4009: 226–232. doi: 10. 1007/978-3-540-68947-8_21
43. Tsouloupas G, Dikaiakos MD (2006) Characterization of Computational Grid Resources Using Low-Level Benchmarks. In Proceedings of the 2nd IEEE International Conference on e-Science and Grid Computing (E-SCIENCE '06). IEEE Computer Society, Amsterdam, Netherlands.
44. Mahmoud QH (2004) Getting Started with Java Management Extensions (JMX): Developing Management and Monitoring Solutions. ORACLE, SDN Sun Developer Network, available at http://www. oracle. com/technetwork/articles/javase/jmx-138825. html. Accessed 11 October 2012.
45. Zhou S, Wang J, Zheng X, Delisle P (1993) Utopia: A load-sharing facility for large heterogeneous distributed computing systems. Software - Practice and Experience 23(12): 1305–1336. doi: 10. 1002/spe. 4380231203
46. Action Statistical Software (2012) Available: http:// www. portalaction. com. br/Accessed12 October 2012.

CHAPTER 5

ERROR RATES IN USERS OF AUTOMATIC FACE RECOGNITION SOFTWARE

David White[1], James D. Dunn[1], Alexandra C. Schmid[2] , Richard I. Kemp[1]

[1] School of Psychology, The University of New South Wales, Sydney, Australia

[2] School of Psychology, The University of Sydney, Sydney, Australia

ABSTRACT

In recent years, wide deployment of automatic face recognition systems has been accompanied by substantial gains in algorithm performance. However, benchmarking tests designed to evaluate these systems do not account for the errors of human operators, who are often an integral part of face recognition solutions in forensic and security settings. This causes a mismatch between evaluation tests and operational accuracy. We address this by measuring user performance in a face recognition system used to screen passport applications for identity fraud. Experiment 1 measured target detection accuracy in algorithm-generated 'candidate lists' selected from a large database of passport images. Accuracy was notably poorer than in previous studies of unfamiliar face matching: participants made over 50% errors for adult target faces, and over 60% when matching images of children. Experiment 2 then compared performance of student participants to trained passport officers–who use the system in their daily work–and found equivalent performance in these groups. Encouragingly, a group of highly trained and experienced "facial examiners" outperformed these groups by 20 percentage points. We conclude that human performance curtails accuracy of face recognition systems–potentially reducing benchmark estimates by 50% in operational settings. Mere practise does not attenuate these limits, but superior performance of trained examiners suggests that recruitment and selection of human operators, in combination with effective training and mentorship, can improve the operational accuracy of face recognition systems.

INTRODUCTION

In modern forensic and security practice, automatic face recognition software is often used to augment important identification processes. An increasingly common application of face recognition technology is known as one-to-many identification—whereby pattern matching algorithms are used to compare a single probe image to large databases of facial images [1]. This function can be used to protect against identity fraud when issuing national identity documents such as passports, immigration visas and driving licences—by improving detection of duplicate applications by the same individual [2]. Further, the recent proliferation of image-based evidence from CCTV and mobile devices entails that facial images are often an important source of evidence in criminal investigations. In forensic applications, face recognition software therefore enables police officers to use this image

Citation: White D, Dunn JD, Schmid AC, Kemp RI (2015) Error Rates in Users of Automatic Face Recognition Software. PLoS ONE 10(10): e0139827. doi:10.1371/journal.pone.0139827.

evidence to search large databases of known offenders [3, 4, 5]. Similar technology is also used to enhance user experience in popular social media platforms.

Although the accuracy of face recognition software has improved markedly over the past two decades [1, 6], it is important to note that Automatic Face Recognition (FR) systems do not yet live up to their name—they are not entirely *automatic*. Identification accuracy can be quite poor in cases where image capture conditions are not optimal [7] and where images of a face are captured several years apart [8]. To manage this uncertainty, in many applications algorithms present human users with a 'candidate list' displaying the highest matching images returned from a database and ranked in order of similarity to the probe image. It then falls to the human operator to review this candidate list and check for the presence or absence of matching identities [3, 4, 9]. Similar combinations of computer and human processing are also used in fingerprint identification systems [10, 11].

Standardised benchmarking tests of algorithm accuracy are administered by the US National Institute of Standards and Technology. The most recent Face Recognition Vendor Test (FRVT) reports accuracy of leading commercial "off-the-shelf" algorithms in one-to-many identification [1]. In a particularly challenging test, recent police "mugshots" were used to probe an historic database of 1.6 million mugshot images containing one or more target images of each identity. Leading algorithms performed with a high level of accuracy, returning matching images of the target identity in the top ten ranked matches for between 80% and 97% of targets, depending on the algorithm. Although performance did vary depending on the size of the database being searched, the effect was typically modest, suggesting that accurate searches are also feasible in nation-sized databases, such as those held by passport-issuing agencies. Importantly however, this method only estimates accuracy of the machine component of the total system, ignoring the impact of the decisions made by the human operators—who monitor image galleries containing the highest ranking matches [1]. This is an important limitation because psychological research has shown people make large numbers of errors when matching photos of unfamiliar faces.

In an early demonstration of this problem, Bruce and colleagues [12] constructed police 'line-up' arrays containing ten high-resolution images of young adult male subjects. Participants had to decide if a target face was present in the photo gallery, and if they were, to select the matching identity. Despite target and gallery images being taken only minutes apart, in full frontal pose and under similar lighting conditions, mean error rates on this task were 30%. Subsequent studies have replicated this basic finding across a variety of stimulus sets and task formats [13–16]. Error-prone performance is also observed in people who perform face matching as part of their daily work. For example, White and colleagues [17] tested matching accuracy of passport officers in their workplace. Despite extensive experience in face matching, these staff were no more accurate than a group of university students—on tasks that modeled decisions encountered in their daily duties.

In this paper we describe the first published test of human performance on FR 'candidate lists' that are sampled from operational conditions. The format of this task was specifically designed to emulate workflow of passport issuance officers using FR software to detect fraudulent passport applications. Target images were real passport application images that were used as probes in an FR one-to-many search of a very large database of passport images. The purpose of this one-to-many search in the passport issuance process is to detect existing passports that contain a picture of the applicant, but under a different name, which is indicative of a fraudulent application. This search returns 'candidate lists' of images with highest ranked similarity to the target according to a scoring metric computed by state-of-the-art FR software.

We tested participants' ability to detect images of the target identity in these candidate lists, by inserting images of the applicant from previous applications. Because we had limited time to conduct tests, and our aim was to provide reliable measures of perceptual matching ability on this task, we inserted matching identities on 50% of candidate lists. This was a necessary divergence from the target prevalence rate in many forensic and security applications, where targets appear in candidate lists very rarely [2, 18]. In the first experiment we test a group of untrained student participants on the FR workflow. We then compare performance of control participants to two groups of Passport Officers who operate FR systems as part of their daily work. We refer to these groups as *Facial Review* and *Facial Examiner* staff; corresponding to the different roles that they perform in their work, and the different levels of training and selection that they have received [19]. *Facial review* staff perform many face matching decisions per day, but check FR candidate lists as part of a series of eligibility checks that make up the majority of processing. These passport officers have typically received a small amount of training when commencing employment, and perform a similar role to passport officers tested in previous studies of face matching ability [17]. On the other hand, *Facial Examiners* were part of a smaller set of highly trained staff who perform more detailed forensic-comparison of facial images. In recent studies, similar groups of professional examiners have been shown to have superior face identification abilities [20, 21].

EXPERIMENT 1

In the experiments reported in this paper we measure human accuracy on a user interface based on output from commercial-off-the-shelf face recognition software (Cognitec DBScan 4.1.0 B3). In the most recent international benchmarking test of leading commercial face identification systems, this algorithm correctly returned a matching image in the top eight ranked matches in approximately 90% of cases, when searching a database of 1.6 million police mugshot images of adults [1]. To generate candidate lists that simulated the work of passport issuance officers, in the tests reported here the algorithm searched a large image database of Australian passport holders and returned the eight highest ranking images in the database. Australian passports are valid for up to 10 years, and so the task involved matching by identity across images captured many years apart. Previous research has shown that face aging makes unfamiliar face matching more difficult, increasing error by 20% when images are separated by more than a year [17, 22, 23] and so we expected error rates to be higher than in similar test using images taken on the same day [12].

To test whether their accuracy varied as a function of target face age, participants performed the task with an equal number of child, adolescent and adult applicants. The human face undergoes significant anatomical change during childhood, and the change is both quantitatively [24] and qualitatively [25] different to changes occurring during adulthood. Thus, we also predicted that the effect of face aging on face matching accuracy reported in previous studies would vary across the course of facial development.

Ethics Statement

This study was approved by the Human Research Ethics Committee at the University of New South Wales. All participants provided written informed consent and appropriate photographic release. The individuals shown in Fig 1 have given written informed consent (as outlined in PLOS consent form) to publish their image.

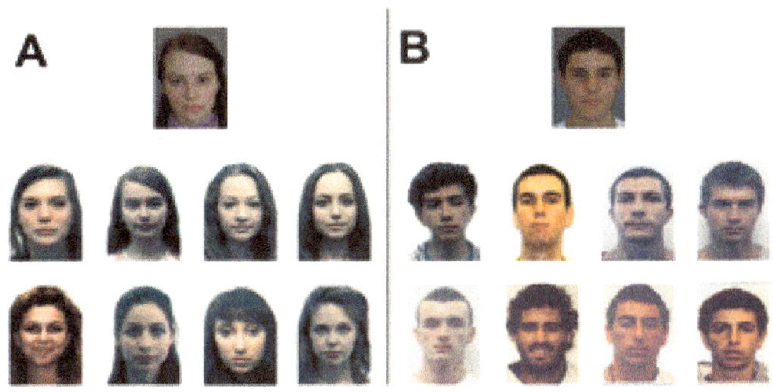

Figure 1. Example one-to-eight face matching arrays used to simulate FR 'candidate lists' in Experiments 1 and 2.

Participants had to decide whether the target (top image) was present in the gallery below, and if so, select the matching identity (for solution to these examples, see Acknowledgements). Images are representative of the stimuli used in the matching task, but for reasons of privacy we are not able to provide examples of the passport images used in our studies.

Method

Participants

Forty-two undergraduate students (32 female) from the University of New South Wales participated in this experiment in exchange for course credit. Participants' age ranged from 17 to 53 years, with a mean of 20.3 years (SD = 6.0). Six participants were excluded from our analysis because they did not finish the experiment in the allocated time of 1 hour and so final analyses were based on data from 36 participants (27 females).

Stimuli

Stimuli used in this study were images of Australian citizens that had consented for their photograph to be used in research during the passport application process. Images were sampled from a database containing passport application images of 20,000 anonymous identities who had at least one previous application image in the database. The database was a random sample of consenting Australian citizens and so demographic composition was reflective of Australian demographics (see S1 Data for item ethnicity and age). On the basis of meta-data generated by face recognition software, we excluded 5810 identities that were wearing glasses or had their mouth open. From the remaining set, we randomly sampled 408 child applicants, selected to have an age at application of between 6 and 13 years (Child condition; M = 10.0, SD = 2.0), 408 adolescent or young adult applicants, aged between 14 and 22 years (Adolescent condition; M = 18.2 SD = 2.65) and 408 adult applicants between 40 and 47 years (Adult condition; M = 43.4 SD = 2.30). An equal number of male and female applicants were sampled in each condition.

For each identity, a set of eight distractor identities were selected by the proprietary FR software. To simulate operational function of this software in an applied context, each application image was used as a probe to return the top eight ranked identities from the passport database (n > 1,000,000). These images were used as foil identities in the 1-to–8 candidate list arrays (see Fig 1). For target present trials, the foil with the lowest ranking match score was replaced by the image from that candidate's previous application. In both target absent and target present trials, position of candidate images in the array was randomised. In Australia, the maximum validity of a passport is 5 years for minors (under 18 years), and 10 years for adults. As a result, the time interval between target image and the image from previous applications shown in the candidate list array varied as a function of condition. For Child applicants the mean was 6.2 years (SD = 1.7) for Adolescents it was 6.3 years (SD = 1.6) and for Adults it was 9.7 years (SD = 2.8).

Design and Procedure

The 1224 target identities were divided into four sets of 306 (consisting of 102 child, 102 adolescent, 102 adult applicants in each set) and each participant was randomly allocated to one of four sets for testing. We used this method to ensure that idiosyncratic properties of the age-defined sets did not confound effects of face age: averaging across many identities ensured that influences of identity-specific properties were 'washed-out'. Each identity appeared once in the experiment, either in a target present or target absent trial (this was randomly determined for each subject). Each participant completed a total of 306 trials including 6 practice trials. Half of trials were target present and half were target absent. All images were presented at size 213 by 268 pixels on a 15" monitor with resolution 1920 by 1080 with each image subtending a visual angle of approximately 3 degrees (see Fig 1).

Participants were tested individually on laptop computers and the experiment was implemented in Psychtoolbox for Matlab [26]. Each participant was presented with 6 practice trials followed by 300 experimental trials. Practice trials were included to familiarise participants with response keys and so no feedback was provided on any trial.

On each trial, participants were presented with the photograph of the applicant (target face) and asked to decide if the target identity was present in the array and if they were present, to select the matching identity. On half of trials an image of the target face was present in the array and on the other half of trials the target was absent from the array, although this was not revealed to participants. Stimuli remained on the screen until the participant made a response and trial order was randomised for each participant. Trials were presented in three blocks of 100 trials with a short break provided between blocks. On average, the experiment lasted 50 minutes.

Results

Overall percent correct was 45.1% (SD = 11.7%) for adult target images, 41.1% (SD = 11.7%) for adolescent target images and 39.0% (SD = 10.6%) for child target images. The main effect of applicant age on overall accuracy was significant [$F(2,70) = 19.49$, $p < .05$, $\eta_p^2 = .358$] with planned contrasts confirming lower accuracy in matching child and adolescent applicants compared to adult applicants [child V adult: $t(35) = -6.87$, $p < .05$, Cohen's $d = 1.17$; adolescent V adult: $t(35) = -4.06$, $p < .05$, Cohen's $d = 0.68$; child V adolescent: $t(35) = -1.91$, $p = .064$, Cohen's $d = 0.32$].

We analysed performance separately for the following response types. For target absent trials, correct 'absent' responses were classified as *correct rejections* (false alarms were not analysed as they are the complement of this measure). For target present trials a *hit*response was registered when the correct identity was selected. Participants could make two types of error in target present trials: *misidentifications*, by selecting the wrong identity, and *misses* by indicating that the target is not present in the array. We analyzed the effect of target age separately for each of these four response types. Mean proportions of each response type are shown separately for each stimulus condition in Fig 2.

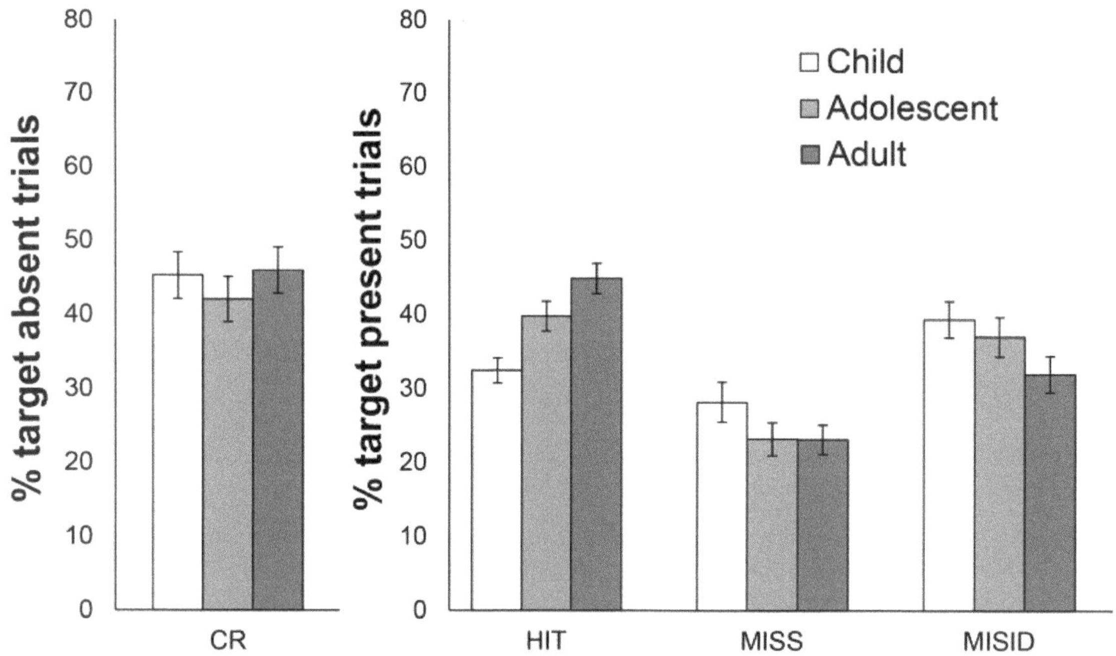

Figure 2. Face matching performance by age of target face in Experiment 1. Performance is expressed as correct rejection (CR), hit, miss and misidentification (MISID) rates. Error bars denote standard error.

For correct rejections, there was a marginally significant effect of Applicant Age [$F(2,70) = 2.95$, $p = .059$, $\eta_p^2 = .078$], with planned comparisons confirming that participants made fewer correct rejections for adolescent compared to child [$t(35) = 3.25$, $p < 0.05$, Cohen's $d = 0.39$] and adult applicants [$t(35) = 3.96$, $p < 0.05$, Cohen's $d = 0.37$] but no difference between for child and adult applicants [$t(35) = 0.71$, $p > 0.05$, Cohen's $d = 0.06$].

For hits, participants were less likely to find younger target identities when present in a candidate list. The main effect of Applicant Age was significant [$F(2,70) = 27.15$, $p < 0.05$, $\eta_p^2 = .437$], with planned comparisons confirming that participants made fewer hits for child compared to adolescent applicants [$t(35) = 4.12$, $p < 0.05$, Cohen's $d = 0.69$] and for adolescent compared to adult applicants [$t(35) = 3.02$, $p < 0.05$, Cohen's $d = 0.44$].

The main effect of applicant age was also significant for misses [$F(2,70) = 6.70$, $p < 0.05$, $\eta_p^2 = .161$] and misidentifications [$F(2,70) = 11.54$, $p < 0.01$, $\eta_p^2 = .248$]. Planned comparisons show more misses in child compared to adolescent [$t(35) = 3.11$, $p < 0.05$, Cohen's $d = 0.55$] and adult arrays [$t(35) = 2.90$, $p < 0.05$, Cohen's $d = 0.56$] but no difference between adolescents and adults ($t < 1$). For misidentifications, the difference between child and adolescent applicants was non-significant [$t(35) = 1.33$, $p > 0.05$, Cohen's $d = 0.22$]. Children [$t(35) = 4.75$, $p < 0.05$, Cohen's $d = 0.79$] and adolescents [$t(35) = 3.63$, $p < 0.05$, Cohen's $d = 0.62$] were misidentified more often than adult applicants. Thus, lower hit rates for younger applicants was caused by an increase in both miss and misidentification errors.

Discussion

Overall, performance on the FR candidate list task was very poor. For adult target faces, participants were incorrect on over *half* of all trials, suggesting that previous studies of unfamiliar face matching may overestimate human accuracy in a variety of modern applied settings. Error rates were especially poor for images of adolescents and children, despite the shorter average time interval between target and array images for children (6.2 years) and adolescents (6.3 years) compared to adults (9.7 years). This suggests that accelerated growth of facial structure in childhood and adolescence [24, 25] increases task difficulty for humans; as has previously been shown for machine recognition [27]. Further, consistent with the effect of face aging on matching adult faces [23], poorer performance for younger compared to older targets was only evident in target present trials.

Given the very low overall accuracy in this test, it becomes important to ask whether these levels of performance are also observed in people who use FR software in their daily work. If error rates in Experiment 1 reflect error in professional operators, realistic estimates of overall accuracy in systems employing both FR algorithms and human operators would be*half* that reported in benchmark tests of the machine component in FR systems. This result has significant implications for critical identity verification processes in forensic and security settings. However, it is possible that in workplaces where staff routinely use this software, performance is improved through experience and training. In the next study we addressed this question by comparing performance of trained passport officers to a control group of untrained students.

EXPERIMENT 2

In Experiment 2, we tested performance of passport issuance officers on a task that modeled the FR system used by these staff their daily work. All images used in the study were real passport images, and the algorithm that selected images to be displayed in candidate lists was the same as that used to check for identity fraud in passport applications in their workplace. Because of their experience and training in this task we expected that they would outperform groups of untrained novice participants. We tested two groups of passport officers: *Facial Review* staff, and a more specialist group of *Facial Examination* staff (for definitions of these roles see [19]). Facial examiners perform more detailed facial image comparisons, receive more training and spend more time each day performing face matching tasks than facial review staff. In recent studies, facial examiners were more accurate in one-to-one facial image comparison compared to control groups [20, 21] and so we expected that examiners would outperform the other groups.

Ethics Statement

This study was approved by the Human Research Ethics Committee at the University of New South Wales. All participants provided written informed consent and appropriate photographic release.

Method

Participants

We tested two groups of passport issuance staff, and a comparison group of untrained participants. The group of 24 *Facial Review* staff (18 Females, Mean Age = 45.9, SD = 12.4) were passport issuance officers who had received limited training and whose primary role was to assess the eligibility of passport applications (similar to participants in [17]). Verifying whether a passport applicant is present in the FR candidate list is one of many tasks that make up the passport eligibility checking process. Employment duration of this group varied between 2 months to 26 years, with the mean duration being 8.2 years (SD = 6.4).

The second group of passport officers, *Facial Examiners*, were a group of 7 specialist staff (4 Females, Mean Age = 40.9, SD = 10.9) who examine facial images in cases of suspected fraud that had been flagged during the eligibility checking process (i.e. by *Facial Reviewers*). These staff spend a significant part of their working day carrying out detailed analysis of facial images, and include court-practicing forensic examiners with many years' experience in making face matching decisions. Employment duration with the Australian Passport Office varied between 2 and 8 years (M = 4.3; SD = 2.4) and two facial examiners had additional experience (> 15 years) performing facial image comparison and document examination for other agencies. Performance of these groups were compared with performance of 48 untrained university students and members of the general public (29 Females, Mean Age = 27.2, SD = 8.9).

Stimuli

720 target identities were randomly selected from the passport image database using the same sampling procedure as in the previous experiment. These stimuli were used to create four versions of the matching task, with counterbalancing ensuring equal assignment of participants to stimulus sets across participant groups. As before, we included an equal number of child, adolescent and adult target identities to ensure that stimuli were representative of daily work of passport officers. However, as the primary aim of this study was to compare performance of users of face recognition software to untrained university students, we were not specifically interested in the effect of applicant age in this experiment. A list of stimulus items coded for face age and ethnicity used in this study, in addition to itemised performance measures, are provided in S1 Data.

Design and Procedure

Design and procedure were identical to the previous experiment. However, because we tested passport officers during their normal working day—making it necessary to reduce the length of the experimental session—each participant completed only 180 trials in a random order (half target present, half target absent). In addition, we limited presentation of each stimulus array to 18 seconds for all participants; after this time had elapsed participants were forced to make a response. Trials were presented in three blocks of 60 trials with a short break provided between blocks, and the experiment lasted approximately forty minutes.

Results

Group Performance

Examiners made substantially fewer errors compared to the other groups. Overall accuracy in facial examiners (M = 69.1%, SD = 16.9%) was substantially better than both facial review staff (M = 48.1%, SD = 15.9%; $t(29) = 3.04$, $p < 0.05$, Cohen's d = 1.13) and students (M = 47.6%, SD = 12.8%; $t(53) = 4.01$, $p < 0.05$, Cohen's d = 1.10). The difference between review staff and students was non-significant (t <

1, Cohen's d = 0.035). Analysis of response bias revealed no significant differences between criterion scores (F < 1) for students (M = -.09, SD = .39), facial review staff (M = -.03, SD = .46) or examiners (M = .06, SD = .33). To examine accuracy differences in greater detail, we carried out separate one-way ANOVAs for the four response types described in Experiment 1: *Correct Rejections,Hits, Misses* and *Misidentifications.* Mean proportions of each response type are shown inFig 3.

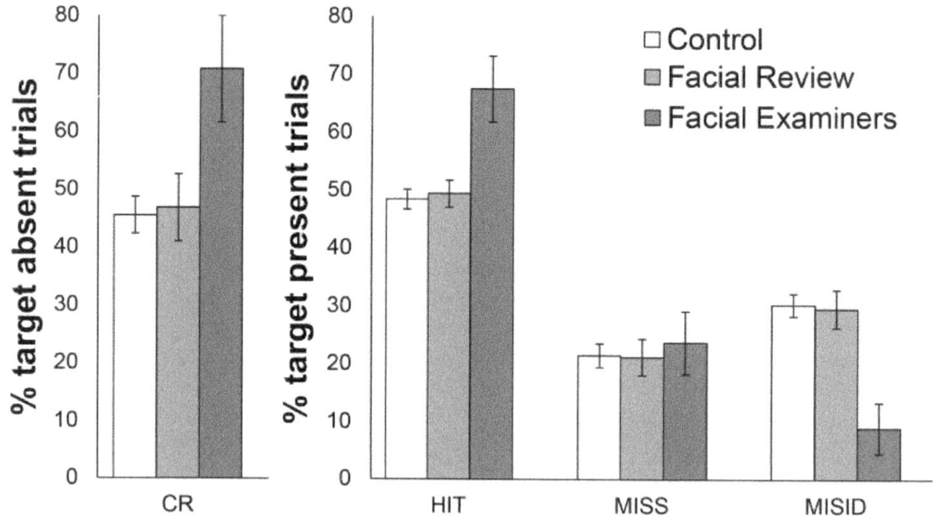

Figure 3. Face matching performance of participant groups in Experiment 2. Performance is expressed as correct rejection (CR), hit, miss and misidentification (MISID) rates. Error bars denote standard error.

For target absent trials there was a significant main effect of group on correct rejections, [F (2,76) = 3.37, p < .05, η_p^2 = .081]. As is evident from visual inspection of Fig 3, this main effect was driven by superior performance in facial examiners—who made 25% less errors in target absent trials compared with both control participants [t (53) = 2.81, p < 0.05, Cohen's d = 0.77] and facial review staff [t (29) = 2.02, p = 0.053, Cohen's d = 0.75], with the latter difference being marginally significant. The difference between facial review staff and control participants was non-significant [t (70) = .220, p > 0.05, Cohen's d = 0.05].

For target present trials, there was a main effect of Group on hit responses [F (2,76) = 7.82, p < 0.05, η_p^2 = .171], which was again driven by examiner's superior performance—making 18% more hits than both facial review staff and control participants [Examiners vs. Review: t (29) = 3.43, p < 0.05, Cohen's d = 1.27; Examiners vs. Control: t (53) = 2.81, p < 0.05, Cohen's d = 0.77; Facial Review V Control: t < 1].

Superior performance in target present trials for the examiner group was driven by a selective reduction in misidentification errors. The significant main effect of group [F (2,76) = 6.94, p < .05, η_p^2 = .154] was driven by 20% fewer misidentifications in examiners compared with other groups [Examiners vs. Review: t (29) = 3.12, p < 0.05, Cohen's d = 1.16; Examiners vs. Control: t (53) = 3.94, p < 0.05, Cohen's d = 1.08; Facial Review V Control: t < 1]. Interestingly, the main effect of Group in miss responses was non-significant (F < 1). Thus, examiners were equally likely to miss matching faces in the candidate list compared to other groups, but were less likely to select non-matching faces when the target was present.

Relationship between Professional Experience and Face Matching Accuracy

To examine whether experience performing the FR candidate list task was predictive of accuracy, we correlated overall accuracy on the task with number of years employed at the Australian Passport Office. This relationship is plotted in Fig 4. Consistent with earlier work [17], there was no relationship between employment duration and face matching accuracy either for facial review staff [n = 24, Spearman's rho = -.248, p > 0.05], or for facial examiners [n = 7, Spearman's rho = .000, p > 0.05]. Although unrelated to professional experience, there was nevertheless a large range of individual differences in accuracy (ranging from 20% to 85% correct), which is also consistent with previous studies of novices [15] and passport officers [17].

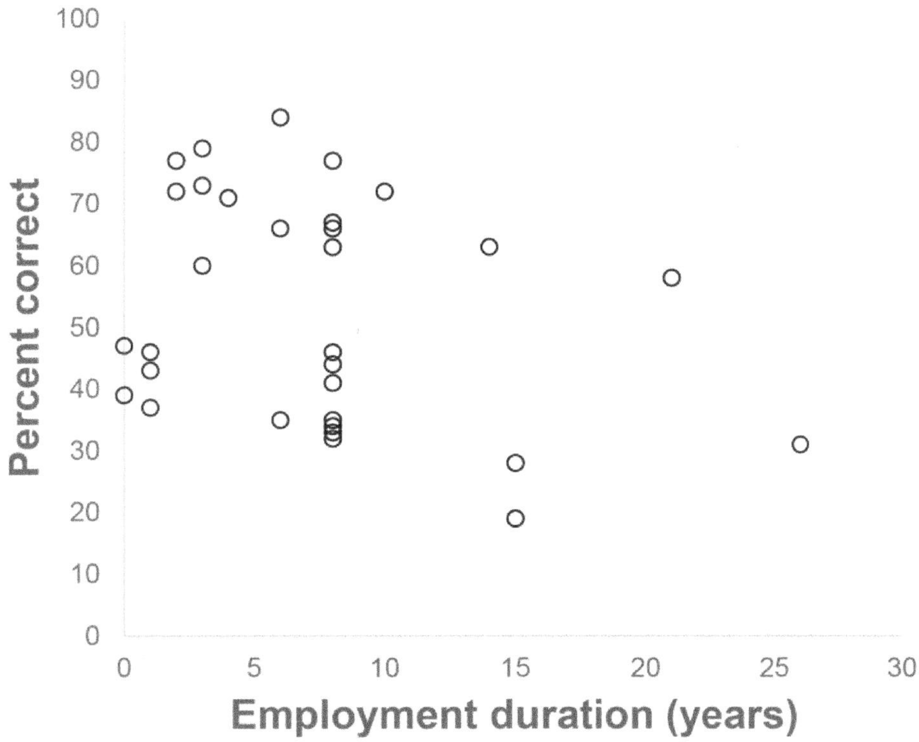

Figure 4. Scatterplot showing non-significant correlation between Passport Officers' employment duration and overall face matching accuracy. The graph does not differentiate facial review staff from facial examiners to protect participant anonymity.

The Effect of Face Ethnicity on Face Matching Accuracy

Previous studies show poorer accuracy when matching faces that are of a different ethnicity to the viewer [16]. Although we did not set out to test this, given the ethnic diversity of Australian citizens used as stimuli in this study, we conducted a post-hoc comparison of face matching accuracy for Caucasian and non-Caucasian faces. Three independent judges coded the ethnicity of target faces and we then compared item accuracy for Caucasian and non-Caucasian target subsets (see S1 Data for coding criteria, item ethnicity and itemised accuracy). Surprisingly, this analysis revealed higher overall accuracy for*non*-Caucasian targets (n = 133; M = 52.3%; SD = 19.0%) compared to Caucasian targets (n = 587; M = 48.1%; SD = 17.7%) [t (726) = 2.45, p <0.05, Cohen's d = 0.23]. We then performed a subject-level analysis by computing face matching performance on Caucasian and non-Caucasian subsets separately for each participant. Analysis of subject performance also revealed higher accuracy on non-Caucasian compared with Caucasian target faces, driven by non-Caucasian foil faces attracting fewer False Alarm [F (1,76) = 3.92, p = .052, η_p^2 = .049] and Misidentification errors [F (1,76) = 10.64, p < 0.05, η_p^2 = .123]. All interactions between target ethnicity and group were non-significant (F < 1; for full details of this analysis see S1 Text).

This result is opposite to that reported in similar face matching studies, where other race faces attract *more* matching errors than own-race faces [16]. One possible explanation for this discrepancy is that the FR algorithm selected more confusable foils when searching for Caucasian targets compared to non-Caucasian targets. Previous studies show that accuracy of face recognition algorithms is sensitive to the demographic composition of both training and test image databases [28, 29]. Moreover, approximately three-quarters of Australian Passport holders are Caucasian, and so the foil stimuli in Caucasian target arrays were selected from a much larger database, making it more likely that the algorithm would identify highly confusable non-matching images. It is not certain that this contributed to the effect of target ethnicity here. However, FR software is often used by ethnically diverse workforces to search ethnically diverse databases, and so the nuanced interaction between ethnicity of human users, algorithms, image databases and target faces is an important topic for future work.

GENERAL DISCUSSION

Overall, our results show very poor face matching performance in a realistic photo-to-photo matching task based on the output of commercial off-the-shelf face recognition software. This task used real passport application images and was designed to model face matching decisions made by FR operators in a passport issuance workflow. In both experiments, untrained participants made over 50% identification errors. More importantly, trained passport officers who use this software in their daily work—making an average of 60 candidate list checks per day—were no better on the task than untrained student participants. These results have clear implications for the reliability of identity verification systems that employ human operators to monitor the output of FR software. In systems implementing one-to-many algorithm checks, it is human users that are required to make final identity decisions, and so the accuracy of the system as a whole is heavily constrained by human accuracy. Performance data reported here equate to errors on average in 1 of every 2 candidate lists. Thus, estimates of operational FR system accuracy, in the conditions we have tested here, can be computed by *halving* scores attained on recent benchmark tests [1].

This level of performance was observed despite using real passport photographs in the FR candidate list task, which are subject to strict quality control measures designed to ensure that they are truthful representations of appearance [30]. Despite these constraints, error rates were substantially higher than in previous studies of face matching performance using one-in-ten face matching arrays [12]. To account for this, and consistent with recent work [17, 23] we suggest that face aging caused poorer performance compared to similar tasks where images were taken on the same day [12]. However, face age only affected accuracy in target present trials, both here and in previous work [17, 23], and so does not account for the equivalent error rates we observed in target *absent* arrays. Comparable error rates when targets did not appear in candidate lists suggests that 'foil candidates'–selected by the computerised FR engine from a database of millions of passport images—were more easily mistaken for the target identity than foils selected by humans from much smaller databases in previous studies [12]. Therefore the capability of FR software to search enormous databases of facial images comes at a cost: it significantly increases the difficulty of the task faced by the human operator.

It is important to note that the task performed by participants in this study, although specifically designed to estimate accuracy rates in users of FR systems, differs from operational conditions. To derive reliable measures of perceptual performance in the limited time we had to test passport officers, target images appeared in candidate lists on half of trials. In many operational settings where the task is to find a matching face in an array—such as when using FR software to search for identity fraud in passport applications—it is very rare that target identities appear in candidate lists. This is because base rates of identity fraud are very low, with some reports estimating 1 in 400 passport applications to be fraudulent [18]. Estimating match detection accuracy at these prevalence rates presents a practical challenge. However, lab based studies that model the task of checking photo-ID for secure access show that non-match prevalence rates of 10% lead to poorer detection accuracy [31] suggesting that performance in operational conditions may be substantially poorer than reported here. Future work that measures match detection in the workplace, perhaps by inserting known matches into candidate lists, may be necessary to provide accurate estimates of user error in face recognition systems [2].

Encouragingly, specialist facial examiners performed far better on the candidate list task than untrained students and the non-specialist passport officers—making 20% fewer errors as a group. However, as is typical in studies of expert populations [32], our data do not isolate the factors that cause their superior performance. One potential cause is that examiners were naturally better at the task. This would be consistent with previous studies showing that some people perform very well in face matching tasks while others perform very poorly [15, 33, 34] and that these individual differences are stable across tests [33–35].

However, at the time this experiment was carried out, the Australian Passport Office did not use formal selection processes to recruit facial reviewers, nor to select facial examiners. However, it is possible that informal selection processes occurred. For example examiners may have been motivated to continue in their role because they believed they were good at the task. Alternatively, recent work has shown that providing feedback on the accuracy of face matching decisions [36, 37] and performing face matching decisions in groups [38] can improve accuracy in face matching tasks. Therefore, by working alongside other facial examination specialists, receiving feedback and discussing their work, examiners may also have developed more effective strategies for face matching. Future work should aim to clarify precisely what aspects of training and experience cause improvement in performance on face matching tasks. Whilst guidelines for training in facial comparison do exist [19, 39, 40], these have not yet been subject to empirical validation. Indeed, some recommended methods have been shown to be ineffective in improving accuracy [41, 42].

Notwithstanding, trained facial examiners have outperformed control participants both here and in recent studies [20, 21]. Further, differences between facial forensic examiners and standard experimental groups are not limited to quantitative differences in overall accuracy–*qualitative* differences also point towards differences in the cognitive processing they deploy. In the present study we found that superior performance in examiners resulted from a reduction in false alarm and misidentification errors (i.e. choosing errors). Examiners made the same proportion of *miss* responses as other groups (i.e. non-choosing errors), raising the possibility that their expertise is tuned towards detecting differences between faces. More generally, this result builds on recent reports of other qualitative differences in performance of forensic facial examiners. For instance, expertise of examiners is most evident at longer exposure durations [20] and when comparing high-quality images [21]. Examiners also show less impairment by image inversion [20] in comparison to university students. These qualitative differences offer important insights into the nature of expertise that can be used to inform development of training methods and workflow systems for facial image comparison.

Finally, given the very clear limits that human performance imposes on the reliability of systems employing 'automatic' face recognition software, computer scientists and psychologists should work together to improve total system accuracy. Studies reported here and in previous work show large and stable individual differences in face matching accuracy that are unrelated to length professional experience [15, 17, 32]. We therefore propose that selection of staff based on face matching performance can provide substantial gains in the reliability of FR systems at little cost. Testing staff on face recognition workflow simulations, as we have here, enables selection tests to be tailored to the precise task demands faced by users in daily work and to monitor their performance over time. Technical solutions that build human testing capabilities into face recognition software may therefore be useful in selecting individuals best suited to operating this software, and in evaluating training and mentorship programs. More broadly, face recognition software developers, user experience designers and system administrators should give careful consideration to the abilities of human operators when designing face recognition systems.

SUPPORTING INFORMATION

SUBJECT #	DEMOGRAPHICS		OVERALL		(%)					LATENCY (s)				
	SEX	*AGE*	*ACCURACY (%)*	*LATENCY (s)*	*CR*	*FA*	*HIT*	*MISS*	*MISID*	*CR*	*FA*	*HIT*	*MISS*	*MISID*
101	Male	36	44.4	11.9	54.4	45.6	34.4	31.1	34.4	12.4	11.6	10.7	14.0	11.0
102	Male	33	33.3	12.3	7.8	92.2	58.9	5.6	35.6	18.0	12.2	11.1	16.0	12.5
103	Female	31	43.3	14.8	44.4	55.6	42.2	20.0	37.8	15.9	15.3	12.6	14.1	15.5
104	Female	31	41.7	16.5	28.9	71.1	54.4	12.2	33.3	17.2	17.3	14.2	18.7	17.1
105	Female	36	56.1	13.3	58.9	41.1	53.3	28.9	17.8	13.2	15.1	11.0	12.5	18.1
106	Female	39	31.4	13.6	19.3	80.7	43.0	7.0	50.0	15.0	14.5	12.1	15.8	12.6
107	Male	37	53.3	10.6	51.1	48.9	55.6	24.4	20.0	12.2	10.3	9.5	11.5	8.7
108	Male	39	43.3	13.4	28.9	71.1	57.8	8.9	33.3	13.8	14.2	11.4	14.7	14.6
109	Female	32	62.2	14.0	52.2	47.8	72.2	13.3	14.4	17.2	15.2	10.6	16.7	13.8
110	Male	35	64.4	14.9	65.6	34.4	63.3	20.0	16.7	15.3	16.8	12.8	16.0	16.7
111	Female	31	47.8	7.9	43.3	56.7	52.2	16.7	31.1	10.1	7.0	6.6	10.7	7.1
112	Female	48	53.3	13.5	44.4	55.6	62.2	13.3	24.4	15.4	15.3	10.4	14.6	13.0
113	Male	30	51.1	14.4	52.2	47.8	50.0	20.0	30.0	14.7	14.7	13.3	14.5	15.2
114	Female	31	18.3	8.8	5.6	94.4	31.1	4.4	64.4	8.8	9.3	8.3	9.8	8.4
115	Female	36	25.0	9.9	0.0	100.0	50.0	0.0	50.0	*	11.1	8.2	*	9.0
116	Female	31	58.3	8.3	77.8	22.2	38.9	50.0	11.1	6.9	11.9	9.1	7.0	14.3
117	Female	30	28.9	12.3	15.6	84.4	42.2	5.6	52.2	12.5	12.4	11.1	12.5	13.1
118	Male	51	43.9	15.4	56.7	43.3	31.1	37.8	31.1	13.8	16.8	13.9	15.8	17.3
119	Male	30	31.7	10.3	37.8	62.2	25.6	33.3	41.1	15.8	8.9	9.3	8.9	9.3
120	Female	32	36.7	13.3	22.2	77.8	51.1	8.9	40.0	15.3	14.4	10.2	19.6	12.9
121	Male	30	39.4	14.9	20.0	80.0	58.9	3.3	37.8	18.8	14.7	13.0	19.6	15.7
122	Male	41	37.2	16.1	16.7	83.3	57.8	3.3	38.9	19.2	16.6	12.1	47.5	16.6
123	Male	19	40.0	10.9	38.9	61.1	41.1	27.8	31.1	11.7	11.4	8.7	11.8	10.7
124	Male	19	38.3	6.2	32.2	67.8	44.4	15.6	40.0	8.0	6.4	5.4	6.9	5.3
125	Female	18	50.6	6.0	62.2	37.8	38.9	43.3	17.8	6.0	6.5	4.5	6.3	7.2

126	Female	19	57.2	15.0	67.8	32.2	46.7	38.9	14.4	13.1	19.7	15.4	14.4	13.7
127	Female	20	61.7	13.0	63.3	36.7	60.0	24.4	15.6	13.0	14.7	11.5	11.9	16.7
128	Female	21	38.9	5.9	41.1	58.9	36.7	20.0	43.3	5.9	5.8	9.2	4.9	3.8
129	Female	18	47.8	9.8	36.7	63.3	58.9	13.3	27.8	11.2	11.1	7.7	10.1	9.5
130	Female	18	50.6	15.0	60.0	40.0	41.1	24.4	34.4	14.7	16.2	13.2	16.5	15.0
132	Male	19	39.4	4.8	63.3	36.7	15.6	55.6	28.9	5.2	4.6	5.2	4.5	4.7
133	Female	22	66.7	12.0	88.9	11.1	44.4	45.6	10.0	13.4	11.0	8.4	12.2	15.2
134	Female	20	53.9	13.3	50.0	50.0	57.8	16.7	25.6	14.6	14.0	11.3	11.5	14.9
135	Male	19	31.7	10.9	20.0	80.0	43.3	5.6	51.1	15.8	10.6	9.1	15.2	10.3
136	Female	18	57.2	17.4	51.1	48.9	63.3	14.4	22.2	20.1	18.5	12.9	25.9	16.5
137	Female	20	68.9	8.0	70.0	30.0	67.8	17.8	14.4	8.2	8.9	7.0	9.0	9.0
138	Female	22	68.3	11.9	65.6	34.4	71.1	10.0	18.9	14.0	11.1	9.3	12.4	15.5
139	Female	21	36.1	10.1	22.2	77.8	50.0	6.7	43.3	12.6	10.2	9.0	11.5	9.6
140	Female	19	34.4	13.2	15.6	84.4	53.3	5.6	41.1	15.9	13.8	11.7	14.4	12.7
141	Female	18	57.8	9.5	74.4	25.6	41.1	45.6	13.3	9.4	11.1	10.7	8.1	7.8
142	Female	19	51.1	10.0	66.7	33.3	35.6	35.6	28.9	9.1	14.3	8.8	9.1	9.6
143	Male	18	60.6	13.2	83.3	16.7	37.8	52.2	10.0	12.2	18.6	11.6	13.0	19.0
144	Male	19	50.0	11.3	51.1	48.9	48.9	25.6	25.6	11.8	12.0	9.7	12.3	10.9
145	Female	21	65.0	10.5	65.6	34.4	64.4	24.4	11.1	11.0	13.8	7.8	12.0	9.7
146	Male	19	43.9	10.2	45.6	54.4	42.2	17.8	40.0	11.6	10.1	7.6	12.6	10.4
147	Male	20	27.2	9.5	12.2	87.8	42.2	4.4	53.3	11.6	9.6	8.5	11.9	9.6
148	Female	19	41.1	13.0	42.2	57.8	40.0	20.0	40.0	15.6	12.5	10.2	16.1	12.5
201	Male	37	72.8	14.8	80.0	20.0	65.6	23.3	11.1	15.1	15.8	13.9	14.8	16.0
202	Female	58	28.3	10.6	8.9	91.1	47.8	2.2	50.0	20.0	10.6	9.2	10.5	10.2
203	Male	59	62.8	11.4	96.7	3.3	28.9	62.2	8.9	10.8	16.3	13.4	10.4	16.9
204	Female	30	47.2	13.0	33.3	66.7	61.1	11.1	27.8	12.0	14.4	11.3	15.9	13.8
205	Male	28	72.2	11.0	90.0	10.0	54.4	36.7	8.9	10.2	13.8	11.4	11.1	13.5
206	Female	59	34.4	17.1	33.3	66.7	35.6	27.8	36.7	18.5	17.4	15.2	18.5	16.3

207	Female	63	30.6	18.5	5.6	94.4	55.6	3.3	41.1	19.6	19.3	16.8	18.7	18.9
208	Female	42	19.4	18.1	10.0	90.0	28.9	5.6	65.6	18.7	18.2	17.4	19.3	18.2
209	Female	40	65.6	10.7	70.0	30.0	61.1	24.4	14.4	11.8	11.7	8.2	12.4	10.4
210	Female	52	31.7	11.6	31.1	68.9	32.2	7.8	60.0	10.8	11.5	12.6	10.1	11.8
211	Female	25	39.4	14.1	32.2	67.8	46.7	23.3	30.0	17.4	13.1	11.8	18.7	12.8
212	Female	56	46.1	17.0	28.9	71.1	63.3	7.8	28.9	19.5	18.2	13.7	17.9	18.5
213	Female	63	35.0	11.2	31.1	68.9	38.9	24.4	36.7	10.9	11.7	10.8	11.5	10.9
214	Male	35	37.2	15.7	27.8	72.2	46.7	12.2	41.1	16.6	16.6	13.7	18.3	15.2
215	Female	35	43.3	19.8	32.2	67.8	54.4	5.6	40.0	20.7	20.2	18.4	21.1	20.2
216	Female	54	62.8	9.7	81.1	18.9	44.4	41.1	14.4	9.5	11.2	8.7	10.1	10.7
217	Female	55	44.4	16.2	35.6	64.4	53.3	11.1	35.6	19.2	16.5	13.3	20.9	15.4
218	Female	57	65.6	14.7	76.7	23.3	54.4	28.9	16.7	15.2	15.8	12.8	14.8	16.8
219	Male	31	66.7	18.4	88.9	11.1	44.4	45.6	10.0	18.5	20.4	17.2	18.6	19.5
220	Male	32	70.6	16.6	80.0	20.0	61.1	30.0	8.9	16.2	18.8	16.5	15.9	19.1
221	Female	53	58.3	13.5	51.1	48.9	65.6	17.8	16.7	14.6	13.7	11.8	14.8	14.1
222	Female	34	45.6	15.6	36.7	63.3	54.4	8.9	36.7	17.2	15.8	13.6	19.0	15.7
223	Female	54	40.6	17.1	46.7	53.3	34.4	35.6	30.0	17.2	17.6	16.6	17.4	16.5
224	Female	49	33.3	15.6	15.6	84.4	51.1	10.0	38.9	18.4	15.8	13.3	17.6	16.7
301	witheld	witheld	77.2	15.2	71.1	28.9	83.3	8.9	7.8	18.3	17.1	11.3	19.2	16.6
302	witheld	witheld	78.9	11.4	85.6	14.4	72.2	25.6	2.2	11.3	17.8	8.9	15.0	10.7
303	witheld	witheld	35.0	14.0	17.8	82.2	52.2	13.3	34.4	18.5	14.3	10.8	17.6	14.4
304	witheld	witheld	71.7	12.9	70.0	30.0	73.3	17.8	8.9	14.3	14.9	10.4	14.6	12.3
305	witheld	witheld	84.4	9.9	87.8	12.2	81.1	17.8	1.1	9.9	12.1	9.3	11.6	6.7
306	witheld	witheld	76.7	13.8	85.6	14.4	67.8	30.0	2.2	16.6	12.3	9.0	17.0	19.2
307	witheld	witheld	60.0	14.0	77.8	22.2	42.2	52.2	5.6	12.7	17.6	14.6	13.5	17.1

S1 Data. Subject and item data. Excel spreadsheet containing performance data from Experiments 1 and 2, separately for each participant (by-subject) and for each target identity (by-item). Target identities used in Experiment 2 are coded for ethnicity.

S1 Text. Analysis of target face ethnicity. Details of post-hoc analysis of face matching accuracy as a function of target ethnicity in Experiment 2.

	Caucasian Targets				non-Caucasian Targets			
	CR	*Hits*	*Miss*	*MisID*	*CR*	*Hits*	*Miss*	*MisID*
Control	43.3 (23.1)	47.2 (13.7)	19.8 (15.0)	33.1 (15.8)	44.7 (24.9)	50.6 (14.8)	22.6 (17.4)	26.8 (16.0)
FR Reviewers	45.7 (28.5)	48.7 (11.9)	20.7 (15.6)	30.7 (15.8)	51.6 (30.0)	52.3 (12.9)	23.4 (16.6)	24.3 (19.8)
FR Examiners	69.9 (23.9)	67.4 (15.4)	23.1 (14.9)	9.5 (12.4)	74.6 (27.1)	67.1 (15.7)	26.2 (15.1)	6.71 (9.4)

ACKNOWLEDGMENTS

This research was supported by Australian Research Council grants to Kemp and White (LP110100448, LP130100702). The authors thank Manuela Tan for help collecting data in Experiment 1 and staff at the Australian Passport Office and Westbourne Group for assistance implementing experimental protocol and recruiting participants. The solution toFig 1A is top row, second from left; Fig 1B is a target absent array.

AUTHOR CONTRIBUTIONS

Conceived and designed the experiments: DW RK AS. Performed the experiments: DW JD AS. Analyzed the data: DW JD. Contributed reagents/materials/analysis tools: DW JD AS. Wrote the paper: DW JD AS RK.

REFERENCES

1. Grother PJ, Ngan M. Face Recognition Vendor Test (FRVT). NIST Interagency Report (8009). 2014. Available:http://biometrics. nist. gov/cs_links/face/frvt/frvt2013/NIST_8009. pdf
2. Undercover tests show passport issuance process remains vulnerable to fraud. US Government Accountability Office, State Department. 2010. Available:http://www. gao. gov/products/GAO-10-922T. Assessed 1 August 2015.
3. Jain AK, Klare B, Park U. Face matching and retrieval in forensics applications. IEEE MultiMedia. 2012;19: 20–28. doi: 10. 1109/mmul. 2012. 4
4. Jain AK, Ross A. Bridging the gap: from biometrics to forensics. Phil Trans R Soc B. 2015;370: 20140254. doi: 10. 1098/rstb. 2014. 0254. pmid:26101280
5. FBI announces full operational capability of Next Generation Identification system. FBI Criminal Justice Information Services Division [Press release]. 2014. Available:http://www. fbi. gov/news/pressrel/press-releases/fbi-announces-full-operational-capability-of-the-next-generation-identification-system. Accessed 1 August 2015.
6. Philips PJ, O'Toole AJ. Comparison of human and computer performance across face recognition experiments. Image Vision Comput. 2014;32: 74–85. doi: 10. 1016/j. imavis. 2013. 12. 002
7. O'Toole AJ, An X, Dunlop J, Natu V. Comparing face recognition algorithms to humans on challenging tasks. ACM Appl Percept. 2012;9: 16. doi: 10. 1145/2355598. 2355599
8. Ricanek K, Tesafaye T. MORPH: A Longitudinal Image Database of Normal Adult Age-Progression. IEEE 7th International Conference on Automatic Face and Gesture Recognition. 2006: 341–345. doi: 10. 1109/fgr. 2006. 78
9. Graves I, Butavicius M, MacLeod V, Heyer R, Parsons K, Kuester N, et al. The Role of the Human Operator in Image-Based Airport Security Technologies. Stud Comp Intell. 2011;338: 147–181. doi: 10. 1007/978-3-642-17764-4_5
10. Dror IE, Mnookin JL. The use of technology in human expert domains: challenges and risks arising from the use of automated fingerprint identification systems in forensic science. Law Prob Ris. 2010;9: 47–67. doi: 10. 1093/lpr/mgp031
11. Dror IE, Wertheim K, Fraser-Mackenzie P, Walajtys J. The Impact of Human-Technology Cooperation and Distributed Cognition in Forensic Science: Biasing Effects of AFIS Contextual Information on Human Experts. J Forensic Sci. 2011;57: 343–352. doi: 10. 1111/j. 1556-4029. 2011. 02013. x. pmid:22212067
12. Bruce V, Henderson Z, Greenwood K, Hancock PJ, Burton AM, Miller P. Verification of face identities from images captured on video. J Exp Psychol Appl. 1999;5: 339–360. doi: 10. 1037//1076-898x. 5. 4. 339
13. Kemp R, Towell N, Pike G. When seeing should not be believing: Photographs, credit cards and fraud. Appl Cognitive Psych. 1997;14: 211–222. doi: 10. 1002/(sici)1099-0720(199706)11:3<211::aid-acp430>3. 0. co;2-o
14. Burton AM, Wilson S, Cowan M, Bruce V. Face recognition in poor-quality video: Evidence from security surveillance. Psychol Sci. 1999;10: 243–248. doi: 10. 1111/1467-9280. 00144
15. Burton AM, White D, McNeill A. The Glasgow Face Matching Test. Behav Res Methods. 2010;42: 286–291. doi: 10. 3758/BRM. 42. 1. 286. pmid:20160307
16. Megreya AM, White D, Burton AM. The other race effect does not rely on memory: Evidence from a matching task. Q J Exp Psychol. 2011;64: 1473–1483. doi: 10. 1080/17470218. 2011. 575228
17. White D, Kemp RI, Jenkins R, Matheson M, Burton AM. Passport Officers' errors in face matching. PLoS ONE. 2014;9: e103510. doi: 10. 1371/journal. pone. 0103510. pmid:25133682
18. 10,000 passports go to frausters. British Broadcasting Corporation. 20 March 2007. Available: http://news. bbc. co. uk/2/hi/uk_news/politics/6470179. stm. Accessed

August 2015.

19. Guidelines and recommendations for facial comparison training to competency. Facial Identification Scientific Working Group. 2011. Available:www. fiswg. org/ document.

20. Norell K, Läthén KB, Bergström P, Rice A, Natu V, O'Toole AJ. The effect of image quality and forensic expertise in facial image comparisons. J Forensic Sci. 2015;60: 331–340. doi: 10. 1111/1556-4029. 12660. pmid:25537273

21. White D, Phillips PJ, Hahn CA, Hill M, O'Toole AJ. Perceptual expertise in forensic facial image comparison. P Roy Soc Lon B Biol. 2015;282: 1814–1822. doi: 10. 1098/rspb. 2015. 1292

22. Davis JP, Valentine T. CCTV on trial: Matching video images with the defendant in the dock. Appl Cognitive Psych. 2009;23: 482–505. doi: 10. 1002/acp. 1490

23. Megreya AM, Sandford A, Burton AM. Matching Face Images Taken on the Same Day or Months Apart: the Limitations of Photo ID. Appl Cognitive Psych. 2013;27: 700–706. doi: 10. 1002/acp. 2965

24. Ferrario VF, Sforza C, Serrao G, Colombo A. Soft tissue facial growth and development as assessed by the three-dimensional computerized mesh diagram analysis. Am J Orthod Dentofac. 1999;116: 215–226. doi: 10. 1016/ s0889-5406(99)70220-9

25. Chakravarty MM, Aleong R, Leonard G, Perron M. Automated analysis of craniofacial morphology using magnetic resonance images. PLoS ONE. 2011;6: e20241. doi: 10. 1371/journal. pone. 0020241. pmid:21655288

26. Brainard DH. The Psychophysics Toolbox. Spat Vis. 1997;10: 433–436. pmid:9176952 doi: 10. 1163/156856897x00357

27. Ling H, Soatto S, Ramanathan N. A study of face recognition as people age. IEEE 11th International Conference on Computer Vision. 2007:1887–1894. doi: 10. 1109/iccv. 2007. 4409069

28. Phillips PJ, Jiang F, Narvekar A, Ayyad J, O'Toole AJ. An other-race effect for face recognition algorithms. ACM Appl Percept. 2011;8: 14. doi: 10. 1145/1870076. 1870082

29. Klare B, Burge MJ, Klontz JC, Vorder Bruegge RW, Jain Anil K. Face Recognition Performance: Role of Demographic Information. IEEE T Inf Foren Sec. 2012;7: 1789–1801. doi: 10. 1109/tifs. 2012. 2214212

30. Photograph Guidelines. Australian Passport Office. 2012. Available:https://www. passports. gov. au/images/ photo_guidelines. pdf. Accessed 1 August 2015.

31. Papesh MH, Goldinger SD. Infrequent identity mismatches are frequently undetected. Atten Percept Psycho. 2014;76: 1135–1349. doi: 10. 3758/s13414-014-0630-6

32. Sternberg RJ. Costs of expertise. In: Ericsson KA, editor. The road to excellence: The acquisition of expert performance in the arts and sciences, sports, and games. Erlbaum, Hillsdale, NJ. 1996. pp. 347–354.

33. Megreya AM, Burton AM. Unfamiliar faces are not faces: Evidence from a matching task. Mem Cognition. 2006;34: 865–876. doi: 10. 3758/bf03193433

34. Russell R, Duchaine B, Nakayama K. Super-recognizers: People with extraordinary face recognition ability. Psychon B Rev. 2009;16: 252–257. doi: 10. 3758/pbr. 16. 2. 252

35. Wilmer JB, Germine L, Chabris CF, Chatterjee G, Williams M, Loken E, et al. Human face recognition ability is specific and highly heritable. P Natl Acad Sci USA. 2010;107: 5238–5241. doi: 10. 1073/pnas. 0913053107

36. White D, Kemp RI, Jenkins R, Burton AM. Feedback training for facial image comparison. Psychon B Rev. 2014;21: 100–106. doi: 10. 3758/s13423-013-0475-3

37. Alenezi HM, Bindemann M. The Effect of Feedback on Face-Matching Accuracy. Appl Cognitive Psych. 2013;27: 735–753. doi: 10. 1002/acp. 2968

38. Dowsett AJ, Burton AM. Unfamiliar face matching: Pairs out-perform individuals and provide a route to training. Brit J Psychol. In press. doi: 10. 1111/bjop. 12103.

39. Spaun NA. Facial comparisons by subject matter experts: Their role in biometrics and their training. In: Tistarelli M, Nixon MS, editors. Advances in Biometrics. Springer-Verlag, Heidelberg. 2009. pp. 161–168.

40. Heyer R, Semmler C. Forensic confirmation bias: the case of facial image comparison. J Appl Res Mem Cog. 2013;2: 68–70. doi: 10. 1016/j. jarmac. 2013. 01. 008

41. Woodhead MM, Baddeley AD, Simmonds DCV. On training people to recognize faces. Ergonomics. 1979;22: 333–343. doi: 10. 1080/00140137908924617

42. Towler A, White D, Kemp RI. Evaluating training methods for facial image comparison: The face shape strategy does not work. Perception. 2014;43: 214–218. pmid:24919354 doi: 10. 1068/p7676

CHAPTER 6

STAKEMETER: VALUE-BASED STAKEHOLDER IDENTIFICATION AND QUANTIFICATION FRAMEWORK FOR VALUE-BASED SOFTWARE SYSTEMS

Muhammad Imran Babar[1] , Masitah Ghazali[1], Dayang N. A. Jawawi[1] , Kashif Bin Zaheer[2]

[1] Department of Software Engineering, Universiti Teknologi Malaysia, Johor, Malaysia

[2] Department of Mathematical Sciences, Universiti Teknologi Malaysia, Johor, Malaysia

ABSTRACT

Value-based requirements engineering plays a vital role in the development of value-based software (VBS). Stakeholders are the key players in the requirements engineering process, and the selection of critical stakeholders for the VBS systems is highly desirable. Based on the stakeholder requirements, the innovative or value-based idea is realized. The quality of the VBS system is associated with the concrete set of valuable requirements, and the valuable requirements can only be obtained if all the relevant valuable stakeholders participate in the requirements elicitation phase. The existing value-based approaches focus on the design of the VBS systems. However, the focus on the valuable stakeholders and requirements is inadequate. The current stakeholder identification and quantification (SIQ) approaches are neither state-of-the-art nor systematic for the VBS systems. The existing approaches are time-consuming, complex and inconsistent which makes the initiation process difficult. Moreover, the main motivation of this research is that the existing SIQ approaches do not provide the low level implementation details for SIQ initiation and stakeholder metrics for quantification. Hence, keeping in view the existing SIQ problems, this research contributes in the form of a new SIQ framework called '*StakeMeter*'. The*StakeMeter* framework is verified and validated through case studies. The proposed framework provides low-level implementation guidelines, attributes, metrics, quantification criteria and application procedure as compared to the other methods. The proposed framework solves the issues of stakeholder quantification or prioritization, higher time consumption, complexity, and process initiation. The framework helps in the selection of highly critical stakeholders for the VBS systems with less judgmental error.

INTRODUCTION

In the Requirements Engineering (RE), the functional and non-functional goals are documented and analyzed in order to develop a new system [1, 2]{Wiegers, 1999 #64}. The well documented and right requirements have a prominent effect on the quality of the software [3, 4]. The RE process is a combination of different activities or phases which when performed in collaboration results in a requirements document. The different phases of the RE process are elicitation, analysis, specification, validation and management [5, 6].

The VBS systems are the part of value-based software engineering (VBSE). The definition of VBSE given by Barry

Citation: Babar MI, Ghazali M, Jawawi DNA, Zaheer KB (2015) StakeMeter: Value-Based Stakeholder Identification and Quantification Framework for Value-Based Software Systems. PLoS ONE 10(3): e0121344. doi:10.1371/journal.pone.0121344.

Boehm is "the explicit concern with value concerns in the application of science and mathematics by which properties of computer software are made useful to the people" [7]. Hence, a VBS system is one that provides useful software properties to the intended stakeholders. The VBS systems are based on an innovative or value-based idea and are associated with the economic leverage. The implementation of an innovative or value-based idea is difficult in terms of high uncertainty. It is difficult to guess that either the innovative or value-based idea will yield the economic benefit or not. In the VBS systems, the involvement of relevant stakeholders can play a vital role in the quality improvement [8] and value-based software requirements engineering (VBSRE) practices. The case of the VBS systems is very sensitive because they are usually part of the distributed environments due to the diverse locations of the stakeholders. In such cases, it is very difficult to consider all the stakeholders who have little stakes in the development of the VBS system. (Fig. 1) summarizes the research on the VBS systems and shows the frequency of the research conducted on different issues in order to design high-quality VBS systems. The research in the domain of VBS development mainly focuses on requirements, profitability, cost and decision-making. The VBSRE approaches do not focus on the stakeholder analysis. There are few studies that focus on the significance of the stakeholders for the VBS systems, but do not propose any framework or approach for the stakeholder identification and quantification (SIQ) process. There is the need to integrate the stakeholder analysis with the VBSRE for better RE practices.

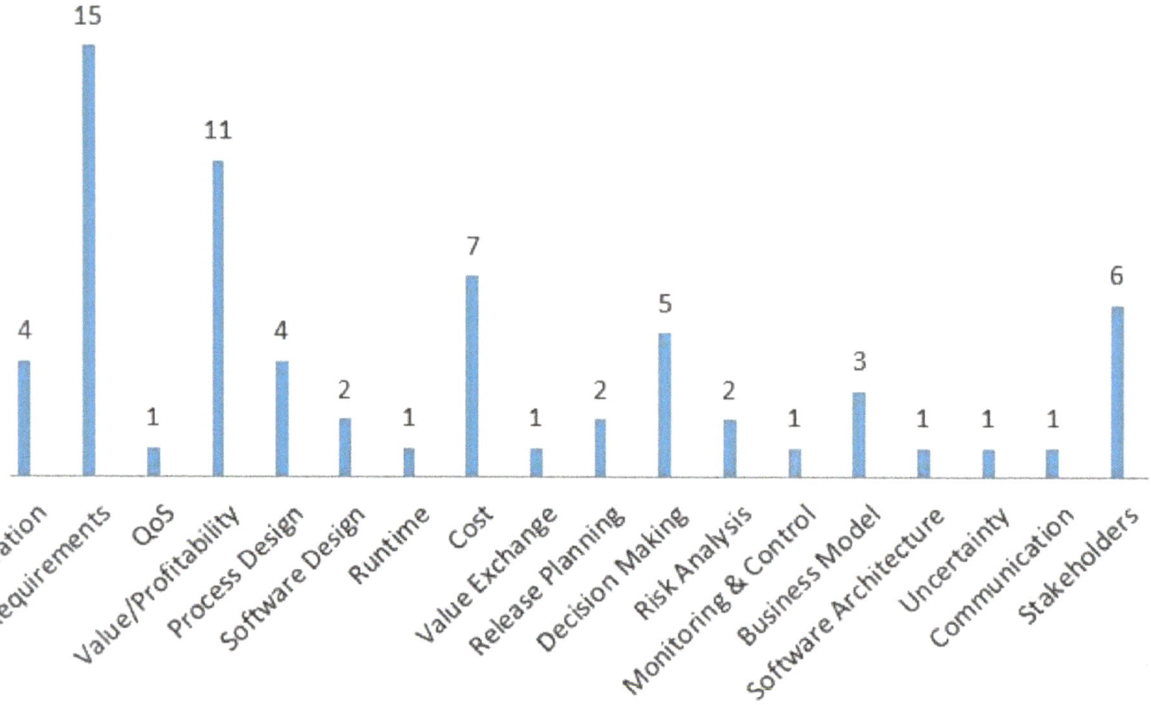

Figure 1. Issues highlighted in the VBS Research.

Stakeholders are the key element in the success and failure of the software. Hence, the high priority is given to the stakeholders in the Star Triangle in [9]. A comprehensive analysis of the SIQ problems is discussed in [10] for the VBS development and it is forced that "to characterise the stakeholders based on the responsibilities", "to propose the stakeholders' metrics to make the SIQ process easy" and "to propose an SIQ framework in easy steps" for the VBS systems. Freeman defines a stakeholder as "any group or individual who can affect or is affected by the achievement of the organization's objectives" [11]. Tom Gilb defines a stakeholder as "any person or organizational group with an interest in, or ability to affect, the system or its environment"[12]. The stakeholder or customer satisfaction related to the VBS system mainly depends on the selection of highly critical requirements. In order to satisfy the customers, the selection of highly valuable stakeholders is essential in the requirements elicitation phase (REP). In order to gain the market leverage, the trustworthiness of the system must be high. The VBS trustworthiness or reliability is taken as a quality measure as trustworthiness or reliability of cloud service is considered as a quantitative quality measure in the case of cloud computing [13]. The cloud computing is also a part of the value-based paradigm and the trustworthiness of the cloud services is highly desirable. Same is the case with the stakeholders with respect to the trustworthiness. However, the current SIQ techniques cannot be adopted as a standard because they are not standardized, applied and tested in a real time environment. Hence, the suitability of the existing SIQ techniques for the VBS systems is questionable. The VBS systems are associated with the economic leverage, thus all the entities cannot be taken at par. For the VBS systems, only the key stakeholders are considered during the requirements analysis phase. It is not easy to decide which technique is suitable for the VBS development. The selection of a technique as a model is very difficult because some methods are just characterizing the stakeholders instead of the quantification [14, 15]. Enough work is done with respect to the value-based requirements prioritization or quantification in different research studies like [16–19]. However, the work in the domain of value-based stakeholder prioritization or quantification is not sufficient.

The rest of the paper is divided into 9 sections. Section 2 discusses the SIQ research background. The detail of the proposed SIQ framework *StakeMeter* is given in Section 3. Section 4 is about stakeholder factor formulation. The description of inclusion and exclusion criteria of stakeholders is given in Section 5. Section 6 describes the implementation guidelines. The details of the case studies are given in Section 7. The details of performance analysis of the *StakeMeter* are given in Section 8. Section 9 highlights the future research directions. The last section, Section 10 concludes this study.

RESEARCH BACKGROUND

Different techniques and methodologies are presented to identify and quantify the stakeholders. Currently there is a lack of uniformity in the existing techniques. There is no existence of a uniform SIQ framework and the selection of the existing approaches is complex [14, 15]. The current methods and techniques do not provide clear guidelines, thus the identification and selection of valuable stakeholders is very difficult. The current techniques identify the stakeholders based on their relationships, roles and influence [20–23]. They provide a very high level picture of the business entities instead of focusing on low level details. There are some techniques that do not consider the aspects of relationships, roles and influence [24, 25] which shows the non-uniformity of the existing techniques. The attributes of power, legitimacy, and urgency are taken into account in the Mitchell's theory. These attributes are used to divide the stakeholders into eight categories like dormant stakeholders, discretionary stakeholders, demanding stakeholders, dominant stakeholders, dependent stakeholders, dangerous stakeholders, definitive stakeholders and non-stakeholders [21]. Mitchell's model is a very basic initial model for stakeholders' identification and lacks in low level details.

Ballejos and Montagna presented a technique based on the roles and types for the SIQ at inter-organizational level [26–28]. The stakeholders are quantified based on key attributes of function, knowledge abilities, geographical position and hierarchy level. The technique induces the problem of competency measurement among all four aspects. Moreover, the technique is not cost-effective in terms of time utilization.

The PisoSIA (Stakeholder Identification and Analysis) technique is an extension in an existing technique called PISO (Process Improvement for Strategic Objectives) [29]. The technique does not focus on the SIQ process. The technique focuses on the identification of new stakeholders when a change is required in the existing functionality of a system. However, the importance of the stakeholders is not denied. Boonstra (2006) conducted a research called "ERP-implementation project from a stakeholder perspective". In this research, a technique is presented based on the Mitchell's model to classify the stakeholders at a higher level of abstraction [30]. In this technique, the new stakeholders are identified based on the induced change and the impact of the change is measured on the existing stakeholders.

Glinz and Wieringa quantified stakeholders into three major categories i.e. critical, major and minor [31]. However, the process level details are not given for the SIQ. An abstract picture of the identification and classification model is depicted. Thus, it is difficult to adopt the model when a project or product requires an agile environment in terms of its execution, implementation or development. Woolridge *et al.* (2007) divide stakeholders into high level major categories based on their induced risk. The research does not provide in depth process level details for classification of stakeholders. The reported stakeholder categories are financial supporters, customers, internal stakeholders, external stakeholders, special interest stakeholders and influencer stakeholders [32].

The research motivation is based on the findings which state that the current techniques are complex, provide a description of stakeholders at a higher level of abstraction, and do not provide process level details in order to quantify the stakeholders [29], incorrect early findings [29], are not uniform [33], cannot be adopted as a framework [33], and are time consuming and costly [26–28]. The VBS systems mainly focus on the economic leverage and this thing differentiates the VBS from traditional software applications. There is the need to propose a new SIQ framework for the VBS systems. The proposed framework will help in finding out a critical set of stakeholders and decision making. The framework provides clear and easy guidelines to initiate the SIQ process. The concept of multi-attribute and multi-metrics as proposed in [34, 35] is introduced in order to evaluate the trustworthiness or reliability of the stakeholders. The selected critical stakeholders will help the requirement engineers in the elicitation of precise and accurate requirements in terms of system's functionality and usability. The clear and profound requirements will help the developers to develop a useful system of high quality as per needs of the stakeholders. (Fig. 2) describes the different issues of the SIQ. There are two types of problems named as process problems and technical problems of the SIQ. The green lightning sign in (Fig. 2) indicates the requirements gathered from the success critical stakeholders while the red lightning sign indicates the requirements which may cause a high risk. In order to solve the SIQ problems this research contributes in the form of a new SIQ framework called as *StakeMeter*. The proposed framework *StakeMeter* comprises responsibilities of stakeholders, attributes and metrics as key contribution elements.

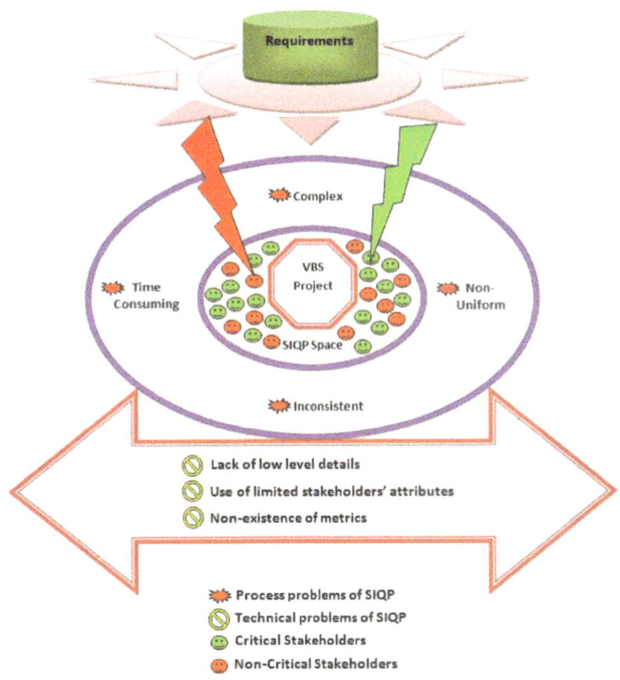

Figure 2. Problems of the SIQP.

PROPOSED FRAMEWORK STAKEMETER

The proposed SIQ framework called *StakeMeter* comprises 6 steps. The main steps of the framework are stakeholder responsibilities, stakeholder groups, stakeholder aspects or attributes, stakeholder factors, stakeholder values and inclusion and exclusion criteria. (Fig. 3) shows the different steps of the proposed framework *StakeMeter*.

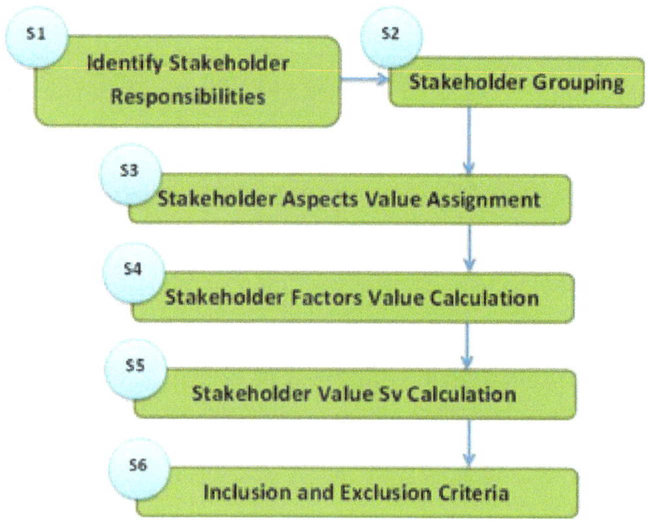

Figure 3. Flowchart of StakeMeter.

Stakeholder Responsibilities

The organizations mostly define the responsibilities of their employees from higher level to the lower level including their authorities. The overview of such documents may help in understanding the responsibilities of the stakeholders of an organization. If the responsibility documents are not available, then there is the need to create them. The responsibilities of stakeholders play a vital role in identification of different stakeholders who may contribute in the development of the VBS systems.

Stakeholder Groups

In this step, the stakeholders are identified and divided into different groups based on their responsibilities. Stakeholders or people working in the same vicinity and professional area are placed in the same group. Moreover, based on the job relationships the stakeholders may also be placed in the similar groups. However, their level of professionalism is defined using stakeholder factors or metrics which are described in Section 4.

Stakeholder Aspects or Attributes

An initial estimation of all the factors is based on the stakeholder aspects or attributes which are taken into account during quantification of the stakeholders. These aspects are taken from literature and industry professionals. Some of the stakeholder aspects are communication, interpretation, decision making, cognitive load, complexity, clarity, objectivity, self-confidence, language barriers, time and geographical differences. The description of some of the stakeholder aspects is given in Table 1. However, the selected stakeholder aspects are described in detail in Section 4.

Table 1. Stakeholders' aspects.

Aspect Name	Aspect Description
Communication	The stakeholders' ability to communicate properly.
Interpretation	Stakeholders' ability to describe the economic benefit of the required needs.
Decision Making	The stakeholder has a prominent role in decision making or not.
Cognitive Load	This shows the stakeholder's ability related to memory stress.
Complexity	Stakeholder's ability to present the complex needs in an elaborative way.
Clarity	Stakeholder's ability to describe the intended needs In a clear manner.
Objectivity	Stakeholder's ability to describe the intended meanings of the needs properly.
Self Confidence	It represents the level of self-confidence of the stakeholder.

doi:10.1371/journal.pone.0121344.t001

Stakeholder Factors

In this step, the individual value of each of the stakeholder factor or metric is calculated to find out the value of a stakeholder. These individual values are given as an input to the *Sv*function as shown in Section 4, and the final value of the stakeholder *Sv* is calculated. This step of the framework comprises different stakeholder factors that must be considered during the SIQ to select the most critical stakeholders. The value of these factors is calculated to find out the importance of an entity for a given VBS system. Table 2 describes the proposed factors in detail.

Table 2. Factor description.

Factor Name	Acronym	Factor Description
Risk Factor	F_{SR}	Depicts the risk imposed by a stakeholder.
Instability Factor	F_{SI}	Helps in calculating the instability in stakeholder's nature.
Communication Factor	F_{SC}	Vital in finding out stakeholder's fluency about the ideas.
Skill Factor	F_{SS}	Helps in finding out stakeholders' professional abilities.
Interest Factor	F_{SIT}	Helpful in knowing the stakeholder's interests in system.
Personality Factor	F_{SP}	Helps in observing the personality of a stakeholder.
Hierarchy Factor	F_{SH}	The F_{SH} helps to find out that at which extent the level of hierarchy is dominant on the personality of a stakeholder.
Legitimacy Factor	F_{SLG}	Depicts the stakeholder have some legitimate need or not.
Environment Factor	F_{SE}	Helpful in finding out the professional ethics.

doi:10.1371/journal.pone.0121344.t002

The factors given in Table 2 consist of stakeholder aspects and the output is in the form of number values obtained from mathematical formulations as described in Section 4. The values obtained from all these factors serve as an input to the final computational logic in order to find out the worth or value of a stakeholder, which is denoted by *Sv*, for the VBS development. (Fig. 4) depicts the computational model for stakeholder quantification in which stakeholder factors serve as an input to the Computational Logic Unit (CLU) or Blackbox and returns the value of the intended stakeholder based on the proposed computational logic.

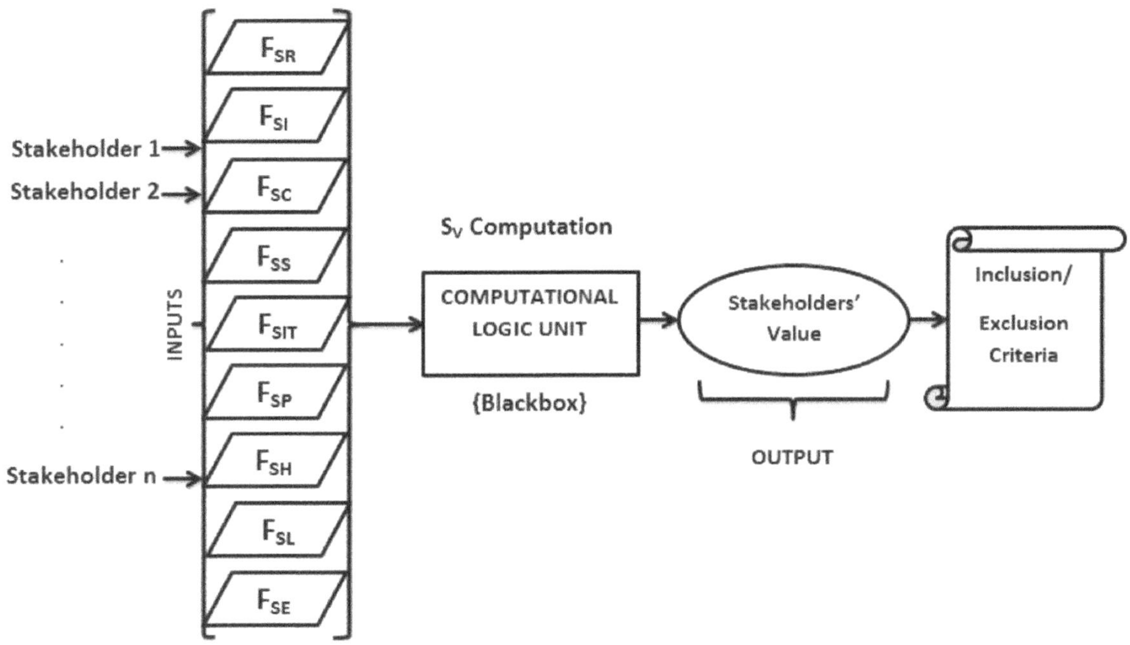

Figure 4. Computational model of stakeholders' quantification.

Stakeholder Values

The value of stakeholder *Sv* is calculated by using all the stakeholder factor values as a variable. The values of stakeholder factors are given to the final *Sv* equation and quantified value *Sv* of a stakeholder is obtained. The *Sv* is explained in Section 4. The *Sv* is the result of a function which can be written as:

$$Sv = f(x)$$

$$x = \{F_{SR}, F_{SC}, F_{SS}, F_{SI}, F_{SIT}, F_{SP}, F_{SH}, F_{SLG}, F_{SE}\}$$

The output of *f(x)* results in the *Sv* which is used to quantify the stakeholders in order to know the stakeholder importance for the VBS project. The value of '*x*' is based on the values of stakeholder factors. In mathematical notations, *Sv* is a function of *x*. The different factors are taken into consideration in order to quantify the stakeholders which serve as an input to the function. For the calculation of all these factors, different stakeholder aspects are taken into account. These aspects help in finding out the value of a given factor for a given stakeholder. Based on the values of all these factors, the overall value of a stakeholder is calculated which is denoted by the *Sv*.

Inclusion and Exclusion Criteria

The inclusion and exclusion criteria are based on the quantification value of stakeholders obtained from individual stakeholder factors after computation. The inclusion and exclusion criteria depend on the *Sv*. The *Sv* defines that either the involvement of a stakeholder is essential for the success of the system or not in terms of market leverage. The inclusion and exclusion criteria are described in Section 5.

STAKEHOLDER FACTOR FORMULATION

The stakeholder selection is based on the stakeholder metrics, which are termed as 'factors' in this study. The stakeholder factors are proposed after long discussions and meetings with the industry professionals. Each of the factor value is calculated by using stakeholder attributes that are stated as 'aspects' in this study. In this stage, the experts are heavily involved, and the significance of the stakeholder aspects is defined for different stakeholder factors. A consensus was made by the experts on the use of the terms factors and aspects instead of metrics and attributes. The values of all the proposed factors are calculated by assigning them the values of stakeholder aspects. Different aspects are used for different factors to evaluate the stakeholders thoroughly in order to know their worth for the VBS project. However, in the existing approaches, the use of few aspects does not help in thorough evaluation of the stakeholders and this limitation results in confusion and biases. Thus, a wide range of aspects is evaluated in order to know the worth of a stakeholder for the VBS project. F denotes the stakeholder factor or metric and T denotes the stakeholder attribute or aspect in this research. The values of the aspects are taken as an input on a Likert scale of 0 to 5.

Factor→F

Aspect→T

Stakeholder Risk Factor (F_{SR})

The aspects that are considered for stakeholder risk factor are communication (T_{CM}), interpretation (T_{IT}), decision-making (T_{DM}), cognitive load (T_{CL}), complexity (T_{CP}), language barriers (T_{LB}), time and geographic differences (T_{TG}). The selected aspects represent the effect of a stakeholder on the RE and it may be positive or adverse. The details of the selected aspects are as follows:

- Communication (T_{CM}): The aspect of communication is taken into consideration in order to judge that at which level the stakeholder is able to communicate the functional objectives of the project.
- Interpretation (T_{IT}): The aspect of interpretation helps in evaluation of the descriptions given by a stakeholder related to a particular functional aspect of the system.
- Decision-making (T_{DM}): The stakeholder has a prominent role in decision-making or not.
- Cognitive Load (T_{CL}): At which level the stakeholder is able to bear the memory stress.
- Complexity (T_{CP}): To which extent the stakeholder is able to present the complex needs and decisions in a more elaborative way.
- Language Barriers (T_{LB}): The impact of language of the intended stakeholder.
- Time & Geographic Differences (T_{TG}): The impact of time and geographical differences related to the stakeholder.

The bad communication and interpretation may result in high risk in the form of changes or project failure. Same is the case with other aspects in order to judge the risk factor. Initially, the partial effect of each of the aspect is taken in the form of a value and the cumulative effect of the different aspects is calculated by summing up the partial effects of all the aspects. The summation as shown in Equation 1 also helps in reducing the expert biases due to the fact that it prevents from mere numbers game. The same technique is used in all other proposed factors in order to obtain a linear dataset. In the case of F_{SR}, if the aspect value is 0 then it means low risk, otherwise 5 means high risk.

$$F_{SR} = 0.2(T_{CM} + T_{IT} + T_{DM} + T_{CL} + T_{CP} + T_{LB} + T_{TG}) + 0.2$$

$$F_{SR} = 0.2\left(\sum_{i=1}^{n} F_{SR_i}\right) + 0.2 \qquad (1)$$

The expert assigns the value to each aspect in the range of 0 to 5. For example if the expert assigns the following values to all seven aspects of F_{SR}:

$$F_{SR} = 0.2(3 + 2 + 4 + 3 + 1 + 2 + 3) + 0.2$$

Then the value of F_{SR} for a given stakeholder is 3.8. In the same way, the values of all other stakeholder factors are calculated based on the aspect values. In Equation 1, i denotes an aspect of F_{SR} and n is the total number of aspects. After inserting the aspect values in the range of 0 to 5, the output of F_{SR} is in the range of 0.2 to 7.2.

Stakeholder Instability Factor (F_{SI})

The aspects that are considered for stakeholder instability factor are immune to challenges (T_{CH}), workload (T_{WL}), and fatigue management (T_{FM}). These aspects are described as follows:

- Immune to Challenges (T_{CH}): The stakeholder has the ability to face the new challenges.
- Work Load (T_{WL}): The stakeholder is able to bear the extra workload.
- Fatigue Management (T_{FM}): The stakeholder's expression of fatigue.

In the case of F_{SI}, if the aspect value is 0 then it means low risk, otherwise 5 means high risk.

$$F_{SI} = 0.2(T_{CH} + T_{WL} + T_{FM}) + 0.2$$

$$F_{SI} = 0.2\left(\sum_{i=1}^{n} F_{SI_i}\right) + 0.2 \qquad (2)$$

In Equation 2, i denotes an aspect of F_{SI} and n is the total number of aspects. After inserting the aspect values in the range of 0 to 5, the output of F_{SI} is in the range of 0.2 to 3.2.

Stakeholder Communication Factor (F_{SC})

The aspects that are considered for stakeholder communication factor are clarity (T_{CR}), objectivity (T_{OB}), and self-confidence (T_{SC}). The description of the aspects is given as follows:

- Clarity (T_{CR}): The stakeholder is able to clearly describe the intended needs of the VBS system.
- Objectivity (T_{OB}): The stakeholder is able to properly describe the intended meaning of the required needs in terms of economic benefit.
- Self-confidence (T_{SC}): The level of self-confidence of the stakeholder.

In the case of F_{SC}, if the aspect value is 0 then it means that the stakeholder is non-critical, otherwise 5 means critical.

$$F_{SC} = 0.2\,(T_{CR} + T_{OB} + T_{SC}) + 0.2$$

$$F_{SC} = 0.2\left(\sum_{i=1}^{n} F_{SC_i}\right) + 0.2 \tag{3}$$

In Equation 3, i denotes an aspect of F_{SC} and n is the total number of aspects. After inserting the aspect values in the range of 0 to 5, the output of F_{SC} is in the range of 0.2 to 3.2.

Stakeholder Skill Factor (F_{SS})

The aspects that are considered for stakeholder skill factor are experience (T_{EX}), managerial abilities (T_{MA}), domain knowledge (T_{DK}), domain training (T_{DT}), and self-esteem (T_{SE}). These aspects are described as follows:

- Experience (T_{EX}): The stakeholder's prior experience or related experience in the domain of VBS systems.
- Managerial Abilities (T_{MA}): The stakeholder's level of management in their respective professional area.
- Domain Knowledge (T_{DK}): The current level of domain knowledge of the stakeholder.
- Domain Training (T_{DT}): The stakeholder is properly trained or not.
- Self-esteem (T_{SE}): The stakeholder is holding the status as per his or her required skills.

In the case of F_{SS}, if the aspect value is 0 then it means that the stakeholder is non-critical, otherwise 5 means critical.

$$F_{SS} = 0.2\,(T_{EX} + T_{MA} + T_{DK} + T_{DT} + T_{SE}) + 0.2$$

$$F_{SS} = 0.2\left(\sum_{i=1}^{n} F_{SS_i}\right) + 0.2 \tag{4}$$

In Equation 4, i denotes an aspect of F_{SS} and n is the total number of aspects. After inserting the aspect values in the range of 0 to 5, the output of F_{SS} is in the range of 0.2 to 5.2.

Stakeholder Interest Factor (F_{SIT})

The aspects that are considered for stakeholder interest factor are domain scope knowledge (T_{DSK}), business knowledge (T_{BK}), and objectivity (T_{OB}). These aspects are described as follows:

- Domain Scope Knowledge (T_{DSK}): The stakeholder has the knowledge of most relevant subject matter of the domain.
- Business Knowledge (T_{BK}): The stakeholder knows well about the business domain.
- Objectivity (T_{OB}): The knowledge shared by the stakeholder is meaningful in terms of financial value.

In the case of F_{SIT}, if the aspect value is 0 then it means that the stakeholder is non-critical, otherwise 5 means critical.

$$F_{SIT} = 0.2\,(T_{DSK} + T_{BK} + T_{OB}) + 0.2$$

$$F_{SIT} = 0.2\left(\sum_{i=1}^{n} F_{SIT_i}\right) + 0.2 \tag{5}$$

In Equation 5, i denotes an aspect of F_{SIT} and n is the total number of aspects. After inserting the aspect values in the range of 0 to 5, the output of F_{SIT} is in the range of 0.2 to 3.2.

Stakeholder Personality Factor (F_{SP})

The aspects that are considered for stakeholder personality factor are cooperative (T_{CO}), visionary (T_{VI}), inspirer (T_{IN}), performer (T_{PR}), knowledge sharer (T_{KS}), role model (T_{RM}), and influence (T_{INF}). These aspects are described as follows:

- Cooperative (T_{CO}): The extent of cooperation of a stakeholder with other team members.
- Visionary (T_{VI}): The stakeholder's level of deep insight of the business.
- Inspirer (T_{IN}): The stakeholder has the ability to do something creative.
- Performer (T_{PR}): The stakeholder has the ability to do something as an achiever in order to make something successful.
- Knowledge Sharer (T_{KS}): The stakeholder shares ideas and experiences with others.
- Role Model (T_{RM}): The stakeholder's abilities make him or her prominent among team members and other stakeholders consider him or her as a role model.
- Influence (T_{INF}): The stakeholder's effect on other members in terms of creative thinking, development and behavioral aspects.

In the case of F_{SP}, if the aspect value is 0 then it means that the stakeholder is non-critical, otherwise five means critical.

$$F_{SP} = 0.2\,(T_{CO} + T_{VI} + T_{IN} + T_{PR} + T_{KS} + T_{RM} + T_{INF}) + 0.2$$

$$F_{SP} = 0.2\left(\sum_{i=1}^{n} F_{SP_i}\right) + 0.2 \tag{6}$$

In Equation 6, i denotes an aspect of F_{SP} and n is the total number of aspects. After inserting the aspect values in the range of 0 to 5, the output of F_{SP} is in the range of 0.2 to 7.2.

Stakeholder Hierarchy Factor (F_{SH})

The aspects that are considered for stakeholder hierarchy factor are executive position (T_{EP}), mid-career (T_{MC}), and entry-career (T_{EC}). The stakeholder's hierarchy is rated in terms of high, average and low. The details of these aspects are given as follows:

- Executive (T_{EP}): The stakeholder's highest level of power based on experience.
- Mid-Career (T_{MC}): The stakeholder's power level with good experience.
- Entry Career (T_{EC}): The stakeholder is serving as a new team member.

The value of F_{SH} is considered based on the current position of the stakeholders.

$T_{EP} = \text{High} = 4$

$T_{MC} = \text{Average} = 3$

$T_{EC} = \text{Low} = 2$

$F_{SH} = T_{Val}$

$T_{Val} = \textit{Value of Hierarcy Aspects}$

Stakeholder Legitimacy Factor (F_{SLG})

The legitimacy shows that either the stakeholder is a legitimate one in terms of system needs or not. The intensity of legitimacy is described in terms of high, average, and low.

$$\text{High} = 4$$

$$\text{Average} = 3$$

$$\text{Low} = 2$$

$$F_{SLG} = T_{Val}$$

$$T_{Val} = \text{Intensity of Legitimacy}$$

Stakeholder Environment Factor (FSE)

The aspects that are considered for stakeholder environment factor are cognitive load (T_{CL}), fatigue management (T_{FM}), inspirer (T_{IN}), and knowledge sharer (T_{KS}). There are some of the aspects which are also common in other factors. The commonality exists due to the dual role of these aspects under different scenarios. The detail of these aspects is given as follows:

- Cognitive Load (T_{CL}): At which level the stakeholder is able to bear the memory stress.
- Fatigue Management (T_{FM}): The stakeholder's expression of fatigue during work hours.
- Inspirer (T_{IN}): The stakeholder has the ability to do something creative.
- Knowledge Sharer (T_{KS}): The stakeholder shares ideas and experiences with others.

In the case of F_{SE}, if the aspect value is 0 then it means that the stakeholder is non-critical, otherwise 5 means critical.

$$F_{SE} = 0.2\,(T_{CL} + T_{FM} + T_{IN} + T_{KS}) + 0.2$$

$$F_{SE} = 0.2\left(\sum_{i=1}^{n} F_{SE_i}\right) + 0.2 \quad (7)$$

In Equation 7, i denotes an aspect of F_{SE} and n is the total number of aspects. After inserting the aspects' values in the range of 0 to 5, the output of F_{SE} is in the range of 0.2 to 4.2.

In all factors, the sum of all different aspects is taken into account and is multiplied by a weight factor of 0.2 and then a weight factor of 0.2 is added to the equation. The summation of the values of all factors is taken into account in order to calculate the accumulative effect of all aspects on the dependant variables of stakeholder factor values. Hence, each factor value is calculated as a linear combination or summation of all the aspects. The weight factor 0.2 is applied in order to get a smaller range of value and to get a linear solution for each factor. The weight factors, greater than 0.2, are problematic in terms of higher values of the *Sv*. Moreover, the weight factor 0.2 is used to standardize the data in a manageable range with upper and lower bounds. The weight factors lower than 0.2 are problematic in terms of fuzzification. Fuzzification causes the problem of uncertainty in the selection process of the stakeholders. Different weight factors are applied and evaluated in the range of 0.1 to 0.9 and it is found that if a factor is applied in this range, the number of quantification values remain the same. However, as the value of the factor is going to increase from 0.1 to 0.9 the values of stakeholder factors are also going to increase. The higher values of stakeholder factors are difficult to manage. Thus, the weight factor of 0.2 is chosen as a solution in order to obtain the normalized and manageable data values. The*Sv* range increases due to the application of a large number of stakeholder aspects. The final *Sv* of a stakeholder is calculated by using the following formula.

$$S_V = (F_{SC} + F_{SS} + F_{SIT} + F_{SP} + F_{SH} + F_{SLG} + F_{SE}) - (F_{SR} + F_{SI})$$

$$S_V = \sum_{i=1}^{n} \beta_i - \sum_{j=1}^{m} \gamma_j \quad (8)$$

$$\beta = \{F_{SC} + F_{SS} + F_{SIT} + F_{SP} + F_{SH} + F_{SLG} + F_{SE}\} \quad (9)$$

$$\gamma = \{F_{SR} + F_{SI}\} \quad (10)$$

In Equation 8, β refers to the values of stakeholder factors that are used to calculate the positive impact of a stakeholder on the system and i refers to the β factors, where n is the total number of β factors. However, γ refers to the values of stakeholder factors that are used to calculate the negative impact of a stakeholder on the system and j refers to the γ factors, where m is the total number of γ factors. After inserting the factor values, the output of β is in the range of 5.0 to 31.0 with a geometric progression of 0.2. After inserting the factor values, the output of γ is in the range of 0.4 to 10.4 with a geometric progression of 0.2. *Sv* is the value of stakeholder that is calculated after taking a summation of the β values of the factors and negating the summation of the γ values of the factors. The *Sv* is in the range of-5.4 to 30.6 with a geometric progression of 0.2. Equation 9 and Equation 10 shows the β and γ factors.

INCLUSION AND EXCLUSION CRITERION

The inclusion and exclusion of a stakeholder in the RE process depends on the *Sv*. In case of the *Sv*, the two exceptions are very prominent:

- The values of β and γ cannot be high at the same time.
- The values of β and γ cannot be low at the same time.

These two exceptions show the contradiction of the results. If values of β and γ are high at the same time, it means that the stakeholder is highly valuable and highly risky, thus it is not acceptable. On the other hand, if the values of β and γ are low at the same time, it means that the stakeholder has low positive value and low risk or negative value, thus it is also not acceptable. Moreover, the requirements engineer may define their own criteria based on the *Sv* of a stakeholder. This makes the proposed framework flexible in terms of stakeholder selection based on the *Sv*.

IMPLEMENTATION GUIDELINES

In order to implement the *StakeMeter* framework, the implementers must adhere to some rules and regulations. In this section, some of the key application principles are given in order to implement the proposed framework *StakeMeter*. The application principles are stated as follows:

- In order to achieve the optimum results of the *StakeMeter* a team of professionals, comprising at least 4 members, must be selected.
- Get knowledge of the business practices of the organization early for which the product is going to be developed.
- Apply all steps of the *StakeMeter* in a rigorous way
- The team members must avoid conflicts and measure the value of each stakeholder based on the proposed framework *StakeMeter*.
- The team members may divide the organizational units based on their key expertise in order to implement the framework *StakeMeter*.

CASE STUDIES

Three teams, comprising five members each, are made in order to implement the framework as per given implementation guidelines which are given in Section 6. The purpose to choose the three teams is to evaluate the framework in a true sense and to reduce the extent of biasness. Two members of each team were working on analysis of the stakeholders based on the proposed SIQ framework and on the requirements in order to get the requirements from the intended stakeholders. Two members of the teams were working as developers in order to realize the requirements of the stakeholders into a working system and one member of each team was working on documentation of the system. The teams are made in order to get the unbiased results and to analyse the real worth of the proposed SIQ framework. The description of the projects is given in Table 3.

Table 3. Case study descriptions.

Case Study	Acronym	Description
Online Car Show Room	OCSR	An OCSR system is used to sell and purchase new and old cars and also related to the maintenance of the vehicles. The owner possesses a dealership contract with manufacturer. The system is a VBS system in terms of cost benefit.
Hospital Management System	HMS	The system provides better process to manage the day to day activities of the hospital and to provide better medical services to patients. The system is helpful in financial management and is termed as a VBS system.
Restaurant Management System	RMS	The RMS is a business oriented system that is normally used to provide better services to its customers. The system is normally used to keep track of all the transactions that are related to food sales and room bookings by the customers.

doi:10.1371/journal.pone.0121344.t003

The process is initiated by the teams after taking into consideration the total number of stakeholders who are related to the system directly or indirectly. The teams initially met with the top management of the business organizations in order to find out the total number of stakeholders in the given organization. Table 4 lists all the possible stakeholders of an organization.

Table 4. Total number of stakeholders.

Organization Name	OCSR	HMS	RMS
Total Stakeholders	23	63	121
Assigned To	Team 1	Team 2	Team 3

doi:10.1371/journal.pone.0121344.t004

Number of stakeholders

In this section, the number of stakeholders of three case studies is described in detail.

Case study: 1 Online Car Show Room

The main purpose of an Online Car Show Room (OCSR) management system is to sell and purchase cars or vehicles, and is normally used by the vehicle dealers. Team 1 who was working on the OCSR found a total of 23 main stakeholders at higher level of abstraction. The car showroom team is presided by one director and two deputy directors. The four stakeholders work on the front desk in order to oversee the customer requests and out of these four, one member works as a cashier. There is one front desk manager who controls the front desk activities. The administration team of car showroom consists of three admin assistants, two accountants and one admin officer. The technical store consists of one store officer, two store assistants, one clerk and five maintenance in-charges. There are 13 mechanics working under these maintenance in-charges who are not directly affected by the system thus, they are not included in the list of stakeholders. Table 5 lists all the stakeholders in the OCSR.

Table 5. List of the OCSR stakeholders.

OCSR CASE STUDY		
#	Stakeholders	To
	Director	1
	Deputy Director	2
	Admin Officer	1
	Front Desk Manager	1
	Store Officer	1
	Store Assistant	2
	Admin Assistant	3
	Accountant	2
	Front Desk Employee	4
	Clerk	1
	Maintenance In-charge	5

10.1371/journal.pone.0121344.t005

Case study 2: Hospital Management System

The Hospital Management System (HMS) is used in order to manage the day-to-day activities of a hospital like administrative affairs, patient administration, billing, and other related activities. The helpful properties of the system are used by all stakeholders from higher ranks to lower ranks in a hospital. Patient is considered as one of the most important entity in this system. There is the need to incorporate all critical needs or requirements of the stakeholders in the intended system. In order to make the HMS beneficial for the intended community, the system should be flexible, reliable, and easy to adopt. The main flow of the information totally depends upon the requirements gathered from the stakeholders. For an automated HMS, there is the need to identify the key stakeholders of the system in order to gather requirements. In the HMS, there is a long list of stakeholders who control different activities of the hospital. The proposed SIQ framework is applied and the stakeholders are quantified based on the *Sv*.

Team 2 was working on the HMS and found a total of 63 stakeholders at a higher level of abstraction. There was one director of the hospital and one administrative officer. The medical departments are governed by four head of departments. In the front desk team, there are five employees headed by a front desk officer. There are a total of 13 medical officers who work in the hospital. The medical laboratory is comprised of three technicians with one lab officer and the X-ray department has two technicians with one X-Ray medical officer. There are a total of 18 male and female nurses. There are two medical equipment maintenance in-charges and three technicians. The admin team consists of one cashier, one accountant, two admin assistants and one clerk. Medical store is controlled by one medical store in-charge and two salesmen. There is one technical store officer and two store assistants. Table 6 lists all the stakeholders in the HMS.

Table 6. List of the HMS stakeholders.

HMS CASE STUDY		
ID #	Stakeholders	Total
1.	Director	1
2.	Admin Officer	1
3.	Head of Departments	4
4.	Medical Officers	13
5.	Medical Lab Officer	1
6.	X-Ray Lab Officer	1
7.	Technical Store Officer	1
8.	Nurses	18
9.	Front Desk Officer	1
10.	Front Desk Employee	5
11.	Maintenance In-charge	2
12.	Maintenance Technician	3
13.	Medical Lab Technician	3
14.	X-Ray Technician	2
15.	Technical Store Assistant	2
16.	Medical Store In-charge	1
17.	Accountant	1
18.	Cashier	1
19.	Admin Assistant	1
20.	Clerk	1

doi:10.1371/journal.pone.0121344.t006

Case study 3: Restaurant Management System

The Restaurant Management System (RMS) is assigned to Team 3 and they have listed a total of 121 stakeholders who are working at the restaurant. However, only 21 stakeholders are selected out of 121 and are listed here based on the core responsibilities of the stakeholders. The focused restaurant is supervised by a general manager who is responsible for overall activities of the restaurant. The food manager manages the food supply chains, and the housekeeping manager keeps the maintenance of the building. There is one administrative officer who handles the administrative affairs of the restaurant, two admin assistants and two clerks are working under his supervision. The financial matters are looked by one cashier and one accountant who supervise two assistants. Three supervisors are responsible for the in-house maintenance or needs of the restaurant that should be informed to senior management. The front desk team consists of three employees who guide the guests about room booking and other services and are supervised by one front desk officer. There is one store officer and one store-assistant.Table 7 describes the total stakeholders in the RMS.

Table 7. List of the RMS stakeholders.

RMS CASE STUDY		
ID #	**Stakeholders**	**Total**
1.	General Manager	1
2.	Food Manager	1
3.	Housekeeping Manager	1
4.	Admin Officer	1
5.	Supervisors	3
6.	Store Officer	1
7.	Store Assistant	1
8.	Accountant	1
9.	Account Assistant	2
10.	Front Desk Executive	1
11.	Front Desk Employee	3
12.	Cashier	1
13.	Admin Assistant	2
14.	Clerk	2

doi:10.1371/journal.pone.0121344.t007

Stakeholders' Responsibilities and Grouping

The responsibilities of the stakeholders play a vital role in description of the different business activities. After counting the total number of stakeholders of all three case studies namely OCSR, HMS and RMS, all of the teams asked the lists of responsibilities of all the stakeholders from the respective business organization. Based on these responsibilities, the teams have found dependencies of different stakeholders on each other and the working relationships between all the entities. The teams have divided the stakeholders into different groups based on their responsibilities, especially based on similar responsibilities.

Online Car Show Room

Team 1 has divided the stakeholders of the OCSR into five main categories namely executive group, administration group, front desk group, maintenance group and technical store group. These groups help in finding out the hierarchies of the stakeholders in terms of their relative position in the organization. Team 1 has included the director and deputy directors into the executive group who mainly handle the financial issues and overall infrastructure of the showroom. The administration group deals with the administrative affairs of the showroom, thus the administrative officer and staff come in the boundaries of this group. The front desk group comprises front desk officer or manager and the related staff who handle similar activities in the showroom. The maintenance group is related to the maintenance of the old and new vehicles and comprises maintenance in-charges and technicians. The technical store group consists of the store officer and working staff. The technical store group handles the inventory of spare parts in the store of the showroom. (Fig. 5) describes the different groups in the OCSR case study.

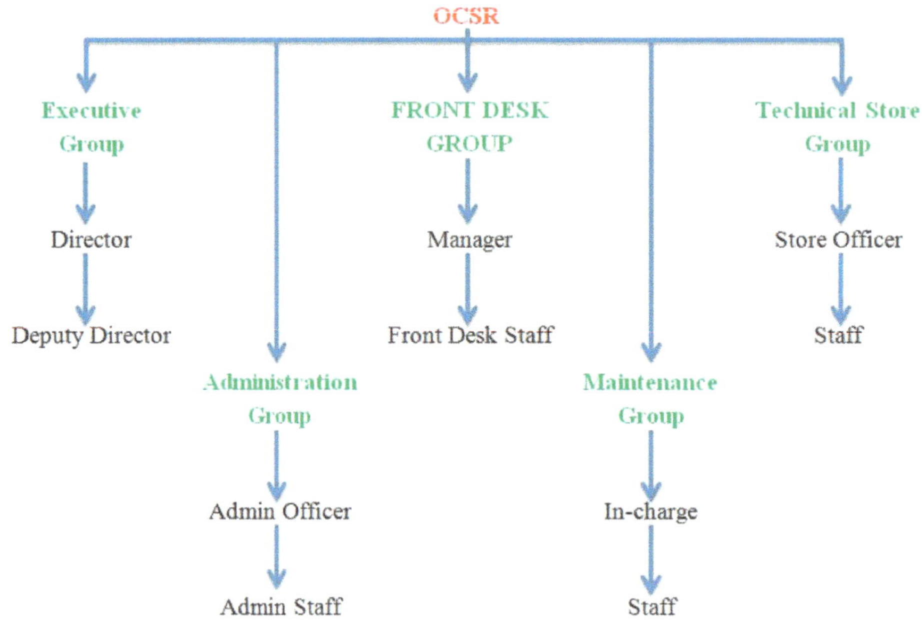

Figure 5. Stakeholders' groups in OCSR.

Hospital Management System

The team who worked on the HMS divided the stakeholders into nine major groups. The list of groups is comprised of executive group, front desk group, treatment group, administration group, maintenance group, laboratory group, medical store group, technical store group and x-ray lab group. (Fig. 6) lists all the groups of the HMS stakeholders. Executive group consists of director and head of departments. Front desk group contains the list of front desk officer and front desk staff. The treatment group is related to the treatment of the patients and is comprised of medical officers and nurses. The elements of administration group are admin officer and admin staff. Maintenance group contains in-charge and technicians. Laboratory group is related to pathological tests and consists of lab officer and technicians. X-ray laboratory group consists of lab officer and technicians. The medical store group contains store in-charge and salesman. Finally, the technical store group is a set of store officer and store assistants.

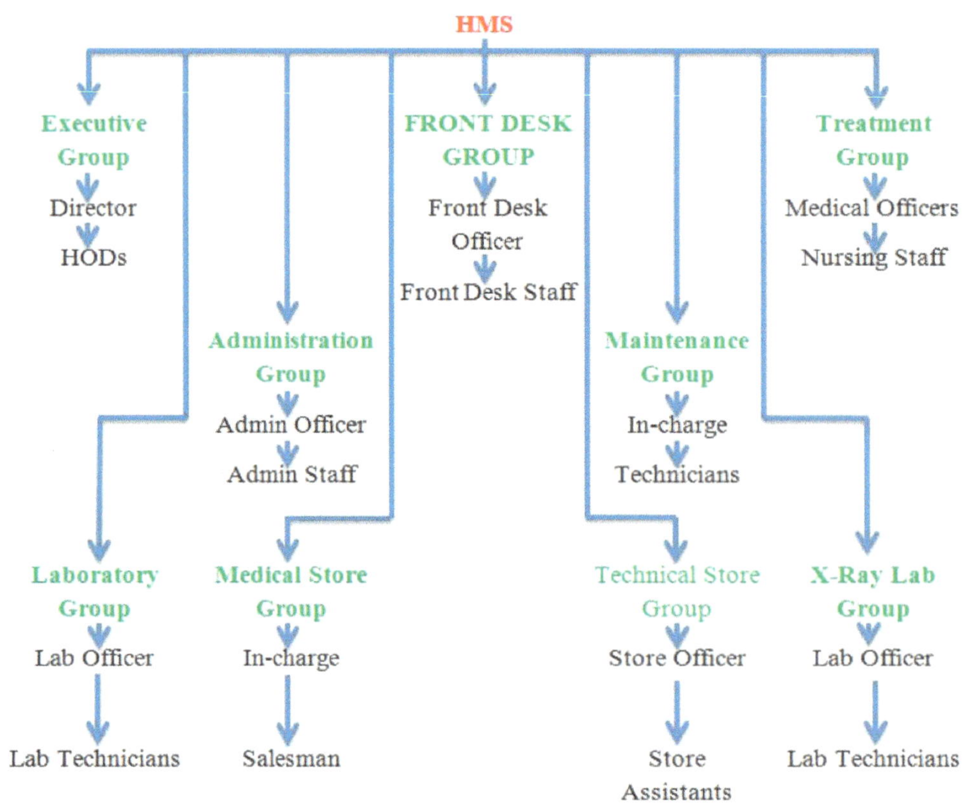

Figure 6. Stakeholders' groups in HMS.

Restaurant Management System

The software team who worked on the RMS reported five groups of stakeholders, namely executive group, front desk group, technical store group, administration group and maintenance group. (Fig. 7) describes all the possible groups of the stakeholders in the RMS. Executive group contains Managers. Front desk group consists of front desk officer and staff. The technical store group consists of store officer and staff. The administration group consists of admin officer and related staff. The maintenance group is comprised of supervisors and staff.

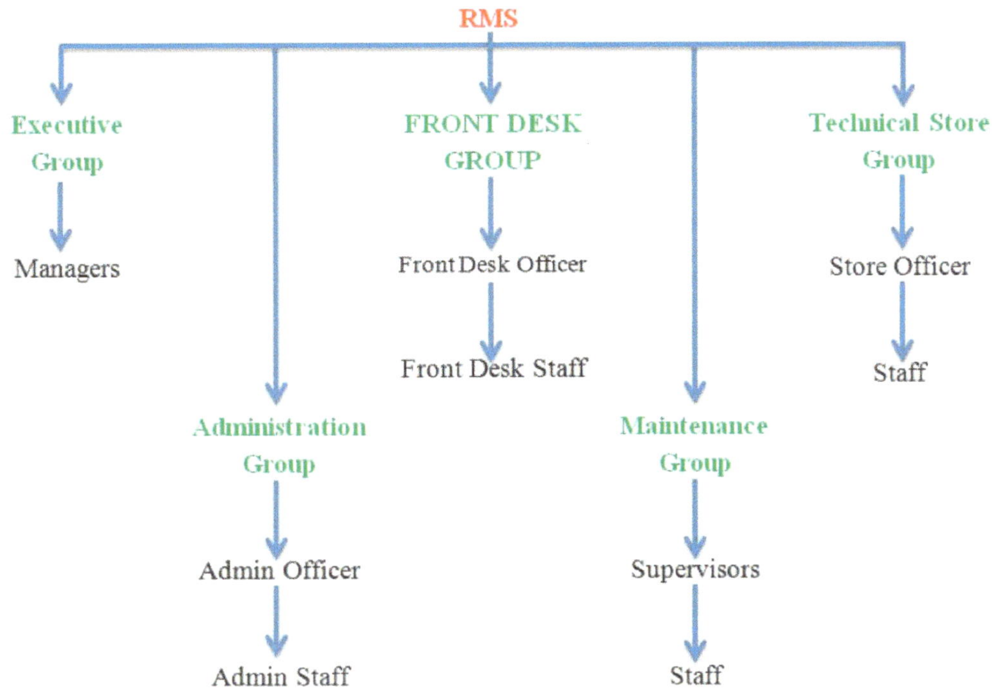

Figure 7. Stakeholders' groups in RMS.

Stakeholder Quantification Results and Analysis

The stakeholder quantification is performed by applying the proposed factors. Every team has used the proposed nine factors and quantified the stakeholders based on the key attributes. The value of each stakeholder is calculated by using the *Sv* equation. Later, for each project a critical set of stakeholders is selected by the professionals. Table 8 describes the selection and quantification of the OCSR stakeholders based on the proposed factor values and *Sv*. Team 1 of the OCSR selected 13 stakeholders based on the *Sv* of each stakeholder. The *Sv* decreases quickly in the case of the OCSR project, which shows that only few stakeholders are beneficial for this project. The rest of the stakeholders in the case of the OCSR are not included due to the low *Sv*.

Table 8. OCSR stakeholder Sv.

Sr. No:	Stakeholder	Group	β Values	γ Values	S_V
1.	Director	Executive	26.4	0.8	25.6
2.	Dy. Director	Executive	23.0	1.2	21.8
3.	Front Desk Manager	Front Desk	20.6	1.0	19.6
4.	AO	Administration	18.8	0.8	18.0
5.	SO	TechStore	19.2	1.6	17.6
6.	SA1	TechStore	18.2	1.2	17.0
7.	SA2	TechStore	17.4	0.8	16.6
8.	MI1	Maintenance	17.6	0.8	16.8
9.	MI2	Maintenance	18.8	2.4	16.4
10.	MECH1	Maintenance	16.4	2.0	14.4
11.	MECH2	Maintenance	14.6	1.8	12.8
12.	MECH3	Maintenance	15.2	2.6	12.6
13.	MECH4	Maintenance	12.8	3.2	9.6

doi:10.1371/journal.pone.0121344.t008

Table 9 describes the *Sv* value of the HMS stakeholders. The team has selected 32 stakeholders out of 63 based on the *Sv*. The software development team 2 has considered all those executive stakeholders who have *Sv* greater than 19. The other non-executive stakeholders with *Sv* greater than 15 are included in the set of key stakeholders. The remaining stakeholders are not considered as key stakeholders for the HMS project, and they do not have legitimate needs. The requirements should be gathered from the selected key stakeholders.

Table 9. HMS stakeholders' Sv.

Sr. No:	Stakeholder	Group	β	γ	S_V
1.	Director	Executive	24.4	0.6	23.8
2.	Admin Officer	Administration	22.2	0.4	21.8
3.	HOD 1	Executive	25.2	0.8	24.4
4.	HOD 2	Executive	21.6	0.6	21.0
5.	HOD 3	Executive	20.4	0.4	20.0
6.	HOD 4	Executive	22.8	0.6	22.2
7.	FDO	Front Desk	19.2	0.8	18.4
8.	Front Desk Employee 1	Front Desk	20.2	2.2	18.0
9.	Front Desk Employee 2	Front Desk	18.6	1.2	17.4
10.	MO 1	Treatment	21.0	0.8	20.2
11.	MO 2	Treatment	22.4	0.6	21.8
12.	MO 3	Treatment	23.0	0.4	22.6
13.	MO 4	Treatment	20.8	0.6	20.2
14.	MO 5	Treatment	19.8	1.2	18.6
15.	MO 6	Treatment	21.4	0.8	20.6
16.	Lab Officer	Laboratory	18.2	1.0	17.2
17.	Lab Technician	Laboratory	18.4	0.6	17.8
18.	X-Ray Technician	X-Ray Lab	21.2	1.6	19.6
19.	X-Ray MO	X-Ray Lab	17.8	1.2	16.6
20.	Nurse 1	Treatment	19.2	1.2	18.0
21.	Nurse 2	Treatment	22.4	0.6	21.8
22.	Nurse 3	Treatment	21.0	1.2	19.8
23.	Nurse 4	Treatment	22.8	2.2	20.6
24.	Nurse 5	Treatment	18.8	1.6	17.2
25.	Nurse 6	Treatment	23.2	0.4	22.8
26.	Nurse 7	Treatment	17.8	2.4	15.4
27.	Cashier	Admin	21.2	1.0	20.2
28.	Accountant	Admin	22.6	2.4	20.2
29.	Admin Assistant	Admin	19.6	2.6	17.0
30.	Medical Store In-charge	Medical Store	17.8	1.6	16.2
31.	Technical Store Officer	Technical Store	18.0	0.6	17.4
32.	Store Assistant	Technical Store	19.2	1.0	18.2

doi:10.1371/journal.pone.0121344.t009

The description of the *Sv* of the selected stakeholders for the RMS is given in Table 10. Team 3 has selected 21 stakeholders out of 121. The remaining stakeholders are reported as non-critical stakeholders based on the different key aspects as given in the *StakeMeter*framework.

Table 10. RMS stakeholder Sv.

Sr. No:	Stakeholder	Group	β Values	γ Values	S_V
1.	General Manager	Executive	20.6	1.8	18.8
2.	Food Manager	Executive	22.4	1.6	20.8
3.	Housekeeping Manager	Executive	23.6	1.0	22.6
4.	Admin Officer	Administration	19.8	2.2	17.6
5.	Store Officer	TechStore	18.2	2.0	16.2
6.	Supervisor 1	Maintenance	18.0	2.4	15.6
7.	Supervisor 2	Maintenance	17.8	1.8	16.0
8.	Supervisor 3	Maintenance	19.2	2.8	16.4
9.	Accountant	Administration	18.4	1.2	17.2
10.	Store Assistant	Maintenance	17.6	1.6	16.0
11.	Account Assistant 1	Administration	19.8	2.4	17.4
12.	Account Assistant 2	Administration	18.4	2.0	16.4
13.	Admin Assistant 1	Administration	16.6	2.4	14.2
14.	Admin Assistant 2	Administration	15.2	2.0	13.2
15.	Front Desk Executive	Front Desk	19.8	2.6	17.2
16.	Front Desk Employee 1	Front Desk	15.6	1.8	13.8
17.	Front Desk Employee 2	Front Desk	16.2	2.0	14.2
18.	Front Desk Employee 3	Front Desk	15.4	2.4	13.0
19.	Cashier	Administration	17.8	2.6	15.2
20.	Clerk 1	Administration	16.2	3.0	13.2
21.	Clerk 2	Administration	17.0	2.2	14.8

doi:10.1371/journal.pone.0121344.t010

Software project team 3 who worked on the RMS has selected a total of 21 stakeholders based on the *Sv* of the stakeholders. The trend, which is observed here, is the similarity in the γ values of the stakeholders at all levels, to some extent, and this makes most of the stakeholders significant.

In all of the three case studies, the stakeholders with higher *Sv* are included in the critical set. The *Sv* of each key stakeholder is obtained by using the key attributes of the stakeholder factors. The consultation with these stakeholders proved highly beneficial. The clarity of the ideas of the stakeholders is appreciated by the development team. The emphasis is given on the participation of the highly critical stakeholders in the case of value-driven software systems. Previously, the existing stakeholder analysis approaches are unable to provide a framework that may be adopted for the VBS systems. The empirical findings report that the proposed stakeholder analysis framework has a deeper effect on the success of the VBS system. It is verified by the results that the proposed stakeholder analysis framework is superior in terms of proposed steps, activities and proposed metrics as reported by the team members. The results show that the quantification of key stakeholders depends on the stakeholder aspects or attributes. The existing approaches do not cover the key aspects or attributes in a uniform way due to which the software professionals face different barriers. These barriers make the initiation process obscure. However, the proposed framework makes the initiation of the SIQ easy. During the implementation of the proposed framework, the professionals accepted that the proposed framework focuses on the stakeholders in a vigorous way. The proposed *StakeMeter* framework reduces the burden of software professionals by providing a step by step guide for stakeholder analysis. Hence, the key contribution of the *StakeMeter* framework is based on clear guidelines, adequacy of the attributes, proposed metrics, and implementation details. However, the existing SIQ approaches do not provide support in terms of clear guidelines, attributes and stakeholder metrics. A comparative analysis of the *StakeMeter* framework, based on the key contributions, is shown in Section 8 with respect to the existing SIQ approaches and methods.

PERFORMANCE ANALYSIS OF THE STAKEMETER

In order to measure the performance of the *StakeMeter* framework three existing methods are selected for comparative analysis. One is very initial method called as Mitchells' method (1997) and the second is a matured method as compared to the Mitchells' method and is called as Ballejos & Montagna method [28]. The third method is a latest one and is based on the bi-metric and fuzzy c-means algorithm [36]. The comparative analysis is based on the number of explored stakeholders, time consumption in terms of total man hours for stakeholder analysis, clearly defined priorities and detailed guidelines. The time less than 24 man hours is considered as low, the time greater than 24 and less than or equal to 48 man hours is considered as medium and lastly the time greater than 48 man hours is considered as high. Table 11 shows the comparative analysis of the proposed *StakeMeter* framework with the selected SIQ methods.

Table 11. Comparative analysis.

	Stakeholders			Time-consumption			Defined-Priorities of the Stakeholders	Detailed Guidelines
	OCSR	HMS	RMS	OCSR	HMS	RMS		
Mitchells' Method	18	43	39	High	High	High	×	×
Ballejos & Montagna Method	15	46	53	Medium	High	High	×	Yes
Bi-Metric & Fuzzy C-Means Method	8	22	13	Low	Low	Low	Yes	Partial
StakeMeter	13	32	21	Low	Low	Medium	Yes	Yes

doi:10.1371/journal.pone.0121344.t011

Table 11 shows the comparative analysis of the three case studies of the OCSR, HMS, and RMS. Along with the application of *StakeMeter* the teams have applied Mitchells' method, the method proposed by Ballejos and Montagna and lastly the bi-metric and fuzzy c-means method in order to analyse the stakeholders of the selected case studies. However, the Mitchells' method is applied first of all. Secondly, the method proposed by Ballejos and Montagna is applied. Thirdly, the bi-metric and fuzzy c-means based method is applied. The main purpose to apply the three methods, prior to the *StakeMeter* application, is to find out the performance of the three methods and latter their performance is compared with the*StakeMeter* framework. Moreover, the teams are assigned every time a new case study in order to avoid expert biases.

Applications of the Mitchells' method

Initially, in the first step Mitchells' method is applied. The team working on the OCSR case study has found 18 stakeholders and it is reported that the time-consumption is very high. In the case of Mitchells' method, it is difficult to define the individual priorities of the stakeholders. Moreover, the guidelines of Mitchells' method are too abstract. There is a lack of low level details of the activities. The team working on the HMS case study has applied Mitchells' method and explored 43 stakeholders and the time taken during stakeholder analysis is high. Later, the Mitchells' method is applied on the RMS study. The team working on the RMS case study has found 39 stakeholders. The time-consumption is also high. The guidelines in the case of Mitchells' method are not clear and this results in higher time-consumption and large number of stakeholders is explored in each case study. It is observed that most of the stakeholders are treated at par instead of quantifying them individually.

Applications of the Ballejos and Montagna Method

Before application of Ballejos and Montagna method [28] all three teams are shuffled on different projects in order to avoid any bias and to measure the performance of the*StakeMeter* effectively. Team working on the OCSR case study has reported 15 stakeholders and the time taken to analyse the stakeholders is medium. The team working on the HMS case study has found 46 stakeholders and the time consumed in the case of HMS case study is high in terms of total man hours. The team of the RMS case study explored 53 stakeholders by applying Ballejos and Montagna method. The time reported by the team in terms of total man hours is high. In the case of Ballejos and Montagna method, it is also observed that more stakeholders are the part of game as compared to the Mitchells' method. Later, it is analyzed by the experts in each case study which stakeholders are not the key stakeholders and all these stakeholders are not considered as vital for the VBS development.

Application of the bi-Metric and Fuzzy c-Means Method

The bi-metric and fuzzy c-means based stakeholder analysis method is a most recent method. The details of the application of this method are given in [36]. The quantification of the stakeholders is based on two stakeholder metrics named as stakeholder skill factor and stakeholder interest factor. It is reported by the professionals that the given skill and interest factors result in selection of only those stakeholders who possess an executive role in the community and many other stakeholders are neglected. The two metrics mainly focus on the domain and its knowledge. However, the requirements of the stakeholders may vary under different contexts which make the suitability of the proposed metrics questionable for the projects with the large number of stakeholders. In this method, few stakeholders are selected based on the proposed metrics as shown in Table 11. However, it is also reported that the use of fuzzy c-means method may serve well in dividing the stakeholders into different clusters based on their proposed values. The proposed method is efficient, but some of the stakeholders are missing in this case and are not the part of critical stakeholders. The team working on the OCSR has reported eight key stakeholders. The team working on the HMS case study explored 22 stakeholders as key stakeholders. However, the RMS team explored a total of 13 stakeholders as critical. The bi-metric and fuzzy c-means method neglects the stakeholders due to the focused attributes which mainly help in the selection of executive members only. This problem is solved by the *StakeMeter*framework in which stakeholder factors or metrics are divided into two main categories of $\beta$and γ factors. The β and γ factors cover a wide range of the stakeholder aspects and make the stakeholder analysis process lenient. The proposed factors of the *StakeMeter* help in evaluation of the stakeholders at different levels who are interested in the development of the VBS project. In the case of *StakeMeter* framework, a range of stakeholder factors mitigates the extent of expert biases too.

The bi-metric and fuzzy c-means based method [36] does not provide the low level implementation details in order to initiate the SIQ. The problem of lack of low level details is highlighted in (Fig. 1). The proposed stakeholder quantification framework *StakeMeter*provides a set of guidelines for industry professionals in order to quantify or prioritize the stakeholders. However, the bi-metric and fuzzy c-means based method is unable to provide easy to adopt guidelines for industry professionals. In the *StakeMeter*, the divide and conquer approach is applied in which the stakeholders are grouped into different categories based on their responsibilities. The responsibilities are assessed through job cards. Based on these responsibilities it becomes easy to find out the initial worth of a stakeholder. However, it is not so in the case of bi-metric and fuzzy c-means based method. Later, in *StakeMeter* the entities are evaluated based on the key aspects and factors that are discussed in Section 4. The proposed framework *StakeMeter* adds new knowledge to software engineering body of knowledge (SWEBOK) and provides full support to industry professionals in the SIQ initiation.

Application of the StakeMeter framework

The details of the application of the *StakeMeter* framework are given in Section 7. The team working on the OCSR has explored 13 key stakeholders and the time consumed in this case is low. In the case of HMS case study, the team has reported 32 stakeholders and the reported time is low again. Moreover, in the case of RMS case study the number of reported stakeholders is 21 and the time taken to analyse the stakeholders is medium as compared to the other three methods. The total number of stakeholders explored by the Mitchells' method, and Ballejos & Montagna method in the case of RMS is high as compared to the*StakeMeter* framework. The *StakeMeter* framework has identified the critical stakeholders only. In the case of bi-metric and fuzzy c-means method, the effort in man hours is less but some of the key stakeholders are missing as compared to the *StakeMeter* framework. However, in the case of the *StakeMeter* framework the overall man hours are less as compared to the Mitchells' method, and Ballejos & Montagna method.

The performance analysis of the three research studies is shown in (Fig. 8). In (Fig. 8), the effectiveness of the three research studies is measured in terms of time and it is obvious from the graph that the efficiency of the proposed *StakeMeter* is higher as compared to the other studies.

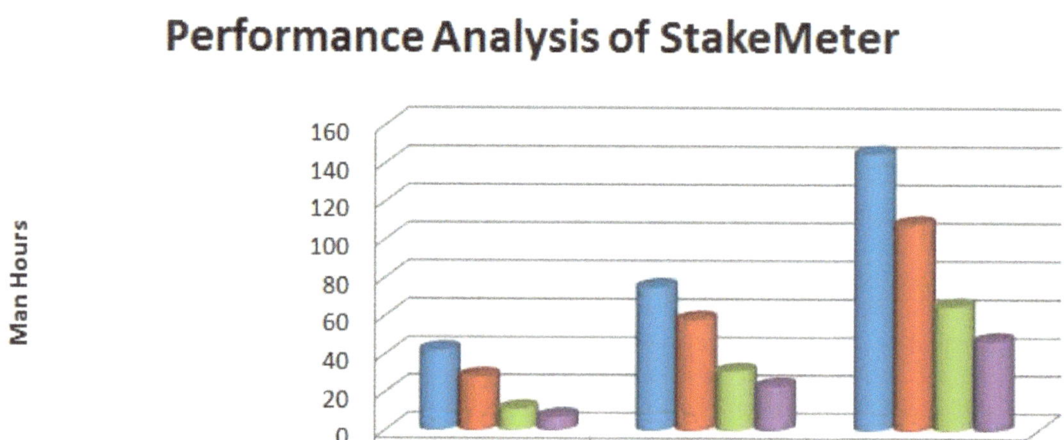

	OCSR	HMS	RMS
Mitchells' Method	42	75	145
Ballejos & Montagna Method	28	58	108
Bi-Metric & Fuzzy C-Means	11	31	65
StakeMeter	7	23	47

Figure 8. Performance analysis of StakeMeter.

The experts of all three teams later analyzed the results and reported their observations. It is observed that due to the lack of clear quantification criteria it is difficult to define the baseline for inclusion and exclusion of stakeholders in the case of Mitchells' method, Ballejos and Montagna method and bi-metric fuzzy c-means method for the VBS development process. Initially, the results of the *StakeMeter* framework are analyzed by the experts. It is reported that in the case of OCSR one stakeholder MECH4 has high risk and low *Sv* as compared to the other mechanics. Hence, it is decided that it is not an element of the set of success critical stakeholders. At this initial stage this stakeholder is eliminated from the key stakeholder set. In the case of HMS, experts have also eliminated one stakeholder Nurse 7 due to the high risk and low *Sv*. However, in the case of RMS 3 stakeholders were eliminated by the experts in the first scrutiny due to the low *Sv*. Hence, in the final dataset of the stakeholders there are 12 key stakeholders in the OCSR, 31 in the HMS, and 18 in the case of RMS.

In the case of Mitchells' method, the number of selected stakeholders is high as compared to the *StakeMeter*. As compared to *StakeMeter* six non-key stakeholders are selected with the application of Mitchells' method in the case of OCSR. In the case of HMS, 12 non-key stakeholders are selected and in the case of RMS 21 non-key stakeholders are selected.

The number of explored stakeholders in the case of Ballejos and Montagna method is also high as compared to the *StakeMeter* framework. In the case of OCSR, three non-key stakeholders are identified as key stakeholders. In the case of HMS, 15 non-key stakeholders are identified as key stakeholders and in the RMS case study 35 non-key stakeholders are reported as success critical stakeholders.

In the case of bi-metric and fuzzy c-means method, the number of selected stakeholders is less as compared to the *StakeMeter* framework. In the OCSR case study four key stakeholders are missing. In the case of HMS case study nine key stakeholders are missing while in the case of RMS case study five key stakeholders are missing. This method mainly selects the executive or influential stakeholders of the VBS system and ignores others. Hence, in this method the error is based on the less number of selected stakeholders and some of the key stakeholders are neglected. In this case the error is higher than the*StakeMeter*. The identification error in the case of *StakeMeter* is very low as compared to the two other methods. Based on the three, case studies the judgmental errors of the three research studies are shown in (Fig. 9) in the form of percentages. (Fig. 9) shows that the error in the case of *StakeMeter* framework is very low as compared to the other studies.

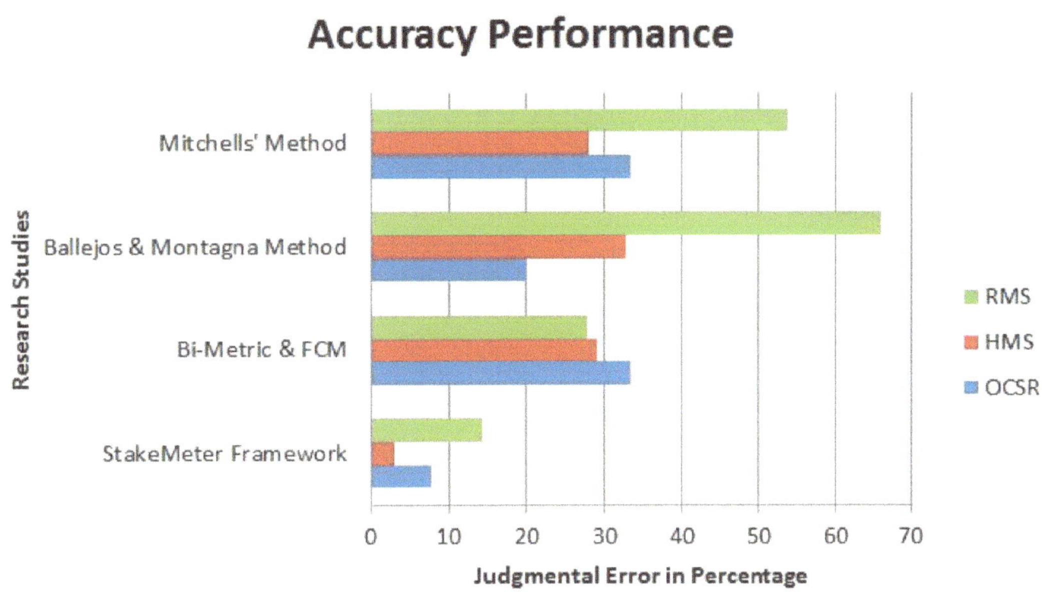

Figure 9. Accuracy analysis of StakeMeter.

Moreover, in order to measure the performance of the proposed SIQ framework *StakeMeter*the industry professionals are also involved for better understanding. Industry professionals have analyzed and evaluated the framework by applying it on different projects. The data is gathered from the industry professionals about performance of the proposed framework*StakeMeter* using survey questionnaire. Two surveys are conducted in this study one before application of *StakeMeter* and one after application of *StakeMeter*. The questionnaire is based on the five key parameters of standardization, easiness, efficiency with respect to time, ambiguity or lack of clarity of the proposed framework. The questionnaire is sent to 25 industry professionals in order to record the data about performance analysis of the proposed framework. The response rate of the different reviewers, before and after application of *StakeMeter*, is shown in Table 12. Previously it is reported by 95.40% of the respondents, that the existing SIQ approaches are not standardized. However, in the current survey, it was reported by 80% of the respondents that the proposed framework *StakeMeter*can be adopted as a framework and 20% of the respondents found that it is still difficult. It was reported by 80% of the respondents in the previous survey that the existing SIQ approaches are not easy to carryout. About the proposed framework *StakeMeter* it is reported by 84% of the respondents that the proposed framework is easy to understand and implement. Moreover, 16% of the respondents reported that the framework is difficult. Previously, it is reported by 72.42% of the respondents that the existing SIQ approaches are difficult to apply in terms of lack of clear guidelines. However, about 88% of the respondents reported that the proposed framework *StakeMeter* provides clear and easy to understand guidelines and 12% are of the view that the framework is not easy. The responses given by most of the respondents show that the proposed framework *StakeMeter* is easy, efficient in terms of time, clear and can be standardized. Table 12 shows the performance of the proposed framework *StakeMeter*.

Table 12. Response rate of StakeMeter performance.

Sr. No:	Problem	Before Response	After Response
1	Lack of Standardization	95.40%	20.0%
2	Not Easy	80.0%	16.0%
3	Time-consuming	78.0%	12.0%
4	Ambiguity or lack of clarity	72.42%	12.0%

doi:10.1371/journal.pone.0121344.t012

The comparison of the *StakeMeter* framework is also made with different methods and is shown in Table 13. The key elements that are taken into account in the comparison are personality metrics, technical metrics, inclusion/exclusion criteria, attribute adequacy, complexity, low level descriptions or guidelines and cost effectiveness in terms of time consumption. The proposed framework *StakeMeter* deals with all the key issues of stakeholder analysis. However, there are some methods which provide partial or limited support for the different key parameters that are focused during comparative analysis and most of the key parameters are not focused by the other methods and approaches.

Table 13. Comparative Analysis of Different Methods.

Method	PersonalityMetrics	Technical Metrics	Selection Criteria	Attribute Adequacy	Complexity	Guidelines	Cost Effective
StakeMeter	Yes	Yes	Yes	Yes	Yes	Yes	Yes
Ballejos & Montagna [39]	Partial	×	Partial	×	×	Yes	×
Fuentes et al. [40]	×	×	×	×	×	×	×
Ballejos & Montagna [28]	×	×	×	×	×	Partial	×
Press & Wegmann [22]	×	×	×	×	×	Limited	×
Babar et al. [36]	Limited	Limited	Partial	Partial	Yes	Partial	Yes
Boonstra [30]	×	×	×	×	×	×	×
Mitchel et al. [21]	×	×	×	×	×	Partial	×
Coakes & Elliman [24]	×	×	×	×	×	×	×
Pan [41]	×	×	×	×	×	×	×
Pouloudi [42]	×	×	×	×	×	Limited	×
Whitley et al. [43]	×	×	×	×	×	×	×
McManus [20]	×	×	×	×	×	Partial	×
Glinz & Wieringa [31]	×	×	×	×	×	Partial	×
Razali & Anwar [44]	×	×	×	×	×	Partial	×
Power [45]	×	×	×	×	×	Partial	×
Lim et al. [46]	×	×	×	×	Partial	Yes	Partial

doi:10.1371/journal.pone.0121344.t013

FUTURE RESEARCH DIRECTIONS

The future research is based on two phases. The first phase is to calculate the trustworthiness of all existing stakeholder analysis approaches in a rigorous way. The second phase of the research is to design an intelligent solution in order to reduce the extent of complexity and expert biases. The proposed framework *StakeMeter* is given for industry professionals. In order to evaluate the trustworthiness of the proposed *StakeMeter*, there is a need to evaluate the trustworthiness of all the existing stakeholder analysis approaches. By finding out the support given by each approach it will be easy to measure the level of expert satisfaction. Hence, in order to measure the satisfaction of the industry professionals or experts in terms of stakeholder analysis approaches we hereby suggest the key satisfaction estimation metrics as proposed in [13].

In the first step, the similarity between the two approaches is calculated by applying Pearson Correlation Coefficient (PCC). Let us suppose, there are N experts and K stakeholder approaches. The expert-approach matrix (EAM) for efficiency (e) value prediction is defined as:

$$EAM = \begin{bmatrix} e_{1.1} & \cdots & e_{1.K} \\ \vdots & \ddots & \vdots \\ e_{N.1} & \cdots & e_{N.K} \end{bmatrix}$$

For two approaches SA_i and SA_k the PCC is applied in order to calculate the similarity between the two by using the following formula:

$$Sim(SA_i, SA_k) = \frac{\sum_{n\in U}(e_{n,i} - \bar{e}_i)(e_{n,k} - \bar{e}_k)}{\sqrt{\sum_{n\in U}(e_{n,i} - \bar{e}_i)^2}\sqrt{\sum_{n\in U}(e_{n,k} - \bar{e}_k)^2}} \quad (11)$$

The similarity value between the two approaches is used to predict the value of the target approach which is *StakeMeter* in this research. Ding et al. (2013) have later identified customer satisfaction, related to a cloud service, as a linear combination of perception function f_p and disconfirmation function f_d as proposed in the CSAT model [37]. Hence, the same function is suggested here in this research in order to estimate the satisfaction of an industry professional or expert with respect to the efficiency of the existing stakeholder approaches. Let us suppose, for a target stakeholder approach SA_i the expert satisfaction is denoted as:

$$EX_n(r_t) = f_p(r_t) + f_d\left(\frac{r_t - r_t^-}{r_t^+ - r_t^-}\right) \quad (12)$$

In order to evaluate the utility of the approach the constant relative risk aversion (CRAA) function can be applied as proposed in [38]. Lastly, the trustworthiness of an approach can be calculated by using the $trust_n$ equation as given in [13].

The next phase for future research is to propose the multi-criteria based neuro-fuzzy inspired intelligent decision support system in order to reduce the extent of complexity and expert biases.

CONCLUSION

The existing stakeholder quantification approaches are non-uniform, inconsistent, and time consuming. Moreover, the existing approaches do not provide the low level implementation details and stakeholder quantification metrics or factors. All these SIQ issues serve as a motivation for this research. Hence, this research study contributes in the form of a new SIQ framework called *StakeMeter* based on the stakeholders' aspects and factors for the VBS systems. The framework is highly beneficial in terms of elaborated activities defined in the process. Moreover, the framework can also be used generically in the industry. The proposed SIQ framework provides professional support in stakeholder analysis and RE to business analysts and developers. The proposed framework *StakeMeter* provides an easy way to initiate it as compared to the other proposed approaches and methods. Due to the unclear guidelines of the existing approaches the time spent on stakeholder analysis spans over several months and years. However, the time taken by the said framework *StakeMeter*is very less as compared to the other SIQ approaches and methods. The proposed stakeholder factors add knowledge to the SWEBOK and also support industry professionals.

However, still the study has some limitations and threats. Firstly, the threat is associated with the validity of the *StakeMeter* if there is a lack of expertise in the stakeholder analysis. The framework requires good expertise in stakeholder analysis domain in order to understand and interpret the requirements. Expert analysts can only evaluate the stakeholders based on the proposed framework and key factors. The professional expertise is highly desirable in order to initiate the framework. Secondly, the framework needs to be implemented in large projects with hundreds of stakeholders and requirements in order to check its performance. So far, the framework is applied on projects with small number of stakeholders. The application in larger projects will help in better evaluation of latency issues in terms of time and other stakeholder management problems. Thirdly, the framework is not tested for the remote stakeholders. There is also the need to apply it in global software engineering practices for better applicability. Lastly, there are chances of the biases induced by the experts which can be reduced by proposing an intelligent solution for the SIQ process.

ACKNOWLEDGMENTS

This research was initiated at the Universiti Teknologi Malaysia by the Software Engineering Research Group (SERG) in which innovative research is under way to solve different software engineering problems. Research is also ongoing into different high profile embedded software applications at the Embedded and Real-Time Software Engineering Laboratory (EReTSEL) Universiti Teknologi Malaysia. The authors give special thanks to Sir, Tom Gilb and all members of the SERG and EReTSEL for their kind support and to the anonymous reviewers for their valuable comments.

AUTHOR CONTRIBUTIONS

Conceived and designed the experiments: MIB. Performed the experiments: MIB. Analyzed the data: MIB MG. Contributed reagents/materials/analysis tools: MIB MG DNAJ KBZ. Wrote the paper: MIB MG.

REFERENCES

1. Wiegers K. Software Requirements, Microsoft Press. Redmond, WA. 1999.
2. Wiegers K. First things first: prioritizing requirements. Software Development. 1999;7(9):48–53.
3. Group S. The CHAOS Report 2012 [July 2012]. Available from:http://www. standishgroup. com/.
4. Babar MI, Ramzan M, Ghayyur S, editors. Challenges and future trends in software requirements prioritization. International Conference on Computer Networks and Information Technology (ICCNIT); 2011; Abbottabad, Pakistan: IEEE.
5. Roger P. Software Engineering a Practitioner's Approach. McGraw-Hill International Edition. 2005.
6. Sommerville Sawyer P. Requirements Engineering-A Good Practice Guide. Chichester, UK. : John Wiley and Sons; 1997.
7. Boehm B. Value-based software engineering: reinventing. ACM SIGSOFT Software Engineering Notes. 2003;28(2):3. doi: 10. 1145/638750. 638775
8. Emam KE, Quintin S, Madhavji NH. User participation in the requirements engineering process: An empirical study. Requirements engineering. 1996;1(1):4–26. doi: 10. 1007/bf01235763
9. Babar MI, Ghazali M, Dayang NA, Jawawi DN. Software quality enhancement for value based systems through stakeholders quantification. Journal of Theoretical & Applied Information Technology. 2013;55(3).
10. Babar MI, Ghazali M, Jawawi DN, Elsafi A. Stakeholder management in value-based software development: systematic review. IET Software. 2014.
11. Freeman RE. Strategic management, a stakeholder approach. Boston: Pitman; 1984.

12. Gilb T. Competitive engineering: a handbook for systems engineering, requirements engineering, and software engineering using Planguage: Butterworth-Heinemann; 2005.
13. Ding S, Yang S, Zhang Y, Liang C, Xia C. Combining QoS prediction and customer satisfaction estimation to solve cloud service trustworthiness evaluation problems. Knowledge-Based Systems. 2014;56:216–25. doi: 10. 1016/j. knosys. 2013. 11. 014
14. Pacheco C, Garcia I, editors. Stakeholder Identification Methods in Software Requirements: Empirical Findings Derived from a Systematic Review. The Third International Conference on Software Engineering Advances; 2008: IEEE.
15. Pacheco C, Garcia I, editors. Effectiveness of Stakeholder Identification Methods in Requirements Elicitation: Experimental Results Derived from a Methodical Review. Eighth IEEE/ACIS International Conference on Computer and Information Science; 2009: IEEE.
16. Ramzan M. Intelligent Requirement Prioritization using Fuzzy Logic: National University; 2010.
17. Ramzan M, Anwar S, Shahid AA, editors. Need to Redefine "Value" and Case for a New "Software Valuation" Technique: An Analytical Study. Proceedings of International Conference on Computer Engineering and Applications (ICCEA 2009); 2009.
18. Ramzan M, Jaffar MA, Iqbal MA, Anwar S, Shahid AA, editors. Value based fuzzy requirement prioritization and its evaluation framework. Fourth International Conference on Innovative Computing, Information and Control (ICICIC); 2009: IEEE.
19. Ramzan M, Jaffar MA, Shahid AA. Value based intelligent requirement prioritization (VIRP): expert driven fuzzy logic based prioritization technique. International Journal Of Innovative Computing, Information And Control. 2011;7(3). doi: 10. 1109/icicic. 2009. 375
20. McManus J, editor A stakeholder perspective within software engineering projects. IEEE International Engineering Management Conference; 2004: IEEE.
21. Mitchell RK, Agle BR, Wood DJ. Toward a theory of stakeholder identification and salience: Defining the principle of who and what really counts. Academy of management review. 1997:853–86.
22. Preiss O, Wegmann A, editors. Stakeholder discovery and classification based on systems science principles. Second Asia-Pacific Conference on Quality Software; 2001; Hong Kong: IEEE.
23. Young SM, McDonald S, Edwards HM, Thompson JB, editors. Quality and people in the development of situationally specific methods. Second Asia-Pacific Conference on Quality Software; 2001; Hong Kong: IEEE.
24. Coakes E, Elliman T. Focus issue on legacy information systems and business process engineering: the role of stakeholders in managing change. Communications of the AIS. 1999;2(1es):4.
25. Sharp H, Finkelstein A, Galal G, editors. Stakeholder identification in the requirements engineering process. Tenth International Workshop on Database and Expert Systems Applications; 1999: IEEE.
26. Ballejos LC, Gonnet SM, Montagna JM. A Stakeholder Model for Interorganizational Information Systems. Requirements Engineering: Foundation for Software Quality. 5025/2008. Berlin / Heidelberg: Springer; 2008b. p. 73–87.
27. Ballejos LC, Montagna JM. Stakeholders Selection for Interorganizational Systems: A Systematic Approach. In: David Avison SE, John Krogstie, Jan Pries-Heje, editor. The Past and Future of Information Systems: 1976–2006 and Beyond: Springer; 2006. p. 39–50. doi: 10. 3402/ ljm. v8i0. 20567. pmid:23537612
28. Ballejos LC, Montagna JM. Method for stakeholder identification in interorganizational environments. Requirements engineering. 2008a;13(4):281–97. doi: 10. 1007/s00766-008-0069-1
29. Davison J, Thompson JB, Deeks DA, Lejk M. PisoSIA a stakeholder approach to assist change in information systems development projects and aid process improvement. Software Quality Journal. 2006;14(1):25–36. doi: 10. 1007/s11219-006-5999-6
30. Boonstra A. Interpreting an ERP-implementation project from a stakeholder perspective. International Journal of Project Management. 2006;24(1):38–52. doi: 10. 1016/j. ijproman. 2005. 06. 003
31. Glinz M, Wieringa RJ. Guest Editor's Introduction: Stakeholders in Requirements Engineering. IEEE Software. 2007;24(2):18–20. doi: 10. 1109/ms. 2007. 42
32. Woolridge RW, McManus DJ, Hale JE. Stakeholder risk assessment: An outcome-based approach. IEEE SOFTWARE. 2007;24(2):36–45. doi: 10. 1109/ms. 2007. 54
33. Pacheco C, Garcia I. A systematic literature review of stakeholder identification methods in requirements elicitation. Journal of Systems and Software. 2012;85(9):2171–81. doi: 10. 1016/j. jss. 2012. 04. 075
34. Ding S, Xia C-Y, Zhou K-L, Yang S-L, Shang JS. Decision Support for Personalized Cloud Service Selection through Multi-Attribute Trustworthiness Evaluation. PloS one. 2014;9(6):e97762. doi: 10. 1371/ journal. pone. 0097762. pmid:24972237
35. Ding S, Xia C, Cai Q, Zhou K, Yang S. QoS-aware resource matching and recommendation for cloud computing systems. Applied Mathematics and Computation. 2014;247:941–50. doi: 10. 1016/j. amc. 2014. 09. 058
36. Babar MI, Ghazali M, Dayang NA, Jawawi DN. A bi-metric and fuzzy c-means based intelligent stakeholder quantification system for value-based software. In: Fujita H, Selamat A. , Haron H. , editor. New Trends in Software Methodologies, Tools and Techniques. 265. Langkwai, Malaysia. : IOS International Publisher; 2014.
37. Xiao J, Boutaba R. Assessing network service profitability: Modeling from market science perspective. IEEE/ACM Transactions on Networking (TON). 2007;15(6):1307–20. doi: 10. 1109/tnet. 2007. 896535

38. Chiu MC, Wong HY. Optimal investment for an insurer with cointegrated assets: CRRA utility. Insurance: Mathematics and Economics. 2013;52(1):52–64. doi: 10. 1016/j. insmatheco. 2012. 11. 004

39. Ballejos LC, Montagna JM. Modeling stakeholders for information systems design processes. Requirements Engineering. 2011;16(4):281–96. doi: 10. 1007/s00766-011-0123-2

40. Fuentes-Fernández R, Gómez-Sanz JJ, Pavón J. Understanding the human context in requirements elicitation. Requirements engineering. 2010;15(3):267–83. doi: 10. 1007/s00766-009-0087-7

41. Pan GS. Information systems project abandonment: a stakeholder analysis. International Journal of Information Management. 2005;25(2):173–84. doi: 10. 1016/j. ijinfomgt. 2004. 12. 003

42. Pouloudi A. Stakeholder analysis as a front-end to knowledge elicitation. AI & Society. 1997;11(1):122–37. doi: 10. 1007/bf02812443

43. Whitley EA, Poulymenakou A, Cornford T. The spring model for knowledge-based systems analysis: a case study. ACM SIGMIS Database. 1992;23(2):1–5. doi: 10. 1145/141342. 141343

44. Razali R, Anwar F. Selecting the Right Stakeholders for Requirements Elicitation: A Systematic Approach. Journal of Theoretical and Applied Information Technology. 2011;33(2).

45. Power K, editor Stakeholder Identification in Agile Software Product Development Organizations: A Model for Understanding Who and What Really Counts. Agile Conference (AGILE); 2010: IEEE.

46. Lim SL, Quercia D, Finkelstein A, editors. StakeNet: using social networks to analyse the stakeholders of large-scale software projects. 32nd ACM/IEEE International Conference on Software Engineering; 2010: ACM.

CHAPTER 7

A WEB RESOURCE FOR STANDARDIZED BENCHMARK DATASETS, METRICS, AND ROSETTA PROTOCOLS FOR MACROMOLECULAR MODELING AND DESIGN

Shane Ó Conchúir[1,2], Kyle A. Barlow[3], Roland A. Pache[1,2], Noah Ollikainen[3], Kale Kundert[4], Matthew J. O'Meara[5], Colin A. Smith[1,2,3], Tanja Kortemme[1,2,3,4]

[1] California Institute for Quantitative Biosciences (QB3), University of California San Francisco, San Francisco, California, United States of America

[2] Department of Bioengineering and Therapeutic Sciences, University of California San Francisco, San Francisco, California, United States of America

[3] Graduate Program in Bioinformatics, University of California San Francisco, San Francisco, California, United States of America

[4] Graduate Program in Biophysics, University of California San Francisco, San Francisco, California, United States of America

[5] Department of Pharmaceutical Chemistry, University of California San Francisco, San Francisco, California, United States of America

ABSTRACT

The development and validation of computational macromolecular modeling and design methods depend on suitable benchmark datasets and informative metrics for comparing protocols. In addition, if a method is intended to be adopted broadly in diverse biological applications, there needs to be information on appropriate parameters for each protocol, as well as metrics describing the expected accuracy compared to experimental data. In certain disciplines, there exist established benchmarks and public resources where experts in a particular methodology are encouraged to supply their most efficient implementation of each particular benchmark. We aim to provide such a resource for protocols in macromolecular modeling and design. We present a freely accessible web resource (https://kortemmelab.ucsf.edu/benchmarks) to guide the development of protocols for protein modeling and design. The site provides benchmark datasets and metrics to compare the performance of a variety of modeling protocols using different computational sampling methods and energy functions, providing a "best practice" set of parameters for each method. Each benchmark has an associated downloadable benchmark capture archive containing the input files, analysis scripts, and tutorials for running the benchmark. The captures may be run with any suitable modeling method; we supply command lines for running the benchmarks using the Rosetta software suite. We have compiled initial benchmarks for the resource spanning three key areas: prediction of energetic effects of mutations, protein design, and protein structure prediction, each with associated state-of-the-art modeling protocols. With the help of the wider macromolecular modeling community, we hope to expand the variety of benchmarks included on the website and continue to evaluate new iterations of current methods as they become available.

Citation: Ó Conchúir S, Barlow KA, Pache RA, Ollikainen N, Kundert K, O'Meara MJ, et al. (2015) A Web Resource for Standardized Benchmark Datasets, Metrics, and Rosetta Protocols for Macromolecular Modeling and Design. PLoS ONE 10(9): e0130433. doi:10.1371/journal.pone.0130433.

INTRODUCTION

Structure-based modeling and design of biological macromolecules have become rich areas of computational research and method development [1–5]. The accuracy of these modeling protocols on diverse applications can be assessed via use of increasingly available, high quality curated experimental datasets [6–10]. Demonstration of the utility of a new prediction or design method requires, at the very least, a proof-of-concept case that exhibits initial success. Further widespread adoption of the method requires more extensive validation: demonstrated success and careful evaluation of key limitations on multiple, diverse, test cases. This general utility can be shown through the use of a suitable benchmark set.

Even though the compilation of these benchmarks is often essential to the creation of novel computational methods, the successful application of a method can often overshadow the critical role of benchmarking during its development. Furthermore, the associated publication of a new method may not contain a description of the dataset or statistical analysis in a format that is readily usable for developers of alternate methods, creating additional obstacles for a direct comparison. Organizations such as CASP [11] and CAPRI [12] create blind prediction tests for problems in protein structure prediction, protein-protein docking, and other applications, but many questions in the field of macromolecular modeling and design could also benefit from canonical benchmarks such as those that exist for protein-protein docking [10,13]. To facilitate rapid, iterative development, it is convenient to make benchmarks available for retrospective testing (although it is essential to pay attention to issues of overfitting to a particular target problem, even for large and diverse datasets).

Even in cases where an effective benchmark has been defined and the efficacy of a modeling protocol has been measured and published, it may be difficult to reproduce similar results post-publication as the method evolves. Protocols in large, complex software suites, such as Rosetta, are highly dependent on core functionality. For example, a sampling algorithm may yield varying results as changes are made to its accompanying score function. Regular benchmarking to track changes in performance is desirable both when core functionality is altered and when the specific protocol has been modified directly. To determine what constitutes the best practice, a user needs access to current benchmarking results, or at the very least, clear instructions on how to benchmark against the latest version of the protocol.

Here we present a web resource (https://kortemmelab.ucsf.edu/benchmarks) to address some of the aforementioned difficulties associated with informative benchmarking. We define the following criteria for a benchmark set in this resource: First, the scientific question or modeling problem posed by the benchmark must be clearly defined. Second, the input dataset should contain numerous, varied test cases that cover a broad range of possible inputs a user might use in a protocol. Success is easier to find when only a small subset of potential test cases is employed; a more general set indicates a correspondingly more generally useful method, and ameliorates issues with over-fitting a method to perform well on a specific test case. To be suitable for comparison against predictions, this input data set should be made up of experimentally validated data (we will refer to predicted data as "predictions" and experimentally determined data as "experiments"). Third, instructions on how to run each computational method should be provided with enough detail and clarity such that researchers other than the developers of a given method are able to use the resource. Finally, each benchmark set should be accompanied both by an appropriate set of defined metrics to quantify how successfully the method addresses the modeling problem and by a set of analysis tools which, given input in a defined format, computes these metrics.

We have used these guidelines to collect benchmark sets for commonly encountered problems in the following three areas (Fig 1): (1) estimation of energetic effects of mutations (protein stability ($\Delta\Delta G$) and computational alanine scanning); (2) protein design predictions (native sequence recovery, evolutionary profile recovery, sequence covariation recovery, and prediction of recognition specificity); and (3) protein structure prediction (loop modeling). We also present corresponding state-of-the-art Rosetta protocols, parameters and command lines applicable to each problem. Each benchmark capture can be downloaded from the web resource either as a self-contained zip file/bundle or as a version-controlled repository. Each bundle contains the input data and documentation describing the given modeling problem, explains how the accompanying methods solve that problem, lists the metrics we use to measure success, includes the Rosetta protocol, and provides analysis scripts to generate these metrics from output data. In the sequel, we describe the technical details of the website we have created for open access and dissemination of benchmarking results.

(A) $\Delta\Delta G$ / Alanine scanning—predicting the energetic effect of point mutations on folding or binding. REU: Rosetta energy units. The dashed line represents the best linear fit model ($y = 0.93x + 0.43$). (B) Native sequence recovery—measuring the similarity between designed and native sequences for a given structure. Boxplots compare fixed to flexible backbone design performance, and designed residues that are identical to the native sequence are highlighted in yellow. (C) Sequence profile recovery—measuring the similarity between designed and natural sequence profiles of protein families. Boxplots compare fixed to flexible backbone design performance in recovering the natural sequence profile. (D) Amino acid covariation—predicting pairs of naturally covarying residues in protein families. Boxplots compare fixed to flexible backbone design performance, and covarying pairs in the multiple sequence alignment are highlighted in green and magenta. (E) Recognition specificity—predicting the tolerated sequence space in a protein-protein interface. The sequence logos [14] visualize the similarities and differences between the predicted and experimentally determined sequence profiles. (F) Loop reconstruction—predicting the backbone conformation of loops in protein structures. Here the scatterplot shows a minimum in the Rosetta energy landscape for the given loop, with the five lowest energy models shown in yellow and the one closest to the experimentally determined (native) structure highlighted in red.

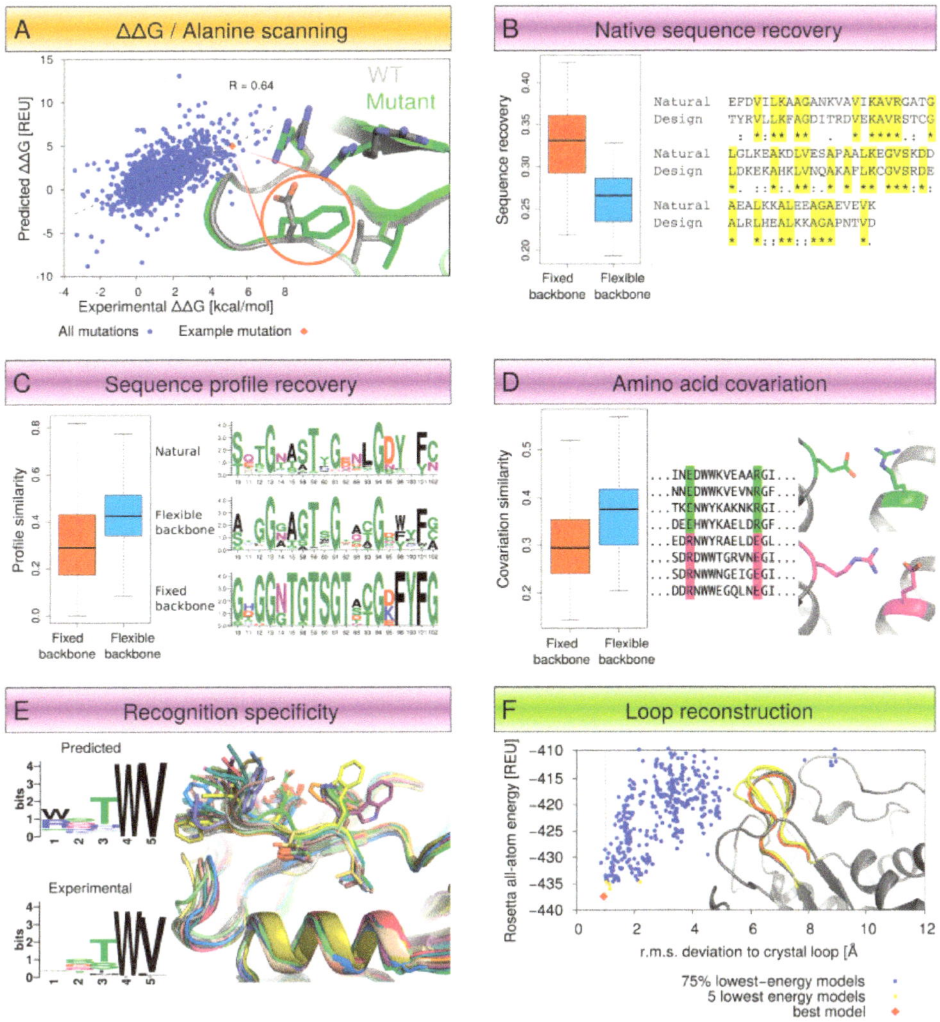

Figure 1. Types of benchmarks and protocols currently included in the web resource. Tests estimating energetic effects of mutation (orange, A), design tests (purple, B-E) and structure prediction tests (green, F).

BENCHMARKS (METHODS)

The web resource currently contains benchmark captures, Rosetta protocols, and performance information for five different benchmarks, which we have grouped below in three different areas (Fig 1): (1) tests estimating energetic effects of mutations, (2) design tests, and (3) structure prediction tests. Each subsection describes, for each benchmark, its purpose (the modeling problem addressed), the benchmark dataset, a Rosetta protocol addressing the modeling problem, metrics of success, key results, and notes on limitations and caveats.

Tests Estimating Energetic Effects of Mutation

Protein Stability (ΔΔG)

Purpose of this test: The purpose of this benchmark is to predict the change in stability (ΔΔG) of a monomeric protein caused by single point mutations (Fig 1A). The predicted stability change is given as the difference in predicted energy between the modeled wild-type and mutant structures. The benchmark compares the predicted energy differences against experimentally measured ΔΔG values in kcal/mol.

Benchmark dataset: In previous studies, protein stability prediction methods have been benchmarked against multiple curated datasets: a set of 1030 mutants collected by Guerois et al. [15]; a set of 2156 mutants collected by Potapov et al. [16]; a set of 1210 mutants collected by Kellogg et al. [17]; and a set of 582 mutants collected by Benedix et al. [18]. The records in these datasets mainly originate from the ProTherm database [7]—a large, manually curated collection of thermostability data from the literature—and are mostly single point mutations. Our benchmark capture collects the Guerois, Potapov, and Kellogg datasets together and adds a fourth dataset of 2971 point mutants from ProTherm. This last dataset is lightly curated; it contains most of the single point mutations available in ProTherm excepting records where: (i) there is no corresponding structure determined via X-ray crystallography with a resolution of at least 2.5Å; (ii) there are multiple experimental ΔΔG values for an individual mutation that differ by more than 2.5 kcal/mol in the experimental values; or (iii) the mutated protein is a transmembrane protein.

ProTherm contains details of the publications from which the thermodynamic data originated. These explicit references were omitted in the previously published datasets mentioned above but we have determined the source of the mutations for each record in the benchmark capture and reformatted the datasets into a standardized format. This refactoring has allowed us to determine the overlap between the datasets in terms of mutations and experimental assays to a large degree. These refactored datasets are included in the benchmark capture.

Rosetta protocol: The benchmark capture currently includes scripts that can be used to run the best-performing protocol described by Kellogg et al. as protocol 16 (see row 16 in Table 1 in reference [17]). This protocol combines a soft-repulsive potential for conformational sampling of side-chains with a standard hard-repulsive potential for minimization to achieve higher prediction accuracy, following the observation that predictive methods are more accurate when the resolution of the force field is matched to the granularity of the sampling method. There are two steps in the protocol. First, the input structure is minimized. Next, fifty pairs of wild-type and mutant structural models are generated using the sampling strategy described above. The ΔΔG value is calculated as the difference between the three best-scoring wild-type structural models and the three best-scoring mutant structural models as measured in Rosetta energy units (REU).

Performance metrics: Three metrics are used for measuring the accuracy of the computational methods, each with a separate focus.

Pearson's correlation coefficient measures the linear correlation between experimentally determined ΔΔG values and their corresponding computationally predicted values. The coefficient is invariant to the scale of the predicted values.

The mean absolute error (MAE) is defined as the mean of the absolute differences between experimental and predicted ΔΔG values. MAE is sensitive to the scale of the predicted values and is an important metric for protein design; high error reduces confidence in the predicted stability of individual cases.

Finally, the *stability classification accuracy* or *fraction correct* metric measures whether a mutation is correctly predicted to be (de)stabilizing or neutral, for a given definition of what constitutes a neutral mutation. Depending on this definition, it is possible to get a relatively high value for this metric with a set of random predicted values. Therefore this metric, while a useful metric for reporting whether a method can correctly classify the stability of a mutant, should be considered alongside the correlation and MAE.

Key results: It has been previously reported that the latest Rosetta score function (Talaris) improves the performance of the Rosetta ΔΔG protocol on the Kellogg dataset compared to the older score function, termed Score12 [19]. We have tested the protocol on the three other curated datasets and found that Talaris improves the correlation with comparable MAE values for these datasets as well, compared to Score12. However, the performance measured by the same metric differs significantly between the different datasets, suggesting that the datasets represent different levels of prediction difficulty. These data are presented on the website.

Notes: (i) We have made some modifications to the datasets from the original publications, such as updating deprecated PDB identifiers and correcting PDB IDs, PDB residue IDs, and ΔΔG values based on cross-referencing to the respective publications. We now attribute each record of a dataset with publications from which the ΔΔG values originate. This information was not present in some of the published datasets. (ii) Neutral experimental ΔΔG values are defined as values within +/-1 kcal/mol, as used by Kellogg et al. We define neutral predicted ΔΔG values as values within +/-1 score unit which differs from their definition (see [17] supporting information; neutral predicted is defined to be in the range [-3, 1.1]).

Alanine Scanning

Purpose of this test: A frequent application of modeling methods is the prediction of energetically important interactions ("hotspots") in protein-protein interfaces. By systematically mutating protein interface residues to alanine ("alanine scanning") and measuring the effect on binding, Wells and coworkers [20] showed that not all residues with interface contacts, but only a smaller subset of 'hotspot' residues contribute significantly to the binding free energy of human growth hormone to its receptor. Subsequent studies suggested that such hotspots may be a general characteristic of many protein-protein interfaces [21–23]. This benchmark tests the ability of computational alanine scanning protocols to recapitulate the results of measurements of changes in binding affinity (ΔΔG values) produced by experimental alanine scanning. A computational protocol performing well on this test set can then be used for additional applications, for instance, as a design tool to disrupt protein-protein interactions by mutations or through targeting small molecules to hotspots, or to analyze the effect of disease mutations.

Benchmark dataset: The protocol has been benchmarked on a previously published set of the energetic effects of 233 mutations to alanine in 19 different protein-protein interfaces with known crystal structures [24].

Rosetta protocol: We have re-implemented a previously published alanine scanning protocol [24,25] in the current version of Rosetta to determine the current performance of this method. Unlike the generalized ΔΔG protocol described above, which performs side chain optimization and side chain and backbone minimization over the entire protein structure, the alanine scanning protocol does not model perturbation of the backbone or side chains other than the side chain of the residue replaced with alanine.

The ΔΔG of binding upon mutation to alanine is calculated using the following equation, in which Rosetta total energy is used to estimate the ΔG of folding of each of the six terms:

$$\Delta\Delta G_{bind} = \left(\Delta G^{MUT}_{complex} - \Delta G^{MUT}_{partnerA} - \Delta G^{MUT}_{partnerB}\right) - \left(\Delta G^{WT}_{complex} - \Delta G^{WT}_{partnerA} - \Delta G^{WT}_{partnerB}\right)$$

Alanine scanning uses a version of Rosetta's Talaris energy function with modified weights intended for scoring mutations to alanine within interfaces, where the score term representing repulsive electrostatic interactions is down-weighted.

The previously published protocol [24,25] is available via the Robetta webserver athttp://robetta.bakerlab.org/alascansubmit.jsp, which has provided more than 20,000 predictions to date. The implementation described here will allow users to run predictions off-line and on large datasets, and implement and test modifications to the protocol.

Performance metrics: Performance can be measured using the same metrics as in the generalized case of the ΔΔG protocol described above, including the Pearson's correlation of predicted ΔΔG values to experimental ΔΔG values, mean absolute error (MAE), and fraction correct (see previous section for descriptions of these metrics).

Key results: Alanine scanning performance has not shown improvement when used with modern Rosetta score functions and aggressive side chain/backbone minimization methods; performance of the protocol described here is comparable to that shown in earlier publications [24,25] and available on the Robetta server.

Notes/Limitations: (i) As the alanine scanning protocol does not perturb the protein backbone or side chains (other than the mutant residue), this protocol is not suitable for use on mutations outside of the interface. A mutation outside of the interface will not change the predicted interaction energy without the use of a more intensive sampling protocol. (ii) As the backbone structure of the wild-type crystal structure is assumed to be a close approximation of the backbone structure of the mutant, this protocol is not useful in situations where this assumption does not hold. This includes testing of many simultaneous mutations that may result in larger structural rearrangements.

DESIGN TESTS

Protein design methods are difficult to test rigorously because an ideal benchmark set would contain both successful and unsuccessful designs, however, the number of cases where both have been characterized functionally and structurally is small and not yet diverse enough. Until the amount of available data of this nature greatly increases, other datasets, in particular the diversity of sequences present in naturally evolved protein families or selected in large-scale experimental screens, can provide informative benchmarks that have been used in the past to assess and compare design methods [26,27]. In the following sections, we first focus on design tests using evolutionary information, and then describe a benchmark testing prediction of protein recognition specificity using data from comprehensive phage display experiments. In each case, we compare designed and evolutionary or experimentally selected sequences using metrics comparing not individual sequences (as the number of possible sequences is large and hence the chance of an exact match at all sequence positions extremely small), but instead predicted and observed amino acid distributions.

Using Evolutionary Information

Purpose of this Test

Evolutionary pressures on protein structure and function have shaped the amino acid sequences of today's naturally occurring proteins [28]. Consequently, the sequences of natural proteins are nearly optimal for their structures [29]. Natural protein sequences therefore provide valuable information for evaluating the accuracy of computational protein design in predicting sequences consistent with a given protein structure and function. We expect that an ideal computational protein design method should be able to recapitulate properties of naturally occurring proteins, including amino acid sequence preferences ("sequence profiles") and patterns of amino acid covariation. In particular the latter tests whether computational protein design methods are capable of recapitulating the precise details of specific residue-residue interactions in proteins.

Benchmark Dataset

To evaluate to what extent protein design methods can recapitulate properties of naturally evolved proteins, we first characterized amino acid sequence profiles and amino acid covariation in 40 diverse protein domain families. Protein domains for this benchmark were selected from Pfam [30] based on the following criteria: (i) there is at least one crystal structure of the domain available from the PDB; (ii) there were at least 500 sequences of the domain family available from Pfam; and (iii) the domain had 150 or fewer amino acids. We selected 40 structurally diverse domains that satisfied these criteria. Sequence profiles were calculated by determining the amino acid distribution at each position and amino acid covariation was calculated for all pairs of amino acids using a mutual information based metric [31].

Rosetta Protocol

We designed 500 sequences for each domain using a variety of protein design methods that used the same energy function but differed in how they modeled protein backbone flexibility. As a baseline, we performed fixed backbone protein design, which does not allow the backbone to be moved. Flexible backbone design simulations were performed multiple times using different temperatures and different types of backbone moves to assess how the magnitude and mechanism of backbone variation affects the recapitulation of natural sequence properties. The different types of backbone moves included Backrub, Kinematic Closure (KIC), small phi/psi moves and all atom minimization (Relax). We also tested fixed backbone design using a soft-repulsive energy function. Additional details on the different methods are described in [26] and Rosetta command lines are provided on the web resource, along with a performance comparison.

Notes/Limitations

This benchmark makes the assumption that naturally occurring proteins are optimized for stability given their particular three-dimensional structures used as input. However, there certainly exist cases where proteins trade stability for function, such as hydrophobic patches that act as protein-protein binding interfaces or charged residues in the protein core used for catalyzing chemical reactions. We therefore expect to observe some differences between naturally occurring sequences and sequences predicted by an accurate protein design method (even if it were perfect). The benchmark assumes that methods that predict more "native-like" sequences overall are more accurate and thus more useful for experimental design applications [29]. In these applications, functional constraints, such as binding and catalysis, are usually explicitly represented by including functional binding partners or specifying certain key catalytic groups and their conformations.

Native Sequence Recovery

Performance Metrics

Native sequence recovery [29] measures the ability of computational protein design to predict the amino acid sequence of a protein given its backbone conformation (Fig 1B). This is simply calculated as the percent identity between the native sequence and a designed sequence.

Key Results

We found that adding a small degree of backbone flexibility prior to design increased sequence recovery on average, however, further increasing the amount of backbone flexibility led to worse sequence recovery scores. A possible explanation for this decrease in recovery is that allowing more backbone flexibility resulted in sequences with a greater diversity in their amino acid sequences and consequently greater divergence from the native sequence. To confirm this, we calculated sequence entropy for the designed sequences and found that structural variation is positively correlated with sequence diversity. These results highlight a caveat with using native sequence recovery as a test of protein design accuracy, which is that protein sequences can be very different from each other but still be consistent with the same protein fold [32], and it is this sequence divergence that can be utilized to evolve existing proteins for new functions.

Sequence Profile Recovery of Protein Families

Performance Metrics

Sequence profiles represent the distribution of amino acids at each position in a multiple sequence alignment of a protein family (Fig 1C). To compare natural and designed sequence profiles, we computed the divergence between the amino acid distributions at corresponding positions in the natural and designed sequences, as described in [32]. Briefly, profile similarity is the product of two scores: (i) the estimated probability that two amino acid distributions represent the same source distribution; and (ii) the *a priori*probability of the source distribution. It is defined as:

$$\textit{Profile Similarity}(p,q) = \frac{1}{2}(1 - D^{JS}[p\|q])(1 + D^{JS}[r\|P_0])$$

where p and q are amino acid probability distributions at corresponding positions in natural and designed sequences, r is the average of p and q, P_0 is the background distribution, and D^{JS} is the Jensen-Shannon divergence. Using this metric, positions in designed sequences receive high profile similarity scores if both: (i) their amino acid distribution is similar to the amino acid distribution at the corresponding position in the natural alignment; and (ii) their amino acid distribution is different than the background amino acid distribution.

Key Results

We observed that backbone flexibility improved our ability to recapitulate sequence profiles of naturally occurring protein families relative to fixed backbone design, and that there exists an optimal magnitude of backbone flexibility (using Rosetta kT = 0.9 in "backrub" simulations, [26]) given that low or high temperature simulations performed worse than medium temperature simulations. This analysis also revealed an important pathology in the designed sequences, which showed an unrealistically high percentage of designed buried polar residues when compared to the natural sequences. To overcome this problem, we repeated the benchmark using a newer Rosetta energy function, Talaris [19] that has stricter definitions for hydrogen-bonding geometries. We found that this decreased the percentage of buried polar residues, including serine, threonine and histidine, although it remained higher than in the natural sequences (Fig 2 and S1 Fig). These results can be quite sensitive to the reference energies in the applied energy function (which allow energetic evaluation of mutations). Existing automated tools [33] that reweight reference energy terms can be used to develop alternative energy functions. Future improvements to sampling and scoring will be required to further reduce the percentage of buried polar groups to levels found in naturally occurring proteins.

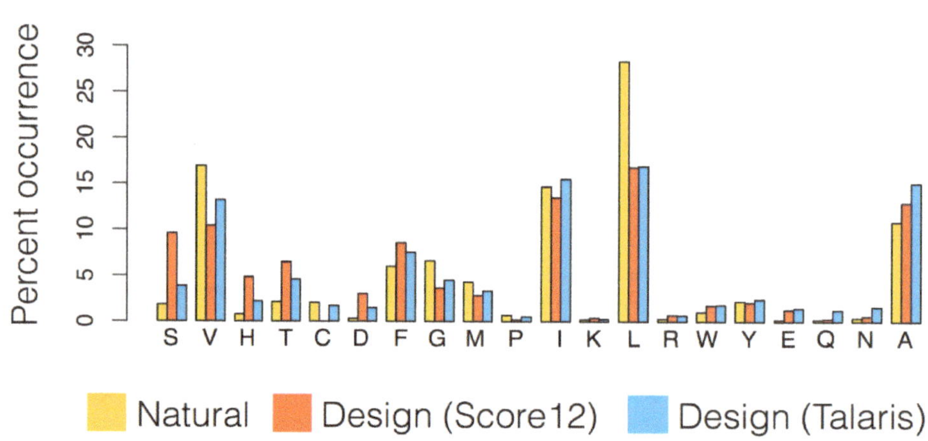

Figure 2. Comparison of occurrences of different amino acid residue types observed at buried positions between natural sequences and sequences designed with two different Rosetta energy functions. Barplot showing the percent occurrence of each type of amino acid found at

buried positions in natural and designed sequences across 40 diverse protein families. Buried positions are defined as positions with greater than 14 neighboring positions, where neighboring positions have C-β atoms within 8Å of the C-β atom of the residue of interest. The X-axis is sorted by the magnitude of improvement of the Talaris energy function relative to the previous Score12 energy function with respect to the similarity to the natural percent occurrences.

Amino Acid Covariation

Performance Metrics

To evaluate how well a given protein design method could recapitulate natural amino acid covariation, we designed 500 sequences for each protein domain in the benchmark and calculated the covariation between all pairs of positions in the designed sequences (Fig 1D). Covariation is calculated based on a mutual-information based metric described in [31]. The mutual information (MI) between each pair of columns in a multiple sequence alignment, i and j, was calculated as the difference between individual entropies (H_i, H_j) and the joint entropy ($H_{i,j}$):

$$MI_{i,j} = H_i + H_j - H_{i,j}$$

The background mutual information due to random noise and shared ancestry is then subtracted to obtain the product corrected mutual information (MIp) [34]:

$$MIp_{i,j} = MI_{i,j} - \frac{\overline{MI_i} \times \overline{MI_j}}{\overline{MI}}$$

where $\overline{MI_i}$ is the mean MI of position i with all other positions and $\overline{MI}$ is the overall mean value. Next this value is converted to two Z-scores, one for each column, which are then multiplied together:

$$Z_{i \times y} = \frac{MIp_{i,j} - \overline{MIp_i}}{\sigma(MIp_i)} \times \frac{MIp_{i,j} - \overline{MIp_j}}{\sigma(MIp_i)}$$

The final covariation score, called Zpx, is calculated as the square root of the absolute value of $Z_{i \times y}$. (If $Z_{i \times y}$ is negative, then Zpx is multiplied by-1.) This normalization was previously shown to reduce sensitivity to potential misaligned regions in multiple sequence alignments, which otherwise result in artificially high MI scores [31]. Similarity between natural and designed covariation was calculated as the percent overlap between the highly covarying pairs in the natural sequences and in the designed sequences. We considered pairs with covariation scores greater than two standard deviations from the mean to be highly covarying [26].

Key Results

We used this metric for quantifying the similarity of natural and designed covariation in order to compare different flexible backbone protein design methods that varied in either the magnitude or mechanism of backbone flexibility. As with sequence profile recovery, we observed that backbone flexibility improved our ability to recapitulate naturally occurring amino acid covariation relative to fixed backbone design, and that there exists an optimal magnitude of backbone flexibility (in the range of kT = 0.6 to kT = 0.9 in Rosetta simulations). We also found that flexible backbone design methods which incorporate backbone flexibility via iteratively applying local backbone moves (*e.g.* Backrub [35] or Kinematic Closure [36]) performed better than Rosetta methods that globally alter the backbone of the entire protein (*e.g.* Relax or AbInitioRelax) [26].

Using Large-Scale Experimental Data

Recognition Specificity

Purpose of this test: "Sequence tolerance" refers to the concept that a certain profile of allowed residues can accommodate the evolved structure and function of a protein (Fig 1E). The computational sequence tolerance protocol attempts to predict the allowed sequence profile in protein-protein interfaces. The predictions are tested for their ability to recapitulate the sequence specificity preferences of protein recognition domains that have been determined by comprehensive phage display experiments. In contrast to the comparison to sequences of evolutionary families in the previous section, the experimentally determined profiles were selected primarily based on the same criterion (most stable binding) as in the design simulations.

Benchmark dataset: The experimental data used for comparison in this benchmark set come from phage display specificity profiles for naturally occurring PDZ domains [37], as well as phage display profiles for peptide interactions with synthetic variants of the Erbin PDZ domain [37,38], comprising over 8000 peptide sequences tested against 169 natural and synthetic PDZ domains total.

Rosetta protocol: There are two main computational steps: (i) the Rosetta Backrub application [35] uses Monte Carlo sampling starting from a single input structure to create an ensemble of near-native conformations; (ii) the sequence tolerance application [39,40] then uses a genetic algorithm to sample and score a large number of sequences for each member of the ensemble. An input file defines the sequence positions to be designed, and interactions within and between different parts of the structure can be individually reweighted, depending on the desired objective.

Performance metrics: The analysis scripts use Boltzmann weighting to generate a predicted position weight matrix (PWM) for the specified sequence positions. This predicted PWM can be compared to known sequence profiles via these metrics described in the previous sequence tolerance publications [39,40]: (i) AAD, average absolute deviation, defined as $\frac{1}{N}\sum_{i=1}^{N}|E_i - P_i|$ and (ii) Frobenius distance, defined as $\sqrt{\sum_{i=1}^{N}(E_i - P_i)^2}$, where E is the vector of experimentally determined amino acid frequencies and P is the corresponding vector of predictions. (iii) AUC, or area under the receiver operator characteristic curve, measures the ability of the predictions to match the experimental values on a known scale, where 0.5 indicates random predictions and 1.0 is perfect. (iv) "Rank top" measures the predicted rank of the most frequent experimentally determined amino acid.

Key results: Recognition specificity performance with Talaris is comparable to the originally published performance of the protocol with Score12 [39,40].

Notes/Limitations: (i) Although the sequence tolerance protocol is capable of generating backbone flexibility, which improves performance, it still relies on known input starting structures. Mutations can be made to these starting structures in order to predict the recognition specificity of experimentally characterized mutated proteins, but the additional mutation step might reduce the overall performance of the protocol. (ii) The backrub phase of the protocol must be run at a reasonable temperature (see protocol capture) to generate an appropriately matching amount of backbone flexibility in the sequence tolerance step. (iii) Due to limitations in the sequence space sampled by the genetic algorithm, it is not recommended to try and sample more than about 4–6 design positions simultaneously. (iv) Sequence profiles produced by this method may accurately predict the most frequently observed amino acid at a design position without containing enough total variation at that same position. (v) The performance metrics described above ignore potential co-variation in predicted or experimentally selected sequences.

Structure Prediction Tests

Loop Reconstruction

Purpose of this test: Being able to correctly model loop conformations (Fig 1F) is crucial because of their functional importance in many proteins, such as in forming the complementarity-determining regions in antibodies or in controlling substrate access and product release in enzyme active sites. However, since many loops in protein structures are flexible, loop modeling is computationally hard, because the many backbone degrees of freedom (depending on the length of the loop) result in a vast conformational search space. The purpose of this test is to reconstruct known native loop conformations, as observed in crystal structures, in non-redundant benchmark sets of different loop lengths.

Benchmark dataset: The Rosetta loop modeling benchmark [36,41] tests the ability of a protocol to reconstruct the backbone conformation of 12-residue loop segments in protein structures. The benchmark set consists of 45 non-redundant protein segments without regular secondary structure, curated from two previously described datasets [42–47]

In each case, the given segment is deleted from the protein structure and then reconstructed *de novo*, given a fixed backbone environment for the rest of the protein. All segment side chains and those within 10Å of the segment are modeled based on a side chain rotamer library [48] that does not include the native side chain conformations.

The long loops benchmark [41] analogously tests whether protocols are able to reconstruct loop segments of 14–17 residues. This benchmark set consists of 27 non-redundant long loops, extracted and manually curated from the dataset described in [49], by requiring at most five residues within 6Å of symmetry mates in the crystal lattice to minimize the potential impact of crystal contacts on loop conformations. *De novo* loop reconstruction and side chain optimization are performed as described above for the standard loop modeling benchmark.

Rosetta protocol: Several protocols have previously been developed to reconstruct or predict the backbone conformation of loops in protein structures. The CCD protocol in Rosetta [43] uses insertion of fragments from proteins of known structure to sample the loop backbone degrees of freedom, followed by torsion angle adjustments via cyclic coordinate descent (CCD) to close the resulting chain break [50]. The kinematic closure (KIC) protocol [36] samples all but six loop backbone degrees of freedom probabilistically from Ramachandran space. These remaining three pairs of φ/ψ torsion angles are then solved analytically through kinematic closure to close the chain break [51]. Next-generation KIC (NGK) [41] adds four additional sampling strategies to the standard KIC protocol: (i) the selection of pairs of φ/ψ torsions from neighbor-dependent Ramachandran distributions; (ii) sampling of ω degrees of freedom; as well as annealing methods that gradually ramp the weights of (iii) the repulsive terms; and (iv) the Ramachandran terms of the Rosetta energy function to overcome energy barriers. All three loop modeling protocols use Monte-Carlo simulated annealing for rotamer-based side-chain optimization ("repacking") of the loop residues and those within 10 Å of the loop, followed by gradient-based minimization.

Performance metrics: With each loop modeling protocol, hundreds of models are generated per benchmark case. Each model is then superposed onto the native structure (excluding the reconstructed loop), followed by calculating the loop backbone heavy-atom root mean square deviation (RMSD) of the model to the native loop conformation. The overall benchmark performance of each protocol is then evaluated using two different metrics across the entire benchmark set: (i) the median loop backbone RMSD of the lowest-energy model to the native structure (or median lowest loop backbone RMSD of the 5 lowest-energy models, which is less susceptible to stochastic fluctuations [33]); and (ii) the median percentage of models generated that have a loop backbone RMSD below 1Å (sub-angstrom predictions).

Key results: With the Rosetta Score12 energy function (the standard before the switch to the Talaris2013 energy function in revision 55274), only the KIC [36] and NGK [41] protocols successfully sampled sub-angstrom loop conformations in many cases, achieving a median RMSD across the entire 12-residue loop benchmark set of <1Å. NGK significantly outperformed standard KIC in the sampling of sub-Å loop conformations, with NGK reaching a median of 16.3% sub-Å models compared to 4.3% for standard KIC [41]. Since the advent of the Talaris2013 score function [19,33], the CCD protocol now also achieves a median RMSD < 1Å on the 12-residue loop dataset. The median percentage of models with sub-Å RMSD is still significantly higher for NGK (13.4%) than for standard KIC (6.4%) and CCD (1.8%). For the more difficult sampling problem in the long loops benchmark, the sub-Å sampling performance of NGK improved from Score12 (0.53%) to Talaris2013 (1.0%).

Notes/Limitations: (i) Flexible loops are often better described by a conformational ensemble rather than a single conformation, and some simulations indeed reveal several clusters of different low-energy conformations. (ii) Crystal contacts can influence loop conformations, and the absence of those contacts during modeling can result in predictions differing from the crystallographic conformation. (iii) There are similar considerations for the presence of water molecules, ions or other small molecules, which might influence loop conformations. (iv) For the KIC and NGK protocols, the start and end points of loops are assumed fixed during the simulations; this simplifies the sampling problem in the context of "native" loop endpoints (*i.e.* taken from a crystal structure), but complicates the situation when the conformation of loop endpoints may not be known exactly, *e.g.* when building loops in homology models. In these cases, protocols that sample the positions of the endpoints or apply KIC moves over several overlapping regions may be more suitable. (v) Modeling long loops is difficult for current protocols, due to the large conformational search space, which is apparent from the considerably lower fraction of sub-angstrom models in the 14–17 residues loop benchmark. (vi) The KIC and NGK protocols do not preserve protein secondary structure, due to probabilistic sampling of φ/ψ torsions from Ramachandran space. Additional sampling constraints could be included to preserve secondary structure.

WEBSITE DESCRIPTION

The benchmark captures are collected and presented online athttps://kortemmelab.ucsf.edu/benchmarks. The purposes of the website are to: (i) describe specific and well-defined problems in computational modeling; (ii) describe and provide benchmarks which can be used to measure the success of methods designed to address these problems; (iii) publish the performance of methods using parameters provided by experienced users; and (iv) act as a unified portal for downloading the benchmark captures.

On the main benchmark page (Fig 3A), we describe each benchmark—its purpose, application, and the currently considered datasets—and publish results of benchmark runs so that users can quickly gauge the performance of different methods. Relevant command lines are provided to promote best practice for each method when using the Rosetta software suite.

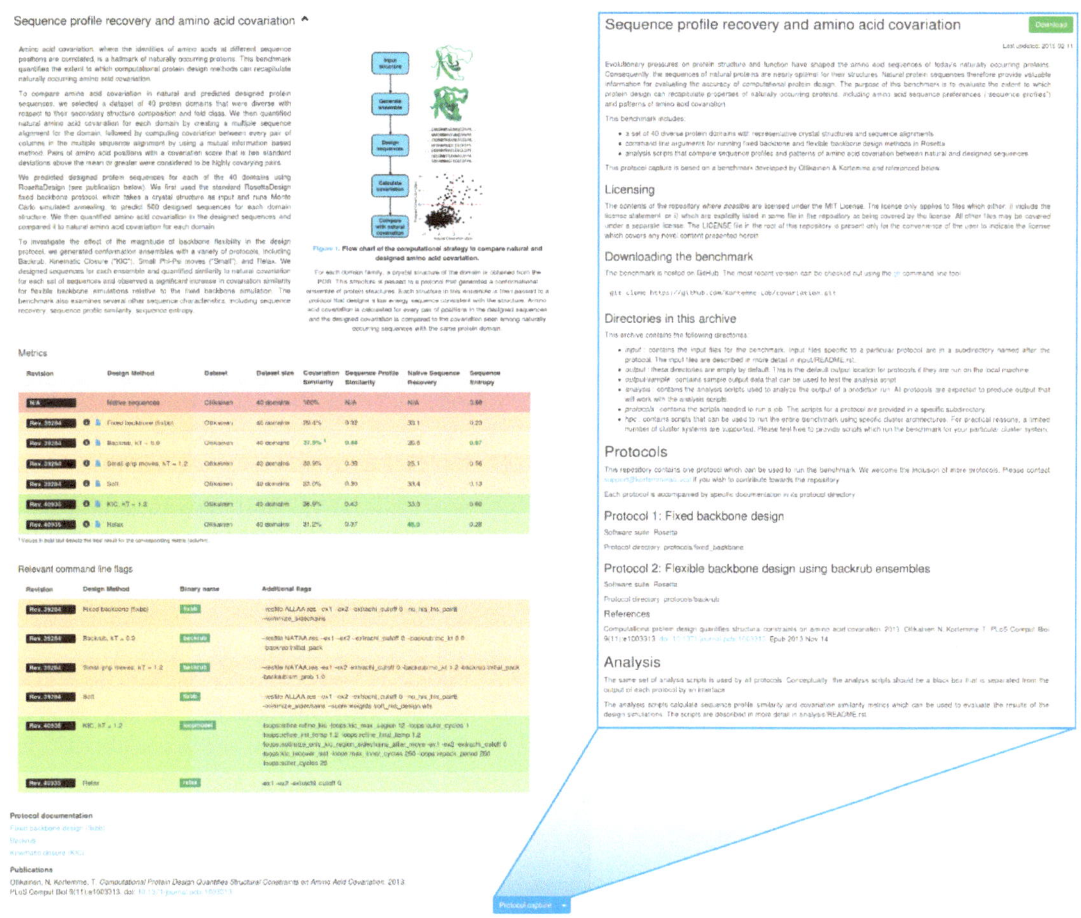

Figure 3. Benchmark and protocols capture website. Left: The website presents an overview of each benchmark and publishes the performance of different methods using a set of standardized metrics. Parameters important to the protocol performance are also provided. Right: Each benchmark capture is stored in a documented version-controlled archive. The most recent version can be downloaded directly from the website.

Each capture has been compiled as a version-controlled, publicly-accessible, open-source archive (currently hosted on GitHub), containing both the associated benchmark datasets and scripts to analyze benchmark output in a specific format. Execution scripts to run the benchmark using at least one computational method are provided. Both the analysis and execution scripts are documented in detail within the capture, and this documentation can be viewed online on GitHub. For convenience, these captures are available for download directly from the web resource (Fig 3B).

As our intention is to provide a dynamic resource, it may be appropriate to refine or expand certain datasets as new data become available in the future. Version control allows us to update the contents while allowing users to track changes in the datasets or analysis metrics. Major changes to repositories will be tagged and referred to in the website text. Following the philosophy of the computer language benchmark projects [52,53], the parameters used for each method should reflect the best practice. For this reason, they should be ideally contributed by a developer or experienced user, and we encourage users to submit their methods, parameters, and results for inclusion on the website.

We have aimed to provide rich, user-friendly datasets. For example, the protein stability datasets are provided in both JSON and CSV formats. The former is readily integrated with multiple programming languages and web frameworks whereas the latter is human-readable and easily imported into spreadsheet applications. In both of these datasets, each record is now associated with experimental values taken from the literature—which we were able to determine using the rich source of data provided by the ProTherm database [7]—so that outliers in the predicted set can be investigated using the original experimental data.

DISCUSSION

We have presented our implementation of a benchmarking and protocol capture web resource which currently describes five diverse benchmarks and their expected performance when tested using a known best-practice methods from the Rosetta software suite. The web site functions as an openly accessible, online, and version-controlled collection of a variety of benchmarks and macromolecular modeling and design protocols, providing a summary of the evolution of the protocols and indicating their expected performance on the associated benchmarks.

The web resource was motivated by previous work [52,53] which has fostered, and continues to foster, competition and innovation in computer language development through the open communication of standardized benchmarks which allow for direct and fair comparison between competing computer languages. In those projects, knowledge of the performance of each language for the particular problem and the open communication of the most efficient code is important for both software developers when choosing which language to use for a particular project and for the language developers so that they can identify parts of the language for optimization. By providing both curated diverse datasets for benchmarking and analysis scripts to generate a set of appropriate metrics, we hope that we can help developers to evaluate new methods in informative ways, which is critically needed for continued progress in many areas of structure-based modeling and design.

ACKNOWLEDGMENTS

We would like to thank the general Rosetta Commons community for continuing, helpful development, support, and discussion. We thank Liz Kellogg, Rebecca Alford, and Julia Koehler Leman for support with developing the $\Delta\Delta G$ benchmark, and Amelie Stein for contributions to loop modeling.

AUTHOR CONTRIBUTIONS

Conceived and designed the experiments: SOC KAB RAP NO KK CAS TK. Performed the experiments: SOC KAB RAP NO KK MJO CAS TK. Analyzed the data: SOC KAB RAP NO KK MJO CAS TK. Contributed reagents/materials/analysis tools: SOC KAB RAP NO KK CAS. Wrote the paper: SOC KAB RAP NO MJO TK. Website design and implementation: SOC TK.

REFERENCES

1. Leaver-Fay A, Tyka M, Lewis SM, Lange OF, Thompson J, Jacak R, et al. Rosetta3: An Object-Oriented Software Suite for the Simulation and Design of Macromolecules. Brand MLJ and L , editor. Methods Enzymol. 2011;487: 545–574. doi: 10. 1016/B978–0–12–381270–4. 00019–6. pmid:21187238
2. Webb B, Sali A. Comparative Protein Structure Modeling Using MODELLER. Curr Protoc Bioinforma. 2002; doi: 10. 1002/0471250953. bi0506s47.
3. Brooks BR, Brooks CL, Mackerell AD, Nilsson L, Petrella RJ, Roux B, et al. CHARMM: The biomolecular simulation program. J Comput Chem. 2009;30: 1545–1614. doi: 10. 1002/jcc. 21287. pmid:19444816
4. Case DA, Cheatham TE, Darden T, Gohlke H, Luo R, Merz KM, et al. The Amber biomolecular simulation programs. J Comput Chem. 2005;26: 1668–1688. doi: 10. 1002/jcc. 20290. pmid:16200636
5. Jorgensen WL, Maxwell DS, Tirado-Rives J. Development and Testing of the OPLS All-Atom Force Field on Conformational Energetics and Properties of Organic Liquids. J Am Chem Soc. 1996;118: 11225–11236. doi: 10. 1021/ja9621760.
6. Berman HM, Westbrook J, Feng Z, Gilliland G, Bhat TN, Weissig H, et al. The Protein Data Bank. Nucleic Acids Res. 2000;28: 235–242. doi: 10. 1093/nar/28. 1. 235. pmid:10592235
7. Kumar MDS, Bava KA, Gromiha MM, Prabakaran P, Kitajima K, Uedaira H, et al. ProTherm and ProNIT: thermodynamic databases for proteins and protein–nucleic acid interactions. Nucleic Acids Res. 2006;34: D204–D206. doi: 10. 1093/nar/gkj103. pmid:16381846
8. Bento AP, Gaulton A, Hersey A, Bellis LJ, Chambers J, Davies M, et al. The ChEMBL bioactivity database: an update. Nucleic Acids Res. 2014;42: D1083–D1090. doi: 10. 1093/nar/gkt1031. pmid:24214965
9. Moal IH, Fernández-Recio J. SKEMPI: a Structural Kinetic and Energetic database of Mutant Protein Interactions and its use in empirical models. Bioinformatics. 2012;28: 2600–2607. doi: 10. 1093/bioinformatics/bts489. pmid:22859501
10. Mintseris J, Wiehe K, Pierce B, Anderson R, Chen R, Janin J, et al. Protein–protein docking benchmark 2. 0: An update. Proteins Struct Funct Bioinforma. 2005;60: 214–216. doi: 10. 1002/prot. 20560.
11. Moult J, Fidelis K, Kryshtafovych A, Schwede T, Tramontano A. Critical assessment of methods of protein

structure prediction (CASP)—round x. Proteins Struct Funct Bioinforma. 2014;82: 1–6. doi: 10. 1002/prot. 24452.

12. Janin J, Wodak S. The Third CAPRI Assessment Meeting Toronto, Canada, April 20–21, 2007. Structure. 2007;15: 755–759. doi: 10. 1016/j. str. 2007. 06. 007. pmid:17637336
13. Hwang H, Vreven T, Janin J, Weng Z. Protein–protein docking benchmark version 4. 0. Proteins Struct Funct Bioinforma. 2010;78: 3111–3114. doi: 10. 1002/prot. 22830.
14. Crooks GE, Hon G, Chandonia J-M, Brenner SE. WebLogo: A Sequence Logo Generator. Genome Res. 2004;14: 1188–1190. doi: 10. 1101/gr. 849004. pmid:15173120
15. Guerois R, Nielsen JE, Serrano L. Predicting Changes in the Stability of Proteins and Protein Complexes: A Study of More Than 1000 Mutations. J Mol Biol. 2002;320: 369–387. doi: 10. 1016/S0022–2836(02)00442–4. pmid:12079393
16. Potapov V, Cohen M, Schreiber G. Assessing computational methods for predicting protein stability upon mutation: good on average but not in the details. Protein Eng Des Sel. 2009;22: 553–560. doi: 10. 1093/ protein/gzp030. pmid:19561092
17. Kellogg EH, Leaver-Fay A, Baker D. Role of conformational sampling in computing mutation-induced changes in protein structure and stability. Proteins Struct Funct Bioinforma. 2011;79: 830–838. doi: 10. 1002/ prot. 22921.
18. Benedix A, Becker CM, de Groot BL, Caflisch A, Böckmann RA. Predicting free energy changes using structural ensembles. Nat Methods. 2009;6: 3–4. doi: 10. 1038/nmeth0109–3. pmid:19116609
19. O'Meara MJ, Leaver-Fay A, Tyka MD, Stein A, Houlihan K, DiMaio F, et al. Combined Covalent-Electrostatic Model of Hydrogen Bonding Improves Structure Prediction with Rosetta. J Chem Theory Comput. 2015;11: 609–622. doi: 10. 1021/ct500864r. pmid:25866491
20. Clackson T, Wells JA. A hot spot of binding energy in a hormone-receptor interface. Science. 1995;267: 383–386. doi: 10. 1126/science. 7529940. pmid:7529940
21. Bogan AA, Thorn KS. Anatomy of hot spots in protein interfaces1. J Mol Biol. 1998;280: 1–9. doi: 10. 1006/ jmbi. 1998. 1843. pmid:9653027
22. Darnell SJ, LeGault L, Mitchell JC. KFC Server: interactive forecasting of protein interaction hot spots. Nucleic Acids Res. 2008;36: W265–W269. doi: 10. 1093/nar/gkn346. pmid:18539611
23. Zhu X, Mitchell JC. KFC2: A knowledge-based hot spot prediction method based on interface solvation, atomic density, and plasticity features. Proteins Struct Funct Bioinforma. 2011;79: 2671–2683. doi: 10. 1002/prot. 23094.
24. Kortemme T, Baker D. A simple physical model for binding energy hot spots in protein–protein complexes. Proc Natl Acad Sci. 2002;99: 14116–14121. doi: 10. 1073/pnas. 202485799. pmid:12381794
25. Kortemme T, Kim DE, Baker D. Computational Alanine Scanning of Protein-Protein Interfaces. Sci Signal. 2004;2004: pl2–pl2. doi: 10. 1126/stke. 2192004pl2.
26. Ollikainen N, Kortemme T. Computational Protein Design Quantifies Structural Constraints on Amino Acid Covariation. PLoS Comput Biol. 2013;9: e1003313. doi: 10. 1371/journal. pcbi. 1003313. pmid:24244128
27. Ollikainen N, Smith CA, Fraser JS, Kortemme T. Chapter Four—Flexible Backbone Sampling Methods to Model and Design Protein Alternative Conformations. Keating AE, editor. Methods Enzymol. 2013;523: 61–85. doi: 10. 1016/B978–0–12–394292–0. 00004–7. pmid:23422426
28. Dokholyan NV, Shakhnovich EI. Understanding hierarchical protein evolution from first principles. J Mol Biol. 2001;312: 289–307. doi: 10. 1006/jmbi. 2001. 4949. pmid:11545603
29. Kuhlman B, Baker D. Native protein sequences are close to optimal for their structures. Proc Natl Acad Sci U S A. 2000;97: 10383–10388. doi: 10. 1073/pnas. 97. 19. 10383. pmid:10984534
30. Finn RD, Bateman A, Clements J, Coggill P, Eberhardt RY, Eddy SR, et al. Pfam: the protein families database. Nucleic Acids Res. 2014;42: D222–D230. doi: 10. 1093/ nar/gkt1223. pmid:24288371
31. Dickson RJ, Wahl LM, Fernandes AD, Gloor GB. Identifying and Seeing beyond Multiple Sequence Alignment Errors Using Intra-Molecular Protein Covariation. PLoS ONE. 2010;5: e11082. doi: 10. 1371/ journal. pone. 0011082. pmid:20596526
32. Yona G, Levitt M. Within the twilight zone: a sensitive profile-profile comparison tool based on information theory1. J Mol Biol. 2002;315: 1257–1275. doi: 10. 1006/jmbi. 2001. 5293. pmid:11827492
33. Leaver-Fay A, O'Meara MJ, Tyka M, Jacak R, Song Y, Kellogg EH, et al. Chapter Six—Scientific Benchmarks for Guiding Macromolecular Energy Function Improvement. Keating AE, editor. Methods Enzymol. 2013;523: 109–143. doi: 10. 1016/B978–0–12–394292–0. 00006–0. pmid:23422428
34. Dunn SD, Wahl LM, Gloor GB. Mutual information without the influence of phylogeny or entropy dramatically improves residue contact prediction. Bioinformatics. 2008;24: 333–340. doi: 10. 1093/ bioinformatics/btm604. pmid:18057019
35. Smith CA, Kortemme T. Backrub-Like Backbone Simulation Recapitulates Natural Protein Conformational Variability and Improves Mutant Side-Chain Prediction. J Mol Biol. 2008;380: 742–756. doi: 10. 1016/j. jmb. 2008. 05. 023. pmid:18547585
36. Mandell DJ, Coutsias EA, Kortemme T. Sub-angstrom accuracy in protein loop reconstruction by robotics-inspired conformational sampling. Nat Methods. 2009;6: 551–552. doi: 10. 1038/nmeth0809–551. pmid:19644455
37. Tonikian R, Zhang Y, Sazinsky SL, Currell B, Yeh J-H, Reva B, et al. A Specificity Map for the PDZ Domain Family. PLoS Biol. 2008;6: e239. doi: 10. 1371/journal. pbio. 0060239. pmid:18828675

38. Ernst A, Sazinsky SL, Hui S, Currell B, Dharsee M, Seshagiri S, et al. Rapid Evolution of Functional Complexity in a Domain Family. Sci Signal. 2009;2: ra50–ra50. doi: 10. 1126/scisignal. 2000416. pmid:19738200

39. Smith CA, Kortemme T. Predicting the Tolerated Sequences for Proteins and Protein Interfaces Using RosettaBackrub Flexible Backbone Design. PLoS ONE. 2011;6: e20451. doi: 10. 1371/journal. pone. 0020451.

40. Smith CA, Kortemme T. Structure-Based Prediction of the Peptide Sequence Space Recognized by Natural and Synthetic PDZ Domains. J Mol Biol. 2010;402: 460–474. doi: 10. 1016/j. jmb. 2010. 07. 032. pmid:20654621

41. Stein A, Kortemme T. Improvements to Robotics-Inspired Conformational Sampling in Rosetta. PLoS ONE. 2013;8: e63090. doi: 10. 1371/journal. pone. 0063090. pmid:23704889

42. Sellers BD, Zhu K, Zhao S, Friesner RA, Jacobson MP. Toward better refinement of comparative models: Predicting loops in inexact environments. Proteins Struct Funct Bioinforma. 2008;72: 959–971. doi: 10. 1002/ prot. 21990.

43. Wang C, Bradley P, Baker D. Protein–Protein Docking with Backbone Flexibility. J Mol Biol. 2007;373: 503–519. doi: 10. 1016/j. jmb. 2007. 07. 050. pmid:17825317

44. Fiser A, Do RKG, Šali A. Modeling of loops in protein structures. Protein Sci. 2000;9: 1753–1773. doi: 10. 1110/ps. 9. 9. 1753. pmid:11045621

45. Rohl CA, Strauss CEM, Chivian D, Baker D. Modeling structurally variable regions in homologous proteins with rosetta. Proteins Struct Funct Bioinforma. 2004;55: 656–677. doi: 10. 1002/prot. 10629.

46. Zhu K, Pincus DL, Zhao S, Friesner RA. Long loop prediction using the protein local optimization program. Proteins Struct Funct Bioinforma. 2006;65: 438–452. doi: 10. 1002/prot. 21040.

47. Jacobson MP, Pincus DL, Rapp CS, Day TJF, Honig B, Shaw DE, et al. A hierarchical approach to all-atom protein loop prediction. Proteins Struct Funct Bioinforma. 2004;55: 351–367. doi: 10. 1002/prot. 10613.

48. Shapovalov MV, Dunbrack RL Jr. A Smoothed Backbone-Dependent Rotamer Library for Proteins Derived from Adaptive Kernel Density Estimates and Regressions. Structure. 2011;19: 844–858. doi: 10. 1016/j. str. 2011. 03. 019. pmid:21645855

49. Zhao S, Zhu K, Li J, Friesner RA. Progress in super long loop prediction. Proteins Struct Funct Bioinforma. 2011;79: 2920–2935. doi: 10. 1002/prot. 23129.

50. Canutescu AA, Dunbrack RL. Cyclic coordinate descent: A robotics algorithm for protein loop closure. Protein Sci. 2003;12: 963–972. doi: 10. 1110/ps. 0242703. pmid:12717019

51. Coutsias EA, Seok C, Jacobson MP, Dill KA. A kinematic view of loop closure. J Comput Chem. 2004;25: 510–528. doi: 10. 1002/jcc. 10416. pmid:14735570

52. Bagley D, Fulgham B, Gouy I. The Computer Language Benchmarks Game [Internet]. 2004. Available: http:// benchmarksgame. alioth. debian. org/.

53. Calpini A. The Great Win32 Computer Language Shootout [Internet]. 2003. Available: http://dada. perl. it/ shootout/.

CHAPTER 8

SDMDATA: A WEB-BASED SOFTWARE TOOL FOR COLLECTING SPECIES OCCURRENCE RECORDS

Xiaoquan Kong, Minyi Huang, Renyan Duan

Department of Life Science, Anqing Normal University, Anqing, Anhui, 246011, PR China

ABSTRACT

It is important to easily and efficiently obtain high quality species distribution data for predicting the potential distribution of species using species distribution models (SDMs). There is a need for a powerful software tool to automatically or semi-automatically assist in identifying and correcting errors. Here, we use Python to develop a web-based software tool (SDMdata) to easily collect occurrence data from the Global Biodiversity Information Facility (GBIF) and check species names and the accuracy of coordinates (latitude and longitude). It is an open source software (GNU Affero General Public License/AGPL licensed) allowing anyone to access and manipulate the source code. SDMdata is available online free of charge from <http://www.sdmserialsoftware.org/sdmdata/>.

INTRODUCTION

Species occurrence records are very important for building species distribution models (SDMs) for use in assessing the potential niches of species [1], testing conservation applications, evolutionary and biogeographical hypotheses [2–4], projecting species invasion risk and proliferation [5], assessing the impact of climate change, land use, urbanization and other environmental changes [6–8], suggesting potential suitable sites for rare species [9], and supporting appropriate conservation planning and reserve selection [10].

The majority of species distribution data sets come from databases, museums, herbaria, and field workers [11]. Among these, the Global Biodiversity Information Facility (GBIF;http://www.gbif.rog/) is the largest provider of species distribution records, with a web-based API (Application Programming Interface) to help users efficiently fetch data. GBIF's API is program-oriented, and several software packages provide functions to help users connect to it. For example, rgbif is a small, open source package linking to GBIF based on R language [12]. However, using R language consumes a large amount of memory, and some users are not familiar with this sometimes idiosyncratic language. Another software providing GBIF API function is modestR. ModestR is a powerful and fully-stacked software to download, import and clean species distribution records [13]. ModestR is a huge software package

Citation: Kong X, Huang M, Duan R (2015) SDMdata: A Web-Based Software Tool for Collecting Species Occurrence Records. PLoS ONE 10(6): e0128295. doi:10.1371/journal.pone.0128295.

(the size is more than 4.6GB in the latest version) written in C# language that can only be used in a Windows operating system in the current version, which limits its application.

With the development of species distribution models, studying the effect of environmental change or reserve size on species distribution requires a large number of species distribution data [14,15]. For example, Munguía et al. [14] used the distribution data of 5544 amphibian species to measure how equilibrium varies between species distributions and climate across taxa and regions at a global scale. Cantú-Salazar and Gaston [15] obtained geographical range maps for 1878 terrestrial mammal, 4100 bird and 3096 amphibian species to explore discrepancies between species richness and geographical range maps and test possible effects of reserve size on range maps. In general, one species has 10~10,000 data records, such that significant time is required to obtain and check the accuracy of many records. There is a need for a powerful but easy-to-use, web-based software to meet the requirements of big data. Python is a widely used programming language (https://www.python.org/) that is often used in writing science software not based on C (e.g. C#, C++, Objective-C), serving as a scripting language for web applications such as those from Google, Yahoo, CERN (European Organisation for Nuclear Research) and NASA (National Aeronautics and Space Administration) [16]. The high-level and high-performance Python language can be installed in many operating systems supporting multiple programming paradigms (e.g. object-oriented, imperative and procedural styles). It is more effective than conventional languages (such as C and Java) in string manipulation, searching and cloud computing with lower memory consumption than Java, C and C++ [16]. Here, we use Python to develop a web-based open source software (SDMdata) for automatically or semi-automatically assisting in identifying and correcting errors from GBIF. The SDMdata web interface allows the process to be performed on any platform with a JavaScript-capable Internet browser. The output of the software is a file in CSV (comma separated values) format that can be widely used in other applications.

SDMdata

SDMdata is designed for researchers to collect occurrence data from GBIF. After users import a file containing a list of species names, SDMdata will check the accuracy of species names against the GBIF database. The program will only proceed to collect species occurrence records if all of the species names are correct. After the collection job is complete, users can choose to do a check on the records to determine whether the coordinates have potential errors. See Fig 1 for whole system structures. SDMdata has some advantages over other software packages including: 1) SDMdata is based on Python, and thus has all the advantages of Python including high-performance and lower memory consumption. 2) The basic workflow of SDMdata is very easy, similar to the online submission system of academic periodicals, familiar to researchers. 3) SDMdata is web-based, meaning that users can access SDMdata from a web browser on any computer without any additional setup. 4) SDMdata has a user-friendly interface such that it can be used on many platforms (different operating systems) and many devices (e.g. desktop computer, tablet computer, or even a mobile phone). 5) SDMdata is released under an AGPL (GNU Affero General Public License) license. It is open source meaning that it is not only free to use, but its full source code is also freely accessible.

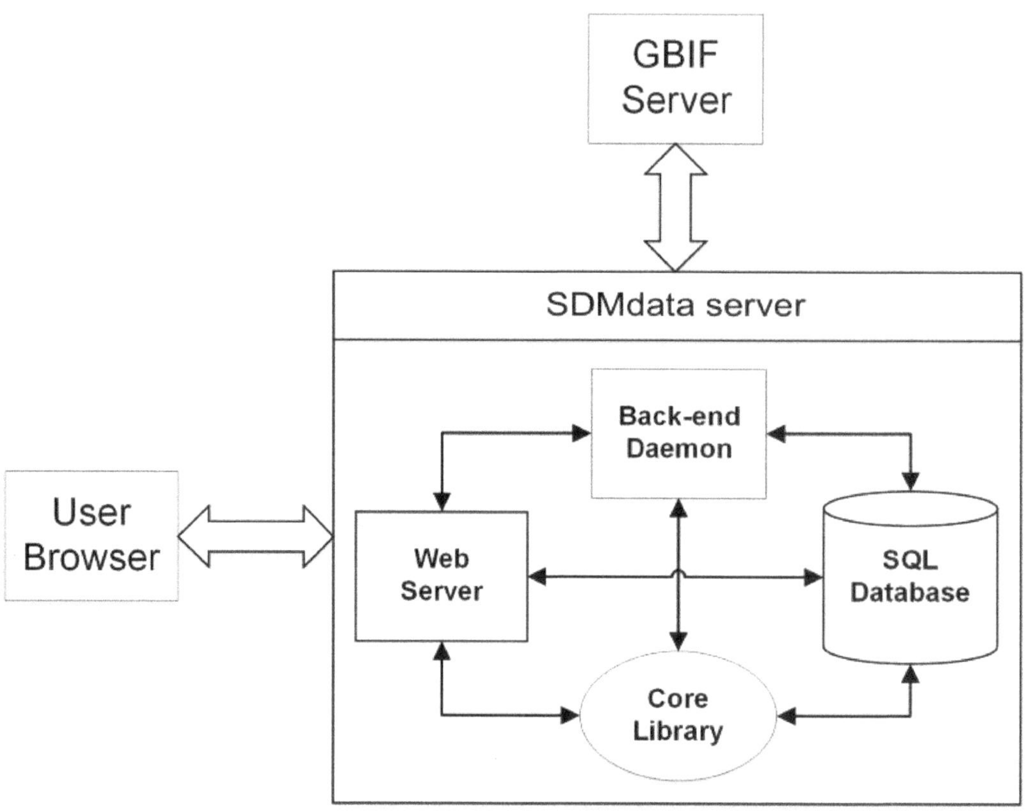

Figure 1. Structure of SDMdata.

THE BASIC WORKFLOW OF SDMDATA

SDMdata has six basic steps within its workflow: 1) uploading a CSV file, 2) cleaning up, checking the species list, and importing the species list into the database, 3) checking the species name with GBIF, 4) collecting species occurrence data, 5) cross-checking occurrence data, and 6) exporting occurrence data (Fig 2). Steps 3–5 are somewhat complicated, and are described below in detail.

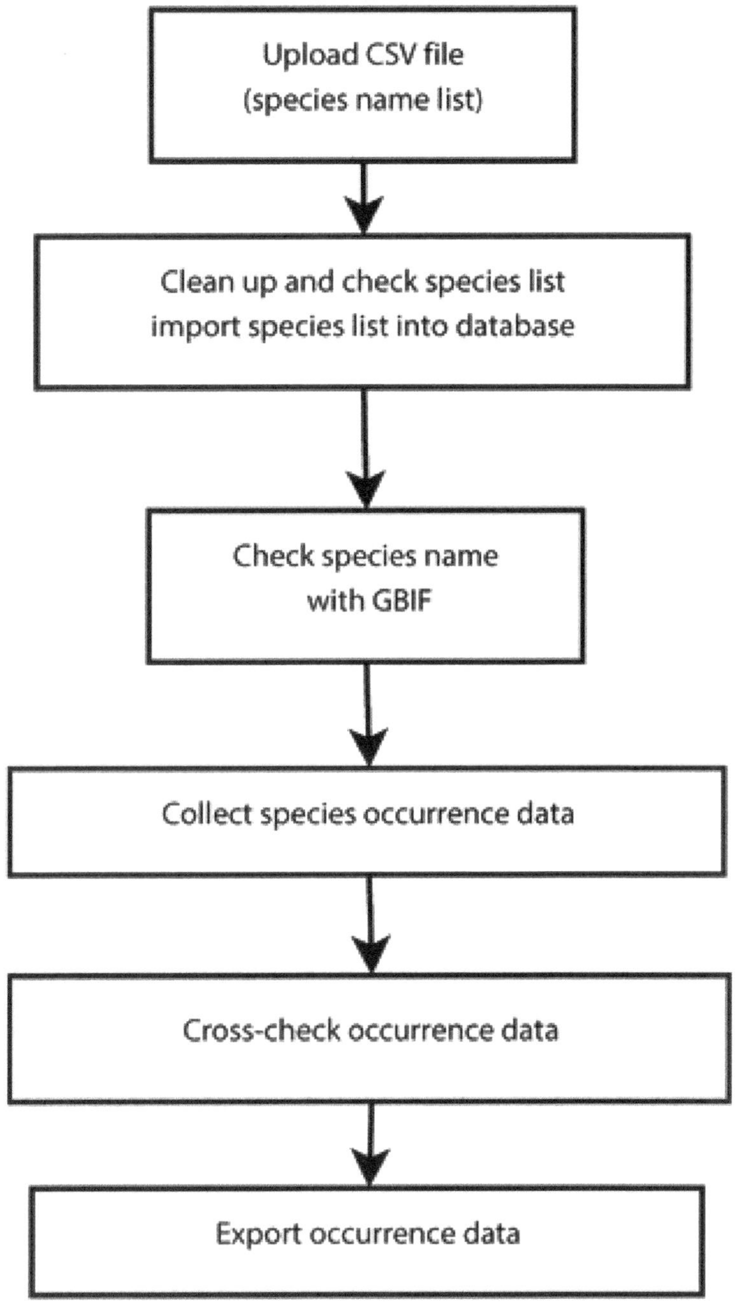

Figure 2. Workflow of SDMdata.

Checking Species Names with GBIF

Inputting species names is the first critical step to obtain species distribution information from species-occurrence databases. However, most ecologists and biogeographers have not completely mastered taxonomic knowledge, especially when many species are needed, and there may be some errors in species names (e.g. formatting errors or misspellings), which leads to problems in obtaining species information. SDMdata provides a function to check and extend species name information by using GBIF's backbone taxonomy as the backend database (S1 Appendix). GBIF's backbone taxonomy, often called the Nub taxonomy, is the largest species taxonomy database with a single synthetic management classification with the goal of covering all names in GBIF. It checks species names first, before the software collects the occurrence record, with two steps: 1) It checks whether users inputted incorrect species names (e.g. wrong spelling, changed species name). This is a common problem when researchers are dealing with tens of thousands of species. 2) It enhances species names with complete taxonomic information (including kingdom, phylum, class, order, family and genus). This is always useful in comparing the distribution of taxa (Fig 3).

Species name	Kingdom	Phylum	Class	Order	Superfamily	Family	Genus
Atelopus oxyrhynchus	Animalia	Chordata	Amphibia	Anura		Bufonidae	Atelopus
Atelopus spurrelli	Animalia	Chordata	Amphibia	Anura		Bufonidae	Atelopus
Atelopus carrikeri	Animalia	Chordata	Amphibia	Anura		Bufonidae	Atelopus
Atelopus spumarius	Animalia	Chordata	Amphibia	Anura		Bufonidae	Atelopus
Anomaloglossus tepuyensis	Animalia	Chordata	Amphibia	Anura		Aromobatidae	Anomaloglossus
Arthroleptis variabilis	Animalia	Chordata	Amphibia	Anura		Arthroleptidae	Arthroleptis
Austrochaperina basipalmata	Animalia	Chordata	Amphibia	Anura		Microhylidae	Austrochaperina
Arthroleptis wahlbergii	Animalia	Chordata	Amphibia	Anura		Arthroleptidae	Arthroleptis
Atelopus andinus	Animalia	Chordata	Amphibia	Anura		Bufonidae	Atelopus
Atelopus pachydermus	Animalia	Chordata	Amphibia	Anura		Bufonidae	Atelopus

Figure 3. Species names with complete taxonomy information from GBIF.

The core function of SDMdata is to fetch species occurrence points. This is the common function in similar software (e.g. rgbif, modestR), but SDMdata improves upon these with an independent daemon program. GBIF provides a web-based API to fetch occurrence points. It is easily impacted by the network and problems with DNS (Domain Name Service) or the network connection. This becomes important when data must be fetched for a long time without a break. All key functions of SDMdata (including checking species name, fetching occurrence records and crossing-checking) are written in an independent daemon program. All key functions have break-point memory protection. This means that it does not matter if the function is stopped at any time, and the software will simply finish the process upon restarting. This is useful when the user needs to stop the process or the network connection encounters a problem. All of the key functions are saved, meaning that an unexpected software or operating system crash or other fatal error will not prevent the software from completing its task.

Cross-checking Occurrence Data

Many occurrence records from observational data, survey data, as well as museum and herbarium data, have little geographic information or inaccurate geographic coordinates (latitude and longitude). Data errors are common and error rates can be up to 1~5% [17]. For data to meet the needs of users, error detection, validation and cleaning are essential parts of the data management process to improve data validation and correctness [18]. The two major errors in species occurrence points are spatial position (geographic coordinates) and identification error resulting for any number of reasons (e.g. GPS device errors, the exchange of longitude with latitude). We use cross-checking to find potential errors. There are many types of cross-checking, for example the quartiles method, jackknife method or autoselect best method [13]. SDMdata implements the most commonly used cross-check function for land-based species, which checks the geographic coordinates (latitude and longitude) with the geographic information of a specific country to identify potential errors [19]. Species occurrence records from GBIF have a country code recording the location of the sample. When the coordinate does not match the country code (the coordinate is not located in the country), this occurrence record may have an error (country border map is provided by GADM; http://www.gadm.org/). Note that a cross-check failure does not mean that this record is incorrect, but indicates to the researcher that this record is likely to be incorrect and requires closer inspection for errors. The accuracy of a country's borders on the map, the accuracy of the GPS device, or other factors may mean that records located near the country's border appear to be outside of the country. Our software will flag species occurrence records with problem for further checking (Fig 4, S2 Appendix).

Longitude	Latitude	Flag
31.0333	-29.7	1
30.5667	-30.2667	1
32.35	-28.3833	1
32.35	-28.35	1
32.4294	-28.3728	0
32.4294	-28.3728	0
32.4294	-28.3728	0
32.4294	-28.3728	0
32.4294	-28.3728	0
32.4294	-28.3728	0
30.85	-28.9667	1
30.85	-28.9667	1

Figure 4. Result of cross-checking (0 indicates that geographic co-ordinates may be wrong, 1 indicates that geographic coordinates are correct).

TECHNICAL IMPLEMENTATION

SDMdata is written in Python language with the geospatial process portion using GDAL library (http://www.gdal.org/) and the web server portion using the flask framework (http://flask.pocoo.org/). GDAL is widely used and the most important open source geospatial process library. SDMdata is currently available at <http://www.sdmserialsoftware.org/sdmdata/>.

SUPPORTING INFORMATION

(1) Upload species name CSV file

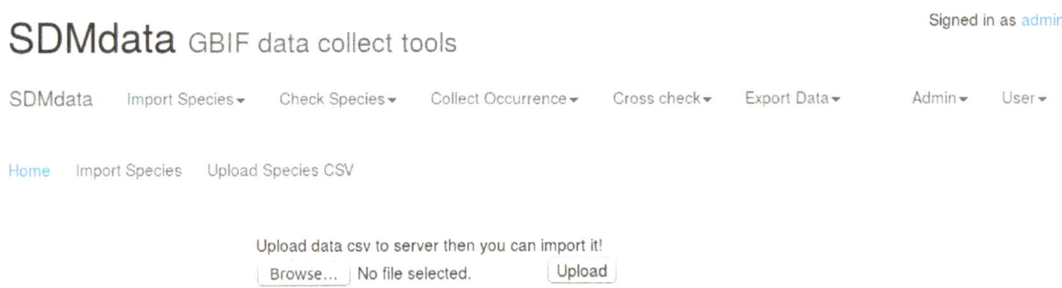

(2) Import species name into software

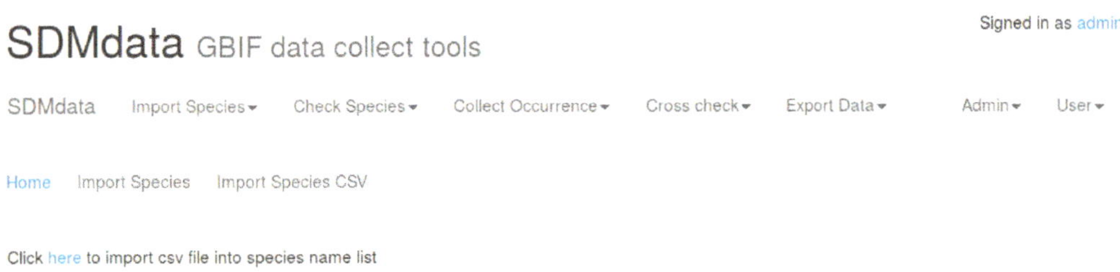

(3) View imported species name (optional)

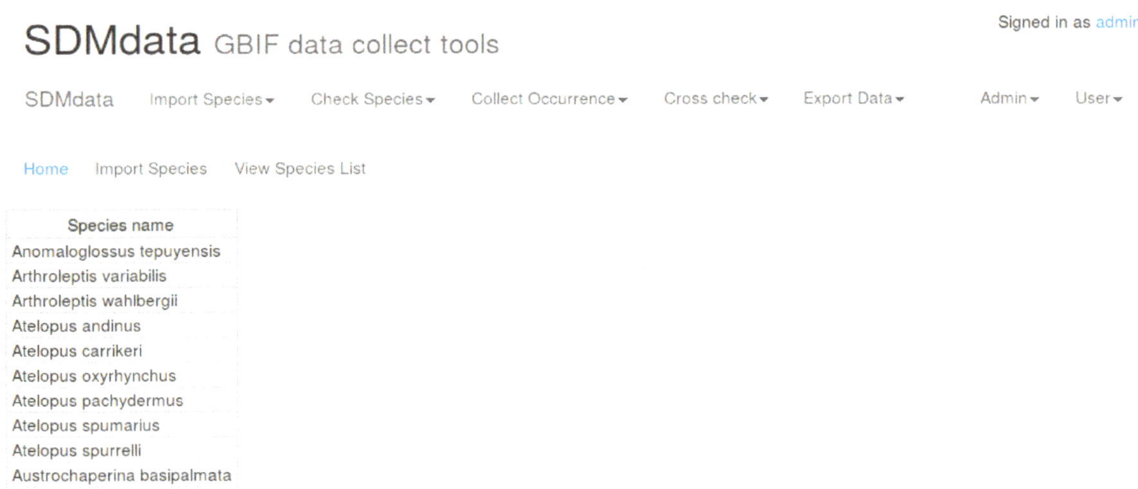

(4) Check species name with GBIF

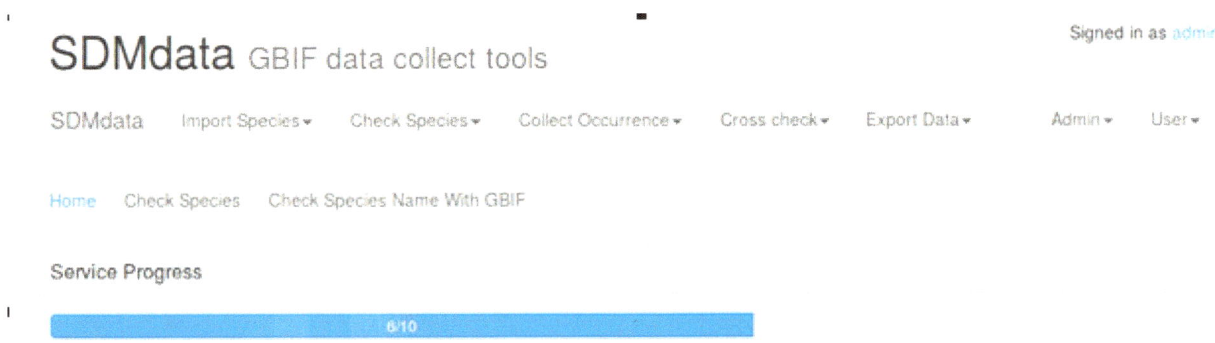

(5) View checked species name (optional)

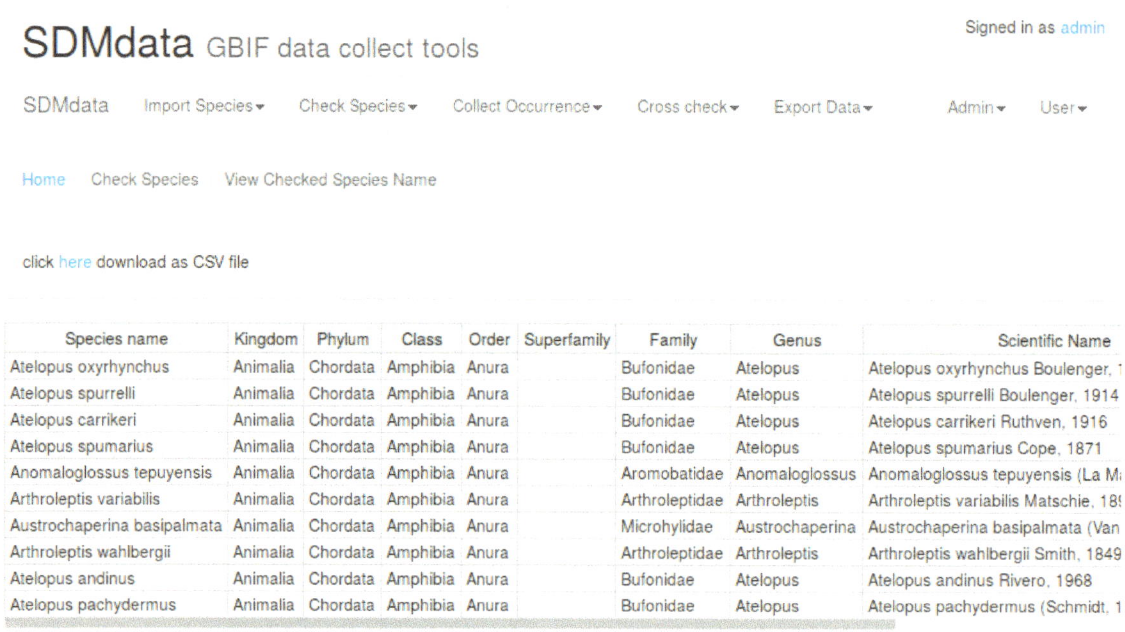

Species name	Kingdom	Phylum	Class	Order	Superfamily	Family	Genus	Scientific Name
Atelopus oxyrhynchus	Animalia	Chordata	Amphibia	Anura		Bufonidae	Atelopus	Atelopus oxyrhynchus Boulenger, 1
Atelopus spurrelli	Animalia	Chordata	Amphibia	Anura		Bufonidae	Atelopus	Atelopus spurrelli Boulenger, 1914
Atelopus carrikeri	Animalia	Chordata	Amphibia	Anura		Bufonidae	Atelopus	Atelopus carrikeri Ruthven, 1916
Atelopus spumarius	Animalia	Chordata	Amphibia	Anura		Bufonidae	Atelopus	Atelopus spumarius Cope, 1871
Anomaloglossus tepuyensis	Animalia	Chordata	Amphibia	Anura		Aromobatidae	Anomaloglossus	Anomaloglossus tepuyensis (La M
Arthroleptis variabilis	Animalia	Chordata	Amphibia	Anura		Arthroleptidae	Arthroleptis	Arthroleptis variabilis Matschie, 18
Austrochaperina basipalmata	Animalia	Chordata	Amphibia	Anura		Microhylidae	Austrochaperina	Austrochaperina basipalmata (Van
Arthroleptis wahlbergii	Animalia	Chordata	Amphibia	Anura		Arthroleptidae	Arthroleptis	Arthroleptis wahlbergii Smith, 1849
Atelopus andinus	Animalia	Chordata	Amphibia	Anura		Bufonidae	Atelopus	Atelopus andinus Rivero, 1968
Atelopus pachydermus	Animalia	Chordata	Amphibia	Anura		Bufonidae	Atelopus	Atelopus pachydermus (Schmidt, 1

(6) View error species name (optional)

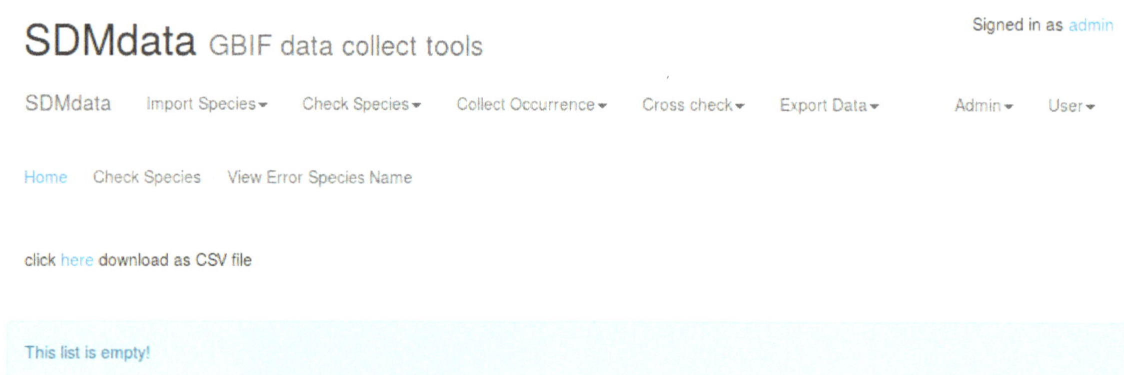

S1 Appendix. Workflow of uploading, importing and checking species names.
doi:10.1371/journal.pone.0128295.s001

(1)Fetching occurrence record

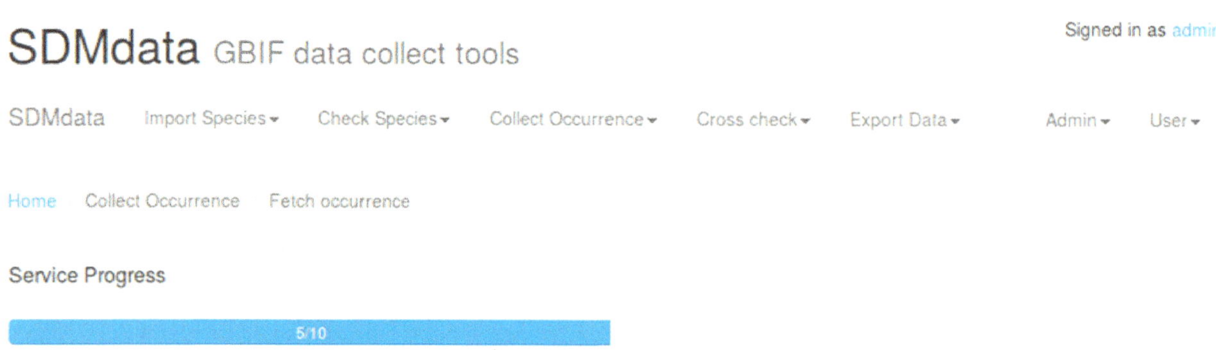

(2) Viewing species with no occurrence record

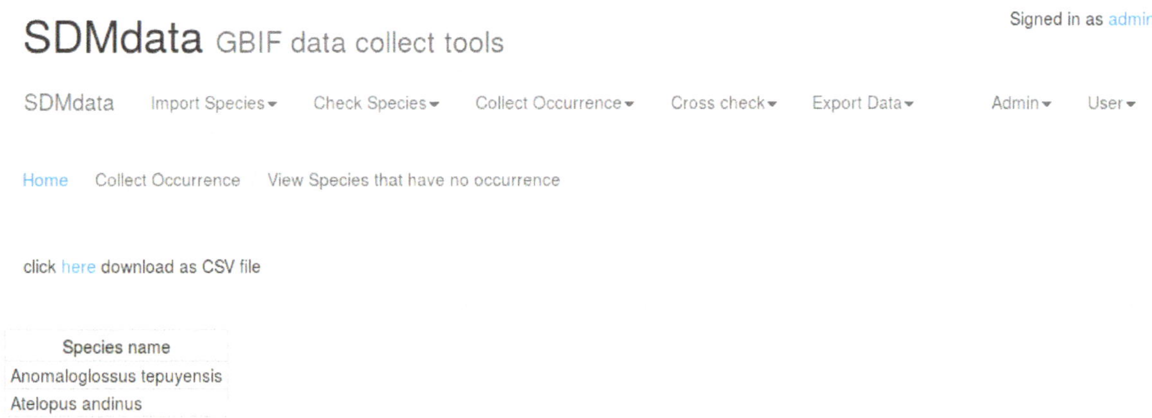

(3)Viewing species with un-coordinate occurrence record

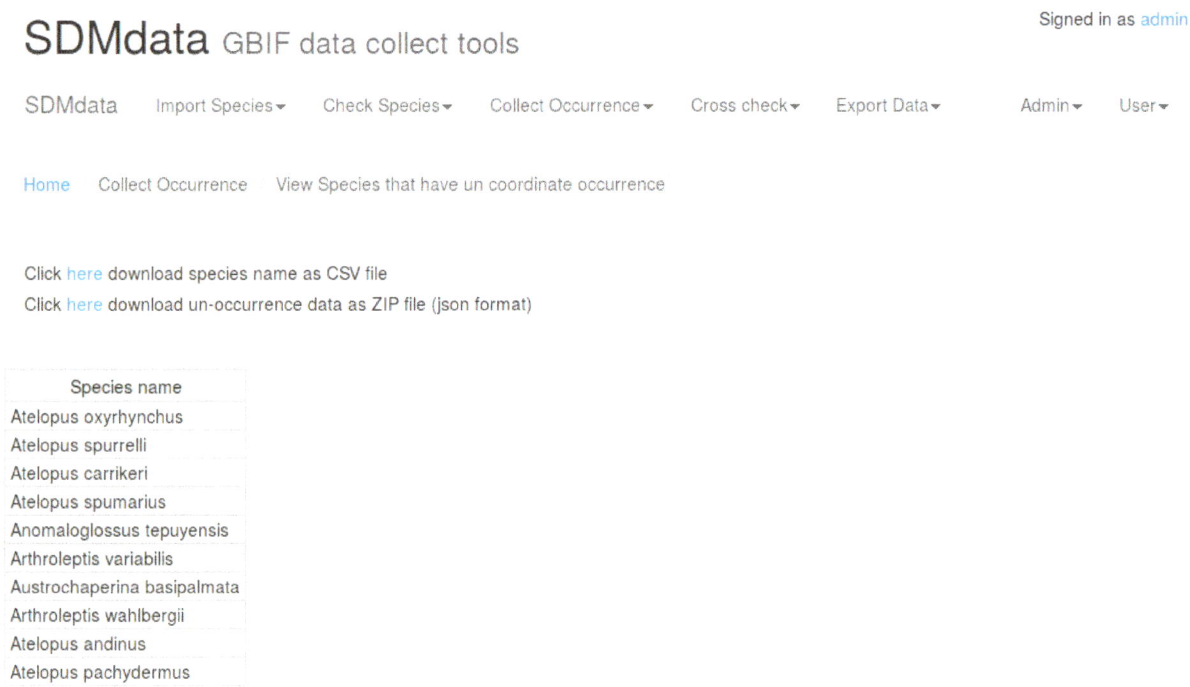

(4) Crossing check the occurrence progress

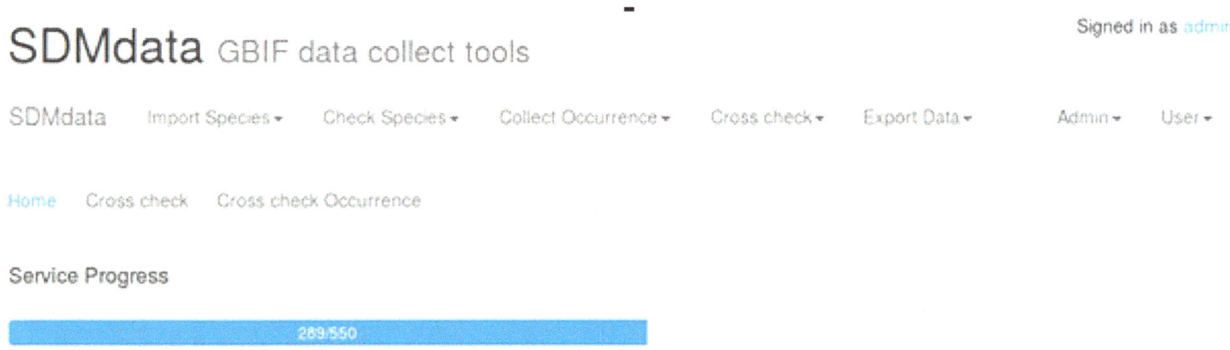

(5) Viewing the status of crossing check

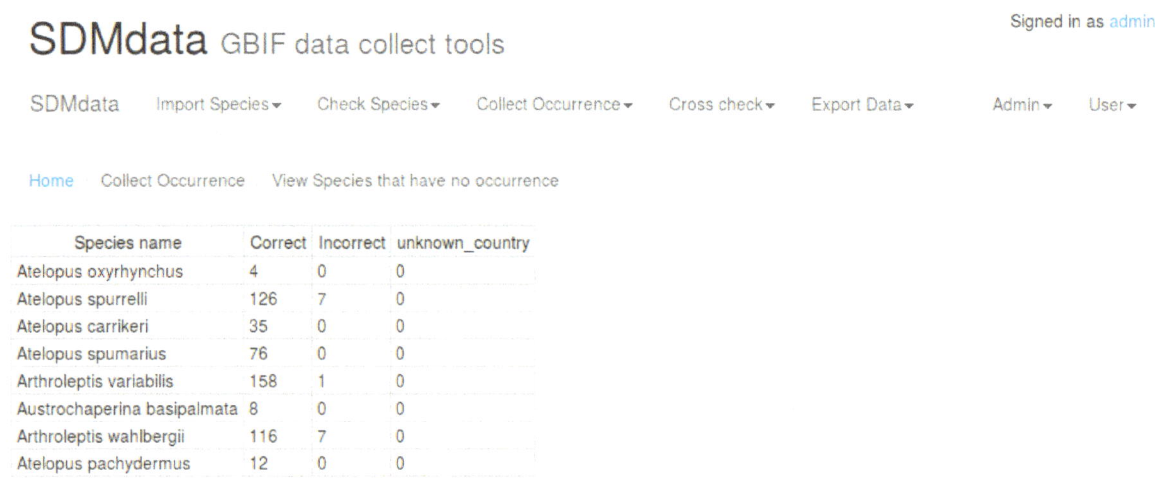

Species name	Correct	Incorrect	unknown_country
Atelopus oxyrhynchus	4	0	0
Atelopus spurrelli	126	7	0
Atelopus carrikeri	35	0	0
Atelopus spumarius	76	0	0
Arthroleptis variabilis	158	1	0
Austrochaperina basipalmata	8	0	0
Arthroleptis wahlbergii	116	7	0
Atelopus pachydermus	12	0	0

(6) Viewing the export data

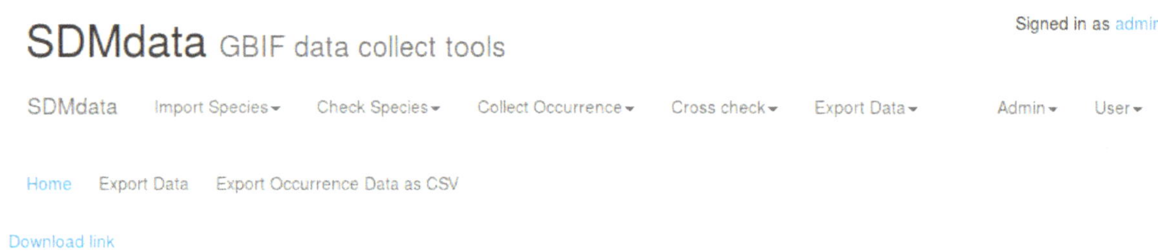

S2 Appendix. Workflow of fetching occurrence and cross-checking occurrence process.
doi:10.1371/journal.pone.0128295.s002

ACKNOWLEDGMENTS

This work was supported by the National Natural Science Foundation of China (31300342, 31100311) and China Postdoctoral Science Foundation (2014M561683).

AUTHOR CONTRIBUTIONS

Conceived and designed the experiments: XQK MYH. Performed the experiments: XQK. Analyzed the data: XQK. Contributed reagents/materials/analysis tools: XQK RYD. Wrote the paper: XQK MYH RYD. Edited and provided suggestions for readability and clarity: MYH RYD. Developed the research framework and provided guidance throughout the project: MYH RYD.

REFERENCES

1. Vetaas OR (2002) Realized and potential climate niches: a comparison of four Rhododendron tree species. Journal of Biogeography 29: 545–554. doi: 10.1046/j.1365-2699.2002.00694.x
2. Andelman SJ, Willig MR (2002) Alternative configurations of conservation reserves for Paraguayan bats: considerations of spatial scale. Conservation Biology 16: 1352–1363. doi: 10.1046/j.1523-1739.2002.01119.x
3. Eskildsen A, Roux PC, Heikkinen RK, Høye TT, Kissling WD, Pöyry J, et al. (2013) Testing species distribution models across space and time: high latitude butterflies and recent warming. Global Ecology and Biogeography 22: 1293–1303. doi: 10.1111/geb.12078
4. Graham CH, Ron SR, Santos JC, Schneider CJ, Moritz C (2004) Integrating phylogenetics and environmental niche models to explore speciation mechanisms in dendrobatid frogs. Evolution 58: 1781–1793. pmid:15446430 doi: 10.1111/j.0014-3820.2004.tb00461.x
5. Rose JP, Todd BD (2014) Projecting invasion risk of non-native watersnakes (*Nerodia fasciata* and *Nerodia sipedon*) in the Western United States. PLoS One 9: e100277. doi: 10.1371/journal.pone.0100277. pmid:24964204
6. Guisan A, Tingley R, Baumgartner JB, Naujokaitis-Lewis I, Sutcliffe PR, Tulloch AI, et al. (2013) Predicting species distributions for conservation decisions. Ecology Letters 16: 1424–1435. doi: 10.1111/ele.12189. pmid:24134332
7. Ochoa-Ochoa LM, Rodríguez P, Mora F, Flores-Villela O, Whittaker RJ (2012) Climate change and amphibian diversity patterns in Mexico. Biological Conservation 150: 94–102. doi: 10.1016/j.biocon.2012.03.010
8. Peterson AT (2011) Ecological niche conservatism: a time-structured review of evidence. Journal of

Biogeography 38: 817–827. doi: 10.1111/j.1365-2699.2010.02456.x

9. Engler R, Guisan A, Rechsteiner L (2004) An improved approach for predicting the distribution of rare and endangered species from occurrence and pseudo-absence data. Journal of Applied Ecology 41: 263–274. doi: 10.1111/j.0021-8901.2004.00881.x

10. Araújo MB, Cabeza M, Thuiller W, Hannah L, Williams PH (2004) Would climate change drive species out of reserves? An assessment of existing reserve-selection methods. Global Change Biology 10: 1618–1626. doi: 10.1111/j.1365-2486.2004.00828.x

11. Feeley KJ, Silman MR (2010) Modelling the responses of Andean and Amazonian plant species to climate change: the effects of georeferencing errors and the importance of data filtering. Journal of Biogeography 37: 733–740. doi: 10.1111/j.1365-2699.2009.02240.x

12. Chamberlain S, Ram K, Barve V, Mcglinn D (2014) rgbif: Interface to the Global Biodiversity Information Facility API. Available: https://github.com/ropensci/rgbif.

13. García-Roselló E, Guisande C, Heine J, Pelayo-Villamil P, Manjarrés-Hernández A, González Vilas L, et al. (2014) Using ModestR to download, import and clean species distribution records. Methods in Ecology and Evolution 5:708–713. doi: 10.1111/2041-210x.12209

14. Munguía M, Rahbek C, Rangel TF, Diniz-Filho JAF, Araújo MB (2012) Equilibrium of global amphibian species distributions with climate. PLoS One 7: e34420. doi: 10.1371/journal.pone.0034420. pmid:22511938

15. Cantú-Salazar L, Gaston KJ (2013) Species richness and representation in protected areas of the Western hemisphere: discrepancies between checklists and range maps. Diversity and Distributions 19: 782–793. doi: 10.1111/ddi.12034

16. Lutz M (2013) Learning python. O'Reilly Media, Inc.

17. Redman TC, Blanton A (1997) Data quality for the information age. Artech House, Inc.

18. Chapman AD (2005) Principles and methods of data cleaning—Primary species and speciesoccurrence data, version 1.0. Report for the Global Biodiversity Information Facility, Copenhagen, Denmark.

19. Hijmans RJ, Elith J (2014) Species distribution modeling with R. Available:http://cran.r-project.org/web/packages/dismo/vignettes/dm.pdf.

CHAPTER 9

TRACEABLE CALIBRATION, PERFORMANCE METRICS, AND UNCERTAINTY ESTIMATES OF MINIRHIZOTRON DIGITAL IMAGERY FOR FINE-ROOT MEASUREMENTS

Joshua A. Roberti[1], Michael D. SanClements[1,2], Henry W. Loescher[1,2], Edward Ayres[1,2]

[1] National Ecological Observatory Network (NEON), Boulder, Colorado, United States of America

[2] Institute of Arctic and Alpine Research (INSTAAR), University of Colorado, Boulder, Colorado, United States of America

ABSTRACT

Even though fine-root turnover is a highly studied topic, it is often poorly understood as a result of uncertainties inherent in its sampling, e.g., quantifying spatial and temporal variability. While many methods exist to quantify fine-root turnover, use of minirhizotrons has increased over the last two decades, making sensor errors another source of uncertainty. Currently, no standardized methodology exists to test and compare minirhizotron camera capability, imagery, and performance. This paper presents a reproducible, laboratory-based method by which minirhizotron cameras can be tested and validated in a traceable manner. The performance of camera characteristics was identified and test criteria were developed: we quantified the precision of camera location for successive images, estimated the trueness and precision of each camera's ability to quantify root diameter and root color, and also assessed the influence of heat dissipation introduced by the minirhizotron cameras and electrical components. We report detailed and defensible metrology analyses that examine the performance of two commercially available minirhizotron cameras. These cameras performed differently with regard to the various test criteria and uncertainty analyses. We recommend a defensible metrology approach to quantify the performance of minirhizotron camera characteristics and determine sensor-related measurement uncertainties prior to field use. This approach is also extensible to other digital imagery technologies. In turn, these approaches facilitate a greater understanding of measurement uncertainties (signal-to-noise ratio) inherent in the camera performance and allow such uncertainties to be quantified and mitigated so that estimates of fine-root turnover can be more confidently quantified.

INTRODUCTION

The growth, senescence, and mortality of fine-roots, collectively referred to as fine-root turnover is key to estimate belowground nutrient and carbon cycling and ecosystem productivity [1], [2]. Production of fine-roots accounts for a third of the Earth's annual net primary production [3], supporting the notion that fine-root mortality returns more carbon and nitrogen to the soil than litterfall [1], [4]. Unlike aboveground primary production, fine-root production has only been measured at a limited number of sites and over relatively short timescales, in part, because of short-comings associated with sampling methods[5]–[7]. Currently, there is no standardized method or

Citation: Roberti JA, SanClements MD, Loescher HW, Ayres E (2014) Traceable Calibration, Performance Metrics, and Uncertainty Estimates of Minirhizotron Digital Imagery for Fine-Root Measurements. PLoS ONE 9(11): e112362. doi:10.1371/journal.pone.0112362.

'best community practice' for evaluating fine-root turnover [8], even though a number of approaches have been used in the past. For example, radiocarbon ^{14}C measurements of fine-roots, although fundamentally sound in theory, provide estimates of mean carbon age based on modeled results that are often under question [9]. Methods such as sequential soil coring and ingrowth cores are reliable for quantifying the stocks of root biomass but embody large spatial and temporal uncertainties when assessing fine-root turnover as a result of sampling at different locations at each sampling event [8], [10], [11]. Moreover, root production and mortality of the same root size, and in some cases, species, cannot be observed successively as these methods are based on destructive sampling [12]–[14]. Today, the minirhizotron is the only nondestructive, *in-situ* sampling method for quantification of fine-root turnover at fine temporal scales.

The first rhizotron was a large, underground room constructed with glass walls allowing for observations of root growth and decay [15]. Cost and area of disturbance in the installation of these large rhizotrons was prohibitive, resulting in a modified approach: the minirhizotron, *i.e.*, buried cameras installed within transparent tubes that emerged in the 1980s [16]. Minirhizotrons are more cost effective, cause less disturbance, and allow for the analyses of successive root images to assess fine-root turnover through time [16], [17], from many species across multiple ecosystems [2], [8], [18].

Like all sampling methods, uncertainties in the minirhizotron approach have been identified. For example, Hendrick and Pregitzer [19] indicated fine-root production and mortality can be underestimated due to the time between sampling (*i.e.*, imaging of fine-roots) intervals. Villordon *et al.* [20] noted that a scanner-based minirhizotron grossly underestimated adventitious root quantity when compared to root quantity as measured by other methods. The limitations of minirhizotron cameras may also hinder accurate and precise estimates of fine-root stocks, turnover and biomass [21]. And even though measurement limitations such as these and others exist (*e.g.*, uncertainties in automated image analysis), minirhizotrons represent a robust and practical approach for quantification of fine-root turnover [22]. Here, we argue that the performance of minirhizotron cameras must be quantified in a reproducible and traceable manner to best quantify fine-root standing stock and turnover, and the processes they inform.

Some minirhizotron camera performances have been previously assessed [22], [23], yet a direct comparison of performance between different commercially available minirhizotrons has not been made. Standardized calibration methods and 'best community practices' for quantifying measurement uncertainties of many environmental sensors (*e.g.*, resistance thermometers, pyranometers, etc.) exist, but such is not the case for minirhizotron cameras and their digital imagery. The absence of establishing such criteria from both the scientific community as well as standards-holding bodies hinder advances in design, deployment and data collection of minirhizotrons. The objectives of this paper are to present a reproducible, statistically traceable and defensible, steady-state approach for quantifying uncertainty and comparing key characteristics of minirhizotron camera performance (*i.e.*, digital imagery). We present measurement uncertainties for an array of performance metrics for two minirhizotron cameras. We also test for sources of human error and the potential for biases due to heating of the soil environment.

MATERIALS AND METHODS

Selected Minirhizotrons

To our knowledge only three companies commercially produced minirhizotrons at the time of our study; i) Bartz Technology Corporation, Carpinteria, CA, USA, ii) CID-BioScience Inc., Camas, WA, USA, and iii) RhizoSystems LLC, Idyllwild, CA, USA. Minirhizotrons from two of the companies: the CI-600 In-Situ Root Imager (CID-BioScience), and the Automated Mini-rhizotron version A (AMR-A; RhizoSystems LLC) were used in developing a steady-state, laboratory approach to compare key functions of minirhizotron cameras and to quantify associated uncertainties. The AMR-A and CI-600 employ fundamentally different but common technologies for root imaging. The AMR-A is a fully automated, programmable instrument that uses a digital microscopic camera, and operates in a closed, sealed system[24]. The CI-600 is a manually controlled minirhizotron that relies upon scanner-based digital technology, and operates as an open system [25]. Choosing to analyze the performance of two different minirhizotrons also reflects the current range (albeit two) of technologies used.

Quantification of Measurement Uncertainty

We assessed four key functions of minirhizotron cameras and propose methods to quantify and reduce associated uncertainties. We follow a traceable and statistically defensible approach (presented below) to quantify measurement uncertainty as proposed by the Joint Committee for Guides in Metrology [26]. Definitions of metrological terms used here are also consistent with the Standards-holding body (Table 1). The first step in calculating a measurement's uncertainty is to identify all input quantities, X_i, on which Y (the measurand) depends:

$$Y = f(X_1, X_2, \ldots, X_n). \tag{1}$$

Table 1. Metrology terms and definitions.

Variable	Definition (is the-)
Accuracy	closeness of agreement between a measured quantity value and a true quantity value of a measurand; the concept 'measurement Accuracy' is not a quantity and is not given a numerical quantity Value
Precision	closeness of agreement between indications or measured quantity values obtained by replicate measurements on the same or similar objects under specified conditions; the 'specified conditions' can be, for example, repeatability conditions of measurement etc.
Relative uncertainty	standard measurement uncertainty divided by the absolute value of the measured quantity value
Repeatability condition	condition of measurement, out of a set of conditions that includes the same measurement procedure, same operators, same measuring system, same operating conditions and same location, and replicate measurements on the same or similar objects over a short period of time
Reproducibility condition	condition of measurement, out of a set of conditions that includes different locations, operators, measurement systems, and replicate measurements on the same or similar objects
Resolution	smallest change in a quantity being measured that causes a perceptible change in the corresponding indication
Resolvable limit	minimum distance at which neighboring objects of the same intensity are resolved as two objects [28,29]
Sensitivity	quotient of the change in an indication of a measuring system and the corresponding change in a value of a quantity being measured
Standard uncertainty	measurement uncertainty expressed as a standard deviation
Trueness	closeness of agreement between the average of an infinite number of replicate measured quantity values and a reference quantity Value
Type A evaluation	evaluation of a component of measurement uncertainty by a statistical analysis of measured quantity values obtained under defined measurement conditions, *e.g.*, repeatability condition
Type B evaluation	evaluation of a component of measurement uncertainty determined by means other than a Type A evaluation

All definitions are provided by JGCM [27] standards-holding body unless otherwise specified.
doi:10.1371/journal.pone.0112362.t001

Because the measurement uncertainty of a measurand is a function of the uncertainty of its input quantities, the function f should contain every known, not necessarily quantifiable, source of measurement uncertainty, including all corrections and correction factors, unit conversions, etc. The standard uncertainty of each input quantity is quantified by two different uncertainty evaluation "Types". Type A evaluation of uncertainty is based on first-hand statistical analyses and quantifies the distribution of n independent observations taken under controlled, often steady-state, conditions. Type B evaluation assumes *a priori* distribution for data and is not based on first-hand statistical analyses. In many cases, Type B uncertainties are taken directly from calibration specifications, typically provided by a manufacturer, or are arrived at using best scientific judgment. Here, we give a mathematical overview of a typical Type A evaluation. First, the mean of n independent observations is calculated:

$$x=\overline{x}=\frac{1}{n}\sum_{i-1}^{n} x_i. \quad (2)$$

Second, the experimental standard deviation is calculated:

$$s(x_i)=\left(\frac{1}{n-1}\sum_{i-1}^{n}(x_i-\overline{x})^2\right)^{\frac{1}{2}}. \quad (3)$$

The standard uncertainty of the input quantity X_i can either be the experimental standard deviation of the sample if quantifying the expected variance of an individual observation *or*the standard deviation of the mean (standard error) if quantifying the expected variance of a mean, such that,

$$u(x_i)=\frac{s(x_i)}{n^{\frac{1}{2}}}. \quad (4)$$

Each individual source of uncertainty (represented here by the standard deviation of the mean) then propagates to a final, combined uncertainty,

$$u_c(y)=\left(\sum_{i-1}^{N}\left(\frac{\partial f}{\partial x_i}\right)^2 u^2(x_i)+ 2\sum_{i=1}^{N-1}\sum_{j=1+1}^{N}\left(\frac{\partial f}{\partial x_i}\right)\left(\frac{\partial f}{\partial x_j}\right) r(x_i,x_j)u(x_i)u(x_j)\right)^{\frac{1}{2}} \quad (5)$$

where, $\frac{\partial f}{\partial x_i}$ is the partial derivative of the function, f, with respect to the input quantity, X_i; $r(x_i,x_j)$ is the correlation coefficient computed by dividing the covariance, $u(x_i,x_j)$, of the respective input terms by the product of their individual uncertainties,

$$r(x_i,x_j)=\frac{u(x_i,x_j)}{u(x_i)u(x_j)}. \quad (6)$$

When input quantities are *uncorrelated*, the second term of Eq. (5) can be dismissed. However, for the case where the input quantities share a correlation of +1, Eq. (5) decreases to the linear sum of terms,

$$u_c(y) = \sum_{i=1}^{N} \left(\frac{\partial f}{\partial x_i}\right) u(x_i). \quad (7)$$

It is common practice to expand the combined uncertainty to a larger confidence level, usually 95%. To do so, the function (Eq. (5)) is estimated by a normal distribution with an effective degrees of freedom, $v_{eff}(y)$, attained by the Welch-Satterthwaite formula,

$$v_{eff}(y) = \frac{u_c^4(y)}{\sum_{i=1}^{N} \frac{u_i^4(y)}{v_i}}, \quad (8)$$

where, $u_i(y) = \left(\frac{\partial f}{\partial x_i}\right) u(x_i)$ represents the individual, partial uncertainties of the combined uncertainty, and $v_i = n-1$, represents the degrees of freedom of each input variable. The expanded uncertainty at 95% confidence, $U_{95}(y)$, is then obtained by,

$$U_{95}(y) = k_{95} u_c(y), \quad (9)$$

where, k_{95} is the coverage factor (found in Table G.2 of [26]). It should be noted that deriving an expanded uncertainty using the Welch-Satterthwaite formula assumes input quantities are uncorrelated and independent. While this assumption typically holds true when measuring *in-situ* phenomena, it is widely applied for steady-state calibrations using repeated measures which further assumes the conditions of instrument uncertainty under*in-situ* and steady-state conditions remain the same. Currently, there is no metrological or statistical alternative to using the Welch-Satterthwaite formula that is accepted by the standards-holding body, and addressing this issue is an active area of research [30], [31]. The reader should also note that unless otherwise specified, all uncertainties presented in this manuscript are given in expanded form at 95% confidence.

Assessing the Spatial Uncertainty of Camera Positioning

Repeated images of the same area provide a measure of how well *the same* root (stocks) and their turnover (a time delta) can be estimated [32]. In all minirhizotrons, the camera moves within an access tube to image the belowground environment. Hence, the ability to assess the spatial variability or precision of a moving camera to repeatedly image the same area is potentially a large source of uncertainty. In some cases, researchers have engraved marks onto minirhizotron tubes or utilized automatic indexing post-manufacture to quantify and possibly account for spatial uncertainties of camera location between sequential sampling times [22]. The minirhizotron tubes of the AMR-A and CI-600, however, did not include reference marks. The AMR-A camera has the ability to 'auto-index' image locations[24], and once the AMR-A completes a full pre-programmed scan of the tube the camera returns to a '*home*' position located at the top of the minirhizotron tube. One method to assess the spatial variance would be to examine the AMR-A camera's auto indexed position for subsequent scans, however, at the time of this study, RhizoSystems LLC's Root View software did not record or archive such information. Because it is a manual minirhizotron, auto indexing was not available in the CI-600.

Here, we quantify the spatial uncertainty among a set of sequential images from each instrument. A stationary target (Kodak TL-5003 imaging test chart, Eastman Kodak Co., Rochester, NY, USA) was secured to an arbitrary location on the outside of each minirhizotron tube. The target was scanned thirty times ($n = 30$, noted throughout the remainder of the text as "test") at manufacturer-specified default settings (Table 2). In total, five tests were completed independently, three with the AMR-A (tests A1, A2, and A3), and two with the CI-600 (tests C1 and C2; Table 3).

Table 2. Specifications and manufacturer recommended default settings of each minirhizotron

Specification/Settings	CI-600	AMR-A
Tube length (cm)	182.0 (Others available)	156.8 (including handle and fin)
Tube diameter (cm)	6.4	10.8
Tube circumference (cm)	20.1	33.9
Operating range (°C)	Dependent on laptop	−12 to 45
Power requirements	Powered by laptop	5A @ 120 VAC
Removable camera	Yes	No
Operations	On site; field technician	Remotely; automated
Image dimensions (cm)	21.6×19.6	0.226×0.301
[a]resolution (im)	42.3×42.3 (~24 pixels (p) mm^{-1})	4.7×4.7 (~212 p mm^{-1})
Pixels/image	2.356×10^{7}	3.07×10^{5}
Images/full-tube scan	8 (with 182.0 cm tube)	3.2928×10^{4}
Software	CI-600 Root Scanner v.3.1.22	Root View v3.0.0.7
[b]Default camera settings	Brightness = 0; (50%)	Camera Exposure = 8; (60%)
	Contrast = 0; (50%)	LED camera lights = 192; (100%)
	Threshold = 0; (50%)	Dwell time = 100 ms

[a]manufacturer recommended resolutions (B Meyer, CID-BioScience Inc., pers. comm.; M Taggart RhizoSystems, LLC, pers. comm.)
[b]settings provided with percentage relative to the maximum range of the particular setting [24,25]
doi:10.1371/journal.pone.0112362.t002

Table 3. Description of camera position tests.

Test	Condition of measurement	Description
A1	Reproducibility	AMR-A: Camera homed between subsequent scans; deviation from home location *was greater than* the manufacturer recommended 20 μm
A2	Reproducibility	AMR-A: Camera homed between subsequent scans; deviation from home location *was equal to or less than* the manufacturer recommended 20 μm
A3	Repeatability	AMR-A: Camera not homed between subsequent scans
C1	Reproducibility	CI-600: Removal and replacement of camera
C2	Repeatability	CI-600: No removal and replacement of camera

Each test had $n = 30$.
doi:10.1371/journal.pone.0112362.t003

To quantify the reproducibility of the AMR-A camera, two tests were conducted under conditions where the camera was programmed to return to its '*home*' position, *i.e.*, the manufacturer's reference location, between subsequent scans of the target. For best results the manufacturer recommends the camera returns to within ±20 μm of its '*home*' position among subsequent scans, thereby managing the reproducibility. The first test (A1) comprised scans where the radial (around the tube) and vertical (along the tube) distances between the camera's actual position and its '*home*' position exceeded ±20 μm among subsequent scans. The second test (A2) comprised scans where the radial and vertical distances between the camera's actual position and its '*home*' position were ≤±20 μm among subsequent scans.

To quantify the repeatability of the AMR-A's camera position, the A3 test was conducted such that the camera was preprogrammed to image a 1 cm^2 area starting at predetermined x (radial) and y (vertical) coordinates within the tube. Between subsequent scans, the camera was not programmed to return to its '*home*' position. This test was designed to assess the variability of the camera's location independent of sending the camera to its '*home*' position among subsequent scans.

Under field conditions, the CI-600 is manually installed into its tube. Hence, the C1 test simulated field conditions where measurements would be prone to human error through the removal and replacement of the camera by the operator (*i.e.*, reproducibility). This test consisted of i) aligning the CI-600's reference dots with a fixed location at the tube's inlet, as recommended by the manufacturer [25], ii) placing the CI-600 camera inside the minirhizotron tube, iii) pushing it to a predetermined depth of the tube (target location) where the camera "locked" into place via its attached placement rod (the camera was pushed to the same depth for all scans), iv) allowing the camera to complete a full, ~360°radial scan, and then rotate back to ~0° from its starting position (an automated process among subsequent scans [25]), and v) removing the CI-600 camera from the tube; this method was repeated thirty times. The C2 test followed the same method as C1 with the exception that thirty successive images were taken under identical and stable conditions without removing the CI-600 from the tube (*i.e.*, repeatability). Test C2 was intended to quantify the spatial uncertainty of the camera free of external factors such as the influence of human error introduced in estimating reproducibility via test C1.

Because the image size of each minirhizotron camera is different (Table 2), two different sized targets of the Kodak TL-5003 test chart, a crosshair and a line-segment, were imaged by the CI-600 and AMR-A cameras, respectively. This ensured that the entire target was captured within an individual image rather than a mosaic of images, thus eliminating another potential source of uncertainty.

The Interactive Data Language (IDL) v8.1 (Exelis Visual Information Solutions, Inc., Boulder, CO, USA) was used to assess each image in grayscale format, and using the *thresholding*and *contouring* functions [33], discern pixels that comprise the target of interest from background pixels. To do so, the pixel intensity (0 (black) to 255 (white)) threshold was initially set to 253 and the pixels that comprised intensities less than this threshold test were then outlined with the contour function. Contouring was used here to ensure that only *one*outline for the entire black colored target was identified, *i.e.*, pixels not part of the target were excluded, and that *only* the coordinates of the pixels that included the target were identified. We then tallied the number of contours that were returned. If more than one contour was identified, the threshold value was lowered by one and the process was repeated until only*one* contour was identified in each image, *i.e.*, dynamic thresholding. Once the final threshold was determined (in this case, it was lowered by a total of 3, thus determining the final threshold of 250), the x and y coordinates of each pixel comprising the target from all images (*i.e.*, those with intensities less than the final threshold value) were outputted to separate data files and labeled by the test and image number.

We then quantified the central position of the respective object's location in each image by calculating the mean x and y coordinates of those pixels passing the threshold test. This was completed using Perl (v5.10, www.perl.org). By computing the object's central location in sequential images (at time one, time two, time n), we were then able to determine the difference in this central location among images and hence, determine the ability of the sensor to repetitively sample the same point(s) in space. We present the spatial uncertainty of the camera via one standard deviation (SD), because in this case, we think it is more informative to do so in the context of the sample variance, rather than the variance of the sample mean, *i.e.*, standard error. The standard deviation can then be used in part to compute the expected spatial uncertainty of the camera (for an individual scan) relative to the camera's "true" location.

Digital Imaging Performance

Evaluating Camera Sensitivity

Accurately quantifying the size of fine-roots may be limited by camera sensitivity and pixelation inherent in digital imagery. The pixelation process averages the signals across a given area, which subsequently decreases the overall sensitivity of a given technology, and can cause large uncertainties when fine-roots are imaged with cameras comprising low resolution, *i.e.*, large pixels [34]. To assess the cameras' abilities to quantify root diameter, we determined the sensitivity of each minirhizotron camera, quantified measurement trueness over a range of known diameters, and computed the precision of such measurements.

Individual, black line segment widths of a truncated fan pattern (Kodak TL-5003 imaging test chart) were measured at the thirteen designated points (Table 4) by a Model 1602 Filar Micrometer (Los Angeles Scientific Instrument Company, Los Angeles, CA, USA), traceable to National Institute of Standards and Technology's (NIST) standards (NIST Test# 821/253660-94) at Applied Image Inc. (Rochester, NY, USA). These measurements were used to calibrate the minirhizotron measurements.

Table 4. Line widths and expanded uncertainties as measured by the NIST traceable micrometer.

Line Width (μm)	±U_{95} (μm)
409.63	2.22
348.21	1.64
303.53	1.64
268.48	1.64
242.62	1.64
194.06	1.64
161.95	1.38
120.27	1.38
100.15	1.38
73.81	1.38
57.99	1.38
43.66	1.38
39.29	1.38

doi:10.1371/journal.pone.0112362.t004

Each minirhizotron camera imaged the truncated fan pattern under steady-state conditions (*i.e.*, no camera removal) and operated with the highest manufacturer recommended resolution. For the AMR-A this was ~212 pixels (p) mm^{-1} with pixel sizes of 4.7×4.7 μm [24], and for the CI-600, this was ~24 p mm^{-1} with pixel sizes of 42.3×42.3 μm [25]. Each minirhizotron camera operated inside a larger opaque tube to mimic underground conditions and eliminate exposure to extraneous sources of light. The resultant images were saved in bitmap (*.bmp) format to avoid data compression.

We assessed the minirhizotron images using IDL. The intensities and coordinates of each pixel residing within the thirteen rows perpendicular to the truncated fan pattern (*i.e.*, those points measured by the NIST traceable micrometer) were outputted to a *.csv file. Data were then normalized with respect to the neighboring maxima. We followed the Rayleigh Criterion to quantify the resolvable limit (sensitivity) of each minirhizotron (Figure 1). This criterion can be thought of as defining the minimum distance between two objects that can be individually resolved by a camera [28], [29]. More specifically, we also define this minimum distance when a contrast of 26.4% exists between two neighboring maxima with identical magnitudes [35]. In the case of pixelated images, *magnitudes* relates to pixel intensities (signals). Pixel intensity graphs (Figure 1) were generated via Microsoft Excel 2010 (Microsoft Inc., Redmond, VA, USA) to assess sensitivity and quantify the Rayleigh Criterion.

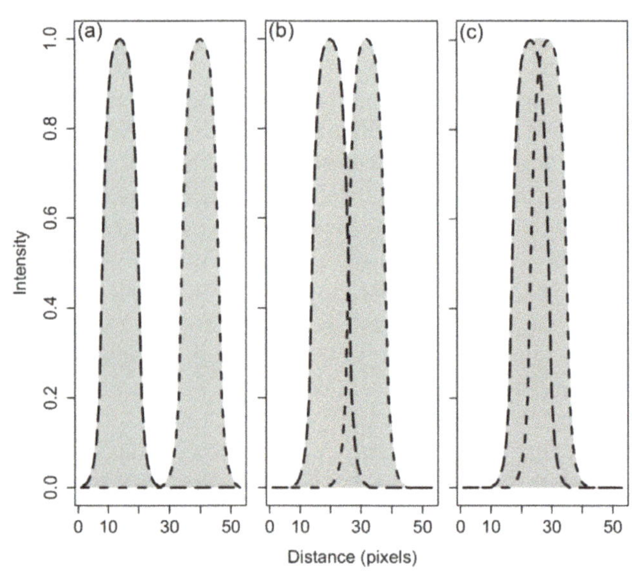

Figure 1. Conceptual diagram depicting the resolution of two objects (smooth contours) with equal intensities at varying distances. The

dashed lines denote two conceptual objects of equal intensity, and the shaded, gray area represents what the camera resolves; (a) fully resolvable, (b) just resolvable (Rayleigh Criterion), and (c) unresolvable, *i.e.*, both objects are resolved as a single object.

Quantifying Root Diameter

Measurement trueness was quantified through a number of steps. First, pixel intensity data (outputted by IDL) of the six widest lines measured by the micrometer (Table 4) were ingested into a Perl script. These six points were chosen because they did not reside near the resolvable limit of either minirhizotron camera. Thus, we standardized the approach to make robust comparisons between both minirhizotron cameras. Second, we used two separate test methods to estimate trueness of line thickness; we tallied the number of successive pixels with intensities less than i) the threshold of 250 (as determined by the camera positioning tests), and ii) half of the maximum intensity of an individual group of successive, black pixels. The latter follows the Full Width at Half Maximum (FWHM) approach, a common method used in optics [28]. The maximum intensity value for FWHM was independently calculated for each group of successive, black pixels. Successive, black pixels from each test were tallied separately, thus quantifying the width of a black line-segment in two different manners. Third, the mean line segment widths of all the black line segments at each of the six points were calculated in units of microns following Eq. (2). Fourth, the standard errors of these six mean line thicknesses were calculated following Eq. (3) and (4). Mean data from each of the minirhizotrons were then fit to a calibration curve against those values quantified by the micrometer.

Uncertainty estimates for uncorrected and corrected (*i.e.*, those data not fit and fit to the calibration curve, respectively) data were estimated and compared. In both cases, input data were considered uncorrelated and independent. Combined uncertainties were derived following Eq. (5). Sources of quantifiable uncertainties of each minirhizotron dataset included: i) uncertainty of the micrometer measurements (Type B uncertainties taken from calibration specifications), ii) measurement trueness (uncorrected or corrected), and iii) the precision of the minirhizotron measurements. The average of the computed standard errors over the entire measurement range was used to calculate the precision of each camera's ability to quantify root diameter. Individual uncertainties were summed in quadrature following Eq. (5), and resulting combined uncertainties were then expanded following Eq.(8) and (9).

Assumptions

It should be noted that two assumptions were made when determining the resolvable limit of each camera and their ability to quantify root diameter. First, we assumed each camera operated using a constant focal length, such that the focal point was always positioned at the outer edge of the respective minirhizotron tube, i.e., where the truncated fan pattern was secured, and not at some distance d (mm) away from the outer edge of the tube. Second, it was assumed that the measured widths of the line segments (two-dimensional objects) were representative of root diameters (three dimensional objects; see [23]). We cannot discount the possibility that these assumptions may lead to additional uncertainties. Regardless, the presented approach is reproducible, statistically traceable, and serves as a guideline for future researchers to build upon.

Quantifying Root Color

Overestimation of fine-root lifespan and subsequent underestimation of fine-root turnover are possible if fine-roots are only classified as dead once they disappear from the view of the minirhizotron camera [10]. To address this problem, some researchers quantify the age and/or health of fine-roots as a function of color. However, the color nomenclature used by researchers to define root health is unstandardized and ambiguous. For example, the terms*white* [10], [36]–[38] and/or *cream* [32] are used to designate living and/or new roots, *brown*[32], [36]–[38], or *woody* [32] to describe dying/aging roots, *dark* to describe older roots [10], and *dark brown*, *very dark brown* [39] or *black* to describe dead roots [32], [37], [39]. Interestingly, the term *brown* is used to describe the colors *orange* and/or *dark yellow*imaged at low luminance [40]. In a recent paper, Dannoura *et al.* [36] quantified root-color changes via digital imagery to discern between living and dying/dead roots, but did not provide an estimate of the imager's ability to quantify color with a known trueness and precision. The color space vectors outputted by digital cameras, *e.g.*, RGB, are device-dependent, do not usually adhere to the fundamentals of Colorimetry [41], and the spectral response to color among a population of cameras can vary greatly [42]. In other words, the same root stock may appear *brown* when imaged by camera A, *cream* colored when imaged by camera B, and *dark brown* when imaged by camera C. "True" root colors cannot be known and comparisons cannot be made using device-dependent imagery (and qualitative color terms). To our knowledge no researchers have identified device-independent color space, *e.g.*, CIE XYZ, CIE L*a*b*, etc., thresholds for digital imagery to discern among new/living, dying/aging, or dead roots, nor have they provided color space uncertainty estimates.

JCGM [26] notes that any measurement is not complete without a supplementary uncertainty estimate; this is especially true for color measurements, as many factors, such as the lighting and the geometry of measurement, can influence the uncertainty of its measurement [43]. Here, we present an uncertainty analysis of color quantification of the two minirhizotron cameras and also stress the importance of monitoring root age and/or health in a quantitative manner via a device-independent color space.

In many cases, spectral reflectance of a sample is quantified by concurrently measuring signals of a sample and a standard under identical measurement conditions [44]. For this study, however, spectral reflectance of the samples and the standards were quantified independently, as this is becoming a more common approach (Gary Reif, Applied Image Inc., Personal Comm. 2014). A Color Test Chart (QA-69-P-RM, Applied Image Inc.) containing eight color patches was measured by a NIST traceable X-Rite eXact densitometer (X-Rite Inc., Grand Rapids, MI, USA) at Applied Image Inc. This densitometer directly measured reflectance of the sample over a spectrum of 400 to 700 nm λ at 10 nm increments while operating with International Commission on Illumination (CIE) [45]Illuminant D50, 0/45° geometry of measurement, and the CIE 1931 2° standard observer. This was completed five separate times for each of the color patches to inform uncertainty of the reflectance measurements. In total, five datasets of n=31 (reflectance data from 400–700 nm λ at 10 nm increments) *for each* of the eight colors were generated. The five datasets of reflectance data for each color patch were then averaged together at each wavelength. Although the CIE [45] recommend that data should be captured at or interpolated to 5 or 1 nm increments to avoid uncertainties due to gaps, research shows that the increase of uncertainty in reflectance data when capturing data at 10 nm increments is likely trivial compared to data captured at 5 or 1 nm [46]. Moreover, interpolating to these increments can actually lead to larger uncertainties (than the 10 nm data) depending on the interpolation scheme (*e.g.*, linear, Lagrange). Therefore, we chose not to interpolate the reflectance data. Following recommendations from the CIE [45] and the American Society for Testing and Materials (ASTM) [47], reflectance data were then converted to the CIE 1931 XYZ color space with the following equations,

$$T_c = k\sum_{\lambda} R_i S_i t_{c,i} \Delta\lambda, \tag{10}$$

where, T_c represents the tristiumulus values: X, Y, and Z; t_c represents the color matching functions: x, y, and z associated with the appropriate tristiumulus value, R represents reflectance, S is the relative spectral power distribution of the illuminant, i is the individual wavelength, and $\Delta\lambda$ represents the wavelength interval. The variable k is a normalizing constant defined by:

$$k = \frac{100}{\sum_{\lambda} S_i y_i \Delta\lambda}. \tag{11}$$

Resulting tristiumulus values were then converted to x and y chromaticity coordinates via:

$$x = \frac{X}{X+Y+Z}, \tag{12}$$

and

$$y = \frac{Y}{X+Y+Z}. \tag{13}$$

Tristiumulus values and resulting chromaticity coordinates were then used to characterize (calibrate) the minirhizotron data.

Each minirhizotron was characterized independently. The Color Scanner Test Chart was secured to the outside of the respective minirhizotron tube, and the minirhizotron was placed inside of a larger opaque tube to eliminate ambient light. The Color Scanner Test Chart was imaged once while each minirhizotron operated at manufacturer-specified default settings (Table 2). The images captured at default settings were then analyzed for over-saturation (over-exposure). If the colors imaged by the minirhizotron were over-exposed, we adjusted the camera settings and reimaged the chart until the influence of saturation was mitigated. We utilized bitmap (*.bmp) format for all the images to avoid data compression. After the optimal camera settings were derived, the Color Scanner Test Chart was imaged five separate times by each minirhizotron camera. Images were uploaded to Adobe Photoshop (Adobe Systems, San Jose, California, USA) to inform the respective device-dependent color space used by each camera. The digital color space of images from both minirhizotrons could not be verified. As such, the individual vector intensities of each of the eight colors imaged by the two minirhizotrons were assumed to be standard RGB (sRGB), and were analyzed using IDL. Pixels residing along the boundaries of each color patch were discarded from the analysis to avoid inadvertent quantification of merged colors. Standard RGB data from each minirhizotron were then characterized (calibrated) to the CIE XYZ data of the densitometer following a linear transformation [48]:

$$\begin{aligned} X_1 &= a_{11}R_1 + a_{12}G_1 + a_{13}B_1, \\ X_2 &= a_{11}R_2 + a_{12}G_2 + a_{13}B_2, \\ X_3 &= a_{11}R_3 + a_{12}G_3 + a_{13}B_3, \end{aligned} \tag{14}$$

where, X_i is a tristiumulus value of an individual color patch (converted from spectral reflectance data measured by the densitometer), R_i, G_i, and B_i are the values outputted by the minirhizotron camera for the same color patch, and a_{11}, a_{12}, and a_{13} are empirical coefficients. The same calculations were carried out for Y and Z, for a total of nine equations. Three colors: *white*, *amber* (a mixture of *orange* and *yellow*), and *yellow*, were used for the linear transformation (Table 5). These colors were chosen as they best represent the region of expected root colors relative to the other five colors of the test chart. The resultant tristiumulus values were then converted to chromatic coordinates following Eq. (12) and (13).

Table 5. Mean chromaticity coordinates (and expanded uncertainties) converted from reflectance data measured by the densitometer.

Color	x	$\pm U_{95}(x)$	y	$\pm U_{95}(y)$
Yellow	0.463	0.001	0.494	0.001
Amber	0.424	0.001	0.397	0.001
White	0.349	0.001	0.363	0.002

doi:10.1371/journal.pone.0112362.t005

Color space characterization, especially for applications relying on digital imagery (RGB), is an active area of research. Various techniques to characterize RGB to a CIE color space have been investigated [48]–[50]. As cautioned by these studies, the use of a linear calibration using only three colors will cause large uncertainties when attempting to characterize other colors via the derived coefficients a_{11}, a_{12}, and a_{13}. Here, we acknowledge this issue; however, one goal of this study was to develop a method of traceable, standard, and defensible means to estimate the uncertainties in minirhizotron imagery. The extent of our characterization was limited by the number of colors on our test chart, and thus a characterization that includes the many possible combinations of tristiumulus values and higher order polynomial modeling was beyond the scope of this investigation.

An uncertainty analysis for color is estimated following the JCGM [26], Early and Nadal [44], the CIE [45], and Sándor *et al.* [46]. Uncertainty estimates of the spectral reflectance data (as measured by the densitometer) were provided as relative values by Applied Image Inc. and are considered Type B uncertainties. Because the spectral reflectance data are the rawest form of data obtained from the densitometer, we assumed that the corresponding uncertainty values provided by Applied Image Inc. encompassed any correlations among the signals of the standard and the sample, and are corrected for any systematic uncertainties inherent in reflectance data (as mentioned in [44]). Correlations among wavelengths and among tristiumulus values were quantified following Eq. (5), and the equations in [44]. Combined uncertainties of each tristiumulus value, T_c, and each chromaticity coordinate, v_c, respectively, were derived via,

$$u_c(T_c) = \left(\sum_{i-1}^{N} \left(\frac{\partial T_c}{\partial R_i} \right)^2 u^2(R_i) + 2\sum_{i=1}^{N-1} \sum_{j=1+1}^{N} \left(\frac{\partial T_c}{\partial R_i} \right) \left(\frac{\partial T_c}{\partial R_j} \right) r(R_i,R_j) u(R_i) u(R_j) \right)^{\frac{1}{2}}, \quad (15)$$

and,

$$u_c(v_c) = \begin{pmatrix} \left(\frac{\partial v_c}{\partial X} \right)^2 u^2(X) + \left(\frac{\partial v_c}{\partial Y} \right)^2 u^2(Y) + \left(\frac{\partial v_c}{\partial Z} \right)^2 u^2(Z) \\ +2\left(\frac{\partial v_c}{\partial X} \right) \left(\frac{\partial v_c}{\partial Y} \right) r(X,Y) u(X) u(Y) \\ +2\left(\frac{\partial v_c}{\partial X} \right) \left(\frac{\partial v_c}{\partial Z} \right) r(X,Z) u(X) u(Z) \\ +2\left(\frac{\partial v_c}{\partial Y} \right) \left(\frac{\partial v_c}{\partial Z} \right) r(Y,Z) u(Y) u(Z) \end{pmatrix}^{\frac{1}{2}} \quad (16)$$

We present uncertainty estimates of uncharacterized (*i.e.*, sRGB vectors), and characterized (*i.e.*, x and y chromaticity coordinates) in expanded form. The act of characterizing from sRGB to the chromatic coordinates is a calibration procedure, and thus, we cannot display uncharacterized minirhizotron data in the form of x and y chromatic coordinates.

Estimating Heat Dissipation

It is well known that temperature controls many enzymatically-driven metabolic processes in the soils [51]–[53]. Artificial changes in soil temperature could, in turn, change plant and microbial responses. For example, a meta-analysis by Rustad *et al.* [54] concluded that nearly all soil warming experiments increased soil respiration, N mineralization, and plant productivity. The AMR-A operates as a closed system and uses the ground as a heat sink[24], which may impact fine-root turnover. To assess the potential impact of heat additions to the soil environment, we measured the soil temperatures surrounding the installation of the AMR-A. We did not measure the soil temperatures around the CI-600 as it is not a closed system and we assumed its scanner-based imager dissipated a negligible amount of heat to the surrounding environment during the time it takes the CI-600 to complete a full-tube scan (*i.e.*, roughly thirty-minutes).

The AMR-A was placed into a 118 cm (L) x 30 cm (ID) QUIK-TUBE (part number 6922, QUIKRETE, Atlanta, GA, USA) and the area between the exterior of AMR-A's tube and interior of the QUIK-TUBE was filled with dry, QUIKRETE, All-Purpose sand (part number 1152). Dry sand was chosen because of its uniformity and low specific heat capacity, thus ensuring that our approach quantified a "worst case" scenario with regard to temperature increase due to heat dissipation from the AMR-A. A pair of holes was drilled at three different levels, and on opposing sides of the QUIK-TUBE. The location of these holes coincided with the AMR-A camera's home position (top), mid-level of the AMR-A's tube (middle) and the lowest possible camera scanning level achieved by the AMR-A (bottom; Figure 2). One four-Wire Platinum Resistance Thermometer (100 Ω PRT; Thermometrics Inc., Northridge, CA, USA) was inserted into each hole, thus allowing each PRT to reside perpendicular to the AMR-A's tube. At each level, the tip of one PRT was positioned 0.5 cm away from the edge of the AMR-A tube. This suite of 6 PRTs remained fixed for this entire heat dissipation test (*A*through *F* in Figure 2). We then positioned another suite of 6 PRTs at the same locations and in the same manner, but inserted them at constant distances of 7.0, 3.0, and 2.0 cm from the AMR-A's tube during three sequential tests, respectively. We then mounted two PRTs 0.5 cm from the AMR-A's tube at heights of 10 and 30 cm above the surface of the sand to measure temperature changes of ambient air near the AMR-A's electrical components and motor. Prior to testing, all PRTs were calibrated against NIST's standards (*i.e.*, the triple point of mercury and water, and melting point of gallium) and uncertainty analyses were generated following JCGM [26]. Data from these fourteen, calibrated, PRTs were acquired with a datalogger (CR3000, Campbell Scientific Inc., Logan, UT, USA) at 0.1 Hz. Before testing began the QUIK-TUBE and AMR-A were collectively tilted at an angle of 60° from horizontal (plane) to mimic the angle minirhizotrons are usually installed in the field [22]. This allowed our setup to mimic the dynamics of heat flow similar to those encountered in the field.

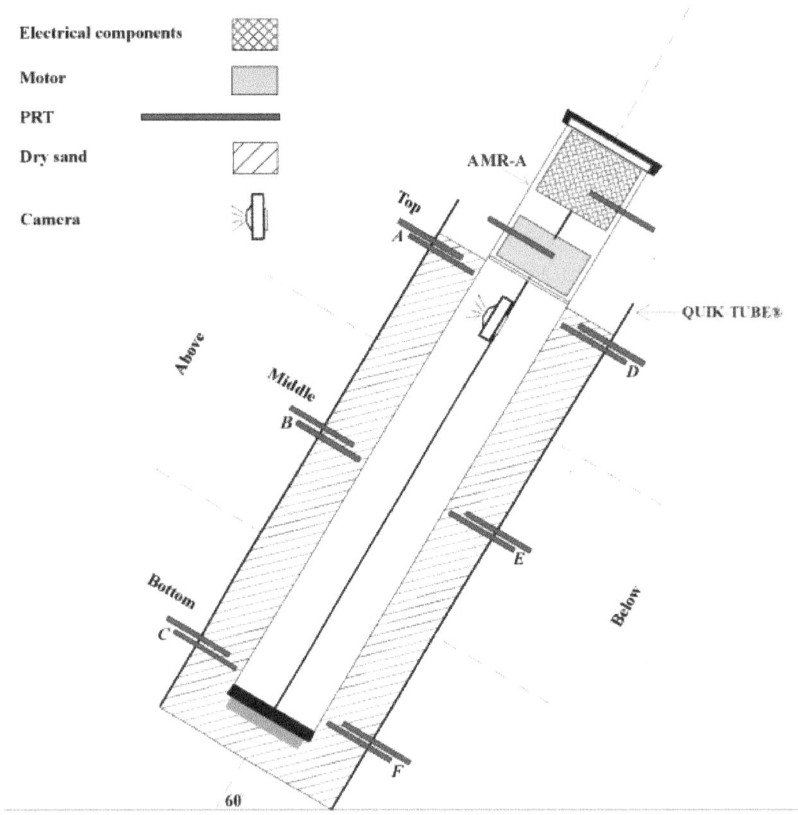

Figure 2. Experimental design to determine heat dissipation. A cross-section schematic of the experimental design used to assess heat dissipation (not to scale) for the AMR-A. The three depths: *Top*, *Middle*, and *Bottom*, correspond to depths of 5, 48, and 86 cm below the sand surface, respectively. The locations of the PRTs residing 0.5 cm from the minirhizotron are denoted by letters *A*through *F*, and correspond to the results shown in Figure 5. The LED lights reside on the body of the camera. The 60° angle refers to the overall installation relative to the horizontal (plane).

Three, individual, full-tube scans were conducted over a ten-day period. During testing, the AMR-A operated with manufacturer-specified, default camera settings (Table 2). Upon completion of each full-tube scan, the camera of the AMR-A was programmed to return to its home position and was powered down. We allowed for the thermal mass of the sand/tube assembly to equilibrate with ambient conditions for a minimum of 48 hours between each test scans. Mean, ambient lab temperature was 23.21±0.21°C (mean ± 1 SD).

Temperature data were split into three different groups, one for each test. Temperature change at each location was quantified relative to the temperature of the respective PRT at the start time of each full-tube scan.

RESULTS AND DISCUSSION

A Caveat

Because we did not test a population of minirhizotron cameras, we cannot rule out that our findings are a function of camera-specific characteristics. We did, however, receive assurances from the manufacturers that the tested cameras were representative of a larger population. Two separate CI-600 In-Situ Root Imagers were used during testing. Both experienced mechanical failures that required replacement or manufacturer repair.

Spatial Uncertainties of Camera Positioning

Both the repeatability and reproducibility of the AMR-A camera's position were significantly better than that of the CI- 600 (Table 6). Regarding reproducibility, the radial and vertical uncertainties of the CI-600 camera (test C1) were *two to three orders of magnitude larger*than the radial and vertical uncertainties of the AMR-A's camera (*i.e.*, A1, and A2). The larger spatial uncertainty of the CI-600's camera position for test C1 is most likely a result of the extraction and replacement of the camera between subsequent scans, a task that mimics how the CI-600 is actually used in the field. The discrepancies of spatial uncertainties for tests A1 and A2 are most likely due to the camera's ability to consistently return to the home position between subsequent scans. In regards to repeatability, the differences between the spatial camera uncertainty of tests A3 and C2 were not as large as those of the reproducibility tests. However, the uncertainties quantified during test C2 were still larger in the radial and vertical dimensions when compared to test A3 (see Table 6). The differences in spatial uncertainties between these two cameras were most likely a result of the operational characteristics of the minirhizotrons, *i.e.*, automated vs. manual camera positioning. That said, we also interpret the large difference between the spatial uncertainties of camera location during tests C1 and C2, is due to the CI-600's removal and replacement from the tube. In other words, the influence of human sources of error is evident in test C1, and the potential magnitude of this error can be quite large. When human interaction was completely removed from testing (*i.e.*, C2) results improved (Table 6).

Table 6. Precision of minirhizotron camera location for each sampling method; values are provided as *one standard deviation*.

Test	Precision	
	Radial (degrees)	Vertical (μm)
A1	0.12	24.87
A2	0.01	4.32
A3	0.01	38.37
C1	13.72	1942.23
C2	0.22	84.06

doi:10.1371/journal.pone.0112362.t006

Human operation and interaction with the technology is an essential aspect of the CI-600 performance. The CI-600 camera needs to be physically moved among field-deployed tubes and moved to different depths of a tube during sampling. Although such an approach can be beneficial in terms of cost, it leads to additional uncertainties. In working with the C1-600, precautions were taken to minimize misalignments of the camera with respect to a reference point at the tube's inlet, as recommended by CID-BioSience Inc. [25]. We assume that our carefully controlled laboratory conditions would result in performance superior to those obtained under field conditions.

An underlying goal was to provide a traceable method to assure the same area of roots is imaged across successive sampling intervals. One solution is creating reference points along the tube via indexed marks or etchings [32], [55]. Given the large spatial uncertainties in the CI-600 camera found in this study (Table 6), the CI-600 is currently incapable of imaging the same area of root stocks at sequential sampling intervals without the use of etchings or reference points along the tube. Providing such indexed etchings to all minirhizotron tubes, including the AMR-A, provides the ability to assess the instrument's spatial uncertainty *a posteri*, as well as manage any changes that occur over time, *e.g.*, mechanical wear. Etchings on the tube would also aid in the alignment of neighboring images when producing a larger ensemble of images, however, estimating the uncertainties of combining neighboring images into a larger mosaic were outside the scope of this study.

Digital Imaging Performance

Camera Sensitivity

The AMR-A was capable of resolving smaller objects than the CI-600. The CI-600 was able to resolve line widths at 100.15±1.38 μm, but was unable to resolve line widths at 73.81±1.38 μm. Since the minirhizotron cameras were calibrated at points, we cannot state (empirically) the exact location where the CI-600 reached its resolvable limit, however, we empirically bound its resolvable limit between 72.43 and 101.53 μm. Vamerali *et al.* [56]found that at least two pixels are needed to resolve the diameter of an object. Thus, it is reasonable to conclude that the resolvable limit of the CI-600's camera is 84.6 μm, *i.e.*, the width of two of its pixels. The ARM-A camera's resolvable limit was unable to be empirically quantified because the camera was able to resolve the narrowest line widths, 39.29±1.38 μm, of the truncated fan pattern. Provided the same reasoning as above, we conclude that the resolvable limit of the AMR-A is 9.4 μm.

Although fine-root diameters can be resolved with two pixels, this does not guarantee that fine-roots of 84.6 μm (CI-600), and 9.4 μm (AMR-A) will be resolvable in the field with varying environmental conditions, root orientations, and potential camera photocell degradation. This is also true if the object is not aligned with the pixels themselves. Zobel[23] states that, ideally, pixel size should be 25% of the diameter of the smallest root being imaged. When we follow Zobel's [23] research and incorporate our findings, the conservative resolvable limits of the CI-600 and AMR-A for operational use in the field would be 169.2 μm and 18.8 μm, respectively (with the given instrument settings used in this study, Table 2). As noted previously, Villordon *et al.* [20], underestimated root quantity using a scanner based minirhizotron (*i.e.*, the CI-600). Given the CI-600 settings that the researchers utilized (*i.e.*, 78 dots (d) cm^{-1} or ~8 p mm^{-1}, with pixel sizes of 127×127 μm), the resolvable limit using the Rayleigh Criterion would be 254 μm. Applying Zobel's [23] findings (above) to the research of Villordon *et al.* [20] would result in fine-roots with diameters <508 μm to go virtually undetected; this may provide insight as to why root quantity was underestimated, and stresses the importance of knowing the limits of digital imagery prior to field use.

Neighboring Objects of Different Sizes

Mean, fine-root diameters have been estimated globally as 220, 440, and 580 μm for grasses, shrubs, and trees, respectively [57], while the range of fine-root diameters are often defined as 0–3000 μm [8], [34], [58], [59], and fungal hyphae diameters range from ~2–80 μm [60]. Given that fine-root diameters can be quite small, argues that the resolvable limit should be reported for such studies. This is the first study to report a defensible and traceable means to determine the resolvable limit of current, commercially available, minirhizotron cameras.

Interestingly, we found a change in the cameras› responses to contrast. The signals of the black line segments became progressively more saturated as the test lines became narrowed. In other words, the signals of the black line segments became larger, *i.e.*, moving away from the lower end of the 0–255 intensity range, and the contrast between the black and white line segments decreased. At a line width of 409.63±2.22 μm the mean pixel intensities were 133.02±2.39 and 121.51±1.02, as imaged by the CI-600 and AMR-A, respectively. At a line width of 194.06±1.64 μm the mean pixel intensities were 146.20±3.53 and 139.25±1.41, as imaged by the CI-600 and AMR-A. We interpret the change in the cameras' abilities to consistently detect contrast to i) the backscattering of light caused by the increased area of white background surrounding the truncated fan pattern as it narrowed, and the ii) signal averaging inherent in the pixelation process. It may also be a result of the analysis software's ability (in this case, IDL) to convert color images to grayscale. Our finding poses a challenge, as it suggests that the two cameras have difficultly resolving neighboring objects of different sizes, *i.e.*, they may have difficulty resolving and quantifying neighboring fine-roots with different colors or brightness, or when there is a range of root diameters.

Root Diameter Measurements

Prior to calibration both minirhizotrons exhibited measurement bias when quantifying root diameter. Using the 250 threshold method, the AMR-A overestimated (*i.e.*, a positive bias) root diameter by an average of 32.03±3.06 μm (Figure 3a), while the CI-600 overestimated by an average of 117.16±13.97 μm (Figure 3c). Using the FWHM method, the AMR-A underestimated (*i.e.*, a negative bias) root diameter by an average of 15.51±12.50 μm (Figure 3b), while the CI-600 underestimated, on average, by 12.47±7.68 μm (Figure 3d). At first glance it may seem that using the FWHM method yielded better results because the absolute bias is smaller than that of the 250 method. Interestingly, however, using the FWHM method, the AMR-A camera grossly underestimated approximately 6% (*i.e.*, 6 of 101) of the samples and skewed the dataset; the result of which was reflected not only in the average systematic bias of -15.51 μm, but also in the large standard error of ±12.50 μm. However, these same 6 samples (line widths) were not significantly different than the other 95 samples when using the signal threshold of 250. The results of the FWHM test suggest a skewed distribution and a potential systematic bias if the products are used for turnover and below ground productivity estimates. If the degree of systematic bias is constant, then the delta calculation of root growth and/or senescence between sequential images in time will be small. If the bias is not constant, the contributing uncertainties will be difficult to quantify over time.

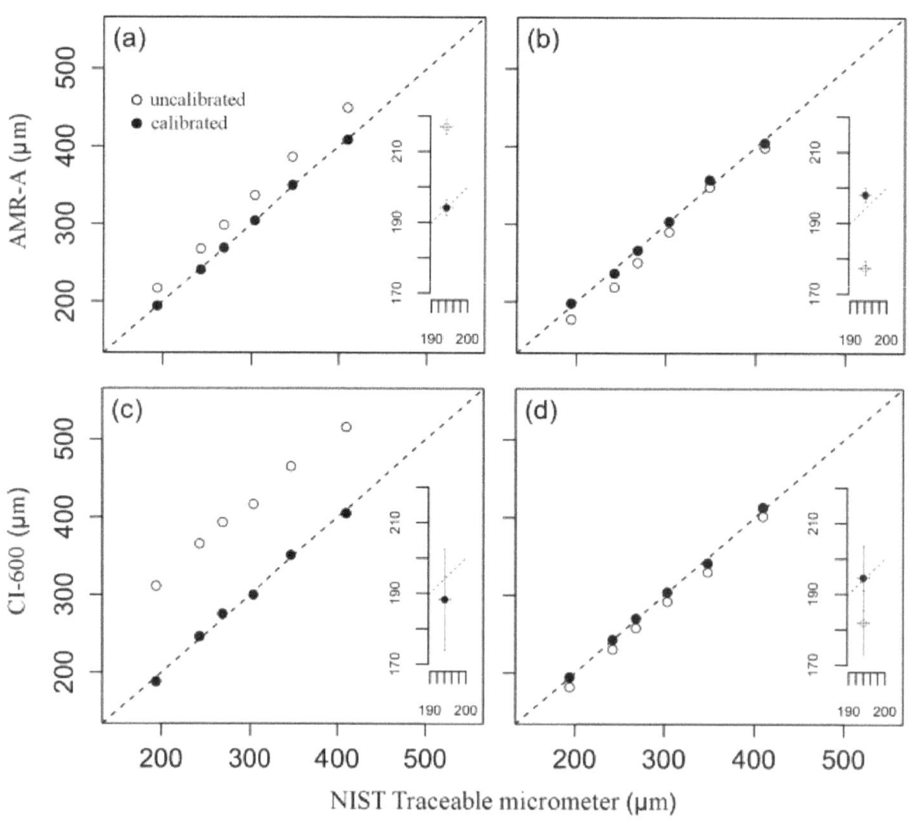

Figure 3. Line widths as measured by both minirhizotrons. Estimated line widths as determined by both minirhizotrons cameras against those of the NIST traceable micrometer. Results of the AMR-A are shown in (a) using the 250 pixel intensity threshold ($n = 101$), and (b) using the FWHM threshold ($n = 101$). Results of the CI-600 are shown in (c) using the 250 pixel intensity threshold ($n = 114$), and (d) using the FWHM threshold ($n = 120$). A 1:1 line is shown on each graph. Inset plots are provided at the 194.06±1.64 μm calibration point to emphasize the magnitude of random uncertainty and show that calibration can correct for bias, but not random uncertainty. Error bars are given as ±2 SE for uncalibrated data and $\pm U_{95}(y)$ for calibrated data.

The ability of each minirhizotron camera to quantify root diameter was greatly improved after calibration. The systematic biases of both cameras were corrected and resultant expanded uncertainties for both minirhizotron cameras using either analysis method reduced to within ±17.00 µm of the estimated "truth". The largest fraction of the expanded uncertainty for the calibrated data resulted from the reproducibility of the cameras' abilities to quantify root diameter. Calibration can correct bias, but it cannot mitigate the estimate of uncertainty in the form of repeatability and/or reproducibility (see inset plots of Figure 3).

Root Color Measurements

When compared to one another, both minirhizotrons exhibited significant differences in quantifying the sRGB vector intensities of each of the eight colors (Table 7, Table 8). At first, we operated using the manufacturer-specified default settings, and three of the color patches: *magenta*, *yellow*, and *amber*, imaged by the AMR-A were over-exposed and all sRGB vectors were 255, *i.e.*, the highest possible pixel intensity. To mitigate over-saturation, the exposure of the camera was adjusted. We empirically determined that the AMR-A was capable of quantifying all eight colors (within reason) when operating at a lower camera exposure of 12, (*i.e.*, not the recommended, default exposure; Table 7). Moreover, many of the AMR-A images were also prone to areas of overexposure in the top left corner of each image, regardless of which exposure was used. The CI-600 also exhibited signs of over-saturation while operating at default settings. Specifically, the R vectors of *magenta*, *yellow*, and *amber*, all registered 255 (Table 8). Although we were aware of this over-saturation, all color characterization tests of the CI-600 were completed using default settings because the CI-600 encountered systematic communication problems with its software during testing, and we were unable to alter the settings.

Table 7. Mean sRGB values (and expanded uncertainties) as measured by the AMR-A.

Color	R	±2SE (R)	G	±2SE (G)	B	±2SE (B)
Cyan	0	N/A	107.529	0.059	244.23	0.026
Magenta	206.423	0.035	123.219	0.048	200.561	0.041
Yellow	232.684	0.022	251.412	0.019	17.079	0.127
Amber	231.734	0.024	234.742	0.011	202.499	0.033
Red	130.17	0.048	0	N/A	0	N/A
Green	0	N/A	89.485	0.061	23.089	0.089
Blue	0	N/A	0	N/A	193.347	0.054
White	245.703	0.025	255	N/A	255	N/A

Expanded uncertainties represent the repeatability of the camera for the specific color patch. Uncertainties for values at the limits of the sRGB spectrum are not provided. $n = 40{,}805$ per color patch.
doi:10.1371/journal.pone.0112362.t007

Table 8. Mean sRGB values (and expanded uncertainties) as measured by the CI-600.

Color	R	±2SE (R)	G	±2SE (G)	B	±2SE (B)
Cyan	90.406	0.026	179.614	0.013	217.403	0.013
Magenta	255	N/A	167.971	0.012	200.864	0.011
Yellow	255	N/A	249.617	0.013	177.415	0.019
Amber	255	N/A	232.644	0.025	214.657	0.033
Red	231.103	0.015	95.250	0.027	95.827	0.029
Green	87.799	0.024	171.210	0.011	119.531	0.015
Blue	78.508	0.047	128.516	0.024	188.291	0.014
White	255	N/A	255	N/A	255	N/A

Expanded uncertainties represent the repeatability of the camera for the specific color patch. Uncertainties for values at the limits of the sRGB spectrum are not provided. $n = 33{,}836$ per color patch.
doi:10.1371/journal.pone.0112362.t008

Both minirhizotron cameras had the ability to repeatedly image the same color with a high degree of precision. The largest estimate of AMR-A imprecision was at 0.127, which was at the B vector of the *yellow* color patch. In terms of relative uncertainty, this result equates to ~0.7%, *i.e.*, the signal-to-noise ratio is 99.3:0.7% (standard error at 95% confidence level). The largest estimate of imprecision in the CI-600, was 0.06% of the signal, which was found at the R vector of the blue color patch. Thus, the signal-to-noise ratio when imaging the eight colors of the specified target was better with the CI-600. But because we did not test over a range of exposures, different lighting etc., we cannot be conclusive if this result is consistent across all colors, or if this is indicative of a population of sensors, but if it is important to the end-user, it should be examined further.

A noted difference among the device-dependent color vectors imaged by the AMR-A and CI-600 was expected. Characterizing the device-dependent sRGB color spaces to the device-independent chromaticity coordinates provided a means by which root colors can be quantified and compared among a group of minirhizotrons with a known accuracy (Table 9;Figure 4). Given the results found here and elsewhere [42], [48]–[50], we recommend that minirhizotron cameras be characterized prior to field deployment with a traceable color test target using the approach presented here and by others [26], [44], [45]. We note that the linear characterization used here may result in different response functions when tested with different cameras (photocells) over a broader color spectrum. The use of colorimetric cameras, and/or a higher order, non-linear characterization, as well as characterizing with a test card comprised of *hundreds* of colors should be explored further [48]–[50]. The resultant coefficients from characterizations should be applied to minirhizotron cameras prior to any type of color analysis. This will allow for traceable quantification of color and will also facilitate estimation of root age and health. We recommend that minirhizotron cameras' are also periodically validated while in the field, as this will aid in quantifying color drift of the camera and photocell degradation over time. Such a task can be completed by installing a color test chart within the minirhizotron tube, preferably at the bottom as to avoid direct interaction with sunlight, and imaging the chart on a periodic basis. Lastly, and possibly most importantly, the natural variation in species-specific relationships between root color and health are likely large, and quite possibly the same magnitude or larger than the variation in color exhibited by these technologies. Only once species and site specific tests are conducted relating root health to chromaticity, do we advise that the classification of root age and or health be defined by chromaticity coordinates. In all cases, however, we highly discourage classifying root age and or health by qualitative, loose nomenclature, such as *white*, *brown*, *cream*, or *black*. This method should also be extended to other camera-based phenological measures and the like.

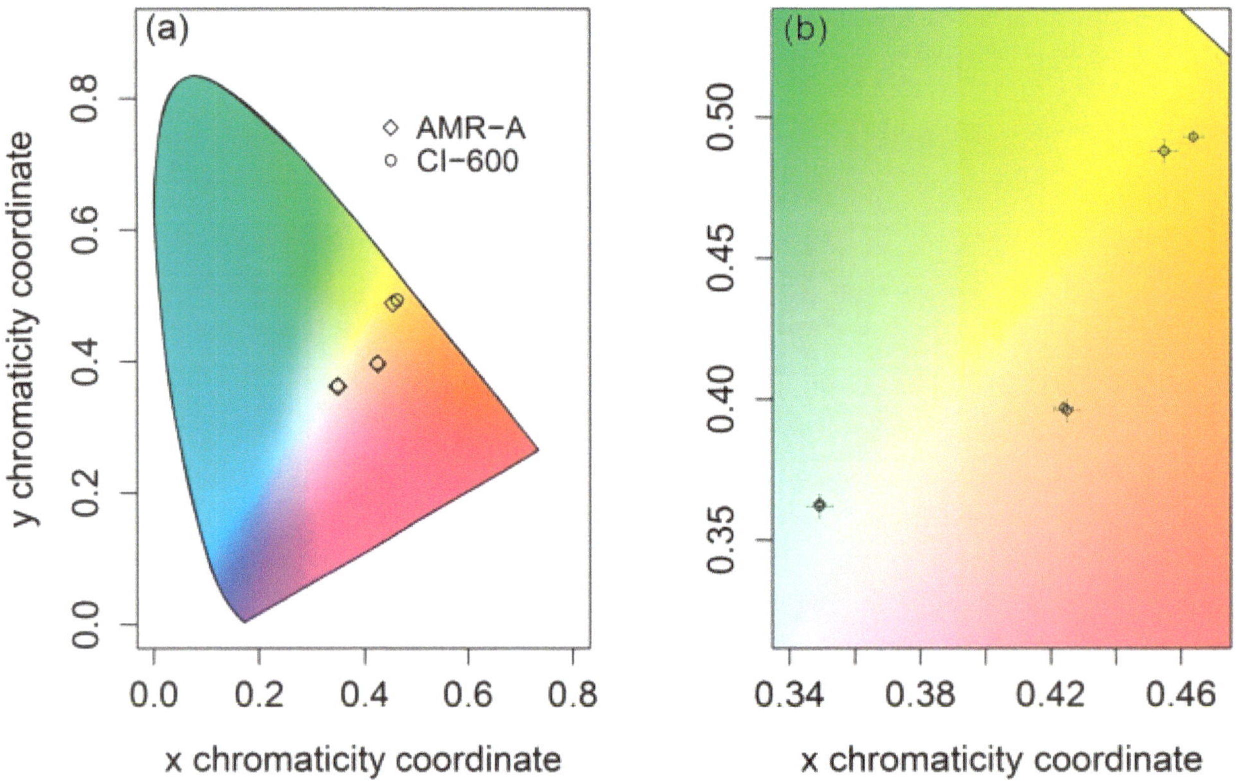

Figure 4. Characterized CIE chromaticity coordinates. CIE chromaticity coordinates of the (a) three characterization points relative to the entire chromaticity coordinate space (as denoted by the horseshoe shaped outline), (b) a zoomed version of the same data in (a) that also depicts the expanded uncertainties of the three characterization points. Error bars are given as $\pm U_{95}(y)$.This figure is presented in addition to Table 9 to demonstrate the spatial (color-space) limitations of the linear characterization performed in this analysis. The overlaid color gamut is for illustrative purposes only.

Table 9. Mean, characterized chromatic coordinates (and expanded uncertainties) of each minirhizotron camera.

	AMR-A				CI-600			
Color	x	$\pm U_{95}(x)$	y	$\pm U_{95}(y)$	x	$\pm U_{95}(x)$	y	$\pm U_{95}(x)$
Yellow	0.455	0.004	0.488	0.004	0.464	0.003	0.493	0.002
Amber	0.425	0.004	0.396	0.004	0.424	0.003	0.397	0.002
White	0.349	0.004	0.362	0.004	0.349	0.002	0.363	0.002

doi:10.1371/journal.pone.0112362.t009

Heat Dissipation Estimates

When operational, the AMR-A increased temperatures in the environment immediately adjacent to its tube, and away from the tube to a distance of 7.0 cm at all measured depths. These temperature increases, however, were not uniform in time or space. The maximum and mean ambient air temperature increases near the AMR-A's motor (located 10 cm above the sand surface) were 6.74 °C and 3.29±0.05 °C, respectively. Similarly, the maximum and mean ambient air temperature increases near the AMR-A's electrical components (located 30 cm above the sand surface) were 9.36 °C and 7.5±0.05 °C, respectively. The largest temperature increases in the sand were found at shallower depths (*i.e.*, closest to the surface; *top* level), *above* (Figure 2), and at a distance of 0.5 cm from the AMR-A's tube (Figure 5). Specifically, the maximum and mean sand temperature increases at this location (point *A*), were 3.25 °C and 1.81±0.02 °C, respectively. The smallest temperature change occurred at the *bottom* level, *below* the AMR-A, and at a distance of 7.0 cm (not shown inFigure 5). The maximum temperature increase at this location was 0.22 °C. However, the mean temperature change at this location was negligible.

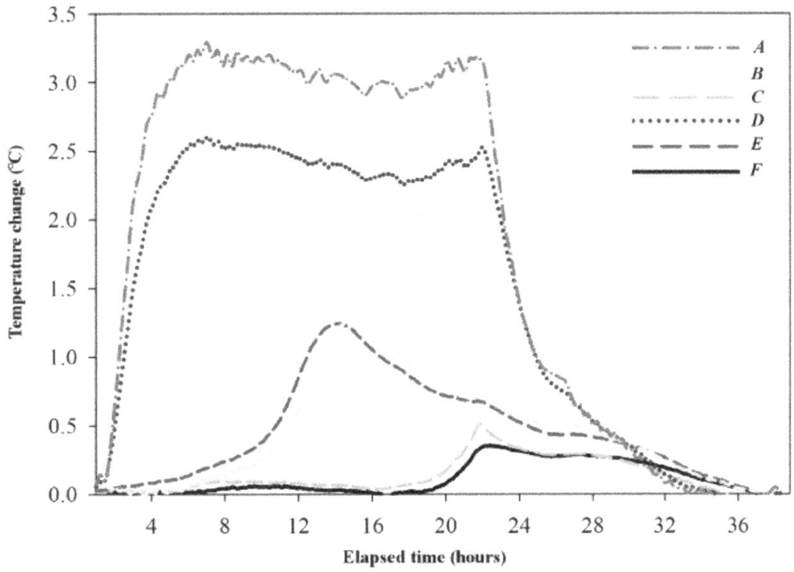

Figure 5. Time series of temperature change at six profile locations. Temperature measurements were made at the three depths (5 [top], 48 [middle], and 86 [bottom] cm) below the surface of the sand and at 0.5 cm away from the AMR-A's tube, the locations of the PRTs *A* through *F* are shown in Figure 2. Temperature change at each location was quantified relative to the temperature of the respective PRT at the start time of each full-tube scan.

The increases in temperatures were not transient, and occurred well before the camera passed a monitored area. Sand temperatures began increasing prior to the camera's passing at PRT locations, and continued to increase for a short period of time after the camera passed. Once reaching their maxima, temperatures persisted above pre-scan values for extended periods of time. For instance, sand temperatures at distances of 0.5 cm away from the AMR-A's tube remained above ambient levels for approximately 28, 23, and 15 hours once maximum temperature change occurred at the *top*, *middle* and *bottom*levels, respectively (Figure 5).

The motor, camera's LED lights, and electrical components of the AMR-A were the major sources of heat. The camera's LED lights, which were attached to the roving camera, were a continuous heat source within the tube. The motor and electronics, which were stationary, were a source of constant heat at the top of the tube. We assumed internal chimney effects within the minirhizotron tube also caused heat to convect to the highest section of tube. Hence, we infer that even if the camera was programmed to image a small and specific region (*i.e.*, not a full tube scan), temperatures generated by the camera's LED lights would rise within the tube, conduct through the AMR-A's tube and warm the surrounding soil.

Clearly, dry sand has a more similar heat capacity to soil than to air, and stores heat similar to that found in soil warming experiments [54], which are designed to alter the soil microclimate in the surrounding rhizosphere. In moist soils, the AMR-A would likely increase the soil vapor pressure and enhance the evaporation of the soil water content around the tube. Given the long operational time it takes the AMR-A to image an entire tube (duration of 25.08±0.43 hours observed during testing; mean ±1 SD), and output of heat from the instrument to the soil, it will likely alter the soil properties, respiration, and likely the measurement of representative root mass (and fine-root turnover) if measurements are conducted frequently, *i.e.*, daily, weekly, monthly or longer pending the ecosystem type.

CONCLUSIONS

Currently, minirhizotrons represent the best non-destructive method for measuring *in-situ*fine-root production, mortality, and turnover. The spatial heterogeneity of fine-root turnover however is typically large [61]–[63], difficult to quantify [64]–[66], and becomes a sample size problem [32], [67]–[69]. Determining seasonal and interannual variability, and long term trends, is a product of matching one's ability to detect a phenomenon with the spatial and temporal signal-to-noise of the phenomenon, in this case fine-root turnover. This is a particularly difficult task because we expect the behavior of fine-roots to change non-linearly in time and space with changes in climate, species composition, nutrient and water availabillty, etc. As we have shown here, if uncalibrated minirhizotrons are used to estimate standing stocks, the risk of improper quantification of fine-root turnover, combined with the amount of undectable roots using scanner-based technologies, have large implications to understand allocation patterns. Knowing the uncertainties of measurements *a priori* is becoming increasingly important as more and more Bayesian and data assimilation approaches are being used in modeling these processes.

Without a traceable and reproducible approach to quantify the measurement uncertainty of minirhizotron camera performance, the signal-to-noise ratio cannot be properly quantified. Once this ratio is quantified, root measurements made by minirhizotrons will be better understood and have increased scientific utilty. Being able to understand and reduce measurement uncertainties in minirhizotrons is key to monitoring root turnover over time and space with minirhizotrons.

Prior to this study no uniform and reproducible method for quantifying and comparing minirhizotron performance existed in the literature. To address this issue, we identified essential, objective, test parameters to assess the minirhizotron cameras' signal-to-noise ratio. We were able to quantify and compare the capabilities of manual and fully automated minirhizotrons to repeatedly image a test target in space, quantify root size and color, and dissipate heat. Because we estimated the signal-to-noise ratio these data can be used as a benchmark to generate sample size requirements given the expected signal-to-noise of fine-root turnover or other ecological processes.

Each minirhizotron camera tested has tradeoffs inherent in their hardware and operating procedures. This included the unavoidable presence of human error in the removal and replacement of the manual minirhizotron camera (CI-600), or the unintended heating of the soil environment (AMR-A). The potential heating effects associated with the AMR-A should, however, be weighed against the much greater sensitivity and repeatability afforded by a fully automated microscopic camera. Additionally, the benefit-to-cost ratio of using a portable camera that can be moved among multiple minirhizotron tubes, such as the CI-600, should be weighed against utilizing a non-portable camera, such as the AMR-A. Regardless, our results suggest that effects of the known, random and systematic uncertainties need to be taken into account when interpreting minirhizotron images and represent an opportunity for new technological advances to increase our knowledge of belowground processes.

In final recommendations; i) one should consider adopting standardized calibration methods (*i.e.*, JCGM [26], CIE [45]) of minirhizotron cameras prior to field deployment, and ii) we suggest that known, traceable targets be used in the calibration process and buried with the minirhizotron tubes. Imaging these targets before and after a full-tube scan would help inform the current state of camera health, as the size and color of the targets can be quantified over time and help post correct fine-root data for any optical drift inherent in the camera.

Lastly, the approaches used here are not just germane to minirhizotrons, but to all digital imaging devices used in the scientific process. Approaches and findings presented here have large relevance to other applications, for example, digital microscopy, phenological cameras, digital biodiversity archives, forensics, and others that also intentionally employ device-dependent color imaging.

ACKNOWLEDGMENTS

The Authors thank the two previous reviewers who helped the clarity of this manuscript. We extend thanks to M LeBlanc and M Pursley for calibrating the PRT sensors, and also to K Sacca and J Taylor for providing helpful insight regarding optical systems. Special thanks to J Csavina and S Streett for providing expertise in uncertainty analyses, L Goldman for graphic support, and also to K Sand for editorial assistance. We are grateful and appreciative of the assistance from M Taggart (RhizoSystems LLC), B Meyer (CID-BioScience Inc.), and G Reif (Applied Image Inc.). This paper would not have taken shape if it were not the guidance, lifetime work, and for many a conversation with leaders in the soils community, and to Albert Einstein who stated "… as far as the laws of mathematics refer to reality, they are not certain; and as far as they are certain, they do not refer to reality". Geometry and Experience, Lecture before the Prussian Academy of Sciences, January 27, 1921.

AUTHOR CONTRIBUTIONS

Conceived and designed the experiments: JAR MDS HWL EA. Performed the experiments: JAR MDS. Analyzed the data: JAR MDS HWL EA. Contributed reagents/materials/analysis tools: JAR MDS HWL EA. Wrote the paper: JAR MDS HWL EA.

REFERENCES

1. Cox TL, Hams WF, Asmus BS, Edwards NT (1978) The role of roots in biogeochemical cycles in an eastern deciduous forest. Pedobiologia 18: 264–271.
2. Pregitzer KS, Zak DR, Curtis PS, Kubiske ME, Teeri JA, et al. (1995) Atmospheric CO_2, soil nitrogen and turnover of fine roots. New Phytol 129: 579–585. doi: 10. 1111/j. 1469-8137. 1995. tb03025. x
3. Gill RA, Jackson RB (2000) Global patterns of root turnover for terrestrial ecosystems. New Phytol 147: 13–31. doi: 10. 1046/j. 1469-8137. 2000. 00681. x
4. Joslin JD, Henderson GS (1987) Organic matter and nutrients associated with fine-root production in a white oak stand. For Sci 33: 330–346.
5. Majdi H, Andersson P (2005) Fine root production and turnover in a Norway spruce stand in northern Sweeden: effects of nitrogen and water manipulation. Ecosyst 8: 191–199. doi: 10. 1007/s10021-004-0246-0
6. Ostertag R (2001) Effects of nitrogen and phosphorus availability on fine-root dynamics in Hawaiian montane forests. Ecol 82: 485–499. doi: 10. 2307/2679874
7. Ruess RW, Van Cleve K, Yarie J, Viereck LA (1996) Contributions of fine root production and turnover to the carbon and nitrogen cycling in taiga forests of the Alaskan Interior. Can J For Res 26: 1326–1336. doi: 10. 1139/x26-148
8. Majdi H, Pregitzer K, Morén AS, Nylund JE, Ågren GI (2005) Measuring fine root turnover in forest ecosystems. Plant Soil 276: 1–8. doi: 10. 1007/s11104-005-3104-8
9. Gaudinski JB, Trumbone SE, Davidson A, Cook AC, Markewitz D, et al. (2001) The age of fine-root carbon in three forests of the eastern United States measured by radiocarbon. Oecologia 129: 420–429.
10. Lukac M (2012) Fine root turnover, In: Mancuso S, editor. Measuring Roots: Springer, Berlin. pp. 363–373.
11. Majdi H (1996) Root sampling methods: applications and limitations of the minirhizotron technique. Plant Soil 185: 255–258. doi: 10. 1007/bf02257530
12. Joslin JD, Henderson GS (1982) A test of the budget method: a refined approach to measurement of the root

turnover, In: Muller RN, editor. Central Hardwood Forest Conference. pp. 220–228.

13. Kurz WA, Kimmins JP (1987) Analysis of error in methods used to determine fine root production in forest ecosystems: a simulation approach. Can J For Res 17: 909–912. doi: 10. 1139/x87-142

14. Sanantonio D, Grace JC (1987) Estimating fine-root production and turnover from biomass and decomposition data: a compartment flow model. Can J For Res 17: 900–908. doi: 10. 1139/x87-141

15. Bates GH (1937) A device for the observation of root growth in the soil. Nature 139: 966–967. doi: 10. 1038/139966b0

16. McMichael BL, Taylor HM (1987) Applications and limitations of rhizotrons and minirhizotrons, In: American Association of Agronomy, editors. Minirhizotron observation tubes: methods and applications for measuring rhizosphere dynamics, ASA Special Publication 50: 1–13. doi: 10. 2134/asaspecpub50. c1

17. Cheng W, Coleman DC, Box Jr JE (1991) Measuring root turnover with the minirhizotron technique. Agr Ecosyst Environ 34: 261–267. doi: 10. 1016/0167-8809(91)90113-c

18. Cheng W, Coleman DC, Box Jr JE (1990) Root dynamics, production and distribution in agroecosystems on the Georgia Piedmont using minirhizotrons. J Appl Ecol 27: 592–604. doi: 10. 2307/2404304

19. Hendrick RL, Pregitzer KS (1996) Temporal and depth-related patterns of fine root dynamics in northern hardwood forests. J Ecol 84: 167–176. doi: 10. 2307/2261352

20. Villordon A, LaBonte D, Solis J (2011) Using a scanner based minirhizotron system to characterize sweet potato adventitious root development during initial storage root bulking stage. Hortic Sci 46: 513–517.

21. Pierret A, Moran CJ, Doussan C (2005) Conventional detection methodology is limiting our ability to understand the roles and functions of fine roots. New Phytol 166: 967–980. doi: 10. 1111/j. 1469-8137. 2005. 01389. x

22. Johnson MG, Tingey DT, Phillips DL, Storm MJ (2001) Review: Advancing fine root research with minirhizotrons. Env Exp Bot 45: 263–289. doi: 10. 1016/ s0098-8472(01)00077-6

23. Zobel RW (2003) Sensitivity analysis of computer-based diameter measurement from digital images. Crop Sci 43: 583–591. doi: 10. 2135/cropsci2003. 0583

24. RhizoSystems LLC (2012) Specifications for the automated mini-rhizotron. Available: http://www. rhizosystems. com/Specifications. html. Accessed 10 April 2012.

25. CID Bio-Science Inc. (2012) In-Situ Root Imager CI-600 Instruction Manual. Available: http://www. cid-inc. com/docs/CI-600_Manual. pdf. Accessed 10 April 2012.

26. Joint Committee for Guides in Metrology (JCGM) (2008) Evaluation of measurement data – Guide to the expression of uncertainty in measurement. 120 p.

27. Joint Committee for Guides in Metrology (JCGM) (2012) International vocabulary of metrology – Basic and general concepts and associated terms (VIM). 3rd Edition. 92 p.

28. Hecht E (2002) Optics. Boston: Addison-Wesley Longman. 680 p.

29. Wilson JD (1990) College Physics. Englewood Cliffs: Prentice-Hall. 875 p.

30. Willink R (2007) A generalization of the Welch-Satterwaithe formula for use with correlated uncertainty components. Metrologia 44: 340–349. doi: 10. 1088/0026-1394/44/5/010

31. Ballico M (2000) Limitations of the Welch-Satterthwaite approximation for measurement uncertainty calculations. Metrologia 37: 61–70. doi: 10. 1088/0026-1394/37/1/8

32. Hendrick RL, Pregitzer KS (1992) The demography of fine roots in a northern hardwood forest. Ecol 73: 1094–1104. doi: 10. 2307/1940183

33. Research Systems Inc. (RSI) (2004) Image Processing in IDL. Available:http://vis. lbl. gov/NERSC/Software/idl/ help6. 1/image. pdf. Accessed 1 June 2012

34. Bauhus J, Messier C (1999) Evaluation of fine root length and diameter measurements obtained using RHIZO image analysis. J Agron 91: 142–147. doi: 10. 2134/agronj1999. 00021962009100010022x

35. Jonkman JEN, Swoger J, Kress H, Rohrbach A, Stelzer EHK (2003) Resolution in optical microscopy, In: Marriot G, Parker I, editors, Methods in Enzymology: Biophotonics Part A. Elsevier Science. pp. 416–446.

36. Dannoura M, Kominami Y, Oguma H, Kanazawa Y (2008) The development of an optical scanner method for observation of plant root dynamics. Plantroot 2: 14–18. doi: 10. 3117/plantroot. 2. 14

37. Comas LH, Eissenstat DM, Lasko AN (2000) Assessing root death and root system dynamics in a study of grape canopy pruning. New Phytol 147: 171–178. doi: 10. 1046/j. 1469-8137. 2000. 00679. x

38. Wells CE, Eissenstat DM (2001) Marked differences in survivorship among apple roots of different diameters. Ecol 82: 882–892. doi: 10. 2307/2680206

39. Wang Z, Burch WH, Mou P, Jones RH, Mitchell RJ (1995) Accuracy of visible and ultraviolet light for estimating live root proportions with minirhizotrons. Ecol 76: 2230–2334. doi: 10. 2307/1941705

40. Strutt J W (1871) Some experiments on colour. Nature 3: 234–236. doi: 10. 1038/003234a0

41. Hong G, Luo MR, Rhodes PA (2001) A study of digital camera colorimetric characterization based on polynomial modeling. Color Res Appl 26: 76–84. doi: 10. 1002/1520-6378(200102)26:1<76::aid-col8>3. 0. co;2-3

42. Ilie A, Welch G (2005) Ensuring color consistency across multiple cameras. Proc. Conf. of the tenth IEEE international conference on computer vision 2: 1268–1275. doi: 10. 1109/iccv. 2005. 88

43. Gardner JL (2000) Uncertainty estimation in colour measurement. Col Res Appl 25: 349–355. doi: 10.

1002/1520-6378(200010)25:5<349::aid-col5>3.3. co;2-e

44. Early EA, Nadal ME (2004) Uncertainty analysis for reflectance colorimetry. Col Res Appl 29: 205–216. doi: 10. 1002/col. 20006

45. International Commission on Illumination (CIE) (2004) Technical report: colorimetry. 3rd Ed. 75 p.

46. Sándor N, Ondró T, Schanda J (2005) Spectral interpolation errors. Col Res Appl 30: 348–353. doi: 10. 1002/col. 20136

47. American Society for Testing and Materials (ASTM) (1999) Standard practice for computing the colors of objects by using the CIE system, E 308. 32 p.

48. Johnson T (1996) Methods for characterizing colour scanners and digital cameras. Displays 14: 183–191. doi: 10. 1016/0141-9382(96)01012-8

49. Hung PC (1993) Colorimetric calibration in electronic imaging devices using a look up table model and interpolations. J Electron Imaging 2: 53–61. doi: 10. 1117/12. 132391

50. Hong G, Luo MR, Rhodes PA (2001) A study of digital camera colorimetric characterization based on polynomial modeling. Col Res Appl 26: 76–84. doi: 10. 1002/1520-6378(200102)26:1<76::aid-col8>3. 0. co;2-3

51. Lloyd J, Taylor JA (1994) On the temperature dependence of soil respiration. Funct Ecol 8: 315–323. doi: 10. 2307/2389824

52. Ryan MG (1991) The effects of climate change on plant respiration. Ecol Appl 1: 157–167. doi: 10. 2307/1941808

53. Starr G, Staudhammer CL, Loescher HW, Mitchell R, Whelan A, et al. . (2014) Fire's role in Longleaf pine forest carbon dynamics: Evidence of resiliency in physiological estimates following prescribed fire. New Forests (in press).

54. Rustad LE, Campbell JL, Marion GM, Norby RJ, Mitchell MJ, et al. (2001) A Meta-analysis of the response of soil respiration, net nitrogen mineralization, and aboveground plant growth to experimental ecosystem warming. Oceologia 126: 543–562. doi: 10. 1007/s004420000544

55. Weber EP, Day FP (1996) The effect of nitrogen fertilization on the phenology of roots in a barrier island sand dune community. Plant Soil 182: 139–148. doi: 10. 1007/bf00011002

56. Vamerali T, Bandiera M, Mosca G (2012) Minirhizotrons in modern root studies, In: Mancuso S, editor. Measuring Roots: Springer, Berlin. pp. 341–362.

57. Jackson RB, Mooney HA, Schulze E-D (1997) A global budget for fine root biomass, surface area, and nutrient contents. Proc. Natl. Acad. Sci. 94: 7362–7366. doi: 10. 1073/pnas. 94. 14. 7362

58. McClaugherty CA, Aber JD, Melillo JM (1982) The role of fine roots in the organic matter and nitrogen budgets of two forested systems. Ecol. 63: 1481–1490. doi: 10. 2307/1938874

59. Kucbel S, Jalovair P, Špisšák J (2011) Quantity, vertical distribution and morphology of fine roots in Norway spruce stands with different stem density. Plant Root. 5: 46–55. doi: 10. 3117/plantroot. 5. 46

60. Swift MJ, Heal OW, Anderson JM (1979) Decomposition in Terrestrial Ecosystems. University of California Press, Berkeley.

61. Comas LH, Bauerle TL, Eissenstat DM (2010) Biological and environmental factors controlling root dynamics and function: Effects of root ageing and soil moisture. Aust J Grape Wine R 16: 131–137. doi: 10. 1111/j. 1755-0238. 2009. 00078. x

62. Comas LH, Anderson LJ, Dunst RM, Lakso AN, Eissenstat DM (2005) Canopy and environmental control of root dynamics in a longterm study of 'Concord' grape. New Phytol 167: 829–840. doi: 10. 1111/j. 1469-8137. 2005. 01456. x

63. Norby RJ, Ledford J, Reilly CD, Miller NE, O'Neill EG (2004) Fine-root production dominates response of a deciduous forest to atmospheric CO2 enrichment. Proc National Academy of Sciences, USA 101: 9689–9693. doi: 10. 1073/pnas. 0403491101

64. Fahey TJ, Bledsoe CS, Day FP, Ruess RW, Smucker AJM (1999) Fine root production and demography, In: Robertson GP, Coleman DC, Bledsoe CS, Sollins P, editors. Standard Soil Methods for Long-Term Ecological Research, Oxford University Press, Oxford, pp. 437–455.

65. Jackson RB, Canadell J, Ehleringer JR, Mooney HA, Sala OE, et al. (1996) A global analysis of root distributions for terrestrial biomes. Oecologia 108: 389–411. doi: 10. 1007/bf00333714

66. Vargas R, Allen MF (2008) Dynamics of fine root, fungal rhizomorphs, and soil respiration in a mixed temperate forest: Integrating sensors and observations. Vadose Zone J 7: 1055–1064. doi: 10. 2136/vzj2007. 0138

67. Fitter AH, Graves JD, Self GK, Brown TK, Bogie DS, et al. (1998) Root production, turnover and respiration under two grassland types along an altitudinal gradient: influence of temperature and solar radiation. Oecologia 114: 20–30. doi: 10. 1007/s004420050415

68. Loescher HW, Law BE, Mahrt L, Hollinger DY, Campbell JL, et al. . (2006) Uncertainties in, and interpretation of carbon flux estimates using the eddy covariance technique. J. Geophys. Res. -Atmos 111: D21S90, 1–19.

69. Vargas R, Allen MF (2008) Environmental controls and the influence of vegetation type, fine roots and rhizomorphs on diel and seasonal variation in soil respiration. New Phytol 179: 460–471. doi: 10. 1111/j. 1469-8137. 2008. 02481. x

CHAPTER 10

EVALUATING THE GOOD ONTOLOGY DESIGN GUIDELINE (GOODOD) WITH THE ONTOLOGY QUALITY REQUIREMENTS AND EVALUATION METHOD AND METRICS (OQUARE)

Astrid Duque-Ramos[1], Martin Boeker[2], Ludger Jansen[3], Stefan Schulz[4], Miguela Iniesta[5], Jesualdo Tomás Ferna´ndez-Breis[1]

[1] Departamento de Informa´tica y Sistemas, Facultad de Informa´tica, Universidad de Murcia, Murcia, Spain

[2] Department of Medical Biometry and Medical Informatics, University of Freiburg, Freiburg, Germany

[3] Department of Philosophy, University of Muenster, Muenster, Germany

[4] Institute of Medical Informatics, Statistics and Documentation Medical University of Graz, Graz, Austria

[5] Departamento de Estadı´stica e Investigacio´n Operativa, Universidad de Murcia, Murcia, Spain

ABSTRACT

Objective

To (1) evaluate the GoodOD guideline for ontology development by applying the OQuaRE evaluation method and metrics to the ontology artefacts that were produced by students in a randomized controlled trial, and (2) informally compare the OQuaRE evaluation method with gold standard and competency questions based evaluation methods, respectively.

Background

In the last decades many methods for ontology construction and ontology evaluation have been proposed. However, none of them has become a standard and there is no empirical evidence of comparative evaluation of such methods. This paper brings together GoodOD and OQuaRE. GoodOD is a guideline for developing robust ontologies. It was previously evaluated in a randomized controlled trial employing metrics based on gold standard ontologies and competency questions as outcome parameters. OQuaRE is a method for ontology quality evaluation which adapts the SQuaRE standard for software product quality to ontologies and has been successfully used for evaluating the quality of ontologies.

Methods

In this paper, we evaluate the effect of training in ontology construction based on the GoodOD guideline within the OQuaRE quality evaluation framework and compare the results with those obtained for the previous studies based on the same data.

Citation: Duque-Ramos A, Boeker M, Jansen L, Schulz S, Iniesta M, Fernández-Breis JT (2014) Evaluating the Good Ontology Design Guideline (GoodOD) with the Ontology Quality Requirements and Evaluation Method and Metrics (OQuaRE). PLoS ONE 9(8): e104463. doi:10.1371/journal.pone.0104463.

Results

Our results show a significant effect of the GoodOD training over developed ontologies by topics: (a) a highly significant effect was detected in three topics from the analysis of the ontologies of untrained and trained students; (b) both positive and negative training effects with respect to the gold standard were found for five topics.

Conclusion

The GoodOD guideline had a significant effect over the quality of the ontologies developed. Our results show that GoodOD ontologies can be effectively evaluated using OQuaRE and that OQuaRE is able to provide additional useful information about the quality of the GoodOD ontologies.

INTRODUCTION

In recent years, ontologies have been successfully applied in different domains including e-commerce [1], biomedicine [2], [3], e-learning [4] or geospatial data [5]. Their success is based mainly on the provision of a well-structured list of terms that are needed to describe a specific domain. Most ontology development efforts have required not only the participation of ontology engineers but also of domain experts. However, the quality of ontologies varies widely due to absent integration of one or more of such expert competencies [6]. Different kinds of quality indicators of ontologies are affected: structural, logical, correct representation of domain knowledge and coverage.

As engineering discipline, the ontology development requires the existence and application of methodologies and standards. In the last decades, different processes, strategies, and ontology development methods have been proposed. Among the methods proposed in the nineties we can highlight TOVE (TOronto Virtual Enterprise) [7], the Enterprise Model Approach [8], or Methontology [9]. More recently, approaches based on best practices like Ontology Design Patterns (http://ontologydesignpatterns.org), principles like the OBO Principles (http://www.obofoundry.org/crit.shtml) or guidelines like GoodOD [10] have been proposed.

Apart from the availability of development methodologies, measuring the quality of the resulting ontologies is necessary in order to monitor to which extent and how good methodologies, practices and guidelines are being applied. Consequently, methods for ontology evaluation have been developed by the ontology community, which can, roughly, be divided into three groups: ontology ranking [11]–[13], formal correctness of the ontology contents [14]–[17]; and ontology quality frameworks [18]–[22].

Despite the differences between these groups, many of the approaches share some evaluation instruments like the use of quality models or metrics. Some methods use a gold standard to which the ontology is compared using ontology similarity metrics [23]–[25]. Gold standards are an important resource, but they are rarely available, especially for those domains for which new ontologies are developed.

Another evaluation approach is the use of competency questions, which can be understood as the formulation of ontology requirements as questions, for which correct answers are created by domain experts. A good ontology has to provide the correct answers to these questions with the help of automated reasoning [26]. This technique has also been mentioned by ontology evaluation [27] and construction [28] approaches. The main reason for this is that ontology development and evaluation methods are related. The final report of the Ontology Summit 2013 [29] proposes a method for developing and evaluating ontologies. The method focuses on the requirements traceability from development life cycle to quality evaluation. Five ontology quality characteristics were identified and combined in a model for ontology life cycle [29]: Requirements Development, Ontological Analysis, System Design, Ontology Development, System Development and Integration. For each phase of the model, a set of ontology evaluation criteria in terms of competency questions were defined.

Hence, it can be said that the alignment of ontology construction and evaluation methods is a current challenge that would be an important contribution to the progress in ontology engineering, although there is *only little empirical evidence* for the effectiveness of this approach. Besides, to our knowledge there are no empirical studies that compare different ontology evaluation methods. In this work we will try to make contributions to these areas by analyzing and comparing the results achieved with the GoodOD ontology construction approach [10], which promotes an ontology construction guideline and has been applied to ontology building tasks under lab conditions. We perform the analysis within the ontology evaluation framework OQuaRE and compare the results with the outcome of previous analyses of the GoodOD method [30], [31].

The ontology quality framework OQuaRE [21] addresses the traceability between requirements and metrics. Ontology requirements are traced to quality characteristics, which in turn are associated with quality subcharacteristics. Each subcharacteristic is measured through a set of metrics. At the end, each (sub)characteristic is given a score in the range 1 (worst) to 5 (best). OQuaRE has demonstrated its usefulness for evaluating existing biomedical ontologies [21], [32], but its usefulness for evaluating ontologies that had been specifically developed following good practices has not been studied so far.

The GoodOD [10] guideline for good ontology design focuses on ontology engineering principles in the spirit of the new reference discipline "Applied Ontology", and methodological principles. This guideline provides a basic understanding required by a user with limited knowledge in logics, computer science or philosophy "to be able to solve ontology engineering problems in a foreseeable and non-arbitrary way" (http://purl.org/goodod/guideline). The effectiveness of the guideline was evaluated in a randomized controlled trial.

The objectives of this paper are (1) to employ the metrics of the OQuaRE framework as outcome parameter for the evaluation of the result ontologies derived from the GoodOD randomized controlled trial, and (2) to specify whether OQuaRE is able to provide additional useful information in addition to similarity and competency question based metrics.

METHODS

The OQuaRE Quality Model

Ontology quality evaluation and Requirements (OQuaRE) is a framework for Ontology Quality Evaluation, based on the software product quality ISO 25000:2005 named as SQuaRE. The OQuaRE framework defines all the elements required for ontology evaluation: evaluation support, evaluation process and metrics. OQuaRE combines a quality model and quality metrics. It also addresses the traceability between ontology requirements and metrics.

Currently, OQuaRE includes the quality model which defines a set of quality characteristics such as structural, reliability, operability, maintainability, compatibility, transferability and functional adequacy, for evaluating ontologies. Such characteristics have been adapted from SQuaRE to ontologies except for the structural one, which has been included due to its importance in measuring ontology quality, according to requirements, principles and characteristics of ontologies. Every quality characteristic has a set of quality subcharacteristics associated, which are measured by quality metrics.

The ontology requirements as such are not defined in OQuaRE but they could be traced to the Quality Characteristics which are presented in terms of the capability of the ontology to fulfill some criteria. Figure 1 shows the OQuaRE model with an example of the traceability from Ontology Requirements to Metrics.

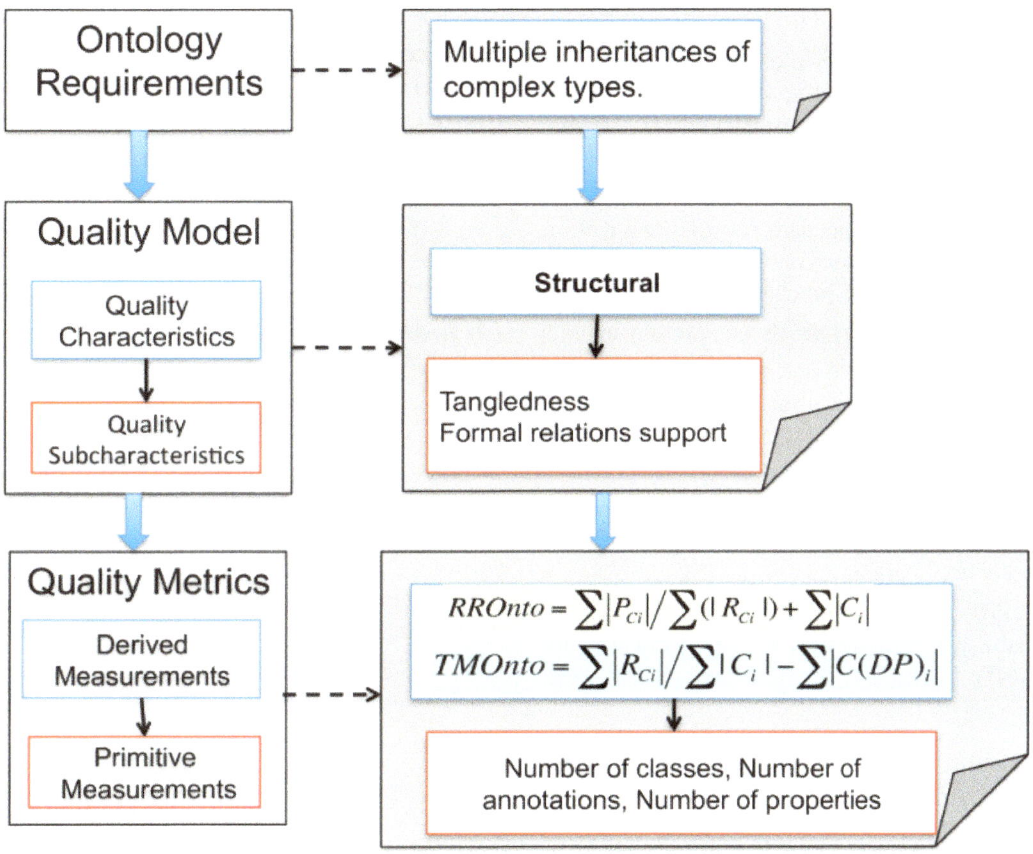

Figure 1. OQuaRE framework. The left side shows the components of the OQuaRE framework (Ontology Requirements, Quality Model and Quality Metrics) and the right side presents an example of traceability from ontology requeriments to metrics in OQuaRE.

The complete description of the OQuaRE quality model is available athttp://miuras.inf.um.es/oquarewiki. The most important characteristics for this study (Structural, Functional Adequacy, Compatibility, Operability, Reliability and Maintainability) and some of its subcharacteristics are described next:

STRUCTURAL: Formal and semantic important ontological properties that are widely used in state of-the-art evaluation approaches. Some subcharacteristics are:

- Cohesion: The degree of relation between the classes. An ontology has a high cohesion if the classes are strongly related.
- Redundancy: Capability of the ontology to be informative.
- Formal relations support: Capability of the ontology to represent relations supported by formal theories different from the formal support for taxonomy.
- Tangledness: This measures the distribution of multiple parent categories, so that it is related to the existence of multiple inheritance.
- FUNCTIONAL ADEQUACY: The capability of the ontologies to be deployed fulfilling functional requirements. Some subcharacteristics are:
- Controlled vocabulary: Capability of the ontology to avoid heterogeneity of the terms.
- Consistent search and query: The degree to which the formal model and structure of the ontology provides a semantic context to determine the result set wanted

by the users, allowing better querying and method searching.

- Knowledge acquisition and representation: Capability of the Ontology to represent the knowledge acquired (ability to support a knowledge base of ontology individuals).
- Knowledge reuse: The degree to which the content of the ontology can be used to build other ontologies.
- COMPATIBILITY: The capability of two or more software components to exchange information and/ or to perform their required functions while sharing the same hardware or software environment. Some subcharacteristics are:
- Replaceability: The degree to which the ontology can be used in place of another specified ontology for the same purpose in the same environment.
- Adaptability: The degree to which the ontology can be adapted for different specified environments (languages, expressivity levels) without applying actions or means other than those provided for this purpose for the ontology considered.
- OPERABILITY: Effort needed for the application. Individual assessment of such application by a stated or implied set of users. Some subcharacteristics are:
- Learnability: The degree to which the ontology enables users to learn its application.
- RELIABILITY: Capability of an ontology to maintain its level of performance under stated conditions for a given period of time.
- Availability: The degree to which an ontology, or part of it, is operational and available when required for use with different applications.
- Recoverability: The degree to which the ontology can re-establish a specified level of performance and recover the data directly affected in the case of a failure.
- MAINTAINABILITY: Capability of ontologies to be modified for changes in environments, in requirements or in functional specifications. Some subcharacteristics are:
- Modularity: The degree to which the ontology is composed of discrete components such that a change to one component has minimal impact on other components.
- Reusability: The degree to which an asset (part of) the ontology can be used in more than one ontology, or in building other assets.
- Analysability: The degree to which the ontology can be diagnosed for deficiencies or causes of failures (inconsistences), or for the parts to be modified to be identified.
- Changeability: The degree to which the ontology enables a specified modification to be implemented. The ease with which an ontology can be modified.
- Modification stability: The degree to which the ontology can avoid unexpected effects from modifications of the knowledge (terms, classes, properties, etc.).
- Testability: The degree to which the modified ontology can be validated.

OQuaRE quality metrics

Quality metrics are composed of primitive and derived measurements. Primitive measurements correspond to metrics that can be measured directly on the ontology, such as number of classes, number of relations, etc, whereas derived ones combine some primitive measurements. A set of quality metrics has been reused and adapted from both ontology and software engineering communities. Some metrics adapted from software engineering are presented in Table 1 (all abbreviations introduced there): RFCOnto, NACOnto, NOCOnto [33], [34], and some metrics adapted from the ontology community are LCOMOnto, RROnto, AROnto, CROnto [13], [35].

Table 1. OQuaRE Metrics.

LCOMOnto (Lack of Cohesion in Methods): Length of the path from the leaf class to Thing, divided by the total number of paths in the ontology
WMCOnto (Weighted Method Count): Average number of Datatype Properties, Object Properties and subclasses per class
DITOnto (Depth of Inheritance Tree): Length of the largest path from Thing to a leaf class of the ontology
NACOnto (Number of Ancestor Classes): Average number of superclasses per leaf class
NOCOnto (Number of Children): Average number of the direct superclasses per class minus the subclasses of Thing
RFCOnto (Response for a Class): Number of Datatype Properties and Object Properties that can be directly accessed from the class
NOMOnto (Number of Properties): Average number of Datatype Properties and Object Properties per class
PROnto (Property Richness): Ratio of the number of Datatype Properties and Object Properties defined in the ontology divided by the number of subclasses, Datatype Properties and Object Properties
AROnto (Attribute Richness): Number of restrictions of the ontology divided by the number of classes
INROnto (Relationships per Class): Average number of subclasses per class
CROnto (Inheritance Relationships Richness): Average number of individuals per class
ANOnto (Annotation Richness): Average number of annotation properties per class

Definition of the metrics used in OQuaRE. In the definition of the metrics, number refers to assertions in the ontology and not to the number of entities defined in the ontology.
doi:10.1371/journal.pone.0104463.t001

The evaluation of an ontology in the OQuaRE framework comprises a score for each quality characteristic, which depends on the evaluation of the set of associated subcharacteristics. The evaluation of a particular subcharacteristic depends on its associated metrics.

One metric can be associated with one or more subcharacteristics, and therefore may contribute to the score of more than one subcharacteristic. For instance, ANOnto "Annotation properties per class" contributes to knowledge reuse (of functional adequacy) and Redundancy (of structural), because annotation properties represent additional knowledge useful for reusing, so it is more informative and helps to be less redundant. Consequently, ANOnto contributes to Structural and Functional Adequacy characteristics.

The metrics are presented in different scales. For instance, RFCOnto and ANOnto generate absolute values whereas CROnto and INROnto produce relative values. Hence, in order to measure a quality subcharacteristic, those values are mapped onto the range 1 to 5. This mapping is based on the SQUaRE scores of the quality characteristics and subcharacteristics where values are ranged between 1 and 5. A value of 1 means "not acceptable", 3 is "minimally acceptable", and 5 is "exceeds the requirements" [36].

It should be noted that high values in the metrics might not correspond to a high quality score. For this purpose we apply the recommendations and best practices of the Software Engineering community for software metrics and ontology evaluation metrics.

Finally, the score of each subcharacteristic is calculated by the weighted average of the scores for its metrics. Likewise, the score of each characteristic is calculated by the weighted average of the scores of its subcharacteristics. The scoring mechanism based on weights provides a flexibility which permits to adapt the method to the need of a particular community.

The Good Ontology Design (GoodOD) Guideline

In the Good Ontology Design (GoodOD) project a guideline was formulated describing principles of good ontology design (http://purl.org/goodod/guideline). The main objective of this guideline is to help domain experts to develop good ontologies focusing on good practices. The GoodOD guideline brings together good practice rules, ontology design patterns and top-level categories, in order to provide ontology developers with standard solutions to recurrent modelling tasks.

The guideline comprises information on the definition of the basic elements of an ontology, its taxonomic structure, the formal language used to develop ontologies, and description logics (DL). The most important classes and relations from the upper domain ontology BioTop [3] are introduced to provide a framework for practical modeling tasks from the biomedical domain. This guideline combines foundations from philosophical ontology and logics, with the representational language OWL DL, and is rooted in the domain top-level ontology BioTop [10].

The effectiveness of the GoodOD guideline was evaluated in a randomized controlled trial in which the performance of ontology developers was compared after specific and unspecific training. As outcome parameters gold-standard based similarity measures [30]and a competency question based approach [31] were adopted. The study is described in more detail in the following sections.

Main results and conclusions from the study were that in the gold-standard based evaluation approach no significant effect of the specific training on the quality of ontologies could be detected. However, these results are not sufficient to conclude that there are generally no effects of the GoodOD principles. With the competency-question based approach a small but significant effect of the guideline-based training over the unspecific training could be shown (about 10% better). However, when analyzed on the level of single topics, a significant effect was measureable only for one topic.

Due to the high complexity and the educational nature of the study, the results should be carefully interpreted. The small effects of this study do not mean that construction principles should be abolished. They indicate that better evaluation methods must be developed. It is also optimistic to expect that significant training effects can be measured already after a one-week training phase. To our knowledge, the GoodOD study is the only empirical study investigating the effects of construction principles and ontology development guidelines on the quality of resulting ontologies so far.

Study Design

In this study the results of a randomized controlled trial are re-assessed by a complementary ontology evaluation framework (OQuaRE) and compared with prior results.

Randomized Controlled Trial on the Effectiveness of Guideline-based Ontology Training

The objective of this trial was to investigate whether guideline-based ontology training has an effect on the performance of ontology developers. The intervention of this trial was a curriculum implementing the principles of the GoodOD-guideline.

DESIGN: The study was conducted as a randomized controlled trial with a crossed intervention in a post-test only design.

POPULATION AND SAMPLE: The target population of the study were students with a combination of subjects from the Life Sciences and Computer Sciences. 24 students with a proven combination of the subjects in Biology or the Life Sciences and Computer Science from Austria, Germany, Slovenia and Switzerland were recruited. The study was conducted in summer 2011 at the Department of Medical Biometry and Medical Informatics of the University of Freiburg, Germany.

ALLOCATION: The students were randomized and allocated to one of two intervention groups.

INTERVENTION: A curriculum implementing the GoodOD-guideline (see above) in 16 modules was used as intervention. After a 2.5 days training in which both groups received the same training, the groups were randomized and received differential training for 1.5 days.

In the differential training phase, modules with different content but balanced in difficulty and duration were taught to each group (see Table 2). Group A was trained on the subject-matters *Process and Participation* (PRO), *Immaterial object* (IMM) and the *Closure* ODP (CLO), whereas group B was trained on *Collective material entity* (CME), *Information object*(INF) and the *Spatial disjointness* ODP (SPA).

Table 2. Intervention of the study, ontology topics and modules.

Module type	Topic	Group Trained
Top-level categories	Process and Participation (PRO)	A
	Immaterial object (IMM)	A
	Collective material entity (CME)	B
	Information object (INF)	B
Ontology design patterns	Closure ODP (CLO)	A
	Spatial disjointness ODP (SPA)	B

doi:10.1371/journal.pone.0104463.t002

OUTCOME PARAMETERS AND DATA COLLECTION: After the training phase, the students were asked to fulfill 12 modeling tasks with different content. Each student developed 12 test ontologies, six ontologies for the three topics in which they had received specific guideline based training and six ontologies for the three topics in which they only received unspecific training. It should be noted that the assessment of each topic included two different ontology development tasks. The students developed the test ontologies with the Protégé ontology editor, so that 12 OWL ontologies were collected from each student in 12 individual OWL files resulting in a total of 288 files.

The outcome parameter of the study was the quality of the resulting ontologies. The main outcome parameter was the quality of the ontologies measured as the similarity with gold standard ontologies and the secondary outcome parameter was the quality of the ontologies measured with a competency-question based approach.

In this work, OQuaRE is introduced as a new set of secondary outcome parameters. The authors of the GoodOD study see this extension of outcome parameters, although not declared in the original study protocol, as a legitimate and valuable application of further quality measures on the original research question of the study. For the detailed application of OQuaRE see the next section.

ANALYSIS AND REPORTING: For the calculation of similarity between students' ontologies and gold standard ontologies, a set of gold standard ontologies was developed by the authors of the GoodOD study. A software, the Good Similarity Evaluator [37], automated the process of similarity calculation on the basis of prior work [23], [25], [38], [39].

For the competency-question based measurement a set of questions and their allowed answers were designed by the experts. They were expressed in Manchester OWL 2 Syntax as DL axioms. The competency questions were used to check different aspects of the ontologies, such as the correctness of the asserted hierarchy, the correct and exhaustive introduction of disjointness axioms, the correct usage of classes and relations of top-level ontologies and the correct usage of ODPs.

The reporting of the study follows the CONSORT statement for the reporting of randomized controlled trials [40].

ETHICAL APPROVAL: Ethical approval was requested from the ethical authority of the University of Freiburg, Freiburg, Germany. The chair of the University of Freiburg ethics committee reviewed the project and concluded that a full formal ethics committee statement was not required due to the educational nature of the study. It was designed according to the general requirements for educational studies at the University Medical Center Freiburg, Freiburg, Germany, and was performed with written informed consent of the participants.

Application of OQuaRE as an Outcome Parameter of the GoodOD Study

In this experiment, 288 OWL files corresponding to 12 ontologies developed by 24 students were reused. Each ontology was evaluated using a predetermined OQuaRE configuration that will make use of 29 OQuaRE subcharacteristics. The application of OQuaRE was done using a home-made Java tool, which calculates the corresponding scores and returns a score in the range 1 to 5 for each characteristic, subcharacteristic and metric.

A random selection of ontologies was performed to obtain independent ontology samples with equal sample sizes in each of the 12 combinations of untrained and trained students by topic, balancing the inability of the tool to process all of the 288 OWL files; 6 randomly selected OWL files per ontology from different students were discarded from the study. The process assured that the data contained ontologies from all of the 24 students. Consequently, the final set of data consisted of 216 OWL files corresponding to 12 ontology construction tasks, each one tackled by 18 different students (9 trained, 9 untrained) randomly selected from a set of 24 students, and supplemented by two gold standard ontologies.

Next, we describe the methodological approach followed to perform the statistical analysis of the data which was done using R packages. Firstly, using data from the evaluation of students' ontologies, a two-way ANOVA model [41] with balanced independent samples design was used to identify the effect of the main factor training by topic in each of the 29 OQuaRE subcharacteristics. The interaction mean plot allowed to visualize the effect of the training along the topics and, in the situation where the interaction term was significant, the Student's t-test was performed to analyse the differences between the means of untrained and trained groups.

Secondly, to compare the gold standard against the students, the mean distances from both untrained and trained students to the gold standard were used. This distance was computed by means of the difference in absolute value of the gold standard measure minus the untrained and trained students observed scores, respectively.

Additionally, descriptive multivariate analysis was used to analyse the 29 OQuaRE subcharacteristics together. Clustering methods were applied to describe, through internally homogeneous groups of subcharacteristics, the change of those groups from untrained to trained case. Principal Component Analysis was applied to quantify and describe in detail this change.

RESULTS

In this section we present the main results of our data analysis. For the sake of simplicity, we do not show the OQuaRE scores for all of the ontologies, which can be accessed athttp://miuras.inf.um.es/oquarewiki.

Analysis of the Effect of the GoodOD Guideline over the Quality of the Ontologies Developed

To analyse the training effect over the ontologies developed by the students, a training by topic two-way ANOVA model with interaction term and balanced design for everyone of the 29 evaluated subcharacteristics was applied. The 216 observations from 24 untrained and trained students, corresponding to 36 ontologies for each of the six topics (PRO, CLO, IMM, INF, CME and SPA) were reused. This analysis showed that there is a significant effect of the interaction training by topic for 22 OQuaRE subcharacteristics (.000<*p–value*<0.03) (Figure 2). This means that the effect of the training could be different depending on the topic for those 22 selected subcharacteristics. For the other seven subcharacteristics there is no effect of the interaction training by topic, neither by topic neither by training (see Table 3 and Figure 3).

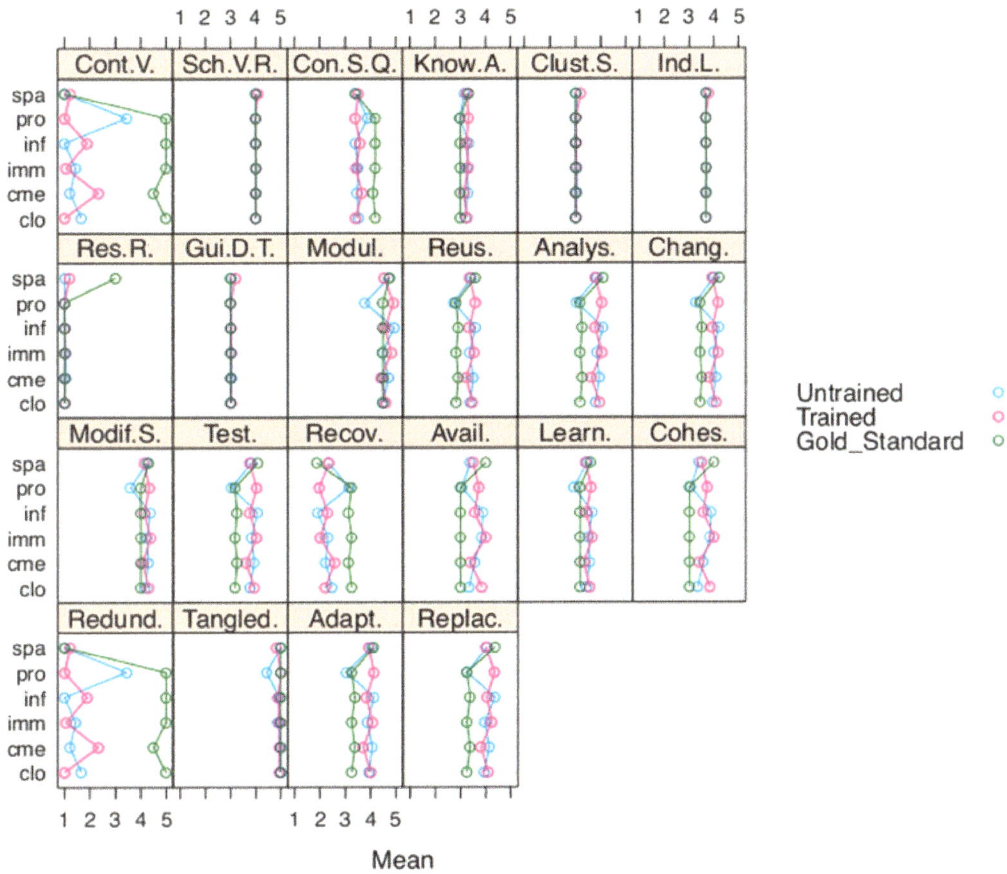

Figure 2. Significant effect of training in some topics. 22 subcharacteristics presented significant effect due to the GoodOD based training for some topics (PRO, IMM, CLO, CME, INF, SPA).

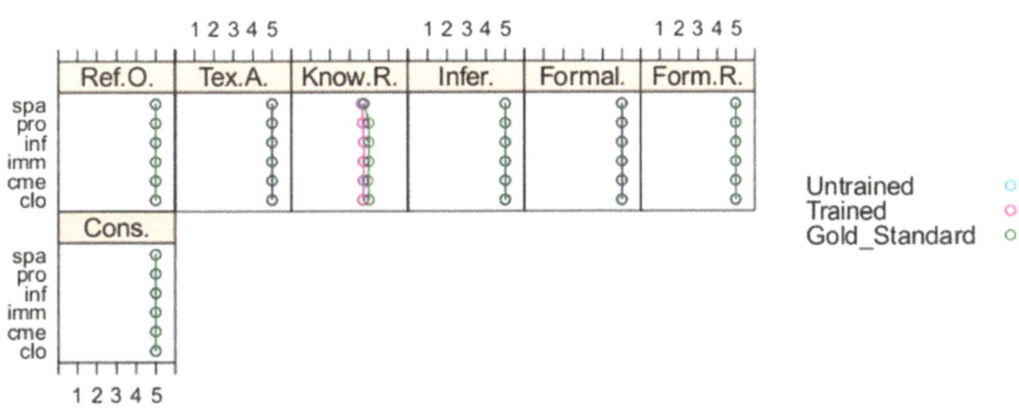

Figure 3. No significant effect of training in any topic. Seven OQuaRE subcharacteristics presented no significant effect of the training for any topic (PRO, IMM, CLO, CME, INF, SPA), and their mean values were similar for students and the gold standard.

Table 3. P-values associated with the main effects in the two-way ANOVA with no effect of the interaction training by topic.

Sub-characteristic	Trained	Topic	Trained X Topic
Reference Ontology	0.318	0.418	0.418
Text Analysis	0.318	0.418	0.418
Knowledge Reuse	0.586	0.069	0.952
Infering	0.318	0.418	0.418
Formalisation	0.318	0.418	0.418
Formal Relation Support	0.318	0.418	0.418
Consistency	0.318	0.418	0.418

doi:10.1371/journal.pone.0104463.t003

Figure 3 represents the mean values of the subcharacteristics by topic, for untrained students, trained students and the gold standard. The graph shows that the seven subcharacteristics with no significant effect of the training for any topic presented similar mean values for students and gold standard.

For the 22 subcharacteristics with significant interaction effect (see Figure 2), new analysis to identify the main effect of the training were done. For those analyses, the topic factor was fixed and Student's t-tests were applied. The results show that there are no significant differences between untrained and trained students for topic SPA for none of the 22 subcharacteristics. Significant differences (*p–value*<0.03) were found for topics CME, IMM, CLO, INF and PRO. Concretely, IMM and CLO presented significant effect of training for one and two subcharacteristics respectively. INF presented significant effect of training for six subcharacteristics and CME presented significant effect of training for eleven subcharacteristics with significance levels less than 0.05 (0.02<*p–values*<0.05). Finally, in PRO, 17 subcharacteristics presented significant effect of training and 12 of them with a high significance level less than 0.000 (*p–values*<.000).

The left side of Figure 4 shows the differences between untrained and trained students through the 95% confidence interval for its mean values for the 22 studied subcharacteristics in topic PRO. The untrained group shows wider intervals than the trained one, so that, the mean of the untrained group has a greater standard error than the trained one.

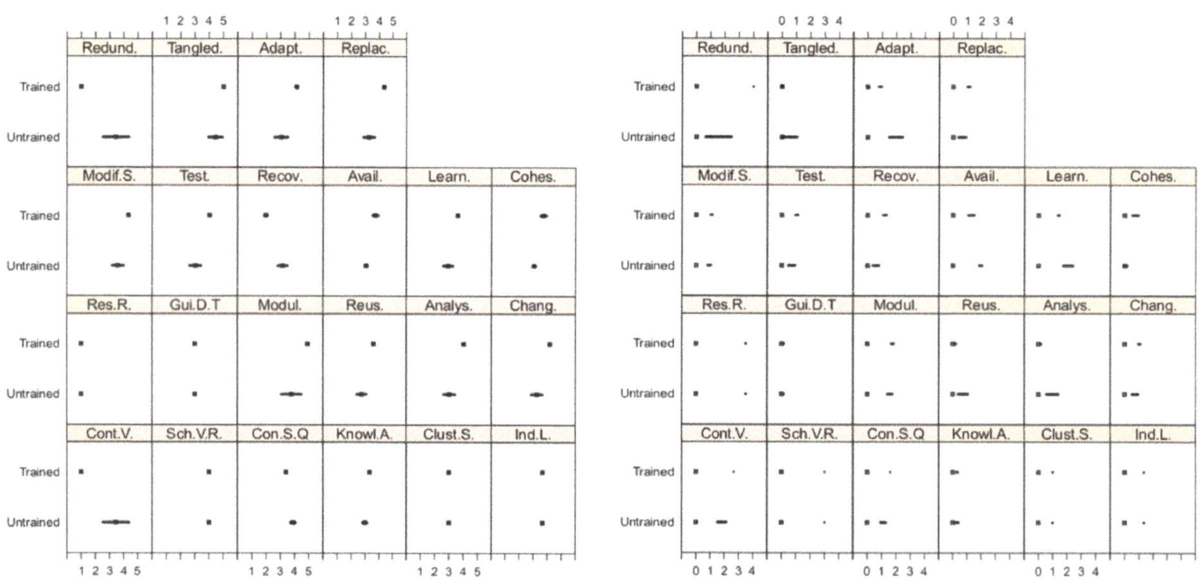

Figure 4. Confidence intervals for Topic PRO: for trained and untrained students (left side); distances to gold standard (right side).

In summary, twelve subcharacteristics did not reveal any training effect in any of the topics (see Table 4). However, the effect of training was significant for the remaining 17 subcharacteristics for topic PRO and some of them for topics CME, INF, CLO and IMM. The effect of training was not significant for any subcharacteristics in topic SPA. These results provide support to say that the GoodOD training presented important effect over the quality of the developed ontologies for PRO and CME, medium effect for INF, low effect for CLO and IMM and no significant effect for SPA. Comparing trained against untrained students, PRO showed a positive effect (higher OQuaRE subcharacteristics score) for 12 of the 17 subcharacteristics (see Figure 2). Additionally, the training effect for PRO can be analyzed using the dispersion (see Figure 4), which is greater for untrained students than for trained ones, except for Cohesion. This shows that the set of ontologies developed by trained students is more homogeneous than the set developed by untrained ones.

Table 4. Significance levels of testing difference of means.

SubCharacteristic	CLO	CME	IMM	INF	PRO	SPA
Reference Ontology	- -	- -	- -	- -	- -	- -
Text Analysis	- -	- -	- -	- -	- -	- -
Infering	- -	- -	- -	- -	- -	- -
Formalisation	- -	- -	- -	-	- -	- -
Formal Relation Support	- -	- -	- -	- -	- -	- -
Consistency	- -	- -	- -	- -	- -	- -
Schema And Value Reconciliation	- -	- -	- -	- -	- -	- -
Indexing And Linking	- -	- -	- -	- -	- -	- -
Clustering And Similarity	- -	- -	- -	- -	- -	- -
Guidance And Decision Trees	- -	- -	- -	- -	- -	- -
Results Representation	- -	- -	- -	- -	- -	- -
Knowledge Reuse	- -	- -	- -	- -	- -	- -
Tangledness	- [***]	- -	- -	- -	(*)[*]	- -
Modularity	- -	- -	- -	- -	(**)	- -
Knowledge Acquisition	- -	- [*]	- [*]	- [*]	(**)	- -
Modification Stability	- [*]	- -	- -	- -	(**)[*]	- -
Learnability	- -	- -	- -	- -	(**)[**]	- -
Reusability	- -	- -	- -	- -	(***)[**]	- -
Changeability	- -	(*) -	- -	- -	(***)[*]	- -
Availability	(**)[**]	(*) -	- -	(*)[*]	(***)[***]	- -
Cohesion	(**)[**]	(*) -	- -	(*)[*]	(***)[***]	- -
Analysability	- -	(*) -	- -	- [*]	(***)[**]	- -
Testability	- -	(*) -	- -	- -	(***)[*]	- -
Adaptability	- -	(*)[***]	- -	- -	(***)[***]	- -
Consistent Search And Query	- -	(*)[*]	- -	(*)[*]	(***)[***]	- -
Replaceability	- -	(*)[***]	- -	- -	(***)[**]	- -
Recoverability	- -	(*) -	(*)[*]	(*) -	(***)[***]	- -
Controlled Vocabulary	- -	(*)[*]	- -	(*)[*]	(***)[***]	- -
Redundancy	- -	(*)[*]	- -	(*)[*]	(***)[***]	- -
Total Significant differences	(2)[4]	(11)[7]	(1)[2]	(6)[7]	(17)[15]	(0)[0]

Differences between means of untrained and trained groups () and mean distances to the gold standard of trained and untrained groups []: The character * is used to indicate the significance level of the differences: * significant, ** very significant and *** highly significant.
doi:10.1371/journal.pone.0104463.t004

Analysis of the Distances Between the Students and the Gold Standard

The mean distances from both, untrained and trained students to the gold standard were obtained and the difference analyzed for every topic (PRO, CME, CLO, IMM, INF and SPA). In each case, the distance was computed by means of the difference in absolute value of the gold standard measure minus the observed score from students.

As previously mentioned, Figures 3 and 2 also represent the mean values of the subcharacteristics for the gold standard ontologies and Figure 3 showed that the gold standard and students had similar behaviour for seven subcharacteristics in all of the topics. In fact, for those subcharacteristics, there are no significant differences between the mean of the distances from untrained and trained students to the gold standard in any topic. For the remaining 22 subcharacteristics (see Figure 2) the analyzed differences provide enough evidence that training had significant effect in some subcharacteristics for CLO, CME, INF, IMM and PRO; but none for SPA. For PRO, significant differences between the mean distances from untrained and trained students to the gold standard were found for 15 subcharacteristics; confidence intervals are shown in the right side of Figure 4.

The effect of the training is summarized in Table 4, where ( ) and [ ] represent the significance level of the difference between the means of untrained and trained students, and between the means distances from untrained and trained students to the gold standard, respectively. The last row of the table shows the total number of significant differences. The highest effect of the training was found for PRO, followed by CME and INF which presented the second and third highest effect respectively.

In conclusion, the effect of the training was significant in 17 subcharacteristics, either due to differences between untrained and trained means, or between untrained and trained mean distances to the gold standard. We consider that this effect is high for PRO, intermediate for CME and INF, and small for CLO, IMM, and no effect was found for SPA.

Analysis of Quality of the Ontologies by Classifying and Sorting the sub-Characteristics

We have performed a multivariate analysis of the means distances from untrained and trained students to the gold standard in the set of the six topics (CLO, CME, IMM, INF, PRO, SPA), to describe the 29 OQuaRE subcharacteristics together. First, the original data were transformed by equation 1, where x_1, x_2 and G represent the mean values of the ontologies from untrained students, trained students and the gold standard ontologies respectively.

$$D(x_j) = 1 - e^{-|G - x_j|}; \quad with \quad 0 \le D(x_j) < 1; \quad j = 1,2; \tag{1}$$

This transformation was applied to all of the subcharacteristics for the six topics, obtaining two 29*x*6 data matrices, namely, D_1 and D_2. These matrices correspond to the mean distances from untrained and trained students to the gold standard respectively. Classification and sort methods were applied to the matrices to identify similar behaviours between subcharacteristics for both untrained and trained cases with respect to their distance to the gold standard.

CLASSIFYING SUBCHARACTERISTICS. Based on the Euclidean distance between subcharacteristics and Ward's minimum variance method of linkage criteria, hierarchical clustering was applied for both cases. The hierarchical cluster allowed to classify the subcharacteristics in four homogeneous groups for untrained and trained cases (see Table 5 and Figure 5).

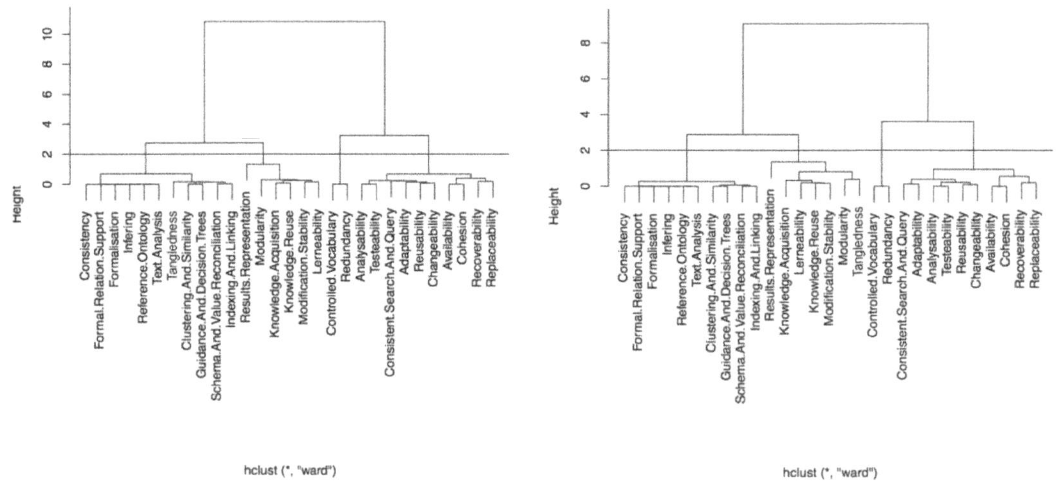

Figure 5. Subcharacteristics classification for untrained and trained students, respectively.

Table 5. Cluster centers.

Group	CLO	CME	IMM	INF	PRO	SPA
			UNTRAINED GROUP			
1	0.00	0.02	0.02	0.00	0.00	0.01
2	0.96	0.96	0.97	0.98	0.79	0.00
3	0.43	0.48	0.50	0.57	0.12	0.24
4	0.12	0.18	0.16	0.23	0.25	0.19
			TRAINED GROUP			
Group	**CLO**	**CME**	**IMM**	**INF**	**PRO**	**SPA**
1	0.01	0.01	0.01	0.02	0.00	0.07
2	0.98	0.89	0.98	0.96	0.98	0.20
3	0.54	0.32	0.59	0.42	0.58	0.28
4	0.20	0.10	0.25	0.15	0.25	0.25

doi:10.1371/journal.pone.0104463.t005

- Group 1 includes ten subcharacteristics for the untrained students plus Tangledness for the trained ones. The means distances from untrained and trained students to the gold standard are low for the six topics.
- Group 2 includes only two subcharacteristics for both untrained and trained students. The distances to the gold standard were high for all topics except for SPA, which were zero for the untrained students and low for the trained ones.
- Group 3 includes ten subcharacteristics in both untrained and trained students. The distances to the gold standard decrease from untrained to trained in CME and INF but increase for the other four topics, the highest one being found for PRO.
- Group 4 includes the same seven subcharacteristics for both untrained and trained cases, except for Tangledness which appears in group 1 for the trained students. This group presented the same behaviour as group 3 but with shorter distances for both trained and untrained students for all of the topics, except for PRO which presented the same value for both untrained and trained students.

In summary, the classification of subcharacteristics were the same along the topics, except for Tangledness which changed from group four in untrained case to group one in trained one, the distances to gold standard being larger for untrained students than for trained ones.

Additionally, a K-means classification with four groups obtained the same distribution of subcharacteristics as hierarchical cluster except for *Results Representation* and*Tangledness*. In contrast to hierarchical clustering, they were classified in group one for both untrained and trained students. The quality of this classification was measured by the percentage of total variance explained (between groups) which was 93% for untrained students and 87% for trained ones. The unexplained variance (within groups) was 4.9%, 0.0%, 1.9% and 0.6% for untrained students and 5.6%, 0.0%, 3.5% and 3.4% for trained ones, respectively in each group.

SORTING SUBCHARACTERISTICS. Principal Component Analysis (PCA) was applied to order the subcharacteristics by distance between untrained or trained groups to the gold standard for every topic. PCA was applied to the D_1 and D_2 matrices to represent the subcharacteristics in two dimensions. The representations obtained were of high quality: more than 98% of total variance was explained for untrained students, and more than 92% of total variance for trained ones, as is shown in Figure 6. This figure also represents the correlations between the topics and the principal components for both cases.

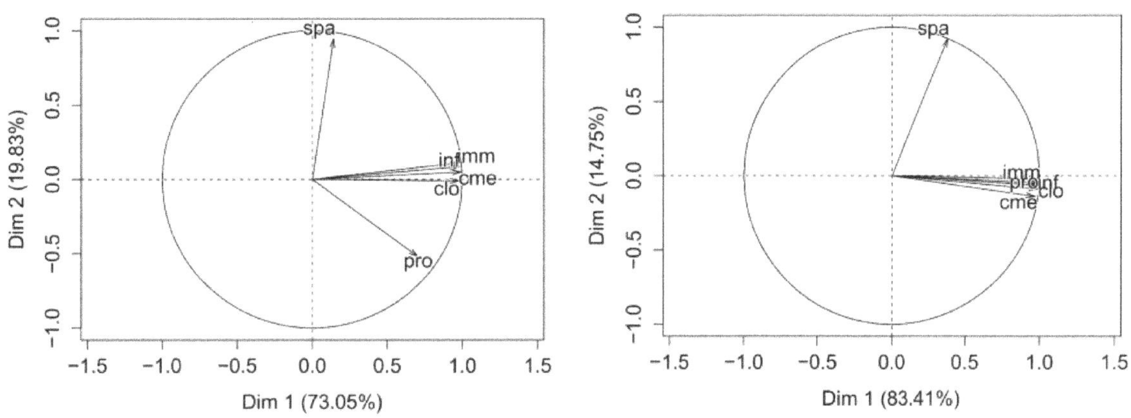

Figure 6. Factor loadings of topics in Principal Component Analysis. Untrained case (left) and trained case (right). With the two more important components, more than 98% of total variance was explained for untrained students, and more than 92% of total variance for trained ones.

The first component was highly correlated with CLO, CME, IMM, INF and PRO for both untrained and trained students. Therefore, subcharacteristics with highest positive values in this component presented the highest mean distances to the gold standard for those topics.

The second component was highly and positively correlated with SPA for both untrained and trained cases and highly negatively correlated with PRO for untrained case. Consequently, subcharacteristics with high positive values in this component presented the largest differences in distance to the gold standard, for both untrained and trained cases for SPA. Additionally, for the untrained case, subcharacteristics with high negative values in this second component presented the largest distances to the gold standard for PRO.

Values for first and second principal components and membership clusters are displayed inTable 6, where subcharacteristics are ordered by the first component for the untrained cases (PC1_U).

Table 6. Sorting and classification of the 29 OQuaRE subcharacteristics for untrained (U) and trained (T) cases, respectively.

Subcharacteristics	PC1 U	PC2 U	Cluster U	PC1 T	PC2 T	Cluster T
Text Analysis	−2.1415	−0.4745	1	−2.3298	−0.7121	1
Infering	−2.1415	−0.4745	1	−2.3298	−0.7121	1
Formalisation	−2.1415	−0.4745	1	−2.3298	−0.7121	1
Formal Relation Support	−2.1415	−0.4745	1	−2.3298	−0.7121	1
Consistency	−2.1415	−0.4745	1	−2.3298	−0.7121	1
Reference Ontology	−2.1415	−0.4745	1	−2.3298	−0.7121	1
Schema And Value Reconciliation	−2.0443	−0.3984	1	−2.1722	−0.1843	1
Indexing And Linking	−2.0099	−0.3925	1	−2.1285	−0.0359	1
Clustering And Similarity	−1.9497	−0.3236	1	−2.0242	0.2940	1
Guidance And Decision Trees	−1.9497	−0.3236	1	−2.0242	0.2940	1
Results Representation	−1.6551	3.4082	4	−1.3535	4.1078	4
Tangledness	−1.2330	−1.3450	4	−1.7404	0.0911	1
Knowledge Acquisition	−0.5027	0.3478	4	−0.5424	−0.5982	4
Modularity	−0.4209	−1.4542	4	−0.8249	0.1186	4
Knowledge Reuse	−0.1599	−0.2951	4	−0.4159	−0.5302	4
Modification Stability	−0.0551	−0.8153	4	−0.5887	−0.1009	4
Learnability	0.1805	−0.1507	4	−0.0425	−0.0061	4
Reusability	0.9643	0.2956	3	1.1085	−0.1203	3
Changeability	1.0905	0.3954	3	1.1980	0.2042	3
Availability	1.1399	1.8666	3	1.8513	0.9520	3
Cohesion	1.1399	1.8666	3	1.8513	0.9520	3
Analysability	1.4098	0.6158	3	1.6183	0.2622	3
Testability	1.4098	0.6158	3	1.6183	0.2622	3
Adaptability	1.4423	−0.1577	3	1.4247	−0.2628	3
Replaceability	1.5039	1.1593	3	2.1282	0.4131	3
Consistent Search And Query	1.5533	−0.6265	3	1.5650	−0.6867	3
Recoverability	2.1280	1.4822	3	2.7585	0.6801	3
Redundancy	5.4335	−1.4619	2	5.3570	−0.9166	2
Controlled Vocabulary	5.4335	−1.4619	2	5.3570	−0.9166	2

doi:10.1371/journal.pone.0104463.t006

The first component of the untrained case is significantly correlated with the first one of the trained case, consequently, a relation between behaviours for both cases was observed for CLO, CME, IMM, INF and PRO:

- Redundancy and Controlled Vocabulary obtained positive and atypical values in the first component, which means that distances to the gold standard were high in both cases.
- Tangledness and Modification stability presented the largest decrease of mean distances to the gold standard from untrained to trained cases. Conversely, Recoverability, Cohesion, Availability and Replaceability presented the highest increase in distance to the gold standard from untrained to trained case.
- The second component showed that:
- Result Representation obtained highest and atypical values in both untrained and trained cases, and the distances to the gold standard were high for SPA.
- Tangledness, Modification Stability, Result Representation, Modularity, Clustering and Similarity, Guidance and Decision Trees had the highest increase of the mean distances to the gold standard from untrained to trained cases. Conversely, Knowledge Acquisition, Availability, Cohesion, Replaceability and Recoverability presented the highest decrease from untrained to trained case.

In conclusion, the first principal component sorting showed that PRO, IMM, CLO, CME, and INF are highly correlated. The mean distance for these topics decreased from the untrained cases to the trained cases for 19 subcharacteristics, most of them with negative values in both cases (this means that mean distance are lower than the general mean). In contrast, this mean distance increased from untrained to trained for the other 10 subcharacteristics, and most of them presented positive larger distance to the gold standard (this means that mean distance is larger than the general mean), except for Result Representation, for which distances were negative.

The second component presented a high correlation with SPA for both untrained and trained cases, and with PRO for the untrained ones. The first and second components are uncorrelated, therefore, the behaviour of SPA is independent of the behaviour of the rest of topics in both untrained and trained cases.

DISCUSSION

In this study, OQuaRE was used to evaluate a set of biomedical ontologies developed by 24 students after guideline-based training. To measure the effect of the training over the properties of the ontologies, two different studies were carried out: (1) comparative analysis of the properties of the ontologies developed by untrained and trained students; (2) analysis of the distances of both sets of ontologies with respect to a set of gold standard ontologies. Additionally, the subcharacteristics have been ordered and classified according to the respective distances to the gold standard solutions.

Comparison with Previous Evaluations of the GoodOD Guideline

Our research objectives were inspired by the work presented in [30], [31]. Consequently we compare the present results with these two studies. We first analyzed the effect of training over the quality of the ontologies. In [31], the evaluation was based on competency questions metrics and found an effect of training for two topics, PRO and CME, and the differences were significant only for the first one. In our study, we have analyzed the effect of the training for 22 subcharacteristics, where the effect of topic by training interaction was significant. The effect was highly significant for six subcharacteristics in INF, 11 in CME and 17 in PRO. Additionally, in this last topic, ontologies developed by trained students were more homogeneous than the set developed by untrained ones. Hence, both studies draw similar conclusions.

Second, we have tested whether the ontologies developed by trained students were closer to the gold standard than those developed by the untrained ones were. In [30], a set of similarity measures of the ontology artifacts revealed that the ontologies developed by trained students were not significantly more similar to the gold standard than those developed by untrained students. Our findings reveal that there is a significant effect of training with respect to the gold standard (Table 4), in both negative and positive directions for PRO, IMM, CLO, CME and INF. SPA did not present significant differences from trained neither untrained students to the gold standard. Additionally, the classification and sorting of subcharacteristics showed that students reached values more similar to the gold standard after training with respect to 19 subcharacteristics, whereas their results were less similar to gold standard after training with respect to the 10 other subcharacteristics (see Table 6). Such conclusions were drawn for PRO, IMM, CLO, CME and INF, which are highly correlated in pairs and with the first component (see Figure 6). On the other hand, SPA is uncorrelated with the rest of the topics, behaving differently for both untrained and trained cases. After training, 18 subcharacteristics reached in SPA values more similar to the gold standard and 11 were less similar.

Consequently, we believe that these results permit to say that OQuaRE is able to capture the findings of the previous GoodOD evaluations, which was one major objective of this work.

Findings in the Ontologies Produced by the Students

A second objective was to study what additional information OQuaRE could provide about the quality of the ontologies developed and the effectiveness of GoodOD. According to our results, the GoodOD training had a significant effect on 59% of OQuaRE subcharacteristics and therefore on the quality of the ontologies developed by the students, and these differences were identified between ontologies developed by specific training and those without it.

Mean values for ontologies developed by untrained students and trained students, and for the gold standard ontologies were similar and high for seven subcharacteristics (see Figure 3). The highest quality scores were obtained for Tangledness for all topics except for PRO, in which Tangledness obtained a better value after the training. These subcharacteristics are associated with the general training of the GoodOD guideline, which seems to have been effective.

In general terms, Tangledness and Modification Stability obtained the highest positive effects of the training. The ontologies developed after the training presented less multiple inheritance and were more stable for changes in their classes, properties and terms. This effect might be due to the training of the GoodOD guideline, where a quality criterion is to construct ontologies in a way that multiple parenthood is inferred and not asserted.

Additionally, Recoverability, Cohesion, Availability and Replaceability obtained the most negative effects of the training. Such subcharacteristics are associated with the dependence between ontology classes.

More findings can be described when focusing on specific topics. Comparing the data for PRO in Figure 4 and Table 4, training had a significant effect on all the Maintainability subcharacteristics: Analysability, Changeability, Modification Stability, Testability and Reusability. Such differences might be induced by the training. A similar conclusion may be drawn for the rest of the subcharacteristics for which the training effect was significant. It should be noted that the most notable evidence of the effect of training is the homogeneity of the results of the trained students compared to those of the untrained students (seeFigure 4).

For CME, Figure 4, shows the effect of the training on subcharacteristics such as Redundancy, Control Vocabulary, Availability, Recoverability, Adaptability, Replaceability, Learnability and Knowledge Acquisition. Thus, the scores of the ontologies from trained students are more similar to the gold standard than those from untrained students.

In Table 6, the largest difference between the gold standard and mean values for untrained and trained students was found in two subcharacteristics: (1) *Redundancy*, which is the capability of the ontology to be informative; and (2) *Controlled vocabulary*, defined as the capability of the ontology to avoid heterogeneity of the terms. Both subcharacteristics are related to the number of annotations per class. We have found that ontologies of trained students included annotations for less than 10% of the classes, whereas the gold standard included them for almost 100%. For topics SPA, INF and CME, untrained students presented lower values than trained ones for those subcharacteristics. This means that training had a positive effect with respect to those specific subcharacteristics. For topics PRO, IMM and CLO, the training effect was negative. This might be due to the annotations created by the students before and after the training. Although finding an explanation for such behaviour is out of the scope of this work, we believe that such information would provide an interesting feedback for further developments and applications of the GoodOD guideline.

These findings lead to the conclusion that OQuaRE is able to provide fine-grained information about the quality of the ontologies because of its organization in quality characteristics and subcharacteristics.

Limitations and Future Work

As it has been aforementioned, due to technical limitations, we have not been able to work with the complete original dataset. Consequently, the study was designed to reduce potential biases. Our design was based on independent samples with equal sample sizes to use an F statistic in the ANOVA analysis less sensitive to the eventual non-compliance of the normality and homocedasticity hypotheses of the sample. In a different situation, we would have needed to test the hypotheses the ANOVA model is based on and to deal with the non-uniqueness of the solution.

The current version of OQuaRE lacks a module for the definition of a set of Ontology Quality requirements which would permit a more direct traceability between competency questions and quality metrics, allowing the measurement of the ontologies from the development phase. Additionally, we are working on including new axiom-based metrics in the framework. Besides, new experiments involving both OQuaRE and GoodOD would permit a coordinated evolution of approaches for guiding the construction of the ontologies and to evaluating those ontologies.

It should be noted that neither the OQuaRE metrics nor the GoodOD methods are meant to be sufficient for a full picture of the quality of an ontology, even when combined. Nevertheless, the work that we present in this paper is one of the very first efforts to combine different methods and our results suggest that it is a promising way to proceed. We aim at extending our approach with new metrics and combining our results with other ontology quality approaches; a possible candidate for such an extension could be the measurement of the cognitive quality of ontologies [22], which could also be included as part of the OQuaRE measurements. This approach proposes a method for evaluating the relationship between a cognitive conceptualization and an explicit specification, but assumes that the quality of an ontology is relevant and useful only in relation to that of another ontology. Consequently, it might provide additional information for studying similarities between the gold standard and the students' ontologies.

CONCLUSION

In this work, OQuaRE was used to evaluate the quality of a set of ontologies developed using the GoodOD guideline for good ontology design. The quality of the ontologies was previously measured a competency-question based approach and the measurement of the similarity to gold-standard ontologies. A comparison of OQuaRE with the two previous evaluations was done.

OQuaRE results showed a significant difference in terms of quality between untrained and trained students for three topics. Additionally, compared to the gold standard, training resulted in both positive and negative effects on five topics. OQuaRE was able to draw similar conclusions as the original GoodOD evaluations, and to provide specific results such as correlations between different topics, the set of subcharacteristics affected by training, and the differences, by subcharacteristics, among ontologies developed by untrained and trained students and gold-standard ontologies.

Summarized, GoodOD and OQuaRE can be used together to take advantage of their respective strengths to develop and evaluate ontologies. To the best of our knowledge, this is one of the very first studies that attempts to compare and combine independent ontology development and evaluation methods. We believe this to be an important contribution to the progress of the ontology engineering community.

AUTHOR CONTRIBUTIONS

Conceived and designed the experiments: AR MI MB LJ SS JTFB. Performed the experiments: AR MI MB LJ SS JTFB. Analyzed the data: AR MI MB LJ SS JTFB. Contributed reagents/materials/analysis tools: AR MI MB LJ SS JTFB. Contributed to the writing of the manuscript: AR MI MB LJ SS JTFB.

REFERENCES

1. Hepp M (2008) GoodRelations: An Ontology for Describing Products and Services Offers on the Web. In: Proceedings of the 16th international conference on Knowledge Engineering: Practice and Patterns. Berlin, Heidelberg: Springer-Verlag, EKAW '08, pp. 329–346.
2. Ashburner M, Ball CA, Blake JA, Botstein D, Butler H, et al. (2000) Gene Ontology: tool for the unification of biology. The Gene Ontology Consortium. Nature genetics 25: 25–29. doi: 10. 1038/75556
3. Beisswanger E, Schulz S, Stenzhorn H, Hahn U (2008) Biotop: An upper domain ontology for the life sciences: A description of its current structure, contents and interfaces to obo ontologies. Appl Ontol 3: 205–212.
4. Sánchez-Vera MM, Fernández-Breis JT, Castellanos-Nieves D, Frutos-Morales F, Prendes-Espinosa MP (2012) Semantic web technologies for generating feedback in online assessment environments. Knowledge-Based Systems 33: 152–165. doi: 10. 1016/j. knosys. 2012. 03. 010
5. Tian Y, Huang M (2012) Enhance discovery and retrieval of geospatial data using soa and semantic web technologies. Expert Syst Appl 39: 12522–12535. doi: 10. 1016/j. eswa. 2012. 04. 061
6. d'Aquin M, Gangemi A (2011) Is there beauty in ontologies? Applied Ontology 6: 165–175.
7. Gruninger M, Fox MS (1994). The design and evaluation of ontologies for enterprise engineering.
8. Uschold M, Gruninger M, Uschold M, Gruninger M (1996) Ontologies: Principles, methods and applications. Knowledge Engineering Review 11: 93–136. doi: 10. 1017/s0269888900007797
9. Lopez MF, Gomez-Perez A, Sierra JP, Sierra AP (1999) Building a chemical ontology using methontology and the ontology design environment. IEEE Intelligent Systems 14: 37–46. doi: 10. 1109/5254. 747904
10. Boeker M, Schober D, Raufie D, Grewe N, Röhl J, et al. . (2012) Teaching good biomedical ontology design. In: Cornet R, Stevens R, editors, ICBO. CEUR-WS. org, volume 897 of *CEUR Workshop Proceedings*.
11. Lozano-Tello A, Gomez-Perez A (2004) Ontometric: A method to choose the appropriate ontology. Journal of Database Management Special Issue on Ontological Analysis, Evaluation, and Engineering of Business Systems Analysis Methods 15: 1–18. doi: 10. 4018/jdm. 2004040101
12. Alani H, Brewster C, Shadbolt N (2006) Ranking ontologies with aktiverank. In: The 5th International Semantic Web Conference (ISWC). Springer Berlin Heidelberg, pp. 1–15.
13. Tartir S, Arpinar IB (2007) Ontology evaluation and ranking using ontoqa. In: ICSC '07: Proceedings of the International Conference on Semantic Computing. Washington, DC, USA: IEEE Computer Society, pp. 185–192.
14. Corcho O, Gómez-Pérez A, González-Cabero R, Suárez-Figueroa MC (2004) ODEVAL: A Tool for Evaluating RDF(S), DAML+OIL and OWL Concept Taxonomies. In: Artificial Intelligence Applications and Innovations. Springer US, pp. 369–382.
15. Guarino N, Welty CA (2004) An overview of ontoclean. In: Staab S, Studer R, editors, Handbook on Ontologies, Springer, International Handbooks on Information Systems. pp. 151–172.
16. Sleeman D, Reul Q (2006) Cleanonto: Evaluating taxonomic relationships in ontologies. In: Workshop on Evaluating Ontologies.
17. Vrandecic D (2010) Ontology Evaluation. Ph. D. thesis, Institute of Applied Informatics and Formal Description Methods AIFB.
18. Gangemi A, Catenacci C, Ciaramita M, Lehmann J (2006) Modelling ontology evaluation and validation. In: Sure Y, Domingue J, editors, ESWC. Springer, volume 4011 of *Lecture Notes in Computer Science*, pp. 140–154.
19. Rogers JE (2006) Quality assurance of medical ontologies. Methods Inf Med 45: 267–274.
20. Stvilia B (2007) A model for ontology quality evaluation. First Monday 12. .
21. Duque-Ramos A, Fernández-Breis JT, Stevens R, Aussenac-Gilles N (2011) Oquare: a square-based approach for evaluating the quality of ontologies. Journal of Research and Practice in Information Technology 43: 159–73.
22. Evermann J, Fang J (2010) Evaluating ontologies: Towards a cognitive measure of quality. Information Systems 35: 391–403. doi: 10. 1016/j. is. 2008. 09. 001
23. David J, Euzenat J (2008) Comparison between ontology distances (preliminary results). In: Sheth A, Staab S, Dean M, Paolucci M, Maynard D, et al. . , editors, The Semantic Web - ISWC 2008, Springer Berlin Heidelberg, volume 5318 of *Lecture Notes in Computer Science*. pp. 245–260.
24. Maedche A, Staab S (2002) Measuring similarity between ontologies. In: Knowledge engineering and knowledge management: Ontologies and the semantic web, Springer. pp. 251–263.
25. Dellschaft K, Staab S (2006) On how to perform a gold standard based evaluation of ontology learning. In: Cruz I, Decker S, Allemang D, Preist C, Schwabe D, et al. . , editors, The Semantic Web - ISWC 2006, Springer Berlin Heidelberg, volume 4273 of *Lecture Notes in Computer Science*. pp. 228–241.
26. Fox MS, Barbuceanu M, Gruninger M, Lin J (1997) An organization ontology for enterprise modelling. In: Modeling, In: International Conference on Enterprise Integration Modelling Technology 97. Springer.

27. Obrst L, Ceusters W, Mani I, Ray S, Smith B (2007) The evaluation of ontologies. In: Semantic Web, Springer US. pp. 139–158.

28. Gruninger M, Fox M (1995) Methodology for the design and evaluation of ontologies. In: IJCAI'95, Workshop on Basic Ontological Issues in Knowledge Sharing, April 13, 1995.

29. Neuhaus F, Vizedom A, Baclawski K, Bennett M, Dean M, et al. (2013) Towards ontology evaluation across the life cycle the ontology summit 2013. Applied Ontology 8: 179–194.

30. Boeker M, Jansen L, Grewe N, Röhl J, Schober D, et al. (2013) Effects of guideline-based training on the quality of formal ontologies: A randomized controlled trial. PLOS One 8: e61425. doi: 10. 1371/journal. pone. 0061425

31. Boeker M, Grewe N, Röhl J, Schober D, Schulz S, et al. . (2013) Measuring the effect of a guideline-based training on ontology design with a competency questions based evaluation approach. In: Informatik 2013, 43. Jahrestagung der Gesellschaft für Informatik e. V. (GI), Informatik angepasst an Mensch, Matthias Horbach, GI, Lecture Notes in Informatics, pp. 1783–1795.

32. Duque-Ramos A, Fernández-Breis JT, Iniesta M, Dumontier M, Aranguren ME, et al. (2013) Evaluation of the oquare framework for ontology quality. Expert Systems with Applications 40: 2696–2703. doi: 10. 1016/j. eswa. 2012. 11. 004

33. Chidamber S, Kemerer C (1994) A metric suite for object oriented design. IEEE Transactions on Software Engineering: 467–493.

34. Li W, Henry S (1993) Object-oriented metrics that predict maintainability. J Sys Software 23: 11–122. doi: 10. 1016/0164-1212(93)90077-b

35. Yao H, Orme AM, Etzkorn L (2005) Cohesion metrics for ontology design and application. Journal of Computer Science 1: 107–113. doi: 10. 3844/jcssp. 2005. 107. 113

36. ISO (2005) ISO/IEC 25000:2005, Software Engineering - Software Product Quality Requirements and Evaluation (SQuaRE) - Guide to SQuaRE (ISO/IEC 25000), Geneva, Switzerland: International Organization for Standardization.

37. Grewe N, Schober D, Boeker M (2012) Comparing closely related, semantically rich ontologies: The GoodOD Similarity Evaluator. In: 4th Workshop Ontologies in Biomedicine and Life Sciences.

38. Vrandečić D, Sure Y (2007) How to design better ontology metrics. In: Proceedings of the 4th European conference on The Semantic Web: Research and Applications. Berlin, Heidelberg: Springer-Verlag, ESWC '07, pp. 311–325.

39. Euzenat J, Allocca C, David J, d'Aquin M, Le Duc C, et al. . (2009). NeOn:Lifecycle Support for Networked Ontologies - D3. 3. 4: Ontology distances for contextualization.

40. Moher D, Hopewell S, Schulz K, Montori V, Goetzsche P, et al. (2010) CONSORT 2010 Explanation and Elaboration: Updated guidelines for reporting parallel group randomised trials. Journal of Clinical Epidemiology 63: e1–37. doi: 10. 1016/j. jclinepi. 2010. 03. 004

41. Everitt BS, Hothorn T (2011) An Introduction to Applied Multivariate Analysis with R. New York: Springer-Verlag. doi:10. 1007/978-1-4419-9650-3.

CHAPTER 11

COMPREHENSIVE QUANTITATIVE ANALYSIS ON PRIVACY LEAK BEHAVIOR

Lejun Fan, Yuanzhuo Wang, Xiaolong Jin, Jingyuan Li, Xueqi Cheng, Shuyuan Jin

Institute of Computing Technology, Chinese Academy of Sciences, Beijing, China

ABSTRACT

Privacy information is prone to be leaked by illegal software providers with various motivations. Privacy leak behavior has thus become an important research issue of cyber security. However, existing approaches can only qualitatively analyze privacy leak behavior of software applications. No quantitative approach, to the best of our knowledge, has been developed in the open literature. To fill this gap, in this paper we propose for the first time four quantitative metrics, namely, possibility, severity, crypticity, and manipulability, for privacy leak behavior analysis based on Privacy Petri Net (PPN). In order to compare the privacy leak behavior among different software, we further propose a comprehensive metric, namely, overall leak degree, based on these four metrics. Finally, we validate the effectiveness of the proposed approach using real-world software applications. The experimental results demonstrate that our approach can quantitatively analyze the privacy leak behaviors of various software types and reveal their characteristics from different aspects.

INTRODUCTION

Privacy leak behavior invading users' data privacy has been widely discovered in different types of software and has thus become a very important research issue of cyber security. Existing approaches to analyzing privacy leak behavior can be classified into two categories: black-box approaches and white-box approaches. The black-box approaches focus on the input data and output network traffic of software, which rapidly find privacy data with well-defined format (e.g., credit card number) by evaluating the variation of privacy information between input and output data [1]–[2]. However, these approaches face the limitation of packet obfuscating techniques (e.g., encrypted connections, message reordering and traffic randomization) [1]. In comparison to the black-box approaches, the white-box approaches can accurately analyze privacy leak behavior in detail [3]. These approaches can be further divided into static analysis approaches and dynamic analysis approaches. Static analysis approaches reveal the accurate data flow from binary executable files of the target software [4], which also confront code obfuscating problems (e.g., code morphing, packer and opaque constant) [5]. Dynamic analysis approaches,

Citation: Fan L, Wang Y, Jin X, Li J, Cheng X, Jin S (2013) Comprehensive Quantitative Analysis on Privacy Leak Behavior. PLoS ONE 8(9): e73410. doi:10.1371/journal.pone.0073410.

which detect the runtime data flow by tracing the execution of the target software, are widely used in software behavior analysis [6]–[7]. Unfortunately, dynamic analysis approaches have their shortages in solving problems such as multiple paths [8] and dormant functionality [9]. Although the above black-box and white-box approaches have been proposed for years, privacy leak behavior analysis still suffers from two common problems. First, there are no quantitative evaluation metrics for analyzing privacy leak behavior. Second, there is no metric for comprehensively comparing the overall degree of privacy leak of different software applications. Such a metric is very important, because it can indicate the overall threat level of the tested software application.

To overcome these two problems, we propose, for the first time, a set of desired quantitative metrics based on an abstract model called Privacy Petri Net (PPN) presented in [10], which characterizes the entire privacy leak procedure with more high-level description. Specifically, we propose and define four quantitative metrics, i.e., possibility, severity,crypticity, and manipulability, to characterize different aspects of privacy leak behavior and make the analysis more understandable. In order to compare the privacy leak behavior of different software applications, we further present a comprehensive metric, i.e., the overall privacy leak degree, by virtue of the above four metrics. Finally, we apply the proposed approach to real-world software applications and show that it can quantitatively analyze the privacy leak behavior of various software types and find their characteristics from different aspects.

MODEL

Privacy Petri Net (PPN) is a high-level Petri net dedicated to privacy leak behavior analysis[10], which has three main features. Firstly, PPN has formal mathematical definitions of syntax and semantics, which provide a precise specification on the target software behavior, so as to essentially define various behavior properties. Secondly, PPN has powerful modeling primitives of graphical abstraction. Specific graph structures can be used to identify unique private information leak behavior. Finally, PPN is modularized and can thus be used to build hierarchical models. By virtue of these features, we can use PPN to model different types of privacy leak behaviors and construct more complicated and powerful models. Here we first make a brief introduction to PPN and then present seven typical modules of PPN.

Definition of Privacy Petri Net (PPN)

Fig. 1 presents a schematic diagram of a PPN that can be formally defined as follows.

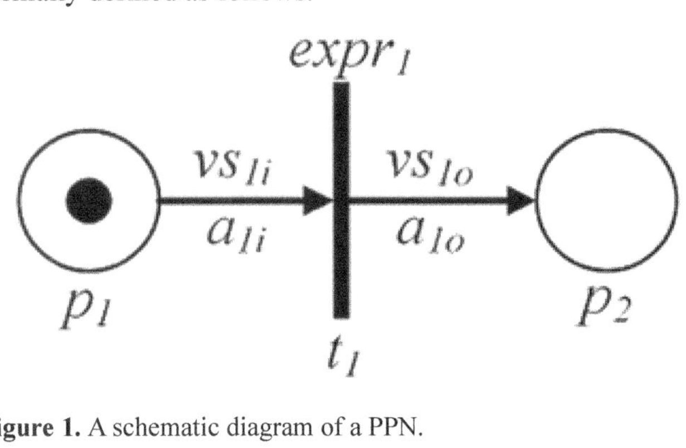

Figure 1. A schematic diagram of a PPN.

Definition 1. A Privacy Petri Net (PPN) is a seven-tuple, PPN=(P, T, A, INST, f_{pos}, f_{tran}, f_{arc}), where:

- P is a finite set of positions. Each position in P denotes a local status of a subroutine of software execution.
- T is a finite set of transitions. Each transition in T denotes a system call or an API call.
- $A \subseteq \{P \times T\} \cup \{T \times P\}$ is a set of directed arcs that connect positions and transitions. The arcs heading to and emiting from a transition are called input and output arcs of the transition, respectively (e.g., a_{1i} and a_{1o} in Fig. 1).
- INST={(Ctg, Cont, Proc)} is the set of instances of privacy data sources in each access. Each instance in INST can be denoted by a token with three special attributes, Ctg, Cont, and Proc. Ctg is the category of data sources, taking possible values from the set, {"File", "Application", "System", "Dynamic"}. Cont is the content of privacy data which differs according to its category. For example, for a file, Cont is its name or path, while for a system, Cont is the registry key name and key value. Procdenotes the steps/path that the token traverses through the whole PPN, which is a sequence of positions and transitions, denoted as Proc=$p_1 t_1 p_2 \ldots p_{n-1} t_{n-1} p_n$ ($n \geq 1$), where $p_i \in P$ (i=1, 2, …, n) and $t_j \in T$ (j=1, 2, …, n−1). These attributes depict the fundamental information of the privacy leakage, which are initialized with an empty value when the token is created.
- f_{pos} is a mapping f_{pos} *: P→{"Start", "Source", "Absorb", "Mid",* "Discrim"}. It assigns a property to each position to indicate its role in privacy leak. In a PPN, different positions are indicated with distinct icons as depicted in Fig. 2. A "Start" position spawns new tokens with unassigned privacy attributes. A "Source" position denotes the access point of a privacy data source. A "Discrim" position means that the privacy leak behavior can be discriminated when a token reaches it. An "Absorb" position implies that the operation on the related data source has been checked and is not considered as privacy leak behavior. "Mid" positions indicate all other positions. In order to implement the modularization of PPNs, a few PPN module will be defined later for the privacy leak procedure. Each PPN module must have at least one "start" position, one "absorb" position, one "source" position and one "discrim" position to depict a complete privacy leak procedure.
- f_{arc} is an arc function set that assigns a set of variables to each arc and is denoted byf_{arc} : A→VARSET. The variable set assigned to an input arc is called an input variable set (e.g., vs_{1i} in Fig. 1), while the one assigned to an output arc is called anoutput variable set (e.g., vs_{1o} in Fig. 1). All variables can be categorized into two main kinds. One is the parameters used to support the system or API calls, such as, integer, float, handle, pointer, string and struct. The other is used to support the privacy attributes. They are mainly calculated from the parameter variables.
- f_{tran} is a transition function that maps an expression to each transition and is denoted by f_{tran}: T→EXPR. EXPR is a Boolean operation of some conditions on checking privacy leak, which intrigue the corresponding

transition. These conditions include many categories, such as, the name checking of the current system call or API call, the value checking of the current system environment variable, globe system configuration checking, and other predefined constraint conditions. There must be at least one condition checking the name of the current system call or API call, because we characterize the software behavior mainly by the call sequence.

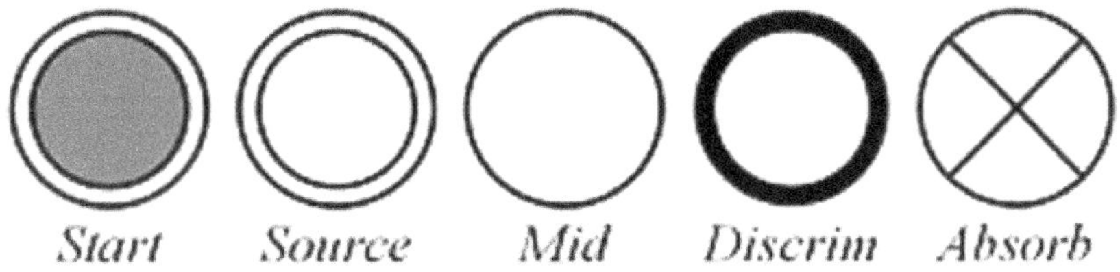

Figure 2. Position icons.

Next, we present two concepts and an important theorem about PPN for checking the privacy leak behavior.

Definiton 2. Behavior path set

Let $C=c_1c_2...c_n$ $(n\geq1)$ be a call sequence of the target software application and $inst_1$, $inst_2$, …, $inst_m$ $(m\geq1)$ be privacy instances spawned when the calls in C are checked to trigger the transitions. The behavior path set, BPS, is the set of move traces of all privacy instances, denoted as BPS=$\{inst_1.proc, inst_2.proc, ..., inst_m.proc\}$. Each call sequence C can be mapped to a unique BPS to describe the privacy leak related behavior of the target software application.

Definiton 3. Leak path and leak reachability

A leak path is a special move trace of a privacy instance in BPS, where there must exist a source position and a discrimination position. Let $inst_k.proc=p_1t_1p_2...p_{n-1}t_{n-1}p_n$ and$inst_k.proc\in BPS$. We have: $inst_k.proc$ is a leak path $\Leftrightarrow$ the privacy instance $inst_k$ has leak reachability$\Leftrightarrow\exists i, j : f_{pos}(p_i)=$"source"$\wedge f_{pos}(p_j)=$"discrim".

With the leak reachability property we can verify whether a certain type of private information contained in the target software application is leaked as presented in Theorem 1.

Theorem 1. (Discrimination Theorem) If a privacy instance, inst, spawned in a PPN module, m, has leak reachability, then the call sequence C of the target software application contains a privacy leak behavior procedure that modeled by the PPN module.

The proof of Theorem 1 can be found in our previous work [10].

Typical Modules of PPN

In PPN, there are a few typical PPN modules corresponding to sub-procedures of privacy leak behavior of Windows software. Specifically, there are four typical PPN modules corresponding to unauthorized data access (see Fig. 3) and three PPN modules for covert network transmission (see Fig. 4). The integration of some typical PPN modules may generate more complicated PPNs.

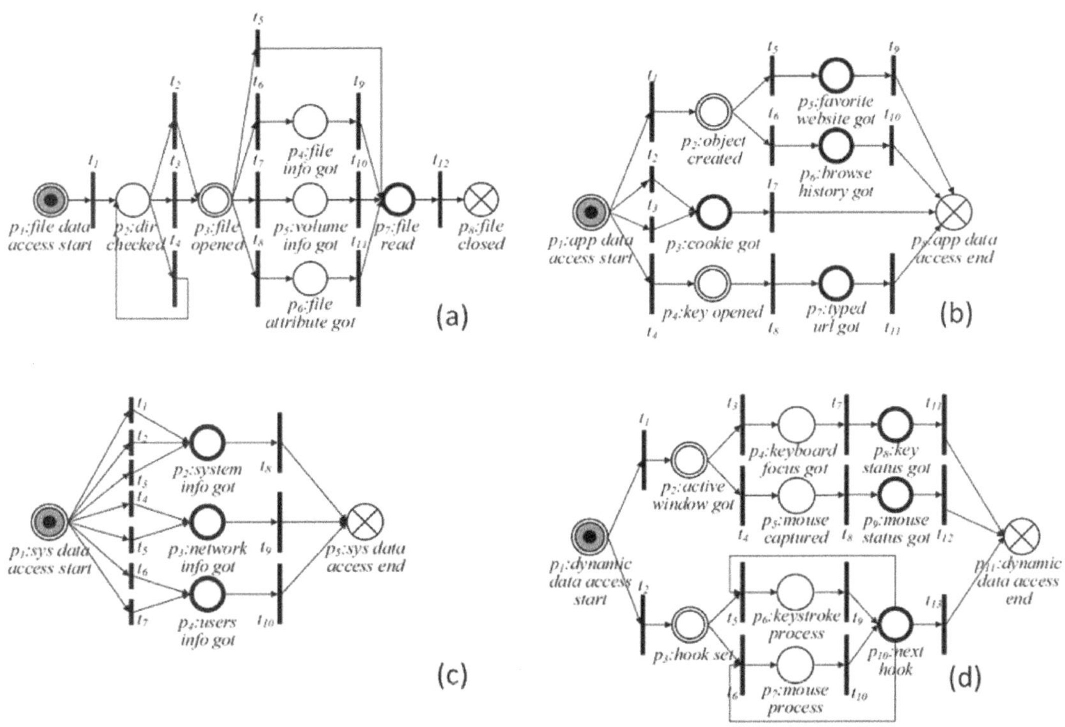

Figure 3. Typical module for privacy data accessing. (a) Module m_{nfda} : PPN module for ordinary file data access; (b)Module m_{ada} : PPN module for application data access; (c) Module m_{sda} : PPN module for system data access; (d) Module m_{dda} : PPN module for dynamic data access.

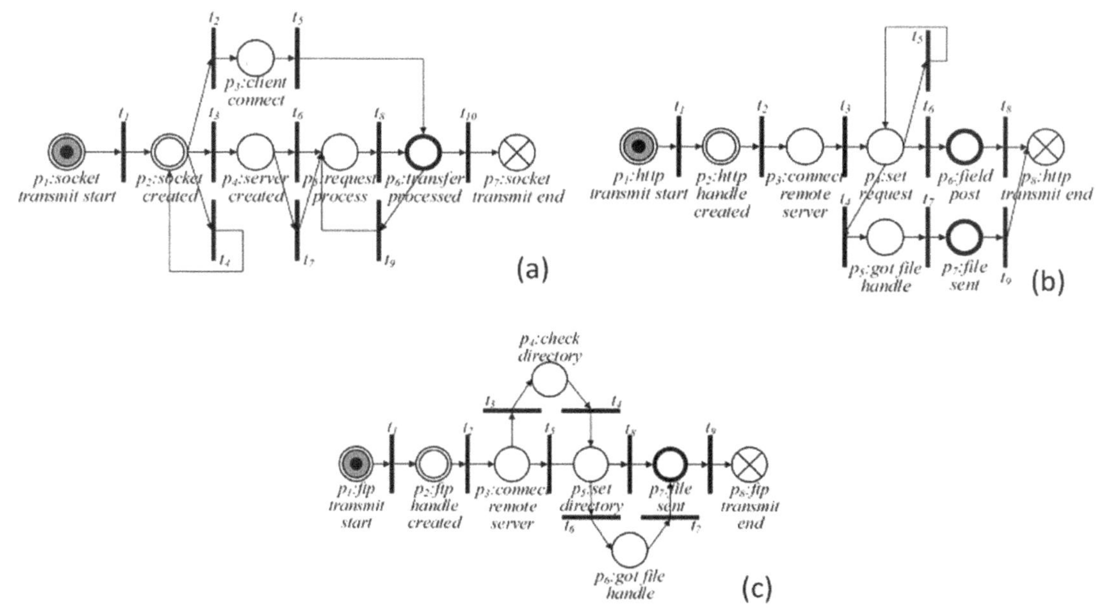

Figure 4. Typical module for privacy data transmission. (a)Module m_{socket} : PPN module for socket connection; (b)Module m_{http} **: PPN module for HTTP connection; (c) Module** m_{ftp} **: PPN module for FTP connection.**

The PPN modules presented in Fig. 3 (a)–(d) correspond to the behavior of software for accessing ordinary files, application data, system data and dynamic data, respectively. It can be seen from Fig. 3(a) that to access data in an ordinary file: (1) The target software should check the possible directories to find the file by "NtQueryDirectoryFile" or "NtNotifyChangeDirectoryFile", which can be found in Table 1. Then the corresponding transitions t_1 or t_4 are triggered and the token moves to position p_2; (2) The software application acquires the file handle by "NtCreateFile" or "NtOpenFile". Then the corresponding transitions t_2 or t_3 are triggered and the token moves to position p_3; (3) Finally, the application obtains the properties or content of the file by "NtFsControlFile". Then the corresponding transition t_5 is triggered and the token moves to position p_7. There are also three other possible leak paths from position p_3 to position p_7: $p_3t_6p_4t_9p_7$, $p_3t_7p_5t_{10}p_7$and $p_3t_8p_6t_{11}p_7$. To differentiate from the legitimate file access, we have to check the file path for further verification. For example in Table 1, the "Path Check" in the EXPR of t_2 and t_3, only software installation path, system path and pathes created by software are permitted to be accessed. For the sake of space limitation, we do not describe the other three modules in Fig. 3 in detail.

Table 1. Details Of **The Module Presented In** Fig. 3(A).

	EXPR	Input VarSet	Output VarSet
t_1	"NtQueryDirectoryFile"	Dir name	"Ctg"
t_2	"NtCreateFile"^Path Check	File name	File handle
t_3	"NtOpenFile"^ Path Check	File name	File handle
t_4	"NtNotifyChangeDirectoryFile"	Dir name	File handle
t_5	"NtFsControlFile"	Ctl Code	Pointer,"Cont"
t_6, t_7, t_8	"NtQueryInformationFile" "NtQueryAttributeFile" "NtQueryVolumeInformationFile	File handle	Pointer,"Cont"
t_9,t_{10},t_{11}	"NtReadFile"	File handle	Pointer,"Cont"
t_{12}	"NtClose"	File handle	NULL

doi:10.1371/journal.pone.0073410.t001

The PPN modules presented in Fig. 4 (a)–(c) for coverting network transmission correspond to three kinds of connections, namely, socket connection, FTP connection, and HTTP connection, respectively. In Fig. 4(a), it can be observed that to build a socket connection, the target software application should first create a socket and further build the server side or the client side. The application can then send privacy data and receive remote data. InFig. 4(b), for building an HTTP connection to leak privacy data, the target software application has to first create an Internet handle and set up a connection to a remote HTTP server. Next, it creates an HTTP request and adds HTTP headers. Finally, it sends data by posting an HTTP request. As depicted in Fig. 4(c), an FTP connection is used to transfer privacy data in files. It is especially suitable for a large number of files or a single large file. The leak procedure is similar to that of an HTTP connection: An Internet handle and connection are created first. Then, the work directory for file transmission is set. After these two steps, privacy data is leaked.

METHODS

Privacy leak can mainly be described from four aspects, namely, content, source, procedure and destination. Leak content refers to which kind of privacy data is leaked. Leak source means the storage form of privacy data. Leak procedure records the related system call sequence and the final destination of privacy data. Finally, leak destination is the remote server to which the privacy data is sent. In this paper, we propose to analyze privacy leak behavior from the above four aspects using PPN. We will not only qualitatively but also quantitatively analyze privacy leak behavior by proposing four metrics, i.e., possibility,severity, manipulability, and crypticity. Possibility is a basic metric denoting the probability that privacy leak behavior may occur. Severity denotes the negative consequence of an actual privacy leak behavior. Manipulability implies the tendency that the software application may be used by, or cooperated with, other applications to leak privacy data. Crypticity indicates the difficulty to detect the corresponding privacy leak behavior. These quantitative metrics characterize different aspects of privacy leak behavior, the combination of which makes the analysis more understandable and comprehensive. They are calculated mainly based on the output of PPN, i.e., the behavior path set (BPS). As presented in Definition 3, software behavior can be mapped to a set of traces of privacy instances moving across positions and transitions in the PPN corresponding to the execution of the target software application.

Weights of Transitions and PPN Modules

For a behavior path σ_{pathi}=inst$_i$.proc=$p_{i1}t_{i1}p_{i2}\ldots p_{i(n-1)}t_{i(n-1)}p_{in}$, we first assign a weight to each transition t_j ($1 \le j \le n-1$) according to its importance in the privacy leak procedure. A high weight means that the corresponding transition is more likely to be triggered in existing malware and is more important to privacy leak behavior. The weights are actually the statistical probabilities of these transitions. Specifically, given a set of software applications, they are run for a long enough period of time such that no more type of transitions can be observed. Assume that there are totally N types of transitions. In this situation, let w_{t_j}($0 \le w_{tj} \le 1$, $1 \le j \le N$) be the weight of transition t_j. If the corresponding system/API call is invoked, its call counter c_j increases by 1. Consequently, w_{t_j} can be calculated by

$$w_{t_j} = \frac{c_j}{\sum_{k=1}^{N} c_k} \quad (1)$$

Additionally, we divide the entire behavior path into different parts based on the typical PPN modules. Assume that a behavior path σ_{path_i} passes through m modules. σ_{path_i} can then be denoted as $\sigma_{path_i}=\sigma_1\sigma_2\ldots\sigma_m$, where $\sigma_i=p_{i1}t_{i1}p_{i2}\ldots p_{i(n-1)}t_{i(n-1)}p_{in}$ ($1 \le i \le m$). We also assign a weight w_{σ_i} to the path fragment σ_i according to the negative consequence of the corresponding PPN module. Such a negative consequence is affected by many factors, including the content, source and final destination of the leaked privacy data. Furthermore, the application scenario of the software application also influences the severity of the negative consequence. For instance, for a business server, the leak of the system data may expose the vulnerability of the system and make the server more vulnerable to network intrusion. For a personal computer, the leak of some dynamic data (e.g., bank account information and password) may cause financial loss. Considering all these factors, we sort the typical PPN modules in an ascending order based on the severity of their negative consequences and assign the module weight w_{σ_i} accordingly. More specifically, in this paper the seven PPN modules are sorted as m_{sda}, m_{nfda}, m_{ada}, m_{dda}, m_{http}, m_{socket}, m_{ftp}. Therefore, since σ_{path_i} contains m predefined PPN modules, their weights w_{σ_i} are assigned values from 1 to m in an ascending order. These weights will be used to calculate the severity and manipulability of privacy leak behavior.

Calculation of Quantitative Metrics

In this subsection, we show how to calculate the four metrics based on the aforementioned behavior paths.

Possibility

Possibility implies the probability that the paths in the BPS actually form leak paths. It is the fundamental metric for evaluating privacy leak behavior. Assume that σ_{path} is a behavior path in the BPS that contains n_j transitions and n_j+1 positions. Then, the possibility $p(\sigma_{pathj})$ can be calculated as: $p(\sigma_{path_j}) = \frac{1}{n_j}\sum_{i=1}^{n_j} w_{t_i}$. If there are N behavior paths in the BPS, the corresponding possibility can be obtained by:

$$P(BPS) = \frac{1}{N}\sum_{j}^{N} p(\sigma_{path_j}) \quad (2)$$

Severity

The calculation of severity is also based on the leak paths in the BPS. Assume that leak path σ_{path_j} contains m_j PPN modules. Its severity $s(\sigma_{path_j})$ can be calculated as $s(\sigma_{path_j}) = \frac{1}{m_j}\sum_{i=1}^{m_j} w_{\sigma_i}$. Further, the overall severity of the application under test can be denoted as:

$$S(BPS) = \frac{1}{N}\sum_{j=1}^{N} s(\sigma_{path_j})p(\sigma_{path_j}) \quad (3)$$

where N is the numbers of leak paths in the BPS. Severity is a comprehensive and intuitive metric for evaluating privacy leak behavior. The higher the severity, the severer the loss caused by the leak behavior.

Manipulability

Manipulability concerns whether the software application can be manipulated by other applications. Although some application only performs sub-procedure of a privacy leak behavior and thus has low possibility and severity, they may become a component of other malicious software in the multi-process collaborative work mode. Typically, manipulability has two modes, the relay race mode and the master/slave mode. The former splits its main functionality flow into two or more consequent parts, while the latter uses a master process to create and control slave processes. A feature they both have is that they split the leak behavior into several partial procedures. Therefore, manipulability should be evaluated for the leak behavior that is only partially completed. Specifically, it can be calculated for the paths that are not leak paths but still contain a source position or a discrimination position. And such paths should also be weighted by their severity. In general, manipulability can be calculated as

$$M(BPS) = \frac{1}{N_{PL}} \sum_{i=1}^{N_{PL}} s(\sigma_{path_i}) p(\sigma_{path_i}) \quad (4)$$

where N_{PL} is the number of partial leak paths in the BPS. The above definition of manipulability simplifies the metric in practice, but still captures the core of manipulation techniques. Although high manipulability does not lead to direct damage to privacy data, it is still necessary to pay special attention to it.

Crypticity

Crypticity is to evaluate the ability of privacy leak behavior to avoiding detection. Dedicately designed software applications always employ hiding and obfuscating techniques to improve their resistance against anti-virus software. There are many hiding and obfuscating techniques that privacy leak software applications often use. Most of them employ additional operations to disguise obvious malicious behavior. Assume that within the system call sequence of the target software application, n_{ei} extra system calls are traced but not represented by transitions between the start position and the end position of a behavior path σ_{path_i}. The crypticity can then be calculated by

$$C(BPS, n_{e_i}) = \frac{1}{N} \sum_{i=1}^{N} \frac{n_{e_i}}{n_i} p(\sigma_{path_i}) \quad (5)$$

Equation (5) indicates that the more the obfuscating or hiding operations for disguising the privacy leak behavior, the higher crypticity. Crypticity is essentially a complementary metric to severity. The software application with high severity may be easily detected and removed by anti-virus software, although high crypticity may help the privacy leak software application be active for a longer time and thus amplify its damage significantly.

Although the four metrics describe privacy leak behavior from different aspects, they have interrelations between each other. Fig. 5 summarizes the interrelationship, where the plus and minus signs indicate the positive and negative correlation between two metrics, respectively. The "+/–" signs denote the uncertain but potential interrelations. We can see from Fig. 5 that the four metrics constitute a closely linked entirety.

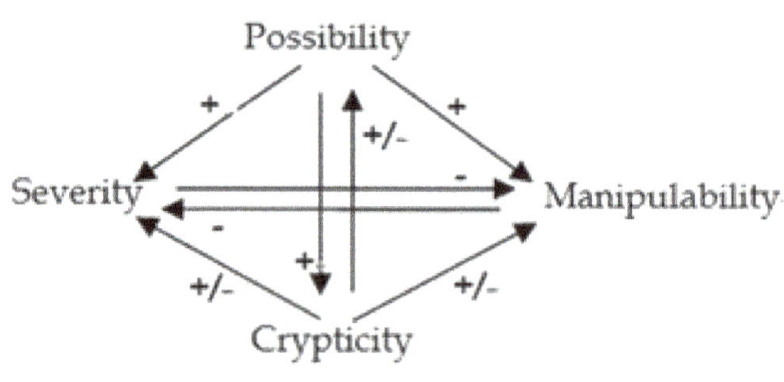

Figure 5. Interrelationship among the four metrics.

Possibility is a fundamental metric for evaluating privacy leak behavior. High possibility means a large probability $p(\sigma_{path_i})$ that the behavior path exists. Because only if a privacy leak behavior probably occurs, severity, manipulability and crypticity make sense. Therefore, possibility is a prerequisite of severity, manipulability and crypticity and $p(\sigma_{path_i})$ thus appears in their formulae as a factor. Severity and manipulability are complementary to each other, which characterize the straightforward and potential negative consequence of the privacy leak behavior of the software application under consideration, respectively. Crypticity is more special than other metrics. It may have an indirect impact on other metrics, because the obfuscating technique can conceal extra malicious operations. For example, it may cause unknown negative consequences, and thus increase severity and manipulability. Therefore, even if the other metrics are trivial, a software application with high cypticity is still likely to exhibit privacy leak behavior.

The Overall Leak Degree

In order to compare the overall degree of privacy leak behavior of different software applications, a comprehensive metric need to be proposed based on the possibility, severity, manipulability and crypticity metrics. Quantifying the overall degree of privacy leak behavior can be abstracted as a Multiple Attribute Decision Making (MADM) problem. An MADM problem aims to choose an item from a set of alternatives characterized by multiple attributes. Consider an MADM problem with n alternatives that denote the values of the four metrics of n software applications under test. A matrix corresponding to privacy leak metric is shown in Fig. 6, where the rows, denoted as P, S, M, C, correspond to the four metrics, and the columes, denoted as $A_1, A_2, \ldots, A_n$, correspond to n alternative, i.e., the n software applications, respectively.

$$\begin{array}{c} P \\ S \\ M \\ C \\ \\ \end{array} \begin{array}{c} \begin{pmatrix} p_1 & p_2 & \cdots & p_n \\ s_1 & s_2 & \cdots & s_n \\ m_1 & m_2 & \cdots & m_n \\ c_1 & c_2 & \cdots & c_n \end{pmatrix} \\ \begin{matrix} A_1 & A_2 & \cdots & A_n \end{matrix} \end{array}$$

Figure 6. Privacy leak metric matrix.

As aforementioned, the four metrics are interrelated. Therefore, in order to evaluate the overall degree of privacy leak behavior of the software application under test, we propose an algorithm, called PLEAS (Privacy Leak ovErall quAntitative analysiS), based on the Principal Component Analysis (PCA) to solve the above MADM problem. PCA is a method for identifying patterns in interrelated data and expressing the data in a way that highlights their similarities and differences. PCA can guarantee that PLEAS is able to obtain the most meaningful overall degree based on four metrics for comparative analysis between different software applications. With PLEAS, the alternatives $A_1, A_2, \ldots, A_n$ will be finally ranked. The higher the ranking value is, the more severe the privacy leak behavior of the corresponding software application will be. Readers are referred to Supporting Information S1 for more details about PLEAS.

RESULTS

This section validates the proposed PPN based approach to quantitative analysis on privacy leak behavior. Specifically, we first present an overview of the analysis environment and software set used for experiments. Next, we show a case study on an Internet software tool in order to demonstrate the effectiveness of the developed approach. Finally, as a direct application, we adopt the approach to carry out a comparative analysis on different software categories and discuss the experimental results.

Analysis Environment

In the experiments, VMware Workstation 7.0 is used as a virtual machine platform to build a Windows OS image. The core algorithm of the PPN model is implemented by Python 3.1. API monitor2 r9 is adopted to extract runtime execution traces of the set of software tools under test. All the software tools are installed and tested in different snapshots of the virtual host to avoid mutual interference.

We selected the programs contained in the Windows OS (WIN 7 Professional Edition) as the evaluation baseline environment. This program set includes system utilities under the system path "C:\\Windows\\System32" and the preinstalled software applications under the program path "C:\\Program Files". For some software tools that need user interaction, we tested them manually for 10 minutes. We then calculated the quantitative metrics of these tools as the baseline values of the baseline environment. After averaging the results of 1,026 benign software tools, the baseline values of the total leak paths, possibility, severity, manipulability and crypticity are 5, 0.35, 2.78, 2.59, and 3.26, respectively.

For the purpose of experiments, we also downloaded seven main categories of software tools from the well-known free software download website, Download.com: (1) entertainment software, including games, music software, video software, etc; (2) operating systems utilities, including file management software, backup software, automation software, desktop enhancement, etc; (3) Internet software, including browsers, email clients, file download/upload software, social networking software, etc; (4) business software, including office suites, account and billing software, E-commerce software, etc; (5) educational software, including E-book software, language software, student tools, science software, etc; (6) developer tools, including IDEs, debugging software, coding utility; (7) security software, including anti-virus software, encryption software, firewalls, etc. Specially, for each category, we downloaded the top ten software applications according to their popularity.

Case Study on a Web Browser

A web browser, referred to as A1 in this paper, has many plug-in enabled functions. Its call sequence fragments are depicted in Fig. 7. If the user installs a plug-in for managing the browse history and the favorite folder, it exposes to leak behavior, such as, collecting the cookies of some websitses and the sensitive system info beyond its authority. According to the call sequence, "GetComputerName, GetUserName, InternetGetCookie, Socket, Bind, Connect, Send", we obtained the PPN model as shown in Fig. 8. By tracing the execution of A1, we collected 15 leak behavior paths within 121 behavior paths. The number of leak behavior paths of A1 is larger than that of the baseline environment. The possibility, P, of the leak paths of A1 is 0.67, which is much higher than the corresponding baseline value, 0.35, indicating that A1 very probably has privacy leak behavior. According to the characteristic of web browsers, system data and application data that contain the browse history, usage habit and favorite websites of users are prone to be leaked. Therefore, the severity S of A1 is obtained to be 4.15. Due to the high percentage of the partial behavior paths, although A1 does not have many complete leak paths, its manipulability M was 3.39, higher than the baseline value. In addition, since a few obfuscating techniques are adopted by A1, its crypticity, P, is 9.51. The above results show that A1 more probably leaks privacy data, causes more severe consequence, and is more probably manipulated by other software tools, than the baseline program set in WIN 7, which is basically a reasonable observation.

Figure 7. The call sequence fragment of A1.

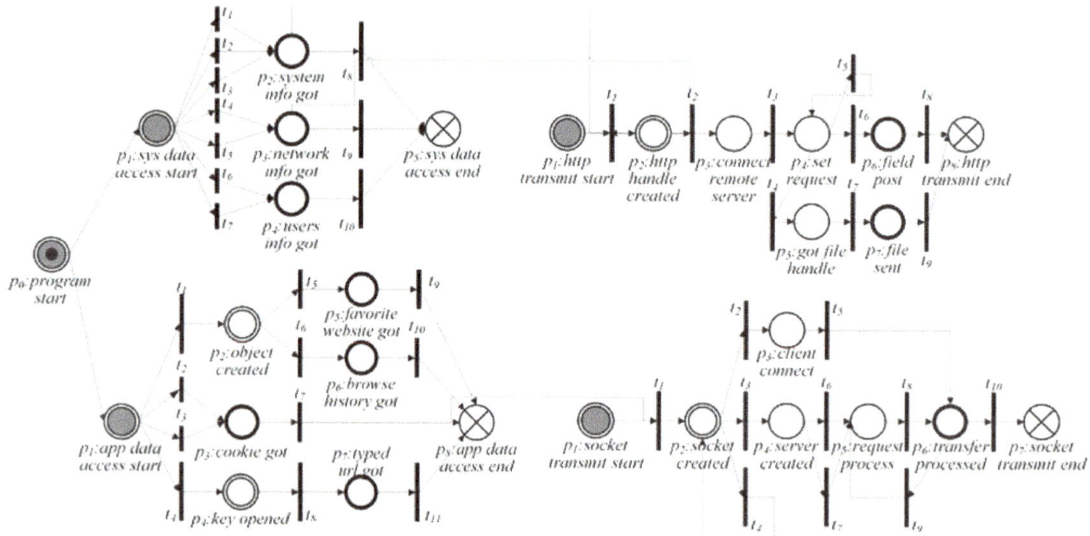

Figure 8. The PPN presenting the privacy leak behavior of A1.

In order to observe the relative performance of A1, we selected 9 other web browsers and calculated the average and variance of the corresponding four metrics. The values of different metrics were further normalized into [0, 1] and compared with those of A1 in Fig. 9. It can be seen that the consequence of privacy leak behavior of A1 is more severe than the average consequence of other browsers, while its manipulability is lower than them. As for possibility and crypticity, A1 and other browers are at the same level.

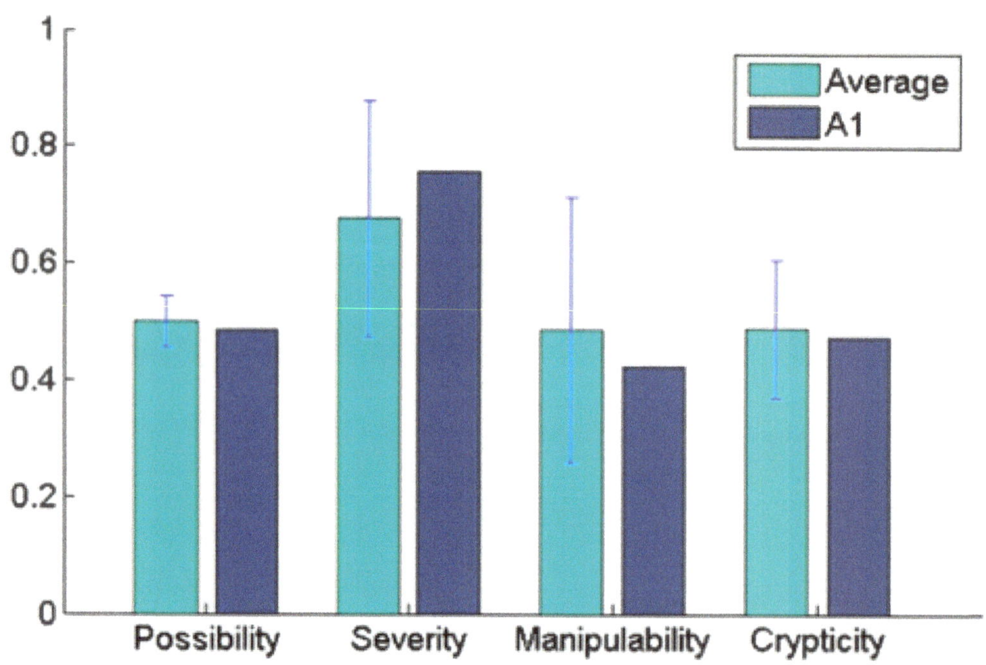

Figure 9. Quantitative values of A1 among browsers.

In summary, this case study has well demonstrated that the developed approach is effectiveness in quatitatively analyzing the privacy leak behavior of software applications.

Comparative Analysis on Different Software Categories

In order to demonstrate the value and merits of the developed PPN based analysis approach, in this subsection we employ it to investigate the privacy leak behavior of different software categories. For each software category, we calculated the average and standard deviation of the four quantitative metrics and futher obtained the overall degree of privacy leak behaviors using the PLEAS algorithm. The results are presented in Table 2.Figure 10 presents the corresponding ordered result for each metric.

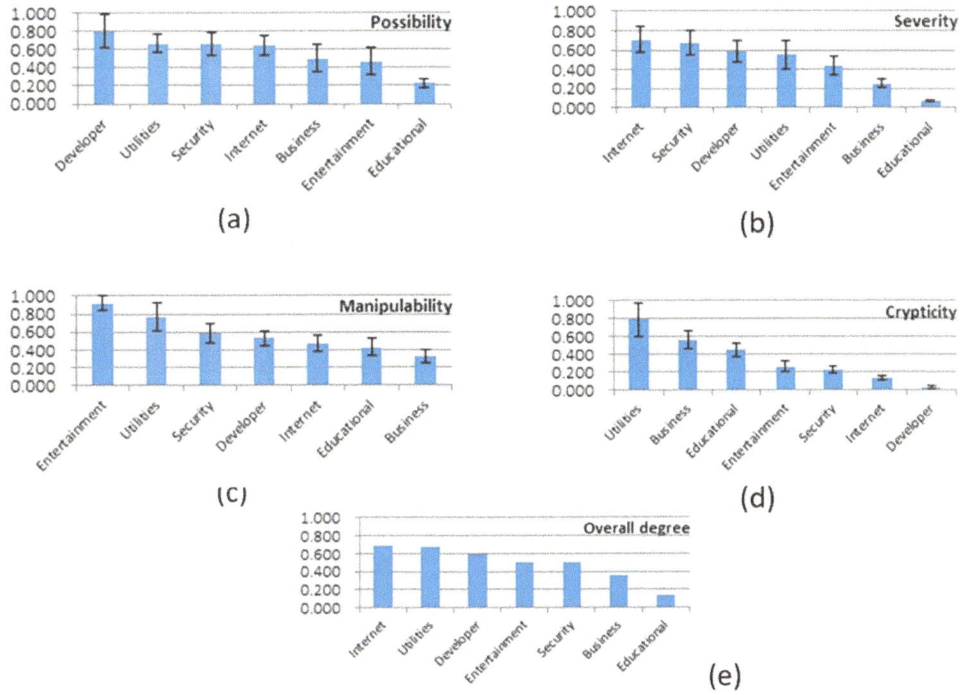

Figure 10. The four metrics and the overall degree of the seven categories of software applications.

Table 2. quantitative metrics of different software categories.

Category	P		S		M		C		O
	avg.	*std.dev.*	*avg.*	*std.dev.*	*avg.*	*std.dev.*	*avg.*	*std.dev.*	
Entertainment	0.473	0.152	0.434	0.095	0.920	0.080	0.265	0.062	0.510
Utilities	0.669	0.102	0.555	0.148	0.534	0.081	0.792	0.185	0.677
Internet	0.649	0.105	0.709	0.130	0.473	0.087	0.135	0.026	0.695
Business	0.503	0.153	0.255	0.042	0.324	0.068	0.036	0.009	0.354
Educational	0.230	0.049	0.075	0.012	0.431	0.095	0.454	0.080	0.145
Developer	0.805	0.176	0.589	0.110	0.765	0.156	0.563	0.097	0.595
Security	0.666	0.121	0.674	0.126	0.588	0.107	0.231	0.035	0.506

doi:10.1371/journal.pone.0073410.t002

Fig. 10 (a) shows that the category with the largest possibility is developer tools, because most developer tools not only manipulate many kinds of system resource such as file, processes and services, but also communicate with their remote servers such as code repository. The system utilities, security software and Internet software also have chances to access different kinds of privacy data and send them out via certain network operations, such as, updating database, getting new versions or communicating with service providers. Business software, entertainment software and educational software usually focus on local operations in their own data spaces and thus have fewer chances to form complete leak paths.

Fig. 10 (b) indicates that Internet software, security software and developer software are able to access most kinds of privacy data and have chances to send them out. Their behavior paths contain leak paths in all kinds of PPN modules such that the severity parameter $s(\sigma_{path_i})$ is usually larger than that of other software categories. Therefore, the severity of these categories is high. Due to similar reasons, entertainment software, business software and educational software have low severity.

High manipulability means that the software has more partial privacy leak paths. Fig. 10 (c)shows that entertainment software and utilities software have high manipulability because they usually collect some privacy data but do not send them out. Therefore, they often contain partial leak paths with only a source position, but without a discrimination position in the corresponding PPNs. Educational software and business software usually do not access privacy data. Consequently, their manipulability is low.

As shown in Fig.10 (d), obfuscating techniques involved in software design are often for the encryption of internal implementation and therefore immune to most of the reverse engineering tools. Software like utilities and business software which are not free usually contain many such techniques so that their crypticity is high. For developer tools that are usually open source, their crypticity is low.

As a comprehensive evaluation metric, the overall privacy leak degree of the seven software categories is presented in Fig.10 (e). It can be observed that Internet software, system utilizes and developer tools have a high privacy leak degree and educational software has the lowest degree. It should be pointed out that this is a general result for different software categories and it may not be appropriate for some special software tools. From this result, we can conclude that privacy leak behavior of software is mainly affected by three factors, namely, the chances that the application has to access important privacy data sources, the network function for transferring privacy data, and the crypticity for concealling the unauthorized operations.

Comparing the order of the seven software categories on different metrics, we find that the relationships between possibility and other three metrics are obviously verified. The possibility of Internet software, developer tools and system utility is high, and other three metrics of them are also higher than other software categories. The relation that severity and manipulability are complementary to each other is also verified. Internet software, security software, developer tools, utilities and entertainment software have reverse orders on severity and manipulability, respetively. The order of different software categories on crypticity implies the relationship we presented in the previous section. Although the other metrics of some software categories are low, they still have privacy leak threats if they have high crypticity. For example, the overall privacy leak degree of entertainment software is high, because its crypticity is high, although it has low possibility and severity.

From the above experimental results and reasonable explanations, we can conclude that the developed PPN based approach is an effective tool for quantitatively analyzeing privacy leak behavior of different software applications.

SUPPORTING INFORMATION

The algorithm of metrics calculation

Algorithm 1: The calculation of the four metrics

Input

CS: The call sequence of the software under test

Output

P: possibility; S: severity; M: manipulability; C: crypticity

Begin

/* Collect and filter the system calls of the tested software application.*/

for c **in** CS

/* if c does not satisfy the condition, drop it from CS. */

if not satisfy(c) **then**

drop(c, CS)

/* Trigger PPN pn with filtered system call sequence. */

else

trigger(c, pn)

/* insert the move path of token into BPS */

insert($inst_c$.proc, BPS)

/* Calculate the metrics by formula (1) to (4) */

[P, S, M, C] = [P(BPS), S(BPS), M(BPS), C(BPS)]

End

Algorithm 1 evaluates the system calls of the tested software application, and outputs the four quantitative metrics. First, we collect the system calls by monitoring the execution of the software on our experiment platform. Next, we check the collected system call sequence by two kinds of conditions. One is to check whether the call name is in the typical PPN modules. The other is to consider whether the parameters are related to our definition in the variable sets. Third, we trigger the PPN with the filtered system call sequence, perform the predefined operations. Fourth, the calls are processed, the moving trace of the tokens forms the BPS of the tested application. Finally, we calculate the four metrics based on the BPS.

Quantification algorithm of overall privacy leak degree

The main steps involved in PLEAS are as follows.

Firstly, we put four metrics of different software into a matrix M as presented in Fig. 11, then normalize the data. For each element m_{ij} in M, we calculate the normalized value $\tilde{m}_{ij}$ and vector $\tilde{X}_i$ as in (5):

$$\tilde{m}_{ij} = \frac{m_{ij} - \mu_{ij}}{s_i}\quad \tilde{X}_i = \frac{X_i - \mu_i}{s_i},\ i = 1, 2, 3, 4 \text{ and } j=1, 2, \dots, n \tag{5}$$

Where

$$\mu_{ij} = \frac{1}{n}\sum_{j=1}^{n} a_{ij}\ ,\quad s_i = \sqrt{\frac{1}{n-1}\sum_{j=1}^{n}(m_{ij} - u_{ij})^2}$$

Secondly, we calculate the covariance matrix $R = r_{ij\,(4\times4)}$ from M:

$$r_{ij} = \frac{\sum_{k=1}^{n} \tilde{m}_{ik}\cdot \tilde{m}_{kj}}{n-1},\ i, j = 1, 2, 3, 4 \tag{6}$$

from which the candidate principal component (PC) with the eigenvalue and eigenvector of R is calculated. Assuming that the eigenvalues are $\lambda_1 \geq \lambda_2 \geq \lambda_3 \geq \lambda_4 \geq 0$, and the corresponding eigenvectors are u_1, u_2, u_3, u_4, where $u_i = [u_{1i}, u_{2i}, u_{3i}, u_{4i}]^T$, then the candidate principal components are:

$$p_i = u_{1i}\tilde{X}_1 + u_{2i}\tilde{X}_2 + u_{3i}\tilde{X}_3 + u_{4i}\tilde{X}_4 \tag{7}$$

Thirdly we select principal components from the candidates. The number of principal components is less than or equal to the number of original variables. This selection is from the information proportion b_i of the pc_i. The first principal component is the most informative, and each succeeding component in turn has a less variance possible. b_i is calculated by eigenvalues:

$$b_i = \frac{\lambda_i}{\sum_{k=1}^{4}\lambda_k} \tag{8}$$

and the cumulative information proportion a_p is calculated based on b_i:

$$a_p = \sum_{k=1}^{p} b_k,\ b_k > b_{k+1} \tag{9}$$

when a_p approaches 1, we select $pc_1, pc_2 \dots pc_p$ as the principal components.

Finally we evaluate the values X of each alternative with the principal components selected in step 7 as in (10):

$$O = \sum_{k=1}^{p} \lambda_k \cdot p_k \tag{10}$$

O is the ranking value to evaluate the overall degree of privacy leak of the tested software application.The whole procedure is presented in Algorithm 2.

Algorithm 2: PLEAS

Input

$A_1, A_2, \ldots, A_n$: metrics tuple of n tested software applications, where $A_i = (p_i, s_i, m_i, c_i)$.

Output

$O_1, O_2, \ldots, O_n$: overall privacy leak degree from A_1 to A_n

Begin

/* Normalize metrics data by formula (5). */

$M = [A_1, A_2, \ldots, A_n]^T$

M' = normalize(M)

/* Calculate the covariance matrix by formula (6). */

R = covariance(M)

/* Calculate the eigenvalue and eigenvector of R. */

$U = [u_1, u_2, u_3, u_4]$ = eigenvector (R)

$\Lambda = [\lambda_1, \lambda_2, \lambda_3, \lambda_4]$ = eigenvalue(R)

/* Select principal component by formula (7) to (9). */

for i = 1 **to** 4

$b_i = b_i + \lambda_i$

$pc_i = u_i \cdot [x_1, x_2, x_3, x_4]^T$

p = i

/* The proportion threshold of principal component is 80% */

if then break

/* Evaluate the alternatives by formula (10). */

for i = 1 **to** n

for j = 1 **to** p

$O_i = O_i + \lambda_i \cdot pc_i$

End

The PCs found by PLEAS can assign the optimal weights of different metrics without the subjective assumption to maximize the variance of the metric vector. Therefore, it can effectively evaluate the overall degree of privacy leak based on the four metrics. Proposition 1 is a formal proof of this characteristic.

Proposition 1. Let $X = [x_1, x_2, \ldots, x_p]$ be variable vector which denotes the metrics of privacy leak behavior, $W = [w_1, w_2, \ldots, w_p]$ be the weight factor of each metric, $\lambda_1 \geq \lambda_2 \geq \ldots \geq \lambda_p \geq 0$ be the eigenvalue of the variance matrix Var(X), the corresponding eigenvector is $u_1, u_2, \ldots, u_p$. We have

$$\max_{W:\|W\|=1} \mathrm{Var}(W^T X) \text{ iff } W = \mu_1.$$

Proof: Assume that $M = \max_{W:\|W\|=1} \mathrm{Var}(W^T X) = \max_{W:\|W\|=1} W^T \mathrm{Var}(X) W$. Let $\Gamma \wedge \Gamma^T$ be the Jordan Decomposition of Var(X), then $\Gamma = (u_1, u_2, \ldots, u_p)$ $\mathrm{diag}(\lambda_1, \lambda_2, \ldots, \lambda_p)$. Let $Y = W^T \Gamma$. Because $Y^T Y = W^T \Gamma\ {}^T W = W^T W = 1$, we have

$$M = \max_{W:\|W\|=1} W^T \Gamma \wedge \Gamma^T W$$

$$= \max_{Y:\|Y\|=1} Y \wedge T^T$$

$$= \max_{Y:\|Y\|=1} \sum_{i=1}^{p} \lambda_i Y_i^2 \leq \lambda_1 \max_{Y:\|Y\|=1} \sum_{i=1}^{p} Y_i^2 = \lambda_1 .$$

The maximum is obtained when $Y = [1, 0, \ldots, 0]^T$, thus . Theorem 2 holds.

$W^T X$ is the first principal component selected based on Equation (7). Similarly, we can select other principals using Equations (8) and (9).

Supporting Information S1. Supporting Materials.

doi:10.1371/journal.pone.0073410.s001

AUTHOR CONTRIBUTIONS

Conceived and designed the experiments: LF. Performed the experiments: LF YW. Analyzed the data: LF YW. Contributed reagents/materials/analysis tools: YW XJ JL XC SJ. Wrote the paper: LF XJ JL.

REFERENCES

1. Jung J, Sheth A, Greenstein B, Wetherall D, Maganis G, et al. (2008) Privacy oracle: a system for finding application leaks with black box differential testing. In the 15th ACM Conference on Computer and Communications Security. Alexandria, Virginia, USA. ACM. pp. 279–288.
2. Borders K, Prakash A (2009) Quantifying Information Leaks in Outbound Web Traffic. In the 30th IEEE Symposium on Security and Privacy. Oakland, California, USA. IEEE. pp. 129–140.
3. Egele M, Kruegel C, Kirda E, Vigna G (2011) PiOS: Detecting Privacy Leaks in iOS Applications. In the 18th Annual Network & Distributed System Security Symposium. San Diego, California, USA. The Internet Society.
4. Kruegel C, Robertson W, Vigna G (2004) Detecting kernel-level rootkits through binary analysis. In the 20th Annual Computer Security Applications Conference. 0006-10-20; Tucson, Arizona, USA. ACM. pp. 91–100.
5. Moser A, Kruegel C, Kirda E (2007) Limits of Static Analysis for Malware Detection. In the 23th Annual Computer Security Applications Conference. Miami Beach, FL, USA. ACM. pp. 421–430.
6. Egele M, Kruegel C, Kirda E, Yin H, Song D (2007) Dynamic spyware analysis. In the 16th USENIX Security

Symposium. Boston, MA, USA. USENIX Association. pp. 233–246.

7. Lanzi A, Sharif MI, Lee W (2009) K-Tracer: A System for Extracting Kernel Malware Behavior. In the 16th Annual Network & Distributed System Security Symposium. 2009; San Diego, California, USA. The Internet Society.

8. Moser A, Kruegel C, Kirda E (2007) Exploring Multiple Execution Paths for Malware Analysis. In the 28th IEEE Symposium on Security and Privacy. 2007; Oakland, California, USA. IEEE. pp. 231–245.

9. Comparetti PM, Salvaneschi G, Kirda E, Kolbitsch C, Kruegel C, et al.. (2010) Identifying Dormant Functionality in Malware Programs. In the 31th IEEE Symposium on Security and Privacy. 2010; Oakland, California, USA. IEEE. pp. 61–76.

10. Fan L, Wang Y, Cheng X, Li J (2012) Analyzing Application Private Information Leaks With Privacy Petri Net. In the 17th IEEE Symposium on Computers and Communication. 2012; Cappadocia, Turkey. IEEE.

CHAPTER 12

DOSIMETRIC VERIFICATION BY USING THE ARCCHECK SYSTEM AND 3DVH SOFTWARE FOR VARIOUS TARGET SIZES

Jin Ho Song[1] , Hun-Joo Shin[2] , Chul Seung Kay[2] , Seok Hyun Son[2]

[1] Department of Radiation Oncology, Seoul St. Mary's Hospital, College of Medicine, The Catholic University of Korea, Seoul, Republic of Korea

[2] Department of Radiation Oncology, Incheon St. Mary's Hospital, College of Medicine, The Catholic University of Korea, Seoul, Republic of Korea

ABSTRACT

Objective

To investigate the usefulness of the 3DVH software with an ArcCHECK 3D diode array detector in newly designed plans with various target sizes.

Methods

The isocenter dose was measured with an ion-chamber and was compared with the planned and 3DVH predicted doses. The 2D gamma passing rates were evaluated at the diode level by using the ArcCHECK detector. The 3D gamma passing rates for specific regions of interest (ROIs) were also evaluated by using the 3DVH software. Several dose-volume histograms (DVH)-based predicted metrics for all structures were also obtained by using the 3DVH software.

Results

The isocenter dose deviation was <1% in all plans except in the case of a 1 cm target. Besides the gamma passing rate at the diode level, the 3D gamma passing rate for specific ROIs tended to decrease with increasing target size; this was more noticeable when a more stringent gamma criterion was applied. No correlation was found with the gamma passing rates and the DVH-based metrics especially in the ROI with high-dose gradients.

Conclusions

Delivery quality assurance by using 3DVH and ArcCHECK can provide substantial information through a simple and easy approach, although the accuracy of this system should be judged cautiously.

Citation: Song JH, Shin H-J, Kay CS, Son SH (2015) Dosimetric Verification by Using the ArcCHECK System and 3DVH Software for Various Target Sizes. PLoS ONE 10(3): e0119937. doi:10.1371/journal.pone.0119937

INTRODUCTION

In order to check the accuracy of radiation delivery in radiotherapy, verification tests such as delivery quality assurance (QA) must be performed prior to patient treatment. Dosimetry verification and QA testing are particularly important in high-precision and complex treatments such as radiosurgery and intensity modulated radiation therapy (IMRT). As these recently developed advanced radiation techniques are characterized according to inherently high dose gradients, even a tiny error can significantly alter the results [1]. Moreover, along with the increasing use of these new radiotherapy techniques, interest in dosimetry verification and QA has been growing.

There are two main methods for evaluating delivery QA: (1) irradiate a plastic phantom that contains an ion-chamber or film with all the beams of the actual treatment plan and measure the actual composite dose; (2) measure each dose of multiple beams by using measuring devices comprising a diode or ion-chamber array. The latter method has been used by several institutions because it can be performed relatively quickly and easily, and can measure all beams. Two-dimensional (2D) detector arrays such as MapCHECK (SunNuclear, Melbourne, FL, USA) and MatriXX (IBA Dosimetry, GmbH, Schwarzenbrook, Germany) were used in the past; these 2D detector array devices had the definite limitation of missing a great portion of the lateral beams because of their individual planar designs [2]. Therefore, three-dimensional (3D) diode array measuring devices such as Delta4 (Scandidos, Uppsala, Sweden) and ArcCHECK (SunNuclear) were recently developed [2–5].

Gamma analysis, which was introduced by Low et al. [6], is used to determine if the measured result is appropriate for comparing and evaluating dose distributions; it uses the following two concepts: dose difference and distance-to-agreement (DTA). The 3% dose difference and 3 mm DTA criterion is commonly used in dosimetric studies as recommended in the American Association of Physicists in Medicine (AAPM) Task Group 119 [7, 8]. When a stricter criterion is required, a 2%/2 mm criterion is often used [4, 9]. The rate that satisfies a gamma criterion is called the gamma passing rate. However, the clinical significance of these criteria is not always clear. For example, even if the gamma passing rate of a specific plan is assumed to be 95%, it cannot ensure that this is actually safer for the patient than another plan with a rate of 85%. Thus, in actual patient treatment, the magnitudes and locations of these dose errors are extremely important.

Several authors recently mentioned that the gamma index obtained through per-beam planar QA can be misleading and insensitive to dosimetric errors [10–12]. In addition, the commercially available 3DVH software from SunNuclear is reported to be able to compensate for the disadvantages. Beam measurements from a treatment plan are input into the 3DVH software, which reconstructs the full 3D dose distribution and allows comparison with the treatment planning system (TPS) calculations. Thus, the 3D distribution of the actually delivered dose can be demonstrated and a dose-volume histogram (DVH) for each target and organ at risk (OAR) can be drawn on the basis of these data [9–13].

Accordingly, in this study, we compared the TPS planned dose to the measured doses by using the ArcCHECK diode array detector and to the predicted doses by using the 3DVH software (2D and 3D gamma analysis) for various target sizes. We also analyzed the 3D DVH-based metrics with the aid of 3DVH software (DVH analysis). Therefore, the usefulness and accuracy of these QA methods has been evaluated.

MATERIALS AND METHODS

Treatment Plan Design and Radiation Delivery

Five treatment plans with various target sizes were newly designed by using the computed tomography (CT) images of a homogenous phantom with the same dimensions (26.5 × 26.5 × 27.0 cm^3) as those of the ArcCHECK (provided by SunNuclear). A circle representing the treatment 'target' was contoured with an isocenter as the center of the axial CT image. Targets of different sizes (1, 3, 5, 7, and 9 cm in diameter) for each plan were established (Fig. 1). We also contoured a donut-shaped region of interest (ROI) with 1 cm thickness around the target and named it the 'adjacent OAR'. The rim of the phantom CT was also contoured in the shape of a donut with a thickness of 1 cm to represent the 'peripheral OAR' (Fig. 1). The lengths of the targets and all OARs were set at 5 cm. The volumes per ROI are shown in Table 1.

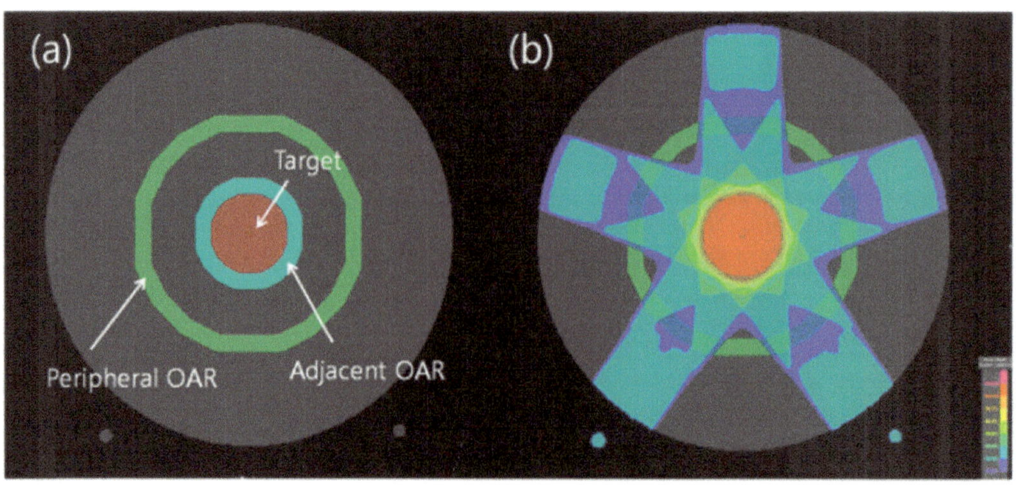

Figure 1. Axial slices of the ArcCHECK CT phantom with the target, adjacent organ at risk (OAR), and peripheral OAR (a). Five portals were used for the planning to cover 95% of the target volume with the prescribed dose. The beam angles were 0°, 72°, 144°, 216° and 288° (b).

Table 1. Volumes of the target, adjacent organ at risk (OAR) and peripheral OAR with respect to target size.

Target size	Target volume (cc)	Adjacent OAR (cc)	Peripheral OAR (cc)
1 cm	4.2	34.3	238.5
3 cm	38.5	68.3	238.5
5 cm	106.8	102.3	238.5
7 cm	209.2	136.4	238.5
9 cm	345.6	170.4	238.5

OAR: organ at risk

All plans used the iPlan (BrainLAB, v.4.1.2) TPS, and the planning goal was set as 95% coverage of the target by using 3D conformal therapy. Five treatment fields were used with 3 mm multi-leaf collimator (MLC) margins from the target. The beam angles were 0°, 72°, 144°, 216°, and 288°. The chosen prescription doses per each target size plan were 200, 400, 600, 800, and 1000 cGy. A pencil-beam algorithm was used for the dose calculations, with dose grids of 1 mm for both axial and coronal planes.

All tests were carried out on a classic Novalis accelerator (BrainLAB, Feldkirchen, Germany). The Novalis is a linear accelerator system with a single 6 MV energy beam specifically manufactured for high-precision radiosurgery. The MLC of Novalis consists of 26 leaf pairs. The 14 central most leaves have a width of 3 mm, the 6 intermediate leaves have a width of 4.5 mm, and the 6 peripheral leaves are of 5.5 mm width. The maximal field size is 10 × 10 cm^2. All plans were delivered with their actual treatment angles to the ArcCHECK 3D diode detector. Each plan was measured 3 consecutive times with 5 different radiation doses. Before the radiation delivery, the absolute dose calibration was performed for a 10 × 10 cm^2 open field at a 100 cm source to skin distance (SSD) according to the TG-51 calibration protocol [14].

Comparison of Isocenter Doses

The first validation test involved comparisons of the isocenter doses. The ArcCHECK has a central cavity into which various inserts and detectors can be plugged in and used. An EXRADIN A16-micro ion-chamber (Standard Imaging, Middleton, WI, USA) was inserted in a CavityPlug acrylic insert, which can directly measure isocenter doses. The doses were read by a SUPERMAX electrometer (Standard Imaging). By this method, a directly measured dose from the ion-chamber was compared with the planned isocenter dose. The planned dose was also compared with the predicted dose calculated by the 3DVH software on the basis of the data measured by the ArcCHECK diodes. For comparisons among individual doses, absolute doses were compared among each other; the significance of differences between mean values was determined by independent t-tests. In addition, dose deviations between the measured or predicted dose and planned dose were identified and compared. Dose deviation is expressed as the absolute value, and it was calculated using the following formula:

$$[\text{Dose deviation } (\%) = \frac{|\text{Measured or Predicted dose } - \text{ Planned dose}|}{\text{Planned dose}} \times 100(\%)]$$

The difference per target size was evaluated by using one-way analysis of variance (ANOVA). All statistical analyses with p values less than 0.05 were considered significant. Statistical analyses were performed by using STATA/IC ver.12 software (StataCorp, College Station, TX, USA).

Analysis of 2D and 3D Gamma Passing Rates

Analysis of 2D gamma passing rates at the diode level.

The ArcCHECK device is a cylindrical water-equivalent phantom with 1,386 diode detectors arranged in a 3D helical fashion at 10 mm intervals within a cylinder with a diameter and length of 21 cm. The angles between the diodes were 5.45 degrees. Each diode in the active detector is 0.8 × 0.8 mm^2 and is positioned 2.9 cm below the surface. A dedicated software program SNC Patient (v.6.1.1, SunNuclear) was used to analyze the ArcCHECK data. A digital imaging and communications in medicine (DICOM) file for the treatment plan is imported in this software, and a dose grid corresponding to diode detector locations is extracted to compare the calculated and measured doses.

With this software, we obtained the gamma passing rate of each plan at the diode level. The global gamma indices were set as the percentage dose differences calculated with respect to the maximum 3D dose. Two gamma criteria were analyzed, 3%/3 mm and 2%/2 mm, in absolute doses with a threshold of 5%. Whether the gamma passing rate differed as per target size was verified by the one-way ANOVA analysis.

Analysis of 3D Gamma Passing Rates For Specific Regions of Interest

One of the advantages of the 3DVH software is that it can calculate the gamma passing rate for the entire radiated volume as well as the gamma passing rate for each corresponding ROI. The data measured in each field by the ArcCHECK diodes are imported into the 3DVH software along with the following 4 other DICOM files from the TPS: the treatment plan, CT images, structures, and calculated dose. The discrepancies between the planned dose and the measured planar dose are calculated, and these calculated errors are back-projected into the original treatment plan. Through this process, we could obtain a newly perturbed 3D dose distribution, which reflects any errors detected by the per-beam planar QA. The proprietary planned dose perturbation (PDP) algorithm was used in the process in this manner [11, 12]. In addition, as the detector pitch between the ArcCHECK diodes was not as dense as those of the planned dose grids, a proprietary interpolation known as Smarterpolation was applied. Through this process, the 3DVH software can calculate the 3D gamma indices for the entire plan as well as the DVH differences for each structure and the 3D gamma indices between the planned and perturbed matrices [11, 12].

With the aid of the 3DVH software, we measured the 3D gamma passing rates for each ROI. The global gamma indices with the two gamma criteria (3%/3 mm and 2%/2 mm) and a threshold of 5% were also used. The 3D gamma passing rates were analyzed according to whether they differed with respect to target size by using the one-way ANOVA and the Pearson correlation analysis.

Analysis of Dose Volume Histogram (DVH)-Based Metrics

Various DVH-based predicted metrics for all ROI structures were obtained by using the 3DVH software. The mean dose and the dose covering 50% of the volume (D50) were obtained, and the dose covering 95% of the volume (D95) was calculated for the 'target' ROI. These predicted dose matrices for each plan were compared with the planned dose matrices in the TPS. The dose deviation was expressed as the absolute value, and it was defined and calculated as follows:

$$\text{Dose deviation } (\%) = \frac{|\text{Predicted dose} - \text{Planned dose}|}{\text{Planned dose}} \times 100(\%)$$

The dose deviation per target size was analyzed by one-way ANOVA, and the Pearson correlation analysis was performed to examine the correlation between the dose deviation of the DVH-based metrics and the 3D gamma passing rate for each ROI.

RESULTS

Comparison of Isocenter Doses

The planned dose at the isocenter was 102.05 ± 1.07% of the prescribed dose. This was not significantly different compared to the dose directly measured by the ion-chamber of 101.81 ± 0.73% (p = 0.359) or the predicted dose calculated by the 3DVH software of 102.65 ± 1.41% (p= 0.099). Table 2 shows the results of the dose deviations according to target size. With a target size of 1 cm, the differences between measured and planned doses, and predicted and planned doses were 0.61% and 1.50%, respectively, which constituted the largest discrepancy; meanwhile, with a target size of 9 cm, the dose deviations decreased to 0.29% and 0.15%, respectively, constituting the smallest discrepancy (Fig. 2). Every dose deviation was below 1%, except for the case of a target of 1 cm. Thus, the 3DVH software could be used to make relatively precise predictions about isocenter doses, although it is important to be cautious when target size is small.

Table 2. Comparison of dose deviations (%) among treatment planning system (TPS)-planned dose, ion-chamber measured isocenter dose, and the 3DVH-predicted isocenter dose

Target size	1 cm	3 cm	5 cm	7 cm	9 cm	*p value*
Measured dose /Planned dose	0.61 ± 0.24	0.67 ± 0.21	0.23 ± 0.17	0.20 ± 0.25	0.15 ± 0.13	*0.001*
Predicted dose /Planned dose	1.50 ± 0.48	0.39 ± 0.32	0.53 ± 0.39	0.47 ± 0.27	0.29 ± 0.08	*<0.001*

There were significant differences with respect to target size verified by one-way ANOVA.

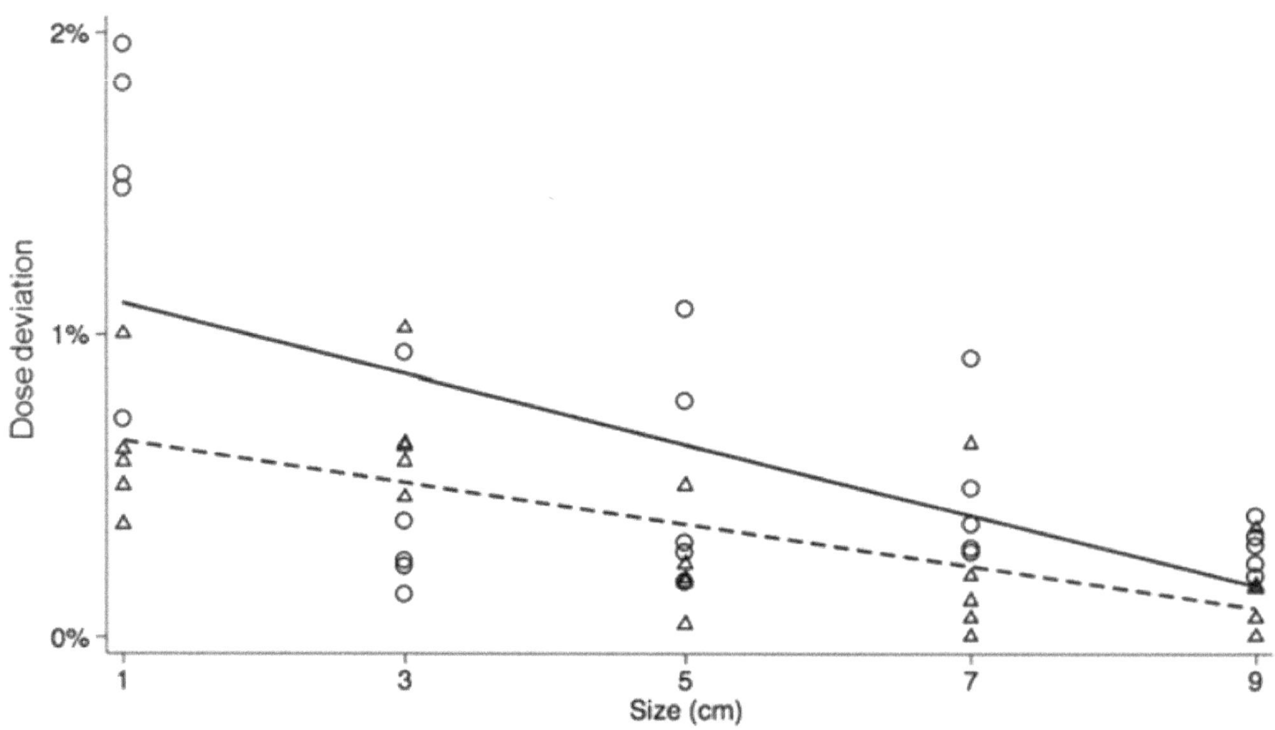

Figure 2. The dose deviation of the isocenter between the 3DVH-predicted dose and the treatment planning system (TPS)-planned dose is plotted as a solid line. The dashed line represents the dose deviation between the ion-chamber measured isocenter dose and planned dose. The dose deviations decreased with increasing target size.

Analysis of 2D and 3D Gamma Passing Rates

Analysis of 2D gamma passing rates at the diode level.

The gamma passing rates at the diode level are presented in Table 3. For the gamma 3%/3 mm criterion, the gamma passing rates were 100% and 98.5% when the target size was 1 and 3 cm. The gamma passing rates decreased to 96.9%, 96.3% and 95.9% with a target size of 5, 7, and 9 cm respectively, and it was statistically significant ($p < 0.001$). As the target size increased, the gamma passing rates at the diode level tended to decrease; this was more prominent when the more stringent gamma 2%/2 mm criterion was applied (Fig. 3).

Table 3. Comparison of gamma passing rates at the diode level according to target size

Target size	1 cm	3 cm	5 cm	7 cm	9 cm	*p value*
3%/3 mm	100	98.5	96.9 ± 0.1	96.3 ± 0.3	95.9 ± 0.3	*<0.001*
2%/2 mm	97.9 ± 0.2	96.1 ± 0.2	92.6 ± 0.3	88.5 ± 0.9	86.0 ± 0.5	*<0.001*

There were significant differences with respect to target size verified by one-way ANOVA.

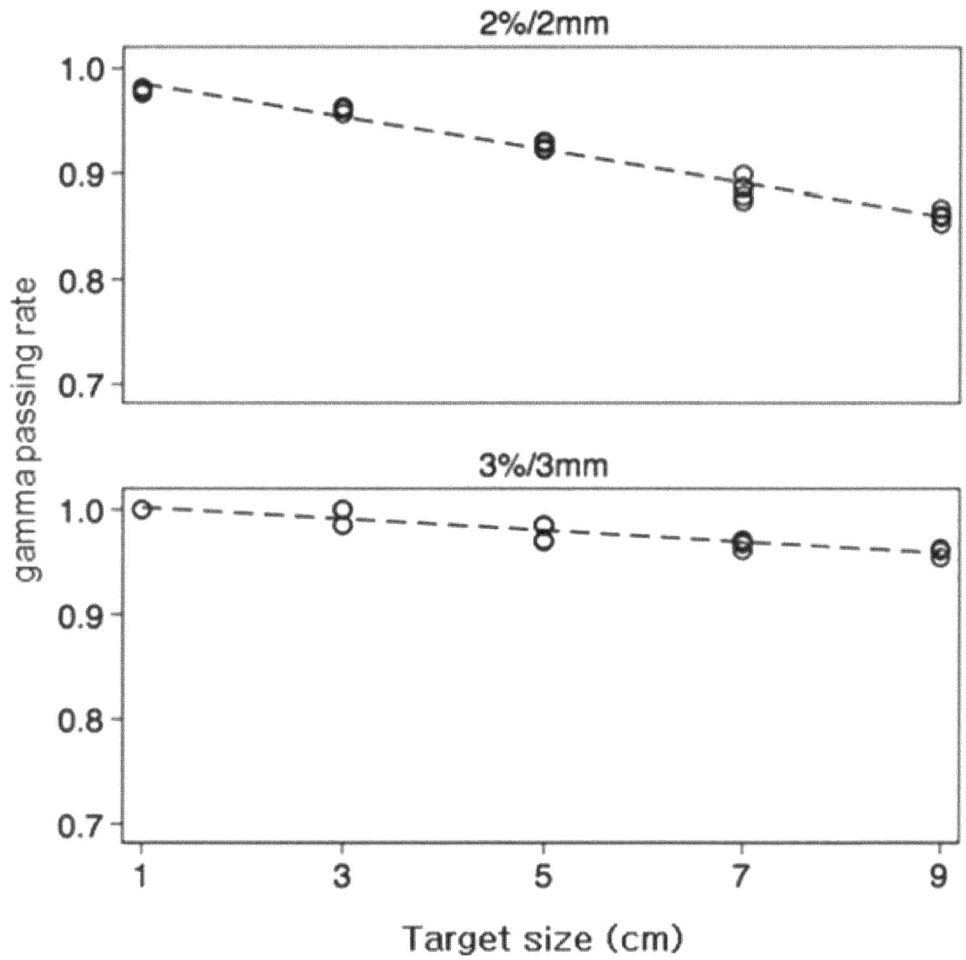

Figure 3. Variations of gamma passing rates at the diode level with various target sizes. The gamma passing rates were calculated with both the 3%/3 mm criterion (lower graph) and the 2%/2 mm criterion (upper graph) in absolute doses with a threshold of 5%. The gamma passing rate decreased as the target size increased.

Analysis of 3D gamma passing rate for specific regions of interest.

The 3D gamma passing rates for specific ROIs were calculated by using the 3DVH software, and they are presented in Table 4. For the gamma 3%/3 mm criterion, the average 3D gamma passing rates of the target, adjacent OAR, and periphery OAR were 96.6%, 98.1%, and 98.8%, respectively; by using the more stringent gamma 2%/2 mm criterion, the average passing rates of each ROI decreased to 85.2%, 89.8%, and 89.7% respectively. As the target size increased, the gamma passing rates tended to decrease in all ROIs; this was more noticeable when the 2%/2 mm criterion was applied (Fig. 4). The correlation analysis with regard to target size and gamma passing rate of each ROI produced correlation coefficient r values of -0.256 ($p = 0.010$) for the target, -0.667 ($p < 0.001$) for the adjacent OAR, -0.853 ($p < 0.001$) for peripheral OAR, respectively, all of which were consistent with negative correlation.

Table 4. Comparison of 3D gamma passing rates of various regions of interest according to target size

Target size		1 cm	3 cm	5 cm	7 cm	9 cm	*p value*
3%/3 mm	Target	97.1 ± 0.7	97.1 ± 1.7	99.8 ± 0.1	96.8 ± 1.1	92.1 ± 1.8	*<0.001*
	Adjacent	99.8 ± 0.1	99.0 ± 0.2	99.6 ± 0.2	98.9 ± 0.2	93.2 ± 0.8	*<0.001*
	Peripheral	100 ± 0.0	100 ± 0.0	99.6 ± 0.2	98.8 ± 0.6	95.8 ± 1.6	*<0.001*
2%/2 mm	Target	88.5 ± 6.0	84.6 ± 4.6	93.3 ± 3.6	82.6 ± 3.3	76.9 ± 3.4	*<0.001*
	Adjacent	99.4 ± 0.1	92.4 ± 1.4	94.8 ± 1.7	87.6 ± 2.0	74.7 ± 2.3	*<0.001*
	Peripheral	100 ± 0.0	100 ± 0.0	93.2 ± 1.5	79.7 ± 1.9	75.9 ± 3.1	*<0.001*

The differences among the groups were verified by one-way ANOVA.

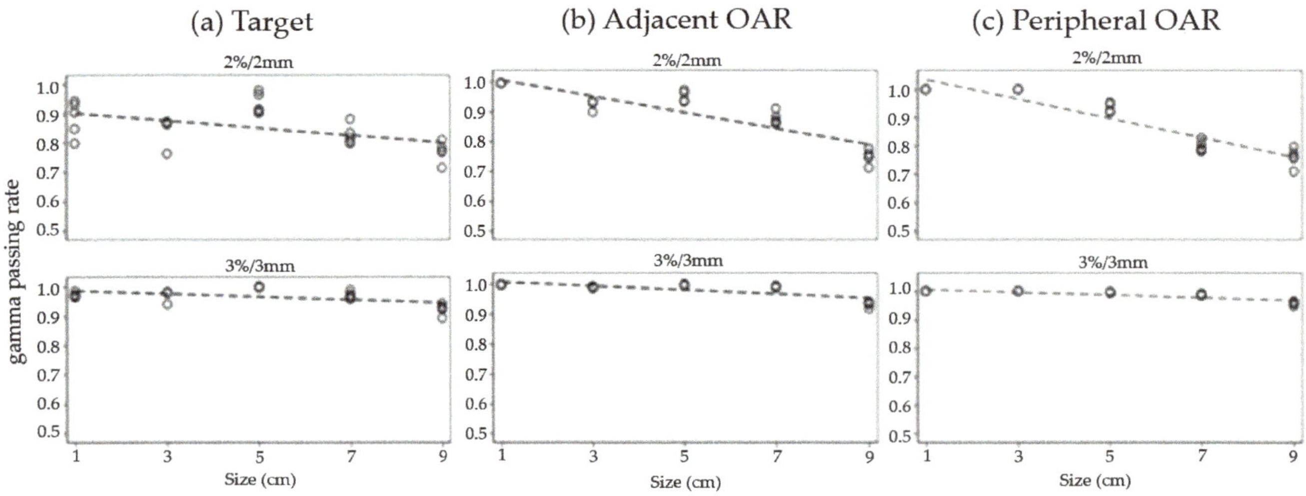

Figure 4. Variation of 3D gamma passing rates for (a) target, (b) adjacent organ at risk (OAR), and (c) peripheral OAR with various target sizes. The gamma passing rates were calculated with both the 3%/3 mm criterion (upper graph) and the 2%/2 mm criterion (lower graph) in absolute doses with a threshold of 5%. The 3D gamma passing rate decreased as the target size increased in all specific regions of interest.

Analysis of Dose Volume Histogram (DVH)-Based Metrics

Table 5 shows the % values of planned and predicted doses for each ROI versus the prescribed doses. For the target, the mean dose, D95, and D50 all differed between the planned and predicted doses. On the other hand, the adjacent and peripheral OARs did not differ significantly between the planned and predicted doses. However, in an example of a real DVH curve, some differences can be observed for all ROIs (Fig. 5).

Table 5. Comparison of the various dose-volume parameters between the treatment planning system (TPS)-planned dose and the 3DVH-predicted dose

		Mean dose (%)	*p value*	D95 (%)	*p value*	D50 (%)	*p value*
Target	Plan	101.82 ± 0.32	*<0.001*	99.32 ± 0.47	*<0.001*	102.17 ± 0.32	*0.025*
	3DVH	101.08 ± 0.83		97.15 ± 0.63		101.72 ± 0.90	
Adjacent	Plan	79.54 ± 9.02	*0.108*	N/A		77.58 ± 11.28	*0.209*
	3DVH	75.46 ± 8.60				73.59 ± 10.86	
Peripheral	Plan	32.29 ± 16.45	*0.776*	N/A		30.95 ± 19.21	*0.842*
	3DVH	31.00 ± 15.36				29.89 ± 18.27	

D95: dose covering 95% of the volume; D50: dose covering 50% of the volume; N/A: not assessed. The mean dose is represented as the relative dose compared to the prescribed dose. The statistical significance of the difference between the planned and predicted dos was calculated by independent t-test.

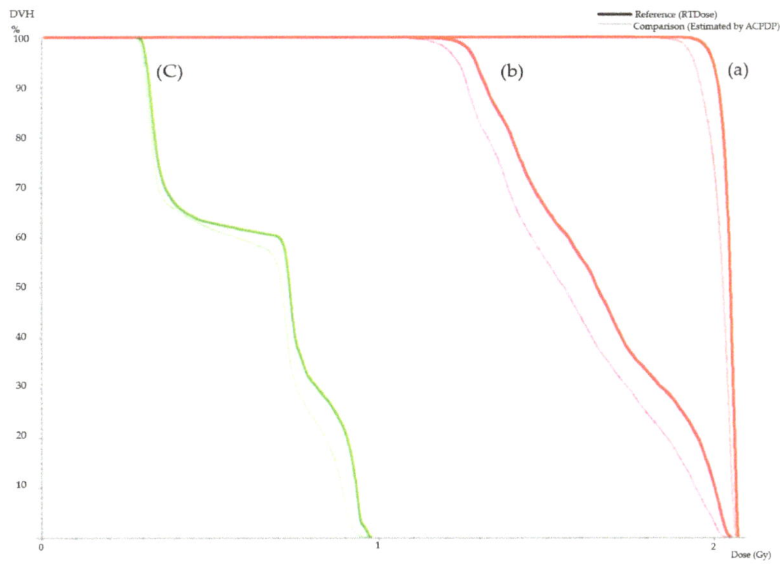

Figure 5. An example of a dose-volume histogram representing the dose distribution for the (a) target, (b) adjacent organ at risk (OAR), and peripheral OAR. The treatment planning system (TPS)-planned doses are plotted as solid lines. The dashed lines represent the 3DVH software-predicted dose, which was calculated on the basis of the ArcCHECK data.

The dose deviations between the planned and the predicted doses of several DVH-based metrics are shown in Table 6. Dose deviations varied in every ROI and every DVH-based dose parameter with respect to varying the target sizes.

Table 6. Dose deviation (%) with various dose parameters between the 3DVH-predicted and planned doses with respect to target size

Target size		1 cm	3 cm	5 cm	7 cm	9 cm	*p value*
Target	mean	0.84 ± 0.49	1.10 ± 0.17	0.78 ± 0.34	1.17 ± 0.18	1.42 ± 0.22	*0.026*
	D95	1.05 ± 0.50	2.72 ± 0.18	2.08 ± 0.33	2.35 ± 0.17	2.71 ± 0.22	*<0.001*
	D50	1.21 ± 0.50	0.70 ± 0.15	0.55 ± 0.35	0.95 ± 0.20	1.20 ± 0.22	*0.011*
Adjacent	mean	5.22 ± 0.26	5.50 ± 0.21	4.49 ± 0.34	5.22 ± 0.21	5.24 ± 0.21	*<0.001*
	D50	5.21 ± 1.13	5.63 ± 0.22	5.70 ± 0.36	4.63 ± 0.21	4.63 ± 0.19	*0.011*
Peripheral	mean	0	0	4.98 ± 0.35	5.08 ± 0.15	4.79 ± 0.22	*<0.001*
	D50	0	0	3.02 ± 0.33	3.99 ± 0.13	4.45 ± 0.22	*<0.001*

D95: dose covering 95% of the volume; D50: dose covering 50% of the volume.

The p values represent the differences among the groups calculated by one-way ANOVA.

Correlation analysis was performed to determine if these dose deviations were related to the 3D gamma passing rates (Table 7). Moderate correlations (i.e., $|r| > 0.4$) were observed for both the target and peripheral OAR. Here, a negative correlation coefficient indicates the dose deviation decreased with an increasing 3D gamma passing rate of a specific ROI. Therefore, the correlations between the 3D gamma passing rate and DVH-based metrics were comparatively confirmed for the target and peripheral OAR. The correlation increased further with the more stringent gamma criterion (2%/2 mm). However, in terms of the adjacent OAR, the mean dose and D50 showed no correlation, indicating a discrepancy between the 3D gamma passing rate and DVH-based metrics.

Table 7. Correlations between the magnitude of dose difference and the gamma passing rate of each region of interest (ROI), calculated with both gamma 3%/3 mm and 2%/2 mm criteria

		Gamma 3%/3 mm		Gamma 2%/2 mm	
		r	*p value*	r	*p value*
Target	mean	-0.723	*<0.001*	-0.878	*<0.001*
	D95	-0.358	*0.079*	-0.455	*0.022*
	D50	-0.651	*<0.001*	-0.677	*<0.001*
Adjacent	mean	-0.237	*0.253*	-0.268	*0.195*
	D50	0.385	*0.057*	0.418	*0.038*
Peripheral	mean	-0.435	*0.030*	-0.812	*<0.001*
	D50	-0.621	*<0.001*	-0.931	*<0.001*

D95: dose covering 95% of the volume; D50: dose covering 50% of the volume.
Pearson correlation coefficient (r) and two-tailed p-values were calculated.

DISCUSSION

Radiation delivery QA has traditionally used a composite irradiation method by using an ion-chamber or film, or a beam-by-beam irradiation method by using diode or ion-chamber arrays. However, neither of these methods can show how the delivery dose errors will affect the actual patient treatments [13]. However, the 3DVH software and a 3D diode array detector such as ArcCHECK can be used to obtain a great amount of information quickly and easily. The use of a 3D rather than a 2D diode array allows the data of each beam's eye view to obtained in every field; both entry and exit dose values can be attained as well [3]. By using the 3DVH software, composite data can be produced with the information obtained from each beam. In addition, the information allows us to determine how the composite data affects the dose distribution of an actual ROI. The present study differs from previous 3DVH software studies using virtual measurement data [11, 12] or 2D diode array detector data [10, 13].

Moreover, this study designed the targets, adjacent OAR, and peripheral OAR directly on the CT phantom, in contrast to several previous studies that have used existing patient plans. In this study, the adjacent OAR was contoured close to the target ROI because an important purpose of performing 3D conformal therapy or IMRT is to reduce the radiation dose to the OARs around the treatment target. The target is a high-dose field, and the adjacent ROI is a field with a high dose-gradient. Clinically, this would allude to the relationship of tumor and normal lung in lung cancer treatment or to a metastatic tumor and the spinal cord in bone metastasis for example. Meanwhile, the peripheral OAR measurements are intended to determine accuracy in the low-dose field, for instance at the chest wall or ribs in patients with lung cancer.

The results of the first trial of isocenter dose measurement showed that neither the measured dose nor the 3DVH-predicted dose differed from the planned dose. The largest dose deviation occurred when the target size was 1 cm. However, even in this case, the average dose deviation between the predicted and planned doses was 1.5%; this was the only instance in which the error exceeded 1%. We attribute this difference to the problems of diode measurement itself rather than algorithmic problems in the 3DVH software. According to the study of Kruse [15], the diode can measure a lower dose for smaller fields than the ion-chamber owing to field size effects due to the differential scatter when the diode is calibrated with a field size of 10×10 cm^2. In the present study, as the ArcCHECK was calibrated with a field dimension of 10×10 cm^2, the largest error is thought to have occurred in the plan with a target size of 1 cm. However, the measured dose deviation was less than 0.7% in every instance except that with a field size 1 cm. Therefore, it appears that measurements of the actual isocenter dose by using an ion-chamber in the ArcCHECK can be substituted by the 3DVH predicted isocenter dose in clinical cases in which the target sizes are usually larger than 1 cm.

It is worth noting that when using the ArcCHECK and 3DVH software in this study, the gamma passing rates decreased with increasing target size. This indicates the accuracy varies with respect to field size instead of target size, as the same phenomenon occurred in peripheral OARs with no variations in volume. There are several possible reasons for this, including problems with the TPS algorithm, the ArcCHECK diode or array itself, or the accuracy of the 3DVH algorithm.

The TPS algorithm used in the present study was the pencil-beam algorithm of iPlan RT. The accuracy of the pencil-beam algorithm used in our study has been verified in several studies [16, 17]. Although some studies show the inferior accuracy of the pencil-beam algorithm compared to Monte Carlo algorithms, especially in inhomogeneous conditions [2, 18], no study has demonstrated the inaccuracy of the pencil-beam algorithm according to field size. Therefore, the differences related to field size cannot be explained by the inaccuracy of the TPS algorithm.

Several studies emphasize the accuracy of Smarterpolation and the PDP algorithm in the 3DVH software [9, 11, 13]. In addition to the 3D gamma passing rate for specific ROIs (calculated by the 3DVH software), the gamma passing rate at the diode level (not calculated by the 3DVH software) tended to decrease with increasing target size. Therefore, the differences associated with field size cannot be attributed to the inaccuracy of the 3DVH algorithm.

The results of the present study collectively suggest that the decreasing gamma passing rates with increasing field size are due to the field size dependence of the ArcCHECK diodes. Feygelman et al. showed that differences between the doses measured by the ArcCHECK diode and ion-chamber existed because of varying field sizes [3]. When the ArcCHECK itself is a homogenous phantom, as was the case in the present study, the percentage difference in the measured dose (ArcCHECK diode versus ion-chamber) ranged from -1.1% for a 5×5 cm^{2}field to +1.3% for a 25×25 cm^2 field. Li et al. reported similar experimental results: the ArcCHECK diode-measured dose with field sizes increasing from 5×5 to 20×20 cm^2 showed errors of 1.2% and 1.7% compared to the TPS-planned dose and ion-chamber measured doses, respectively [4]. Kozelka et al. calibrated the ArcCHECK with a virtual inclinometer algorithm [19]. However, the field size dependence was still observed in our study. It is unclear why the ArcCHECK diode responses are influenced by field sizes. However, Saini and Zhu have suggested that variations in the thickness and design of the buildup around the silicone dye could cause varying field size dependences even for the same diode [20].

It also should be noted that analyses by using gamma indices are not always clinically relevant. The results of several recent studies have indicated that the gamma index is lacking with regard to clinical impact and correlation [10–12, 21]. The present study also failed to demonstrate any definitive correlation between gamma passing rates and DVH-based matrices. In the instances with comparatively homogenous dose distributions, such as the target and peripheral OAR, gamma passing rates were correlated with DVH-based dose parameters; these correlations were stronger with the 2%/2 mm criterion than the 3%/3 mm criterion. On the other hand, regarding the adjacent OAR, no correlations were found between 3D gamma passing rates and DVH-based metrics; instead, the dose deviation decreased with increasing gamma passing rate. This may be because the adjacent OAR represents a field with a high-dose gradient. This situation frequently occurs in clinical cases with inherently high dose gradients, such as IMRT or cases in which normal organs are located close to the target. Therefore, when assessing delivery QA by using ArcCHECK and the 3DVH software, the actual dose distribution must be examined carefully especially in regions with high-dose gradients.

CONCLUSIONS

Delivery QA by using ArcCHECK and the 3DVH software can provide physicians a great deal of information simply and easily, including the previous simple 2D gamma index, the 3D gamma index, the gamma index for each ROI, the perturbed dose distribution, and several DVH-based matrices. The field size dependence of the ArcCHECK diodes requires careful attention; it is recommended that along with the gamma index, various clinically relevant DVH-based matrices should also be examined, especially in regions with high-dose gradients.

AUTHOR CONTRIBUTIONS

Conceived and designed the experiments: SHS JHS CSK. Performed the experiments: HJS CSK SHS. Analyzed the data: HJS SHS. Contributed reagents/materials/analysis tools: SHS. Wrote the paper: JHS SHS.

REFERENCES

1. Ezzell GA, Galvin JM, Low D, Palta JR, Rosen I, Sharpe MB, et al. Guidance document on delivery, treatment planning, and clinical implementation of IMRT: report of the IMRT Subcommittee of the AAPM Radiation Therapy Committee. Med Phys. 2003;30:2089–2115. pmid:12945975 doi: 10.1118/1.1591194
2. Petoukhova AL, van Egmond J, Eenink MG, Wiggenraad RG, van Santvoort JP. The ArcCHECK diode array for dosimetric verification of HybridArc. Phys Med Biol. 2011;56:5411–5428. doi: 10.1088/0031-9155/56/16/021. pmid:21804180
3. Feygelman V, Zhang G, Stevens C, Nelms BE. Evaluation of a new VMAT QA device, or the “X” and “O” array geometries. J Appl Clin Med Phys. 2011;12:3346. pmid:21587178
4. Li G, Zhang Y, Jiang X, Bai S, Peng G, Wu K, et al. Evaluation of the ArcCHECK QA system for IMRT and VMAT verification. Phys Med. 2012;29:295–303. doi: 10.1016/j.ejmp.2012.04.005. pmid:22583979
5. Bedford JL, Lee YK, Wai P, South CP, Warrington AP. Evaluation of the Delta4 phantom for IMRT and VMAT verification. Phys Med Biol. 2009;54:N167–176. doi: 10.1088/0031-9155/54/9/N04. pmid:19384007
6. Low DA, Harms WB, Mutic S, Purdy JA. A technique for the quantitative evaluation of dose distributions. Med Phys. 1998;25:656–661. pmid:9608475 doi: 10.1118/1.598248
7. Ezzell GA, Burmeister JW, Dogan N, LoSasso TJ, Mechalakos JG, Mihailidis D, et al. IMRT commissioning: multiple institution planning and dosimetry comparisons, a report from AAPM Task Group 119. Med Phys. 2009;36:5359–5373. pmid:19994544 doi: 10.1118/1.3238104
8. Nelms BE, Simon JA. A survey on planar IMRT QA analysis. J Appl Clin Med Phys. 2007;8:2448. pmid:17712302 doi: 10.1120/jacmp.v8i3.2448
9. Nelms BE, Opp D, Robinson J, Wolf TK, Zhang G, Moros E, et al. VMAT QA: measurement-guided 4D dose reconstruction on a patient. Med Phys. 2012;39:4228–4238. doi: 10.1118/1.4729709. pmid:22830756
10. Carrasco P, Jornet N, Latorre A, Eudaldo T, Ruiz A, Ribas M. 3D DVH-based metric analysis versus per-beam planar analysis in IMRT pretreatment verification. Med Phys. 2012;39:5040–5049. doi: 10.1118/1.4736949. pmid:22894429
11. Zhen H, Nelms BE, Tome WA. Moving from gamma passing rates to patient DVH-based QA metrics in pretreatment dose QA. Med Phys. 2011;38:5477–5489. doi: 10.1118/1.3633904. pmid:21992366
12. Nelms BE, Zhen H, Tome WA. Per-beam, planar IMRT QA passing rates do not predict clinically relevant patient dose errors. Med Phys. 2011;38:1037–1044. pmid:21452741 doi: 10.1118/1.3544657
13. Olch AJ. Evaluation of the accuracy of 3DVH software estimates of dose to virtual ion chamber and film in composite IMRT QA. Med Phys. 2012;39:81–86. doi: 10.1118/1.3666771. pmid:22225277
14. Almond PR, Biggs PJ, Coursey BM, Hanson WF, Huq MS, Nath R, et al. AAPM’s TG-51 protocol for clinical reference dosimetry of high-energy photon and electron beams. Med Phys. 1999;26:1847–1870. pmid:10505874 doi: 10.1118/1.598691
15. Kruse JJ. On the insensitivity of single field planar dosimetry to IMRT inaccuracies. Med Phys. 2010;37:2516–2524. pmid:20632563 doi: 10.1118/1.3425781
16. Ahnesjo A, Saxner M, Trepp A. A pencil beam model for photon dose calculation. Med Phys. 1992;19:263–273. pmid:1584117 doi: 10.1118/1.596856
17. Bortfeld T, Schlegel W, Rhein B. Decomposition of pencil beam kernels for fast dose calculations in three-dimensional treatment planning. Med Phys. 1993;20:311–318. pmid:8497215 doi: 10.1118/1.597070
18. Ali I, Ahmad S. Quantitative assessment of the accuracy of dose calculation using pencil beam and Monte Carlo algorithms and requirements for clinical quality assurance. Med Dosim. 2013;38:255–261. doi: 10.1016/j.meddos.2013.02.005. pmid:23558145
19. Kozelka J, Robinson J, Nelms B, Zhang G, Savitskij D, Feygelman V. Optimizing the accuracy of a helical diode array dosimeter: a comprehensive calibration methodology coupled with a novel virtual inclinometer. Med Phys. 2011;38:5021–5032. doi: 10.1118/1.3622823. pmid:21978046
20. Saini AS, Zhu TC. Energy dependence of commercially available diode detectors for in-vivo dosimetry. Med Phys. 2007;34:1704–1711. pmid:17555252 doi: 10.1118/1.2719365
21. Chan MF, Li J, Schupak K, Burman C. Using a Novel Dose QA Tool to Quantify the Impact of Systematic Errors Otherwise Undetected by Conventional QA Methods: Clinical Head and Neck Case Studies. Technol Cancer Res Treat. 2013;13:57–67. doi: 10.7785/tcrt.2012.500353. pmid:23819494

CHAPTER 13

ANALYSIS OF LIPID EXPERIMENTS (ALEX): A SOFTWARE FRAMEWORK FOR ANALYSIS OF HIGH-RESOLUTION SHOTGUN LIPIDOMICS DATA

Peter Husen[1], Kirill Tarasov[2], Maciej Katafiasz[1], Elena Sokol[1], Johannes Vogt[3], Jan Baumgart[3], Robert Nitsch[3], Kim Ekroos[2], Christer S. Ejsing[1]

[1] Department of Biochemistry and Molecular Biology, University of Southern Denmark, Odense, Denmark

[2] Zora Biosciences Oy, Espoo, Finland

[3] Institute for Microscopic Anatomy and Neurobiology, Johannes Gutenberg University Mainz, Mainz, Germany

ABSTRACT

Global lipidomics analysis across large sample sizes produces high-content datasets that require dedicated software tools supporting lipid identification and quantification, efficient data management and lipidome visualization. Here we present a novel software-based platform for streamlined data processing, management and visualization of shotgun lipidomics data acquired using high-resolution Orbitrap mass spectrometry. The platform features the ALEX framework designed for automated identification and export of lipid species intensity directly from proprietary mass spectral data files, and an auxiliary workflow using database exploration tools for integration of sample information, computation of lipid abundance and lipidome visualization. A key feature of the platform is the organization of lipidomics data in "database table format" which provides the user with an unsurpassed flexibility for rapid lipidome navigation using selected features within the dataset. To demonstrate the efficacy of the platform, we present a comparative neurolipidomics study of cerebellum, hippocampus and somatosensory barrel cortex (S1BF) from wild-type and knockout mice devoid of the putative lipid phosphate phosphatase PRG-1 (plasticity related gene-1). The presented framework is generic, extendable to processing and integration of other lipidomic data structures, can be interfaced with post-processing protocols supporting statistical testing and multivariate analysis, and can serve as an avenue for disseminating lipidomics data within the scientific community. The ALEX software is available at www.msLipidomics.info.

INTRODUCTION

The lipidome of eukaryotic cells comprises hundreds to thousands of molecular lipid species that constitute and functionalize biomembranes, store metabolic energy in lipid droplets and function as signaling molecules that control cell and organism physiology [1–3]. A key tenet of contemporary mass spectrometry-based lipidomics methodology revolves around the identification and quantification of lipid species on a lipidome-wide scale [4–8]. As such, shotgun lipidomics has emerged as a powerful tool for global lipidome analysis that complements mechanistic studies of lipid metabolism, lipid homeostasis and membrane biology [9–13]. The efficacy of shotgun lipidomics stems from its relative technical simplicity where hundreds of lipid species in sample extracts can be quantitatively monitored at high throughput using direct infusion nanoelectrospray ionization combined with high-

Citation: Husen P, Tarasov K, Katafiasz M, Sokol E, Vogt J, Baumgart J, et al. (2013) Analysis of Lipid Experiments (ALEX): A Software Framework for Analysis of High-Resolution Shotgun Lipidomics Data. PLoS ONE 8(11): e79736. doi:10.1371/journal.pone.0079736.

resolution Fourier transform mass spectrometry (FT MS) or/ and tandem mass spectrometry (MS/MS) [2,14]. Notably, lipidomics analysis on a global scale generates large amounts of (spectral) data that requires software routines for automated lipid identification and quantification, and additional data management for subsequent lipidome visualization and bioinformatics analysis.

Extensive lipidome characterization by shotgun lipidomics can be achieved by executing a systematic program of mass spectrometric analyses of sample extracts in positive and negative ion mode, and by incorporating chemical derivatization procedures to specifically monitor poorly ionizing lipid molecules such as cholesterol [4–7]. Executing such an analytical program generates several mass spectral data files per sample that must be queried for lipid identification, and combined into a single dataset for lipidome quantification and visualization. Numerous software tools have been developed for the identification of lipids: LipidQA[15], LIMSA[16], FAAT[17], lipID[18], LipidSearch[19], LipidView[20], LipidInspector[21] and LipidXplorer[22]. These tools cover a broad range of applications spanning dedicated lipid identification for only certain instrumentations and specific mass analysis routines (MS and MS/MS) to cross-platform software featuring user-specified commands querying spectral data in the open-source .mzXML format. Identified lipid species are typically annotated by a shorthand nomenclature corresponding to the information detail of the mass spectrometric analysis [23,24]. The detection of lipid species by FT MS analysis or by MS/MS analysis for lipid class-specific fragment ions (e.g. *m/z* 184.0733 for phosphatidylcholine (PC) species) supports only "sum composition" annotation (e.g. PC 34:1). In comparison, annotation by the more detailed "molecular composition" (e.g. PC 16:0-18:1) requires MS/MS analysis and detection of structure-specific fragment ions [25]. To support the cataloging of lipid species, the LIPID MAPS Consortium recently developed the "Comprehensive Classification System for Lipids" which outlines an informatics framework for lipidomics [26,27]. Using a classification system enables the design of lipid databases where each lipid species is listed together with a range of accessory lipid features such as lipid category (e.g. glycerophospholipid, sphingolipid, glycerolipid, sterol lipid), lipid class, structural attributes (e.g. number of double bonds, fatty acid chain length), chemical formula, mono-isotopic mass and isotope information. These accessory lipid features can be incorporated into lipidomic data processing routines using database-orientated exploration tools to support computations and visualization of distinct lipidome hallmarks. Notably, none of the currently available software tools comprise streamlined processing routines that integrate lipid intensity data, the accessory lipid features and a full catalog of sample information.

Here we present a platform for processing, management and visualization of high-content shotgun lipidomics datasets acquired using high-resolution Orbitrap mass spectrometry. The platform features a novel software framework termed ALEX (Analysis of Lipid Experiments) that supports automated identification and export of lipid species intensity directly from proprietary mass spectral data files and the integration of accessory lipid features and sample information into a single output structured in "database table format". This design supports swift data processing and lipidome visualization across large sample sizes using an auxiliary workflow powered by the database exploration tools: Orange [28] and Tableau Software. To demonstrate the efficacy of the platform, we present a comparative neurolipidomics analysis of cerebellum, hippocampus and S1BF from wild-type and knockout mice devoid of the PRG-1 gene encoding a putative lipid phosphate phosphatase [29].

MATERIALS AND METHODS

Chemicals and Lipid Standards

Chemicals, solvents and synthetic lipid standards were purchased from Sigma-Aldrich, Rathburn Chemicals, Avanti Polar Lipids and Larodan Fine Chemicals AB.

Mouse Brain Tissue Sampling

Animal experiments were conducted in strict accordance with German law (in congruence with 86/609/EEC) for the use of laboratory animals and approved by the local animal welfare committee at the Johannes Gutenberg University Mainz. Male C57Bl/6 wild-type and PRG-1 knockout mice [29] were euthanized by an intraperitoneal injection of ketamine at an overdose. Subsequently, the mice were perfused intracardially with 4°C 155 mM ammonium acetate, and the cerebellum, hippocampus and S1BF were dissected. The tissues were immediately frozen on dry ice and stored at -80°C until further processing.

Lipid Extraction

Brain tissues were homogenized in 155 mM ammonium acetate and analyzed for total protein concentration using BCA Protein Assay Kit (Thermo Scientific). Aliquots of tissue homogenates corresponding to 10 µg of total protein were subjected to lipid extraction executed at 4°C as previously described [7]. Briefly, the tissue homogenates were spiked with 10 µl of internal mixture (providing a total spike of 54 pmol CE 19:0, 35 pmol TAG 17:1/17:1/17:1, 35 pmol DAG 19:0/19:0, 26 pmol LPA O-16:0, 35 pmol PA 17:0/14:1, 25 pmol LPS 17:1, 13 pmol PS 17:0/20:4, 50 pmol PE O-20:0/O-20:0, 30 pmol LPC O-17:0, 137 pmol PC 18:3/18:3, 35 pmol PI 17:0/20:4, 30 pmol PG 17:0/17:0, 55 pmol Cer 18:1;2/17:0;0, 69 pmol SM 18:1;2/17:0;0, 49 pmol HexCer 18:1;2/12:0;0, 28 pmol SHexCer 18:1;2/12:0;0) and diluted to 200 µl using 155 mM ammonium acetate. Samples were subsequently added 990 µl chloroform/methanol (10:1, v/v) and vigorously mixed for 2 h. The lower organic phase was collected (10:1-phase lipid extract). The remaining aqueous phase was re-extracted with 990 µl of chloroform/methanol (2:1, v/v) for 1 h and the lower organic phase was collected (2:1-phase lipid extract). The collected lower organic phases were vacuum evaporated.

Shotgun Lipidomics Analysis

Lipid extracts were dissolved in 60 µl of chloroform/methanol (1:2, v/v) and subjected to mass spectrometric analysis using an LTQ Orbitrap XL instrument (Thermo Fisher Scientific) equipped with a TriVersa NanoMate (Advion Biosciences) as previously described [4,7]. The 10:1-phase lipid extracts were analyzed by positive ion mode multiplexed FT MS analysis with scan ranges *m/z* 280-580 (monitoring lysophosphatidylcholine

(LPC) and lysophosphatidylethanolamine (LPE) species) and *m/z* 500-1200 (monitoring sphingomyelin (SM), ceramide (Cer), diacylglycerol (DAG), PC, ether-linked PC (PC O-), phosphatidylethanolamine (PE), ether-linked phosphatidylethanolamine (PE O-) and triacylglycerol (TAG) species). The 2:1-phase lipid extracts were analyzed by negative ion mode multiplexed FT MS analysis with scan ranges *m/z* 370-660 (monitoring lysophosphatidic acid (LPA), lysophosphatidylserine (LPS) and lysophosphatidylinositol (LPI) species) and *m/z*550-1700 (monitoring phosphatidic acid (PA), phosphatidylserine (PS), phosphatidylinositol (PI), phosphatidylglycerol (PG) and sulfatide (SHexCer) species). All FT MS spectra were acquired in profile mode using a target mass resolution of 100,000 (fwhm), activation of isolation waveforms, automatic gain control at 1e6, max injection time at 250 ms and acquisition of 2 µscans.

Annotation of Lipid Species

Glycerophospholipid and glycerolipid species were annotated using sum composition: <lipid class><total number of C in the fatty acid moieties>:<total number of double bonds in the fatty acid moieties> (e.g. PI 34:1). Sphingolipid species were annotated as <lipid class><total number of C in the long-chain base and fatty acid moiety>:< total number of double bonds in the long-chain base and fatty acid moiety>;< total number of OH groups in the long-chain base and fatty acid moiety> (e.g. SM 36:1;2) [5,7].

ALEX Software

The individual parts of the ALEX software were programmed using several programming languages, libraries and software frameworks. The ALEX lipid database is implemented using the library based SQLite database engine. The ALEX target list generator is written in C++ and uses the Qt framework for its user interface. The ALEX converter, ALEX extractor and ALEX unifier are written in Python 2.7 and make use of the Python packages PySide, NumPy and SciPy. Furthermore, the ALEX converter uses the package comtypes to interface with the MSFileReader library version 2.2 (Thermo Scientific), which must be installed. Finally, the standalone ALEX lipid calculator is written in common lisp and uses the GTK+ framework for its user interface, while the online version is written in PHP. The ALEX software is available athttp://mslipidomics.info | software along with installation instructions. A sample dataset is also available for testing local installations of the software.

Data Processing and Visualization

Computation of molar abundance (fmol) of lipid species [20] was performed using open source software Orange 2.6 (www.orange.biolab.si) [28]. The Orange workflow is provided as part of the sample dataset available at http://mslipidomics.info | software. In addition, the Orange output with lipidomics data is available as Data S1. Visualization and calculation of mol% values were performed using commercially available Tableau Software (www.tableausoftware.com). Lipidomic data in Tableau file format is available as Data S2 and can be navigated using the freeware Tableau Reader (http://www.tableausoftware.com/products/reader).

RESULTS AND DISCUSSION

Input: High-Resolution Shotgun Lipidomics Data

Shotgun lipidomics platforms based on high-resolution Orbitrap mass spectrometry and automated nanoelectrospray ionization support high throughput analysis with high sensitivity, specificity and extensive lipidome coverage [4,5,7,30]. The extensive lipidome coverage is generated by combined analyses of sample extracts in negative and positive ion mode, and by implementing chemical derivatization procedures to monitor low abundant or poorly ionizing lipid species [31–33]. In order to maximize the sensitivity of Orbitrap mass analysis, we typically record two multiplexed FT MS scans covering a low *m/z* range and high *m/z* range (e.g. +FT MS *m/z* 280-580 and +FT MS *m/z* 500-1200). Each FT MS scan is recorded in profile mode with a target mass resolution of 100,000. The rationale for this multiplexed FT MS analysis is that the instrument injects a user-specified quantum of ions into the Orbitrap for mass analysis (defined by the automated gain control). Hence, multiplexing two or more scan ranges allows separate quanta of ions within specific *m/z* ranges to be analyzed sequentially in the Orbitrap and yields better ion statistics as compared to injecting all ions at the same time when monitoring a wider *m/z* range (e.g. +FT MS *m/z* 200-1200) [34]. We note that the boundaries of the scan ranges should be chosen to cover specific lipid classes and respective internal standards. For example, the scan range +FT MS *m/z* 280-580 is used for monitoring LPC and LPE species whereas +FT MS *m/z* 500-1200 analysis is used for monitoring Cer, SM, HexCer, PC, PC O-, PE, PE O-, DAG and TAG species. The total time of analysis is typically set to 3 min. Within this time we record 25 low *m/z* and 25 high *m/z* range FT MS spectra. Likewise, negative ion mode analysis is also executed using multiplexed FT MS acquisitions to monitor negatively charged glycerophospholipid and SHexCer species (see Material and Methods). Consequently, this lipidomics approach generates four distinct mass spectral datasets per sample (two per polarity) that need to be queried for lipid identification and export of lipid species intensity. We note that this lipidomics approach is designed for high throughput-oriented studies and supports annotation of lipid species by sum composition nomenclature (e.g. PC 34:1). Characterization of molecular lipid species (e.g. PC 16:1-18:0) requires implementation of time-consuming MS/MS analysis and lipid identification by dedicated software such as LipidXplorer [22].

Design of the ALEX Software Framework

The ALEX software framework was designed for processing of shotgun lipidomics datasets obtained by multiplexed high-resolution FT MS. The rationales for the design were: i) that ALEX should support lipidomic studies with large sample sets for which a multitude of multiplexed FT MS acquisitions have been acquired; and ii) that the output format of ALEX should be compatible with an auxiliary workflow that supports robust data processing including computation of molar abundances of lipid species across numerous lipid classes, integration of sample information, implementation of data quality control procedures and rapid lipidome visualization. To this end, we designed the ALEX software framework to utilize distinct modules that identify lipid species from proprietary .RAW spectral file format, incorporate accessory lipid features stored in a lipid database and output lipidomic data in "database table format" (Figure 1). In this format, the lipidomic data is stored in tabulator or comma separated text files structured as database tables with a separate row for each data point. Each row separately contains fields (also termed attributes) reporting for example the originating sample (.RAW file name), the lipid species, adduct information, intensity, peak area, *m/z* values and accessory lipid features derived from the lipid database. This format also easily supports the management of multiple attributes for each data point (e.g. both peak intensity and area) and can be appended with calculated fields such as lipid abundance (e.g. both pmol and fmol, if needed), and sample information and internal standard information supplied by additional text files in database table format. Importantly, this relational database format provides a robust way to manage large datasets programmatically and avoids the need for error-prone manual alignment of data with lists of accessory features and quantification information. We note that the output of most contemporary lipidomics software tools utilizes a "spreadsheet" format where samples/injections are arranged in the columns and lipid species in the rows of a table of with either intensities or peak areas. This "spreadsheet" format is adequate for processing and visualizing simple lipidomic datasets using tools such as Microsoft Excel, but becomes exceedingly cumbersome if sample sets include more than 10 samples and monitor more than 200 lipid species across different FT MS scan ranges.

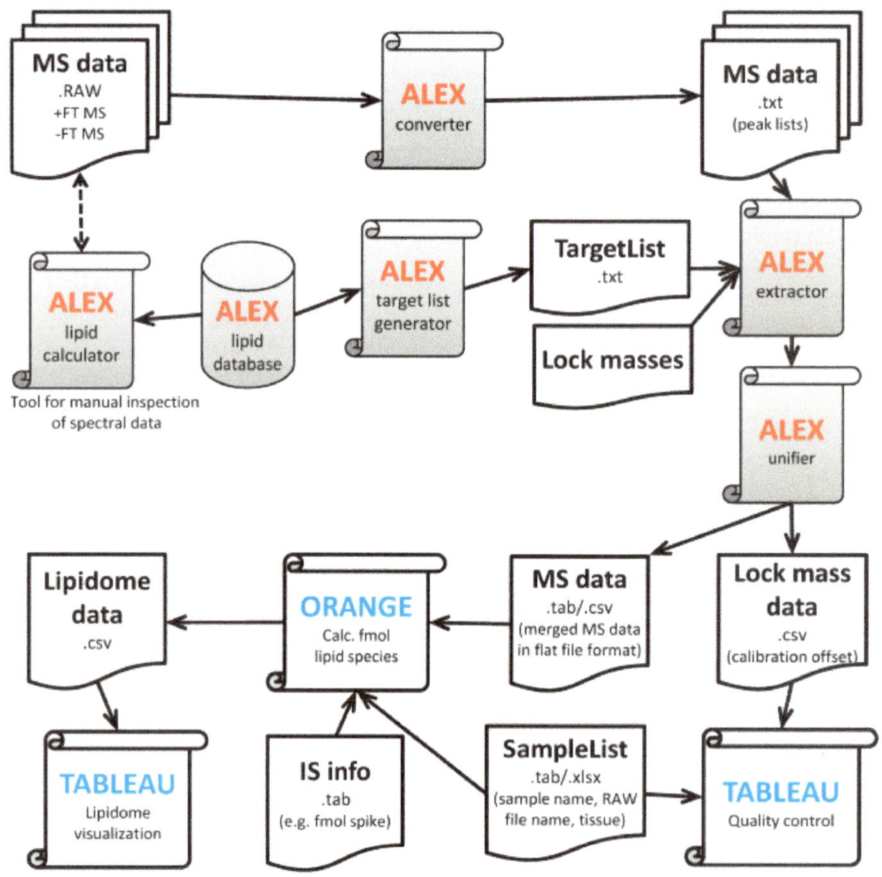

Figure 1. Overview of the ALEX software framework and auxiliary workflow. The ALEX framework comprises six core modules (grey colored boxes). The function of each module is explained in the Results and Discussion section. The output of the ALEX framework includes a data file with identified lipid species, intensities and accessory lipid features across all processed samples and FT MS scan ranges. The ALEX output is organized in database table format that can be accessed and processed by the auxiliary workflow using Orange and Tableau software. The auxiliary workflow is designed to integrate sample information, compute lipid molar abundance, implement quality control procedures and visualize lipidome data.

The ALEX software framework consists of six core modules (Figure 1): i) the ALEX lipid database featuring a comprehensive range of lipid species and accessory lipid features used for lipid identification, data processing and management; ii) the ALEX lipid calculator which supports manual interpretation of mass spectra; iii) the ALEX converter which converts mass spectrometric data in proprietary .RAW format into averaged spectral peak lists in text file format; iv) the ALEX target list generator which queries the ALEX lipid database to compile target lists used for lipid species identification; v) the ALEX extractor which uses the target lists to identify lipid species and export corresponding intensities from spectral peak lists; and vi) the ALEX unifier that merges the multiple ALEX extractor outputs containing lipid species data from different FT MS scan ranges into a single data file. Further information about the function of the ALEX modules and the auxiliary workflow is outlined in the subsequent sections.

ALEX Lipid Database

To support identification of lipid species we constructed the ALEX lipid database. Currently, the database covers more than 20,000 lipid species from more than 85 lipid classes. Each lipid species in the database is annotated by sum composition and contains a range of accessory lipid features denoting its chemical formula, mono-isotopic mass, adduction in positive and negative ion mode, lipid category, lipid class, and the total number of C atoms, double bonds and hydroxyl group in fatty acid and long chain base moieties (termed C index, db index and OH index, respectively). The ALEX lipid database is available as a collection of text files and as a binary SQLite database queried by the ALEX lipid calculator and the ALEX target list generator, respectively (outlined in the next sections). The text version also serves as the source for the binary version (compiled by a supporting Python program) and can be edited by the user. To support the editing of the database, a template Microsoft Excel file can be used to assist the enumeration and calculation of the chemical formula and mass for each species, such that catalogs of entire lipid classes can readily be added. We note that the accessory lipid features serve as important attributes in the final ALEX output that facilitate data processing and lipidome visualization.

ALEX Lipid Calculator

The ALEX lipid calculator was designed to complement manual inspection of FT MS spectra when using proprietary Xcalibur software (Fig. 2). The calculator is available as executable program and as an online application at www.mslipidomics.info/lipid-calc. Both versions of the ALEX lipid calculator support querying *m/z* values of specific lipid species and searching the lipid database for candidate lipid species that match a measured *m/z* value within a user-specified tolerance window. Since the accuracy of lipid identification can be hampered by drifts of the FT MS calibration we also implemented an option to specify an *m/z* offset while querying the lipid database. To accurately specify the calibration offset requires that the user knows the identity of at least one well-characterized "lock mass" ion that can be used for estimating the*m/z* offset (Figure 2). An option to minimize potential problems with FT MS calibration drifts is to apply online lock mass calibration during sample acquisition [35]. However, the online lock mass calibration eliminates the lock mass ion(s) from the recorded FT MS spectra using waveforms that might concomitantly eliminate lipid ions having similar *m/z*. An alternative strategy is to apply an offline lock mass adjustment as implemented in the ALEX extractor (outlined below).

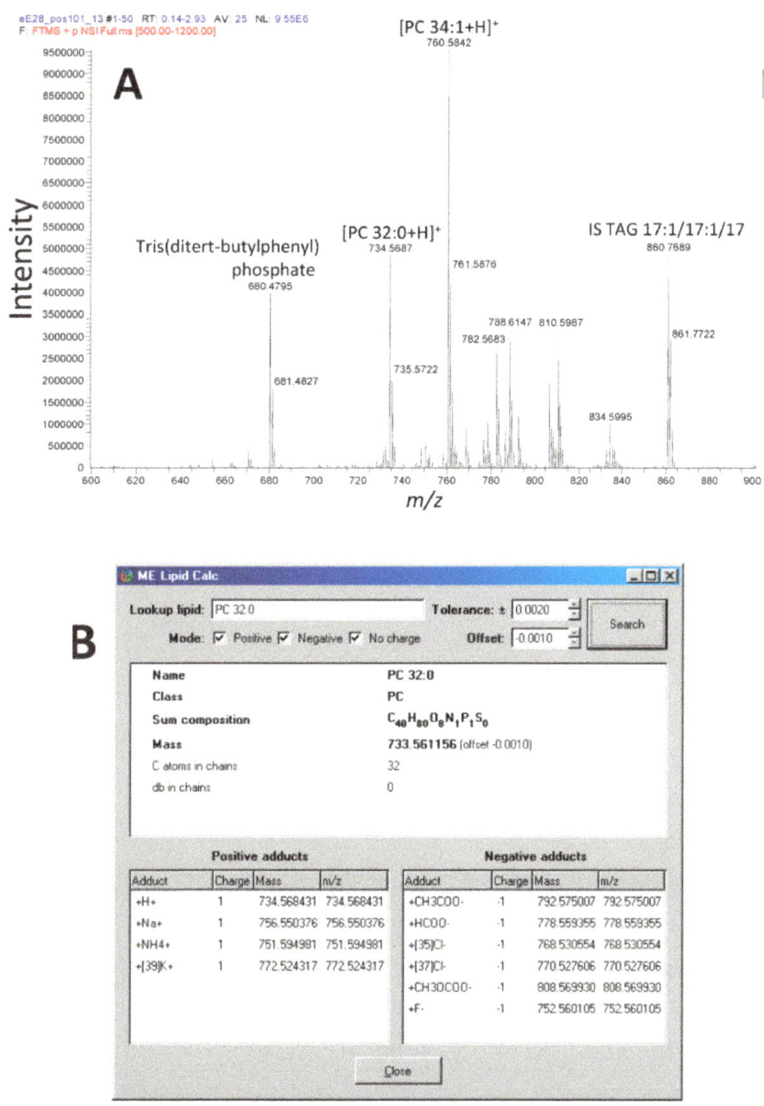

Figure 2. The ALEX lipid calculator. (A) Representative positive ion mode FT MS spectrum of a 10:1-phase lipid extract of hippocampus from a PRG-1 knockout mouse. Note that the detection of selected lock mass ions tris(ditert-butylphenyl) phosphate (chemical background,

[M+NH$_4$]$^+$, calculated *m/z* 680.48022, measured *m/z* 680.47945, *m/z* offset = -0.00077) and TAG 17:1/17:1/17:1 (internal standard (IS), [M+NH$_4$]$^+$, calculated *m/z* 860.77017, measured*m/z* 860.76889 and *m/z* offset = -0.00128). The FT MS calibration offset is estimated as the average of the *m/z* offset for both lock mass ions, i.e. the FT MS calibration offset = -0.0010. (**B**) Screenshot of the ALEX lipid calculator showing information for endogenous lipid species PC 32:0 while applying the FT MS calibration offset = -0.0010. Note that the measured *m/z* of PC 32:0 is 734.56872 and that the calculated *m/z*adjusted for the calibration offset is 734.56843 which yield a *m/z* difference of 0.00029 corresponding to a mass error of 0.4 ppm. Without applying lock mass adjustment the mass error would be 1 ppm.

ALEX Converter

A prerequisite for automated lipid identification and export of intensity is that the mass spectrometric data in proprietary .RAW format are made accessible for querying. To this end, we designed the ALEX converter to interface with the proprietary dynamic-link library MSFileReader. The MSFileReader supports export of all scan information within .RAW files including single and averaged spectral peak lists in either centroid or profile mode format. The ALEX converter was designed to export individual spectral peak lists in profile mode format, to average peak lists for specific FT MS scan ranges and to save these averaged peak lists in .txt format. The ALEX converter output consists of a directory with separate folders named according to each FT MS scan range containing corresponding .txt files named according to the originating .RAW files (i.e. the ALEX converter does not merge overlapping FT MS scan ranges). Output files in these FT MS scan range-dependent folders are queried by the ALEX extractor (outlined below). The rationales for this design were i) that no available software supports export of multiplexed FT MS data in profile mode format; and ii) that a simple output text format reporting averaged peak list data allows users to easily review data as in contrast to accessing data in stored in the encrypted .mzXML format.

ALEX Target List Generator

Lipid identification by the ALEX software framework is based on matching intensity data in the exported peak lists with lipid species information derived from the ALEX lipid database. Important for the design of the identification routine was the ability to accurately identify lipid species, and furthermore to support integration of accessory lipid features and subsequent data management for a multitude of lipid species monitored by various FT MS scan ranges across large sample sets. To this end, the ALEX framework was designed to perform a targeted identification of lipid species and export intensity by querying spectral peak lists using target lists with lipid species and respective *m/z* values. Two modules execute this routine: (i) the ALEX target list generator (Figure 3A) which compiles target lists by querying the ALEX lipid database, and (ii) the ALEX extractor which uses the target lists to identify and extract lipid species intensity (outlined in the next section). We note that a distinct target list with appropriate lipid species should be manually compiled for each FT MS scan range. In addition to listing lipid species and respective *m/z* values, the target lists also include the accessory lipid features derived from the ALEX lipid database. Importantly, these accessory lipid features are incorporated into the final output, and used for processing and visualization by the auxiliary workflow.

A

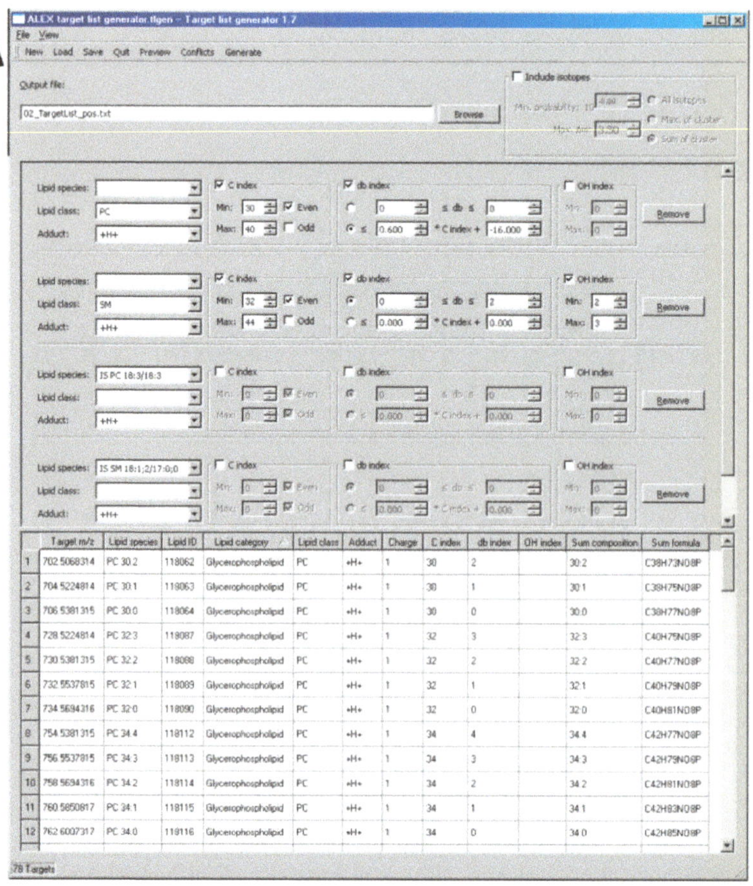

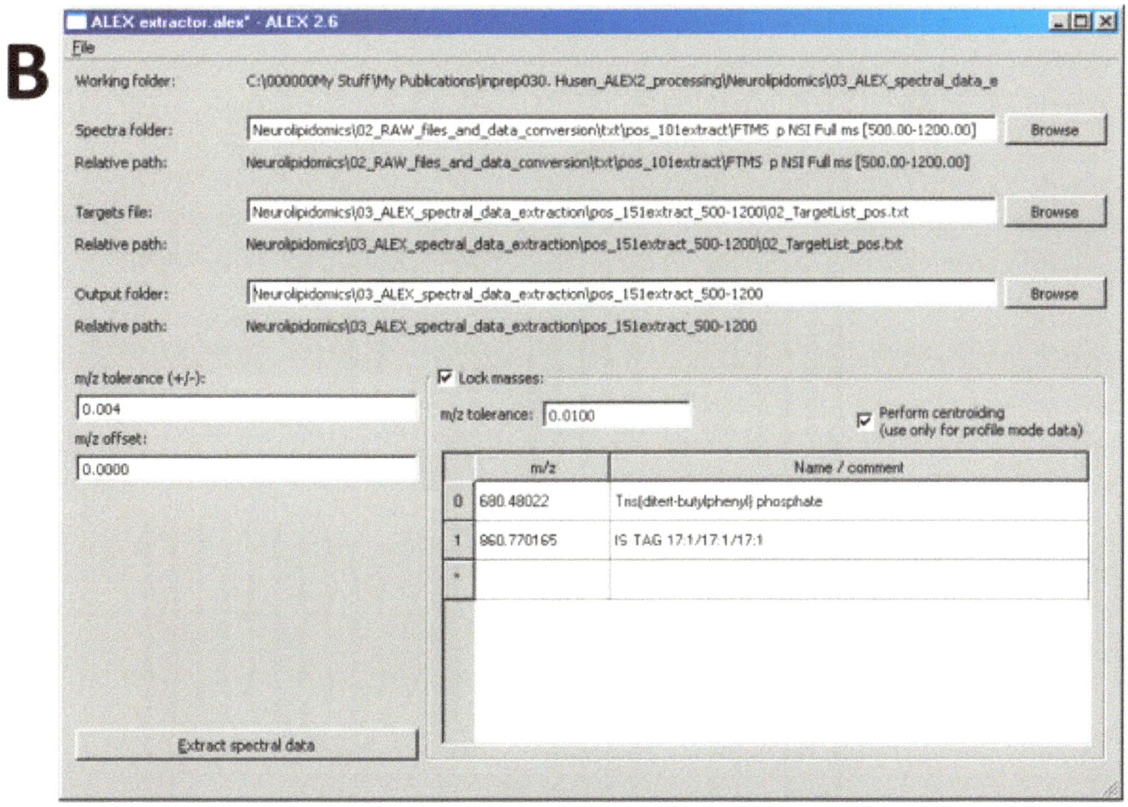

Figure 3. Screenshots of the ALEX target list generator and ALEX extractor. (A) The ALEX target list generator allows users to select lipid classes and species to be identified using criteria such as lipid class, adduction, C index, db index and OH index. Individual lipid species including internal standards can also be selected. The ALEX target list generator output is a .txt file with a shortlist of selected lipid species, respective *m/z* values and accessory lipid features. The ALEX target list generator also supports inclusion of isotope information that can be used for deisotoping and isotope correction [20] by applying algorithms within the auxiliary workflow. (B) The ALEX extractor identifies lipid species, exports intensity data and incorporates accessory lipid features. As input the ALEX extractor requires the location of spectral peak lists generated by the ALEX converter, a target list compiled by the ALEX target list generator and a location to deposit output files. The ALEX extractor features options to specify an *m/z* tolerance window for lipid identification, to apply a constant *m/z* offset to correct lipid searches for a constant FT MS calibration offset or to apply a lock mass adjustment routine that automatically corrects lipid searches for drifts in FT MS calibration. The automated lock mass adjustment routine requires specification of well-characterized and ubiquitous lock mass ions in order to estimate the FT MS calibration offset.

ALEX Extractor and ALEX Unifier

The ALEX extractor identifies lipid species and exports intensities by querying the averaged peak lists produced by the ALEX converter (Figure 3B). As input the ALEX extractor requires the folder location containing averaged peak lists, an appropriate target list (i.e. specific for the FT MS scan range) to query the peak lists and a destination folder to deposit output text files. Notably, the ALEX extractor also requires an *m/z* tolerance window to identify lipid species. This *m/z* tolerance window is dependent on instrumental mass resolution and typically set to ±0.0020 amu when processing FT MS data acquired with a target resolution at 100,000. To export lipid species intensity the ALEX extractor selects the maximum intensity value within the specified tolerance window and reports the corresponding *m/z* bin value. As mentioned above, the FT MS calibration can drift during the sample analysis and depending on the time of analysis can yield either a constant calibration offset or a progressively changing offset (see Figure 4A). In order to monitor and adjust lipid searches for potential calibration drifts, we incorporated a novel feature in the ALEX extractor termed "lock mass adjustment". Lock mass adjustment serves to correct the *m/z* values of targeted lipid species for calibration drifts and thereby support more accurate lipid identification. This lock mass adjustment can be specified as a constant *m/z* offset and applied across all samples being processed. Alternatively, the ALEX extractor features an in-build automatic lock mass adjustment routine that calculates *m/z* calibration offsets for each sample based on selected lock mass ions (Figure 4A). The calculation of calibration offset uses a three-point quadratic interpolation for estimating the centroid *m/z* values of lock mass ions. We note that the automatic lock mass adjustment requires selection of well-characterized and ubiquitous ions as lock masses. For example, by positive ion mode FT MS analysis we always detect both the chemical background ion tris(ditert-butylphenyl) phosphate and the internal standard TAG 17:1/17:1/17:1 (Figure 2). Using these ions as lock masses enables estimation of the FT MS calibration offset for individual samples and correcting lipid searches by adjusting the *m/z* values of targeted lipid species for each sample. As exemplified in Figure 2, using these lock mass ions allows identification of endogenous lipid species with a mass error of 0.4 ppm instead of 1 ppm when ignoring the FT MS calibration offset. Hence, this automated lock mass adjustment routine serves to improve the accuracy of lipid species identification despite drifts in FT MS calibration.

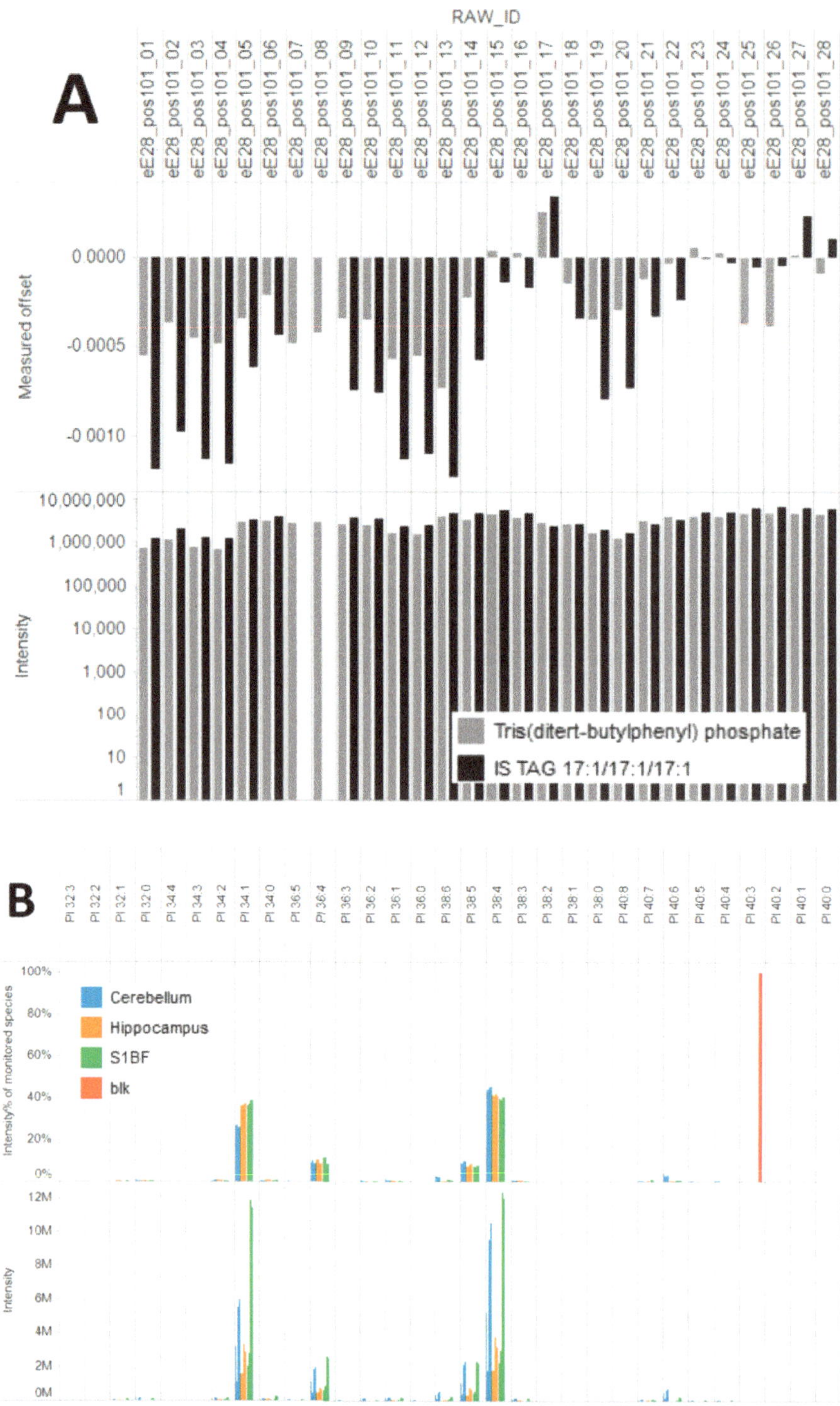

Figure 4. Quality control analysis. (A) Monitoring of lock mass offset and lock mass ion intensity as function of sample injection. Notice that the lock mass and internal standard TAG 17:1/17:1/17:1 is not detected in injection 07 and 08. Manual inspection of FT MS spectra revealed that the particular sample had not been spiked with internal standards. (B) Assessing the specificity of the PI species profile and intensity across all samples from wild-type mice and the negative control blank samples. Note that in the negative control blank sample (red) a low abundant background ion is detected and falsely identified as PI 40:3. Dubious lipid species can be removed using background subtraction and filtering during subsequent processing in Orange.

The ALEX extractor outputs, for each FT MS scan range, several comma-separated value (.csv) files with lipid species intensity data and calculated lock mass adjustments for all processed samples. Notably, the lipid species intensity output is organized in database table format and includes attributes that track the originating .RAW file name, lipid species intensity and peak area, measured *m/z*, calculated *m/z*, the difference between measured and calculated *m/z*, and all the accessory lipid features included on the target list. We note that these sample attributes facilitate subsequent processing and visualization, and implementation of quality control procedures. In order to merge lipid species data from different FT MS ranges, we devised the ALEX unifier to concatenate selected .csv output files into one final .csv file which contains the union of all data and an additional column with an index, "rangeID", that tracks the FT MS scan range of the input .csv files. This output format supports further data processing including computation of lipid abundance by the auxiliary workflow using open-source Orange [28] and Tableau Software.

Application of the ALEX Software Framework

In order to demonstrate the efficacy of the ALEX software framework and describe the auxiliary workflow, we here present a neurolipidomic pilot study. Three brain tissues; cerebellum, hippocampus and S1BF from two control mice and two mice devoid of the PRG-1 gene were subjected to shotgun lipidomics analysis. Homogenates of the tissues (12 samples in total) and two blank samples were spiked with defined amounts of internal lipid standards and subjected to 2-step lipid extraction [7]. The apolar (10:1-) and polar (2:1-phase) lipid extracts were analyzed by multiplexed FT MS analysis in positive and negative ion mode, respectively. Each sample extract was analyzed twice (technical replicates). In total, this analysis produced 56 .RAW files (14 samples analyzed twice per polarity).

First, the ALEX converter was used to convert .RAW files to spectral peak lists (Figure 1). This processing produced a total of 112 peak list files (56 .RAW files, two FT MS scan ranges per polarity). The peak list files were automatically organized into 4 folders named according to polarity and scan range: +FTMS *m/z* 280-580, +FTMS *m/z* 500-1200, -FTMS *m/z* 370-660, and -FTMS *m/z* 550-1700 (each folder having 28 peak list files). Next, target lists with lipid species for each of the four FT MS *m/z* ranges were generated using the ALEX target list generator (See Materials and Methods for details). These target lists were subsequently used by the ALEX extractor to identify lipid species and export corresponding intensities from the peak list files. In addition, the processing by the ALEX extractor was performed using lock mass ions for each FT MS *m/z* range in order to monitor and correct searches for FT MS calibration drifts (Figure 4A). Finally, the ALEX unifier was applied to merge the four ALEX extractor output files into single output files reporting all identified lipid species, intensities and accessory lipid features, and lock mass information and calculated FT MS calibration offsets.

As a first step in the auxiliary workflow we performed a quality control of the neurolipidomics dataset (Figure 1). To this end, we accessed the lock mass information using Tableau Software and displayed the estimated FT MS calibration offsets as function of sample injection. This quality control showed that the calibration offset was not constant across all samples (Figure 4) and thus highlighting the efficacy of the automatic lock mass adjustment. Importantly, for one sample we observed no intensity of the selected lock mass ion TAG 17:1/17:1/17:1. By manual inspection of the .RAW data, we concluded that the investigator in charge had failed to spike internal lipid standards into the particular sample. Consequently, this quality control demonstrated that the particular sample (cerebellum from a knockout mouse) could not be used for computing the molar amount of lipid species. As an additional quality control procedure we also accessed the output file with lipid species intensity data using Tableau Software, and displayed both the absolute intensity and intensity profile of monitored lipid species within lipid classes for all samples analyzed (Figure 4B). This analysis showed that a low abundant ion in the blank samples was falsely identified as PI 40:3. Due to the low intensity of this ion and its presence in the blank samples we concluded that this ion represents a chemical background ion. To minimize bias from falsely identified background ions one can implement a background subtraction during the subsequent computation of molar lipid abundance using the Orange software. Moreover, it is recommendable to perform additional tandem mass analysis to assess the identity of dubious identification.

Outlining the Auxiliary Workflow

In order to compute molar abundance (e.g. fmol) of lipid species we made use of the database exploration tool and open-source software Orange [28]. The molar abundance of lipid species is easily computed via a sequence of processing steps (depicted in Fig. 5). Step (1); the lipid species intensity data generated by the ALEX framework is specified as input (icon (a)) and merged with a second input specifying sample information (e.g. tissue type, genetic information, name of mice; icon (b)). Step (2); an intensity filter is implemented in order to remove intensities below a user-specified threshold if deemed necessary. Step (3); a third input specifying the spiked amount of internal standards is incorporated (icon (c)). Step (4); a new attribute is defined by specifying the intensities of internal standards. This attribute is used in step (6) for computing the molar abundance. Step (5); internal standards and corresponding intensities are defined for the subsequent calculation of molar lipid abundances. Step (6); an equation using the attributes lipid species intensity, internal standard intensity and spiked amount of internal standard is applied for calculating the molar lipid abundance [20]. Step (7); processed data is saved as a .csv output file (in database table format) that can be accessed for computation of mol% and lipidome visualization by Tableau Software. We here note that the Orange schema produced an output file of the neurolipidomics analysis featuring 997 targeted lipid species with accessory information across 56 sample injections producing a data matrix with a total of 1,050,504 data points (Data S1). Notably, managing and processing a dataset of this magnitude is poorly suited for Microsoft Excel and highlights the benefits of managing the data using a database exploration tools.

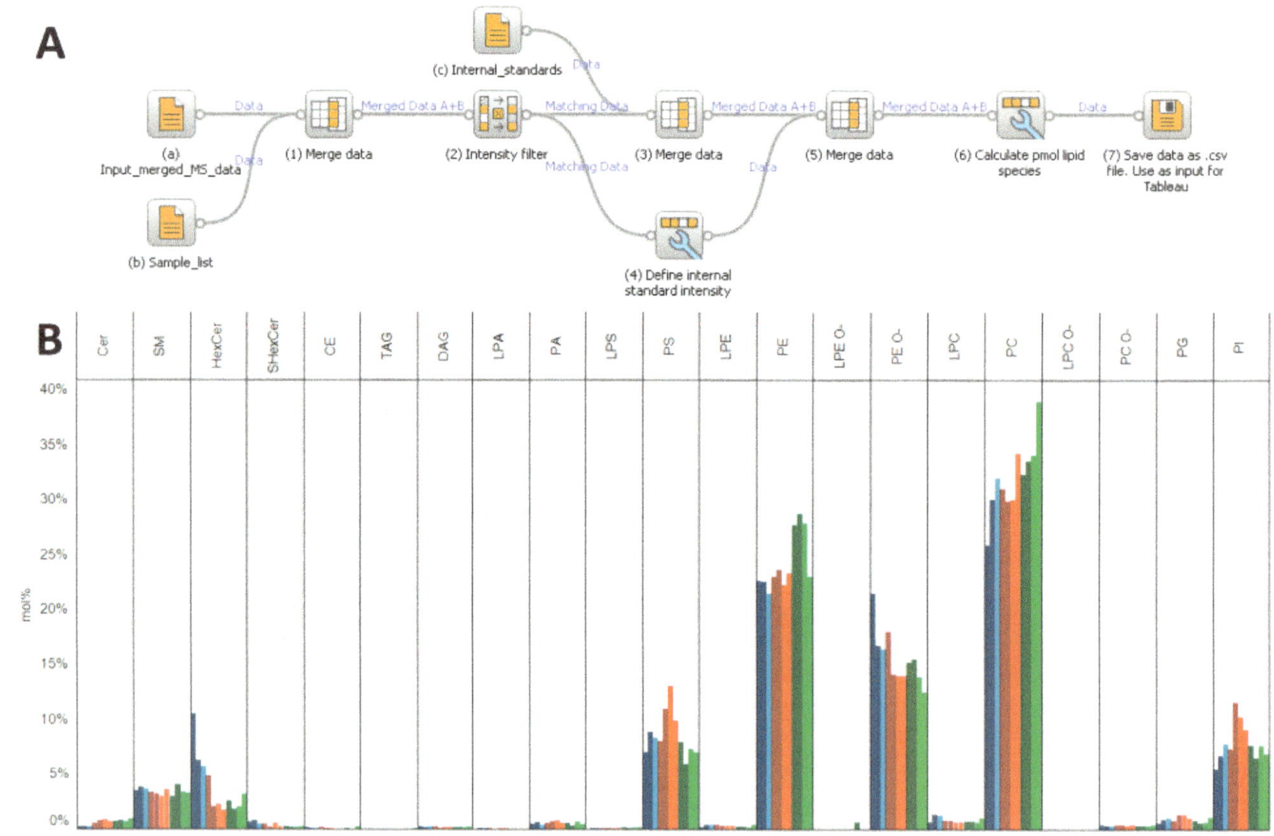

Figure 5. Outline of the auxiliary workflow used for lipidome data processing. (A) A sequence of processing steps executed by the Orange software is used to compute the molar abundance of lipid species. The processing routine utilizes three input files: (a) the output file generated by the ALEX framework specifying lipid intensities, (b) a text file specifying sample information, and (c) a text file specifying internal standards and molar spike amounts. Seven processing steps are executed in order to compute the molar abundances of lipid species for all samples. The data processing generates an output file in database table format featuring the molar abundances of lipid species, originating intensity data, all accessory lipid features and all sample information. (**B**) Lipid class composition of cerebellum, hippocampus and S1BF from wild-type and PRG-1 knockout mice as automatically calculated and displayed using Tableau Software.

To support rapid and efficient visualization of large lipidome datasets, we integrated Tableau Software as part of the auxiliary workflow. Tableau Software can be dynamically linked to the Orange output files such that any potential modifications within the data processing procedure can be visualized simply by updating the Orange output file and the link to Tableau. Notably, the Tableau software includes a feature that easily allows calculation and display of "mol% of lipid species" normalized to any given set of attributes and accessory lipid features in the input file. As such, the user can rapidly display the "mol% of all monitored PE species" (Figure 6C) or "mol% of all monitored glycerophospholipid species" (Figure 6D). We note, that calculation of such data formats would require implementation of additional processing steps within Orange (and equally in Microsoft Excel) in order to calculate and output such data values. We also note that these accessory lipid features provided by the ALEX framework, and consequently the information content in database table format, facilitates lipidome visualization by Tableau software.

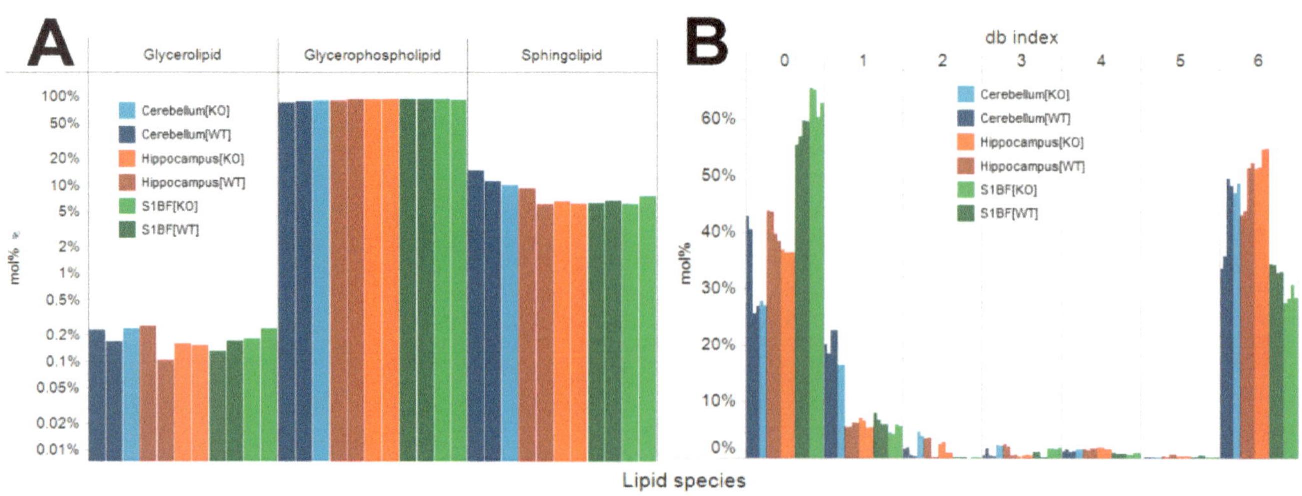

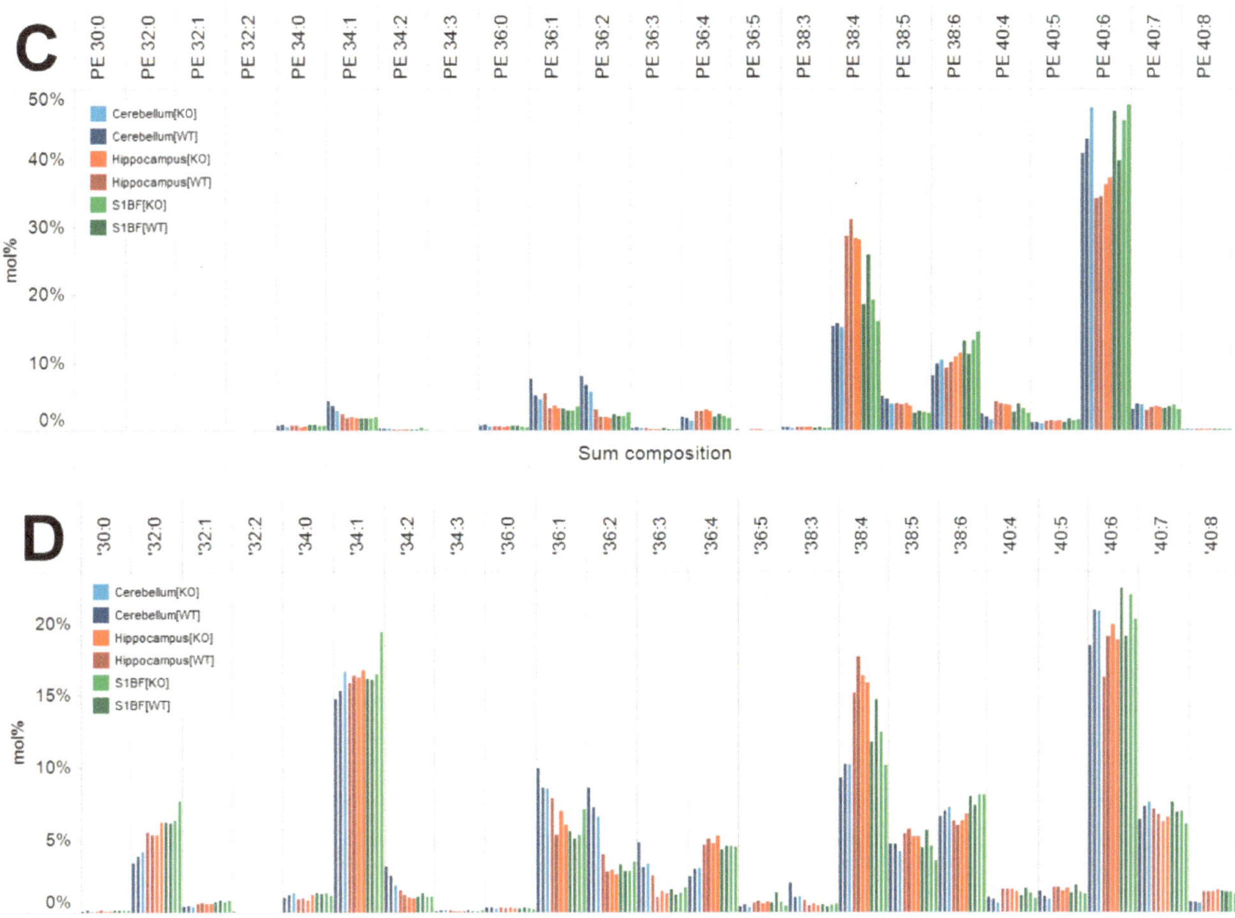

Figure 6. Lipidome visualization using different display formats. (A) mol% lipid category. Notice that the y-axis is logarithmic. Data is displayed as the average of the two technical replicates per sample. (B) mol% of db index of LPS species. Note that histogram include plot for both technical replicates. (**C**) mol% of PE species. Data is displayed as the average of the two technical replicates per sample. (**D**) mol% of all GPL species. Data is displayed as the average of the two technical replicates per sample. Notice that data for only one sample of cerebellum from knockout mice is available due to lack of spiked internal standards as outline in the section "Application of the ALEX software framework". This neurolipidomics dataset is available as supporting information (Data S2).

Application of the Auxiliary Workflow

To illustrate the efficacy of the auxiliary workflow we here present the results of the neurolipidomic pilot study. First, we assessed the lipid class composition of the three mouse brain tissues from wild-type and PRG-1 knockout mice (Figure 5B). The lipid class composition of brain tissues was primarily comprised of PC, PE, PE O-, PS, PI, SM and HexCer lipids. In addition, the analysis also showed a low abundance of Cer, SHexCer, CE and TAG species (Figure 5B). This result corroborates previous reports on brain lipid composition [36–38]. Notably, comparing the lipid class composition of the brain tissues did not show any pronounced differences between the wild-type and PRG-1 knockout mice. Moreover, the analysis also did not show any major difference in lipid class composition between the three brain tissues. To further interrogate the lipidome data, we explored alternative display formats including lipid category composition (e.g. glycerophospholipids, sphingolipids and glycerolipids,Figure 6A), lipid species composition within a defined lipid class (e.g. PE species, Figure 6C), lipid species composition across a defined lipid category (e.g. all glycerophospholipids, Figure 6D) and db index within a defined lipid class (e.g. LPS, Figure 6B). Using the various modes of lipidome visualization, we observed that each of the three mouse brain tissues featured specific signatures of lipid species. Specifically, we observed that the composition of PE species was different between all three tissues; the hippocampus comprised a relatively high level of PE 38:4, the S1BF contained relatively high levels of PE 40:6, and the cerebellum contained a relatively high level of PE 40:6 and minor but systematically higher levels of PE 34:1, PE 36:1 and PE 36:2 as compared to the two other tissues. These distinct lipidome hallmarks could also be observed when assessing the collective lipid species composition across all glycerophospholipids (Figure 6D) albeit with a less pronounced differences as compared to only PE species. The specific lipid compositions of the three brain tissues were further interrogated by visualizing the distribution of double bonds within the fatty acid moieties of LPS species. This visualization revealed that the S1BF comprised relatively high levels of LPS species with 0 double bonds (primarily attributed LPS 18:0) being offset by lower levels of LPS species having 6 double bonds (attributed LPS 22:6). In comparison, the cerebellum showed a characteristic distribution of LPS species with higher levels of species with 1 double bond as compared to the two other tissues. The LPS composition of the hippocampus comprised a double bond distribution intermediate of the S1BF and the cerebellum. We note that the lipidome visualization did not reveal any pronounced differences in lipid species composition between any of the tissues from wild-type and PRG-1 knockout mice. This observation is furthermore substantiated by results of principal component analysis (data not shown).

CONCLUSIONS

Here we presented a platform for streamlined processing, computation and visualization of high-content lipidomics datasets acquired using high-resolution Orbitrap mass spectrometry. The platform features a novel routine for querying proprietary spectral data that supports identification and quantification of lipid species, execution of quality control routines and rapid visualization of lipidome data. The platform utilizes three software modules: the ALEX framework that accesses and queries mass spectral data, the visual programming tool Orange that integrates sample information and computes molar lipid abundances, and the visual analytical tool Tableau Software for lipidome visualization. A key asset of the framework is the storage of lipidome data in "database table format" that enables using a multitude of data attributes for robust data processing and visualization. To demonstrate the efficacy of the platform, we presented a comparative neurolipidomic pilot study of mouse cerebellum, hippocampus and S1BF from wild-type and PRG-1 knockout mice [29]. The analysis demonstrated a distinct lipid species signature for each of the three brain tissues, but failed to ascertain any pronounced perturbations of lipid composition in mice devoid of the PRG-1 gene. This observation can potentially be explained by the localized expression of PRG-1 in the postsynaptic density of glutamatergic synapses. Regional differences in the lipidome composition induced by PRG-1 deficiency might potentially be concealed by the complexity of the macroscopic brain tissues investigated herein. We note that the ALEX framework can easily be adapted for processing of high-resolution shotgun lipidomics data acquired by any type of instrumentation (e.g. LTQ FT, Q Exactive, Orbitrap Fusion, solariX) provided spectral peak lists are stored in .txt file format. Moreover, the Orange processing procedure and Tableau visualization can be extended to include various filters for improved lipid identification, to calculate molar abundance of lipid species per unit of sample material (e.g. pmol lipid/µg protein), to perform statistical testing or multivariate analysis, and to integrate and support processing and visualization of lipidome data acquired by MS/MS analysis. Notably, the auxiliary workflow can also be adapted to use other database-orientated exploration tools than Orange and Tableau software. Finally, we argue that storage of lipidomics data in database table format can be a future avenue for data dissemination since it enables investigators to easily access, inspect and apply such resource data.

ACKNOWLEDGMENTS

We are grateful to Dr. Ole N. Jensen for providing access to Triversa NanoMate. We thank Dr. Albert Casanovas and Reinaldo Almeida for critical reading of the manuscript. We thank Hans Kristian Hannibal-Bach and Nikolai Schmarowski for technical assistance.

AUTHOR CONTRIBUTIONS

Conceived and designed the experiments: PH KT KE CSE. Performed the experiments: PH KT ES CSE. Analyzed the data: PH KT CSE. Contributed reagents/materials/analysis tools: PH KT MK JV JB RN. Wrote the manuscript: CSE.

REFERENCES

1. Yetukuri L, Ekroos K, Vidal-Puig A, Oresic M (2008) Informatics and computational strategies for the study of lipids. Mol Biosyst 4: 121-127. doi:10.1039/b715468b. PubMed: 18213405.
2. Shevchenko A, Simons K (2010) Lipidomics: coming to grips with lipid diversity. Nat Rev Mol Cell Biol 11: 593-598. doi:10.1038/nrg2850. PubMed: 20606693.
3. van Meer G (2005) Cellular lipidomics. EMBO J 24: 3159-3165. doi:10.1038/sj.emboj.7600798. PubMed: 16138081.
4. Ejsing CS, Sampaio JL, Surendranath V, Duchoslav E, Ekroos K et al. (2009) Global analysis of the yeast lipidome by quantitative shotgun mass spectrometry. Proc Natl Acad Sci U S A 106: 2136-2141. doi:10.1073/pnas.0811700106. PubMed: 19174513.
5. Klose C, Surma MA, Gerl MJ, Meyenhofer F, Shevchenko A et al. (2012) Flexibility of a eukaryotic lipidome--insights from yeast lipidomics. PLOS ONE 7: e35063. doi:10.1371/journal.pone.0035063. PubMed: 22529973.
6. Carvalho M, Sampaio JL, Palm W, Brankatschk M, Eaton S et al. (2012) Effects of diet and development on the Drosophila lipidome. Mol Syst Biol 8: 600. PubMed:22864382.
7. Sampaio JL, Gerl MJ, Klose C, Ejsing CS, Beug H et al. (2011) Membrane lipidome of an epithelial cell line. Proc Natl Acad Sci U S A 108: 1903-1907. doi:10.1073/pnas.1019267108. PubMed: 21245337.
8. Dennis EA, Deems RA, Harkewicz R, Quehenberger O, Brown HA et al. (2010) A mouse macrophage lipidome. J Biol Chem 285: 39976-39985. doi:10.1074/jbc.M110.182915. PubMed: 20923771.
9. Breslow DK, Collins SR, Bodenmiller B, Aebersold R, Simons K et al. (2010) Orm family proteins mediate sphingolipid homeostasis. Nature 463: 1048-1053. doi:10.1038/nature08787. PubMed: 20182505.
10. Klemm RW, Ejsing CS, Surma MA, Kaiser HJ, Gerl MJ et al. (2009) Segregation of sphingolipids and sterols during formation of secretory vesicles at the trans-Golgi network. J Cell Biol 185: 601-612. doi:10.1083/jcb.200901145. PubMed: 19433450.
11. Brügger B, Glass B, Haberkant P, Leibrecht I, Wieland FT et al. (2006) The HIV lipidome: a raft with an unusual composition. Proc Natl Acad Sci U S A 103: 2641-2646. doi:10.1073/pnas.0511136103. PubMed: 16481622.
12. Takamori S, Holt M, Stenius K, Lemke EA, Grønborg M et al. (2006) Molecular anatomy of a trafficking organelle. Cell 127: 831-846. doi:10.1016/j.cell.2006.10.030. PubMed: 17110340.
13. Zech T, Ejsing CS, Gaus K, de Wet B, Shevchenko A et al. (2009) Accumulation of raft lipids in T-cell plasma membrane domains engaged in TCR signalling. EMBO J 28: 466-476. doi:10.1038/emboj.2009.6. PubMed: 19177148.
14. Han X, Yang K, Gross RW (2012) Multi-dimensional mass spectrometry-based shotgun lipidomics and novel strategies for lipidomic analyses. Mass Spectrom Rev 31: 134-178. doi:10.1002/mas.20342. PubMed: 21755525.

15. Song H, Hsu FF, Ladenson J, Turk J (2007) Algorithm for processing raw mass spectrometric data to identify and quantitate complex lipid molecular species in mixtures by data-dependent scanning and fragment ion database searching. J Am Soc Mass Spectrom 18: 1848-1858. doi:10.1016/j.jasms.2007.07.023. PubMed: 17720531.

16. Haimi P, Uphoff A, Hermansson M, Somerharju P (2006) Software tools for analysis of mass spectrometric lipidome data. Anal Chem 78: 8324-8331. doi:10.1021/ac061390w. PubMed: 17165823.

17. Leavell MD, Leary JA (2006) Fatty acid analysis tool (FAAT): An FT-ICR MS lipid analysis algorithm. Anal Chem 78: 5497-5503. doi:10.1021/ac0604179. PubMed:16878888.

18. Hübner G, Crone C, Lindner B (2009) lipID--a software tool for automated assignment of lipids in mass spectra. J Mass Spectrom 44: 1676-1683. PubMed: 19816875.

19. Houjou T, Yamatani K, Imagawa M, Shimizu T, Taguchi R (2005) A shotgun tandem mass spectrometric analysis of phospholipids with normal-phase and/or reverse-phase liquid chromatography/electrospray ionization mass spectrometry. Rapid Commun Mass Spectrom 19: 654-666. doi:10.1002/rcm.1836. PubMed: 15700236.

20. Ejsing CS, Duchoslav E, Sampaio J, Simons K, Bonner R et al. (2006) Automated identification and quantification of glycerophospholipid molecular species by multiple precursor ion scanning. Anal Chem 78: 6202-6214. doi:10.1021/ac060545x. PubMed:16944903.

21. Schwudke D, Oegema J, Burton L, Entchev E, Hannich JT et al. (2006) Lipid profiling by multiple precursor and neutral loss scanning driven by the data-dependent acquisition. Anal Chem 78: 585-595. doi:10.1021/ac051605m. PubMed: 16408944.

22. Herzog R, Schwudke D, Schuhmann K, Sampaio JL, Bornstein SR et al. (2011) A novel informatics concept for high-throughput shotgun lipidomics based on the molecular fragmentation query language. Genome Biol 12: R8. doi:10.1186/gb-2011-12-1-r8. PubMed: 21247462.

23. Ejsing CS, Husen P, Tarasov K (2012) In: K. Ekroos. Lipidomics: technologies and applications. Weinheim: Wiley-VCH. pp. 147-174.

24. Liebisch G, Vizcaíno JA, Köfeler H, Trötzmüller M, Griffiths WJ et al. (2013) Shorthand notation for lipid structures derived from mass spectrometry. J Lipid Res 54: 1523-1530. doi:10.1194/jlr.M033506. PubMed: 23549332.

25. Ekroos K, Ejsing CS, Bahr U, Karas M, Simons K et al. (2003) Charting molecular composition of phosphatidylcholines by fatty acid scanning and ion trap MS3 fragmentation. J Lipid Res 44: 2181-2192. doi:10.1194/jlr.D300020-JLR200. PubMed:12923235.

26. Fahy E, Subramaniam S, Brown HA, Glass CK, Merrill AH Jr. et al. (2005) A comprehensive classification system for lipids. J Lipid Res 46: 839-861. doi:10.1194/jlr.E400004-JLR200. PubMed: 15722563.

27. Fahy E, Subramaniam S, Murphy RC, Nishijima M, Raetz CR et al. (2009) Update of the LIPID MAPS comprehensive classification system for lipids. J Lipid Res 50 Suppl: S9-14. PubMed: 19098281.

28. Curk T, Demsar J, Xu Q, Leban G, Petrovic U et al. (2005) Microarray data mining with visual programming. Bioinformatics 21: 396-398. doi:10.1093/bioinformatics/bth474. PubMed: 15308546.

29. Trimbuch T, Beed P, Vogt J, Schuchmann S, Maier N et al. (2009) Synaptic PRG-1 modulates excitatory transmission via lipid phosphate-mediated signaling. Cell 138: 1222-1235. doi:10.1016/j.cell.2009.06.050. PubMed: 19766573.

30. Schwudke D, Hannich JT, Surendranath V, Grimard V, Moehring T et al. (2007) Top-down lipidomic screens by multivariate analysis of high-resolution survey mass spectra. Anal Chem 79: 4083-4093. doi:10.1021/ac062455y. PubMed: 17474710.

31. Liebisch G, Binder M, Schifferer R, Langmann T, Schulz B et al. (2006) High throughput quantification of cholesterol and cholesteryl ester by electrospray ionization tandem mass spectrometry (ESI-MS/MS). Biochim Biophys Acta 1761: 121-128. doi:10.1016/j.bbalip.2005.12.007. PubMed: 16458590.

32. Sandhoff R, Brügger B, Jeckel D, Lehmann WD, Wieland FT (1999) Determination of cholesterol at the low picomole level by nano-electrospray ionization tandem mass spectrometry. J Lipid Res 40: 126-132. PubMed: 9869658.

33. Bilgin M, Markgraf DF, Duchoslav E, Knudsen J, Jensen ON et al. (2011) Quantitative profiling of PE, MMPE, DMPE, and PC lipid species by multiple precursor ion scanning: a tool for monitoring PE metabolism. Biochim Biophys Acta 1811: 1081-1089. doi:10.1016/j.bbalip.2011.09.018. PubMed: 22001639.

34. Southam AD, Payne TG, Cooper HJ, Arvanitis TN, Viant MR (2007) Dynamic range and mass accuracy of wide-scan direct infusion nanoelectrospray fourier transform ion cyclotron resonance mass spectrometry-based metabolomics increased by the spectral stitching method. Anal Chem 79: 4595-4602. doi:10.1021/ac062446p. PubMed:17511421.

35. Schuhmann K, Almeida R, Baumert M, Herzog R, Bornstein SR et al. (2012) Shotgun lipidomics on a LTQ Orbitrap mass spectrometer by successive switching between acquisition polarity modes. J Mass Spectrom 47: 96-104. doi:10.1002/jms.2031. PubMed: 22282095.

36. Chan RB, Oliveira TG, Cortes EP, Honig LS, Duff KE et al. (2012) Comparative lipidomic analysis of mouse and human brain with Alzheimer disease. J Biol Chem 287: 2678-2688. doi:10.1074/jbc.M111.274142. PubMed: 22134919.

37. Rappley I, Myers DS, Milne SB, Ivanova PT, Lavoie MJ et al. (2009) Lipidomic profiling in mouse brain reveals differences between ages and genders, with smaller changes associated with alpha-synuclein genotype. J Neurochem 111: 15-25. doi:10.1111/j.1471-4159.2009.06290.x. PubMed: 19627450.

38. O'Brien JS, Sampson EL (1965) Lipid composition of the normal human brain: gray matter, white matter, and myelin. J Lipid Res 6: 537-544. PubMed: 5865382.

CHAPTER 14

CONFOCALCHECK - A SOFTWARE TOOL FOR THE AUTOMATED MONITORING OF CONFOCAL MICROSCOPE PERFORMANCE

Keng Imm Hng, Dirk Dormann

MRC Clinical Sciences Centre, Faculty of Medicine, Imperial College London, London, United Kingdom

ABSTRACT

Laser scanning confocal microscopy has become an invaluable tool in biomedical research but regular quality testing is vital to maintain the system's performance for diagnostic and research purposes.

Although many methods have been devised over the years to characterize specific aspects of a confocal microscope like measuring the optical point spread function or the field illumination, only very few analysis tools are available. Our aim was to develop a comprehensive quality assurance framework ranging from image acquisition to automated analysis and documentation. We created standardized test data to assess the performance of the lasers, the objective lenses and other key components required for optimum confocal operation.

The ConfocalCheck software presented here analyses the data fully automatically. It creates numerous visual outputs indicating potential issues requiring further investigation. By storing results in a web browser compatible file format the software greatly simplifies record keeping allowing the operator to quickly compare old and new data and to spot developing trends.

We demonstrate that the systematic monitoring of confocal performance is essential in a core facility environment and how the quantitative measurements obtained can be used for the detailed characterization of system components as well as for comparisons across multiple instruments.

INTRODUCTION

Since the release of the first commercially available instruments more than 25 years ago laser scanning confocal microscopy has rapidly become a standard tool in many areas of research in the life sciences and medicine [1,2]. The combination of a diffraction limited spot of laser light - scanning across a fluorescently labelled sample - with the confocal pinhole – an aperture in a conjugate image plane placed in front of the light detector – allows the effective rejection of out-of-focus fluorescence light emanating from excited fluorophores outside the focal volume [3,4]. From these blur-free 'optical sections' the three-dimensional structure of both fixed and living biological samples can be rapidly reconstructed. This

Citation: Hng KI, Dormann D (2013) ConfocalCheck - A Software Tool for the Automated Monitoring of Confocal Microscope Performance. PLoS ONE 8(11): e79879. doi:10.1371/journal.pone.0079879.

has been invaluable in countless studies and to date more than 45600 articles have been published on the subject [5].

Confocal microscopes are complex instruments consisting of many optical, mechanical and electronic components that all need to be properly aligned and calibrated before accurate data can be recorded [4]. Despite their popularity and wide spread use there are very few if any tools provided by the manufacturers themselves to monitor confocal performance following the purchase of a new system. It might just be a slide with a fluorescently labelled section of plant tissue (Convallaria spec., 'lily of the valley') which provides 'pretty' multi-colour images but the use of these biological samples as test specimens for the evaluation of a confocal microscope is very limited [6,7].

While imaging experts and staff of centralised microscopy facilities would be able to recognise many of the issues adversely affecting confocal image acquisition there are far more confocal instruments in individual research labs where this specialised support might not be readily available.

How can the average user, the cell or developmental biologist be confident that the images acquired on a confocal microscope are actually reflecting the biology of the sample rather than the variability of the instrument? Due to the increasing demand for quantitative analysis of biological samples and the complexity of biological research with experiments stretching over many months or years or even spread over several laboratories it is essential to ensure the accuracy and comparability of the data recorded on a confocal microscope [6,8]. When performing quantitative fluorescence imaging the main source of concern would be temporal and spatial signal intensity variations introduced by the instrument itself (which are by no means specific to the confocal microscope) [8,9,10]. Even the probably most common and basic confocal application, studying the spatial distribution or colocalisation of two different fluorescently labelled antibodies could easily be invalidated if the system was misaligned or the wrong objective lens used.

For the systematic analysis of confocal performance a wide range of tests have been developed, mostly relying on inexpensive samples and yet providing a wealth of information on the state of the instrument and individual components [7 ,8,11,12,13,14,15,16,17,18,19,20,21,22,23,24,25,26,27,28,2 9]. Although there are many differences in the design of the commercially available confocal microscopes - and each of them available with a multitude of possible configurations - the following parameters are commonly checked for quality control purposes:

Lasers: Measuring the laser power directly on the microscope stage with a power meter is used to assess not only the status of the lasers themselves but probes the alignment of entire excitation light path with all the intermediate optical elements and light guides [20,21]. Short term laser stability and noise can be measured with time lapse recordings (in fluorescence, reflection or transmitted light mode)[19,24]. The observed intensity fluctuations should ideally be negligible compared to the signal variations that need to be measured in the biological sample.

Field illumination: The field pattern is observed by illuminating a homogeneously fluorescent sample, the intensity distribution should be relatively uniform with the maximum signal in the center but this will depend of the objective lens, alignment of the lasers, any corrective optics for UV/405nm lasers etc. [7,13]. For quantitative measurements any unevenness in the field should be avoided or corrected for.

Image distortion: A grid pattern of small squares is used to test the XY scanning mechanism that moves the laser beam across the sample [13,19]. Any deviation from the square shape would indicate a distortion in the image that would need to be fixed.

Spectral registration: This is tested by imaging multi-color fluorescent beads in three dimensions [7]. For colocalisation experiments the bead images in the different color channels should coincide with very little deviation. Although dependent on the type of objective lens used spectral registration will be affected by the alignment of other components like the lasers as well.

Point spread function (PSF): The PSF is obtained by recording sub-resolution fluorescent beads in three dimensions. It is used to determine the axial and lateral resolution of the microscope and to identify problems in the imaging system in particular the objective lenses [27,30].

Axial resolution: The axial resolution is used to assess the optical sectioning capability of the instrument and can be obtained from imaging a thin fluorescent film [26,28,31] or the reflection of laser light from a mirror [7,13]. Axial resolution has been described as a 'gold standard' and is used by some manufacturers to check whether the system is working according to specifications [7]. By comparing the reflection bands of multiple laser lines the axial chromatic correction of the objective lenses can be revealed - how well light of different wavelengths is focused in the same plane, important again for colocalisation experiments [13,20].

There are many excellent guidelines and protocols included in the literature cited above on how to acquire suitable data sets with the test samples and how to interpret the results. Some parameters like resolution can easily be measured using the basic quantification tools available in the confocal software packages but this can be tedious, subjective and time consuming. And yet there are very few software tools for the automated quantitative analysis of the performance data. Some programs have been developed only for a specialized purpose, for example to analyze the PSF [32], or to provide the detailed quantification of the Z-sectioning capability using the SIPchart methodology [26,31,33]. To date only the MetroloJ plugin for ImageJ can process a wider range of data, measuring the PSF, bead colocalisation, field illumination and axial resolution [34,35].

As none of these tools were able to capture the range of issues we had encountered on the confocal instruments in our microscopy facility over the years we decided to develop the ConfocalCheck software which integrates many previously proposed analysis methods into a single easy to use package. We focused on three general topics - the lasers, the objective lenses and other important mechanical components present on a modern confocal microscope. This comprised the scanning galvos, the Z-focus drives, the motorised microscope stages and the spectral detector units that are specific to Leica SP confocal microscopes. The interplay of all these components is essential for the optimum operation of the microscope and can easily be monitored on a regular basis.

The protocols for the acquisition of the test data were standardized to provide the basis for the fully automated and quantitative analysis with the ConfocalCheck software, without user intervention and bias. A visual output for most parameters assists in the quick detection of potential problems while additional files in the HTML format are created for record keeping and long-term monitoring. This should be of particular benefit to core facility staff involved in the maintenance of multiple confocal units. Even during the initial testing phase on the six single-point scanning confocal systems available in our unit we discovered many issues that required further investigation by service engineers suggesting that there are many underperforming systems out there. This can be a serious problem especially when there is no trained staff carrying out regular system checks. Unless the problem is so severe that it is noted by the average user many faults could remain undetected for some time.

We describe the acquisition and analysis of the confocal test data sets, illustrated with examples from the microscopes available in our facility. Regular and systematic checks using the tools described in this report should assist even the inexperienced user in identifying potential problems that might need to be addressed. Furthermore, the quantitative measurements obtained with ConfocalCheck give the operator the means to characterize and compare individual components across multiple instruments.

MATERIALS AND METHODS

Sources of Slides and Materials

A slide with a reflective square grid pattern (9.9µm x 9.9µm) was taken from a set of Deltavision calibration slides (Applied Precision, Inc.; similar grid slides: planotec silicon test specimen S1934, Agar Scientific). We used the red fluorescent slide of that kit (Excitation 590nm, Emission 650nm) for the field illumination tests of the 543/561/594/633nm laser lines and the blue and green fluorescent Chroma slides (part no. 92001, Chroma technology Corp.) or the equivalent Deltavision slides for testing the 405nm and 488nm field illumination [7,20]. Glass slides (76x26mm) and No 1.5 coverslips (22x22mm, Menzel-Gläser) were obtained from Fisher Scientific. As most modern objective lenses are designed to be used with 170µm coverslips high-precision cover glasses could also be considered for best performance (No. 1.5H, thickness 170µm±5µm; Marienfeld Superior cat.no. 0107052 or Zeiss cat.no. 474030-9020-000).

Front surface mirrors were from Edmund Optics Ltd (part no: 32368, 22x22mm), 175nm green PS-speck beads (P-7220), 1µm Tetraspeck beads (T-7282) and Prolong Gold mounting medium (P36934) from Life Technologies Corporation.

Laser power was measured with a Fieldmaster power meter (part no. 33-0506-000, Coherent Inc.) where the LM-2 VIS sensor (part no. 1098298, wavelength range: 405-1070nm) had been mounted on a custom made slide-sized holder to simplify power measurements directly on the microscope stage (see 21 for possible designs).

Stage temperature was monitored with a 'USB-Temp' PC Thermometer, (31.1026, TFA Dostmann GmbH, Germany), room temperature with a RMS300 Weatherstation (Oregon Scientific).

Preparation of Slides

The mirror slide was prepared by gluing the mirror directly onto a glass slide [7]. 175nm PS-speck beads (green only) and 1µm Tetraspeck bead stock tubes were vortexed, diluted 1:10000 in distilled water and vortexed again. 5µl of each suspension was placed in the center of the same coverslip and allowed to dry [21,32]. The coverslip was carefully lowered on a slide with a 5µl drop of Prolong gold mounting medium which was allowed to cure for 24h at room temperature in darkness. All fluorescent plastic slides and the mirror slide were covered with no 1.5 coverslips held in place with a small drop of immersion oil (n=1.518, Zeiss Immersol 518F) as described [7]. For inexperienced users it might be useful to prepare additional slides with more beads (1:100 dilution) as finding the PS-speck beads can be challenging.

Performance Checks - Data Acquisition

The following confocal systems were available in our microscopy facility and used for evaluation: Leica (Leica Microsystems) SP1 and SP2 with dichroic beamsplitters, 2× Leica SP5 with AOBS (acousto optical beam splitter), Leica SP5 II with AOBS. Additional tests were carried out on a Zeiss LSM510 Meta system (Carl Zeiss Microscopy, Jena, Germany), a Zeiss LSM780 and a Nikon A1R (Nikon Instruments) microscope. On another Deltavision Core (Applied Precision) deconvolution microscope we only measured the motorised stage performance.

The confocal systems including all the lasers were switched on at least 1h prior to testing and all objective lenses were first inspected and cleaned with absolute ethanol as required.

On the Leica systems a single experiment file (.lif/.lei) should be created for each objective lens. For the Zeiss (.lsm/.czi), Nikon (.nd2) and TIFF (.tif) files separate folders should be created for each objective lens with each folder containing the relevant image files eg. "bead.lsm", "psf.nd2", "bead.tif". Importantly, the file and folder names must not contain any spaces as that causes problems with data import in ImageJ/Fiji.

The general procedures are described below.

Lasers – Laser Power.

The power measurements were taken in the specimen plane on the microscope stage using a low magnification 10× objective [20,21] with laser beam blanking disabled. Having direct meter readings was very useful when communicating with service engineers to assess whether a callout is required. Alternatively one could for example measure the reflection of the different laser lines from the mirror slide. By always using the same fixed scan parameters and fixed settings for the detector gain/offset and the laser power changes in image intensity should reflect changes in laser intensity. At fixed laser power settings one could also note the detector gain required to achieve saturation, this could be done with the mirror slide, with a fluorescent sample or even without a slide using the transmitted light detector (see section below).

Lasers – Laser Stability.

Laser stability was measured from time lapse recordings for all lasers using the transmitted light PMT (photomultiplier tube) and the 10× lens [8,19]. First the transmitted light path was properly adjusted according to Köhler. PMT gain and offset were kept the same for all laser lines, with the PMT gain as low as possible to keep detector noise low. Image brightness for each wavelength was adjusted with the AOTF (acousto-optical tunable filter) to an intermediate grey intensity to monitor intensity fluctuations during the time course. Using the sequential scan mode scanning only with one laser line at a time images were recorded every 20s for 2 hours at 256×256 pixels and at the highest zoom settings to avoid intensity variations within the images due to uneven field illumination. Long term laser stability was measured overnight or as required. The image series was renamed *laser* for the subsequent automatic analysis.

Objective Lens – Axial Resolution and Chromatic Correction.

Axial resolution and axial chromatic correction was measured for all objective lenses by using the reflection of laser light from the mirror slide [7,13,21]. To detect the reflected light we used 10-20nm wide detection windows centered on the main laser lines (e.g. 488/561/633nm). Depending on the number of available detection channels between 3 and 5 lasers lines were recorded simultaneously. After focusing on the mirror surface the acquisition was changed to the XZ line scan mode. The confocal pinhole diameter was set to 1 Airy unit, however when trying to obtain the highest possible Z resolution in reflection mode the confocal pinhole was set to its minimum diameter [7]. The zoom factor was increased (about 10-40× zoom to achieve a z step size of 0.015-0.03µm when using a Leica Z-galvo) and the bright horizontal reflection band placed in the middle of the field using the microscope focus control. XZ images were recorded with the following combinations of laser lines (depending on the system configuration):

1. 405/488/543(561)nm; 2. 488/543(561)/633nm. As most instruments only had three PMTs available we performed these two scans to avoid using sequential scanning which would have introduced a time delay and possibly changes in the Z position due to vibration or focus drift. On a 4 or 5 channel system all these laser lines can be evaluated in a single scan. The scans starting with the 405nm line were renamed *axial405*, the scans starting with the 488nm line were renamed *axial488*.

Objective Lens – Field Illumination.

Field illumination was tested for each objective lens and for all the main laser lines (for example 405/488/561/633nm) with the fluorescent plastic slides [8,13,21]. The slides were mounted and the slide surface identified by looking for the brightest fluorescence signal. The actual recordings were taken at an offset focusing 30-75 µm into the slide depending on the objective (10×: 75µm; 20×: 50µm; 40×: 40µm; 63×: 30µm; 100×: 30µm) to reduce the uneven intensity distribution observed on the slide surface [7,8]. The zoom factor was set to 1 to obtain the maximum field size, image size to 512×512 pixel and pinhole size set to 1 Airy unit. Low laser power was used to avoid bleaching and due to high PMT gain images were averaged (4× line/frame average). The recorded images were renamed *field405, field488* etc.

Objective Lenses – Bead Colocalisation.

Spectral registration was measured using 1µm Tetraspeck beads [8]. Beads on the coverslip (closest to the objective lens) were selected using low intensity epi-fluorescence illumination and centered in the field of view.

The pinhole diameter was set to 1 Airy unit, image size to 256×256 pixels and XY resolution to about 0.03µm (zoom factor 16-64×)[7]. Laser power was kept reasonably low to avoid bleaching and gain/offset adjusted to optimize the dynamic range. Very noisy images were averaged four times. Using the XYZ scan mode with sequential scanning for 3-4 wavelengths (eg 405/488/561/633nm) we recorded Z stacks with the total Z height and Z step size depending on the objective lens (eg. 10×: 1µm steps; 63× oil: 0.15µm steps). The oversampling in the XY and in the Z direction is required for analysis and visualization purposes. Stacks were renamed *bead*. Only one bead per stack is permitted as the analysis software does not distinguish between multiple beads within the field of view.

Objective Lenses – Point Spread Function.

The point spread function was measured using green 175nm PS-speck beads excited with the 488nm laser line [13,21,27]. Beads closest to the coverslip were selected and centered in the field of view. The other acquisition settings were the same as for the Tetraspeck beads described above. The 3D image stack was renamed *psf*. Only one bead per stack is permitted as the analysis software does not distinguish between different beads.

Testing other Mechanical Components

Spectrophotometer Accuracy.

The accuracy of the spectral slider movement in the spectrophotometer unit of the Leica SP systems was measured with the 10× lens and the mirror slide for three laser lines - 488, 543 or 561, 633nm – again in reflection mode [13,19]. After focusing on the mirror surface, the confocal pinhole was fully opened, image size set to 256×256 pixel and zoom to 8×.

The lambda scan mode (XYλ) was selected and the detection window width set to 5nm. The PMT offset was left at 0. The detection window was moved to the different laser lines and the gain adjusted for each PMT so that the reflection image at each line was below saturation for the most sensitive PMT. AOTF settings for each laser line were adjusted to obtain similar peak intensities.

The lambda scan was performed from 470 to 670nm in 2nm intervals in 100 steps on the SP1/SP2 systems (SP5: 470-668nm, 3nm intervals, 67 steps). This was repeated for all spectral detectors available keeping the same AOTF settings and the same gain/offset values The AOTF/gain/offset settings should be optimized first by testing the reflection images for all the different detectors and laser lines to ensure that there is no saturation while running the lambda scan. The individual scans were renamed *scanpmt1, scanpmt2*, etc.

XY Scanning Galvos.

The accuracy of the XY scanning galvos was assessed using the 10x lens with the grid slide [13,19]. Using the 488nm line in reflection mode and with the pinhole diameter set to 1 airy unit we focused on the grid pattern. If the grid lines were not parallel to the scan field the slide was rotated either manually or using the scan field rotation optics. The zoom was adjusted (8×) so that the width and the height of the squares in the grid pattern could be properly assessed. A single image was recorded with 1024×1024 pixel and renamed *grid*.

XY Motorised Stage.

The performance of the motorized microscope stages was assessed by repeatedly recording either different fluorescent beads at different locations of the bead slide or the same bead at different locations within the same field of view. We used the 20×/air objective lens to image 1µm Tetraspeck beads with the 633nm line to reduce photobleaching. Pinhole size was set to 1 Airy unit, image size 256x256 pixel, resolution 0.1µm/pixel. To measure unidirectional stage repeatability over a larger area three different beads were defined (5-10mm apart) and a timelapse recording started that visited these positions 100 times. The recordings of the different positions were named *stage1, stage2* and *stage3* in the Leica .lif/.lei experiment files and the TIFF format and *stage* in the other file formats.

To measure stage accuracy as well as repeatability over a small movement range we used one bead and shifted its position once or twice within the field of view by a given value (eg. 10µm in X; 10µm in Y). A timelapse recording visited these positions 100 times. The three bead positions were named *stageacc1, stageacc2* and *stageacc3* in the Leica .lif/.lei experiment files and the TIFF format and *stageacc* in the other file formats. These tests could also be performed at higher magnification or on larger samples like multi-well plates to assess performance over long distances.

Z-Galvo Stability.

The stability of the Z-galvo available on the Leica SP systems was measured similarly to the axial resolution described above except that only the reflection of the 488nm line was used with a high NA 40×-100× objective [7,19,29]. After focusing on the surface of the mirror slide, the scan mode was switched to XZT and the pinhole diameter set to 1 Airy unit (or to the minimum diameter when trying to achieve maximum Z resolution). The horizontal reflection band was placed in the middle of the image at a Z-resolution of 0.015-0.03µm, image size 256x256 pixels. Time-lapse series with 2s interval were recorded for at least 10min but ideally for one hour or longer. The image series was renamed *zgalvo*.

Table 1. Summary of the routine confocal checks performed with different objective lenses

	Performance test									
Objective lens	Laser power	Laser stability	Axial resolution and co-localisation	Field illumination	Bead colocalisation	Point spread function (PSF)nbsp;	Lambda scan(1)	XY galvos	XY stage	Z galvo stability(1)
10×	●	●	●	●	●	●	●	●		
20×			●	●	●	●			●	
40×			●	●	●	●				●*
63×			●	●	●	●				●*
100×			●	●	●	●				●*

* Z galvo stability is only tested with one of the high NA objectives.

(1) These measurements are only applicable to the Leica SP confocal systems SP1/SP2/SP5.

Design and Implementation of the Analysis Software

The processing and analysis of the image data was performed automatically with minimal user intervention using the custom-written ConfocalCheck macro (Macro S1). We tested ConfocalCheck with ImageJ (version 1.46r)[35] and Fiji (version 1.47h)[36] on a Windows XP 32bit Dell Optiplex 620 PC with 2GByte RAM and a Windows 7 64bit Dell Optiplex 980 computer. The LOCI bioformats plugin was required for the import of some of the confocal files and to obtain the metadata (release version 4.4.8, built 1May2013) [38]. This bioformats version works fine, however as there are frequent revisions often affecting the name tags used to obtain the metadata values different versions might require simple changes to the macro code.

Before using ConfocalCheck for the first time some system specific details have to be edited in the configuration file. This only involves providing a list of the installed objective lenses and specifying the lasers used for various performance tests.

A step-by-step guide on running ConfocalCheck, details of the output files and the measurements it creates are provided. Several datasets are available to evaluate the software.

ConfocalCheck searches for the different keywords eg. *laser*, *bead*, *psf* etc in the experiment files (Leica .lif/.lei) or in the experiment folders with the instrument specific data files (Zeiss .lsm/.czi; Nikon .nd2). Once found appropriate metadata are retrieved and the images loaded and processed. TIFF images or stacks acquired on other systems should be labeled by the appropriate keyword followed by the extension *.tif* for example *bead.tif* or *psf.tif.*

All measurements are saved in tab delimited text files that can be opened with any text editor or spreadsheet software.

Additionally HTML files containing the result images and measurements can be created at a user defined location. This is done for each confocal system with a separate HTML file for each objective. The HTML files are amended when a new analysis is carried out at a later date providing a fast and simple way of tracking the different performance parameters over time.

Laser Stability.

For each laser line the average image intensity and the standard deviation are measured at each time point and plotted versus time [19,21]. The minimum and maximum intensities are determined as well as the maximum percentage change. A number of output images are created: a plot containing the mean intensity versus time, a rescaled version to visualize smaller fluctuations and a plot of the standard deviation versus time as a measure of how laser noise changes over time. To measure laser noise on a very short time scale the pixel intensities along a single horizontal line scan in the first image of the time lapse are recorded and mean, standard deviation and CV (coefficient of variation) values calculated [21]. The intensity profiles are plotted as pixel intensity versus pixel position.

To quantify laser intensity fluctuations over time scales from μs to hours we calculated the differences between adjacent data points [24] and created histograms of the percentage changes. For the μ-second time scale we obtained the intensity data from horizontal line plots of the first 100 images, the millisecond time scale was derived from 100 vertical intensity plots from the same images. For the other time scales we compared the mean intensities of images recorded 20s, 1min, 10min and 1 hour apart.

Axial Resolution.

For the axial resolution measurements a line is manually drawn perpendicular to the horizontal reflection pattern [7,13]. Alternatively this can be done automatically through the center of the image. The smoothened intensity profile along this line is derived by averaging over 10 pixels in X direction and the peak Z position and the FWHM (Full Width at Half Maximum) for each laser line is calculated. The output image displays the RGB overlay of the first three channels with the line position indicated and the corresponding intensity plots. The dots on the graphs mark the peak positions and the intensity values used for calculating the FWHM.

Field Illumination.

The image is first smoothened by a mean filter (radius 5 pixel) to reduce noise and to remove small artifacts due to dirt or scratches on the plastic slides. Then the horizontal and vertical intensity profiles through the centre of the image are measured [7,13]. The intensity profiles are further smoothened by reading out the average over 10 adjacent pixels (either in X or Y direction) rather than using a one pixel wide profile. The result image shows the smoothened and contrast enhanced field image with black lines marking where the intensity profiles were measured together with the intensity plotted versus pixel position. Minimum/maximum intensities and the percentage differences are calculated.

Bead Colocalisation.

For the colocalisation analysis with the 1μm Tetraspeck beads the different channels are analyzed separately [7,8,13]. First the images are median filtered (radius 7 pixel) to remove noise and to smoothen the image, then the brightest image in the stack is identified (typically the image with the maximum bead diameter). For the size or resolution measurements of beads one typically records the diameter obtained at the half maximal bead intensity (FWHM – full width at half maximum). We use this half-maximum intensity to set a channel specific threshold for the subsequent binarisation that is applied to the whole Z stack. The 3D centroid is calculated and the procedure repeated for the different channels. The image stack is also re-sliced in XZ and YZ direction at the centroid position. For visualization purposes the original images are overlaid as RGB images in XY, XZ and YZ with the Z views corrected (extended by the ratio of Z step size to XY pixel size) to obtain similar dimensions in XY and Z. The outlines of the thresholded images with the calculated centroids are presented in a similar fashion. The XY and Z distances between all centroids are calculated.

Point Spread Function.

The PSF image stacks are processed similarly, but after the centroid has been calculated we obtain the intensity profiles at the centroid position in XY and Z direction and fit a Gaussian curve to obtain the lateral and axial FWHM as a measure for resolution [13,32,34]. For display purposes XY/XZ/YZ views are calculated and an image montage is created showing all the Z sections. To enhance the visibility of the weaker diffraction patterns the gamma setting is changed (0.1), contrast enhanced and a pseudo-color look-up-table (LUT) applied.

Spectrophotometer Accuracy.

For the lambda scans the average image intensities are plotted versus the wavelength for all PMTs used [13,19]. The wavelengths corresponding to the peak intensities, the actual peak intensity and the FWHM are determined. The wavelengths of the three laser lines used are also indicated.

XY Scanning Galvos.

The reflection image with the grid pattern is currently only contrast enhanced and saved. No further measurements of the square dimensions are implemented yet.

XY Stage Accuracy.

The image series of the fluorescent beads are median filtered to reduce noise and binarised (threshold set to half of maximum pixel brightness, calculated for each image). The binary image is used as mask for the original image, creating a new image where only the above threshold intensities of the bead are displayed while all other pixels are set black (=0 intensity). Then XY centroid coordinates and average intensity of all pixels with values larger than 0 are calculated. The intensity measurements are useful to examine Z focus drift. To assess repeatability average and standard deviation for all the X and Y centroid positions are calculated and a plot is generated showing the scatter of the bead centroids around the average position. For the accuracy measurements we compare the stage movement as recorded in the metadata with the actual bead centroid movement within the same field of view. The actual distance traveled by the bead is calculated and subtracted from the stage movement.

Z-Galvo Stability.

To assess Z-galvo drift the Z position of the reflection peak is measured at each time point from the intensity profile of a vertical line running through the center of the image from top to bottom. The peak position is plotted versus time [29]. Since vibrations during the course of a single Z scan can also affect the width of the main reflection peak the FWHM of the reflection peak is measured and plotted as a simple vibration indicator.

RESULTS AND DISCUSSION

How to use ConfocalCheck

ConfocalCheck was developed to assist with the qualitative and quantitative analysis of confocal microscope performance tests. Figure 1A shows the workflow of the proposed approach. First of all standardized test images are obtained. Image acquisition was simplified as much as possible to deliver reliable and reproducible test data sets. ConfocalCheck analyses the test images and provides a range of output files. ConfocalCheck is not platform specific - we have tested the software with Leica SP1/SP2/SP5 systems, a Zeiss LSM510 Meta and a LSM780 as well as a Nikon A1R confocal microscope. Data from other instruments can be imported as TIFF images.

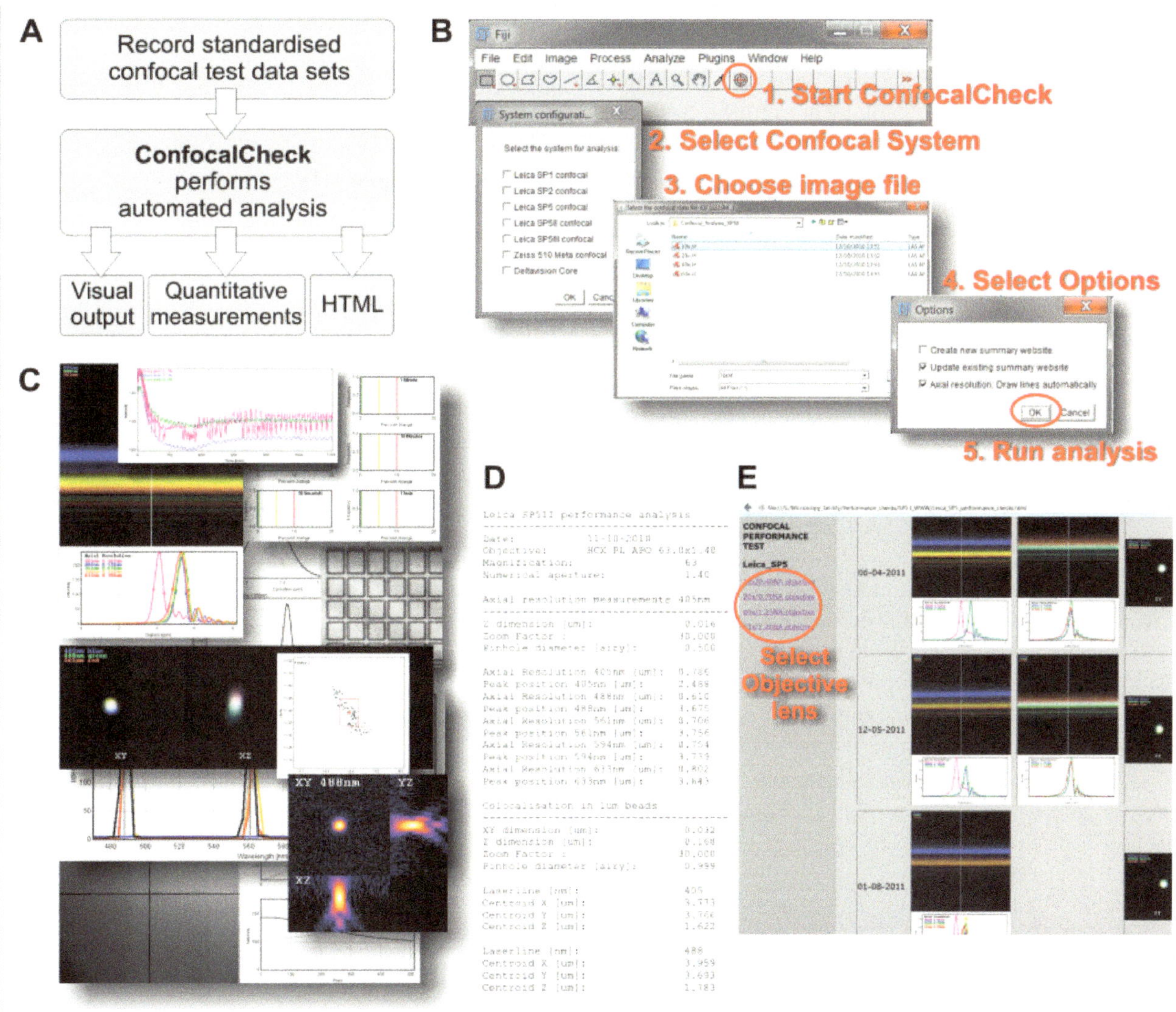

Figure 1. Using ConfocalCheck. A: Workflow of our approach. The analysis of the standardized test data with ConfocalCheck provides a range of numerical and visual outputs to monitor confocal performance. B: Running ConfocalCheck. Once installed in ImageJ/Fiji, click on the target pattern (step 1, marked by red circle) to start the software. Choose a confocal system (step 2), then the data files (step 3). The options window provides choices mainly related to the HTML output. Click OK to run the analysis. C: Collage of some of the output images created to provide quick visual feedback. D: The measurement file contains all the quantitative data used for a more detailed characterization of the system. E: The HTML output is a very useful tool for long term record keeping and monitoring particularly in a facility environment with many confocal instruments. Different objective lenses are selected in the left frame of the browser window, the corresponding test data are displayed on the right.

ConfocalCheck is easy to use, the user interface has been kept very simple. Once the macro has been installed in ImageJ/Fiji a target pattern icon appears on the tool bar (Figure 1B). Click there to start ConfocalCheck. If there are multiple confocal systems, tick the appropriate box. Choose the test data file and select any options. On clicking OK the analysis will commence.

There are three different types of output data (Figure 1A). The images were designed to provide quick visual feedback on many important parameters (a subset of result images is shown in Figure 1C). The quantitative measurements are recorded in tab delimited text files for further analysis (Figure 1D) and the HTML output is an invaluable tool for record keeping (Figure 1E). We have used ConfocalCheck for two purposes: to monitor confocal performance and to compare individual components across different microscopes.

Monitoring Confocal Performance

The main result of testing the confocal microscopes in our microscopy facility over the last three years was that these routine checks are absolutely essential to maintain system performance as many critical parameters changed over time. Most of these problems would not have been noticed by the average facility users with their biological samples. And the confocal microscope cannot be examined in isolation either, the impact of environmental factors like air flow and temperature changes also needs to be considered, for example by measuring room and/or microscope stage temperature in conjunction with some of the performance tests [29,37].

Observing trends in the measurements - for example looking at the changes in laser power or in the alignment of the spectral detectors - can help identifying potential issues which can be rectified before they cause problems for the users. The automated integration of the ConfocalCheck test results with the HTML web site format allows the operator to quickly browse through all the historic data and to spot those gradual changes that could easily be missed if one had to locate and compare the individual images.

Having done all the tests monthly for each system for about two years we re-assessed whether all of them were required in our setting as the recording of all the test data is time consuming. We have now an essential set of five tests:

1. Maximum laser power. 2. Field illumination at 405nm. 3. Colocalisation of 1μm Tetraspeck beads. 4. Lambda scans (spectral sliders on Leica confocal systems). 5. Grid pattern (XY-scanning galvos). The 405nm field illumination and the colocalisation tests are mainly used to check the alignment of the 405nm laser optics, in particular the alignment of the objective specific 405nm correction lenses on our Leica SP5 systems (Fig. S4A/S5A).

Other tests are not routinely performed any more except when problems are suspected. We stopped measuring the PSF as we didn't observe any significant changes in the PSF shape or the derived resolution measurements [27,32]. Although there are plenty of scratches and indentations on the front metal surface of the objective lenses indicating collisions with the metal sample holder and/or the motorized stages maybe the fact that our local users are not swapping or manually handling the objective lenses themselves prevents serious damage. The lens specific axial chromatic correction didn't change either over time and is now only used for characterizing new lenses.

Depending on the local instrument configuration, user needs and demands we would encourage users to choose a set of calibration checks and measure them routinely as good practice. As a minimum requirement the alignment and stability of the illuminating lasers, the detectors, optical performance of the objective lenses, the XY scanner and other important mechanical components of the microscope should be tested. To do nothing is not an option. Even with the most expensive service contract there is typically only one annual service visit by a confocal engineer which would not be sufficient as we have demonstrated. A misaligned system could have detrimental consequences for the acquired images as the observed fluorescence intensity patterns might not reflect the actual dye distribution in the specimen. The subsequent quantitative analysis or colocalisation measurements would also be affected in the worst case invalidating the conclusions drawn from these experiments.

Using ConfocalCheck to compare microscope components

ConfocalCheck is also a useful tool to compare confocal instruments or individual components across multiple instruments as it provides the necessary quantitative measurements (Figure 1D).

We examined in detail the chromatic correction of the objective lenses to illustrate the robustness and reproducibility of the metrics used. Our comparison of two different high performance plan-apochromat lenses from two different Leica microscopes clearly showed the similarity of equivalent lenses across the systems and as well as the differences between the lens types (Figs. S5C/S6D; for a similar comparison of 20× objective lenses on three instruments see Figs. S5D/S6A-B).

Beyond this application, if equipment fails and another instrument needs to be used, if upgrades and changes are made to a piece of equipment, or if different objective lenses are tested before purchasing, the metrics provided by ConfocalCheck could be used for the necessary side by side comparisons.

And if an equivalent objective lens in not available on the replacement instrument knowing the degree of bead displacement at a particular wavelength for example could help to correct this during post acquisition processing. To be able to reliably compare data that have been created over many months or years on the same instrument, or even to combine microscopic data from several laboratories is not trivial, it does require a significant and constant effort to ensure the performance of the confocal setup [10].

ConfocalCheck works well for the standardized data sets but is far from perfect. Anyone with some experience of the ImageJ macro language should be able to extend its capabilities or to adapt the code for specific instruments not currently covered. Significant improvements in speed and functionality could be achieved by rewriting this into a Java plugin for ImageJ and better integration with the LOCI Bioformats plugin [38] to use data from a wider range of microscope manufacturers. A more detailed analysis could be carried out to automatically assess the distortions of the square grid standards or to characterize the nature of the vibrations affecting the confocal setup [39].

Another tool for tracking confocal performance is MetroloJ [34], a freely available plugin developed for ImageJ [35]. It can analyse a limited range of important parameters (detector CV, field illumination, the psf [27], bead colocalisation, axial resolution) and extract very detailed quantitative metrics from the test images. Reports in the PDF file format and output images are created for documentation purposes. Some of the quantitative measurements are similar to the metrics provided by ConfocalCheck, there are however limitations. The colocalisation analysis is restricted to two or three channels, the axial resolution is only determined for one channel. As the user has to load the necessary data sets before starting MetroloJ and enter additional microscope information before the actual analysis MetroloJ would be more suitable for the detailed interactive analysis of smaller data sets while ConfocalCheck could be regarded as a batch processing tool for fully automated processing.

With the increase in quantitative imaging and in medical applications of fluorescence based techniques regular performance checks with standardized samples and defined acquisition protocols will be key to ensure that appropriate experimental data are acquired [6,10]. Efforts are being made to develop suitable calibration and validation standards required to standardize microscopic imaging [6]. This is a major issue that needs to be addressed. Many confocal microscopes are not performing as well as they should as highlighted by a recent study comparing laser stability, field illumination and colocalisation on confocal systems from 23 laboratories spread across eight countries [37]. A large proportion of instruments failed the set acceptance criteria for the various tests. Some steps have been taken by manufacturers to simplify daily maintenance: Zeiss have introduced a special calibration objective lens used for the routine calibration of some instrument parameters like beam path alignment, pinhole adjustment and scanner calibration for their latest range of confocal microscopes. Leica offer a remote sensing system that monitors many instrument parameters for remote diagnostics and repair purposes. But although this could potentially provide valuable feedback directly to the microscope user or facility staff this is currently not implemented. Obtaining even very basic system information like regular laser power readings would be very helpful as our long term analysis has shown. Nevertheless an independent evaluation of the instrument by the user is necessary and any issues uncovered need to be resolved in collaboration with the manufacturer.

Our approach of combining standardized image acquisition with the easy-to-use ConfocalCheck analysis tool presented here should enable even inexperienced microscopists to evaluate and monitor the performance of their local confocal instrument. This is going to be essential given the increasing complexity and functionality of confocal microscopes that are now often combined with super-resolution techniques requiring even more stringent imaging conditions.

ACKNOWLEDGMENTS

We would like to thank Stephen Rothery and Martin Spitaler from the Imperial College FILM facility and John Harris and Jan Soetaert from the Nikon Imaging Centre at Kings College London for providing access and help with the confocal microscopes.

AUTHOR CONTRIBUTIONS

Conceived and designed the experiments: DD. Performed the experiments: KIH DD. Analyzed the data: KIH DD. Wrote the manuscript: DD. Designed and wrote the ConfocalCheck software macro: DD.

REFERENCES

1. Murray JM (2011) Methods for imaging thick specimens: confocal microscopy, deconvolution, and structured illumination. Cold Spring Harbor Protoc 2011: 1399-1437. PubMed: 22135661.
2. Amos WB, White JG (2003) How the confocal laser scanning microscope entered biological research. Biol Cell 95: 335-342. doi:10.1016/S0248-4900(03)00078-9. PubMed: 14519550.
3. McConnell G, Amos W, Wilson T (2012) Confocal microscopy. Comprehensive Biophysics. Elsevier. pp. 3–23.
4. Pawley JB (2006) Handbook of Biological Confocal Microscopy. New York: Springer Verlag.
5. Pubmed website. Available: http://www.ncbi.nlm.nih.gov/pubmed/. Search using the term 'confocal' in title and abstract. Accessed: August 2013.
6. Hoffmann K, Resch-Genger U, Nitschke R (2008) Comparability of Fluorescence Microscopy Data and Need for Instrument Characterization of Spectral Scanning Microscopes. In: OS Wolfbeis. Springer Series on Fluorescence - Standardization and Quality Assurance in Fluorescence Measurements II, Bioanalytical and Biomedical Applications. Berlin Heidelberg: Springer Verlag.
7. Zucker RM, Price OT (1999) Practical confocal microscopy and the evaluation of system performance. Methods 18: 447-458. doi:10.1006/meth.1999.0812. PubMed:10491274.
8. Zucker RM, Price O (2001) Evaluation of confocal microscopy system performance. Cytometry 44: 273-294. doi:10.1002/1097-0320(20010801)44:4. PubMed: 11500845.
9. Dixon A, Heinlein T, Wolleschensky R (2008) Need for standardization of fluorescence measurements from the instrument manufacturer's view. In: OS Wolfbeis. Springer Series on Fluorescence - Standardization and Quality Assurance in Fluorescence Measurements II, Bioanalytical and Biomedical Applications. Berlin Heidelberg: Springer Verlag.
10. Resch-Genger U, Hoffmann K, Nietfeld W, Engel A, Neukammer J et al. (2005) How to improve quality assurance in fluorometry: fluorescence-inherent sources of error and suited fluorescence standards. J Fluoresc 15: 337-362. doi:10.1007/s10895-005-2630-3. PubMed: 15986157.
11. Pawley J (2000) The 39 steps: a cautionary tale of quantitative 3-D fluorescence microscopy. BioTechniques 28: 884-886, 10818693.
12. Centonze V, Pawley J (2006) Tutorial on practical confocal microscopy and use of the confocal test specimen. In: J. Pawley. Handbook of Biological Confocal Microscopy.

3rd ed. New York: Springer Verlag. pp. 627-649.

13. Hibbs AR, MacDonald G, Garsha K (2006) Practical Confocal Microscopy. In: J. Pawley. Handbook of Biological Confocal Microscopy. 3rd ed. New York: Springer Verlag. pp. 650-671.

14. Garsha K (2008) Quantitative Fluorescence Microscopy: Considerations and Controls. In: OS Wolfbeis. Springer Series on Fluorescence - Standardization and Quality Assurance in Fluorescence Measurements II, Bioanalytical and Biomedical Applications. Berlin Heidelberg: Springer Verlag.

15. Zucker RM, Price OT (2001) Statistical evaluation of confocal microscopy images. Cytometry 44: 295-308. doi:10.1002/1097-0320(20010801)44:4. PubMed: 11500846.

16. Lerner JM, Zucker RM (2004) Calibration and validation of confocal spectral imaging systems. Cytometry A J Int Soc Anal Cytol 62: 8-34. PubMed: 15468110.

17. Zucker RM, Lerner JM (2005) Wavelength and alignment tests for confocal spectral imaging systems. Microsc Res Tech 68: 307-319. doi:10.1002/jemt.20249. PubMed:16315239.

18. Zucker RM, Jeffay SC (2006) Confocal laser scanning microscopy of whole mouse ovaries: excellent morphology, apoptosis detection, and spectroscopy. Cytometry A J Int Soc Anal Cytol 69: 930-939. PubMed: 16969804.

19. Zucker RM (2006) Quality assessment of confocal microscopy slide-based systems: instability. Cytometry A J Int Soc Anal Cytol 69: 677-690. PubMed: 16807898.

20. Zucker RM (2006) Quality assessment of confocal microscopy slide based systems: performance. Cytometry A J Int Soc Anal Cytol 69: 659-676. PubMed: 16807897.

21. Zucker RM (2006) Evaluation of confocal microscopy system performance in "Methods in molecular biology - Cell Imaging Techniques, Methods and Protocols". JM Walker. Totowa:: Humana Press Inc.. pp. 77-135.

22. Zucker RM, Rigby P, Clements I, Salmon W, Chua M (2007) Reliability of confocal microscopy spectral imaging systems: use of multispectral beads. Cytometry A J Int Soc Anal Cytol 71: 174-189. PubMed: 17266146.

23. Zucker RM, Chua M (2010) Evaluation and purchase of confocal microscopes: numerous factors to consider. Curr Protoc Cytom. 54: 2.16.1–2.16.12. PubMed:20938918.

24. Swedlow JR, K H, Andrews PD, Roos DS, Murray JM (2002) Measuring tubulin content in Toxoplasma gondii: a comparison of laser-scanning confocal and wide-field fluorescence microscopy. Proc Natl Acad Sci U S A 99: 2014-2019. doi:10.1073/pnas.022554999. PubMed: 11830634.

25. .Murray JM, Appleton PL, Swedlow JR, Waters JC (2007) Evaluating performance in three-dimensional fluorescence microscopy. J Microsc 228: 390-405. doi:10.1111/j.1365-2818.2007.01861.x. PubMed: 18045334.

26. Zwier JM, Oomen L, Brocks L, Jalink K, Brakenhoff GJ (2008) Quantitative image correction and calibration for confocal fluorescence microscopy using thin reference layers and SIPchart-based calibration procedures. J Microsc 231: 59-69. doi:10.1111/j.1365-2818.2008.02017.x. PubMed: 18638190.

27. Cole RW, Jinadasa T, Brown CM (2011) Measuring and interpreting point spread functions to determine confocal microscope resolution and ensure quality control. Nat Protoc 6: 1929-1941. doi:10.1038/nprot.2011.407. PubMed: 22082987.

28. Model MA, Blank JL (2008) Concentrated dyes as a source of two-dimensional fluorescent field for characterization of a confocal microscope. J Microsc 229: 12-16. doi:10.1111/j.1365-2818.2007.01880.x. PubMed: 18173639.

29. Adler J, Pagakis SN (2003) Reducing image distortions due to temperature-related microscope stage drift. J Microsc 210: 131-137. doi:10.1046/j.1365-2818.2003.01160.x. PubMed: 12753095.

30. Hiraoka Y, Sedat JW, Agard DA (1990) Determination of three-dimensional imaging properties of a light microscope system. Partial confocal behavior in epifluorescence microscopy. Biophys J 57: 325-333. doi:10.1016/S0006-3495(90)82534-0. PubMed:2317554.

31. Brakenhoff GJ, Wurpel GW, Jalink K, Oomen L, Brocks L et al. (2005) Characterization of sectioning fluorescence microscopy with thin uniform fluorescent layers: Sectioned Imaging Property or SIPcharts. J Microsc 219: 122-132. doi:10.1111/j.1365-2818.2005.01504.x. PubMed: 16176252.

32. Gelman L, Rietdorf J (2010) Routine Assessment of Fluorescence Microscope Performance. Imaging & Microscopy Website. Available: . http://www.imaging-git.com/science/light-microscopy/routine-assessment-fluorescence-microscope-performance. Accessed. October 2013.

33. Vischer N, Savenije M, Brakenhoff GJ (2013) SIPchart plugin for ImageJ. Website. Available: . http://simon.bio.uva.nl/sipcharts/SIPchart.html. Accessed. October 2013.

34. Matthews C, Cordelieres FP (2010) MetroloJ: an ImageJ plugin to help monitor microscopes' health. ImageJ User and Developer Conference. MetroloJ website. Available: . http://imagejdocu.tudor.lu/doku.php?id=plugin:analysis:metroloj:start. Accessed. October 2013.

35. Schneider CA, Rasband WS, Eliceiri KW (2012) NIH Image to ImageJ: 25 years of image analysis. Nat Methods 9: 671-675. ImageJ website. Available: .http://rsbweb.nih.gov/ij/ . Accessed: October 2013. doi:10.1038/nmeth.2089. PubMed:22930834.

36. Schindelin J, Arganda-Carreras I, Frise E, Kaynig V, Longair M et al. (2012) Fiji: an open-source platform for biological-image analysis. Nat Methods 9: 676–682. Fiji website. Available: http://fiji.sc/Fiji . Accessed: October 2013 PubMed: 22743772.

37. Stack RF, Bayles CJ, Girard AM, Martin K, Opansky C et al. (2011) Quality assurance testing for modern optical imaging systems. Microsc Microanal. 17: 598-606. doi:10.1017/S1431927611000237. PubMed: 21477410.

38. Linkert M, Rueden CT, Allan C, Burel JM, Moore W et al. (2010) Metadata matters: access to image data in the real world. J Cell Biol 189: 777-782. Bio-formats website. Available: http://loci.wisc.edu/software/bio-formats . Accessed: October 2013 doi:10.1083/jcb.201004104. PubMed: 20513764.

39. Vagh HC, VK , Chakrabarty BS, Anand A (2006) Vibration analysis with pinhole confocal technique. Rev Sci Instrum 77: 116113. doi:10.1063/1.2390626.

CHAPTER 15

REPORTING OF SYSTEMATIC REVIEWS: BETTER SOFTWARE REQUIRED

Jan Brogger

University of Bergen Bergen, Norway

This is an important paper and editorial [1,2]. Systematic reviews should be much more widespread, and not only for randomized clinical trials of clinical treatments. A paper on an elegant piece of experimental data or on epidemiological observations would be made all the more interesting if the first table were a high-quality assessment of previous studies. In fact, I would suggest that performing a systematic review should be part of a research protocol for any subject, even before the study is initiated. However, this paper confirms my suspicion that the rising popularity of "systematic reviews" has not been followed by adherence to methodological rigor.

With this background, I would like to point out one weakness that may explain part of the current quality deficit in some systematic reviews. There is a substantial lack of software that can assist in an important part of a systematic review: tracking literature searches and early phase screening. From browsing of the literature and communications with various Norwegian and Danish Cochrane collaborators (including the RevMan developers), there seems to be a limited number of tools for this use. Oftentimes, it is suggested that commercial reference management software be used, such as the popular EndNote. These types of software were not designed with systematic reviews in mind. At later stages of a review, Cochrane's RevMan is useful, but not early on.

As far as I have been able to ascertain, there are only two tools presently available. The first is EPPI-Reviewer (http://eppi.ioe.ac.uk/cms/Default.aspx?tabid=184), which is non-profit, but does not seem to be open source or available for local deployment. The second is TrialStat's SRS software (http://www.trialstat.com), which is commercial and has a substantial price tag.

I would therefore encourage researchers and institutions to contribute to the development of open-source tools for assisting in systematic reviews. I am currently writing such a simple tool, based on the open-source JabRef package (http://sourceforge.net/projects/jabref) and would welcome feedback on perceived needs and other similar projects.

Citation: Brogger J (2007) Reporting of Systematic Reviews: Better Software Required. PLoS Med 4(6): e225. doi:10.1371/journal.pmed.0040225

REFERENCES

1. Moher D, Tetzlaff J, Tricco AC, Sampson M, Altman DG (2007) Epidemiology and reporting characteristics of systematic reviews. PLoS Med 4: e78. doi: 10.1371/journal.pmed.0040078.
2. The *PLoS Medicine* Editors (2007) Many reviews are systematic but some are more transparent and completely reported than others. PLoS Med 4: e147. doi:10.1371/journal.pmed.0040147.

CHAPTER 16 THE QUESTION OF DATA INTEGRITY IN ARTICLE-LEVEL METRICS

1

Gregg Gordon[1] , Jennifer Lin[2], Richard Cave[2,3], Ralph Dandrea

[1] Social Science Research Network, Rochester, New York, United States of America

[2] Public Library of Science, San Francisco, California, United States of America

[3] Independent, San Francisco, California, United States of America

ATRACT

Interest in and use of article-level metrics (ALMs) has grown rapidly amongst the research community, by researchers, publishers, funders, and research institutions. As this happens, it is critical to ensure secure and reliable data that is trustworthy and can be used by all. Two case studies are presented, which illustrate different approaches to establishing ALM data integrity

THE PRICE OF PURPOSE

Scholarly journals had published a cumulative total of 50 million scholarly articles by 2010 [1]. An estimated 114 million scholarly documents currently reside on the web [2]. Moreover, what is considered scholarly research has expanded—boundaries between working manuscripts and accepted papers blur, and scholarly communications take on new forms. Our existing mechanisms for sizing up a research article are sorely inadequate in the face of this acceleration of growth.

The journal in which an article is published has served as the long-standing, default solution, and the Journal Impact Factor (JIF) has become the exclusive proxy for importance in the past few decades. Today, its shortcomings are widely documented [1,3] and its vulnerability to manipulation also well understood [4].

Citation: Gordon G, Lin J, Cave R, Dandrea R (2015) The Question of Data Integrity in Article-Level Metrics. PLoS Biol 13(8): e1002161. doi:10.1371/journal.pbio.1002161.

To redress the inadequacies of journal-level measures of article relevancy, article-level metrics (ALMs) were introduced in the 1990s and expanded greatly in the late 2000s to capture signals from the broad spectrum of ways in which researchers engage with articles: disseminating, accessing, commenting, and citing research. This multidimensional suite of indicators includes citations, article usage (online page views and downloads), and altmetrics (social metrics that incorporate bookmarking and dissemination activity, media and blog coverage, discussion activity, and ratings). With its broad suite of indicators, the ALM framework offers more ways to measure research based on individual and community need. ALMs can help researchers find the literature relevant to their interests with a custom selection of relevancy signals. They may also provide more diverse evidence of research engagement for reporting scholarly contributions as funder and institutional interest continues to grow in this area [5].

But with great promise also comes considerable concern as ALMs continue to develop into formal credentials that are widely adopted and incorporated into systems of evaluation. The science of ALMs—the conceptual and technical foundations—is still being established, but there is general agreement on their potential value amongst funders, institutions, researchers, and bibliometricians who continue to test the hypotheses and assumptions that undergird this enterprise [6]. Gaming citations, the intentional or unintentional attempt to mislead the measure, has long been a worry [7,8]. With the introduction of new metrics, the concern has understandably broadened in step with the expansion of measures available.

THE QUESTION OF DATA INTEGRITY

Public Library of Science (PLOS) (http://articlemetrics.github.io/plos/) and the Social Science Research Network (SSRN) (http://www.ssrn.com/en/index.cfm/ssrn-faq/#download) are early ALM providers for their publications. Since 2009, they have been joined by most major publishers. ALM services (ex: Altmetric, ImpactStory, Plum Analytics, etc.) have significantly contributed to the proliferation of interest in these metrics. The growth of the community-owned, open source software, Lagotto, has also fueled greater publisher adoption and display of ALMs (http://lagotto.github.io/status/). On the downstream end, researchers, institutions, and funders have begun to explore ways in which they can make sense and use of the data in their activities.

But the research community largely still lacks sufficient support for tracking research activity at the level of the article. The secure and reliable provisioning of data remains a prominent need. Infrastructure required to support an ALM-enabled future is just beginning to emerge across the scholarly landscape [9]. The ALM community recognizes the need for complete, consistent, available, authoritative, and trustworthy data as ALMs mature and garner value [10–13]. To develop ALMs into a widespread resource, we must sufficiently address the problems of standardized data generation across providers, widespread community provisioning, and data integrity to ensure valid and reliable measures. The attainment of this future state relies on a number of elements: robust technology that scales to the growing volume of articles tracked, information security controls, high availability, and mechanisms that ensure the accuracy and consistency of data over its entire lifecycle.

Data integrity—valid and reliable data—is an issue inherent in all information systems. As long as data are collected, stored, and shared, any metric reliant on these data is vulnerable to internal and external quality issues. Data integrity is especially critical during this stage of ALM development when establishing trust is of paramount importance, even as the methods necessary to ensure this are developing. Invalid, unreliable ALM data from any service may introduce confounding variables and uncertainty during the analysis of this new measurement science.

STRATEGIES

We believe that advancing the importance of data integrity also needs to entail a conversation on practical approaches to addressing this issue. To date, ALM data providers do not publicize their mechanisms to ensure data integrity. PLOS and SSRN will share the strategies currently in place in our respective systems.

Data integrity begins with continual tracking and analysis of data activity across a diversity of channels. Researchers share, comment, and discuss articles through any number of available channels to reach their communities. The proverbial water cooler takes numerous forms on the web, spanning platforms dedicated to scholarly activity (Mendeley, F1000Prime, CrossRef, etc.) and mainstream, public sites (Wikipedia, Twitter, etc.). All these are part of the ALM ecosystem.

For both SSRN and PLOS, the strategy centers on usage statistics. Activity largely originates at the source where the article is accessed before it is shared, discussed, and cited. The record of page views and downloads loosely serves as an abstraction for baseline activity, which can be checked relative to the rest of the ALM suite. SSRN focuses on preventative antifraud measures as part of content access regulation, while PLOS focuses on activity detection as part of content delivery.

The SSRN Experience

In 2000, SSRN began collecting data about each PDF download request and analyzing the activity patterns. It quickly became apparent there was a significant amount of questionable activity through pattern recognition, which was also influencing its "Top 10" rankings list. In response, and in the absence of any industry-standard rules, SSRN established a set of "fraud rules," which were applied at the time that each download was requested. Initial rules determined if a paper was downloaded more than once from the same IP address within two hours and ensured that the download wasn't coming from a search engine. If the request passed the fraud rules, the download would be counted. If the request failed the fraud rules, the paper was still delivered to the user making the request, but the download was not counted. These first fraud rules removed most of the inadvertent duplicate counting of downloads due to user error or to reasonable user behaviors that resulted in downloading the same file multiple times.

In 2007, SSRN introduced new "fraud gate" measures based on the user's IP address and other data. For example, if the same paper was downloaded a number of times from the same IP address, or the number of papers downloaded from a given IP address exceeded a certain limit, then that IP address was placed on a watch list. In 2010, these rules were expanded based on additional data and "behavioral blacklisting" email spam research [14]. Any future download requests violating the rules would result in a message indicating that "potentially fraudulent activity has been detected." The user would then have three options: sign in using their existing SSRN account, create a new account at SSRN, or accept that the download would not be counted (Fig 1).

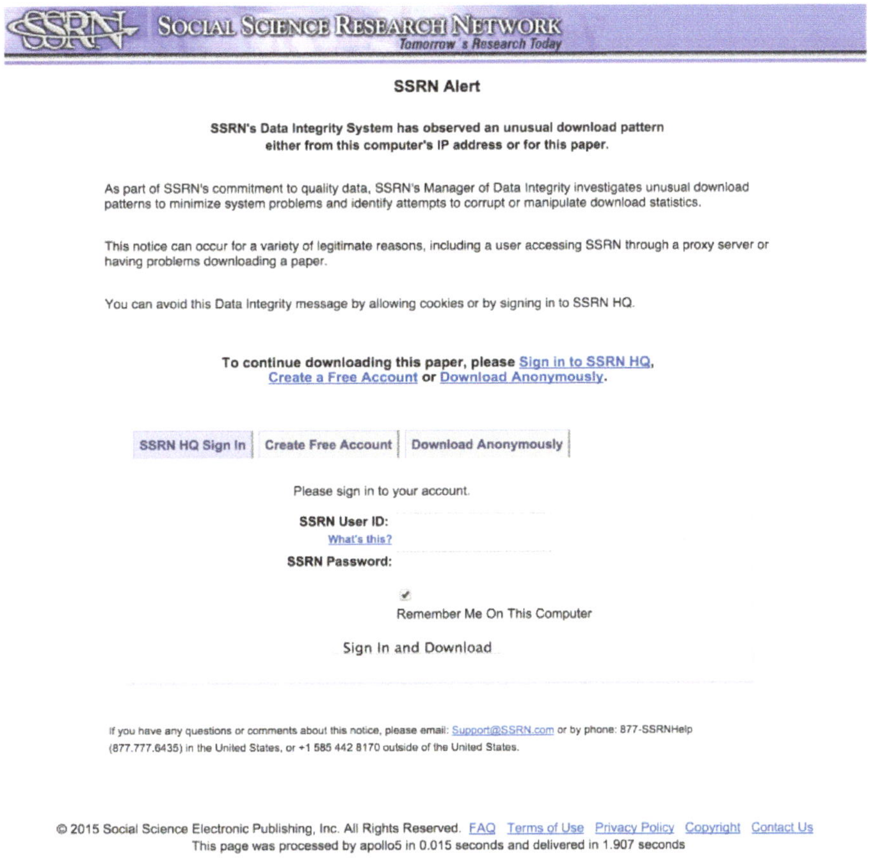
SSRN Social Science Research Network
Tomorrow's Research Today

SSRN Alert

SSRN's Data Integrity System has observed an unusual download pattern either from this computer's IP address or for this paper.

As part of SSRN's commitment to quality data, SSRN's Manager of Data Integrity investigates unusual download patterns to minimize system problems and identify attempts to corrupt or manipulate download statistics.

This notice can occur for a variety of legitimate reasons, including a user accessing SSRN through a proxy server or having problems downloading a paper.

You can avoid this Data Integrity message by allowing cookies or by signing in to SSRN HQ.

To continue downloading this paper, please Sign in to SSRN HQ, Create a Free Account or Download Anonymously.

SSRN HQ Sign In | Create Free Account | Download Anonymously

Please sign in to your account.

SSRN User ID:
What's this?
SSRN Password:

Remember Me On This Computer

Sign In and Download

If you have any questions or comments about this notice, please email: Support@SSRN.com or by phone: 877-SSRNHelp (877.777.6435) in the United States, or +1 585 442 8170 outside of the United States.

© 2015 Social Science Electronic Publishing, Inc. All Rights Reserved. FAQ Terms of Use Privacy Policy Copyright Contact Us
This page was processed by apollo5 in 0.015 seconds and delivered in 1.907 seconds

Figure 1. SSRN fraudulent alert.

The IP-based fraud gates worked so well that most instances of what was, in retrospect, potentially fraudulent activity ceased immediately. Users that had been identified with the inflation of download counts stopped once it became clear that their activity was being monitored. Since the introduction of the fraud rules, the number of downloads counted by SSRN is much less than the actual number of downloads served. Today, even "questionable" downloads are excluded from a paper's metrics. For some months, the downloads that have been excluded can exceed the number of downloads counted by SSRN (Fig 2).

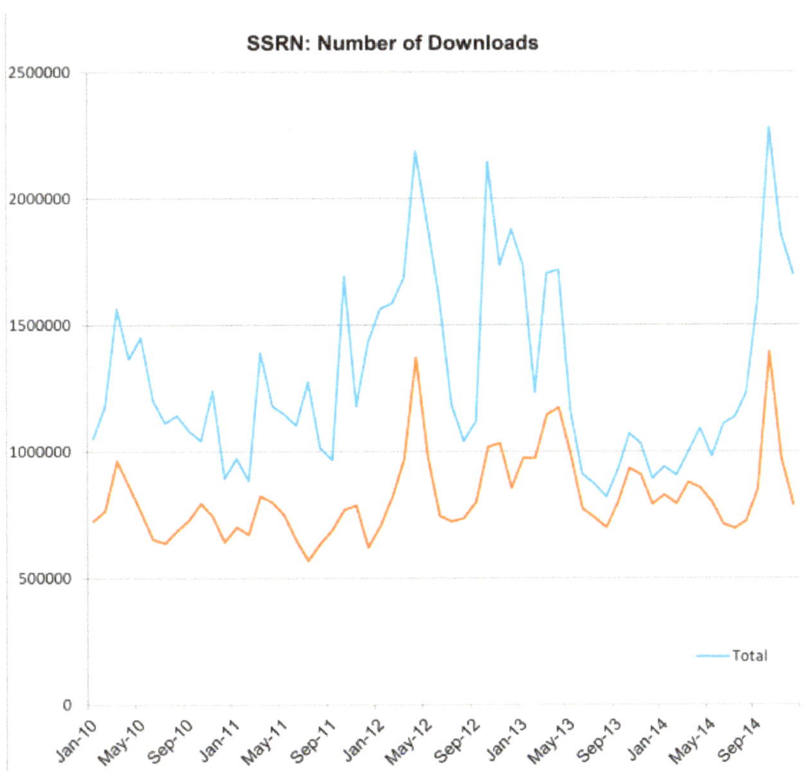

Figure 2. SSRN fraudulent activity detected.

SSRN cannot definitively ascertain that the difference between the total downloads and what is counted is due to intentional fraudulence per se. However, particular patterns may suggest this as a potential occurrence:

- a registered user is downloading a paper that they have already downloaded
- the same IP address is downloading a paper multiple times in a given time period
- the IP address is associated with a known search engine
- the IP address is flagged as having potentially fraudulent activity in the past.

These checks provide additional security measures to ensure that SSRN usage counts are valid.

The PLOS Experience

Since 2009, PLOS has tracked usage for its articles through online views, PDF downloads, and XML downloads on its site. These usage statistics adhere to COUNTER (http://www.projectcounter.org), the scholarly publishing industry standard for recording and reporting online usage statistics. Other article activities tracked include scholarly citations across various indices and a vast range of social web activity (http://alm.plos.org/sources).

The overall approach begins with the proper and complete transfer of the data on article events from the web services where the activity occurred. The PLOS implementation of the Lagotto ALM software provides two levels of checks: a) a dedicated error tracking service to monitor overall system performance and b) filters, an additional layer of scripts that monitor the data collected to detect unusual activity. At the first level, PLOS conducts system error tracking, which requires more detailed monitoring of exception events. Network errors are common, due to the varying states of the many web services involved (e.g., overloaded source server, rate limits exceeded, query time outs, etc.). The system sends an email every 24 hours that summarizes all errors for human follow-up. At the second level, PLOS runs a set of scripts for tracking outliers and pattern recognition analysis to detect unusual activity (usage surges, decreases in cumulative counts, etc.). By tracking typical monthly article activity for a group of articles, a threshold is determined to detect outliers. An algorithmic script is then used to find and identify the outliers. This strategy makes reporting straightforward (Table 1) and provides an efficient approach to monitoring at scale.

Table 1. PLOS page view increases. Dec 10, 2013 to Jan 10, 2014

10.1371/journal.pone.0080347	First Partial Skeleton of a 1.34-Million-Year-Old Paranthropus boisei from Bed II, Olduvai Gorge, Tanzania	34,315
10.1371/journal.pmed.0020124	Why Most Published Research Findings Are False	14,252
10.1371/journal.pone.0069841	Facebook Use Predicts Declines in Subjective Well-Being in Young Adults	13,398
10.1371/journal.pone.0010894	Exon Exchange Approach to Repair Duchenne Dystrophin Transcripts	11,453

doi:10.1371/journal.pbio.1002161.t001

Pattern recognition can be used to detect gaming by reviewing usage activity across multiple sources and provides a more consistent basis for detection. Article views and PDF downloads on PLOS journals along with usage activity on the PubMed Central article repository reveal general patterns of usage over time (Fig 3). In general, page views of a research article will track closely to the number of PDF downloads. When usage statistics fall outside of the correlation, further verification of higher usage statistics is then needed.

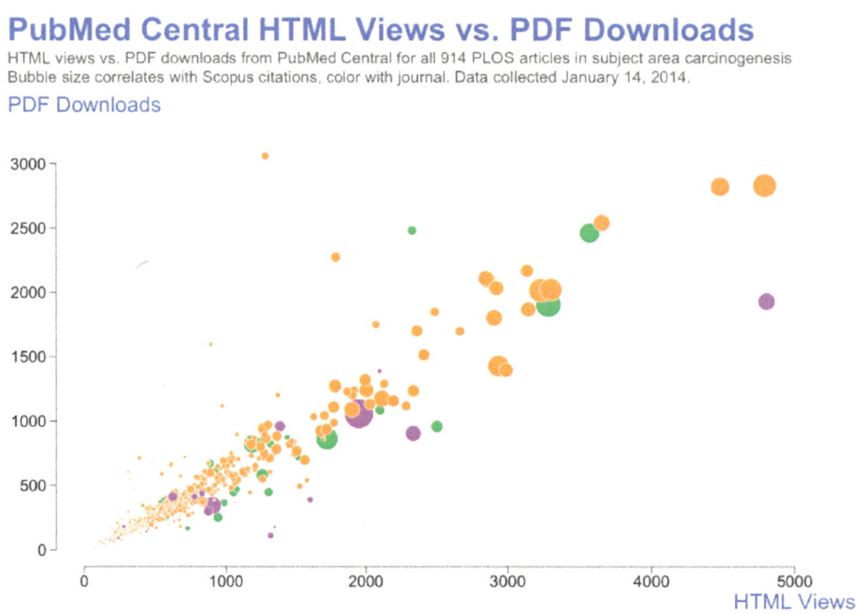

Figure 3. PLOS comparison of PMC page views and downloads.

PLOS also cross validates usage activity with other sources. While a direct correlation between the two activities is not given, an article with high usage activity generally exhibits related activity in another metric. Articles with an abnormal spike in one usage activity without a corresponding spike in another are examined to determine the cause of the discrepancy. Fig 4 shows an article with a typical distribution pattern of usage activity until a significant spike occurred three years after publication. Further investigation may then determine the source of the increased usage. In this instance, article referral traffic reveals that the spike in usage activity was due to a blog post on Nature Blogs that discussed the article, rather than fraudulent activity.

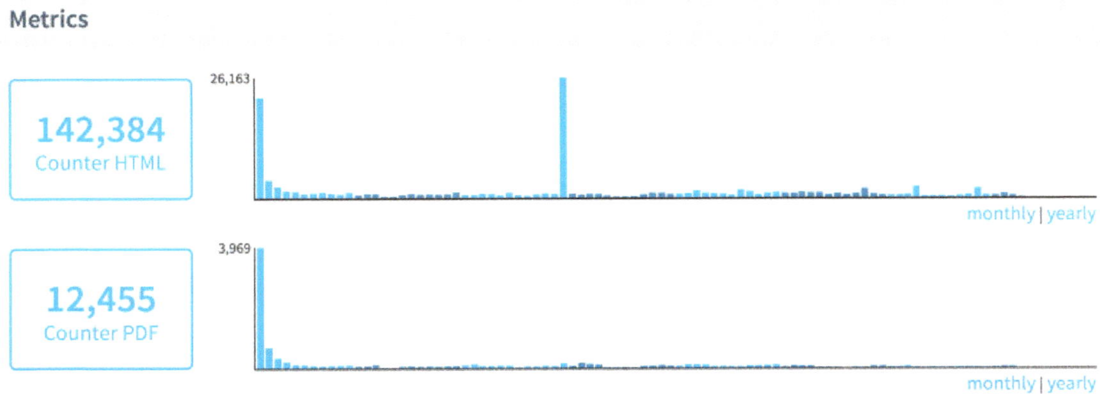

Figure 4. *PLOS Medicine* article with irregular page view activity.

But irregular usage only sometimes correlates with higher traffic driven by other sources. PLOS employs a number of tactics to address and prevent systematic abuse, including more detailed analyses of specific users or IP addresses. Repeated hits from a single IP address (human or machine) in server logs are considered artificial inflation of counts. To ensure valid counting of usage data in this case, PLOS adjusts direct activity accordingly for the article in question from the offending agent.

As a publisher where usage activity is occurring on its own platform, PLOS has a wider scope of means available to ensure data integrity, adhering to proper guidelines of collection and exclusion of counts, as well as correcting counts as appropriate when irregularities are found. But data stewardship entails different degrees of responsibility for each agent according to its role. For the data aggregator who is pulling counts of activity from external sources, data stewardship entails ensuring that ALM data are correctly aggregated. Oversight here is limited to ensuring full and accurate integration of data and complete provisioning of fresh data. PLOS serves both roles for the articles in its corpus—the original source for usage data and the aggregator for all external sources.

The efforts summarized above aim to mitigate some of the concerns about data integrity, but more work needs to be done. Currently, usage profile is static and constructed based on historical patterns. Monitoring thresholds built into the Lagotto filters are also static and not ideal in the face of evolving online behaviors. But there is great potential for progress in this area. The application of statistical computing and visualizations for data integrity is currently being tested by data scientists and shows significant promise [15]. Open source software, which extends the ALM technology toolkit in this area, would significantly contribute to the programmatic operationalization of data integrity across data providers.

CALL TO ACTION

ALMs are spreading as the data become more interesting to the scholarly community. They have been found to be valuable for researchers searching for relevant content, for authors interested in highlighting the reach of their work, and for institutions and funders monitoring the progress of the research they support. For any data to be a valuable part of the research information ecosystem, confidence in the metrics is fundamental. ALMs are no different.

The distributed ALM information environment is a network made up of multiple agents that capture activity originating on their site, data aggregators who collect the data, and distributors who enrich and package the data along with any host of additional intermediaries. To understand data integrity from a network standpoint, we recognize the diversity of players and complex information exchanges across the web that occur at each and every site. In the networked world of the scientific enterprise, data integrity is a shared responsibility of all the players involved.

Policies, processes, and supporting technologies are an integral part of a holistic approach and require the endorsement and participation of the entire scholarly community. ALM providers need to clearly describe how they calculate their measures as well as provide an understanding of how they have kept their data free of error, both intentional and unintentional. Shared conventions for data irregularity resolution (excluded sources, data adjustment practices) are necessary for data quality across providers. Individual users can then determine if a particular ALM is trustworthy and reliable enough to inform their work. Funders and research institutions can play a role in demanding that the data be made available in a standardized fashion across publishers and in a replicable and verifiable manner so that the community can scrutinize its strength and trustworthiness. The entire community can establish guidelines and incentives for good and fair behaviors impacting the collection and use of metrics.

So as to be readily monitored, ALM data need to be open, transparent, and auditable. Academia currently operates well with its existing ethos of community scrutiny for plagiarism or data manipulation. Similar community norms are needed for ALM gaming where willful manipulation ought to be treated as a professional offense and reported to respective institutions for further action. In addition to transparency, accountability is a key ingredient to trust. And as chances of discovering gaming increase, the risk of engaging in such practices would be magnified, thereby lowering the incentive. But the question is not just about gaming. The entire research community has an interest in ensuring the highest level of ALM data integrity at large. This path begins with the first step: taking a broader view of what is required for trust and engaging the entire community to consider their role within this ecosystem.

REFERENCES

1. Amin M, Mabe M. (2000) Impact Factors: Use and Abuse. *Perspectives in Publishing*, 1, 1–6.
2. Khabsa M, Giles CL. (2014) The Number of Scholarly Documents on the Public Web.*PLoS ONE*, 9(5): e93949. doi: 10.1371/journal.pone.0093949
3. Kurmis A. (2003) Understanding the Limitations of the Journal Impact Factor. *The Journal of Bone & Joint Surgery*, 85 (12), 2449–2454.
4. Tort ABL, Targino ZH, Amaral OB (2012) Rising Publication Delays Inflate Journal Impact Factors. *PLoS ONE* 7(12): e53374. doi: 10.1371/journal.pone.0053374
5. Dinsmore A, Allen L, Dolby K (2014) Alternative Perspectives on Impact: The Potential of ALMs and Altmetrics to Inform Funders about Research Impact. *PLoS Biol* 12(11): e1002003. doi: 10.1371/journal.pbio.1002003. pmid:25423184
6. Tattersall, A. 2014 Sep 30 [Cited 2015 Feb 26]. 1AM Altmetrics Conference Review. Available from: http://scharrlibrary.blogspot.com/2014/09/1am-altmetrics-conference-review.html.
7. Wilhite A, Fong E. (2012) Coercive Citation in Academic Publishing. *Science*335(6068): 532–543. doi: 10.1126/science.1212540
8. van Noorden R. (2013) Brazilian citation scheme outed. *Nature News*.http://www.nature.com/news/brazilian-citation-scheme-outed-1.13604.
9. PLOS Article-Level Metrics. 2015 Jan 12 [Cited 2015 Feb 26]. ALM Workshop 2014 Report. figshare. http://dx.doi.org/10.6084/m9.figshare.1287503.
10. National Information Standards Organization. 2014 June 6 [Cited 2015 Feb 26]. NISO Altmetrics Initiative Phase 1 White Paper.http://www.niso.org/apps/group_public/download.php/13809/Altmetrics_project_phase1_white_paper.pdf.
11. Adie, E. 2013 Sep 18 [Cited 2015 Feb 26]. Gaming altmetrics.http://www.altmetric.com/blog/gaming-altmetrics/.
12. Carpenter T. 2012 Nov 14 [Cited 2015 Feb 26]. "Altmetrics—Replacing the Impact Factor is Not the Only Point." *The Scholarly Kitchen*.http://scholarlykitchen.sspnet.org/2012/11/14/altmetrics-replacing-the-impact-factor-is-not-the-only-point.
13. Holmberg K. 2014 Jul 11 [Cited 2015 Feb 26]. "How concerned should we be about gaming altmetrics?" *Social Science Space*.http://www.socialsciencespace.com/2014/07/altmetrics-may-be-able-to-help-in-evaluating-societal-reach-but-research-significance-must-be-peer-reviewed/.
14. Ramachandran A, Feamster N, and Santosh V. "Filtering Spam with Behavioral Blacklisting". 14th ACM Conference on Computer and Communications Security. 29 October –02 November 2007. Ed. New York: ACM, 2007. 342–351. Digital.
15. Chamberlain S. 2015 Jan 14 [Cited 2015 Feb 26]. Summary of ALM data quality work.*PLOS Tech*. http://blogs.plos.org/tech/summary-of-alm-data-quality-work/.

CHAPTER 17

ARTICLE-LEVEL METRICS AND THE EVOLUTION OF SCIENTIFIC IMPACT

Cameron Neylon[1] , Shirley Wu[2]

[1] Science and Technology Facilities Council, Rutherford Appleton Laboratory, Didcot, United Kingdom

[2] 23andMe, Mountain View, California, United States of America

Formally published papers that have been through a traditional prepublication peer review process remain the most important means of communicating science today. Researchers depend on them to learn about the latest advances in their fields and to report their own findings. The intentions of traditional peer review are certainly noble: to ensure methodological integrity and to comment on potential significance of experimental studies through examination by a panel of objective, expert colleagues. In principle, this system enables science to move forward on the collective confidence of previously published work. Unfortunately, the traditional system has inspired methods of measuring impact that are suboptimal for their intended uses.

MEASURING IMPACT

Peer-reviewed journals have served an important purpose in evaluating submitted papers and readying them for publication. In theory, one could browse the pages of the most relevant journals to stay current with research on a particular topic. But as the scientific community has grown, so has the number of journals—to the point where over 800,000 new articles appeared in PubMed in 2008 (http://www.ncbi.nlm.nih.gov/sites/entrez?Db=pubmed&term=2008:2008[dp], archived at http://www.webcitation.org/5k1cbn1WX on 24 September 2009) and the total is now over 19 million (http://www.ncbi.nlm.nih.gov/sites/entrez?Db=pubmed&term=1800:2009[dp], archived at http://www.webcitation.org/5k1crb7Pi on 24 September 2009). The sheer number makes it impossible for any scientist to read every paper relevant to their research, and a difficult choice has to be made about which papers to read. Journals help by categorizing papers by subject, but there remain in most fields far too many journals and papers to follow.

As a result, we need good filters for quality, importance, and relevance to apply to scientific literature. There are many we could use but the majority of scientists filter by preferentially reading articles from specific journals—those they view as the highest quality and the most important. These selections are highly subjective but the authors' personal experience is that most scientists, when pressed, will point to the Thomson ISI Journal Impact Factor [1] as an external and "objective" measure for ranking the impact of specific journals and the individual articles within them.

Yet the impact factor, which averages the number of citations per eligible article in each journal, is deeply flawed both in principle and in practice as a tool for filtering the literature. It is mathematically problematic [2]–[4], with around 80% of a journal impact factor attributable to around 20% of

Citation: Neylon C, Wu S (2009) Article-Level Metrics and the Evolution of Scientific Impact. PLoS Biol 7(11): e1000242. doi:10.1371/journal.pbio.1000242

the papers, even for journals like *Nature* [5]. It is very sensitive to the categorization of papers as "citeable" (e.g., research-based) or "front-matter" (e.g., editorials and commentary) [6], and it is controlled by a private company that does not have any obligation to make the underlying data or processes of analysis available. Attempts to replicate or to predict the reported values have generally failed [5]–[8].

Though the impact factor is flawed, it may be useful for evaluating journals in some contexts, and other more sophisticated metrics for journals are emerging [3],[4],[9],[10]. But for the job of assessing the importance of specific papers, the impact factor—or any other journal-based metric for that matter—cannot escape an even more fundamental problem: it is simply not designed to capture qualities of individual papers.

ARTICLE-LEVEL METRICS

If choosing which articles to read on the basis of journal-level metrics is not effective, then we need a measure of importance that tells us about the article. It makes sense that when choosing which of a set of articles to read, we should turn to "article-level metrics," yet in practice data on individual articles are rarely considered, let alone seriously measured.

Perhaps the main reason for this absence is a practical one. Accurately determining the importance of an article takes years and is very difficult to do objectively. The "gold standard" of article impact is formal citations in the scholarly literature, but citation metrics have their own challenges. One is that citation metrics do not take the "sentiment" of the citation into account, so while an article that is heavily cited for being wrong is perhaps important in its own way [11], using citation counts without any context can be misleading. The biggest problem, though, is the time-delay inherent in citations. The first citations to a paper will appear—at the earliest—months after it is first available; far too late to be useful in the days and weeks after it is published. If we are looking for a way to evaluate recently published papers of potential interest to us, citation-based metrics are not the answer.

THE TROUBLE WITH COMMENTS

A common solution proposed for getting rapid feedback on scientific publications is inspired by the success of many Web-based commenting forums. Sites like Stack Overflow, Wikipedia, and Hacker News each have an expert community that contributes new information and debates its value and accuracy. It is not difficult to imagine translating this dynamic into a scholarly research setting where scientists discuss interesting papers. A spirited, intelligent comment thread can also help raise the profile of an article and engage the broader community in a conversation about the science.

Unfortunately, commenting in the scientific community simply hasn't worked, at least not generally. BioMedCentral, PLoS, and BMJ have all had commenting platforms for several years (see Figures 1 and 2 for examples), and while certain papers have extensive discussions[12]–[15], these are the exception rather than the rule. Moreover, highly commented papers tend to fall under the category of "front matter" rather than primary research (e.g., a recent Perspective article in *PLoS Biology* had 17 comments and over 20,000 page views on 4 October 2009 [16]). Attempts to apply a "Digg-like" mechanism for voting up or down on the basis of perceived value—on the ArXiv preprints service, for instance—have failed to gain traction [17]. At the same time new sites based on similar systems have flourished for communities as diverse as programmers and amateur knitters. Why is community participation apparently easy for some but not for researchers—whose work, after all, depends on constructive feedback from their peers?

Figure 1. Examples of article comments on BioMed Central. The comments shown are for an article published in BMC Medicine [14]. Full names and affiliations are typically given and commenters also indicate conflicts of interest. Readers must also be logged in to comment. Note that conversations are not threaded—meaning that replies cannot be formally directed towards specific comments—though commenters sometimes indicate whether their comment pertains to a specific comment via the "re:" designation in the comment title.

Part of this resistance to commenting may relate to technical issues, but the main reason is likely social. For one thing, researchers are unsure how to behave in this new space. We are used to criticizing articles in the privacy of offices and local journal clubs, not in a public, archived forum. Junior researchers may be concerned about the potential repercussions on their own careers. Anonymity can support more direct and honest discussion but as anyone who has visited popular video or news sites knows, anonymity often degrades discussions to the point where they detract from the original piece.

Another issue is that the majority of people making hiring and granting decisions do not consider commenting a valuable contribution. Stack Overflow, which caters to programmers, works in part because its contributors build up "karma" through a points-based system that translates into greater influence within the community. More importantly, high Stack Overflow karma can be taken beyond the site to add credibility to your resume and directly enhance career opportunities. There is currently no analogous credit system for post-publication commenting in the scientific community. And if there is no reward for quality contribution then people will struggle to justify the time involved in generating high quality comments. It is interesting in this sense that the one commenting system that does appear to obtain reasonable amounts of researcher input is the Faculty of 1000, where senior researchers are selected to become "Faculty" and contribute their opinions on papers they believe are important. Being able to place "Member: Faculty of 1000" on your CV is incentive enough to encourage contributions of sufficient quantity and quality.

Then there is simply the size of the community. There are many more people broadly involved in programming (or knitting) than there are scientists. For community-based social media efforts, there is a well-known 90-9-1 rule: 90% of people merely observe, 9% make minor contributions, and 1% are responsible for the vast majority of original content (http://www.90-9-1.com/). This breakdown need not be a bad thing—on any given article you want the people who care and who have the expertise to be providing critical commentary. But it also means that if only 100 people read a paper, it will be lucky if even one of them leaves a comment.

TECHNICAL SOLUTIONS TO SOCIAL PROBLEMS

Given the lack of incentive, are there ways of capturing article-level metrics from what researchers do anyway? A simple way of measuring interest in a specific paper might be via usage and download statistics; for example, how many times a paper has been viewed or downloaded, how many unique users have shown an interest, or how long they lingered. This method can certainly provide a rapid means of assessing interest in a paper by comparing the trend in downloads and page views against the average. A common objection is that these statistics can be artificially inflated by faking or automating downloads, but this problem has been largely solved by the online advertising industry, which relies on trusted page view and download metrics provided by third parties. These statistics may not be completely accurate but they are consistent, comparable, and considered sufficiently immune to cheating to be the basis for a billion dollar Web advertising industry.

A more important criticism of download statistics is that it is a crude measure of actual use. How many of the downloaded papers are even read, let alone digested in detail and acted upon? What we actually want to measure is how much *influence* an article has, not how many people clicked on the download button thinking they "might read it later." A more valuable metric might be the number of people who have actively chosen to include the paper in their own personal library. Endnote, Refworks, and libraries in BibTex format have been the traditional tools for managing personal reference libraries, but there is a growing set of tools with some significant advantages: the tools are free, easy to use, and can help to provide high value article-level metrics without requiring any additional effort on the part of the researchers.

Examples of such tools are Zotero, Citeulike, Connotea, and Mendeley, which all allow the researcher to collect papers into their library while they are browsing on the Web, often in a single click using convenient "bookmarklets." The user usually has the option of adding tags, comments, or ratings as part of the bookmarking process. From this point on the tools differ in a variety of ways: Zotero and Mendeley allow formatting citations within manuscripts, whereas Citeulike and Connotea are more focused on using tags and feeds to share information. Importantly, however, they all provide information on *how many people have bookmarked a specific paper*. Citeulike, Connotea, and Zotero currently go further by providing information on precisely *who* has bookmarked a specific paper, a piece of information that may be very valuable, although people can choose not to make that information public. Some of these tools may also eventually be able to track the amount of time users spend viewing papers within their interface [18].

Metrics collected by reference management software are especially intriguing because they offer a measure of active interest without requiring researchers to do anything more than what they are already doing. Scientists collect the papers they find interesting, take notes on them, and store the information in a place that is accessible and useful to them. A significant question is why would they share that valuable information with the rest of the world? The data would still be useful even without identities attached, but researchers are more likely to share openly if appropriate incentive structures exist, as in the example of Faculty of 1000.

Rapid Responses to:

RESEARCH:
Wouter de Ruijter, Rudi G J Westendorp, Willem J J Assendelft, Wendy P J den Elzen, Anton J M de Craen, Saskia le Cessie, and Jacobijn Gussekloo
Use of Framingham risk score and new biomarkers to predict cardiovascular mortality in older people: population based observational cohort study
BMJ 2009; 338: a3083 [Abstract] [Full text]

Rapid Responses: Submit a response to this article

Rapid Responses published:

Fatty Acid Profiles, major factor, were omitted
Edward N. Siguel (20 January 2009)

Accurate and Ethical?
Chris C Gunstone, Burton, Staffs DE14 2JA (24 January 2009)

Does the ability of homocysteine to predict mortality of the very elderly merely reflects their reduced renal function?
Michael Bursztyn, Iddo Z Ben-Dov (26 January 2009)

Authors' Reply
Wouter de Ruijter, Rudi G.J. Westendorp, Willem J.J. Assendelft, Wendy P.J. den Elzen, Anton J.M. de Craen, Saskia le Cessie and Jacobijn Gussekloo. (29 January 2009)

New markers predicting mortality in the elderly
Yoram Maaravi, Jeremy M Jacobs, Jochanan Stessman (11 February 2009)

What is the cut-off value of homocysteine that can be considered as biomarker?
Neeru Gupta, A.K. Mathur. Suwarna, Nivedita Gupta. (14 September 2009)

Fatty Acid Profiles, major factor, were omitted

20 January 2009

Edward N. Siguel,
PHysician, lipid research
essentiial fats, MD, USA, 20898
Send response to journal:
Re: Fatty Acid Profiles, major factor, were omitted

Predictor models are functions; Dependent variable = = f(independent variables). Some functions allow relationships to be explicit and clearly understood, such as multivariate regression (not necessarily linear). In a multivariate regression, the predictive value of the equation is (in part) measured by the R square. Writers often misunderstand R square. It is possible to have high predictive value with very low R square (example = circle). However, low R squares usually means the model is a poor predictor. When the R square is below .3 (as it is in most models used to predict cardiovascular disease risk, and as I believe it is with Framingham models), it means that the most important predictor factors have been overlooked.

The methods of communication theory, such as area under receiver operating characteristic curve, must be used with great caution when extrapolated to mean predictive value for cardiovascular disease risk. Communication theory deals with stochastic processes with emphasis on error detection and correction, and predicting the value of a signal transmitted. Receiver operating characteristic curve may be used to analyze the value of comparable tests. However, for predicting risk, authors should at least include a model that more directly reflects the intended purposes, such as multivariate regression or equivalent mathematical functions. Otherwise, the data and interpretation can be

Figure 2. Examples of article comments on *BMJ*. The comments shown are for a research article published in early 2009 [17]. Full names and affiliations are typically given, and commenters indicate conflicts of interest but no login is needed to comment. As with BMC articles, threading is not formally implemented.

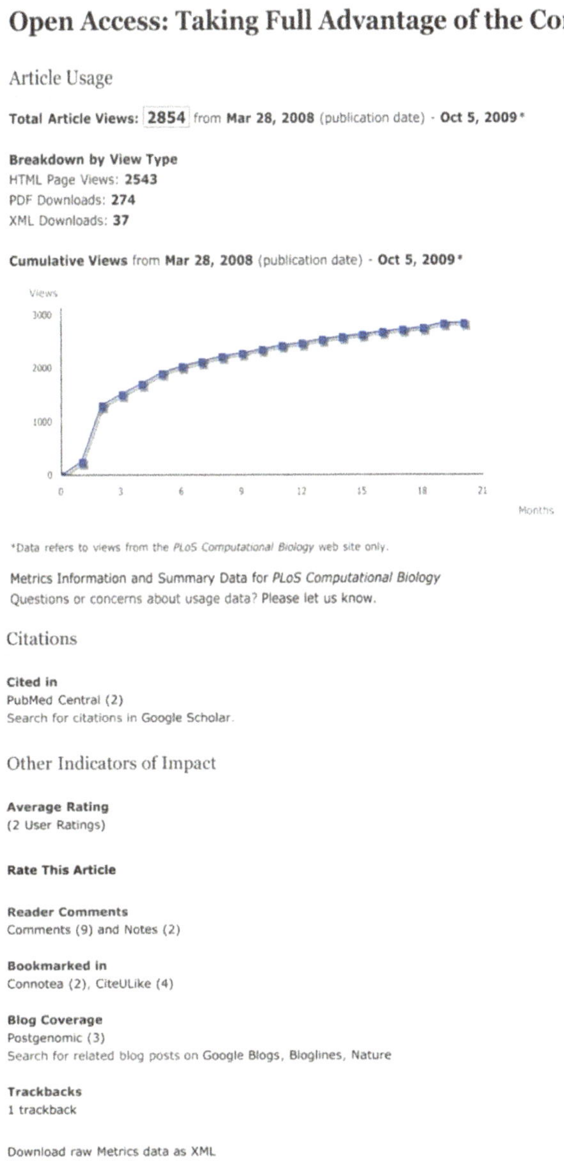

Figure 3. Article-level metrics provided by PLoS. Shown here are article-level metrics for a recent article in *PLoS Comput Biol* [15], accessible by clicking the "Metrics" tab on the article Web page. At the top, page view and download counts provide an immediate measure of the number of times people accessed the article via the journal Web site. The plot showing cumulative views gives a sense of the trend in views over time. Citations are shown next and refer to the number of other articles that have referenced this one as indexed in citation databases; PubMed Central and Google Scholar in this case. Citations typically take months or years to appear, but are better indicators of how many other articles have built upon the work. "Other Indicators of Impact" include ratings and comments, which, like page views, are immediate but may offer more insight because users are more likely to have read the article and found it compelling enough to respond. Additional other indicators are bookmarks, used by some people to keep track of articles of interest to them, and blog posts and trackbacks, which indicate where else on the Web the article has been mentioned and can be useful for linking to a broader discussion. It is clear that all of the types of data provide different dimensions, which together can give a clearer picture of an article's impact.

Part of the solution to encouraging valuable contributions, then, may simply be that the default settings involve sharing and that people rarely change them. A potentially game-changing incentive, however, may be the power to influence peers. By broadcasting what papers they think are important, researchers are directly influencing the research community's choice of reading and discussion material. This type of influence can be both a good thing, in providing the type of recognition that drives career prospects and will enhance the quality of contributions, but also potentially bad in as much as it concentrates power in the hands of the few. In a sense it is a shift in power from one set of editors, those currently in charge of journals, to a new set of "editors" who curate published papers in a different, but possibly just as useful way.

It is too early to tell whether any specific tools will last, but they already demonstrate an important principle: a tool that works within the workflow that researchers are *already using* can more easily capture and aggregate useful information. With researchers constantly pressured for time and attention, approaches that gather information from processes that are already part of the typical research workflow are also much more likely to succeed.

The Great Thing about Metrics...Is That There Are So Many to Choose From

There are numerous article-level metrics (see Figure 3) and each has its own advantages and problems. Citation counts are an excellent measure of influence and impact but are very slow to collect. Download statistics are rapid to collect but may be misleading. Comments can provide valuable and immediate feedback, but are currently sparse and require a change in the research reward culture to become more widespread and to improve quality. Bookmarking statistics can be both rapid to collect and contain high quality information but are largely untested and require the widespread adoption of unfamiliar tools. Alongside these we have "expert ratings" by services such as Faculty of 1000 and simple rating schemes.

The metrics are also useful in different contexts. Indeed, the fundamental problem of which paper to read can also have different contexts. Which new papers are relevant to you? Which papers should you read if you are going to pursue research question X? Which papers do you need to read before submitting your paper? Are you a funder interested in media coverage of work you have paid for or a textbook writer aiming to assess the most important contributions in a field? All of these questions require different information at different times and may be better determined using different measures of article impact. As recently shown [10], scientific impact is not a simple concept that can be described by a single number. The key point is that *journal* impact factor is a very poor measure of *article* impact. And, obviously, the fact that an article is highly influential by any measure does not necessarily mean it should be.

Many researchers will continue to rely on journals as filters, but the more you can incorporate effective filtering tools into your research process, the more you will stay up-to-date with advancing knowledge. The question is not whether you should take article-level metrics seriously but how you can use them most effectively to assist your own research endeavours. We need sophisticated metrics to ask sophisticated questions about different aspects of scientific impact and we need further research into both the most effective measurement techniques and the most effective uses of these in policy and decision making. For this reason we strongly support efforts to collect and present diverse types of article-level metrics without any initial presumptions as to which metric is most valuable. Different users will need different information and it will take time before any metric proves useful.

As Clay Shirky famously said [19], you can complain about information overload but the only way to deal with it is to build and use better filters. It is no longer sufficient to depend on journals as your only filter; instead, it is time to start evaluating papers on their own merits. Our only options are to publish less or to filter more effectively, and any response that favors publishing less doesn't make sense, either logistically, financially, or ethically. The issue is not how to stop people from publishing, it is how to build better filters, both systematically and individually. At the same time, we can use available tools, networks, and tools built on networks to help with this task.

So in the spirit of science, let's keep learning and experimenting, and keep the practice and dissemination of science evolving for the times.

REFERENCES

1. Garfield E (1972) Citation analysis as a tool in journal evaluation. Science 178: 471–479.
2. Bollen J, Rodriquez M. A, Van de Sompel H (2006) Journal status. Scientometrics 69: 669–687.
3. Bergstrom C (2007) Eigenfactor: measuring the value and prestige of scholarly journals. C&RL News 68(5):
4. Bollen J, Van de Sompel H, Hagberg A, Chute R (2009) A principal component analysis of 39 scientific impact measures. PLoS One 4: e6022. doi:10.1371/journal.pone.0006022.
5. Rossner M, Van Epps H, Hill E (2007) Show me the data. J Cell Biol 179: 1091–1092.
6. Rossner M, Van Epps H, Hill E (2008) Irreproducible results: a response to Thomson Scientific. J Cell Biol 180: 254–255.
7. The PLoS Medicine Editors (2006) The impact factor game. PLoS Med 3: e291. doi:10.1371/journal.pmed.0030291.
8. Campbell P (2008) Escape from the impact factor. Ethics Sci Environ Polit 8: 5–7.
9. Chen P, Xie H, Maslov S, Redner S (2007) Finding scientific gems with Google. J Informet 1: 8–15.
10. Bollen J, Van de Sompel H, Hagberg A, Bettencourt L, Chute R, et al. (2009) Clickstream data yields high-resolution maps of science. PLoS One 4: e4803. doi:10.1371/journal.pone.0004803.
11. Bollen J, Rodriquez M. A, Van de Sompel H (2006) Journal status. Scientometrics 69: 669–687.
12. Reeves W. C, Wagner D, Nisenbaum R, et al. (2005) Chronic fatigue syndrome – a clinically empirical approach to its definition and study. BMC Medicine 3: 19.
13. Bourne P. E, Fink J. L, Gerstein M (2008) Open Access: taking full advantage of the content. PLoS Comput Biol 4: e1000037. doi:10.1371/journal.pcbi.1000037.
14. Oleksyk T. K, Zhao K, De La Vega F. M, et al. (2008) Identifying selected regions from heterozygosity and divergence using a light-coverage genomic dataset from two human populations. PLoS One 3: e1712. doi:10.1371/journal.pone.0001721.
15. de Ruijter W, Westendorp R. G. J, Assendelft W. J. J, et al. (2009) Use of Framingham risk score and new biomarkers to predict cardiovascular mortality in older people: population bases cohort study. BMJ 338: a3083.
16. Lawrence P. A (2009) Real lives and white lies in the funding of scientific research. PLoS Biol 7: e1000197. doi:10.1371/journal.pbio.1000197.
17. Nielsen M (2009) Doing science in the open. Physics World May: 30–35.
18. Henning V, Hoyt J, Reichelt J (2009) Usage-based impact metrics in research. In: Masum H, Tovey M, Zhang Y-C, Zimmer M,, editors. The reputation society. Boston: MIT Press.
19. Shirky C (2008) It's not information overload. It's filter failure. Available:http://www.web2expo.com/webexny2008/public/schedule/detail/4817. Accessed 1 October 2009.

CHAPTER 18

I3DREFINE SOFTWARE FOR PROTEIN 3D STRUCTURE REFINEMENT AND ITS ASSESSMENT IN CASP10

Debswapna Bhattacharya[1] , Jianlin Cheng[2]

[1] Department of Computer Science, University of Missouri, Columbia, Missouri, United States of America

[2]Department of Computer Science, Informatics Institute, Bond Life Science Center, University of Missouri, Columbia, Missouri, United States of America

ABSTRACT

Protein structure refinement refers to the process of improving the qualities of protein structures during structure modeling processes to bring them closer to their native states. Structure refinement has been drawing increasing attention in the community-wide Critical Assessment of techniques for Protein Structure prediction (CASP) experiments since its addition in 8th CASP experiment. During the 9th and recently concluded 10th CASP experiments, a consistent growth in number of refinement targets and participating groups has been witnessed. Yet, protein structure refinement still remains a largely unsolved problem with majority of participating groups in CASP refinement category failed to consistently improve the quality of structures issued for refinement. In order to alleviate this need, we developed a completely automated and computationally efficient protein 3D structure refinement method, i3Drefine, based on an iterative and highly convergent energy minimization algorithm with a powerful all-atom composite physics and knowledge-based force fields and hydrogen bonding (HB) network optimization technique. In the recent community-wide blind experiment, CASP10, i3Drefine (as 'MULTICOM-CONSTRUCT') was ranked as the best method in the server section as per the official assessment of CASP10 experiment. Here we provide the community with free access to i3Drefine software and systematically analyze the performance of i3Drefine in strict blind mode on the refinement targets issued in CASP10 refinement category and compare with other state-of-the-art refinement methods participating in CASP10. Our analysis demonstrates that i3Drefine is only fully-automated server participating in CASP10 exhibiting consistent improvement over the initial structures in both global and local structural quality metrics.

INTRODUCTION

The biennial community-wide Critical Assessment of protein Structure Prediction (CASP) experiment aims to evaluate the progress and challenges in the state-of-the-art of protein structure modeling techniques, one of the fundamental problems in computational biology- prediction of the tertiary structure of protein from its sequence information. During the recent CASP experiments, encouraging and consistent progress have witnessed in template-based modeling (TBM) [1]–[4] or ab-initio (free-modeling; FM) [5]–[8] folding of protein structures. The refinement category has been a recent addition to

Citation: Bhattacharya D, Cheng J (2013) i3Drefine Software for Protein 3D Structure Refinement and Its Assessment in CASP10. PLoS ONE 8(7): e69648. doi:10.1371/journal.pone.0069648.

the CASP framework since CASP8, which aims to evaluate whether further improvement is possible to the best predictions made by contemporary structure prediction techniques. In the blind refinement experiment, predictors are given a starting structure evaluated by the organizers as the best submitted model during the structure prediction phase (TS category) along with the sequence information. Occasionally, some hints are also provided to aid the refinement like the focus regions during refinement or the accuracy of the starting structure.

Since its inclusion during CASP8, refinement category has been drawing increasing attention by the community. During recently concluded CASP10 refinement experiment, a 92% increase in the number of refinement targets and 39% increase in the number of participating groups have been observed compared to CASP9. This is not unexpected because a consistent and efficient refinement protocol can serve as a natural end step in almost all the contemporary structure prediction pipelines adding value to the already predicted structures through simultaneous improvement in backbone geometry and correction of local errors like irregular hydrogen bonding, steric clashes, unphysical bond length, unrealistic bond angles, torsion angles and side-chain χ angles. However, structure refinement has proven to extremely challenging as revealed in the assessment of refinement experiments during CASP8 and CASP9 [9], [10] with only a few participating groups were able to improve the model quality consistently. It should be noted, however, that CASP refinement category differs in a slight but significant way from refinement in the context of TBM [11]–[19] where the objective is to refine the best identified template structure(s) to produce better quality prediction. In CASP, on the other hand, the starting models issued for refinement have already been refined by other structure prediction pipelines and judged to be the best among all the submitted models. Thus, attempts to improve qualities of these models would naturally impose more challenges and often the risk of degrading the model quality instead of improving it.

In view of the major difficulties in the field, we developed a consistent and computationally efficient refinement algorithm, called 3Drefine [20] by optimizing the hydrogen bonding network and atomic level energy minimization using a composite physics and knowledge-based force field. We participated in CASP10 refinement category with an iterative version of 3Drefine protocol, i3Drefine. As per the official CASP10 results released during CASP10 meeting in the form of assessors' presentation (http://predictioncenter.org/casp10/docs.cgi?view=presentations), i3Drefine was ranked as the single best refinement server method capable of consistent improvement in qualities of starting structures. The contribution of this article are two-fold: (1) Providing the community with access to a fast, accurate and freely downloadable executable version of refinement software which could be used to improve the qualities of the models coming from variety of protein structure prediction methods, or to act as the end-game strategy in a TBM pipeline and (2) evaluation of its performance in CASP10 refinement experiment to analyse the effectiveness of this method in a strict blind mode. Although CASP10 refinement category includes both human and server predictors, since i3Drefine is a fully automated server, this article will be mainly focused on the assessment of refinement in the context of automated server predictions.

MATERIALS AND METHODS

i3Drefine Algorithm

i3Drefine is an iterative implementation of the energy minimization technique, 3Drefine for protein structure refinement. The details of 3Drefine protocol has been described in [20]. Here, we present a brief overview of 3Drefine algorithm.

3Drefine refinement protocol involves a two-step process: (1) Optimizing hydrogen bonding network and (2) atomic-level energy minimization using a combination of physics and knowledge based force fields; implemented using the molecular modeling package MESHI [21]. Given a starting structure for refinement, a combination of local geometry restraint and a conformational search is first performed in order to optimize the hydrogen bonding network. The optimized structure is called extended atomic model. Subsequently, 200,000 steps of energy minimization is employed on the extended atomic model using highly convergent limited memory Broyden–Fletcher–Goldfarb–Shannon (L-BFGS) [22] algorithm or until convergence to machine precision using a customized all-atom force field. The force field consists of a combination of physics based and knowledge based terms. The energetic contributions of the bonded interactions described in ENCAD potential [23] (bond length, bond angle, and torsion angle) along with tethering term of the C_α and C_β atoms [20] constitute the physics-based part while atomic pairwise potential of mean force [24] and explicit hydrogen bonding potential [25]account for the knowledge-based terms. A detailed analysis of the relative importance of these energy terms has been presented in the published work of 3Drefine [20]. The energy-minimized model is the refined model.

In i3Drefine, we use an iterative version of 3Drefine method. In order to escape from the local minima and move closer to the native structure, the starting model is minimized using 3Drefine protocol and the resulting refined model is again processed by the same method. This iteration is done five times to generate five refined models for the starting structure. Because 3Drefine invokes restrained backbone flexibility during energy minimization due to the inclusion of the knowledge-based terms in the all-atom force field, such an iterative scheme is effective. Furthermore, because of the computationally inexpensive nature of 3Drefine protocol, this iterative strategy does not provide significant computational overhead in i3Drefine pipeline consuming only a few minutes (typically less than 15 minutes) to generate five refined structures at a 2.4 GHz CPU.

Programming Language, Platform and External Programs

The core of i3Drefine is developed in Java (http://www.java.com/en/) on top of MESHI [21]software package and the command-line interface to perform the refinement is developed in Perl programming language (http://www.perl.org/). For a seamless installation and usage of i3Drefine, a Java version 6.0 or above and Perl version 5.8.8 or above is recommended. Also, since some of the energy terms in the customized force fields require the secondary structure assignment of the starting structure for accurate calculations, DSSP program [26] needs to be used in conjunction with i3Drefine. The detailed installation instructions along with typical example of using i3Drefine have been provided in the user manual file supplied with the software. i3Drefine has been tested on 64-bit Linux based platform. However, because of the platform independent nature of Java and versatile platform support of Perl, it can be fairly easily modified to run for Windows or Mac OSX platforms.

Metrics used for Evaluation

We evaluate the quality of the structural refinement using both global and local measures. We focus on GDT-TS [27] and RMSD [28] score to measure of the global positioning of C_α atoms. Global distance cutoff sidechain (GDC-SC) [2] has been used as a global quality metric for sidechain positioning. To assess the local qualities of the models, we use MolProbity score [29]as a local measure of physical correctness of a structure and SphereGrinder [10] as a local all-atom measure of structural similarity. Finally we use a recently introduced contact area difference (CAD) score [30] which quantifies the differences between physical contacts in the models before and after refinement with respect to their native structures.

GDT-TS

GDT-TS [27] is a global quality measure of the correct positioning of backbone based on multiple superpositions of the predicted and experimental structure. It counts the average percentage of residues with C_α atom distance from the native structure residues below 1, 2, 4, and 8 Å, respectively, after optimal structure superposition. GDT-TS ranges from [0, 1] with higher value indicating better accuracy.

RMSD

Similar to GDT-TS, RMSD [28] is a global measure of the correct positioning of the C_α atoms. However, RMSD is based on a single superposition lacking any kind of distance cutoffs. Hence, RMSD and GDT-TS is weekly correlated. Furthermore, unlike GDT-TS, a lower RMSD value indicates that the predicted structure is close to its native state.

GDC-SC

GDC-SC [2] has been used as a global quality metric for sidechain positioning. Unlike GDT-TS, which is focused on C_α atoms, GDC-SC use a single characteristic atom near the end of each sidechain. Also, 10 different superpositions with different weighting schemes are employed to calculate GDC-SC.

MolProbity

In order to evaluate the physical realism and the local errors, we use MolProbity [29] – a single and composite score to measure local model quality. The MolProbity score denotes the expected resolution of the protein model with respect to standard experimental structures and therefore, lower MolProbity score indicates more physically realistic model.

SphereGrinder

We use SphereGrinder to measures the local environment around each residue which was used in the refinement assessment of CASP9 [10]. SphereGrinder is based on an all-atom RMSD fit between the experimental and predicted structures using a sphere constructed by considering the set of atoms within 6 Å of the C_α atoms for each residue in experimental structure.

CAD-AA

CAD score [30] is a newly introduced quality metric which is based on contact area difference between predicted and experimental structure, thereby directly reflecting interactions within the protein structure. The contact area is calculated based on a protein structure tessellation approach [31] and normalized between [0, 1] with higher value indicating better structure. We use the all-atom version of the CAD score, namely, CAD-AA.

Normalizing and Overall Quality Score

Higher value of GDT-TS, GDC-SC, SphereGrinder and CAD-AA scores indicate better models while lower values RMSD and MolProbity scores represent better models. In order to effectively compare the degree of refinement between different groups or targets, a single overall quality score is essential. We use a robust version of Z-score based on median absolute difference (MAD) of the changes in quality of the models induced through refinement. This is a slightly modified approach used in refinement assessment during CASP9 [10].

The difference in the model quality is first calculated to get the delta quality score for a given quality metric (e.g. GDT-TS).

$$\delta_Q(r) = Q(r) - Q(s) \quad (1)$$

where Q(r) and Q(s) denote the quality score for refined and starting structures respectively corresponding to quality measure Q.

For a given target, we calculate the MAD using:

$$MAD_{\delta_Q} = median(|\delta_Q(r) - median(\delta_Q)|) \quad (2)$$

where median(δ_Q) denotes the median of the delta score for the corresponding quality metric and |.| is the absolute value. The robust Z-score is then calculated as:

$$Z_{r,Q} = \frac{\delta_Q(r) - median(\delta_Q)}{1.486 \times MAD_{\delta_Q}} \quad (3)$$

The factor 1.486 scales the MAD to be same as standard deviation of a normal distribution.

Finally, a weighted average of Z-score is taken for all different quality metrics to combine the results of all six scores into a single score, called Q-score.

$$Q_{overall,r} = \frac{5 \times Z_{r,GDT-TS} - Z_{r,RMSD} + Z_{r,GDC-SC} + Z_{r,MP} + Z_{r,SpGr} + Z_{r,CAD-AA}}{10} \quad (4)$$

In this scoring scheme, GDT-TS is given a weight of 5, which makes half of the overall score and other five metrics makes the other half. Although this procedure is arbitrary, it emphasizes the improvement in backbone positioning as judged by GDT-TS score, a widely used metric by CASP assessors, compared to other measures.

RESULTS AND DISCUSSION

The fully automated i3Drefine software was first blindly tested in CASP10 refinement experiment, 2012 with the group name MULTICOM-CONSTRUCT (Server group 222). Since then, we systematically evaluate its performance using global and local quality metrics like GDT-TS, RMSD, GDC-SC, MolProbity, SphereGrinder and CAD-score and perform comparative analysis of i3Drefine against all the groups participating in CASP10 refinement category. Here, we first summarize the targets offered for refinement during CASP10 refinement experiment along with the measures of the initial quality. Secondly, we present the automated server groups participating in CASP10 refinement category and introduce a pseudo group called "Void" as a control. Thirdly, we assess the overall degree of refinement produced by i3Drefine in a strict blind mode. Fourthly, a comparison of i3Drefine against the state-of-the-art refinement server methods participating in CASP10 has been presented along with head-to-head comparison of the scores and their statistical significance. During CASP10, each predictor was asked to submit up to five predictions while ranking submissions from best to worst. We, therefore, perform one set of analysis using the first submitted model, which is the best prediction as per the ranking from the predictor. However, because predictors often fail to correctly rank their submissions, we present a second set of analysis by selecting the best prediction (as evaluated by our overall quality score) from each group for each target. The comparison between the first and the best predicted models by i3Drefine also reveals the advantages of the iterative version of our refinement method (i3Drefine) over the non-iterative version (3Drefine). Finally, we compare i3Drefine with the top five non-server (human) methods and discuss the added benefits of human predictors and the possibility of adopting them in computational structure prediction pipelines.

Targets used for Refinement in CASP10

Table 1 summarizes the targets issued for refinement in CASP10 and the measures of the initial quality of these targets. The occasional "hints" provided by the organizers to focus on certain segment(s) of the structures during refinement has also been reported. These are the starting models for refinement and were chosen from the top submissions during the structure prediction category. These models, therefore, represent one of the best predicted structures submitted by the community for each target and intuitively, consistent refinement of these structures is a nontrivial task.

Table 1. Summary of CASP10 refinement targets

#	Target	Residues	Method	GDT-TS	RMSD (Å)	GDC-SC	MP[a]	SG[b]	CAD-AA	Focus[c]
1	TR644	141	X-ray	0.8422	2.712	0.4346	2.49	0.7518	0.69	–
2	TR655	175	NMR	0.6871	4.654	0.2853	3.83	0.5143	0.58	6–20; 51–64
3	TR661	185	X-ray	0.800	2.743	0.375	1.11	0.7135	0.67	–
4	TR662	75	NMR	0.8267	2.031	0.3364	2.42	0.7600	0.67	–
5	TR663	152	X-ray	0.6908	3.372	0.2626	4.05	0.7697	0.67	53–78; 141–181
6	TR671	88	X-ray	0.5568	7.716	0.1158	3.68	0.4432	0.59	–
7	TR674	132	X-ray	0.8523	3.444	0.4417	2.99	0.7424	0.69	–
8	TR679	199	X-ray	0.7186	3.949	0.3076	1.15	0.5226	0.6	25–45; 146–156; 187–197
9	TR681	191	X-ray	0.7827	2.273	0.3274	2.89	0.6387	0.64	–
10	TR688	185	X-ray	0.7838	2.524	0.4249	1.77	0.7730	0.67	–
11	TR689	214	X-ray	0.8773	1.660	0.4202	3.18	0.8738	0.72	–
12	TR696	100	X-ray	0.7075	3.519	0.2631	2.97	0.5000	0.58	–
13	TR698	119	X-ray	0.6471	4.653	0.2568	2.73	0.6555	0.63	17–35; 90–100
14	TR699	225	X-ray	0.8411	2.211	0.3361	2.77	0.7733	0.66	–
15	TR704	235	X-ray	0.6989	2.78	0.2325	2.89	0.7319	0.64	–
16	TR705	96	X-ray	0.6458	4.709	0.2211	3.63	0.3750	0.52	–
17	TR708	196	X-ray	0.8648	4.630	0.4551	2.65	0.8214	0.71	–
18	TR710	194	X-ray	0.7487	2.440	0.3628	0.50	0.7732	0.72	–
19	TR712	186	X-ray	0.9261	1.992	0.5515	2.69	0.8817	0.77	80–89; 116–129; 141–155
20	TR720	198	X-ray	0.5783	8.515	0.2558	1.33	0.4697	0.58	–
21	TR722	127	X-ray	0.5709	4.422	0.1614	0.88	0.8976	0.72	–
22	TR723	131	X-ray	0.8511	2.232	0.3772	2.21	0.8473	0.68	–
23	TR738	249	X-ray	0.9006	1.396	0.5036	2.38	0.9398	0.75	17–35; 90–100
24	TR747	90	X-ray	0.825	1.956	0.3796	1.95	0.6778	0.63	–
25	TR750	182	X-ray	0.7679	2.125	0.348	2.49	0.7967	0.67	–
26	TR752	148	X-ray	0.9037	1.495	0.4305	1.52	0.7973	0.71	41–50; 100–110; 125–128
27	TR754	68	NMR	0.7794	2.410	0.1997	2.56	0.8235	0.65	–

[a]MolProbity scores of the starting structures.
[b]SphereGrinder scores of the starting structures.
[c]The numbers indicate the range of focus residues as suggested by CASP10 organizers.
doi:10.1371/journal.pone.0069648.t001

Server Groups Participating in CASP10 Refinement Category

A total of fifty groups participated in CASP10 refinement experiment including both human and server predictors. Thirteen groups took part as fully automated server predictors. The server predictors were given a three days deadline to submit the refined structures to the prediction centre as opposed to a three weeks deadline offered for the human predictors. In Table 2, we summarize the server groups participating in CASP10 along with the number of predictions submitted by each predictor. The performance of fully automated i3Drefine method (group name MULTICOM-CONSTRUCT) can be directly compared to these methods on the CASP10 refinement targets. This would enable us to assess the ability of i3Drefine protocol with state-of-the-art automated refinement methods in a strict blind mode. Groups attempting more that 50% of the targets have been highlighted in bold in Table 2.

Table 2. List of server groups participating in CASP10 refinement category

#	Group #	Group Name[a]	Targets attempted	Total submitted models	First submitted model[b]
1	006	**MUFOLD-QA**	22	110	22
2	028	**YASARA**	18	18	18
3	103	PconsM	2	10	2
4	108	**PMS**	27	135	27
5	124	PconsD	2	10	2
6	175	**FRESS_server**	27	135	27
7	179	Lenserver	2	10	2
8	198	**chuo-fams-server**	27	27	27
9	222	**MULTICOM-CONSTRUCT**[c]	27	135	27
10	238	**chuo-repack-server**	26	26	26
11	286	Mufold-MD	1	5	1
12	292	Pcons-net	2	10	2
13	424	**MULTICOM-NOVEL**	27	135	27

[a]Group name in bold indicates the group has attempted more than 50% of refinement targets.
[b]Models submitted with a Model ID of one.
[c]CASP10 group name for i3Drefine.
doi:10.1371/journal.pone.0069648.t002

As a control, we created a pseudo group called "Void" group. This group represents the starting model provided by the CASP organizers for refinement. We judge the success and degree of refinement with respect to the 'Void' group. Groups that perform worse than Void group have on average degraded the quality of starting structures rather than improving it.

Overall Performance of i3Drefine in CASP10 Blind Refinement Experiment

Figure 1 shows the distribution of change in model quality relative to the starting model as judged by the score difference in six quality metrics for all submitted model by i3Drefine method for all CASP10 refinement targets. Positive changes in GDT-TS, GDC-SC, SphereGrinder and CAD-AA scores represent refinement success whereas negative changes in RMSD and MolProbity scores indicate a failure in refinement. In Figure 1, the regions shaded in black indicate improvement in the corresponding quality measure with the numbers above these regions representing the percentage of refinement successes while the regions without shading indicate degradation in the model quality and the numbers specify the percentage of failures in refinement. While for most metrics, the number of improvements significantly outnumbered number of failures, the improvement is typically modest in nature. For example, refinement successes outnumber failures by more than a factor of three in global position of the backbone atoms as judged by GDT-TS and RMSD scores and global quality of sidechain positioning as measured by GDC-SC score. While most of ΔGDT-TS, ΔRMSD and ΔGDC-SC scores lie within ~ ±4%, the distributions are skewed towards improvement. Highly consistent improvement has also been observed in the local quality measures like ΔSphereGrinder and ΔCAD-AA scores and the distributions are highly skewed towards success with over 90% success. However, for MolProbity score, there are more failures than success and the distribution is marginally skewed towards failure. The distributions in Figure 1 are multimodal, which indicate that not all targets are equally easy to refine and the degree of refinement vary with the difficulty of targets.

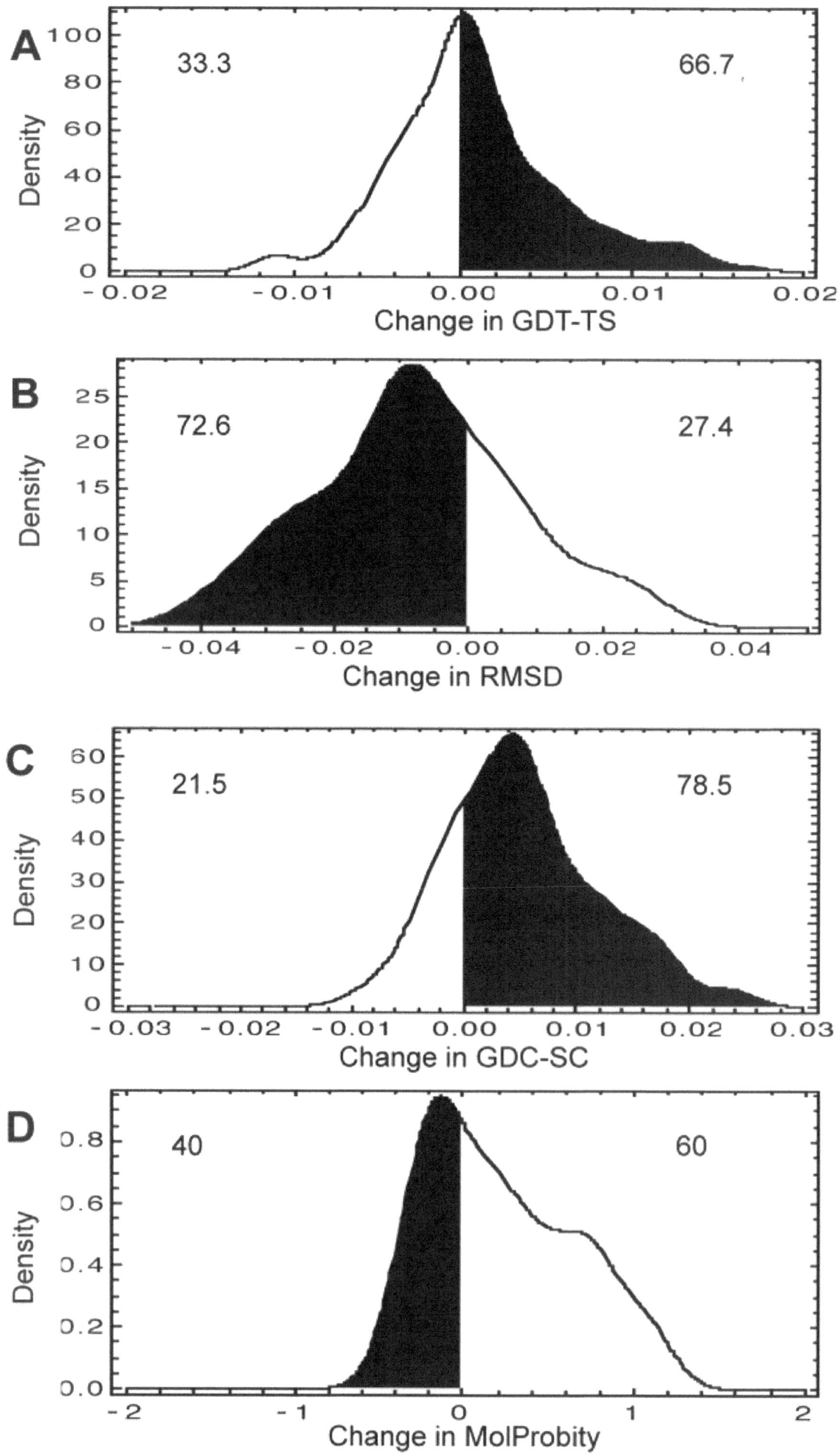
A
33.3
66.7
Density
Change in GDT-TS
B
72.6
27.4
Density
Change in RMSD
C
21.5
78.5
Density
Change in GDC-SC
D
40
60
Density
Change in MolProbity

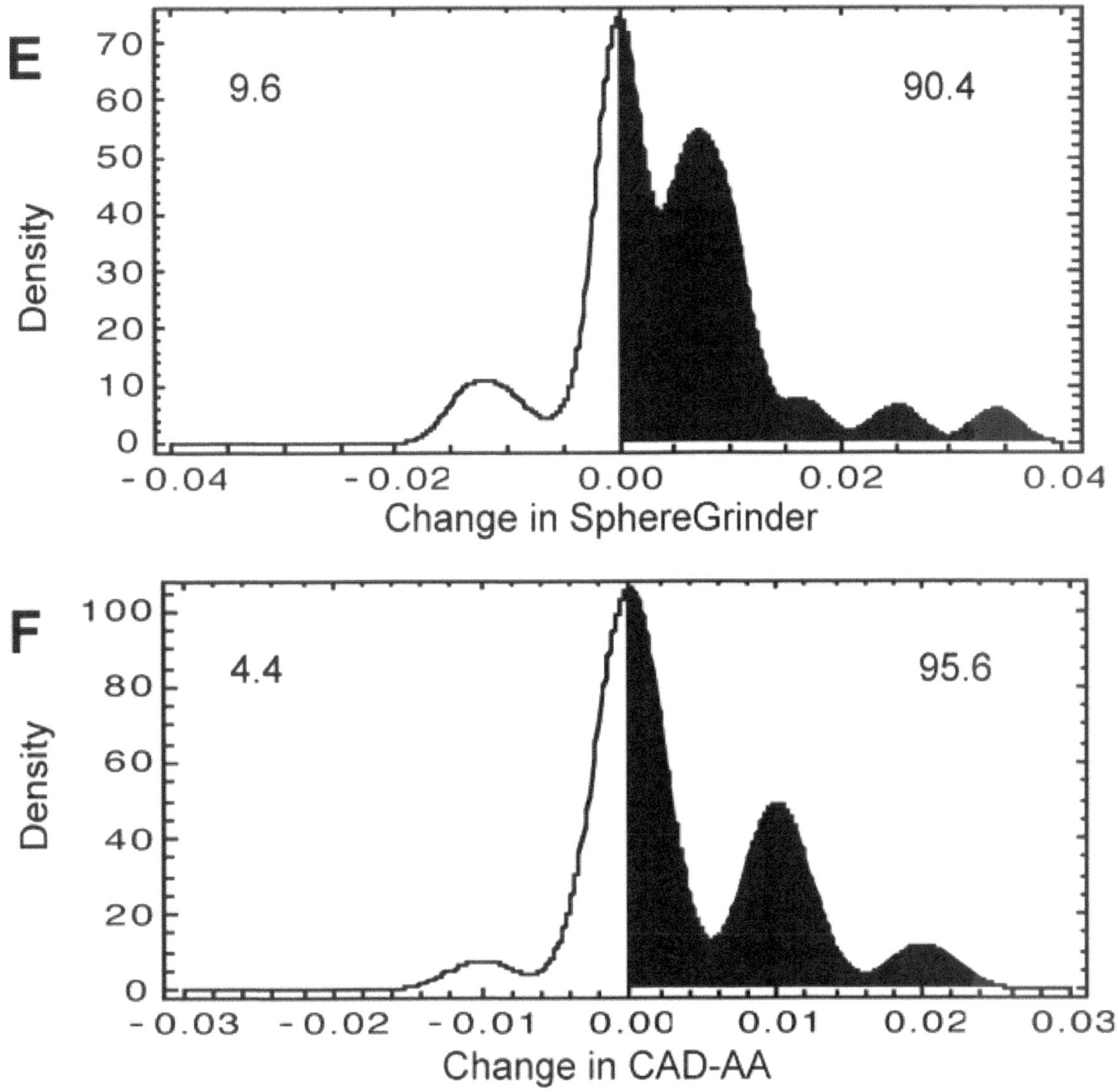

Figure 1. Distribution of i3Drefine refinement for all submitted structures. Distributions of change in quality scores after i3Drefine refinement are shown for these metrics: (A) GDT-TS, (B) RMSD, (C) GDC-SC, (D) MolProbity, (E) SphereGrinder and (F) CAD-AA. Regions shaded in black indicate improvement over the starting model. The numeric values are the percentage of times the structures were made better or worse for each metric.

In Fig. 2, we examine the relationship between the starting score of any of the quality measures and the ability of i3Drefine to improve the starting model. Although, it is difficult to infer a conclusive correlation between them with only 27 targets, some interesting trends can be observed. For example, most of the starting structures have quite accurate backbone positioning with only 7 out of 27 targets have RMSD score more than 4Å and GDT-TS less than 0.7. For these moderate-accuracy targets, i3Drefine always improves the backbone quality by increasing GDT-TS score and reducing RMSD score. For the more accurate starting structures with RMSD ~ 2Å, the RMSD distribution is skewed towards improvement. However, there are approximately as many improvements as failures in GDT-TS score for high-accuracy targets (GDT-TS more than 0.8). The global quality of sidechains, as measured by GDC-SC varies from 0.1 to 0.6 indicating that the starting structure set comprises a wide variety in terms of accuracy of sidechain positioning, although most of the targets are in the range of 0.3 to 0.5. Promisingly, i3Drefine consistently improves the GDC-SC score irrespective of the quality of starting structures. When the initial model has less accurate local quality as measured by MolProbity (MolProbity score is more than 2), we observe consistent improvement in MolProbity. However, i3Drefine almost always increases MolProbity score indicating degradation in local model quality when MolProbity score is less than 2. For other local quality measures like SphereGrinder and CAD-AA, we observe a modest but consistent improvement in the model quality across all target difficulty. In short, more consistent and simultaneous improvements both in global and local quality measures have been observed for moderately accurate targets than high-accuracy targets.

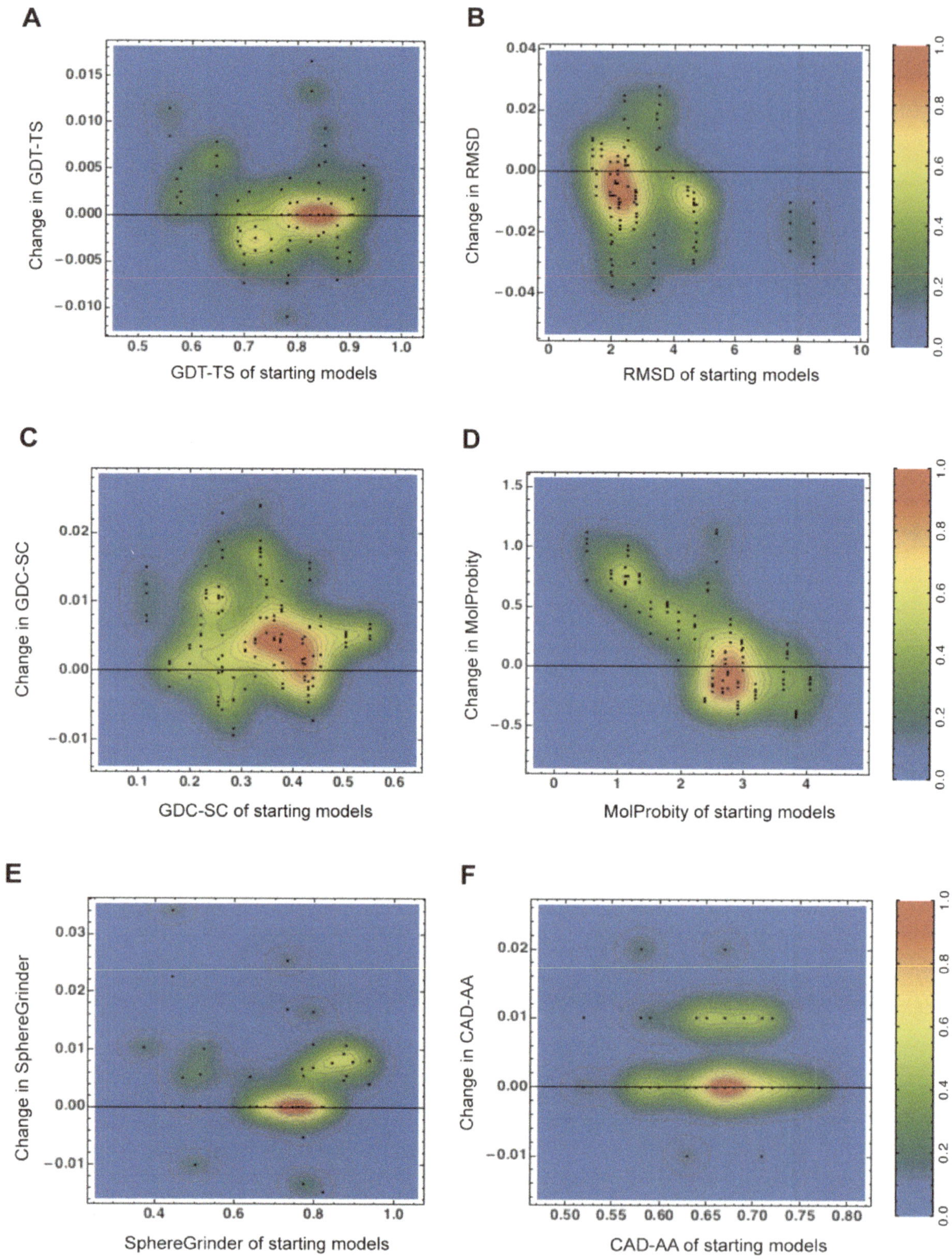

Figure 2. Distributions of score changes with respect to the quality of starting structures. Relationships between changes in quality scores and the quality of the starting models are shown for these metrics: (A) GDT-TS, (B) RMSD, (C) GDC-SC, (D) MolProbity, (E) SphereGrinder and (F) CAD-AA. The Black points indicate the actual data points while the contours are filled with colours that vary from blue for low density to red for high density. The colour function has been scaled between 0 and 1 and the legends are shown on the right.

A representative example of refinement has been presented in Fig. 3 for CASP10 refinement target TR705. i3Drefine refinement results in GST-TS, GDC-SC, SphereGrinder and CAD-AA scores to increase from 0.6458, 0.2211, 0.375 and 0.52 to 0.651, 0.2291, 0.3854 and 0.53 respectively. The RMSD and MolProbity score decreases from 4.709 Å and 3.53 to 4.698 Å to 3.52 respectively. Clearly, a modest yet consistent improvement in all quality measures has been observed. More pronounced structural improvement in terms of backbone positioning has been observed around residue 58 where a disoriented strand region is rearranged to a coil, thereby bringing the refined model closer to the native state.

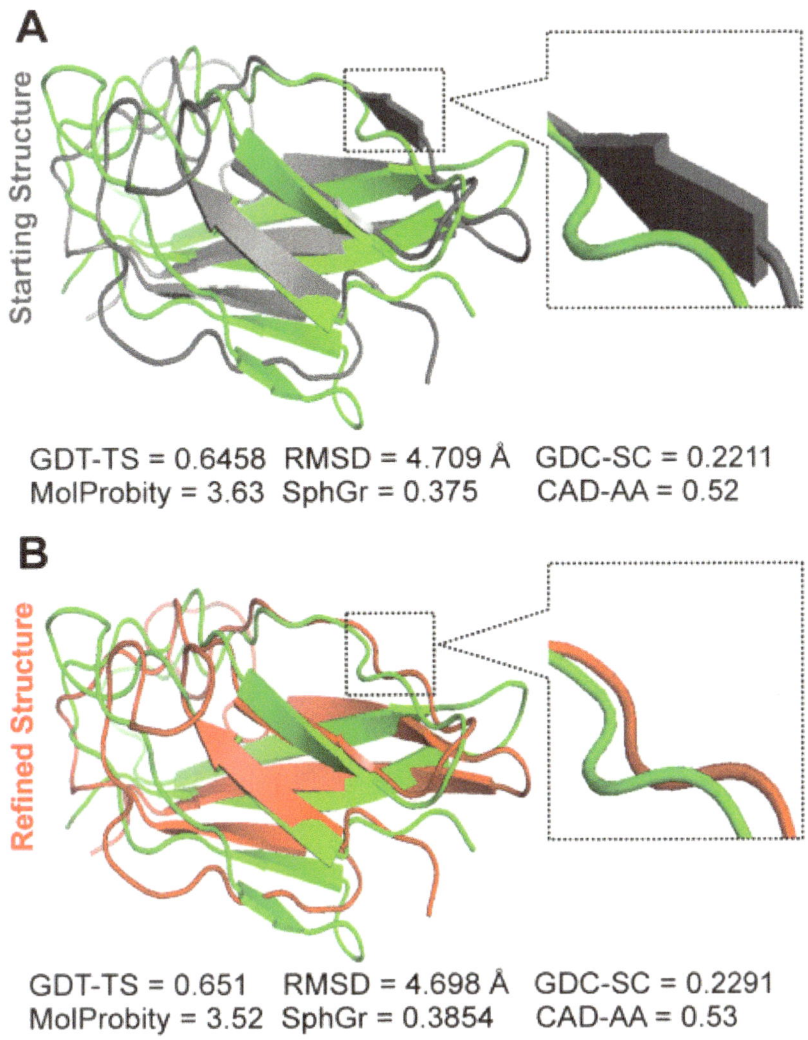

Figure 3. Example of i3Drefine refinement for CASP10 target TR705. (A) Structural superposition of initial model (grey) on native structure (green). (B) Structural superposition of refined model using i3Drefine (red) on native structure (green). The values of the quality measures before and after refinement have been reported under the models. The black dotted square highlights the region with prominent structural improvements and a closer look of the change is shown in the right.

Comparison of i3Drefine with other Server Predictors Participating in CASP10

We compare the performance of i3Drefine with the thirteen server predictors participating in CASP10 refinement category based on the first submitted model and the best submitted model as judged by our overall quality score, $Q_{overall}$. It can be noticed form Table 2 that some of the predictors attempted very few targets and only eight groups (including i3Drefine) submitted prediction for more than 50% of targets (i.e. more than 13 targets). Although we have taken into account all the submitted models by every group while performing our analysis, we choose to focus on these eight predictors for a fair comparison between them. To compare predictors with a single score, we have computed the sum of $Q_{overall}$ for each predictor and ranked groups based on that.

Upper part of Table 3 summarizes cumulative change in all the quality measures with respect to the starting structures (represented as 'Void' group) for eight server predictors. The groups have been ordered based on the cumulative $Q_{overall}$ score for all the submitted targets. The results demonstrate except MolProbity score, i3Drefine improves all the quality measures in terms of cumulative change with respect to the starting structures. In Figure 4, we present the distributions of changes in model quality relative to the starting models for the eight server predictors as measured by six quality metrics. Similar to Figure 1, the regions shaded in black in Figure 4 correspond to refinement successes while the regions without shading indicate failures in refinement. We also report the percentage of successes and failures for each quality measures. The distributions for each predictor are multimodal due to variations in the quality of the starting models. Also, the degree of change in the quality score varies between predictors and type of quality metric. We, therefore, choose to maximally cover the range of score changes for each predictor and each quality measure. Some interesting variations between groups can be observed and often a trade-off exists between the extent of improvement and consistency. For example, groups like i3Drefine and chuo-fams-server perform modest but consistent improvement in almost all the scores. While the delta scores for these predictors usually lie within ~ ±4%, the distributions are skewed towards improvement. On the other hand, there exist more adventurous groups like YASARA and MULTICOM_NOVEL capable of performing larger improvements at the cost of consistency. Also, different server predictors excel at different aspects of refinement. For instance, i3Drefine improves GDT-TS and RMSD, GDC-SC, SphereGrinder and CAD-AA scores more frequently than any other groups. The ability of YASARA to improve the GDC-SC, MolProbity and CAD-AA scores in terms of degree of change and consistency is quite impressive. The most striking feature we observe is the inability of predictors to improve the backbone positioning as judged by GDT-TS and RMSD scores. i3Drefine is the only server method able to perform consistent improvement in backbone quality as measured by a simultaneous improvement in ΔGDT-TS and ΔRMSD scores. Clearly, most of the predictors are better at improving general physicality of the starting structures than at improving the backbone positioning.

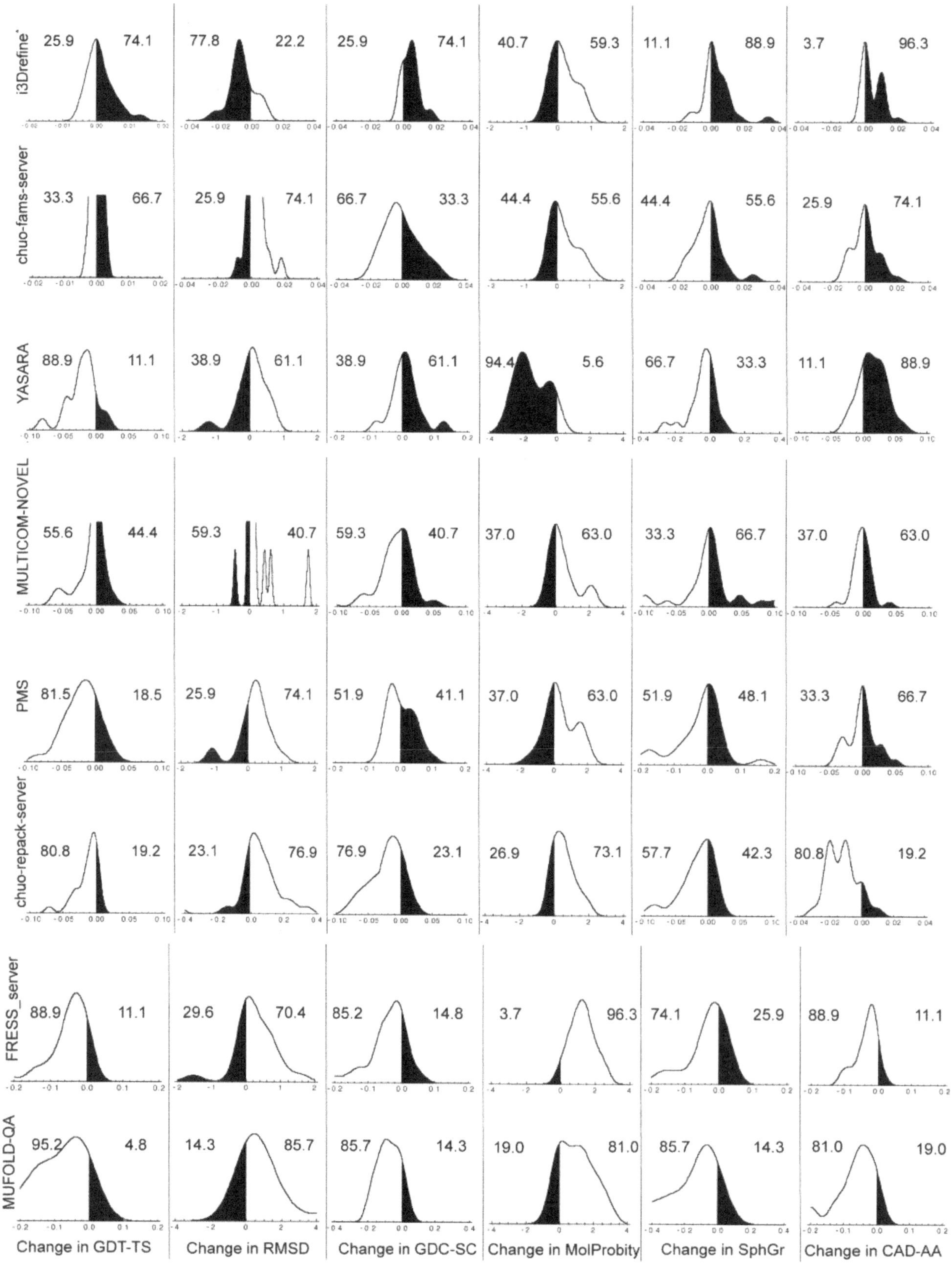

Figure 4. Distribution and degree of refinement for top server groups based on first submitted model. Distribution and degree of score changes relative to starting models for the 8 groups based on the first submitted models. The X-axis shows changes in scores with respect to the starting

model. Regions shaded in black indicate improvement over the starting model. The numeric values are the percentage of times the structures were made better or worse than the starting model for each metric. The groups are ordered by the sum of overall quality score. * CASP10 group name for i3Drefine is MULTICOM-CONSTRUCT.

Table 3. Cumulative improvement relative to starting model for the top server groups in CASP10 refinement experiment*

Selection	Group Name	ΔGDT-TS	ΔRMSD (Å)	ΔGDC-SC	ΔMP[a]	ΔSG[b]	ΔCAD-AA	Q_overall[c]
First Model	MULTICOM-CONSTRUCT[d]	0.036	−0.165	0.120	3.93	0.096	0.120	12.69
	Void	0.000	0.000	0.000	0.00	0.000	0.000	10.91
	chuo-fams-server	0.003	0.074	−0.191	5.05	−0.803	−0.060	5.71
	YASARA	−0.372	−2.138	0.188	−27.75	−0.800	0.270	2.79
	MULTICOM-NOVEL	−0.490	27.479	−0.294	11.72	−0.253	−0.090	−0.97
	PMS	−0.534	9.606	0.097	9.73	−0.624	−0.010	−5.97
	chuo-repack-server	−0.364	1.939	−0.523	13.86	−0.439	−0.430	−8.27
	FRESS_server	−1.574	10.155	−1.102	32.79	−1.512	−0.930	−39.53
	MUFOLD-QA	−2.194	140.087	−1.604	20.37	−3.121	−1.340	−109.18
Best Model	MULTICOM-CONSTRUCT[d]	0.068	−0.224	0.151	4.25	0.124	0.140	13.96
	PMS	−0.162	−2.091	0.382	8.29	−0.025	0.170	13.72
	Void	0.000	0.000	0.000	0.00	0.000	0.000	10.91
	MULTICOM-NOVEL	−0.220	14.010	−0.105	9.79	−0.059	0.010	7.49
	chuo-fams-server	0.003	0.074	−0.191	5.05	−0.803	−0.060	5.71
	YASARA	−0.372	−2.138	0.188	−27.75	−0.800	0.270	2.79
	chuo-repack-server	−0.364	1.939	−0.523	13.86	−0.439	−0.430	−8.27
	FRESS_server	−0.926	4.787	−0.648	30.10	−0.865	−0.520	−21.75
	MUFOLD-QA	−1.968	31.832	−1.289	13.17	−2.436	−0.980	−62.30

*The values for all quality metrics represent the cumulative change relative to the starting structures for all targets.
[a]Cumulative change in MolProbity score.
[b]Cumulative change in SphereGrinder score.
[c]Sum of overall quality score for all targets.
[d]CASP10 group name for i3Drefine.
doi:10.1371/journal.pone.0069648.t003

Because the predictors often face difficulty in correctly ranking their submissions, the first models are often not the best submitted one. To overcome this challenge, we have recalculated the results by examining only the best structure for each group (as judged by $Q_{overall}$) for each target. In case the groups (like YASARA, chuo-fams-server and chuo-repack-server) submitted only one model as prediction, we are left with the only choice to select that as best prediction. When judged by their best model for each target, there are two groups that perform better than the 'Void' pseudo group as shown in the lower part of Table 3. Once again, i3Drefine outperform all the server predictors with a consistent improvement in all the quality measures except MolProbity as evaluated by cumulative change in scores. The only other group that perform better than 'Void' is PMS with an impressive ability to improve the overall RMSD, GDC-SC and CAD-AA scores. We observe a consistent improvement in cumulative scores changes for the predictors submitting multiple predictions when the best models are selected from each group. The distributions of changes in model quality relative to the starting models are captured in Figure 5 with the best submitted model for each predictor as judged by six quality metrics. Once more, we see a clear trade-off between consistency and degree of refinement and different predictors performing well at different aspects of refinement. It can be observed fromFigure 5, that i3Drefine improves GDT-TS and RMSD, GDC-SC, SphereGrinder and CAD-AA scores more frequently than any other groups, indicating its ability for a consistent improvement. The changes are, however, modest in nature. Although the group PMS has an impressive cumulative ΔRMSD score as shown in Table 3, Figure 5 reveals that changes in RMSD score is not consistent for this predictors. The overall RMSD is improved primarily due to large changes made in three targets (TR671, TR720 and TR722) and not because of consistency. When the best models are considered, MULTICOM-NOVEL has been seen to have notable ability to improve backbone positioning as measured by GDT-TS and RMSD scores by performing a consistent and often large improvement. Apart from i3Drefine, MULTICOM-NOVEL is the only other predictor able to achieve a consistent and simultaneous improvement in ΔGDT-TS and ΔRMSD scores. YASARA group is shown to have promising ability to consistently improve MolProbity score and often with a large degree. In short, if we set aside the difficulty of the predictors to correctly rank their submissions and instead focus on the best structures from each group, we see more successes in refinement.

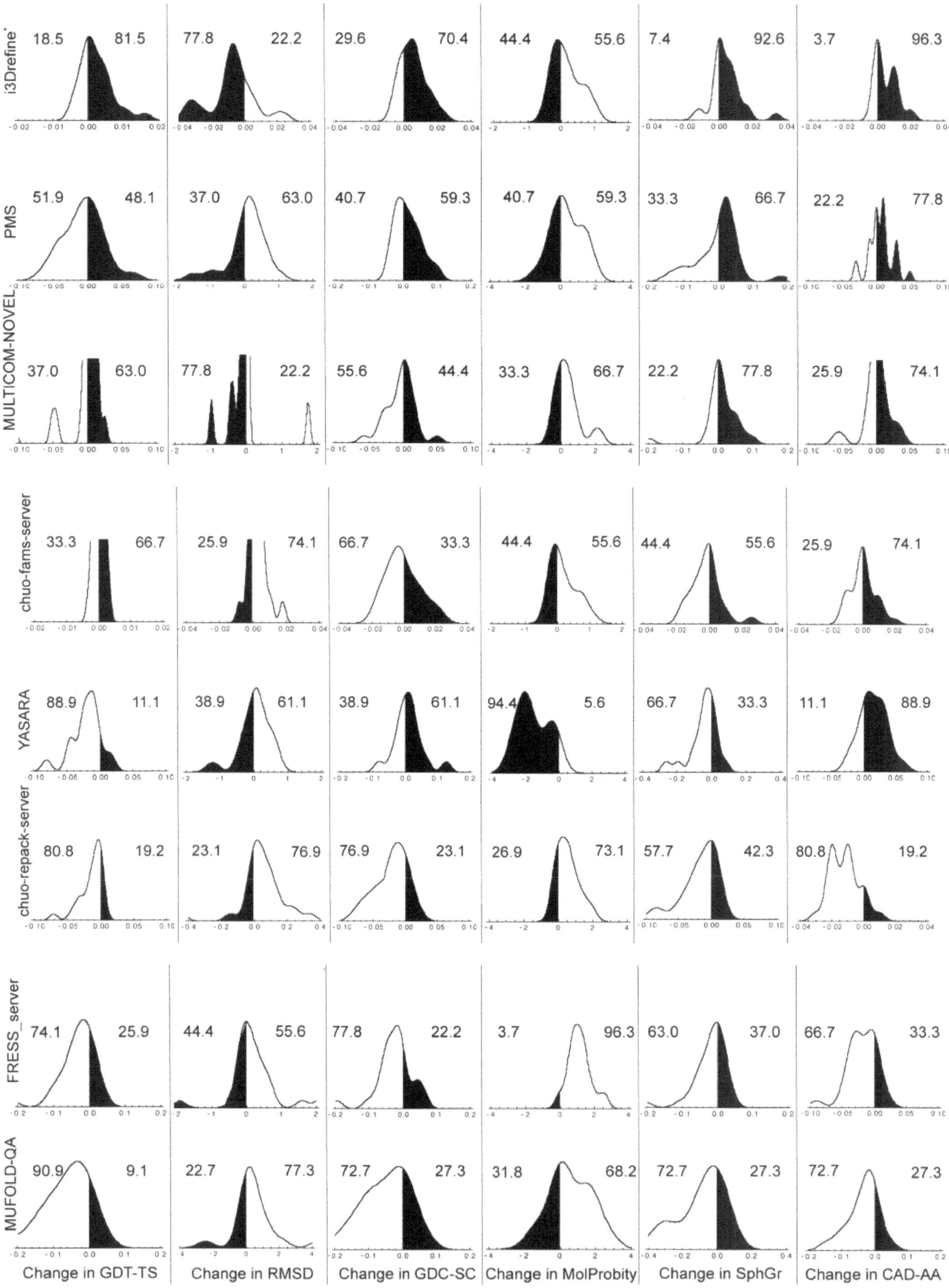

Figure 5. Distribution and degree of refinement for top server groups based on best submitted model. Distribution and degree of score changes relative to starting models for the 8 groups based on the best submitted models as judged by quality score for each target. The X-axis shows changes in scores with respect to the starting model. Regions shaded in black indicate improvement over the starting model. The numeric values are the percentage of times the structures were made better or worse than the starting model for each metric. The groups are ordered by the sum of overall quality score. * CASP10 group name for i3Drefine is MULTICOM-CONSTRUCT.

Overall, i3Drefine method has shown promising ability for a steady improvement in nearly all quality measures both in terms of first or best submitted predictions. The ability of i3Drefine to consistently improve GDT-TS and RMSD scores, which appear to be the most difficult metrics to improve consistently, is also encouraging.

Head-to-head Comparison of Server Predictors and their Statistical Significance

Figure 6 shows the head-to-head comparison in the quality metrics for eight server predictors considering the first model. Upper part of Table 4 summarizes the *p*-values in Wilcoxon signed-rank test with null hypothesis that the refined models are same as the starting structures for eight server predictors. At 5% confidence level, i3Drefine performs statistically significant improvements in RMSD, GDC-SC, MolProbity and CAD-AA scores. The only other group with a statistically significant positive result in for at least one score is YASARA improving MolProbity score significantly. The results remain largely unaffected when judged by the best model for each target. In Figure 7, we present the results for eight server groups considering the overall best models for each target, whose *p*-values of Wilcoxon signed-rank test have been shown in the lower part of Table 4. With the best overall model, i3Drefine performs statistically significant positive result in all quality measures except MolProbity at 5% confidence level. Strikingly, the rest of the server predictors are either indistinguishable from or worse than the 'Void' group although the magnitude of average change in scores differs for each method. Given the small number of targets, a group must perform very consistent improvement to be statistically significant with respect to 'Void' group and promisingly, i3Drefine is the only server method participating in CASP10 refinement experiment capable to achieve statistically distinguishable improvement in most of the quality metrics.

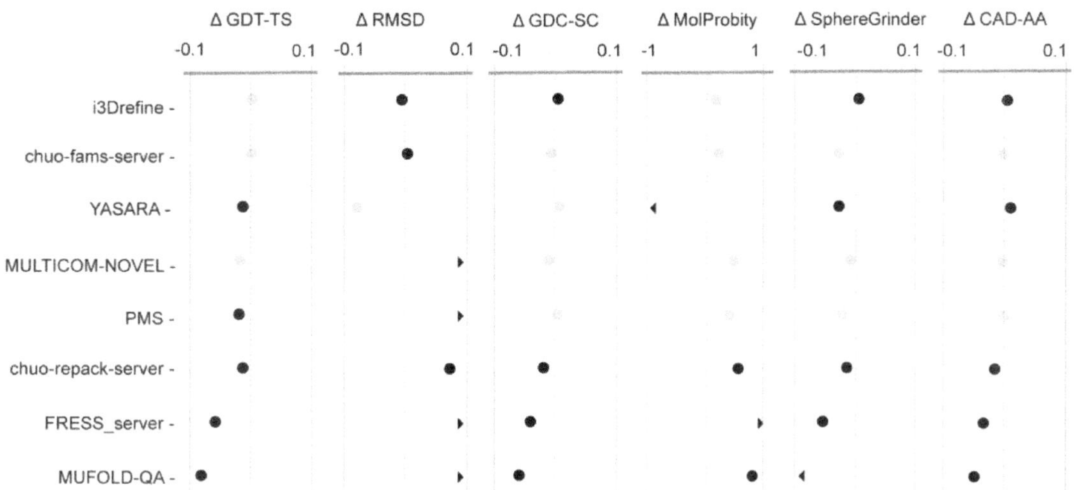

Figure 6. Summary of the average score changes and their statistical significance for top server groups based on best submitted model. Average score changes and their statistical significance relative to starting models for the 8 groups based on the best submitted models as judged by quality score for each target. Each column shows one of the metrics we used to evaluate performance. The scales are marked at ± Average Changes relative to the 'Void' group. For GDT-TS, GDC-SC, SphereGrinder and CAD-AA scores, positive changes indicate the quality of the model has been improved by refinement whereas for RMSD and MolProbity, negative changes represent improvement. Black points are statistically distinguishable from the 'Void' group; gray points are indistinguishable (Wilcoxon signed-rank test, P=0.05). A chevron indicates that the corresponding score is off the scale.

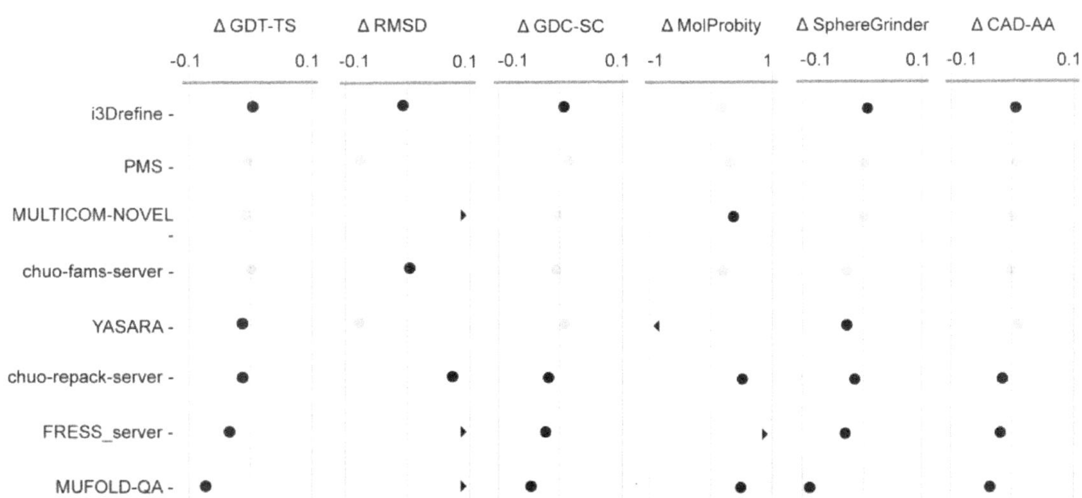

Figure 7. Summary of the average score changes and their statistical significance for top server groups based on best submitted model. Average score changes and their statistical significance relative to starting models for the 8 groups based on the best submitted models as judged

by quality score for each target. Each column shows one of the metrics we used to evaluate performance. The scales are marked at ± Average Changes relative to the 'Void' group. For GDT-TS, GDC-SC, SphereGrinder and CAD-AA scores, positive changes indicate the quality of the model has been improved by refinement whereas for RMSD and MolProbity, negative changes represent improvement. Black points are statistically distinguishable from the Null group; gray points are indistinguishable (Wilcoxon signed-rank test, P=0.05). A chevron indicates that the corresponding score is off the scale.

Table 4. *p*-values of score changes (Wilcoxon signed-rank test) relative to starting model for the top server groups in CASP10 refinement experiment*

Selection	Group Name	P_{GDT-TS}	P_{RMSD} (Å)	P_{GDC-SC}	P_{MP}[a]	P_{SG}[b]	P_{CAD-AA}
First Model	MULTICOM-CONSTRUCT[c]	0.206377	**0.001270**	**0.000196**	0.102297	**0.035156**	**0.000977**
	chuo-fams-server	0.705321	0.002984	0.420913	0.557197	0.075062	1.000000
	YASARA	0.001715	0.663197	0.338008	**0.000232**	0.029442	0.012940
	MULTICOM-NOVEL	0.101554	0.800817	0.075386	0.107752	0.982396	0.629059
	PMS	0.000590	0.046136	0.782327	0.062602	0.248658	0.930290
	chuo-repack-server	0.000123	0.002466	0.000764	0.000526	0.006444	0.000011
	FRESS_server	0.000024	0.005522	0.000618	$6.64*10^{-6}$	0.004414	0.000017
	MUFOLD-QA	0.000021	0.000392	0.000447	0.001226	0.000214	0.000122
Best Model	MULTICOM-CONSTRUCT[c]	**0.011201**	**0.004240**	**0.000108**	0.178480	**0.004181**	**0.000488**
	PMS	0.312444	0.367622	0.121221	0.107443	0.763939	0.115318
	MULTICOM-NOVEL	0.555264	0.009355	0.485959	0.033486	0.146779	0.803619
	chuo-fams-server	0.705321	0.002984	0.420913	0.557197	0.075062	1.000000
	YASARA	0.001715	0.663197	0.338008	**0.000232**	0.029442	0.012940
	chuo-repack-server	0.000123	0.004268	0.000764	0.000526	0.006444	0.000011
	FRESS_server	0.001396	0.085835	0.014257	$7.44*10^{-6}$	0.015651	0.000402
	MUFOLD-QA	0.000112	0.004061	0.004277	0.027268	0.003859	0.001248

*Numbers in bold indicates statistically significant positive results at P = 0.05.
[a]P-values for change in MolProbity score.
[b]P-values for change in SphereGrinder score.
[c]CASP10 group name for i3Drefine.
doi:10.1371/journal.pone.0069648.t004

Comparison between first model and the best model of i3Drefine shows that effectiveness of the iterative version of the protocol against the non-iterative version (3Drefine). Except MolProbity, the iterative version enhances all the quality measures in terms of cumulative improvement relative to starting models as shown in Table 3. Also, the *p*-values of Wilcoxon signed-rank test are lower for the best model compared to the first model in GDT-TS, RMSD, GDC-SC, MolProbity and CAD-AA scores as reported in Table 4. In short, the degree of refinement as well as their statistical significance in the iterative version is, therefore, more pronounced than the non-iterative version of the protocol.

Comparison of i3Drefine with Top Five Human Predictors Participating in CASP10

Figure 8 shows the quartile plots of change in model quality relative to the starting model in six quality metrics for all submitted model by top five human predictors as per the official CASP10 results released during CASP10 meeting and i3Drefine for all CASP10 refinement targets. The most obvious added benefit of human predictors is the ability to perform large improvement in model quality. Groups like FEIG, Seok, Mufold and FLOUDAS seem to perform large changes in starting structures. Although the degree of refinement in these adventurous refinement strategies are much more pronounced than i3Drefine, these methods often lack the ability to perform consistent improvement. Encouragingly, the ability of i3Drefine to perform steady and consistent improvement is noticeable even when it is compared with non-server methods participating in CASP10 refinement experiment. Majority of the times, i3Drefine improves all the quality scores except MolProbity. KnowMIN protocol seems to be more conservative refinement approach than other top-performing human groups. Except SphereGrinder, KnowMIN group improves in the other quality metrics consistently. Among the top-performing human predictors, FEIG group is particularly noteworthy in its ability to improve the backbone positioning as measured by GDT-TS score accompanied by enhancement in local quality measures like MolProbity and CAD-AA. This is possibly achieved through a broader sampling around the starting model. It has to be noted, however, that the human predictors were given three weeks deadline to submit the refined structures to the prediction centre as opposed to three days deadline offered for the server methods and there might be significant human intervention involved in the non-server prediction primarily because of the relaxed submission window. A server group like MULTICOM-CONSTRUCT (i3Drefine), on the other hand, has to be completely automated in order to meet the submission deadline. It is, therefore, unfair to directly compare a server method with human groups especially when the turnaround time for a human predictor is not known. Nevertheless, the ability of human predictors to perform larger improvement can advance the field of protein structure refinement, thereby enhancing the accuracy of contemporary computational protein structure prediction methods provided these methods can be automated providing the prediction within a reasonable amount of time. In addition to being directly implemented in an automated server, human predictors in the CASP experiments often generate valuable insights and guidance for improving protein structure refinement in general.

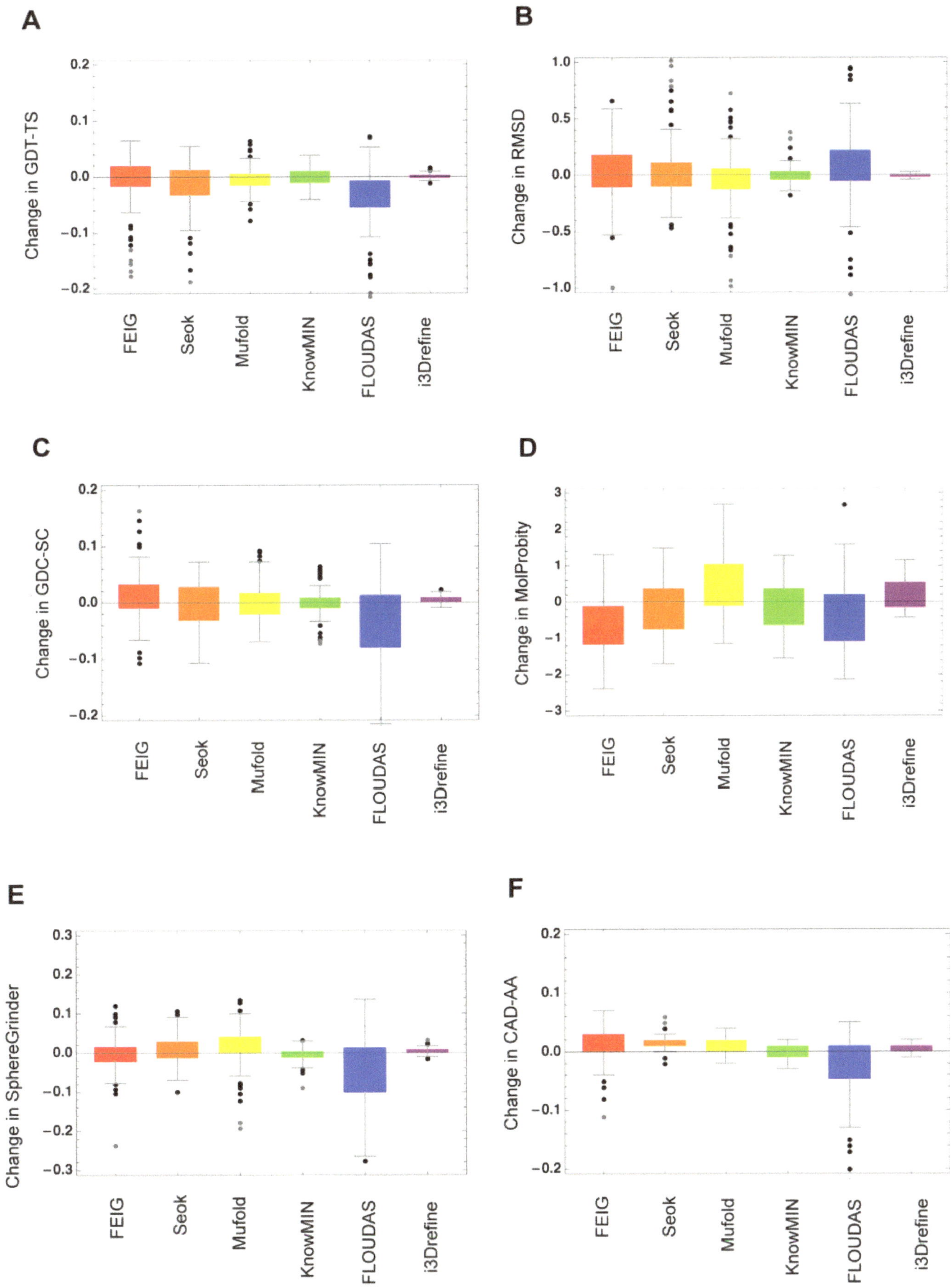

Figure 8. Quartile plots of score changes with respect to the quality of starting structures for top human predictors and i3Drefine. Quartile plots of score changes relative to starting models for 5 human predictors and i3Drefine are shown for these metrics: (A) GDT-TS, (B) RMSD, (C) GDC-SC, (D) MolProbity, (E) SphereGrinder and (F) CAD-AA. The points outside the boxes indicate the outliers.

CONCLUSIONS

In this work, we present a computationally inexpensive and reliable protocol for protein structure refinement, called i3Drefine and systematically analyze its performance in a completely blind mode on the targets issued for refinement category in recently concluded CASP10 experiment based on a diverse set of quality metrics. When compared with other state-of-the-art server predictors participating in CASP10, i3Drefine is observed to perform more consistently than other methods. Future directions would be to explore the possibility of i3Drefine method to perform larger improvement the quality measures by performing a broader sampling around the starting model and possible amendments to the composite force filed. The executable version of i3Drefine software is freely available to the community providing open access to an efficient refinement method. The low computational cost and high accuracy of the i3Drefine protocol will allow this consistent refinement method to be run on a genome scale or be adopted as a final step in computational structure prediction pipeline.

ACKNOWLEDGMENTS

The authors thank Dr. Chen Keasar for making the MESHI software package available.

AUTHOR CONTRIBUTIONS

Conceived and designed the experiments: DB JC. Performed the experiments: DB. Analyzed the data: DB JC. Wrote the paper: DB JC.

REFERENCES

1. Kopp J, Bordoli L, Battey JND, Kiefer F, Schwede T (2007) Assessment of CASP7 predictions for template-based modeling targets. Proteins: Structure, Function, and Bioinformatics 69: 38–56. doi: 10.1002/prot.21753
2. Keedy DA, Williams CJ, Headd JJ, Arendall WB, Chen VB, et al. (2009) The other 90% of the protein: Assessment beyond the Cαs for CASP8 template-based and high-accuracy models. Proteins: Structure, Function, and Bioinformatics 77: 29–49. doi: 10.1002/prot.22551
3. Mariani V, Kiefer F, Schmidt T, Haas J, Schwede T (2011) Assessment of template based protein structure predictions in CASP9. Proteins: Structure, Function, and Bioinformatics.
4. Cozzetto D, Kryshtafovych A, Fidelis K, Moult J, Rost B, et al. (2009) Evaluation of template-based models in CASP8 with standard measures. Proteins: Structure, Function, and Bioinformatics 77: 18–28. doi: 10.1002/prot.22561
5. Jauch R, Yeo HC, Kolatkar PR, Clarke ND (2007) Assessment of CASP7 structure predictions for template free targets. Proteins: Structure, Function, and Bioinformatics 69: 57–67. doi: 10.1002/prot.21771
6. Ben-David M, Noivirt-Brik O, Paz A, Prilusky J, Sussman JL, et al. (2009) Assessment of CASP8 structure predictions for template free targets. Proteins: Structure, Function, and Bioinformatics 77: 50–65. doi: 10.1002/prot.22591
7. Floudas C, Fung H, McAllister S, Mönnigmann M, Rajgaria R (2006) Advances in protein structure prediction and de novo protein design: A review. Chemical Engineering Science 61: 966–988. doi: 10.1016/j.ces.2005.04.009
8. Kinch L, Yong Shi S, Cong Q, Cheng H, Liao Y, et al.. (2011) CASP9 assessment of free modeling target predictions. Proteins: Structure, Function, and Bioinformatics.
9. MacCallum JL, Hua L, Schnieders MJ, Pande VS, Jacobson MP, et al. (2009) Assessment of the protein-structure refinement category in CASP8. Proteins: Structure, Function, and Bioinformatics 77: 66–80. doi: 10.1002/prot.22538
10. MacCallum JL, Pérez A, Schnieders MJ, Hua L, Jacobson MP, et al. (2011) Assessment of protein structure refinement in CASP9. Proteins: Structure, Function, and Bioinformatics 79: 74–90. doi: 10.1002/prot.23131
11. Chen J, Brooks CL (2007) Can molecular dynamics simulations provide high-resolution refinement of protein structure? Proteins: Structure, Function, and Bioinformatics 67: 922–930. doi: 10.1002/prot.21345
12. Fan H, Mark AE (2009) Refinement of homology-based protein structures by molecular dynamics simulation techniques. Protein Science 13: 211–220. doi: 10.1110/ps.03381404
13. Ishitani R, Terada T, Shimizu K (2008) Refinement of comparative models of protein structure by using multicanonical molecular dynamics simulations. Molecular Simulation 34: 327–336. doi: 10.1080/08927020801930539
14. Lee MR, Tsai J, Baker D, Kollman PA (2001) Molecular dynamics in the endgame of protein structure prediction. Journal of molecular biology 313: 417–430. doi: 10.1006/jmbi.2001.5032
15. Misura K, Baker D (2005) Progress and challenges in high-resolution refinement of protein structure models. Proteins: Structure, Function, and Bioinformatics 59: 15–29. doi: 10.1002/prot.20376
16. Sellers BD, Zhu K, Zhao S, Friesner RA, Jacobson MP (2008) Toward better refinement of comparative models: predicting loops in inexact environments. Proteins: Structure, Function, and Bioinformatics 72: 959–971. doi: 10.1002/prot.21990
17. Zhu J, Fan H, Periole X, Honig B, Mark AE (2008) Refining homology models by combining replica-exchange molecular dynamics and statistical potentials. Proteins: Structure, Function, and Bioinformatics 72: 1171–1188. doi: 10.1002/prot.22005
18. Jagielska A, Wroblewska L, Skolnick J (2008) Protein model refinement using an optimized physics-based all-atom force field. Proceedings of the National Academy of Sciences 105: 8268–8273. doi: 10.1073/pnas.0800054105
19. Wroblewska L, Jagielska A, Skolnick J (2008) Development of a physics-based force field for the scoring and refinement of protein models. Biophysical journal 94: 3227–3240. doi: 10.1529/biophysj.107.121947

20. Bhattacharya D, Cheng J (2012) 3Drefine: Consistent protein structure refinement by optimizing hydrogen bonding network and atomic-level energy minimization. Proteins: Structure, Function, and Bioinformatics.

21. Kalisman N, Levi A, Maximova T, Reshef D, Zafriri-Lynn S, et al. (2005) MESHI: a new library of Java classes for molecular modeling. Bioinformatics 21: 3931–3932. doi: 10.1093/bioinformatics/bti630

22. Liu DC, Nocedal J (1989) On the limited memory BFGS method for large scale optimization. Mathematical programming 45: 503–528. doi: 10.1007/bf01589116

23. Levitt M, Hirshberg M, Sharon R, Daggett V (1995) Potential energy function and parameters for simulations of the molecular dynamics of proteins and nucleic acids in solution. Computer Physics Communications 91: 215–231. doi: 10.1016/0010-4655(95)00049-l

24. Summa CM, Levitt M (2007) Near-native structure refinement using in vacuo energy minimization. Proceedings of the National Academy of Sciences 104: 3177–3182. doi: 10.1073/pnas.0611593104

25. Zhang J, Liang Y, Zhang Y (2011) Atomic-level protein structure refinement using fragment-guided molecular dynamics conformation sampling. Structure 19: 1784–1795. doi: 10.1016/j.str.2011.09.022

26. Kabsch W, Sander C (1983) Dictionary of protein secondary structure: pattern recognition of hydrogen-bonded and geometrical features. Biopolymers 22: 2577–2637. doi: 10.1002/bip.360221211

27. Zemla A (2003) LGA: a method for finding 3D similarities in protein structures. Nucleic acids research 31: 3370–3374. doi: 10.1093/nar/gkg571

28. Kabsch W (1976) A solution for the best rotation to relate two sets of vectors. Acta Crystallographica Section A: Crystal Physics, Diffraction, Theoretical and General Crystallography 32: 922–923. doi: 10.1107/s0567739476001873

29. Chen VB, Arendall WB, Headd JJ, Keedy DA, Immormino RM, et al. (2009) MolProbity: all-atom structure validation for macromolecular crystallography. Acta Crystallographica Section D: Biological Crystallography 66: 12–21. doi: 10.1107/s0907444909042073

30. Olechnovič K, Kulberkytė E, Venclovas Č (2012) CAD-score: A new contact area difference-based function for evaluation of protein structural models. Proteins: Structure, Function, and Bioinformatics.

31. Abagyan RA, Totrov MM (1997) Contact area difference (CAD): a robust measure to evaluate accuracy of protein models. Journal of molecular biology 268: 678–685. doi: 10.1006/jmbi.1997.0994

CHAPTER 19

PUTTING THE PIECES TOGETHER: INTEGRATIVE MODELING PLATFORM SOFTWARE FOR STRUCTURE DETERMINATION OF MACROMOLECULAR ASSEMBLIES

Daniel Russel[1], Keren Lasker[1,2], Ben Webb[1], Javier Vela´zquez-Muriel[1], Elina Tjioe[1], Dina Schneidman-Duhovny[1], Bret Peterson[3], Andrej Sali[1]

[1] Department of Bioengineering and Therapeutic Sciences, Department of Pharmaceutical Chemistry, California Institute for Quantitative Biosciences (QB3), University of California, San Francisco, San Francisco, California, United States of America

[2] Raymond and Beverly Sackler Faculty of Exact Sciences, Blavatnik School of Computer Science, Tel Aviv University, Tel-Aviv, Israel

[3] Google, Mountain View, California, United States of America

INTRODUCTION

Building models of a biological system that are consistent with the myriad data available is one of the key challenges in biology. Modeling the structure and dynamics of macromolecular assemblies, for example, can give insights into how biological systems work, evolved, might be controlled, and even designed. Modeling can also suggest future experiments. Unfortunately, current publishing norms make it hard to build on published models, because such models are often not available in usable form and because it is hard to publish refinements of others' models. Here, we present steps towards a future in which a scientist can read a paper, download a script, add new data, and see how the new data improve the published model. Integrative structure modeling casts the building of structural models as a computational optimization problem, for which information about the assembly is encoded into a scoring function that evaluates candidate models. We describe our software suite, Integrated Modeling Platform, and invite members of the scientific community to use it, improve on it, and apply it to their own scientific problems of interest.

Citation: Russel D, Lasker K, Webb B, Velázquez-Muriel J, Tjioe E, Schneidman-Duhovny D, et al. (2012) Putting the Pieces Together: Integrative Modeling Platform Software for Structure Determination of Macromolecular Assemblies. PLoS Biol 10(1): e1001244. doi:10.1371/journal.pbio.1001244

Numerous structures have to date been solved by using an integrative structural modeling approach. The structure of the 26S proteasome was determined from an electron microscopy (EM) map of the whole assembly, proteomics data about its subunit composition, and comparative protein structure models of the component proteins [1]. The structure of the bacterial type II pilus was assembled from sparse nuclear magnetic resonance (NMR) data and X-ray crystallographic structures of constituent proteins [2]. The structure of chromatin around the alpha-globin gene was assembled from so-called 5C data (chromosome conformation capture carbon copy) [3]. The value of integrative modeling is illustrated by its application to the yeast nuclear pore complex (NPC) [4],[5]. The sheer size and flexibility of the NPC makes it all but impossible to solve its molecular architecture by conventional atomic resolution techniques, such as X-ray crystallography. However, integrating information from multiple sources, including stoichiometry from protein quantification, protein proximities from subcomplex purification, protein positions from immuno-EM, sedimentation analysis that sheds light on protein and subcomplex shapes, and the overall NPC shape from EM, resulted in an ensemble of medium-resolution models. The models were summarized by a 3-D probability map, resembling an EM map and localizing the 456 constituent proteins with an average precision of approximately 5 nm. This map has revealed fundamental new insights into the function of the NPC as a gatekeeper controlling the entry into and exit from the nucleus of macromolecules, and also shed light on its evolution [4],[6]–[8].

Integrative modeling entails a computational encoding of the standard scientific cycle of gathering data, proposing hypotheses, and then gathering more data to test and refine those hypotheses. It proceeds through repeated iterations of the stages of gathering information, choosing how to represent and evaluate models, finding models that score well, and analyzing the models and information (Figure 1; Box 1). The cycle terminates when a convergent ensemble of models is found fitting the current information and the models have been judged to be satisfactory [9]. When new information is gathered, whether by other scientists or other techniques, the cycle is resumed.

Box 1. The Four Stages of the Integrative Modeling Cycle

Stage 1: Gathering Information

Information is collected in the form of data from wet lab experiments, as well as statistical tendencies such as atomic statistical potentials, physical laws such as molecular mechanics force fields, and any other feature that can be converted into a score for use to assess features of a structural model.

Stage 2: Choosing How To Represent And Evaluate Models

The resolution of the representation depends on the quantity and resolution of the available information and should be commensurate with the resolution of the final models: different parts of a model may be represented at different resolutions, and one part of the model may be represented at several different resolutions simultaneously. The scoring function evaluates whether or not a given model is consistent with the input information, taking into account the uncertainty in the information.

Stage 3: Finding Models That Score Well

The search for models that score well is performed using any of a variety of sampling and optimization schemes (such as the Monte Carlo method). There may be many models that score well if the data are incomplete or none if the data are inconsistent due to errors or unconsidered states of the assembly.

Stage 4: Analyzing Resulting Models and Information

The ensemble of good-scoring models needs to be clustered and analyzed to ascertain their precision and accuracy, and to check for inconsistent information. Analysis can also suggest what are likely to be the most informative experiments to perform in the next iteration.

Integrative modeling iterates through these stages until a satisfactory model is built. Many iterations of the cycle may be required, given the need to gather more data as well as to resolve errors and inconsistent data.

The integrative approach has a number of advantages over informal or partial consideration of available information (Box 2). Fully realizing these advantages requires encoding modeling efforts into integrative modeling applications that consist of the scripts and the associated information. Adoption of integrative modeling can occur through a tight collaboration between a computational lab and an experimental lab, through direct adoption by an experimental lab, or by experimentalists modifying existing integrative modeling applications. To facilitate widespread adoption, we have developed the Integrative Modeling Platform (IMP) software package.

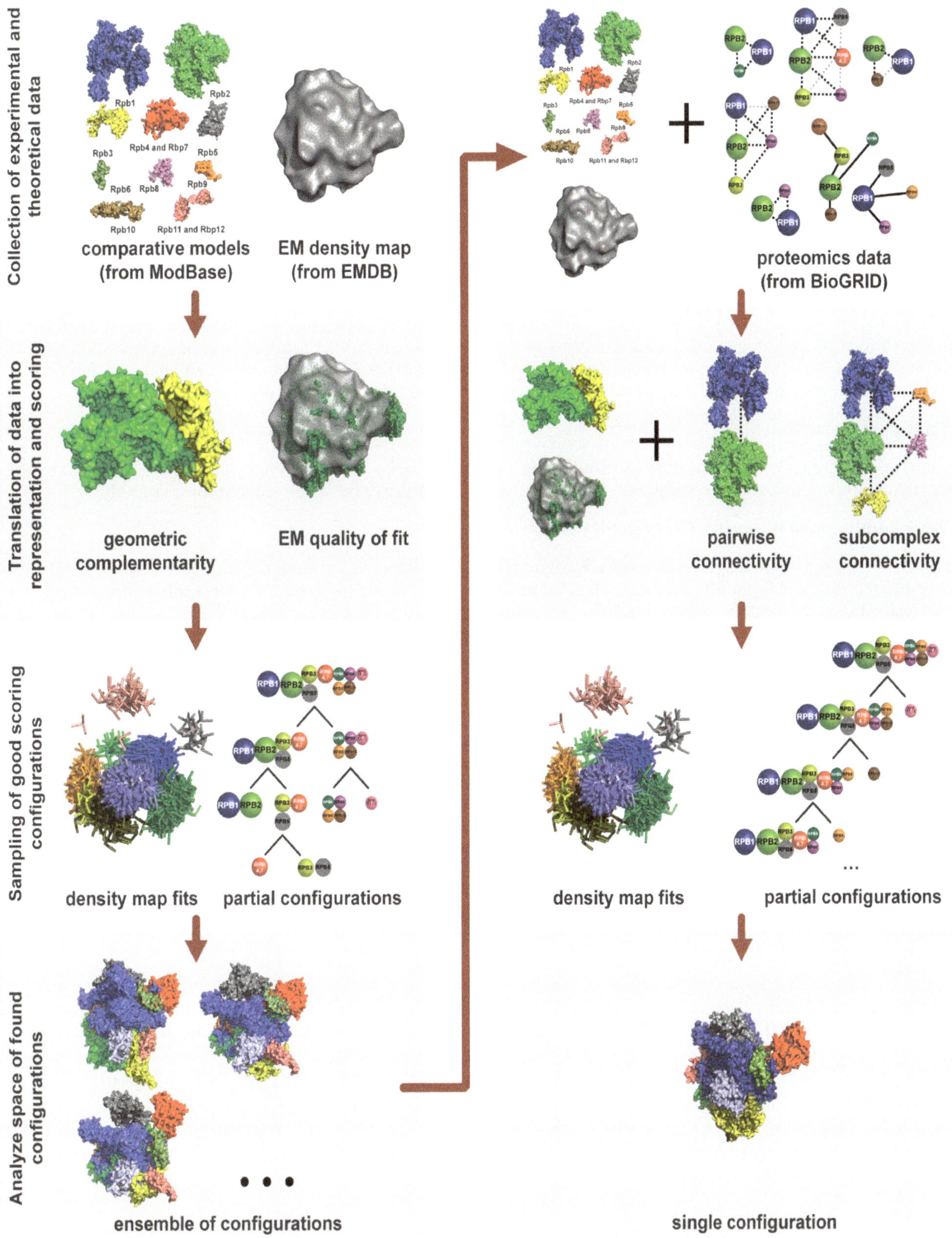

Figure 1. Integrative structure modeling of the human RNA Polymerase II [10]. The first round of modeling was performed using only the 2nm EM density map of the assembly from EMDB [51] and subunit comparative models from ModBase [47], on the basis of the crystallographic structures of the yeast RNAPII proteins. The data were found to be insufficient to uniquely resolve the structure. To overcome this challenge, protein interaction networks extracted from BioGrid [48] were added. The addition of these data resulted in a single structure. The scripts are available as part of IMP.

Box 2. Advantages of the Integrative Structure Modeling Approach

Using New Information

Integrative modeling makes it easy to take advantage of new information and new types of information, resulting in a low barrier for using incremental information that is generally not applied to structure characterization. Even when a single data type is relatively uninformative, multiple types can give a surprisingly complete picture of an assembly [9],[10].

Maximizing Accuracy, Precision and Completeness

Integrative models fit multiple types of information, and can thus be more accurate, precise, and complete than models based on the individual sources.

Understanding and Assessing the Models

By exhaustively sampling the space of models fitting the information, integrative modeling can find all models fitting the information, not only one. A full sampling of the models of a structure can improve the understanding of its function [49]. Because the data are encoded in scoring functions and the full set of models can be found, integrative modeling facilitates assessing the input information and output models in terms of precision and accuracy.

Planning Experiments

Integrative modeling provides feedback to guide future experiments, by computationally testing the impact of hypothetical datasets. As a result, experiments can be chosen to best improve our knowledge of the assembly.

Understanding and Assessing Experimental Accuracy

Data errors present a challenge for all methods of model building. Integrative modeling can detect inconsistent data as no models will exist that fit all the data. In addition, integrative modeling facilitates the application of more sophisticated methods for error estimation, such as Inferential Structure Determination [16].

Box 3. Key Requirements for Integrative Modeling Infrastructure

Modular structure

To allow a community of developers to easily add sources of information, sampling schemes or analysis methods, IMP is structured as a collection of self-contained modules that can be developed and distributed independently.

Simple abstractions

Having a set of simple common abstractions allows independently written modules to be used together. The restraint/scoring function abstraction provides one such, allowing arbitrary data to be combined. Representing models as collections of particles with associated data provides another, allowing easy mixing of coarse grained and atomic models.

Easy sharing

IMP provides a platform-independent high level scripting interface for writing integrative modeling applications from data to analysis; this reduces the burden of supporting the applications and so reduces the cost of sharing.

Higher level entry points

IMP provides a set of high level tools to facilitate application of established protocols to new systems. These include Multifit for assembling multiple subunits based on an EM density map, proteomics data and molecular docking [10], and FoXS for computing a SAXS profile of a given structure [50], both of which can be use via web interfaces, from Chimera [24] or from the command line.

A PLATFORM FOR INTEGRATIVE MODELING

The IMP software package facilitates the writing of integrative modeling applications; the development of new model representations, scoring functions, sampling schemes, and analysis methods; and the distribution of integrative modeling applications.

In IMP, models are encoded as collections of particles, each representing a piece of the system. Depending on the data available, particles can be used to create atomic, coarse-grained, or hierarchical representations. It is straightforward to represent a protein at any resolution, from fully flexible atomic models (one particle per atom), to rigid bodies, to coarse-grained models consisting of only one or a few particles for the whole protein (see Figure 1 for a worked-through example, structural modeling of the human RNA polymerase II [10]). Different parts of the model can be represented differently, as dictated by the available information. Each particle has associated attributes, such as coordinates, radius, atom type, rigid body composition, residue information, and mass. If the attributes already in IMP are not sufficient, new attributes can be created and used similarly to the predefined ones. For example, for coarse-grained small angle X-ray scattering (SAXS) scoring, a scattering factor attribute could be associated with the particles representing amino acid residues.

Candidate models are evaluated by a scoring function composed of terms called restraints, each of which measures how well a model agrees with the information from which the restraint was derived. The restraints encode both what is known about structures in general and what is known about this particular structure. Thus, a candidate model that scores well is consistent with all used information. The precision and accuracy of the resulting model increases with the amount and quality of information that is encoded in the restraints. IMP's ever-growing set of scoring function types includes ones for SAXS profiles [11], proteomics data [9], EM images and density maps [10],[12], NMR spectroscopy [2], the CHARMM force-field [13], alignment with related structures [14], and a variety of statistical potentials [15]. IMP has been designed to make it easy for others to develop, use, and distribute new restraints. Other research groups are currently implementing restraints for various mass spectrometry measurements, SAXS, 5C data [3], and atomic structure prediction.

For experimental data, the scoring is generally implemented using a "forward model" [16], which simulates the measurements on the basis of the candidate model and then compares the simulated measurements to the actual measurements. For example, to evaluate the fit to an EM density map, a restraint uses the coordinates, radii, and masses of a set of particles representing the assembly to simulate its density map and then evaluates the cross-correlation with the experimental map.

As with most computational structure efforts, the main demand for computational time in integrative modeling comes from sampling models that satisfy the restraints (good-scoring models). IMP provides a wide variety of tools for building these sampling protocols, including optimization algorithms such as Monte Carlo [17] and conjugate gradients [18], the simplex optimizer from Gnu Scientific Library (GSL) [19], simulation schemes such as molecular dynamics and Brownian dynamics [20], and the Bullet rigid body dynamics engine (http://www.bulletphysics.com), as well as full sampling schemes such as the Gibbs sampler[16], replica exchange [21], and a divide-and-conquer sampler called DOMINO [22].

Finally, IMP provides a variety of tools for comparing, clustering, and analyzing models. These tools can be used to check for quality-of-fit, the existence of multiple states of the system [3], and inconsistent information. Models can be clustered on the basis of root-mean-square deviation (RMSD), placement score [11], and various other metrics. Supported clustering algorithms include k-means, centrality betweenness clustering [23], and simple binning. The resulting clusters and the constituent models as well as restraints can be exported to Chimera[24] and Pymol [25] for visual inspection and further analysis.

IMP has been used to produce a number of models; for example, a eukaryotic ribosome [26], a mammalian ribosome [27], a ryanodine receptor channel [28], the 26S proteasome [1], the Hsp90 chaperonin [29], the TRiC/CCT chaperonin [30], the actin-scruin complex [31], chromatin[3], and the NPC [4]. More information about IMP can be found athttp://integrativemodeling.org/. The website provides a technical introduction, a tutorial, as well as a variety of examples to help users get started. In addition, it contains nightly tests, user and developer email lists, a wiki, and a bug tracker.

TOWARDS OPEN STRUCTURE MODELING

Publication of macromolecular structures has evolved from printed words and pictures to include deposition of coordinates in the Protein Data Bank [32], and more recently deposition of raw input data such as X-ray scattering factors [32], NMR restraints [33], and EM particle images [34]. However, the conversion of the raw data to the final structures is often only briefly described and all too rarely available in a directly usable form [35]–[37], making reproduction and use of the published results laborious or even impossible.

If published papers included integrative modeling applications, a wide variety of researchers would benefit. In particular, experimental labs, which are unlikely otherwise to go through the effort of modeling systems themselves, would be able to use the state-of-the-art model to plan experiments by simulating potential benefits gained from new data. It would also be easy to see how much each new measurement contributes to and fits with the current model. Other computational groups could more easily experiment with new scoring, sampling, and analysis methods, without having to reimplement the existing methods from scratch. The common abstraction would make it easier to mix and match parts of other modeling packages [13],[14],[16],[38]–[46] to improve the applications of integrative modeling. Finally, the authors themselves would maximize the impact of their work, increasing the odds that their results are incorporated into future modeling.

ACKNOWLEDGMENTS

We thank Frank Alber and Friedrich Förster for their contributions to the development of the integrative modeling paradigm; Ben Schwarz and Yannick Spill for contributing to the IMP code and design; Riccardo Pellarin, Massimiliano Bonomi, and Ben Schwarz for insightful comments on early iterations of the paper; and Jeremy Phillips, Frank Alber, Friedrich Förster, Marc Marti-Renom, and Davide Baù for being early users of the IMP library.

REFERENCES

1. Lasker K, Förster F, Bohn S, Walzthoeni T, Villa E, et al. Molecular architecture of the 26S proteasome holocomplex determined by an integrative approach. Proc Natl Acad Sci U S A.
2. Simon B, Madl T, Mackereth C. D, Nilges M, Sattler M (2010) An efficient protocol for NMR-spectroscopy-based structure determination of protein complexes in solution. Angewandte Chemie (International ed in English) 49: 1967–1970.
3. Baù D, Sanyal A, Lajoie B. R, Capriotti E, Byron M, et al. (2010) The three-dimensional folding of the α-globin gene domain reveals formation of chromatin globules. Nature Struct Biol 18: 107–114.

4. Alber F, Dokudovskaya S, Veenhoff L. M, Zhang W, Kipper J, et al. (2007) The molecular architecture of the nuclear pore complex. Nature 450: 695–701.

5. Alber F, Dokudovskaya S, Veenhoff L. M, Zhang W, Kipper J, et al. (2007) Determining the architectures of macromolecular assemblies. Nature 450: 683–694.

6. Wente S. R, Rout M. P (2010) The nuclear pore complex and nuclear transport. Cold Spring Harb Perspect Biol 2: a000562.

7. Devos D, Dokudovskaya S, Williams R, Alber F, Eswar N, et al. (2006) Simple fold composition and modular architecture of the nuclear pore complex. Proc Natl Acad Sci U S A 103: 2172–2177.

8. DeGrasse J. A, DuBois K. N, Devos D, Siegel T. N, Sali A, et al. (2009) Evidence for a shared nuclear pore complex architecture that is conserved from the last common eukaryotic ancestor. Mol Cell Prot 8: 2119–2130.

9. Alber F, Förster F, Korkin D, Topf M, Sali A (2008) Integrating diverse data for structure determination of macromolecular assemblies. Annu Rev Biochem 77: 443–477.

10. Lasker K, Phillips J. L, Russel D, Velazquez-Muriel J, Schneidman-Duhovny D, et al. (2010) Integrative structure modeling of macromolecular assemblies from proteomics data. Mol Cell Prot 9: 1689–1702.

11. Schneidman-Duhovny D, Hammel M, Sali A (2011) Macromolecular docking restrained by a small angle X-ray scattering profile. J Struct Biol 173: 461–471.

12. Lasker K, Sali A, Wolfson H. J (2010) Determining macromolecular assembly structures by molecular docking and fitting into an electron density map. Proteins 78: 3205–3211.

13. Brooks B. R, Brooks C. L, Mackerell A. D, Nilsson L, Petrella R. J, et al. (2009) CHARMM: the biomolecular simulation program. J Comput Chem 30: 1545–1614.

14. Sali A, Blundell T. L (1993) Comparative protein modelling by satisfaction of spatial restraints. J Mol Biol 234: 779–815.

15. Shen M-Y, Sali A (2006) Statistical potential for assessment and prediction of protein structures. Protein Sci 15: 2507–2524.

16. Rieping W, Nilges M, Habeck M (2008) ISD: a software package for Bayesian NMR structure calculation. Bioinformatics (Oxford, England) 24: 1104–1105.

17. Metropolis N, Rosenbluth A. W, Rosenbluth M. N, Teller A. H, Teller E (1953) Equation of state calculation by fast computing machines. J Chem Phys 21: 1087–1092.

18. Press W. H, Flannery B. P, Teukolsky S. A, Vetterling W. T (1997) Numerical recipes in C. Cambridge: Cambridge University Press.

19. Gough B, editor. (2006) GNU Scientific library reference manual. Network Theory Ltd.

20. Schlick T (2002) Molecular modeling and simulation. New York: Springer.

21. Zhou R (2007) Replica exchange molecular dynamics method for protein folding simulation. Methods Mol Biol 350: 205–223.

22. Lasker K, Topf M, Sali A, Wolfson H. J (2009) Inferential optimization for simultaneous fitting of multiple components into a CryoEM map of their assembly. J Mol Biol 388: 180–194.

23. Freeman L (1977) A set of measures of centrality based on betweenness. Sociometry 40: 35–41.

24. Yang Z, Lasker K, Schneidman-Duhovny D, Webb B, Huang C, et al. UCSF Chimera, MODELLER, and IMP: an Integrated Modeling System. J Struct Biol.

25. DeLano W (2002) The PyMOL molecular graphics system. Available: http://pymol.org.

26. Taylor D. J, Devkota B, Huang A. D, Topf M, Narayanan E, et al. (2009) Comprehensive molecular structure of the eukaryotic ribosome. Structure 17: 1591–1604.

27. Chandramouli P, Topf M, Ménétret J-F, Eswar N, Cannone J. J, et al. (2008) Structure of the mammalian 80S ribosome at 8.7 A resolution. Structure 16: 535–548.

28. Serysheva I. I, Ludtke S. J, Baker M. L, Cong Y, Topf M, et al. (2008) Subnanometer-resolution electron cryomicroscopy-based domain models for the cytoplasmic region of skeletal muscle RyR channel. Proc Natl Acad Sci U S A 105: 9610–9615.

29. Krukenberg K. A, Förster F, Rice L. M, Sali A, Agard D. A (2008) Multiple conformations of E. coli Hsp90 in solution: insights into the conformational dynamics of Hsp90. Structure 16: 755–765.

30. Booth C. R, Meyer A. S, Cong Y, Topf M, Sali A, et al. (2008) Mechanism of lid closure in the eukaryotic chaperonin TRiC/CCT. Nature Struct Mol Biol 15: 746–753.

31. Cong Y, Topf M, Sali A, Matsudaira P, Dougherty M, et al. (2008) Crystallographic conformers of actin in a biologically active bundle of filaments. J Mol Biol 375: 331–336.

32. Berman H. M, Westbrook J, Feng Z, Gilliland G, Bhat T. N, et al. (2000) The Protein Data Bank. Nucleic Acids Res 28: 235–242.

33. Ulrich E. L, Akutsu H, Doreleijers J. F, Harano Y, Ioannidis Y. E, et al. (2008) BioMagResBank. Nucleic Acids Res 36: D402–D408.

34. Lawson C. L, Baker M. L, Best C, Bi C, Dougherty M, et al. (2011) EMDataBank.org: unified data resource for CryoEM. Nucleic Acids Res 39: D456–464.

35. Mesirov J. P (2010) Computer science. Accessible reproducible research. Science 327: 415–416.

36. Barnes N (2010) Publish your computer code: it is good enough. Nature 467: 753.

37. Merali Z (2010) Computational science: ...Error. Nature 467: 775–777.

38. Leaver-Fay A, Tyka M, Lewis S. M, Lange O. F, Thompson J, et al. (2011) Rosetta3 an object-oriented software suite for the simulation and design of macromolecules. Methods Enzymol 487: 545–574.

39. Ludtke S. J (2010) 3-D structures of macromolecules using single-particle analysis in EMAN. Methods Mol Biol 673: 157–173.

40. Shaikh T. R, Gao H, Baxter W. T, Asturias F. J, Boisset N, et al. (2008) SPIDER image processing for single-particle reconstruction of biological macromolecules from electron micrographs. Nat Protoc 3: 1941–1974.

41. Schwieters C. D, Kuszewski J. J, Tjandra N, Clore G. M (2003) The Xplor-NIH NMR molecular structure determination package. J Magn Reson 160: 65–73.

42. Adams P. D, Afonine P. V, Bunkoczi G, Chen V. B, Davis I. W, et al. (2010) PHENIX: a comprehensive Python-based system for macromolecular structure solution. Acta Crystallogr D 66: 213–221.

43. Case D. A, Cheatham T. E 3rd, Darden T, Gohlke H, Luo R, et al. (2005) The Amber biomolecular simulation programs. J Comput Chem 26: 1668–1688.

44. Sharma S, Ding F, Nie H, Watson D, Unnithan A, et al. (2006) iFold: a platform for interactive folding simulations of proteins. Bioinformatics 22: 2693–2694.

45. Hess B, Kutzner C, van der Spoel D, Lindahl E (2008) GROMACS 4: algorithms for highly efficient, load-balanced, and scalable molecular simulation. J Chem Theory and Computation 4: 435–447.

46. Peter E, Vijay P (2010) OpenMM: a hardware-independent framework for molecular simulations. Comput Sci Eng 12: 34–39.

47. Pieper U, Webb B. M, Barkan D. T, Schneidman-Duhovny D, Schlessinger A, et al. (2011) ModBase, a database of annotated comparative protein structure models, and associated resources. Nucleic Acids Res 39: D465–D474.

48. Stark C, Breitkreutz B-J, Chatr-Aryamontri A, Boucher L, Oughtred R, et al. (2011) The BioGRID Interaction Database: 2011 update. Nucleic Acids Res 39: D698–D704.

49. Ma W, Trusina A, El-Samad H, Lim W. A, Tang C (2009) Defining network topologies that can achieve biochemical adaptation. Cell 138: 760–773.

50. Schneidman-Duhovny D, Hammel M, Sali A (2010) FoXS: a web server for rapid computation and fitting of SAXS profiles. Nucleic Acids Res 38: W540–W544.

51. Kostek S. A, Grob P, De Carlo S, Lipscomb J. S, Garczarek F, Nogales E (2006) Molecular architecture and conformational flexibility of human RNA polymerase II. Structure 14: 1691–700.

CHAPTER 20

MARATHON: AN OPEN SOURCE SOFTWARE LIBRARY FOR THE ANALYSIS OF MARKOV-CHAIN MONTE CARLO ALGORITHMS

Steffen Rechner[1], Annabell Berger[1,2]

[1] Institute of Computer Science, Martin Luther University Halle-Wittenberg, Halle (Saale), Germany

[2] German Centre of Integrative Biodiversity Research (idiv) Halle-Jena-Leipzig, Leipzig, Germany

ABSTRACT

We present the software library marathon, which is designed to support the analysis of sampling algorithms that are based on the Markov-Chain Monte Carlo principle. The main application of this library is the computation of properties of so-called state graphs, which represent the structure of Markov chains. We demonstrate applications and the usefulness of marathon by investigating the quality of several bounding methods on four well-known Markov chains for sampling perfect matchings and bipartite graphs. In a set of experiments, we compute the total mixing time and several of its bounds for a large number of input instances. We find that the upper bound gained by the famous canonical path method is often several magnitudes larger than the total mixing time and deteriorates with growing input size. In contrast, the spectral bound is found to be a precise approximation of the total mixing time.

INTRODUCTION

The task of random sampling is to return a randomly selected object from a typically large set of objects according to a specified probability distribution. Such tasks often arise in practical applications like network analysis, where properties of a certain network of interest are to be compared with those of a random null model network [1, 2]. Another application is approximate counting of combinatorial objects. While this is typically a hard problem, the number of solutions of a self-reducible problem, however, can be approximated in polynomial time using randomly sampled objects [3]. We consider sampling methods which follow the so-called Markov-Chain Monte Carlo (MCMC) approach. A MCMC algorithm can be considered as a random walk on a directed graph where the vertices of this graph correspond to the set of objects to be sampled from. Starting at an arbitrary vertex, we go to a randomly chosen adjacent vertex and continue our random walk from this vertex; after some time, we stop the random walk. The object representing the final vertex is returned as a random sample. An overview of the surprisingly versatile applications of the MCMC approach was given by Diaconis [4].

Citation: Rechner S, Berger A (2016) Marathon: An Open Source Software Library for the Analysis of Markov-Chain Monte Carlo Algorithms. PLoS ONE 11(1): e0147935. doi:10.1371/journal.pone.0147935.

Motivation

In general, an infinite number of steps will lead to a truly random sample. But what happens if we stop the random walk after a finite number of steps? The number of steps which are necessary to sample from a probability distribution which is close to the desired distribution is known as the total mixing time of a Markov chain, and is of central interest for the applicability of an MCMC algorithm. There are several methods which are able to gain upper bounds on the total mixing time like the canonical path method. Sinclair [5] gives an excellent overview about different bounding techniques. Sometimes, such bounding methods can successfully be applied to Markov Chains to gain upper bounds on their total mixing times. When applied successfully, such upper bounds most often are high-degree polynomials on the size of the input. This is far too large to be applicable in practice, where more than a linear number of steps is infeasible for large input size. In fact, software tools like mfinder [1], which can be used for motif search in large networks, use a MCMC sampling approach with a linear number of steps as default for generation of null models. This leads to the problem that the sampling result might not be as random as desired, resulting in a non-optimal or even incorrect behavior of the application.

On the other hand, it may be the case that upper bounds on the total mixing time are just too pessimistic. From a purely theoretical perspective it is often already a breakthrough to establish that a given Markov chain is rapidly mixing, that is, to establish a polynomial mixing time bound. Since the bounding techniques in Markov chain analysis are often fairly general and worst-case instances in terms of total mixing time are not known, it is not clear, whether the upper bounds gained by such methods are tight for some worst-case instance. However, for practical applicability, it is of eminent importance to find as sharp bounds as possible. Up to now, there is very little knowledge about the gap between the so established upper bounds and tight bounds for actual worst-case instances. Probably most researches in this field will suspect that a considerable real gap exists, but for specific Markov chains it is in general completely open how many orders of magnitude this gap may be large. By this reason, we believe that the true total mixing time might be much lower than proven by theoretical methods. Therefore, our working questions are: a) Is the total mixing time really as large as the bounding methods propose, or is it possible that the bounding methods are just not precise enough to capture the real total mixing time? b) Which bounding method has the best potential and could lead to better results when further information about the structure of state graphs is given?

Contribution

In trying to answer these questions, we developed the C++ library marathon, which has been designed to compute several structural properties of Markov chains and its corresponding state graphs. The library offers the following features:

- Construction of state graphs from arbitrary input instances for a set of user-definable transition rules.
- Computation of structural properties of state graphs.
  - Computation of the total mixing time for arbitrary ϵ.
  - Computation of the congestion bound gained by the canonical path method with an arbitrary, user-definable, path construction scheme.
  - Computation of the upper and lower spectral bound.
  - Computation of network properties like diameter and average path length.

We built this library to easily add algorithms for network analysis. We expect that our library could be helpful both for theoretical scientists as well as for practitioners, who implement MCMC algorithms and have to choose an appropriate number of steps.

As a demonstration on what kind of research can be done with the help of marathon, we analyzed structural properties and investigated the quality of the total mixing time bounds on the example of four well-known Markov chains. From our experiments, we gained several insights.

- We found that the congestion bound is multiple times larger than the corresponding total mixing time for almost all instances. In addition, the quality of the congestion bound deteriorates with growing input size. This indicates that the congestion bounds are bad approximations of the total mixing time, and, since this bound is often used for theoretical analysis, that the high-degree polynomial bounds from theory may be too pessimistic.
- In contrast, the upper spectral bound is close to the total mixing time for all observations. Even if its quality also deteriorates with growing instance size, the spectral bounds keeps close to the total mixing time much longer than the congestion bound.
- The lower spectral bound can be used as a very good approximation for all input instances we investigated in this work. The data suggests an almost linear relationship between the lower spectral bound and total mixing time.
- We figured out several new structural insights about the Markov chains we investigated. For example, we found that the second largest eigenvalue in magnitude is almost always positive. The total mixing time of instances of the same input size can be very diverse and depends on the vertex degree in the state graphs. This shows that the experimental approach provided by our library may lead to structural insights which may be useful to get new intuitions for developing more precise bounding techniques.

From our experiments we can conclude that the canonical path method will not lead to tight bounds of the total mixing time, even when further information about a state graphs structure is included. Instead, developing new methods based on the spectral gap seems to be more promising.

Structure

The remainder of this article is structured as follows: In the next section we give a brief introduction into the theory of Markov chains, in particular, in the concepts of total mixing time and its bounds. Thereafter, we present the main features of the marathon library. In the second part of this article, we demonstrate the applicability of the library in a set of experiments, while trying to answer the questions described above. The results of these experiments are shown and discussed in the final section.

METHODS AND MATERIALS

An important tool for understanding MCMC based sampling processes are Markov chains. To make the following sections more understandable, we will briefly introduce the most important concepts of the theory of Markov chains. For a less steep introduction into the topic, we recommend the lecture notes of Sinclair [6], the textbook by Levin, Peres and Wilmer [7], and the survey of Lovász [8].

Theory of Markov Chains

A Markov chain can be seen as a random walk on a set Ω of combinatorial objects, the so-called states. Two states x, y $\in$ Ω can be connected via a transition arc (x, y)$\in\Psi$, when x can be transformed into y via small local changes. This definition induces a so-called state graph $\Gamma = (\Omega, \Psi)$, representing the objects and their adjacencies. We define for each pair of states x, y $\in \Omega$ the so-called proposal probability $\kappa: \Omega \times \Omega \to [0, 1]$ and a weight function $w : \Omega \to \mathbb{R}^+$. A step from x to y in a random walk is done with transition probability $P(x, y) = \kappa(x, y) \cdot \min(1,w(y)/w(x))$. The matrix $P = (P(x, y)_{x, y \in \Omega})$ is called transition matrix.

Algorithm 1 shows the classical random walk based sampling method. A random state b $\in \Omega$ is returned, sampled from a probability distribution $p_a^{(t)}$ which describes a state's probability after t steps when starting at state a $\in \Omega$. The fundamental theorem for Markov chains (see for example [7]) says that the distribution $p_a^{(t)}$ converges for $t \to \infty$ to the unique stationary distribution π with $\pi(y) = \frac{w(y)}{\sum_{x\in\Omega} w(x)}$ for all y $\in \Omega$ and initial states a $\in \Omega$, if the state graph Γ is non-bipartite, connected and reversible with respect to π, i.e. $\pi(x) P(x, y) = \pi(y)P(y, x)$ for each pair of states x, y $\in \Omega$. Markov chains which fulfil these properties are called ergodic.

Algorithm 1 Random Walk

Input: State a $\in \Omega$, number t of steps.

Output: State b $\in \Omega$, according to probability distribution $p_a^{(t)}$

.

1: x $\leftarrow$ a

2: **for** i $\leftarrow$ 1 **to** t **do**

3: **Neighbour selection**: Pick a neighbour y of x with probability $\kappa(x, y)$.

4: **Metropolis rule**: x $\leftarrow$ y with probability $\min\left(1, \frac{w(y)}{w(x)}\right)$

5: **end for**

6: **return** x

Total Mixing Time.

The total variation distance measures the distance between two probability distributions μ and η:

$$||\mu - \eta|| := \frac{1}{2}\sum_{x\in\Omega}|\mu(x) - \eta(x)|. \quad (1)$$

We define $\tau_a(\epsilon) := \min\{t \in \mathbb{N}: ||p_a^{(t)} - \pi|| \leq \epsilon\}$ as the minimal number of steps a random walk has to take to reach a distribution which is close to ϵ to its stationary distribution when starting at state a $\in \Omega$. The total mixing time $\tau(\epsilon)$ of a Markov chain is defined as

$$\tau(\epsilon) := \max_{a\in\Omega}\{\tau_a(\epsilon)\}. \quad (2)$$

A Markov chain is known as rapidly mixing, if $\tau(\epsilon)$ can be bounded from above by a polynomial which depends on the input size n and the parameter ϵ^{-1}. The total mixing time can be bounded by several techniques. We briefly present two widely used bounding methods which we investigate in the remainder of this article.

Spectral Bound

Let $1 = \lambda_1 > \lambda_2 \geq \ldots \geq \lambda_{|\Omega|} > -1$ be the real eigenvalues of the transition matrix P and let λ_{max} be defined as $\lambda_{max} = \max\{|\lambda_2|, |\lambda_\Omega|\}$. The total mixing time can be bounded by the lower and upper spectral bound[5], i.e.,

$$\tau(\epsilon) \leq (1 - \lambda_{\max})^{-1} \cdot \left(\ln(\epsilon^{-1}) + \ln(\pi_{\min}^{-1})\right) \quad (3)$$

$$\tau(\epsilon) \geq \frac{1}{2}\lambda_{\max}(1 - \lambda_{\max})^{-1}\ln(2\epsilon)^{-1}, \quad (4)$$

where π_{min} denotes the smallest component of π. The transition matrix P is not necessarily symmetric. However, it can be transformed into a symmetrical matrix:

$$P_{sym} = D^{-1/2} \cdot P \cdot D^{1/2}, \quad (5)$$

where D is the $|\Omega| \times |\Omega|$ diagonal matrix with the components of π on its main diagonal. This transformation relies on the reversibility of a Markov chain. It is a classical result that P_{sym} has the same eigenvalues as P.

Congestion Bound

Sinclair's multi commodity flow method[5] is often used for bounding the total mixing time. Let $\mathcal{P} = \bigcup_{x\neq y}\mathcal{P}_{xy}$ be a family of simple paths in Γ, each P_{xy} consisting of simple paths between x and y $\in \Omega$. The maximum load congestion ρ, with respect to P, is then defined as

$$\rho(\mathcal{P}) = \max_{(u,v)\in\Psi} \frac{\sum_{p\in\mathcal{P}(u,v)\in p}\pi(x)\pi(y)|p|}{\pi(u)P(u, v)}. \quad (6)$$

For any system of paths P the total mixing time of a reversible Markov chain can be bounded by the congestion bound, i.e.,

$$\tau(\epsilon) \leq \rho(\mathcal{P}) \cdot \left(\ln(\epsilon^{-1}) + \ln(\pi_{\min}^{-1})\right). \quad (7)$$

The quality of the congestion bounds depend on the path construction scheme P. The congestion bound is often used to gain theoretical bounds on the total mixing time.

The Marathon Library

In this section, we introduce the main features of the marathon library. Our source code is published under MIT license and freely available at https://github.com/srechner/marathon. To install, just follow the instruction manual at github. Several example programs are available.

The marathon library is designed for the study of structural properties of Markov chains, respectively their corresponding state graphs. One of its current main applications is the computation of the total mixing time and several of its bounds. The suggested way to use our library is to implement the transition rules of a Markov chain and conduct some experiments to quickly learn some properties which are typically hard to find in theory. In particular, we allow the computation of the eigenvalue λ_{max} and the application of the canonical path method to compute the congestion bound with some path congestion scheme. This way, one can quickly evaluate whether a scheme captures the total mixing time closely or if there is a noticeable gap. The marathon library has been designed with two main goals in mind: Performance and Extensibility. Aiming for the first goal, we use the C++ programming language, so that various highly efficient third party libraries become available. In particular, we use CUDA[9] and OpenMP[10] to accelerate compute-intense tasks with the use of multi-core processors and highly parallel graphic processing units. To achieve the second goal, we designed our library for easy extensibility. Our representation of the state graphs is versatile enough to allow the integration of arbitrary graph algorithms. Moreover, we provide interfaces to simplify the programming effort and to hide complexity from the user. For example, adding a new Markov chain is done in a few steps:

Implement a data structure which represents a state, here simply called State.

- Create a class which implements the MarkovChain interface, using State as a template parameter. The following virtual methods have to be overridden:
  - The method MarkovChain::arbitraryState, constructs an arbitrary state from a given input string (e.g. construct a bipartite graph from a given bipartite degree sequence).
  - The method MarkovChain::neighbours, takes an object u of type State and creates a list of adjacent states N_u whose elements are the result of all valid random choices within u plus their corresponding proposal probability κ, according to the set of transition rules.

In many cases this can be done within about 200 lines of code with a high amount of re-usability. Example chains have been included within the library. We will now give a detailed description of the algorithmic ideas behind the most important methods available in the library.

Construction of the State Graph.

Given an instance representation (e.g. a degree sequence), the first step of the analysis is the construction of the state graph for the given instance. The purpose of this step is to gain a sparse representation of the state graph $\Gamma = (\Omega, \Psi)$. Initializing Ω with an arbitrary state generated by the MarkovChain::arbitraryState method, we perform a full graph scan to iteratively enumerate the set of states and transition arcs. In each step, we select a state $u \in \Omega$ and enumerate all its adjacent states N_u via the MarkovChain::neighbors method. We add a transition arc (u, v) with proposal probability κ(u, v) to Ψ for each adjacent state $v \in N_u$ and add v to Ω, if not already included. At the end of this step, we have a complete list Ω of states and an adjacency list representation of the transition arcs Ψ. The probability of each transition $(u, v) \in \Psi$ is subsequently computed as κ(u, v) · min(1, w(v)/w(u)), where the function $w : \Omega \rightarrow \mathbb{R}^+$ can optionally be overridden to enable the Metropolis rule (see Algorithm 1). The construction of the state graph relies on connectedness of the state graph, which is given whenever the Markov chain is irreducible. The construction of the state graph is a sequential process, consuming $O(|\Omega| + |\Psi|)$ time and memory.

Computation of the Total Mixing Time.

We compute the total mixing time τ(ϵ) of a state graph based on the following idea: Let P be the transition matrix of an ergodic Markov chain and let $a \in \Omega$ be an initial state. One step of the random walk changes the probability distribution $p_a^{(t)}$ to $p_a^{(t+1)} = p_a^{(t)}$. Iterating this argument, the distribution after t steps is given by

$$p_a^{(t)} = p_a^{(0)} \cdot P^t, \qquad \textbf{(8)}$$

where $p_a^{(0)}$ is a row vector whose components are $p_a^{(0)}(a) = 1$ for the initial state a and $p_a^{(0)}(i) = 0$, for $i \neq a$. So, each row of the matrix P^t gives the distribution to a certain $p_a^{(t)}$ for $a \in \Omega$. The total mixing time τ(ϵ) can therefore be computed from P by iterated matrix multiplication. The principle can be described as follows: We transform the adjacency list representation of Γ into its adjacency matrix representation. The entries $P_{i,j}$ of this matrix represent the transition probabilities for going from state i to state j, so this matrix is the transition matrix described above. Since the total variation distance decreases monotonically with t, we can find τ(ϵ) with a two-step procedure.

- Starting with i = 0, we iteratively increment i until $\max_{a\in\Omega}||p_a^{(2^i)} - \pi|| \leq \epsilon$. This requires, in fact, just a sequence of $i = \lceil \log_2(\tau(\epsilon)) \rceil$ matrix squaring operations to compute the matrices $P^2, P^4, P^8, \ldots, P^{2i}$. At the end of step one, we know that the total mixing time τ(ϵ) lies in the range $2^{i-1} < \tau(\epsilon) \leq 2^i$.
- We use binary search to find τ(ϵ). We define two variables $l = 2^{i-1}$ and $r = 2^i$ representing respectively lower and upper bounds on τ(ϵ). In a sequence of $\log_2(r - l) = \lceil \log_2(\tau(\epsilon)) \rceil - 1$ iterations, we half the search space in each step by computing the total variation distance $\max_{a\in\Omega}||p_a^{(m)} - \pi||$ with $m = \lfloor (l + r)/2 \rfloor$ from P^m. Although P^m could, in principle, be computed from P with binary exponentiation, we save additional matrix multiplications by reusing P^l to compute $P^m = P^l P^{m-l}$. Maintaining the invariant $\max_{a\in\Omega}||p_a^{(l)} - \pi|| > \epsilon \geq \max_{a\in\Omega}||p_a^{(r)} - \pi||$ we update the lower bound l or the upper bound r, depending, whether the total variation distance is larger than ϵ or not. We stop when $l \geq r$. The value of r is the total mixing time.

Computing the total mixing time requires $O(|\Omega|^2)$ memory and $O(\log(\tau(\epsilon)) \cdot |\Omega|^{\omega})$ time, where ω is the exponent of the matrix multiplication algorithm. (In most libraries, ω is equal to 3. However, the matrix multiplication implementation can be exchanged by using another implementation when building the library.)

Computing the total mixing time is currently by far the most time and memory consuming operation in our library. Due to quadratic memory requirement, it is applicable only for small state graphs with $|\Omega| \leq 30000$ (depending on main memory). Since this method is also very time-consuming, we provide three implementations, which can be used if the appropriate hardware is available:

- A classical CPU implementation on the basis of openBLAS[11], which runs in parallel on multi-core CPUs. This method should be used for very small instances, or if no CUDA-capable GPU is available.
- A cuBLAS[12] based GPU implementation which can be significantly faster than the CPU implementation. Because of the lack of memory on most GPUs, this implementation is designed for small state graphs with $|\Omega| \leq 15000$ (depending on GPU memory).
- A CPU-GPU hybrid implementation using the cuBLASXt[13] library for matrix multiplication. This implementation should be the method of choice if a CUDA capable GPU is available. This method is typically faster than the CPU implementation and has the additional advantage that the CPU is free to be used for other computations.

The three implementations share the same asymptotical running time, but differ greatly in practice (see Fig 1 for a comparison of performance). Since most of the work is matrix multiplication, this comparison almost directly maps to a performance comparison between the corresponding libraries for matrix multiplication. The $O(\log(\tau(\epsilon)))$ invocations of the total variation distance computation, each with time complexity of $O(|\Omega|^2)$, contribute only a little to the running time.

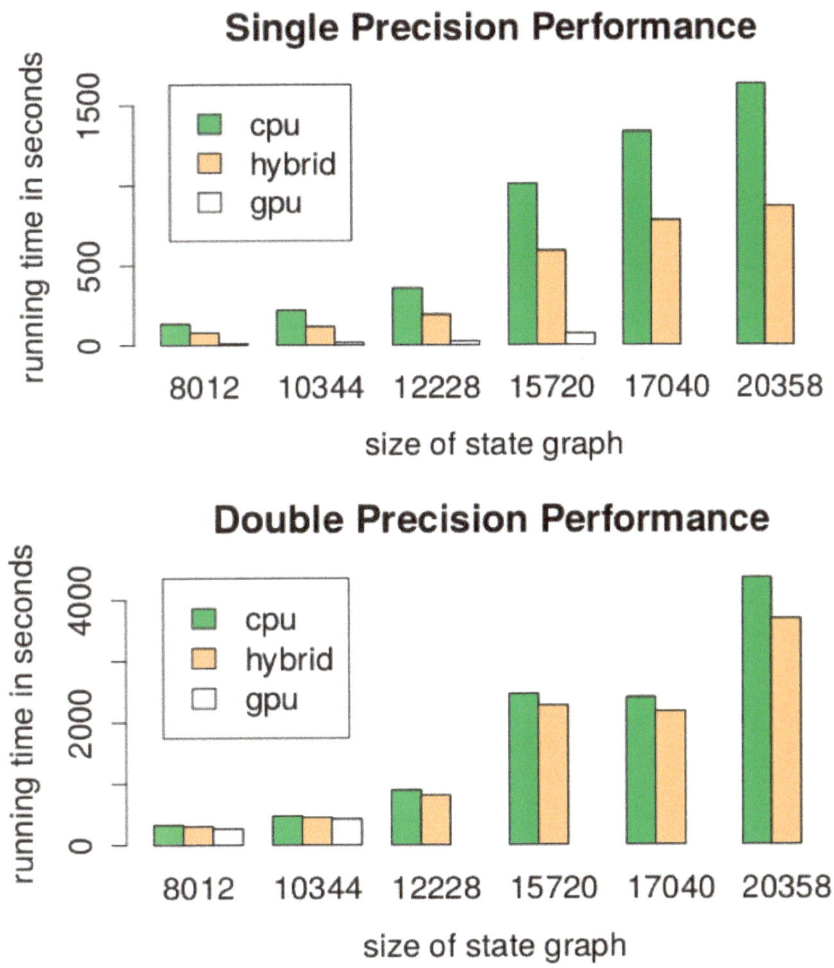

Figure 1. Single and double precision performance of the total mixing time computation. The charts show the running time for the computation of the total mixing time on the example of five state graphs of size 8012 to 20358. Due to the relatively small amount of GPU memory on our test system, only the first four (respectively two) state graphs could be processed by the GPU implementation in single precision mode (respectively double precision mode). The running times were measured on an Ubuntu 14.04 system with a Intel Xeon E3-1231, NVIDIA GeForce GTX 970 (4 GB GPU memory) and 16 GB of main memory, using gcc in version 4.8.4 and CUDA in version 7.0.

Computation of the Spectral Bound.

The difference between the largest and the second largest eigenvalue $(1 - \lambda_{max})$ of a Markov chain's transition matrix is known as the spectral gap and is of central interest in mixing time analysis. To compute this quantity, we use the well-known ARPACK++[14] library to compute the two real eigenvalues with the largest magnitude of the transition matrix P. In case of non-symmetric transition rules, we first transform the transition matrix P into the symmetrical matrix P_{sym} via Eq (5). After computing both eigenvalues with the largest magnitude, we use the second eigenvalue in order to compute the upper and lower spectral bound via Inequalities Eqs(3) and (4). Since this method requires only a sparse representation of the transition matrix, it is also applicable for large state graphs.

Computing the Congestion Bound.

As stated in the introduction, we are also interested in the quality of other bounding techniques. In particular, we are interested in the canonical path method which is often used to gain theoretical bounds. We implemented a method that can be used to gain an upper bound on the mixing time by computing the maximal congestion of a user-definable path construction scheme. Four each pair of states (u, v) $\in \Omega \times \Omega$ we apply the path construction scheme to construct a path p from state u to state v. The congestion of each transition arc lying on this path is increased by $|p|\pi(u)\pi(v)$ (see Eq (6)). Since the construction of $|\Omega|^2$ paths can be done completely independently of each other, we use OpenMP to construct all paths in parallel. The maximal congestion of any transition arc is used for computing the upper bound via InequalityEq (7). This method has a time complexity of $O(|\Omega|^2)$ and a memory complexity of $O(|\Psi|)$.

Network Analysis.

As state graphs can be seen as weighted directed graphs, all kinds of graph algorithms can be integrated into marathon. As an example, we added functions for computing the diameter of a state graph, as well as functions for computing the average path length.

Exemplary Markov-Chains

To demonstrate possible applications of marathon, we will describe a set of experiments in the following section. In our experiments, we focus on two famous sampling problems. The problem of uniformly sampling a perfect matching in a bipartite graph and of uniformly sampling a bipartite graph realization for given vertex degrees. Both problems are based on bipartite graphs. A bipartite graph G = (U, V, E) is an undirected graph with disjoint vertex sets V and U and a set of edges $E \subseteq U \times V$, connecting vertices from U with V. We will refer to the vertices of U as u_i, where i ranges from 1 to n := |U| and to the vertices of V as v_j, where j ranges from 1 ton': = |V|. We analyzed four different chains that can be used for these sampling problems. To make this article self-contained, we give a introduction to the chains.

Markov Chains for Sampling of Perfect Matchings

A perfect matching in a bipartite graph G = (U, V, E), with n = n′, is a subset $M \subseteq E$ of edges such that a) all edges in M are non-adjacent, and b) |M| = n. Uniformly sampling a perfect matching is the problem of choosing one perfect matching from the set of all perfect matchings of G uniformly at random. We describe two important Markov chains which are known to solve the problem of uniformly sampling perfect matchings. These chains origin from applications in statistical physics and are widely known in the field of Markov chain analysis, so they make good examples for our analysis. Both Markov chains use the set of near-perfect matchings as auxiliary states. A near-perfect matching is a subset of non-adjacent edges from E, but with one edge less than a perfect matching. So, being specific, the Markov chains used for sampling are based on the set Ω_M of perfect and near perfect matchings in G.

Matching Chain One.

Broder [15] introduced a Markov chain which can be described as follows. In state $M \in \Omega_M$ we pick a candidate state M′ (line three in Algorithm 1) by choosing an edge e = {u, v} from E uniformly at random. One of five cases occurs:

- If M is a perfect matching and $e \in M$, then remove e from M and select $M' \leftarrow M \setminus \{e\}$.
- If M is a near-perfect matching and $e \notin M$, then add e to M and select $M' \leftarrow M \cup \{e\}$.
- If M is a near-perfect matching, u is not matched in M, and an edge $e' = \{w, v\} \in M$ exists, then remove e′ from M, add e and select $M' \leftarrow (M \setminus \{e'\}) \cup \{e\}$.
- Symmetrically, if M is a near-perfect matching, v is not matched in M, and an edge $e' = \{u, z\} \in M$ exists, then remove e′ from M, add e and select $M' \leftarrow (M \setminus \{e'\}) \cup \{e\}$.

In all other cases, stay at M.

The state M′ is proposed as a candidate state with proposal probability $\kappa(M, M') = 1/|E|$ in line three of Algorithm 1. The proposed state M′ is accepted or refused by line four of Algorithm 1, using unit weights. So, this chain converges to a uniform stationary distribution. In the remainder of this article, we refer to this Markov chain as Matching Chain One. Jerrum and Sinclair [16] proved that Matching Chain One is rapidly mixing for a graph class where the ratio of near-perfect matchings N(G) and perfect matchings M(G) in G is polynomially bounded. Being specific, its total mixing time can be bounded from above:

$$\tau(\epsilon) \leq 16^2|E|^2\left(\frac{|\mathcal{N}(G)|}{|\mathcal{M}(G)|}\right)^4 \ln(|\Omega_M| \cdot \epsilon^{-1}). \tag{9}$$

The class of dense bipartite graphs, i.e. bipartite graphs G = (U, W, E) with |U| = |W| = n and with minimal vertex degree of at least n/2, was shown as a class for which the ratio of near-perfect and perfect matchings is polynomially bounded [16]. For this class of graphs, the following upper bound on the total mixing time can be gained [17]:

$$\tau(\epsilon) \in O(n^7 \ln(|\Omega_M| \cdot \epsilon^{-1})). \tag{10}$$

A main problem of Matching Chain One is the fact that it does not only generate perfect matchings but also near-perfect matchings. In many graphs with 2n vertices the ratio of the number of near-perfect and perfect matchings cannot be bounded by a polynomial which is dependent on n. In such cases, the sampling of a perfect matching needs an exponential number of trials to see a perfect matching at all.

Matching Chain Two.

One way to overcome the problem of an exponential total mixing time has been given by Jerrum, Sinclair and Vigoda [18]. Their main idea is to use a carefully chosen weight function w to sample from a non-uniform distribution. This way, they gained a rapidly mixing Markov chain which can be used to sample perfect matchings from any given bipartite graph. In addition, the transition rules were changed to the following: In a state $M \in \Omega_M$:

- If M is a perfect matching, we choose an edge e = {u, v} from M uniformly at random. Remove e from M and select $M' \leftarrow M \setminus \{e\}$.
- If M is a near-perfect matching where u and v are unmatched vertices, we choose a vertex $z \in U \cup V$ uniformly at random.
  - If z is one of the unmatched vertices u and v and e = {u, v} ∈ E, then add e to M and select $M' \leftarrow M \cup \{e\}$.
  - If z ∈ V, {u, z} ∈ E and {x, z} ∈ M, then remove the edge {x, z} from M, add {u, z} and select $M' \leftarrow (M \setminus \{\{x, z\}\}) \cup \{\{u, z\}\}$.
  - If z ∈ U, {z, v} ∈ E and {z, y} ∈ M, then remove the edge {z, y} from M, add {z, v} and select $M' \leftarrow (M \setminus \{\{z, y\}\}) \cup \{\{z, v\}\}$.

The proposal probability κ(M,M′) for two states M,M′ $\in \Omega_M$ is therefore 1/n when moving between perfect and near-perfect matchings and 1/(2n) when moving between near-perfect matchings. In connection with Algorithm 1, this Markov chain converges to a stationary distribution π which is proportional to the weight function w. Defining M as the set of perfect matchings of G, and $N_{u,v}$ as the set of near perfect matchings in G where u and v are unmatched, the weight function suggested in [18] is defined as:

$$w(M) = \begin{cases} 1, & M \in \mathcal{M} \\ |\mathcal{M}|/|\mathcal{N}_{u,v}|, & M \in \mathcal{N}_{u,v}. \end{cases} \quad \textbf{(11)}$$

Knowing the values of $|\mathcal{M}|$ and $|\mathcal{N}_{u,v}|$, the total mixing time of this chain can be bounded from above by the following polynomial [19]:

$$\tau(\epsilon) \in O(n^4 \ln((\pi_{min} \cdot \epsilon)^{-1})). \quad \textbf{(12)}$$

Unfortunately, $|\mathcal{M}|$ and $|\mathcal{N}_{u,v}|$ are usually not known in practice. Jerrum, Sinclair and Vigoda gave a description of a procedure for approximating these quantities in polynomial time [18]. In our experiments though, we knew the exact values since we had a list of all states. In combination with Algorithm 1, this Markov chain is rapidly mixing for all bipartite graphs and can be used for sampling of perfect matchings. We refer to this chain as Matching Chain Two.

Markov Chains for Sampling of Bipartite Graph Realizations

The bipartite graph realization problem is to find, for a pair of non-increasing integer sequences $(a_1, \ldots, a_n)$, $(b_1, \ldots, b_{n'})$ with $a_i, b_i > 0$, a bipartite graph G = (U, V, E), without loops and parallel edges, such that the vertex degrees of $u_i \in U$ matches the a_i and that the vertex degrees of $v_i \in V$ match the b_i. Such a graph G is then called bipartite graph realization or, shorter still, realization. The set of all realizations of a given degree sequence pair makes the sampling set Ω_R for this sampling problem. The bipartite graph realization problem is so important in many fields that it was reinvented several times. It is also known as the problem of contingency tables with given marginal sums or, as matrices with fixed row and column sums. As a direct application of random bipartite graphs, scientists often use a sampled realization as a null model to prove statistical hypotheses. Since sampling of random bipartite graphs is important in a wide range of fields, we chose it as a second example for our experiments.

In contemporary literature, one can find two possible Markov chains that solve the problem of uniform sampling of a bipartite graph realization. One of these approaches is simply to transform it into the perfect matching sampling problem [20]. This way, it is known that the running time of the sampling procedure is bounded polynomially. However, the very simple and intuitive switch chain, presented by Kannan et al. [21], is widely used in practice.

Switch Chain One.

At a state $G = (U, V, E) \in \Omega_R$, choose four integers i, j, k, l with $1 \le i \le k \le n$ and $1 \le j \le l \le n'$ uniformly at random. One of three cases occur:

- If the edges $e_1 = \{u_i, v_j\}$ and $e_2 = \{u_k, v_l\}$ exist in E but the edges $e_1' = \{u_i, v_l\}$ and $e_2' = \{u_k, v_j\}$ do not, then select G′ = (V, U, E′) with $E' \leftarrow (E \setminus \{e_1, e_2\}) \cup \{e_1', e_2'\}$.
- Symmetrically, if $e_1 = \{u_i, v_j\}$ and $e_2 = \{u_k, v_l\}$ both do not exist in E but the edges $e'_1 = \{u_i, v_l\}$ and $e_2' = \{u_k, v_j\}$ exist, select G′ = (V, U, E′) with $E' \leftarrow (E \setminus \{e_1', e_2'\}) \cup \{e_1, e_2\}$.
- In all other cases, select $G' \leftarrow G$.

Such a switch, i.e. changing the endpoints of two edges, does not change the degree sequence and thus constructs a new bipartite graph realization of S. It turns out, all graph realizations can be generated by starting with a given graph realization and applying a number of switches [22]. The proposal probability κ(G,G′) of a non-loop transition is $\frac{2}{n(n+1)} \cdot \frac{2}{n'(n'+1)}$. Using unit weights w(x) = 1 for all $x \in \Omega_R$ Algorithm 1 converges to a uniform stationary distribution. Kannan et al. [21] proved polynomially bounded mixing times of this chain for regular sequence pairs. Miklós et al. [23] extended the proof to half-regular sequence pairs. For all other sequence classes, the problem of the rapid mixing property is still open. We will refer to this Markov chain as Switch Chain One. Recently, Greenhill gave a proof that the total mixing time of the directed, non-bipartite version of Switch Chain One is bounded by the following polynomial when the largest degree d_{max} of the input sequence lies in the range $3 \le d_{max} \le \frac{1}{4}\sqrt{|E|}$, where |E| is the number of edges in the realization [24]:

$$\tau(\epsilon) \le \frac{1}{10} d_{max}^{14} |E|^9 (|E| \ln |E| + \ln(\epsilon^{-1})). \quad \textbf{(13)}$$

Switch Chain Two.

A modification of Switch Chain One, given by Berger et al. [25] for directed graph sequences, can also be used for the bipartite version. The main idea is to reduce the number of transition loops in the state graph. To avoid non-convergence, an additional additional artificial edge $\{u_0,v_0\}$, which connects two additional vertices u_0 and v_0, is added to the set of edges. In a state $G = (U, V, E) \in \Omega_R$ select a pair of non-adjacent edges e_1

= $\{u_i, v_j\}$ and $e_2 = \{u_k, v_l\}$ from the set$E \cup \{\{u_0, v_0\}\}$.

- If, $e_1 = \{u_0, v_0\}$ or $e_2 = \{u_0, v_0\}$, select $G' \leftarrow G$.
- If $e_1' = \{u_i, v_l\} \notin E$ and $e_2' = \{u_k, v_j\} \notin E$, then switch the edges (e_1, e_1', e_2, e_2') and select $G' = (V, U, E')$ with $E' \leftarrow (E \setminus \{e_1, e_2\}) \cup \{e_1', e_2'\}$.
- In all other cases, select $G' \leftarrow G$.

Without the additional edge, a problem would occur if no adjacent edge pairs existed for each graph realization of a sequence; then, the state graph would not possess loops. Similar arguments like those of Ref. [25] show that this chain converges to the uniform distribution. This chain reduces the average probability of transition loops and, as it will turn out, the average total mixing time. However, the asymptotical total mixing time is the same as for Switch Chain One. We will refer to this chain as Switch Chain Two.

EXPERIMENTS

We demonstrate our library to experimentally analyze the mixing time behavior of the Markov chains. The goal of our experiments is to quantify the gap between the total mixing time and the various bounding methods. We are asking the question, whether the bounding techniques are tight or if there is a huge gap between total mixing time and its bounds. The latter case would support the thesis that the total mixing time actually is far smaller than known in theory. This would be a welcomed message for any programmer who wants to implement a sampling method and does not want to choose a highly polynomial (or even exponential) number of steps. We want to make some general remarks before beginning to describe our experiments.

The Choice of ϵ

Recall, that the total mixing time $\tau(\epsilon)$, as well as its bounds depends on the value of ϵ which defines the distance to the stationary distribution at the end of the random walk. For the purpose of our experiments, we choose $\epsilon = 10^{-3}$. Furthermore, for other values of ϵ we get similar results.

Applying Canonical Paths

To compute the congestion bounds, we use the path construction schemes from the original proofs and apply them to concrete state graphs. As those path construction schemes were used to gain theoretical bounds without full knowledge of a Markov chain's structure, applying them to concrete state graphs shows how sharp such bounds could be if full structural information were available. Consequently, the bounds in general cannot be better than the upper bounds that are gained when applying the scheme on an actual state graph. To understand, how sharp the theoretical bounds can be, we analyze the differences to the actual total mixing times. In the case of matching chains, we use the construction scheme presented in [16] which was used to gain the upper bound given in Eq 10. In case of the switch chains we apply the definition of the canonical paths from [21]. For the definition of the path construction schemes, we refer to the original articles. We tried as close as possible to implement the original canonical path construction rules. However, the definition often relies on an arbitrary order of the vertices, or orderings of cycles. It turned out that changing these orders has an effect on the quality of the congestion bound. However, as the proofs for the upper bounds are valid for all orderings, this is not a problem for our observations.

Hardware Usage

Since we wanted to compute the properties of a large amount of instances, we decided to compute as many properties of a state graph as possible in parallel. As shown before, the computation of the total mixing time is the bottleneck for our computations. For this reason, we decided to transfer this task to the GPU whenever possible. This has the advantage, that the free CPU cores can be used for the computation of other quantities, while the GPU is occupied. With this strategy, we achieve a large throughput of instances. Fig 2 shows the hardware usage while computing the properties of a Markov chain instance.

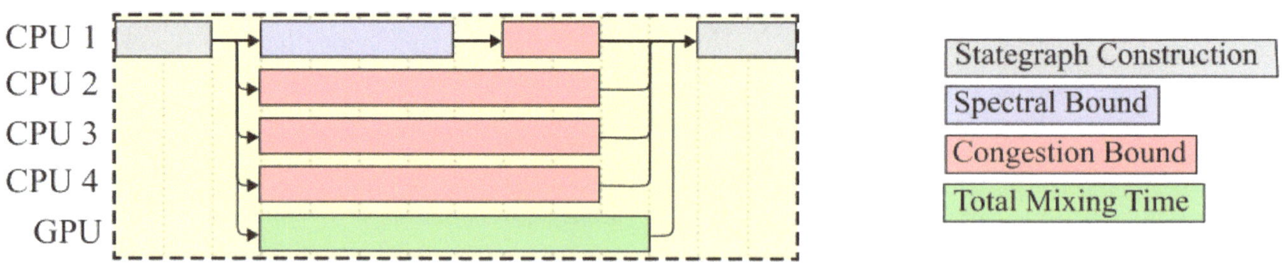

Figure 2. Typical hardware usage for our experiments. At first, the state graph is being constructed as a sequential task. Afterwards, the properties of the state graph are being computed in parallel. When each property is computed the next instance is processed in the same manner.

Enumeration Experiment

In our first experiment, we wanted to gain an impression concerning the dimension of the total mixing time and its bounds.

Experimental Setup.

Firstly, we enumerated all small input instances up to a given limit for each chain. In particular, we enumerated 19,378 bipartite degree sequence pairs with up to 6+6 vertices as input for the switch chains and 89,242 connected non-isomorphic bipartite graphs with 6+6 vertices as input for the matching chains. While the first task was done with a simple backtracking procedure, the latter task was done by the command line tool nauty[26]. These combinatorial objects served as input instances for the Markov chains. Even though the size of input is small, the resulting state graphs can be large. For example, the largest state graph processed in this experiment had 297,200 states and corresponds to the regular degree sequence pair (3, 3, 3, 3, 3, 3),(3, 3, 3, 3, 3, 3). Since both the number of instances, as well as the size of the state graphs grow exponentially, we were not able to perform such an experiment for a much larger instance size. For each instance, we constructed the corresponding state graph. For all state graphs with a maximum of 20,000 states, we computed the following properties: a) total mixing time, b) spectral bound, and c) canonical path congestion bound. Although we could easily compute the latter bounds for much larger state graphs, we did not do so, since we need the total mixing time for comparison.

RESULTS.

In Fig 3, we show the results of the enumeration experiment. Each input instance corresponds to two data points, showing the ratio of the upper spectral bound (green), and congestion bound (blue) with the total mixing time. We immediately observe that the spectral bound is very close to the total mixing time for all instances, in contrast to the congestion bound. More precisely, in case of Matching Chain Two, the congestion bound is up to 800 times larger than the total mixing time. Similar observations can be made for the other chains.

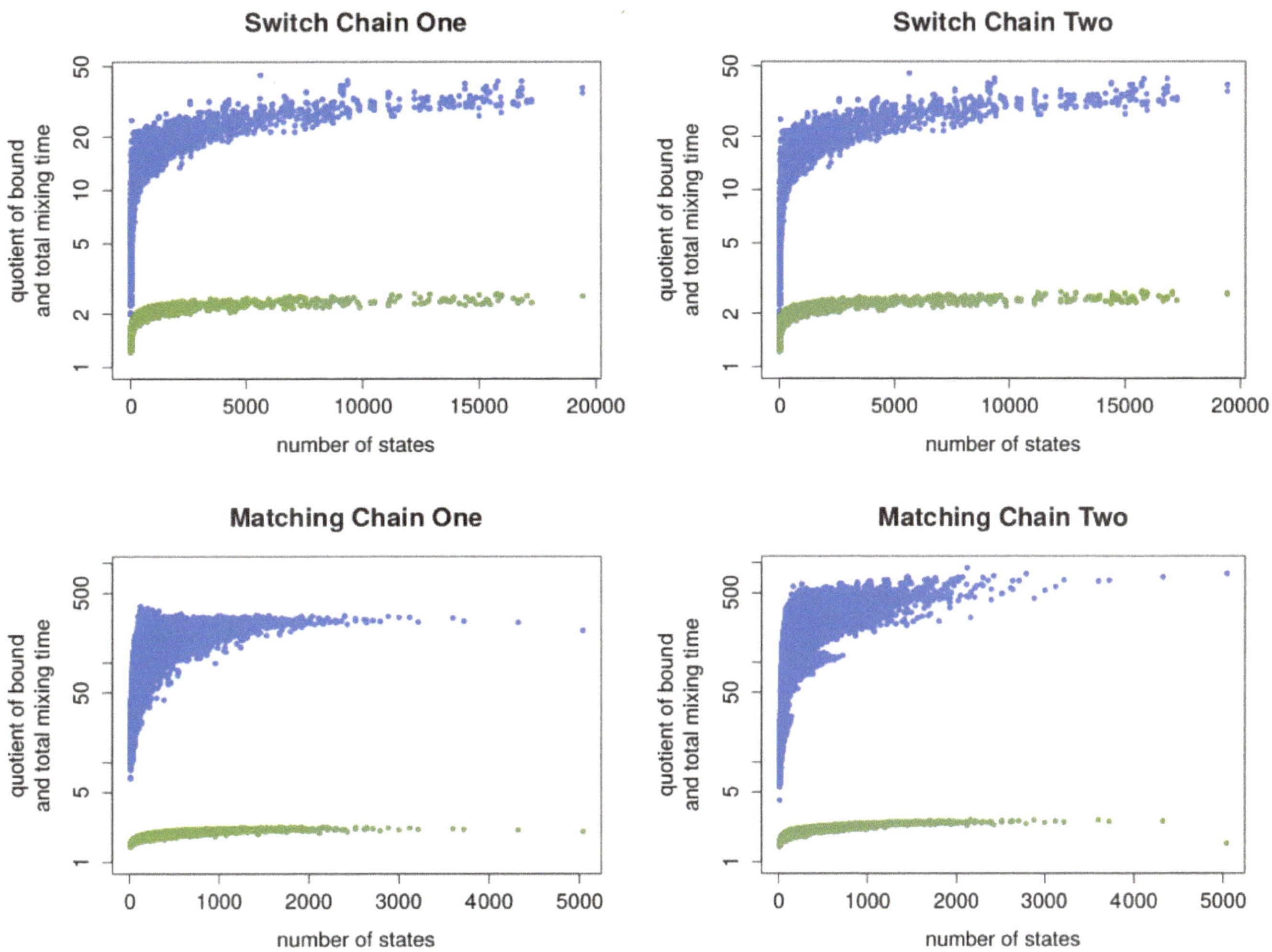

Figure 3. The quality of the upper bounds. The quotient of congestion bound (blue) and total mixing time, respectively upper spectral bound (green) and total mixing time versus the size of the corresponding state graph.

In Fig 4, we highlight the instances which are known to have a polynomial congestion bound. In the case of the switch chains, these are regular and half-regular degree sequences. In the case of Matching Chain One, these are dense bipartite graphs. Matching Chain Two is known to be rapidly mixing for all instances. We find that the observations can also be confirmed within this set.

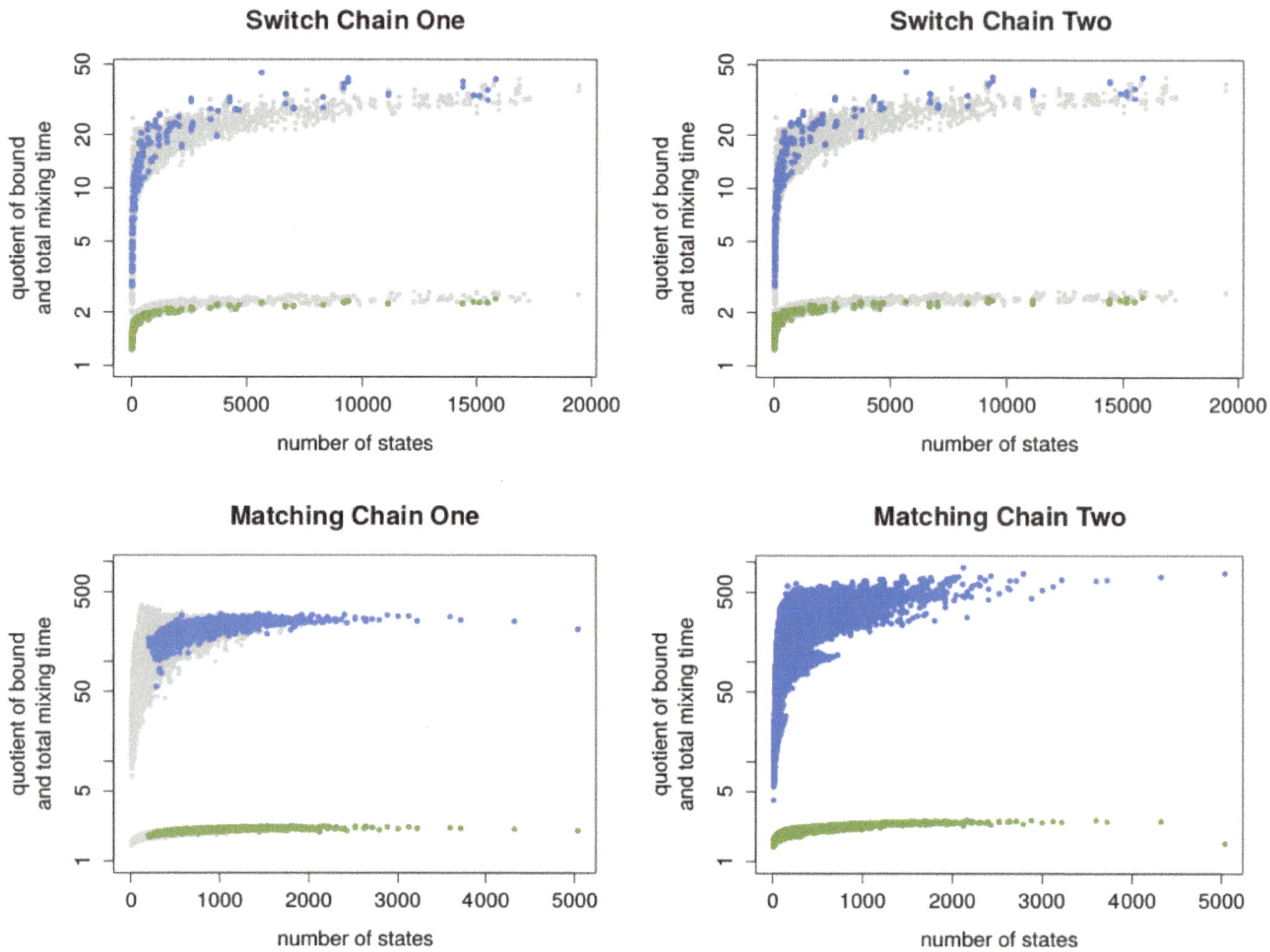

Figure 4. The quality of the upper bounds for rapidly mixing instances. The results of Fig 3 filtered to highlight instances with known polynomial mixing time. Instances with no known polynomial bound are colored gray.

Scaling Experiment

We wanted to know whether the observed effects remain valid for larger instances. The main problem is, that the number of instances for our Markov chains, both degree sequences and bipartite graphs, grows exponentially with input size. So, a complete enumeration becomes infeasible when the instance size grows. To gain some insights, we picked selected instances for the switch chains and scaled them to larger size.

Experimental Setup.

We picked a half-regular sequence pattern (n − 1, n − 2, 2, 1), (2, 2, …, 2), where the number of two's in the second sequence is n. The parameter n can be used to scale the instance to different sizes. In doing so, a bipartite graph which realizes this degree sequences has n + 4 vertices and 2n edges. These sequence pairs are half-regular and so, it is known that the switch chains are rapidly mixing. For each n between 4 and 50, we constructed the corresponding state graph and computed the total mixing time and its bounds. Again, due to the large memory consumption, we stopped computing the total mixing time when $|\Omega|$ exceeded 20,000. To predict missing values of total mixing time for larger state graphs up to about 600,000 states, we used a linear model based on the following observation.

Results.

We observed that the lower spectral bound seems to have a linear relationship with the total mixing time. This allowed us to predict the missing total mixing time values using a simple linear model (see Fig 5 for details).

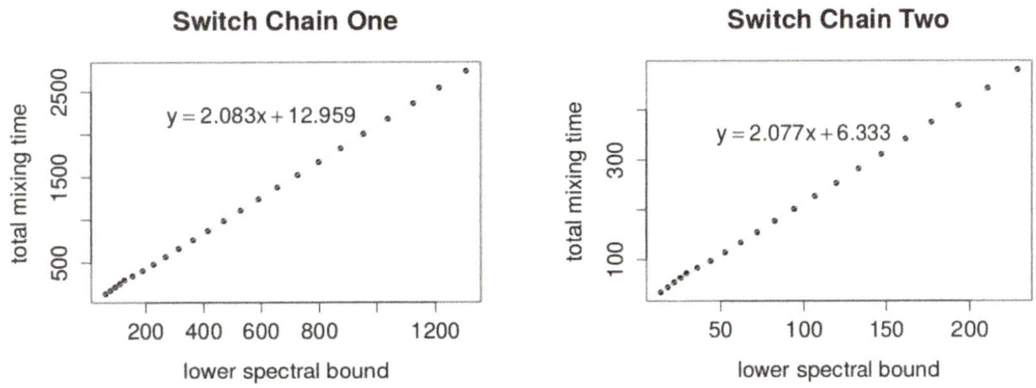

Figure 5. Relationship between the lower spectral bound and the total mixing time. The total mixing time is shown in connection to a corresponding lower spectral bound for sequence pairs of the form (n − 1, n − 2, 2, 1), (2, 2, …, 2). We use the displayed formulas to predict missing values for total mixing time.

To quantify the gap between the bounds and total mixing time, we again divided each bound through the corresponding total mixing time or its predicted value. Fig 6 shows the result of this experiment. We observed that the gap between the congestion bound and the total mixing time grows with input size n. Furthermore, we observed that the same is true for the upper spectral bound, but in a much slower way.

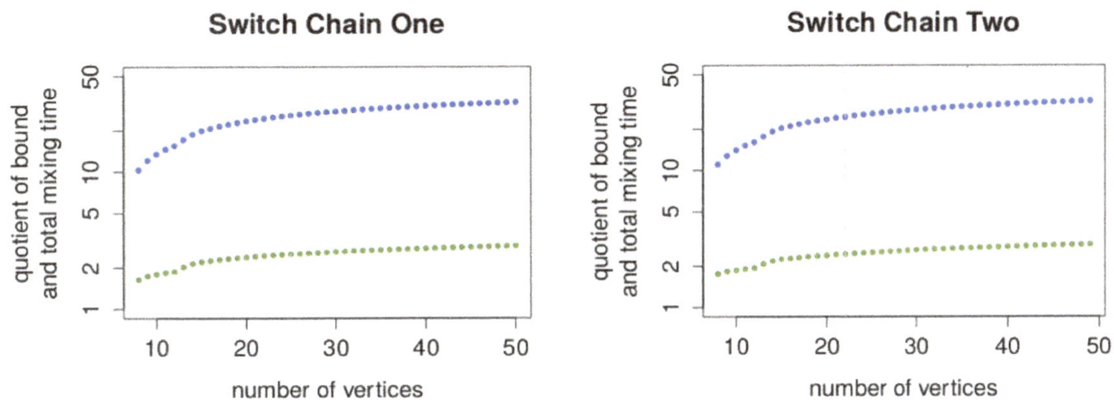

Figure 6. Quality of the upper bounds with growing instance size. The quotient of congestion bound (blue), respectively upper spectral bound (green) with total mixing time is shown as a function of the instance size. A dotted line shows the point where we stop computing the total mixing time and start using the lower spectral bound approximation.

We repeated this experiment with other half-regular sequence patterns and observed similar effects. In particular, we changed our sequence pattern (n − 1, n − 2, 2, 1), (2, 2, …, 2), which we call type A, slightly to the sequences patterns (n − 1, n − 2, 3), (2, 2, …, 2) (type B) and (n − 1, n − 2, 1, 1, 1), (2, 2, …, 2) (type C). Fig 7 shows the, partially estimated, total mixing time for each sequence type. We observed that each type has its own growing asymptotic. The data suggests, in the case of Switch Chain One, the total mixing time of sequence type A grows with $O(n^{2.27})$, of type B with $O(n^{1.16})$, and of type C with $O(n^{2.43})$. In the case of Switch Chain Two, we observe similar effects.

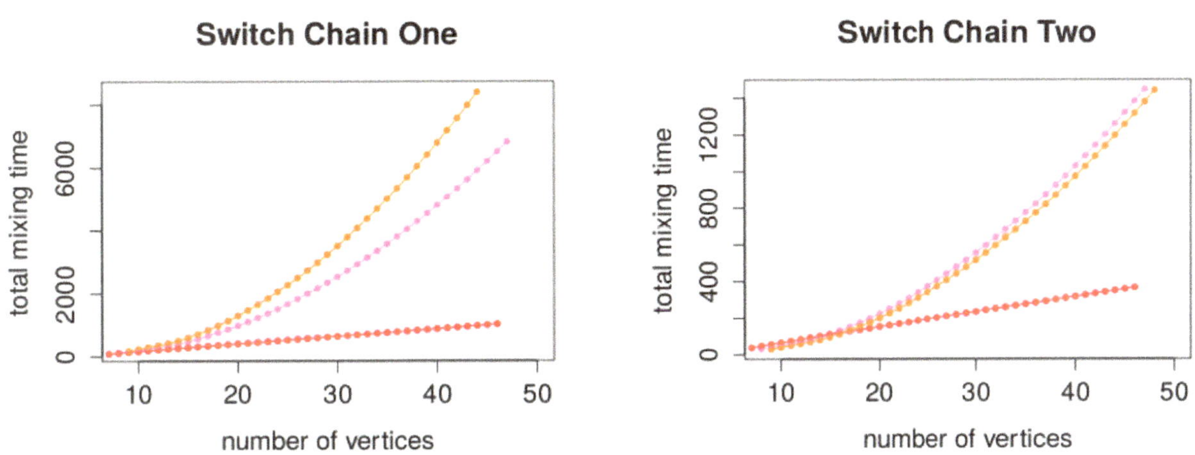

Figure 7. Growing asymptotic for the total mixing time of half-regular sequence pairs. The observed mixing time curves for the degree sequence pairs of type A are colored violet, of type B red, and of type C orange.

These results are interesting because these bounds are lower bounds on the mixing time of the switch chains for all half-regular sequence pairs. Since two of them are clearly super-linear, a random walk with a linear number of steps must ultimately fail and will result in a non-random sample.

Loop Reduction Experiment

From the data of the enumeration experiment, we observed that the total mixing time does not correlate with the size of the state graph (see Fig 8). Instead, the largest mixing time appears at input instances corresponding to small state graphs.

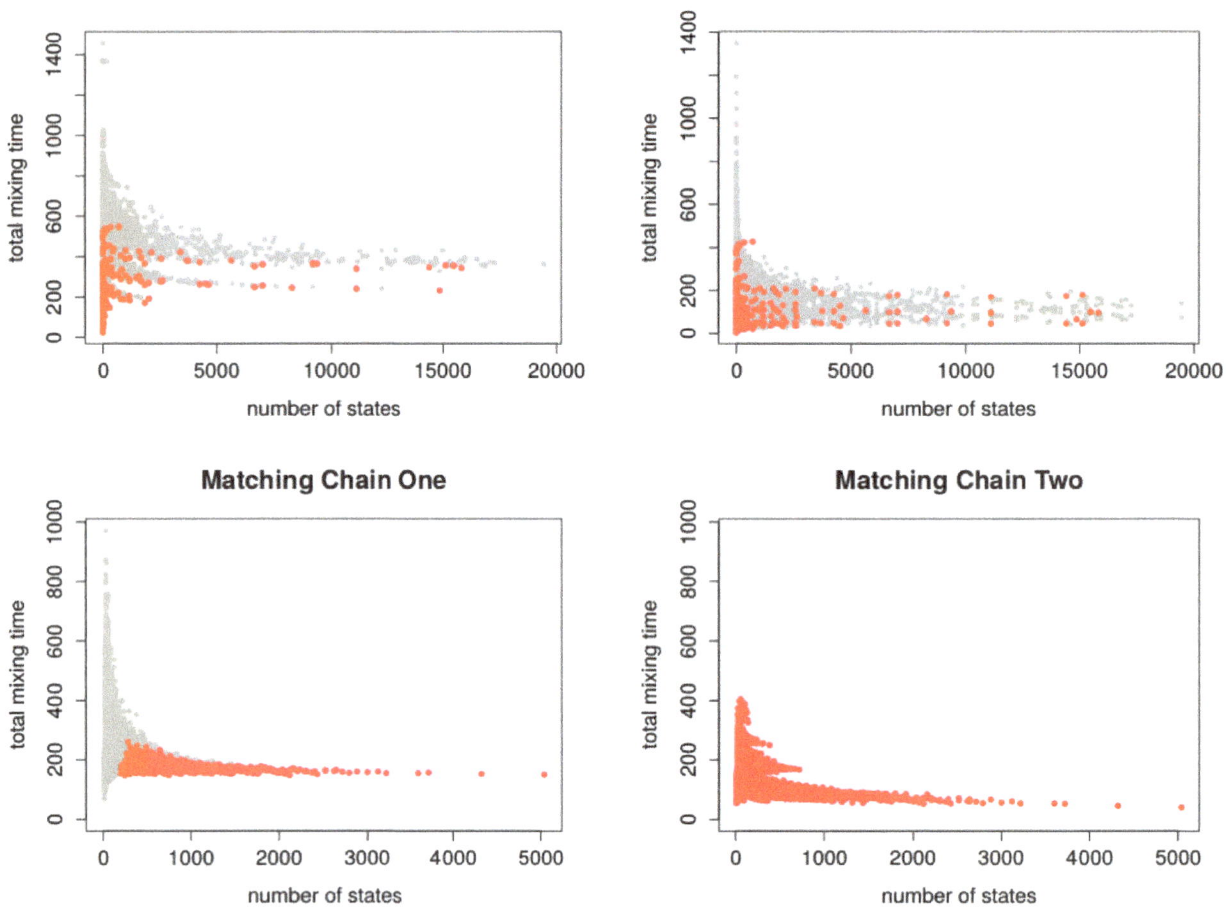

Figure 8. Number of states versus total mixing time. Each data point represents one input instance from our set of input instance. Instances with known polynomial mixing time are highlighted red.

For example, the sequence pair (6, 6, 6, 6, 5, 5),(6, 6, 6, 6, 5, 5), possesses just two different states but is beneath the instances with largest total mixing time in both switch chains. To explain this effect, consider sequence pairs of the general form (n, n,..., n − 1, n − 1), (n, n, ...,n − 1, n − 1), where 2n is the number of vertices in the corresponding bipartite graph. It is apparent that such sequence pairs posses two different realizations, meaning, their state graph have two states. Now consider Switch Chain One; for a given n, the number of ways to choose i, j, k, l is $(n \cdot (n + 1)/2)^2 \in O(n^4)$. Due to the large number of edges in the sequence pairs, all but one of these choices result in loops. As a consequence, the expected number of steps, just to get from one state to the other, is $O(n^4)$, which is immediately a lower bound for the mixing time of Switch Chain One. The fact that an instance with polynomially bounded total mixing time makes the largest mixing time over all instances is likely an effect of the small input size. To better understand this effect, we decided to further reduce the influence of the loops.

Experimental Setup.

We repeated the enumeration experiment but made some artificial modifications on each state graph before computing its properties. For each state graph we determined the minimal loop probability over all states $P_{min} := \min_{i\in\Omega} P_{ii}$. We wanted to reduce the transition probability of each loop in the state graph by this quantity. However, to avoid the removal of all loops and possible problems with convergence, we removed only 99% of this probability from the loops. This way, we gained new transition probabilities of

$$P'_{ii} \leftarrow P_{ii} - .99P_{min} \quad \text{for all} \quad i \in \Omega. \tag{14}$$

The amount of $.99P_{min}$ which was reduced from the probability mass of each state, was restored to the network through rescaling of the remaining transition arcs:

$$P'_{ij} \leftarrow \frac{P_{ij}}{1 - .99P_{min}} \quad \text{for all} \quad i, j \in \Omega. \tag{15}$$

By subtracting the same amount of probability from each loop, we kept the symmetry of the transition matrix so that the chain's stationary distribution was still uniform. The result was a state graph with the same structure but drastically reduced loop probability. In such state graphs, the mixing times are much more dependent on the structure of the state graph than on the number of the loops. We repeated the computation of the total mixing time and its upper bounds with those modified state graphs for Switch Chain One.

Results.

We first observed that the modification indeed had a strong effect on the total mixing time (see Fig 9).

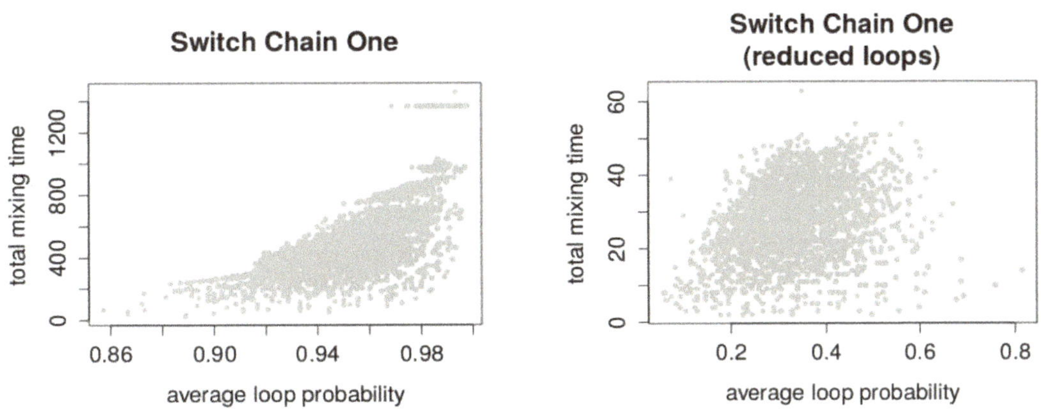

Figure 9. Influence of the average loop probability on the total mixing time. Each data point represents a state graph, for each input instance of Switch Chain One, before and after loop reduction.

While the largest total mixing time in our instance set is about 1400, in the set of reduced state graphs, it is 63. In addition, we observed that the total mixing time after the reduction steps no longer correlates with the average loop probability. So, the effects we observe now are more or less detached from the influence of the loops. We observed, that the effect we observed in the enumeration experiment still remain (see Fig 10). The quality of the congestion bound is still bad while the largest total mixing time occurs at relatively small state graphs.

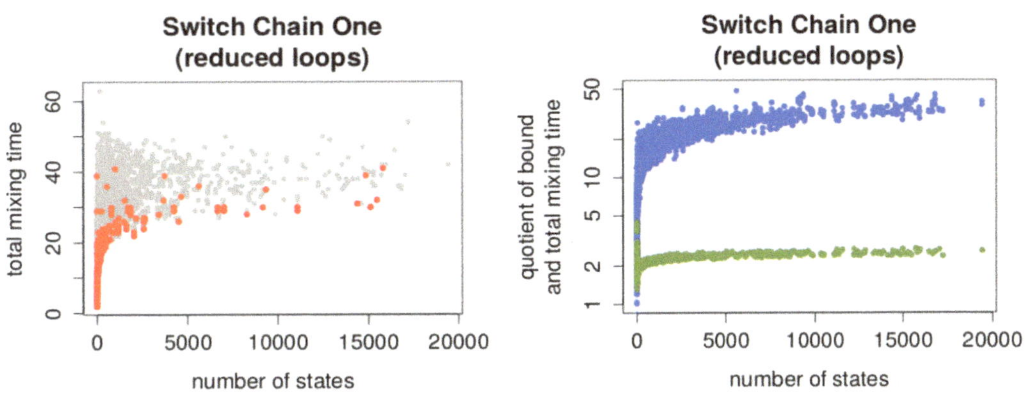

Figure 10. Properties of reduced state graphs. (A) Size of a state graph versus its total mixing time. Regular and half-regular sequence pairs are highlighted red. (B) Quotient of congestion bound (blue) and upper spectral bound (green) with corresponding total mixing time.

We finished our experiments with the observation that the upper spectral bound as well as the congestion bound heavily depend on the average vertex degree of the state graph (see Fig 11). We concluded that the average degree is a structural property of a state graph which has a stronger influence on the total mixing time than its size.

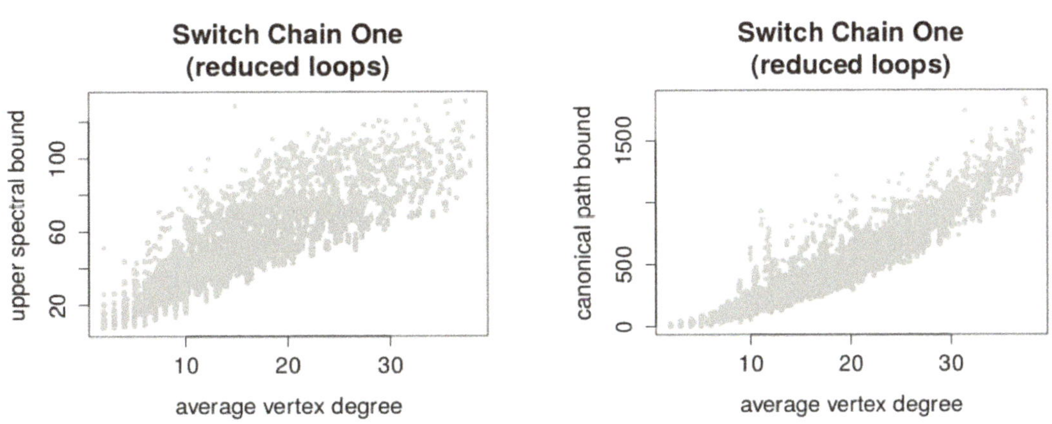

Figure 11. Influence of the average vertex degree. Connection between average vertex degree of a state graph and its total mixing time, respectively canonical path bound.

RESULTS AND DISCUSSION

We introduced the marathon library and demonstrated how it can be used to support the analysis of sampling algorithms by a set of experiments. We briefly summarize the most important observations from our experiments:

- The congestion bound is much larger than the total mixing time in almost all cases. The quality of the congestion bounds deteriorates with growing input size. This observation is made in reduced and non-reduced state graphs.
- The upper spectral bound keeps close to total mixing time even when the input size grows, although it can be observed, that its quality drops slowly. Again, this observation is made in reduced and non-reduced state graphs.
- The lower spectral bound seems to have an almost linear relationship with the total mixing time. This way, it can be used to precisely predict the total mixing time. The search for an explanation of this effect is likely a good subject for further theoretical studies.
- Maybe the most surprising observation made in our experiments is that large total mixing time tends to occur at small state graphs.
- The average vertex degree of a state graph has a strong relationship on its total mixing time. This observation should be investigated further. Figuring out which sequences have a tendency towards more diverse vertex degrees in their state graphs could lead to further interesting rapidly mixing graph classes.

Our observations indicate that the theoretical bound gained by the canonical path method is likely too pessimistic. Moreover, although we know the exact structure of a state graph in our experiments, which can never be the case in a normal practical scenario, the congestion bound is too large. This leads us to the conclusion that the canonical path method will never yield applicable values. Furthermore, this gives hope to the hypothesis, that the true total mixing time is smaller than existing theory is able to prove. So, we are optimistic about the applicability of the switch chains. We think that a promising next step could be to focus on two fields which need one another: investigating and the proving of special structures for state graphs depending on the problem and figuring out new relationships between structures of graphs and its eigenvalues.

Future Work

One of our next steps is to use our new tool very extensively. We want to investigate further chains and test further hypotheses. Moreover, we plan to add further functionality to the marathon library to enable additional research questions. For example, we want to compute the distribution of the mixing time. While the total mixing time displays the maximal number of steps necessary to drop below a total variation distance of ϵ, the mixing time as a function of the starting state would lead to further insights, such as average mixing time. Another additional feature would be the computation of a multi commodity flow congestion scheme, which is a generalization of the canonical path method. Furthermore, we want to improve the performance of existing methods. In particular, we want to add multi GPU support as well as a parallel method for the construction of the state graph. Another topic would be the parallel evaluation of the canonical path congestion method using GPUs.

ACKNOWLEDGMENTS

We would like to thank Matthias Müller-Hannemann for his remarks and suggestions, as well as for the fruitful discussions.

AUTHOR CONTRIBUTIONS

Conceived and designed the experiments: SR AB. Performed the experiments: SR. Analyzed the data: SR AB. Contributed reagents/materials/analysis tools: SR. Wrote the paper: SR AB. Designed the software: SR.

REFERENCES

1. Kashtan N, Itzkovitz S, Milo R, Alon U. mfinder: Network motif detection tool; 2005. Available from: http://www.weizmann.ac.il/mcb/UriAlon/.
2. Gotelli NJ. Null Model Analysis of Species Co-Occurrence Patterns. Ecology. 2000;81(9):2606–2621. Available from: http://www.jstor.org/stable/177478. doi: 10.1890/0012-9658(2000)081%5B2606:NMAOSC%5D2.0.CO;2.
3. Jerrum MR, Valiant LG, Vazirani VV. Random generation of combinatorial structures from a uniform distribution. Theoretical Computer Science. 1986;43:169–188. Available from: http://www.sciencedirect.com/science/article/pii/030439758690174X. doi: 10.1016/0304-3975(86)90174-X.
4. Diaconis P. The markov chain monte carlo revolution. Bulletin of the American Mathematical Society. 2009;46(2):179–205. doi: 10.1090/S0273-0979-08-01238-X.
5. Sinclair A. Improved bounds for mixing rates of Markov chains and multicommodity flow. In: Simon I, editor. LATIN'92. vol. 583 of Lecture Notes in Computer Science. Springer Berlin Heidelberg; 1992. p. 474–487. Available from:http://dx.doi.org/10.1007/BFb0023849.
6. Sinclair A. CS294: Markov Chain Monte Carlo: Foundations & Applications; 2009. Last visited on March 2014. http://www.cs.berkeley.edu/~sinclair/cs294/f09.html.
7. Levin DA, Peres Y, Wilmer EL. Markov chains and mixing times. American Mathematical Society; 2006.
8. Lovász L. Random Walks on Graphs: A Survey. In: Miklós D, Sós VT, Szőnyi T, editors. Combinatorics, Paul Erdős is Eighty. vol. 2. Budapest: János Bolyai Mathematical Society; 1996. p. 353–398.
9. Nvidia. CUDA Toolkit; 2015. Available from: https://developer.nvidia.com/cuda-toolkit.
10. Dagum L, Menon R. OpenMP: An Industry-Standard API for Shared-Memory Programming. IEEE Comput Sci Eng. 1998 Jan;5(1):46–55. doi: 10.1109/99.660313.
11. Xianyi Z. openBLAS; 2015. Available from: http://www.openblas.net/.
12. Nvidia. cuBLAS; 2015. Available from: https://developer.nvidia.com/cublas.

13. Nvidia. cuBLAS-XT; 2015. Available from: https://developer.nvidia.com/cublasxt.

14. Lehoucq RB, Sorensen DC, Yang C. Arpack User's Guide: Solution of Large-Scale Eigenvalue Problems With Implicityly Restorted Arnoldi Methods (Software, Environments, Tools). Soc for Industrial & Applied Math;. Available from:http://www.worldcat.org/isbn/0898714079.

15. Broder AZ. How hard is it to marry at random? (On the approximation of the permanent). In: Proceedings of the Eighteenth Annual ACM Symposium on Theory of Computing. `STOC'86. New York, NY, USA: ACM; 1986. p. 50–58. Available from:http://doi.acm.org/10.1145/12130.12136.

16. Jerrum M, Sinclair A. Approximating the permanent. SIAM J Comput. 1989 Dec;18(6):1149–1178. doi: 10.1137/0218077.

17. Diaconis P, Graham R, Holmes SP. Statistical problems involving permutations with restricted positions. In: IMS Lecture Notes Monogr. Ser; 1999. p. 195–222.

18. Jerrum M, Sinclair A, Vigoda E. A polynomial-time approximation algorithm for the permanent of a matrix with nonnegative entries. Journal of the ACM. 2004;51:671–697. doi: 10.1145/1008731.1008738.

19. Bezáková I, Stefankovič D, Vazirani VV, Vigoda E. Accelerating Simulated Annealing for the Permanent and Combinatorial Counting Problems. In: In Proceedings of the 17th Annual ACM-SIAM Symposium on Discrete Algorithms (SODA). ACM Press; 2006. p. 900–907.

20. Tutte WT. The factors of graphs. Canadian J of Mathematics. 1952;4:314–328. doi: 10.4153/CJM-1952-028-2.

21. Kannan R, Tetali P, Vempala S. Simple Markov-chain algorithms for generating bipartite graphs and tournaments. Random Structures & Algorithms. 1999;14(4):293–308. doi: 10.1002/(SICI)1098-2418(199907)14:4%3C293::AID-RSA1%3E3.3.CO;2-7.

22. Petersen J. Die Theorie der regulären graphs. Acta Mathematica. 1891;15:193–220. doi: 10.1007/BF02392606.

23. Miklós I, Erdös PL, Soukup L. Towards Random Uniform Sampling of Bipartite Graphs with given Degree Sequence. Electr J Comb. 2013;20(1).

24. Greenhill CS. The switch Markov chain for sampling irregular graphs (Extended Abstract). In: Proceedings of the Twenty-Sixth Annual ACM-SIAM Symposium on Discrete Algorithms, SODA 2015, San Diego, CA, USA, January 4-6, 2015; 2015. p. 1564–1572. Available from: http://dx.doi.org/10.1137/1.9781611973730.103.

25. Berger A, Müller-Hannemann M. Uniform sampling of digraphs with a fixed degree sequence. In: Proceedings of the 36th International Conference on Graph-Theoretic Concepts in Computer Science. WG'10. Berlin, Heidelberg: Springer-Verlag; 2010. p. 220–231. Full version available from Arxiv:0912.0685v3.

26. McKay BD, Piperno A. Practical graph isomorphism, (II). Journal of Symbolic Computation. 2014;60(0):94–112. Available from:http://www.sciencedirect.com/science/article/pii/S0747717113001193. doi: 10.1016/j.jsc.2013.09.003.

CHAPTER 21

WHAT DO EYE GAZE METRICS TELL US ABOUT MOTOR IMAGERY?

Elodie Poiroux[1,2], Christine Cavaro-Ménard[1] , Stéphanie Leruez[1,3], Jean Michel Lemée[4,5], Isabelle Richard[2,6], Mickael Dinomais[1,2]

[1] LUNAM, Université d'Angers, Laboratoire Angevin de Recherche en Ingénierie des Systèmes (LARIS), EA 7315 F-49000, Angers, France

[2] LUNAM, Université d'Angers, Département de Médecine Physique et de Réadaptation, CHU d'Angers, 4 rue Larrey, 49933, Angers, Cedex 9, France

[3] LUNAM, Université d'Angers, Département d'Ophtalmologie, CHU d'Angers, 4 rue Larrey, 49933, Angers, Cedex 9, France

[4] LUNAM, Université d'Angers, Département de Neurochirurgie, CHU d'Angers, 4 rue Larrey, 49933, Angers, Cedex 9, France

[5] LUNAM, Université d'Angers, INSERM U1066 « Micro- et nano-médecines biomimétiques », bâtiment IRIS 3e étage, CHU d'Angers, 4 rue Larrey, 49933, Angers, Cedex 9, France

[6] LUNAM, Université d'Angers, Laboratoire d'épidémiologie, ergonomie et santé au travail, EA 4626 F- 49000, Angers, France

ABSTRACT

Many of the brain structures involved in performing real movements also have increased activity during imagined movements or during motor observation, and this could be the neural substrate underlying the effects of motor imagery in motor learning or motor rehabilitation. In the absence of any objective physiological method of measurement, it is currently impossible to be sure that the patient is indeed performing the task as instructed. Eye gaze recording during a motor imagery task could be a possible way to "spy" on the activity an individual is really engaged in. The aim of the present study was to compare the pattern of eye movement metrics during motor observation, visual and kinesthetic motor imagery (VI, KI), target fixation, and mental calculation. Twenty-two healthy subjects (16 females and 6 males), were required to perform tests in five conditions using imagery in the Box and Block Test tasks following the procedure described by Liepert et al. Eye movements were analyzed by a non-invasive oculometric measure (SMI RED250 system). Two parameters describing gaze pattern were calculated: the index of ocular mobility (saccade duration over saccade + fixation duration) and the number of midline crossings (i.e. the number of times the subjects gaze crossed the midline of the screen when performing the different tasks). Both parameters were significantly different between visual imagery and kinesthesic imagery, visual imagery and mental calculation, and visual imagery and target fixation. For the first time we were able to show that eye movement patterns are different during VI and KI tasks. Our results suggest gaze metric parameters could be used as an objective unobtrusive approach to assess engagement in a motor imagery task. Further studies should define how oculomotor parameters could be used as an indicator of the rehabilitation task a patient is engaged in.

Citation: Poiroux E, Cavaro-Ménard C, Leruez S, Lemée JM, Richard I, Dinomais M (2015) What Do Eye Gaze Metrics Tell Us about Motor Imagery? PLoS ONE 10(11): e0143831. doi:10.1371/journal.pone.0143831.

INTRODUCTION

Motor imagery (MI) consists of imagining the execution of a simple or complex movement that is not accompanied by bodily movement. Thus, MI is an active cognitive process in which the action representation is internally reproduced within the working memory, without overt execution [1] [2] but in a way that is similar to when the subject actually performs the movement [3]. At least two different modalities of imagery can be described [4] [5]: 1) the subject produces a visual representation of the movement; this is also known as visual imagery (VI); and 2) the subject carries out a mental simulation of the movement, which is associated with kinesthetic sensations. This requires imagining "feeling" the movement, and is known as kinesthetic imagery (KI). Motor observation (MO) consists of observing an action realized by other subject. At least, two different modalities of MO can be described [6]: 1) a passive observation paradigm where participants observe the movement without any overt aim; and 2) an active observation paradigm where participants observe the movement with the intent to reproduce it.

A growing number of neuroimaging studies have demonstrated that many of the brain structures involved in performing real movements also show increased activity during imagined movements [7] or during motor observation [8]. Although the extent of the shared neural overlap between these motor conditions is the subject of current debate [9], action execution, MO and MI share similar neural networks and mechanisms [10] [11] at least in part, and this might be the neural substrate underlying the effects of MI in motor learning and motor rehabilitation.

One of the applications of MI ability is the use of MI either as a training process in sports [12], or as a rehabilitation process [13] [14] [15] [16]. Sports literature indicates that MI in combination with physical exercise improves motor function more effectively than either MI or exercise [17]. MI has also been studied as a rehabilitation procedure in patients unable to perform active movements [18] [19] [20] or, when possible, in association with performing actual movements. A systematic review concluded that there is evidence that MI combined with physical therapy has additive effects on motor recovery after a stroke [13], while MI alone does not necessarily result in greater performance [21] [22].

Despite these findings, there are a number of differences in the available neuroimagery literature concerning the neural network involved in MI [13] [22] which appears to vary between VI and KI tasks, and also concerning the effects of either type of MI on motor rehabilitation. Some of these differences may be due to methodological limitations, since monitoring of the type of activity a subject is really engaged in when instructed to imagine a movement is difficult. Such monitoring is most often lacking or limited to verbal feedback from the subject on the task, reporting of the vividness of the mental representation of movement [23] or mental chronometry tasks. The mental chronometry method provides information about the temporal congruence between real and imagined movements. This method has been proven to give reliable and replicable results in healthy subjects and stroke patients (for a review see Malouin et al. [24]). Mental chronometry requires the subject to imagine the movement and give "go" and "stop" signals allowing measurement of the time required for the mental procedure. However, in the absence of any objective physiological measurements it remains impossible to be sure that the patient is indeed performing the task as instructed. The combination of existing measurement methods such as mental chronometry and task-related electrophysiological measurements would be necessary to assess objectively the real engagement of the subject in the MI task, which is a covert cognitive task.

Measurement of eye movement during a MI task could be a possible way of "spying" on the activity the patient is really engaged in. Indeed, eye movements have been studied in a variety of motor tasks, including movement performance, MO and MI [11]. The gaze metrics commonly measured in this experimental approach are fixations, the brief periods of time (typically greater than 100ms) when the eyes are stable and consciously focused on a visual cue [25]. Fixation can be described both by spatial and temporal parameters (describing how long the subject fixes a given point in space). McCormick and al. reported significantly longer fixation duration in MO compared to MI tasks [26], and that fixation duration was significantly influenced by target size and task complexity in MO tasks and action execution tasks, but not in MI tasks [25]. Another possible parameter is the measurement of saccades, which are the rapid eye movements between one fixation and another. The saccade time has been studied across a variety of cognitive tasks [27] [28] [29]. Similarities in eye movements across motor conditions has revealed that these tasks share a common representation of movement that also governs the eye movement pattern [30] [11]. Comparison of eye movement parameters between conditions might therefore be a possible measure to monitor whether a subject is sufficiently engaged in a MI task. In other words, determining the degree of similarity between the eye movement pattern during MI and during other cognitive processes might be a monitoring procedure to detect whether the subject is indeed imagining the movement. The aim of the present study was to compare the eye movement patterns during motor observation, visual and kinesthetic motor imagery, target fixation, and mental calculation.

MATERIALS AND METHODS

Subjects

Twenty-two healthy right-handed volunteers (16 females and 6 males) (mean age = 25.09 years, SD = 7.05, range = 20–53 years), with normal or corrected to normal vision, participated in the study after giving informed written consent. Inclusion criteria were: age above 18 years, volunteer status, with no limitation of mobility or movement disorder, and right handed as assessed by the Edinburgh Handedness Inventory Questionnaire. Approval was granted by the local Ethics Committee (University Hospital of Angers, France).

Eye Tracking System (*SMI* (SensoMotoric Instruments) System)

The SMI RED250 system (RED: Remote Eye-tracking Device) was used in this study. This device provides the point of regard or gaze direction in real time without any physical contact with the person being tested. This dark pupil eye tracking system uses infrared illumination; the eye and face reflect this illumination but the pupil absorbs most infrared light and appears as a high contrast dark ellipse. The images of the eyes are analyzed in real time to detect the pupil and the corneal reflection. To determine gaze points, the system measures the vector distance between the center of the pupil and the corneal reflection (the first Purkinje image). The corneal reflection location compensates for small head movements.

The SMI RED250 system has a gaze position accuracy of 0.4° and a spatial resolution of 0.03°. The sampling rate used in this study was 120 Hz.

The RED device was combined with an external 22" TFT monitor (screen resolution of 1680x1050 pixels) and a laptop that monitored the camera equipment and processes using the SMI iView X™ software. The gaze tracking experiment with the presentation of several visual stimuli was created and controlled using SMI Experiment Center™ software. The gaze tracking data were analysed using SMI BeGaze™ software.

A calibration procedure is needed before using eye tracker. During the calibration session, iView X™ software establishes a relationship between the position of the eye in the field of the camera and a point on the stimulus monitor. A calibration session was carried out before each experiment. We used a 9 point calibration, which provided a good compromise between time and accuracy of the calibration. The observer had to fix the calibration points (known locations on the monitor) while the position of the subject's gaze was recorded by SMI iView X™ software in order to create a mapping function relating the positions of the eye to points in the calibration zone.

Experimental Procedure

The eye-tracking session was performed for each subject in five conditions:

- two motor imagery tasks: visual imagery (VI), kinesthetic imagery (KI),
- one motor observation (MO) task: visual observation of the movement video,
- two control conditions: observation of a fixed image (Fix) and mental calculation (MC).

Before the eye-tracking session, all participants completed the French Movement Imagery Questionnaire-Revised Second version (MIQR-S) as described in Loison et al. [31] in order to assess the imagery ability of each subject. Then they executed the Box and Block Test (BBT) following the procedure described by Liepert et al. [32]. Each subject was comfortably seated at a table on which the BBT was installed with 15 blocks in the right hand compartment (Fig 1A). We ensured that the subject could see both compartments and the cubes inside. He/She received the instruction to pick up each block one by one with the right hand and move it to the left hand side of the box as quickly as possible, with advice to start with the first row and finish with the last row. The examiner demonstrated the movement. This condition served as a procedure enabling the subject to learn the movement in order to imagine it.

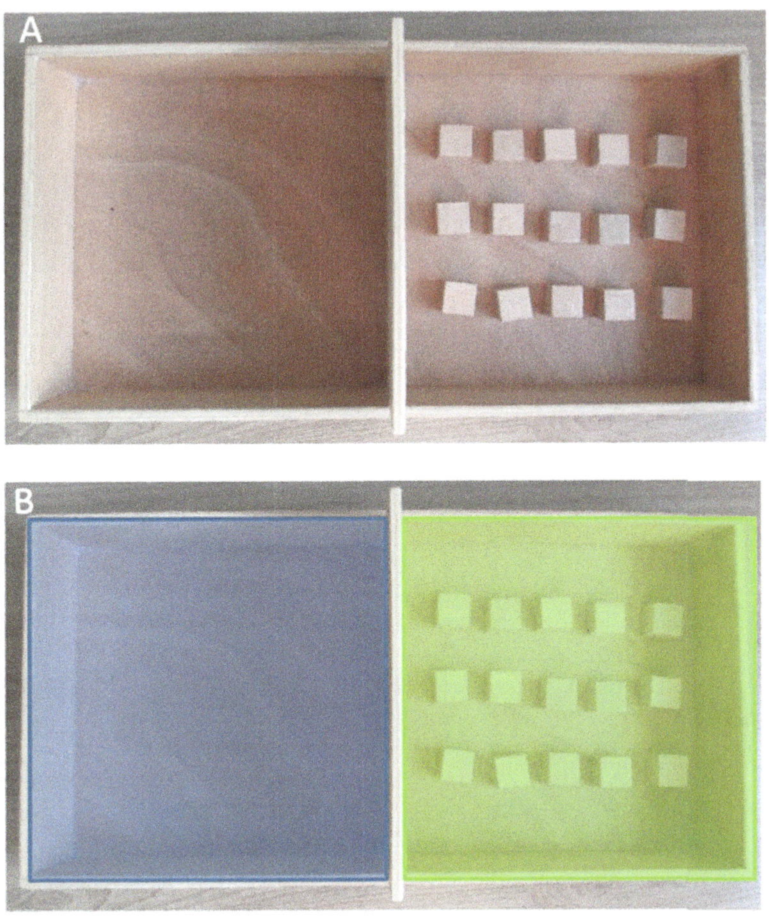

Figure 1. A. Photograph of the Box and Block Test (BBT) used for MC, Fix, KI, and VI conditions, with 15 blocks in the right hand compartment; B. Illustration of the placement of the two Regions of Interest (ROIs) used for counting the number midline crossings.

For the eye-tracking session, the subject was placed in a comfortable sitting position in front of the RED module and the stimulus monitor. The illumination of the testing room was kept constant throughout the testing session. The subject was requested to limit both head movements and speech during the eye-tracking session. The SMI iView XTM software guided the optimal subject placement for good eye tracking, with two white dots representing the eyes and arrows to indicate the optimal position.

The viewing distance was around 70 cm and the visual angle was 45 pixels per degree.

The order for the MI tasks, MC and Fix conditions was selected randomly. The MO task was presented last, to avoid recalling of the observation task when performing other tasks notably MI tasks. Before each task, the subject read the instructions displayed on the screen and pressed the keyboard space bar in order to start the task.

Motor Imagery Tasks

We used imagination of the Box and Block Test (BBT) tasks following the procedure described by Liepert et al. [32] [33], with two MI conditions (KI or VI). The subjects were shown a photograph of the BBT with the 15 blocks in the right hand compartment. The color of the BBT materials was neutral (wood, see Fig 1A), as color has been reported to increase fixation duration [34]. The same BBT equipment was used to create the photograph and to perform real execution of the movement. For the VI task, participants were instructed to "*Attempt to see yourself making with your right hand the BBT just performed with as clear and vivid a visual image as possible*". For the KI task, they were instructed to "*Attempt to feel yourself making with your right hand the BBT just performed, without actually doing it*". These instructions for VI and KI conditions were derived from the French version of the MIQ-RS [31]. Subsequently no instruction on the perspective (First or third person) used to perform MI tasks was explicitly given to the participants.

Motor Observation Task.

During the MO task, each participant observed a video showing the execution of the BBT by a third person, moving the 15 blocks from the right compartment to the left with the right hand. Subjects received the instruction to "*observe the video*". Only the arm and the hand of the actor were visible (for an example see the snapshot of the screen provided in Fig 2). No further instruction and specifically no instruction to imitate the movement was given and the MO task was the last task of the session in order to avoid possible influence of this video on the strategy used by the participants during MI tasks.

Figure 2. Two snapshot of video used for MO task, showing the arm and the hand of the model.

To maintain ecological validity the video was a color video of a model performing the BBT. However, the materials of the box and blocks were neutral, as in the photo (Figs 1 and 2). A video of a model has already been used as an observation task in eye gaze studies [26].

Control Tasks.

Two control conditions were included in the experiment to ensure that the gaze metrics were task-related. The first control task was a fixation task (Fix). The participant observed the photo of the BBT used in the MI tasks for 15 seconds, without any specific instruction other than to watch the screen. The second control task was a mental calculation (MC) task during which the participant was instructed to count mentally forwards from 150 in steps of 3 to the first number above 175, and to give the number obtained while observing the same photo of the BBT.

Data Processing.

The projected Point Of Regard (POR), i.e. the (x,y) coordinates of the user's gaze on the stimulus image or video, was estimated by SMI BeGazeTM software on the basis of gaze tracking data. The software has a built-in saccade, fixation and blink detector. The software considered an out of track period as a blink; this state, in which the eye tracking system cannot determine where the observer is looking, can indeed occur during a blink but also when the observer's head movement exceeds the tracking capabilities of the system setup. Fixation was defined as a stable gaze position (i.e. within 2.23° visual angle) that was maintained for at least 80ms. Saccades were defined as rapid eye movements repositioning the fovea between two successive fixation periods.

The events (fixations, saccades and blinks) were exported to a tab-delimited table in text format to be analyzed with Microsoft Excel® software. The table included the chronological list of events for each event:

- timestamp of the event (start time and end time in microseconds),
- eye position on x, and eye position on y,
- type of event detected (fixation, saccade or blink),
- task and associated stimuli (still images for control conditions and MI tasks, video for MO)

From this information, the total duration of saccades and the total duration of fixations were calculated for each task. We then defined a ratio considered to be the ocular mobility index (OMI) (Eq 1):

$$OMI = 100 * \frac{Saccade\ duration}{Fixation\ duration + Saccade\ duration} \quad (1)$$

In order to characterize further the gaze pattern, we used a Region of Interest (ROI) approach to determine whether there was a difference in the number of times the subjects gaze crossed the midline of the BBT when performing the different tasks. This parameter indicates whether two successive eye fixations were or not located in the same half of the BBT. The screen was divided in two ROIs (Fig 1B) placed on each side of the midline of the BBT. The ROI of each fixation period was defined. We then calculated the number of midline crossings. Midline crossing was defined as the fact that the ROIs of two successive fixation periods were situated alternatively on the right and left side (or inversely).

Mental Chronometry Data

For each MI condition (VI or KI), the difference (time lag) between MI duration (recorded by timestamp of the event (KI or VI)) and the real BBT task duration (performed at the beginning of the experiments) was taken as an absolute error and was chosen as a measure of MI time congruence which is frequently used as a marker of MI ability [23] [33].

Statistical Analysis

Analyses were performed using version 6.01 GraphPad Prism for Windows (GraphPad Software, San Diego California USA, www.graphpad.com).

Estimates of the eye-tracking measures are usually quite noisy and are highly sensible to the negative influence of possible outliers. Before analyzing the eye gaze data recorded and to assess the quality of these data, we calculated for each condition and for each participant the percentage of errors/blinks. Then we performed a statistical approach to identify and remove potential outliers using the ROUT method (Q coefficient = 1%) [35]) available on GraphPad Prism 6.01.

After assessing the normality of distributions using Skewness and Kurtosis tests, we carried out a one-factor analysis of variance (one-way ANOVA) with repeated measures for conditions (5 levels; MC, Fix, KI, VI and MO) as within-subject factors, followed by a post- hoc Holm-Sidak's multiple comparison test to identify the differences between OMI measured in KI and/or VI conditions and in other conditions (MC, Fix and MO). The significance level was set at 5%, adjusted for multiple comparisons. The same analysis was applied to the number of midline crossings.

MIQ-RS results and time lag measures for VI and KI were compared using a paired t test.

RESULTS

For our sample (22 subjects), the mean value of the percentage of errors/blinks was 8.718 (SD = 5.671) for the MC task, 2.958 (SD = 3.203) for the Fix condition, 5.087 (SD = 4.498) for the KI task, 5.373 (SD = 4.453) for the VI task, and 1.875 (SD = 3.233) for the MO. The ROUT method detected and removed four subjects. Eighteen subjects were subsequently analyzed.

MIQ-RS Data

The mean value of the MIQ-RS was 5.728 (SD = 0.7598) for the VI tasks, and 4.741 (SD = 0.8555) for the KI tasks.

The paired t test revealed significantly difference between MIQ-RS-VI and MIQ-RS-KI (mean difference = - 0.9864; t = 4.2940; adjusted p value = 0.0004).

Time Lag Measures in *KI* and *VI* Conditions

The mean value of the time lag was 8.644 seconds (SD = 5.927) for the KI task, and 3.930 seconds (SD = 3.848) for the VI task.

The paired t test revealed significantly difference between KI time lag and VI time lag (mean difference = 4.715 seconds; t = 2.764; adjusted p value = 0.0133).

Ocular Mobility Index (Fig 3)

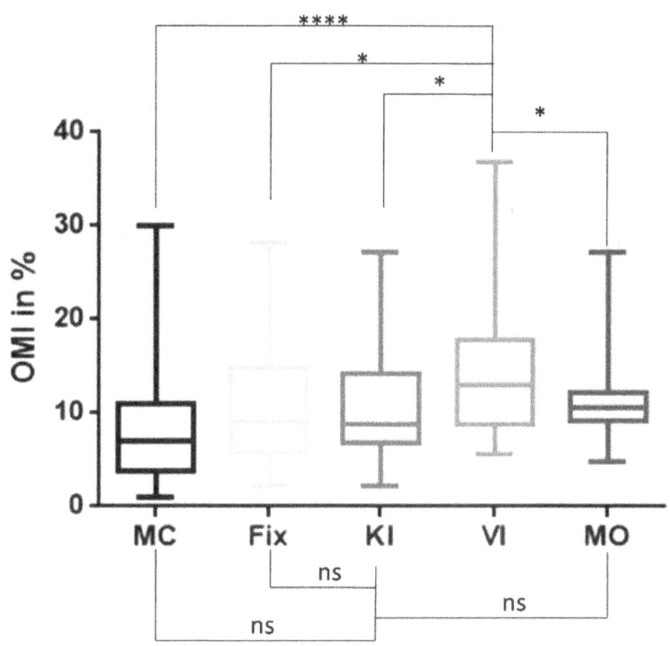

Figure 3. Box plot of the Ocular Mobility Index (OMI = saccade duration/(fixation duration + saccade duration). MC = Mental Calculation, Fix = Fixation task, KI = Kinesthetic motor Imagery, VI = Visual motor Imagery, MO = Motor Observation. The whiskers are drawn down to the 10th percentile and up to the 90th. **** $p < 0.0001$, *$p<0.0500$.

The mean value of the OMI was 7.745 (SD = 6.588) for the MC task, 10.04 (SD = 7.578) for the Fix condition, 9.843 (SD = 5.210) for the KI task, 14.16 (SD = 7.942) for the VI task, and 11.22 (SD = 4.551) for the MO.

The one-factor analysis of variance (ANOVA) with repeated measures for the five conditions (MC, Fix, KI, VI and MO) as within-subject factors showed means were significantly different (F = 5.791, p = 0.0005).

The post-hoc test revealed that OMI was significantly different between VI and KI (mean difference = 4.315; SE of dif = 1.380; t = 3.125; adjusted p value = 0.0156, DF = 68); VI and MC (mean difference = - 6.413; SE of dif = 1.380; t = 4.645; adjusted p value = 0.0001, DF = 68), and VI and Fix (mean difference = 4.119; SE of dif = 1.380; t = 2.984; adjusted p value = 0.0196, DF = 68), but not between VI and MO (mean difference = 2.943; SE of dif = 1.380; t = 2.131; adjusted p value = 0.1388, DF = 68). The Holm-Sidak's multiple comparison test for comparison of OMI between the KI condition and the other conditions did not reveal any significant differences for MC (mean difference = - 2.098; SE of dif = 1.380; t = 1.520; adjusted p value = 0.3487, DF = 68), Fix (mean difference = -0.1958; SE of dif = 1.380; t = 0.1418; adjusted p value = 0.8876, DF = 68), or MO (mean difference = - 1.372; SE of dif = 1.380; t = 0.9939; adjusted p value = 0.5427, DF = 68).

Region of Interest (*ROI*)–Based Approach, Number of Midline Crossings (Fig 4)

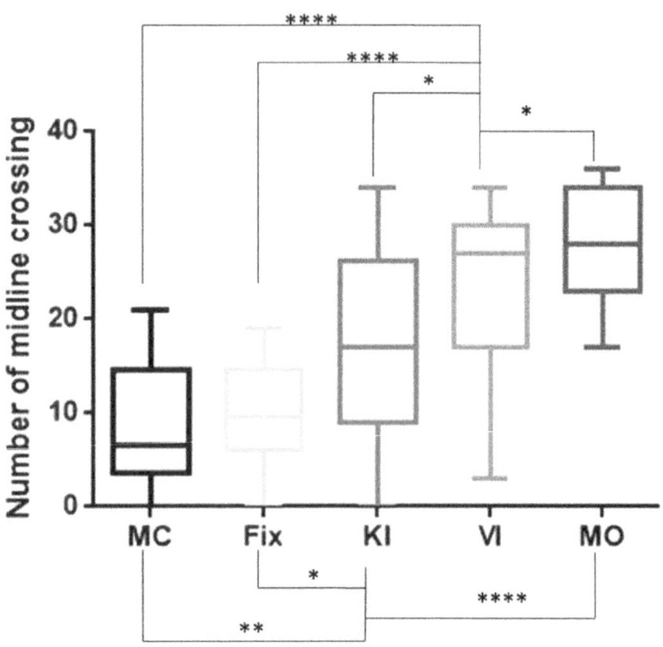

Figure 4. Box plot of the number of midline crossings calculated with the ROIs of the BBT. MC = Mental Calculation, Fix = Fixation task, KI = Kinesthetic motor Imagery, VI = Visual motor Imagery, MO = Motor Observation. The whiskers are drawn down to the 10th percentile and up to the 90th. **** p < 0.0001, *p<0.0500.

When considering the ROI of successive fixation periods, the mean number of midline crossings was 8.444 (SD = 6.252) for the MC task, 9.944 (SD = 5.713) for the Fix condition, 16.83 (SD = 10.29) for the KI task, 23.00 (SD = 9.293) for the VI task, and 28.28 (SD = 5.529) for the MO.

The one-factor analysis of variance (ANOVA) with repeated measures for the five conditions (MC, Fix, KI, VI and MO) as within-subject factors showed means were significantly different (F = 23.77, p < 0.0001).

The post-hoc test (Holm-Sidak's multiple comparison test) revealed that midline crossings were significantly different between VI and KI (mean difference = 6.167; SE of dif = 2.451; t = 2.516; adjusted p value = 0.0283, DF = 68), VI and MC (mean difference = - 14.560; SE of dif = 2.451; t = 5.938; adjusted p value < 0.0001, DF = 68), VI and Fix (mean difference = 13.06; SE of dif = 2.451; t = 5.326; adjusted p value < 0.0001, DF = 68), VI and MO (mean difference = - 5.278; SE of dif = 2.451; t = 2.153; adjusted p value = 0.0349, DF = 68), KI and MC (mean difference = - 8.389; SE of dif = 2.451; t = 3.422; adjusted p value = 0.0042, DF = 68), KI and Fix (mean difference = 6.889; SE of dif = 2.451; t = 2.810; adjusted p value = 0.0193, DF = 68), and KI and MO (mean difference = - 11.44; SE of dif = 2.451; t = 4.668; adjusted p value < 0.0001, DF = 68).

DISCUSSION

Our results showed that the metrics of gaze behavior differed in MI tasks, MO and control tasks and suggest that gaze metric parameters could be used as an objective unobtrusive approach to assess engagement in a motor imagery task, as suggested before [36]. We used a non-invasive oculometric system and, due to the inconspicuous RED device, subjects quickly forgot the gaze acquisition system during the test, increasing the reliability of the results. For the first time we demonstrated that eye movement patterns differ between VI and KI showing that these two MI modalities share different cognitive processes. The differences found in the time lag between VI and KI could also support this view.

Previous studies [26] [37] have already established some eye movement congruency between MI and MO tasks, notably by studying the saccadic eye movements as in our study. Previous studies have focused on fixation rather than saccades. As MI tasks and eye movement (specially saccades) share common neural networks, it seemed relevant to include the parameters describing saccades during different tasks, and this led us to the definition of the OMI, corresponding to the saccade duration over saccade + fixation duration ratio.

Indeed, some of the brain areas activated in MI tasks are also involved in control of eye movements [11]. At least four frontal regions participate in eye movements: the frontal eye field (FEF), which participates in voluntary saccades, the supplementary eye field (SEF) located in the rostral supplementary motor area (SMA), the dorsolateral prefrontal cortex (DLPFC) [38] and the pre-SEF. The 'cingulate eye field' (CEF) in the cingulate cortex, located at the limit between Brodmann areas 23 and 24, is involved in intentional saccade control to act in forthcoming motor behavior [39]. In the parietal lobe, the posterior parietal cortex (PPC) is involved in the control of saccades and attention, and the parietal eye field (PEF) is involved in triggering a reflex saccade.

However, OMI could appear as a rough indicator of gaze behavior because this index focused on ocular saccades and says nothing about the actual pattern of eye movements during the different tasks. Therefore we used a ROI approach which allowed further study of the gaze pattern by calculating the number of midline crossings. This simple parameter appears well adapted to the BBT which requires moving the blocks from one side of the box to the other when performing real movement and one side of the screen to the other when performing visual imagery.

Using these two parameters (both the OMI and the number of midline crossings), we were able to show that eye movement patterns are different during MI, MO and control tasks (MC and Fix). A more in-depth analyze of our results showed differences in eye movement pattern between KI and VI, and this has not, to our knowledge, been previously described. KI and VI are known to be different cognitive processes and rely on different neuronal networks [4] [7]. Our results support this view, when considering that studying gaze behavior is an indirect approach that offers an objective and dynamic marker of neuronal activity [34].

Neuroimagery studies have shown that MI activates brain areas which are also involved in movement execution, such as the SMA, the superior and inferior parietal lobule, dorsal and ventrolateral pre-motor cortices, pre-frontal areas, inferior frontal gyrus, superior temporal gyrus, primary motor cortex (M1), primary sensory cortex, secondary sensory area, insular cortex, anterior cingulate cortex, superior temporal gyrus, basal ganglia and cerebellum [4] [7] [10] [40]. The modality of MI (KI or VI) seems to influence the consistency of brain activation across MI neuroimagery studies [4] [7]. Activation is greater in occipital areas during VI and in sensori-motor areas during KI, suggesting that VI is a visuo-motor task and KI a sensori-motor task [23]. Thus, the difference in terms of eye movement pattern between VI and KI might indicate either an intrinsic difference between the two tasks, VI being a visuo-motor task and KI a sensori-motor task, or the difficulty encountered by the subject in engaging appropriately in KI compared to VI. Indeed, KI is known to be more difficult than VI as confirmed by the lower KI abilities compared to VI abilities found in our sample and already showed [31] [41].

Behavioral data also show slight, but consistent differences between KI and VI. Our healthy sample population demonstrated lower VI than KI time lag, which is coherent with several previous findings [42]. This difference in time lag found here between KI and VI could be interpreted as an indirect marker of previous findings related to the different cognitive and neural processes activated during these two MI tasks (see above). MI consists in a mental transformation of visual and kinesthetic percept's [43] and KI, but not VI seems to be influenced by biomechanical constraints and postural manipulation [44] [45] [46]. During VI tasks the participant does not actually encounter the biomechanical constraints of the movements (the participant does not "feel" the movement during VI), and time duration to perform VI is shorter than the time duration to perform KI. Subsequently compared to the actual performance, the time to perform VI is more accurate than the time to perform KI. Thus our eye gaze data and mental chronometry confirm that KI and VI appear as two separate cognitive processes. This warrants further investigation.

Number of midline crossings show a progressive increase of eye mobility from the MC task to MO, VI being the closest to MO. This could be related to the fact that MI and MO are governed by similar activation of the motor system [47]. The difference between VI and MO remains significant for midline crossings but not for the OMI. The explanation of the apparent contradiction in the parameters of MO and VI tasks is not obvious. Methodological considerations such as the small difference in the apparent size of the BBT in MI tasks (40 cm x 20 cm) and in the MO (30 cm x 15 cm) could play a role. Indeed the size of the target may influence saccade duration (saccades do not conform to Fitt's Law and can decrease in velocity as the distance between two targets decreases). However, the OMI, which used saccade parameters, did not differ between VI and MO. Thus we believe that this possible difference does not dramatically influence our OMI results. Since the result is an absence of difference in OMI despite a difference in target size, this consideration tends to make our result more robust.

The absence of difference in the OMI between these two conditions is in line with previous results. Jacobson [48] and Totten [49] were the first to analyze oculomotor behavior during VI and showed similarities in the production of visual saccades. Hebb [50] later considered VI as a rehearsal of visual perception and hypothesized that VI relied on, and required the production of, ocular movements. Comparison of scanpaths (the resulting series of fixations and saccades) during VI and MO further suggest that internal image representation consists of a sequence of sensory and activities [51] [52] [53]. MI and MO appear to be mediated by the activation of the motor system and organized as motor actions [47]. The oculomotor system would then encode the ocular movements during the perception of a visual scene, and use them to generate the image necessary for VI [54]. The visuo-motor processes activated in MO and VI would therefore be very similar [55] [56], and the ocular movements during VI could be interpreted as an echo of our internal visual representation [37] [57]. In other words VI could be understood as a motor task relying on visual perception in which the subject views his internal representation of movement [26]. This is corroborated by neuroimagery data showing the involvement of the posterior parietal cortex in the visuo-spatial representation of movement [58] [59] [60], and its role in the visual guidance of motor execution [61]. Activation of this area is observed during actual movement execution and also during observation of a third person's movement [62] [63] and VI [7].

While our results suggest a cognitive proximity between VI and MO as previously described [11], the analysis of the number of midline crossing between these two tasks shows a significant difference in the eye gaze pattern. This result suggests that eye gaze pattern are not similar between MO and VI revealing a difference in terms of cognitive demand between these two tasks, even though the visual component is clearly important in VI task [1]. Here, the lack of neurophysiological data does not allow further discussion and further studies are required. Perspective is an important issue that is often overlooked in motor imagery/motor observation studies. Actions can be imagined from a first person perspective and or a third person perspective, and the agent of the action can be the self or other (in either perspectives). In our study participants could have imagined themself from either a first person or third person perspective and the perspective may not have been consistent between VI and KI. This could interfere with the comparison of VI and KI and deserves further studies.

Our results, and their relation to the underlying neural substrate, may mean that the degree of similarity in oculomotor behavior between MO and VI could indicate whether the subject is fully engaged in the VI task. OMI and midline crossings could be a first quantitative approach of the gaze pattern. Further studies, including more sophisticated modelisation of the gaze pattern are necessary to define other parameters of the gaze metrics such as calculation of the entire gaze trajectory, and measurement of parameters describing the similarity of different trajectories such as the Levenshtein distance [64] which has been already proposed by other authors [65] [66] or MultiMatch approach [67]. Moreover, further analyses, with a strict control of the size of the BBT, specifically dedicated to assess eye pattern parameters during VI and MO tasks are required.

CONCLUSION

In conclusion, the metrics of gaze behavior (i.e. OMI and number of midline crossings) differed in MI, MO and control tasks and suggest that these gaze metric parameters could be used as an objective unobtrusive approach to assess engagement in a MI task. For the first time we were able to show that eye movement patterns are different during VI and KI tasks. Our results support this view as VI and KI are known to be different cognitive processes and indicate a potential intrinsic difference between the two tasks: VI being a visuo-motor task and KI, a sensori-motor task. Further studies should define how oculomotor parameters could be used as an indicator of the rehabilitation task a patient is engaged in.

REFERENCES

1. Jeannerod M. Mental imagery in the motor context. Neuropsychologia. 1995 Nov;33(11):1419–32. pmid:8584178 doi: 10.1016/0028-3932(95)00073-c
2. Porro CA, Francescato MP, Cettolo V, Diamond ME, Baraldi P, Zuiani C, et al. Primary Motor and Sensory Cortex Activation during Motor Performance and Motor Imagery: A Functional Magnetic Resonance Imaging Study. J Neurosci. 1996 Dec 1;16(23):7688–98. pmid:8922425 doi: 10.1007/978-88-470-2194-5_11
3. Decety J. Do imagined and executed actions share the same neural substrate? Cogn Brain Res. 1996 Mar;3(2):87–93. doi: 10.1016/0926-6410(95)00033-x
4. Solodkin A, Hlustik P, Chen EE, Small SL. Fine modulation in network activation during motor execution and motor imagery. Cereb Cortex N Y N 1991. 2004 Nov;14(11):1246–55. doi: 10.1093/cercor/bhh086
5. Guillot A, Collet C. Contribution from neurophysiological and psychological methods to the study of motor imagery. Brain Res Brain Res Rev. 2005 Dec 15;50(2):387–97. pmid:16271398 doi: 10.1016/j.brainresrev.2005.09.004
6. Hétu S, Mercier C, Eugène F, Michon P-E, Jackson PL. Modulation of Brain Activity during Action Observation: Influence of Perspective, Transitivity and Meaningfulness. PLoS ONE. 2011 Sep 12;6(9):e24728. doi: 10.1371/journal.pone.0024728. pmid:21931832
7. Hetu S, Gregoire M, Saimpont A, Coll M-P, Eugene F, Michon P-E, et al. The neural network of motor imagery: an ALE meta-analysis. Neurosci Biobehav Rev. 2013 Jun;37(5):930–49. doi: 10.1016/j.neubiorev.2013.03.017. pmid:23583615
8. Chong TT-J, Cunnington R, Williams MA, Kanwisher N, Mattingley JB. fMRI Adaptation Reveals Mirror Neurons in Human Inferior Parietal Cortex. Curr Biol. 2008 Oct 28;18(20):1576–80. doi: 10.1016/j.cub.2008.08.068. pmid:18948009
9. Macuga KL, Frey SH. Neural representation involved in observed, imagined, and imitated actions are dissociable and hierarchically organized. Neuroimage. 2011;2798–807. doi: 10.1016/j.neuroimage.2011.09.083. pmid:22005592
10. Grezes J, Decety J. Functional anatomy of execution, mental simulation, observation, and verb generation of actions: a meta-analysis. Hum Brain Mapp. 2001 Jan;12(1). doi: 10.1002/1097-0193(200101)12:1<1::aid-hbm10>3.0.co;2-v
11. Causer J, McCormick SA, Holmes PS. Congruency of gaze metrics in action, imagery and action observation. Front Hum Neurosci. 2013;7. doi: 10.3389/fnhum.2013.00604
12. Dickstein R, Deutsch JE. Motor imagery in physical therapist practice. Phys Ther. 2007 Jul;87(7):942–53. pmid:17472948 doi: 10.2522/ptj.20060331
13. Braun SM, Beurskens AJ, Borm PJ, Schack T, Wade DT. The effects of mental practice in stroke rehabilitation: a systematic review. Arch Phys Med Rehabil. 2006 Jun;87(6):842–52. pmid:16731221 doi: 10.1016/j.apmr.2006.02.034
14. Sharma N, Pomeroy VM, Baron J-C. Motor imagery: a backdoor to the motor system after stroke? Stroke J Cereb Circ. 2006 Jul;37(7):1941–52. doi: 10.1161/01.str.0000226902.43357.fc
15. Dodakian L, Campbell Stewart J, Cramer SC. Motor imagery during movement activates the brain more than movement alone after stroke: a pilot study. J Rehabil Med. 2014 Oct;46(9):843–8. doi: 10.2340/16501977-1844. pmid:25182189
16. Malouin F, Jackson PL, Richards CL. Towards the integration of mental practice in rehabilitation programs. A critical review. Front Hum Neurosci. 2013;7. doi: 10.3389/fnhum.2013.00576
17. Feltz DL, Landers DM. The effects of mental practice on motor skill learning and performance: a meta-analysis. J Sport Exerc Psych. 1983;5:25–57.
18. Page SJ, Levine P, Leonard A. Mental practice in chronic stroke: results of a randomized, placebo-controlled trial. Stroke J Cereb Circ. 2007 Apr;38(4):1293–7. doi: 10.1161/01.str.0000260205.67348.2b
19. Page SJ, Levine P, Sisto SA, Johnston MV. Mental practice combined with physical practice for upper-limb motor deficit in subacute stroke. Phys Ther. 2001 Aug;81(8):1455–62. pmid:11509075
20. Liu KP, Chan CC, Lee TM, Hui-Chan CW. Mental imagery for promoting relearning for people after stroke: a randomized controlled trial. Arch Phys Med Rehabil. 2004 Sep;85(9):1403–8. pmid:15375808 doi: 10.1016/j.apmr.2003.12.035
21. Ietswaart M, Johnston M, Dijkerman HC, Joice S, Scott CL, MacWalter RS, et al. Mental practice with motor imagery in stroke recovery: randomized controlled trial of efficacy. Brain J Neurol. 2011 May;134(Pt 5):1373–86. doi: 10.1093/brain/awr077

22. Oostra KM, Oomen A, Vanderstraeten G, Vingerhoets G. Influence of motor imagery training on gait rehabilitation in sub-acute stroke: A randomized controlled trial. J Rehabil Med. 2014 Nov 14; doi: 10.2340/16501977-1908
23. Guillot A, Collet C. Duration of mentally simulated movement: a review. J Mot Behav. 2005 Jan;37(1). doi: 10.3200/jmbr.37.1.10-20
24. Malouin F, Richards CL, Durand A, Doyon J. Reliability of mental chronometry for assessing motor imagery ability after stroke. Arch Phys Med Rehabil. 2008 Feb;89(2):311–9. doi: 10.1016/j.apmr.2007.11.006. pmid:18226656
25. McCormick SA, Causer J, Holmes PS. Active Vision during Action Execution, Observation and Imagery: Evidence for Shared Motor Representations. PLoS ONE [Internet]. 2013 Jun 25 [cited 2015 Feb 11];8(6). Available from:http://www.ncbi.nlm.nih.gov/pmc/articles/PMC3692467/
26. McCormick SA, Causer J, Holmes PS. Eye gaze metrics reflect a shared motor representation for action observation and movement imagery. Brain Cogn. 2012 Oct;80(1):83–8. doi: 10.1016/j.bandc.2012.04.010. pmid:22647575
27. Kosilo M, Wuerger SM, Craddock M, Jennings BJ, Hunt AR, Martinovic J. Low-level and high-level modulations of fixational saccades and high frequency oscillatory brain activity in a visual object classification task. Front Psychol. 2013;4. doi: 10.3389/fpsyg.2013.00948
28. Funahashi S. Saccade-related activity in the prefrontal cortex: its role in eye movement control and cognitive functions. Front Integr Neurosci. 2014;8. doi: 10.3389/fnint.2014.00054
29. Siegenthaler E, Costela FM, McCamy MB, Di Stasi LL, Otero-Millan J, Sonderegger A, et al. Task difficulty in mental arithmetic affects microsaccadic rates and magnitudes. Eur J Neurosci. 2014 Jan;39(2):287–94. doi: 10.1111/ejn.12395. pmid:24438491
30. Flanagan JR, Johansson RS. Action plans used in action observation. Nature. 2003 Aug 14;424(6950):769–71. pmid:12917683 doi: 10.1038/nature01861
31. Loison B, Moussaddaq A-S, Cormier J, Richard I, Ferrapie A-L, Ramond A, et al. Translation and validation of the French Movement Imagery Questionnaire—Revised Second Version (MIQ-RS). Ann Phys Rehabil Med. 2013 Apr;56(3):157–73. doi: 10.1016/j.rehab.2013.01.001. pmid:23415992
32. Liepert J, Greiner J, Nedelko V, Dettmers C. Reduced upper limb sensation impairs mental chronometry for motor imagery after stroke: clinical and electrophysiological findings. Neurorehabil Neural Repair. 2012 Jun;26(5):470–8. doi: 10.1177/1545968311425924. pmid:22247502
33. Greiner J, Schoenfeld MA, Liepert J. Assessment of mental chronometry (MC) in healthy subjects. Arch Gerontol Geriatr. 2014 Apr;58(2):226–30. doi: 10.1016/j.archger.2013.09.003. pmid:24275122
34. Henderson JM. Human gaze control during real-world scene perception. Trends Cogn Sci. 2003 Nov;7(11):498–504. pmid:14585447 doi: 10.1016/j.tics.2003.09.006
35. Motulsky HJ, Brown RE. Detecting outliers when fitting data with nonlinear regression—a new method based on robust nonlinear regression and the false discovery rate. BMC Bioinformatics. 2006 Mar 9;7:123. pmid:16526949
36. Gueugneau N, Crognier L, Papaxanthis C. The influence of eye movements on the temporal features of executed and imagined arm movements. Brain Res. 2008 Jan 2;1187:95–102. pmid:18035337 doi: 10.1016/j.brainres.2007.10.042
37. Heremans E, Helsen WF, Feys P. The eyes as a mirror of our thoughts: Quantification of motor imagery of goal-directed movements through eye movement registration. Behav Brain Res. 2008 Mar 5;187(2):351–60. pmid:17977607 doi: 10.1016/j.bbr.2007.09.028
38. Vernet M, Quentin R, Chanes L, Mitsumasu A, Valero-Cabre A. Frontal eye field, where art thou? Anatomy, function, and non-invasive manipulation of frontal regions involved in eye movements and associated cognitive operations. Front Integr Neurosci. 2014;8. doi: 10.3389/fnint.2014.00088
39. Pierrot-Deseilligny C, Müri RM, Ploner CJ, Gaymard B, Demeret S, Rivaud-Pechoux S. Decisional role of the dorsolateral prefrontal cortex in ocular motor behaviour. Brain. 2003 Jun 1;126(6):1460–73. doi: 10.1093/brain/awg148
40. Rizzolatti G, Luppino G, Matelli M. The organization of the cortical motor system: new concepts. Electroencephalogr Clin Neurophysiol. 1998 Apr;106(4):283–96. pmid:9741757 doi: 10.1016/s0013-4694(98)00022-4
41. Gregg M, Hall C, Butler A. The MIQ-RS: A Suitable Option for Examining Movement Imagery Ability. Evid-Based Complement Altern Med ECAM. 2010 Jun;7(2):249–57. doi: 10.1093/ecam/nem170
42. Malouin F, Richards CL, Durand A, Doyon J. Clinical Assessment of Motor Imagery After Stroke. Neurorehabil Neural Repair. 2008 Jul 1;22(4):330–40. doi: 10.1177/1545968307313499. pmid:18326057
43. de Lange FP, Hagoort P, Toni I. Neural Topography and Content of Movement Representations. J Cogn Neurosci. 2005 Jan 1;17(1):97–112. pmid:15701242 doi: 10.1162/0898929052880039
44. Parsons LM. Imagined spatial transformation of one's body. J Exp Psychol Gen. 1987 Jun;116(2):172–91. pmid:2955072 doi: 10.1037/0096-3445.116.2.172
45. Parsons LM. Temporal and kinematic properties of motor behavior reflected in mentally simulated action. J Exp Psychol Hum Percept Perform. 1994 Aug;20(4):709–30. pmid:8083630 doi: 10.1037/0096-1523.20.4.709
46. Ter Horst AC, Cole J, van Lier R, Steenbergen B. The Effect of Chronic Deafferentation on Mental Imagery: A Case Study. PLoS ONE [Internet]. 2012 Aug 7 [cited 2015 Sep 20];7(8). Available from: http://www.ncbi.nlm.nih.gov/pmc/articles/PMC3413668/

47. Jeannerod M. Neural Simulation of Action: A Unifying Mechanism for Motor Cognition. NeuroImage. 2001 Jul;14(1):S103–9. pmid:11373140 doi: 10.1006/nimg.2001.0832

48. Jacobson E. E. Electrical measurements of neuromuscular states during mental activities: VI. A note on mental activities concerning an amputated limb. Am J Physiol. 1931;

49. Totten . Eye movement during visual imagery. Comp Psychol Monogr 1935;11:46.

50. Hebb DO. Concerning imagery. Psychol Rev. 1968 Nov;75(6):466–77. pmid:4973669 doi: 10.1037/h0026771

51. Brandt SA, Stark LW. Spontaneous eye movements during visual imagery reflect the content of the visual scene. J Cogn Neurosci. 1997 Jan;9(1). doi: 10.1162/jocn.1997.9.1.27

52. Noton D, Stark L. Scanpaths in saccadic eye movements while viewing and recognizing patterns. Vision Res. 1971 Sep;11(9):929–42. pmid:5133265 doi: 10.1016/0042-6989(71)90213-6

53. Noton D, Stark L. Scanpaths in eye movements during pattern perception. Science. 1971 Jan 22;171(3968):308–11. pmid:5538847 doi: 10.1126/science.171.3968.308

54. Laeng B, Teodorescu D. Eye scan paths during visual imagery re-enact those of perception of the same visual scene. Cognitive Science. 2002; (26):207–31. doi: 10.1207/s15516709cog2602_3

55. Heremans E, Smits-Engelsman B, Caeyenberghs K, Vercruysse S, Nieuwboer A, Feys P, et al. Keeping an eye on imagery: the role of eye movements during motor imagery training. Neuroscience. 2011 Nov 10;195:37–44. doi: 10.1016/j.neuroscience.2011.07.030. pmid:21884759

56. De' Sperati C. Precise oculomotor correlates of visuospatial mental rotation and circular motion imagery. J Cogn Neurosci. 2003 Nov 15;15(8):1244–59. pmid:14709240 doi: 10.1162/089892903322598184

57. Spivey MJ, Geng JJ. Oculomotor mechanisms activated by imagery and memory: eye movements to absent objects. Psychol Res. 2001 Nov;65(4):235–41. pmid:11789427 doi: 10.1007/s004260100059

58. Lebon F, Lotze M, Stinear CM, Byblow WD. Task-Dependent Interaction between Parietal and Contralateral Primary Motor Cortex during Explicit versus Implicit Motor Imagery. PLoS ONE. 2012 May 31;7(5):e37850. doi: 10.1371/journal.pone.0037850. pmid:22693579

59. Harris IMM, Carlo . Parietal Lobe Contribution to Mental Rotation Demonstrated with rTMS. J Cogn Neurosci. 4/1/2003;15(3):315–23. pmid:12729485 doi: 10.1162/089892903321593054

60. Torres EB, Raymer A, Gonzalez Rothi LJ, Heilman KM, Poizner H. Sensory-Spatial Transformations in the Left Posterior Parietal Cortex May Contribute to Reach Timing. J Neurophysiol. 2010 Nov;104(5):2375–88. doi: 10.1152/jn.00089.2010. pmid:20810686

61. Mutha PK, Sainburg RL, Haaland KY. Left parietal regions are critical for adaptive visuomotor control. J Neurosci Off J Soc Neurosci. 2011 May 11;31(19):6972–81. doi: 10.1523/jneurosci.6432-10.2011

62. Turella L, Erb M, Grodd W, Castiello U. Visual features of an observed agent do not modulate human brain activity during action observation. NeuroImage. 2009 Jul 1;46(3):844–53. doi: 10.1016/j.neuroimage.2009.03.002. pmid:19285143

63. Caspers S, Zilles K, Laird AR, Eickhoff SB. ALE meta-analysis of action observation and imitation in the human brain. NeuroImage. 2010 Apr 15;50(3):1148–67. doi: 10.1016/j.neuroimage.2009.12.112. pmid:20056149

64. Levenshtein V. I. Binary codes capable of correcting deletions, insertions and reversals. Soviet Physics—Doklady. 1966; (6):707–10.

65. Josephson S, Holmes ME. Attention to repeated images on the World-Wide Web: another look at scanpath theory. Behav Res Methods Instrum Comput J Psychon Soc Inc. 2002 Nov;34(4):539–48. doi: 10.3758/bf03195483

66. Privitera C. M., & Stark L. W. Algorithms for defining visual regions-of-interest: Comparison with eye fixations. IEEE Transactions on Pattern Analysis and Machine Intelligence (PAMI). 2000; (22):970–82. doi: 10.1109/34.877520

67. Nyström M, Jarodzka H, Dewhurst R, Foulsham T. Comparing scanpaths during scene encoding and recognition: A multi-dimensional approach. J Eye Mov Res. 2012;5(4:3):1–14.

INDEX

A

Akaike Information Criteria 40, 44
Android software development 34
article-level metrics (ALMs) has grown rapidly amongst the research community, by researchers, publishers, funders, and research institutions. As 201
artificial neural networks (ANNs) 26, 34

B

bibliometricians 202
biogeographers 109
biological macromolecules 96
biomembranes 173
bookmarklets 209
Box and Block Test (BBT) 257, 258
Brownian dynamics 235

C

Collective material entity (CME) 139
computational fluid dynamics (CFD) 26
Computational Logic Unit (CLU) 77
CPU-bound 40, 42, 43, 46, 47, 48, 51, 52, 55
Critical Assessment of protein Structure Prediction (CASP) 213
current stakeholder identification and quantification (SIQ) 73
cyclic coordinate descent (CCD) 102

D

database service 43, 50, 51
decision making 75, 76
description logics (DL) 139
dorsolateral prefrontal cortex (DLPFC) 260
dose-volume histograms (DVH) 163
Dosimetry verification 164

E

e-commerce 136
electron microscopy (EM) 231

F

Face Recognition (FR) 60
face recognition systems 59, 66
Face Recognition Vendor Test (FRVT) 60, 70
facial development 61
frontal eye field (FEF) 260

G

Global Biodiversity Information Facility (GBIF) 107
Gnu Scientific Library (GSL) 235
GoodOD method 136

H

High-Performance Computing 40
Hospital Management System (HMS) 82
hydrogen bonding 213, 214, 229

I

i3Drefine 213, 214, 216, 217, 219, 220, 221, 223, 224, 225, 226, 227, 228
Interactive Data Language (IDL) 121
isocenter 163, 164, 165, 166, 170

J

Java Management Extensions (JMX) 44, 57

K

Kinematic Closure (KIC) 99
kinesthesic imagery 255
kinesthetic imagery (KI) 256, 257

L

Large-scale software systems 1
Laser scanning confocal microscopy 187
lipidome 173, 174, 175, 176, 177, 181, 182, 183, 184, 185
Lipidomic data 175

M

macromolecular 95, 96, 104
Markov-Chain Monte Carlo (MCMC) 239
Markov chains 239, 240, 241, 242, 244, 245, 246, 248, 252
mean absolute error (MAE) 98, 99
mental calculation (MC) 257, 258
metric model 1, 2, 3, 4, 5, 6, 7, 8
minirhizotrons 117, 118, 120, 123, 124, 125, 126, 128, 129, 131, 132, 133
Model Assembly (MA) 15, 19, 20
Multilayer feed-forward neural networks (MLFNs) 26
multi-ring network 3

N

nanoelectrospray 173, 175, 185
National Aeronautics and Space Administration 108
National Institute of Standards and Technology's (NIST) 122
next generation sequencing (NGS) 14
nuclear magnetic resonance (NMR) 231
nuclear pore complex (NPC) 231

O

ocular mobility index (OMI) 259
oculomotor 255, 261, 262, 264
Online Car Show Room (OCSR) 81
Ontological Analysis 136, 148
Ontology Development 136
Ontology quality evaluation and Requirements (OQuaRE) 137
organ at risk (OAR) 164, 165, 168, 169

P

photobleaching 191
planned dose perturbation (PDP) 165
Point Of Regard (POR) 258
Point spread function (PSF) 188
Principal Component Analysis (PCA) 156
Privacy Petri Net (PPN) 151, 152
Process and Participation (PRO) 139
Protein design methods 99
Protein Structure 213
Public Library of Science (PLOS) 202

R

Representative State Transfer 41
requirements elicitation phase (REP) 74
Requirements Engineering (RE) 73
Restaurant Management System (RMS) 83
root mean square deviation (RMSD) 102
root-mean-square deviation (RMSD) 235
Rosetta energy units (REU) 98

S

SDMdata 107, 108, 109, 110
Service-Orientated Architecture 39
simple sequence repeats (SSRs) 14
single nucleotide polymorphisms (SNPs) 14
Smarterpolation 165, 170
Software 1, 2, 8, 10, 11
software networks 1, 2, 5, 11
soil environment 118, 125, 132
solar water 25, 26, 27, 28, 31, 32, 34, 37, 38
source to skin distance (SSD) 165
species distribution models (SDMs) 107
Stakeholders 73, 74, 76, 83, 84, 85, 92, 93
supplementary eye field (SEF) 260
supplementary motor area (SMA) 260
support vector machine (SVM) 26

T

transcriptome data 13, 14, 15, 18, 19, 20, 21

U

Universal Description Discovery and Integration 41

V

value-based software engineering (VBSE) 73
value-based software requirements engineering (VBSRE) 74
value-based software (VBS) 73
visual imagery (VI) 256, 257

W

Web services 39, 40, 42, 57